P9-CRC-390

Formatting Legal Documents
With
Microsoft Word 2010

Tips and Tricks for Working With
Pleadings, Contracts, Mailings,
and Other Complex Documents

Jan Berinstein, Ph.D.

Formatting Legal Documents With Microsoft Word 2010
Tips and Tricks for Working With Pleadings, Contracts, Mailings, and Other Complex Documents

Copyright © 2010, 2012 by Jan Berinstein, Ph.D.
ISBN 061-5-58697-X

All rights reserved. No part of the contents of this book may be reproduced, stored in a retrieval system, or transmitted in any form or by any means—electronic, mechanical, photocopying, photostating, recording, or otherwise—without written permission of the author. No patent liability is assumed with respect to the use of the information contained herein.

Originally published in slightly different form.

Warnings and Disclaimers

The views and opinions expressed in this book are solely those of the author.

Mention herein of a particular product or service does not constitute an endorsement of that product or service.

Although every precaution has been taken in the preparation of this book, the author / publisher assumes no responsibility for errors or omissions. Nor is any liability assumed for damages resulting from the information contained herein, which is provided without any express, statutory, or implied warranties.

Trademarks

Microsoft and Windows are registered trademarks of Microsoft Corporation.

WordPerfect is a registered trademark of Corel Corporation.

Screenshots

Microsoft product screenshots reprinted with permission from Microsoft Corporation.

Printed and bound in the United States of America.

First printing: May, 2010.
Second printing: January, 2012

Revised Edition

For the unsung heroines—my women friends
Who have been there for me, lending support and setting examples,
through it all

Acknowledgments

A book is never a solitary effort, even when there is but one author. This project is no exception to that rule. Although I performed nearly all of the research, the testing, the writing, the design, and the formatting (not to mention taking and inserting the screenshots), I have had many helpers. I've been inspired, enlightened, assisted, encouraged, and generally tended to by an assortment of wonderful people throughout the planning and writing stages of this book. I am grateful to each of them for their succor and support, which have taken a variety of forms.

Both this book and my previous one (<u>Formatting Legal Documents With Microsoft Office Word 2007</u>) sprang from a desire to fill the gap left after the formidable Donna Payne and her company, Payne Consulting, stopped publishing their first-rate <u>Word for Law Firms</u> series. It was only after learning conclusively that Donna did not intend to write a book about Word 2007 that I dared to jump in and try to make my own contribution to the field last year. Although I have taken a somewhat different approach from Donna's, and I don't claim to have inherited her mantle, it would not be terribly far-fetched to call her my muse.

I owe copious, profound thanks (and apologies) to everyone who put up with my singular focus for so many weeks and listened patiently to my promises about all of the ways I would make it up to them "when The Book is done." Among those who deserve extra-special thanks for their forbearance and for a host of other favors—and who can begin to collect on those promises soon—are the following:

My mother, Norma J. Baron, who meticulously (and with eagle eyes!) proofread most of the manuscript, helped me "fact-check" certain items, let me bounce ideas off her, and provided moral support in general.

My sister, Paula Berinstein, a prolific and highly creative writer who has been through this process far more often than I have, who led the way, inspired me, and gave me some terrific publishing pointers.

Marilyn Thomas, who graciously and generously juggled her schedule so that I could take a significant amount of time off work and devote my energies to the book project, and whose steadfastness, wit, and periodic bursts of encouragement helped more than she knows.

Linda Hopkins, who has graced my life with friendship, constancy, a sense of fun, and cheerfulness; who pitched in and returned phone calls for me when I was overwhelmed; and who buoyed my spirits and also contributed a plethora of helpful ideas for both books.

Barry, ever my hero, who lavished me with emotional sustenance (as well as a steady supply of coffee), tickled my funny bone, shifted my attention, reminded me what matters most, and just generally increased my joy quotient.

Angela Carrigan, who selflessly helped out whenever I asked for backup, and who looked out for my best interests (as she always does), all with perennial sweetness and good humor.

Linda Heineman, who listened, took me seriously, lent moral support, and made me feel that I could accomplish anything I set out to do.

Suzanne O'Connell, who regularly interjected "Yays" and other reinforcement that kept my morale high.

Sue Kane, one of my dearest friends and the best legal secretary I know, whose unfailing warmth, impish humor, and infectious sense of fun have kept me smiling for two decades.

And all of my other friends who believed in me and urged me on. Although I haven't mentioned everyone by name (you know who you are!), I am extremely grateful to each of you. I've dedicated the book to my women friends for their daily contributions, as well as their extraordinary "life support" over the years, but my men friends mean the world to me, too.

My neighbors, Sandy and Robbie Patten, deserve mention for their consideration and numerous kindnesses that made my life easier during the last part of my sabbatical, when I was sequestered in my home office, working furiously to finish the book.

Special, and effusive, thanks to Beth Melton, MVP, my "guardian angel," who appeared out of nowhere at a critical moment à la "It's a Wonderful Life." She generously reviewed, critiqued, and helped me rework the co-authoring section (and tweaked some screenshots in that section). (However, I take full—sole—responsibility for any errors, misstatements, etc. therein.) She also provided helpful tips about the AutoComplete feature. And because of Beth, I was able to obtain the RTM version of the software in time to meet my deadline. She has earned her wings many times over.

Thanks, too, to Ayca Yuksel and Jen Gaudette of Microsoft, who forwarded white papers and screenshots to help me get a handle on a couple of features that I wasn't able to test because of the technical limitations of my computer setup.

Lulu staffers Carol Housel and, especially, Nick Popio earned my lasting gratitude for getting back to me with rock-solid information when I imposed on them personally rather than using Lulu's Byzantine support system for answers to my pressing questions about publication.

I'm indebted to my training clients, whose queries prompted me to look ever more closely at the program in order to understand it well enough to be able to explain it to others. They were at the forefront of my thoughts both when I wrote the Word 2007 book and when I started this one. For their sake, I kept honing the book, constantly rereading and reassessing (and re-testing) to try to make the tutorials as clear, and as accurate, as possible.

Thanks as well to the people who bought my Word 2007 book and gave thoughtful feedback that guided me as I worked on this one. You have made a genuine contribution.

And finally, a nod to my late father, Nathan W. Berinstein. Even though he has been gone since 2006, he has remained in my thoughts and, in an indirect way, he helped motivate me to tackle—and complete—the project. I wish he were here to see what I've accomplished.

About the Author

Jan Berinstein has worked as a legal word processor since 1986. She also runs her own software-training company, CompuSavvy Computer Training & Consulting, which provides hands-on classes and on-site training for law firms, government agencies, and corporate legal departments (among other businesses) throughout California. Recently, she has subcontracted with other training companies in order to assist with Office 2010 and Windows 7 upgrades at a number of mid-sized and large law firms in Southern California.

In addition, she has been a UCLA Extension instructor for more than 15 years, designing and teaching computer courses for legal secretaries and paralegals, as well as "computers for seniors" workshops. She has taught similar classes at the University of West Los Angeles and Learning Tree University, and has led "Internet Legal Research" seminars in Los Angeles, San Francisco, and San Jose for the Center for Professional Education / Center for Legal Education.

Ms. Berinstein has given presentations about various computer-related topics at LegalTech Los Angeles, before the Beverly Hills Bar Association, and for several legal secretaries' groups.

A native of Los Angeles, Ms. Berinstein holds a Bachelor's degree in political science from UCLA as well as an M.A. and Ph.D. in government from Cornell University. After working for several years as a freelance writer and editor, she enrolled in UCLA Extension's journalism program and obtained her certification in print journalism in 1993.

In 2009, she wrote and published her first book, <u>Formatting Legal Documents With Microsoft Office Word 2007</u>. Earlier in the decade, she served as a contributing author on Laura Acklen's <u>Absolute Beginner's Guide to WordPerfect 12</u> (Que Publishing, 2005) and as a technical editor on Ms. Acklen's <u>Absolute Beginner's Guide to WordPerfect X3</u> (Que Publishing, 2006).

Ms. Berinstein, who uses both Word and WordPerfect to format legal documents on a daily basis, offers article-length tips about both programs in her popular, well-respected blog at <u>http://compusavvy.wordpress.com</u>. (The American Bar Association included her blog in its "60 Sites in 60 Minutes 2010" list in March of 2010.) She also serves as the webmistress and administrator of the WordPerfect Universe web site, a user-to-user support group (<u>www.wpuniverse.com</u>).

To visit Ms. Berinstein's training company web site, go to <u>www.compusavvy.com</u>.

CONTENTS AT A GLANCE

WORKING WITH MAILINGS AND FORMS

WORKING WITH PLEADINGS AND CONTRACTS

TROUBLESHOOTING TIPS

FILE CONVERSION ISSUES

COPING WITH METADATA

RESOURCES

INDEX

CONTENTS

WORD'S "LOGIC" (AND HOW IT COMPARES WITH WORDPERFECT'S)

GETTING WORD TO WORK THE WAY YOU WANT

DEMYSTIFYING EVERYDAY FEATURES

WORKING SMARTER AND FASTER / AUTOMATING WORD

Introduction

Despite its length, this book is not—and is not intended to be—a "complete" reference for Microsoft Word 2010. Indeed, there are plenty of other tomes that span nearly the full range of topics, from the most basic features of the program to highly advanced, specialized tasks such as blogging, creating web pages, and working with Extensible Markup Language (XML) coding. Those books certainly have their place, but for the most part they don't address the specific needs of the legal profession: to generate and format documents that meet strict formatting rules imposed by courts or other judicial bodies.

By contrast, this book takes a relatively narrow focus. It is designed mainly to help people who work in law firms, government agencies, and corporate legal departments use Word 2010 to prepare the specialized legal documents they work with on a daily basis: briefs, motions, discovery documents, and other documents used in litigation (i.e., pleadings), as well as contracts, wills and trusts, and even multi-page letters. Because of this more limited emphasis, the book covers only selected features of the program—some of them fairly simple and others rather advanced—needed for legal document formatting. I have chosen those features based on my extensive experience (23-plus years) as a legal word processor, as well as on feedback from my training clients (mostly legal secretaries, lawyers, and paralegals) and from people who purchased my Word 2007 book. Obviously, my decisions about which features to include and which to exclude, while far from arbitrary, reflect my own subjective judgment.

Throughout the book, I also offer assorted tips for improving efficiency in general, along with troubleshooting suggestions.

The instructions I provide for formatting pleadings are designed to comport with the California Rules of Court, since California is the jurisdiction with which I am most familiar. However, with minor modifications, the guidelines should work for other jurisdictions as well. In most cases, customizing the general instructions is just a matter of simple tweaks to margin settings and/or line spacing. That holds true even for the tutorial on creating pleading paper from scratch, a task that probably will require a certain amount of trial and error regardless of the jurisdiction.

The book assumes fundamental computer literacy on the part of the readers. As a result, I don't go into much detail about basic tasks such as moving around the screen and applying font attributes like bolding and italics. I make exceptions to that general rule where (1) a commonly used feature has lesser-known aspects that can be useful (such as Paste Special, which allows you to paste text that you have copied from another program or from the Internet without any formatting); (2) a "simple" feature, such as line spacing, actually turns out to be more complicated than it first appears (I'm thinking specifically of the frustration many people experience when they can't get the text in a pleading to align with the line numbers embedded in the pleading paper); or (3) the steps to perform a simple function in Word 2010 differ significantly from those in earlier versions of Word.

Although I've tailored much of the material for legal professionals, the book includes plenty of tips about features that are in wide use. Thus, people in other fields should find the book helpful, too.

One more caution, just to make clear what you realistically can expect from the book. It decidedly is ***not*** an introductory text for aspiring legal word processors. (That is one of the reasons I haven't included samples of legal documents. Another reason is that formatting varies significantly from jurisdiction to jurisdiction; California pleadings look different from those in Florida, which look different from those in Massachusetts, and so on.) Rather, it is meant to assist folks who already work in law firms, corporate legal departments, and government agencies to get the best possible results—and meet deadlines without experiencing undue stress—when they prepare the pleadings, contracts, estate plans, letters of intent, and other papers that constitute the bulk of their daily work.

Genesis of the Book and What's Included

Both my Word 2007 book and this one evolved, at least in part, from handouts I previously wrote for use in my on-site trainings and laboratory classes. For both books, I also wrote quite a bit of original material, ranging from brief introductory and transitional passages to entire new sections.

This book picks up where the Word 2007 book left off. I've added a tremendous amount about features that are brand-new in Word 2010 and features that work differently from the way they worked in Word 2007 or an earlier version of the program. Moreover, I've written a large number of new full-length tutorials, as well as shorter tips, covering topics I didn't go over in the Word 2007 book. For instance, there is a new chapter with instructions for performing merges, using merges to format a sheet of labels addressed to multiple recipients, creating "quick 'n' dirty" labels, and setting up and printing envelopes. You'll find, as well, new tutorials about setting up your own templates and creating pleading paper from scratch, plus a section that explores how to prevent, diagnose, and repair document corruption. I've fleshed out the discussion of features introduced in Word 2007, and I've expanded on and clarified several lessons about features, such as multilevel lists, that haven't changed markedly since Word 2007 but that remain a source of confusion to many people (particularly users upgrading from a pre-Word 2007 version of the program).

Additionally, I've included information about file conversions—how to enable your contacts who don't have Word 2010 or Word 2007 to read .docx files; how to save Word files to PDF; and how to convert between WordPerfect and Word (always with the proviso that you should never round-trip documents between the two formats because of the risk of corruption).

And I've revised the Resources section of the book, incorporating descriptions of a few tools (some specifically geared toward IT people) that Microsoft has made available to help companies migrate to Office 2010, adding some links to help you locate key files (in order to back them up on a regular basis and/or to transfer customizations from an earlier version of Word), and updating—as well as lengthening—the list of useful web sites.

What's Not Included

I'm not a macro guru, so I haven't covered macro writing in great detail. It's relatively easy to create macros that accomplish basic tasks—essentially it's a matter of recording keystrokes—but anything more complex, such as building customized dialog boxes, requires fluency in Visual Basic for Applications (VBA). That is beyond my abilities, and it's also beyond what most of my training clients want (or need) to learn. Instead, I've provided a gentle introduction to macros, illustrating the process with a simple example (creating a macro to print the current page, then adding a keyboard shortcut and toolbar button to run the macro).

Many people use the term "macros" rather loosely to refer to the insertion of boilerplate text such as signature blocks and standard paragraphs in contracts. These items can be created by using the Building Blocks / Quick Parts feature (formerly known as AutoText), something I also cover in the book.

Another feature I have de-emphasized to some degree is styles. A number of trainers and IT people swear by styles, and I agree that the uniform use of styles for headings, body text, and other formatting makes sense in large firms where consistency in the appearance of documents is at once highly desirable and somewhat difficult to accomplish. I believe, as well, that it's important for all Word users to have enough fluency with styles to be able to apply them where necessary, troubleshoot them, and remove them where they're problematic.

However, for some users styles are neither necessary nor desirable. They add a layer of complexity that can make working with Word intimidating and frustrating, which in turn can cause legal staff to resist learning the program. That is particularly true for people who are migrating to Word from WordPerfect—a program that allows for the creation and use of styles but downplays them. Also, in an environment where people often face strict deadlines, taking time to ensure that styles have been applied methodically throughout a given document can mean an unacceptable delay in the work flow. (I'm a firm believer in using particular features of a program like Word only when and to the extent that those features enhance productivity.)

Thus, I have made a conscious—if seemingly heretical—choice to cover only the essentials of working with styles, recognizing that firms that depend heavily on styles can find comprehensive instructions elsewhere. Even so, I think my treatment of styles is sufficiently detailed to give you a solid grounding and avoid some common pitfalls associated with their use.

Screenshots

I have used screenshots as visual aids where I thought they would make it easier to follow the step-by-step instructions. (In fact, I have made much greater use of screenshots in this book than in the Word 2007 book.) Note that images on your screen might not look exactly the same as those in the book as a result of customization (at your end or mine), disparities in printer drivers (which can affect the appearance of text on the screen), and/or differences between the various editions of the program.

Organization of the Book

Although I based this book to some extent on the Word 2007 book, I've modified the organization dramatically. In particular, I have tried to group the tutorials in a more logical fashion and, at the same time, have changed the emphasis in significant ways. Among other changes, I have focused more attention on customizing the interface, both because it is the first thing that people see when they launch the program and because many people who have upgraded say they miss the traditional toolbars and menus from earlier versions of Word. Also, as you will discover, it is much easier to customize the Ribbon in Word 2010 than it was in Word 2007 (in Word 2007, you pretty much had to learn XML programming!).

Moreover, I've devoted a separate section of the book to features that help users automate their documents and that otherwise tend to increase efficiency. I've divided other sections according to the **_functionality_** of particular features: everyday features, features that help you work with mailings and forms, and features that help you work with legal-specific documents (pleadings, contracts, and estate documents).

In large part, the book moves from the general to the specific. It begins with a brief look at some of the most significant differences between Word 2010 and previous versions of the program—new features, modified features, and features that have been removed. Although some readers undoubtedly already are familiar with the drastically changed interface introduced in Word 2007, I have provided a road map for those of you who are upgrading from Word 2003 or an even older edition. I've also listed numerous online resources, including interactive guides, to help you figure out where your frequently used commands have gone.

Additionally, I explore certain features unique to Word 2010—most notably the "Backstage View," an expanded File drop-down that has replaced the Office button; the Navigation Pane, a feature that combines aspects of the Find feature, the Document Map, Browse by Object, and Thumbnails; and Co-authoring, a robust collaboration tool—as well as enhancements (including improved customization options) and altered functionality.

After sketching the key differences between Word 2010 and Word 2007, I review the features that were changed in major respects in Word 2007 but that remain essentially the same in this version. This section of the book is meant mainly to introduce people who are upgrading from Word 2003 (or earlier) to the most significant changes between the "traditional" versions and the "modern" versions of the program.

Next, I cover what I consider the key to success in using Word to format complex documents: understanding the program's "logic." This somewhat theoretical section presents a brief comparison of the essential underpinnings of both Word and WordPerfect, but it is intended for **_all_** users, even those who have never worked with WordPerfect. The discussion that follows about how Word works "under the hood"—and in particular, its singular emphasis on paragraph and section formatting—will give you insights as well as diagnostic tools you'll need to troubleshoot problems that otherwise might be maddeningly obscure.

Once I have gone over those fundamentals, I offer tips to help you make the program more user-friendly—and, in particular, how to get it to work the way <u>you</u> want it to. Some simple customizations to the interface, such as adding buttons to the Quick Access Toolbar, can improve your efficiency dramatically (because it puts the features you use most often within easy reach). Also, Word has lots of built-in keyboard shortcuts that can save you oodles of time and wasteful mouse clicks, and it's easy to set up additional shortcuts of your own.

One aspect of making Word 2010 more user-friendly involves tweaking it so that it works more or less like pre-Word 2007 versions of the program. I provide instructions for modifying the default font face and size and the default line spacing—which Microsoft changed from earlier versions when it introduced Word 2007. And I explain how to set your own defaults by modifying the default Style Set and Theme, as well as the Normal paragraph style, heading styles, and various other elements of the program.

The next part of the book concentrates on selected features legal staffers use every day but often find puzzling—adjusting page margins, inserting and formatting a date code, working with tabs, setting up "Quick Parts" (boilerplate text that you can insert in a document with a couple of keystrokes), indenting (via the Ruler and otherwise), tweaking line spacing and "before" and "after" paragraph spacing, and working with that all-important but somewhat enigmatic feature, headers and footers.

Following the more general sections of the book, I concentrate on legal document formatting. I begin with a new tutorial about creating pleading paper from scratch, then go into considerable detail about setting up and modifying case captions, inserting pleading footers, marking text for inclusion in a Table of Contents (TOC), marking citations for inclusion in a Table of Authorities (TOA), and generating a TOC and a TOA. I also discuss, and provide some workarounds for, the common problem of aligning text with pleading line numbers.

Toward the end of the book, I proffer some general troubleshooting tips. Also, because so many firms are moving from WordPerfect to Word, or use both programs, I touch upon some of the typical issues involved in converting between the two, with some cautions against the ill-advised practice of "round-tripping." And I briefly address concerns about metadata—"private" or confidential information embedded in your documents that can be revealed to others inadvertently unless you take active steps to remove it. (I explain how to use Word 2010's built-in tool for removing metadata, the Document Inspector.)

Finally, I list certain helpful resources, including links to web sites you might find useful as you explore the software.

Conventions Used in the Book

When describing keyboard shortcuts, I follow the convention of mentioning a sequence of keys to be used in combination, such as Ctrl Alt 1, without any linking character such as a plus sign between the keys (Ctrl+Alt+1). The context should make it clear that the keys are intended to be used together.

I have attempted to make it easier to follow step-by-step instructions by using boldface to emphasize items that should be clicked or pressed, such as a particular tab of the Ribbon, a group within a tab, a dialog box or task pane, a button or icon, or a keyboard shortcut.

In places, I use boldface and capital letters to make the following advisories stand out:

TIP or **QUICK TIP**: A helpful hint for using a feature more efficiently or, sometimes, for working around a problem.

WORKAROUND: Just that. A method of bypassing something that you find problematic, whether an actual bug in the program or whether it's "Working As Designed" (a term of art that you'll occasionally see abbreviated—though not in this book—as "WAD").

NOTE: Something to keep in mind—typically advice that might or might not apply to your situation, but is worth taking into account when you are working with a feature.

CAUTION: A warning about a potential glitch or unexpected/unintended result.

SIDEBAR: A brief section that is peripherally related to the previous section or chapter.

An aside about a new convention in this book, the use of so-called "**tiny URLs**." As I reviewed the Word 2007 book, it occurred to me that many of the links to Internet sites, which made use of their original URLs (web addresses), were extremely long. In order to make it easier for readers to use the links, I have translated several of them into shorter URLs, using the free online service "TinyURL," which is located at http://tinyurl.com. When you copy and paste a lengthy web address for conversion to a shorter one, you have the option of letting the site randomly assign a "tiny URL" for you (which usually results in a meaningless assortment of characters)   or you can type a "meaningful" one. Sometimes the meaningful URLs you choose are already taken, in which case you'll have to try again. As always, my goal in providing these tiny URLs, and giving them meaningful names, is ease of use. I hope you find them helpful.

Second Printing

Because of unexpected changes in the policies governing the distribution of my books, I am reprinting/republishing this book as of early 2012. I have made only minor revisions since the first printing/publication in May of 2010. Therefore, the material in the section about the Web Apps might be somewhat out of date. If time permits, I will publish a true second edition of the book, incorporating the latest information about the Web Apps, later this year.

My Style

The book, like my training, is highly task-oriented. My foremost goal is to help you get your work done—as accurately, efficiently, smoothly, and quickly as possible.

I make an effort to use realistic examples (based on my own experience as a legal word processor, as well as issues that my clients have brought to my attention). Mixed in with the realism, I sometimes employ offbeat humor to keep my trainees / students alert during long sessions. It's just a technique; I've tried to use it sparingly so that it doesn't get in the way of the substantive points I'm trying to make.

Typically, my instructions about using a particular feature also include "background" or contextual information about that feature. My intention in providing that additional commentary is to make it easier to understand **when** to use the feature as well as **how** to use it. Often the contextual explanation also helps users recognize the limits of a feature or to help them work around its quirky behavior.

You might notice a certain amount of redundancy. A few tips appear in several places. There are a couple of reasons for the repetition. For one thing, much of the material in this book, as well as in the Word 2007 book, is adapted from training handouts comprising individual tutorials that are intended to stand on their own. Secondly, I recognize that people ordinarily don't read this type of book from cover to cover; instead, they flip through it, looking up particular features that they want to learn or that are causing them trouble. As a result, I have incorporated some tips into individual tutorials—when they seem pertinent—even though the same tips appear in a different context elsewhere in the book. And because it seems to me that the tips are important enough to bear repeating, I haven't attempted to eliminate the duplicates.

In closing, I want to emphasize that there is almost always more than one way to accomplish a particular task in Word. As my clients and my students know, I'm not presumptuous enough to think that my way of doing things is necessarily the "right" way. If you have a favorite method that differs from mine but works well for you, by all means use it. The whole point, after all, is to make the software do your bidding and get your work done in a timely and efficient manner.

We might take disparate approaches at times, but what matters is attaining a desirable end result with minimal frustration. And that, ultimately, is what I'm trying to achieve.

*   *   *   *   *

I hope the book proves useful to you. I welcome your constructive suggestions for ways to improve and enhance it (you can write c/o the e-mail address listed below), and I will incorporate the best ideas in future editions.

Jan Berinstein, Ph.D.
CompuSavvy
Computer Training & Consulting
Northridge, California
compusavvy2@earthlink.net
Winter, 2012

Migrating From an Earlier Version of Word

What's New and/or Different in Word 2010

If you're moving to Word 2010 from WordPerfect or from a version of Word prior to Word 2007, you'll notice some dramatic differences, primarily—but not solely—in the interface. However, if you're upgrading from Word 2007, you're already familiar with the Ribbon and other changes introduced in that version. Even so, Microsoft has made some tweaks to this latest version, many of which will be apparent as soon as you start working with the program.

I'll start by addressing the main differences between the new version and Word 2007. Those of you who are jumping straight from WordPerfect or from Word 2003 (or earlier) to Word 2010 might benefit by skipping ahead to the section about the features introduced in Word 2007 that persist in Word 2010 (starting with the information about the altered interface—the Ribbon and the Quick Access Toolbar) and then backtracking and reading this "What's New and/or Different" section.

Summary of the Major Changes Since Word 2007

Perhaps the most obvious change between Word 2007 and Word 2010 is the "**Backstage View**"—the expanded File drop-down that has replaced Word 2007's Office button (as well as the traditional File menu in previous versions of the program). Because it is one of the first aspects of the program that users encounter, and because of its importance and the fact that it appears in all Office 2010 programs, I'll explore this feature at length.

Other notable new and/or modified features include:

- "**Print Place**" – a radically redesigned full-page version of the Print dialog;

- the **Navigation Pane**, which combines aspects of the Find feature, the Document Map, Browse Objects, and Thumbnails;

- **Co-authoring**, a robust collaboration tool that allows several people to work on the same document simultaneously;

- a new **Save option** that automatically saves temporary drafts of files when you close without saving, in case you change your mind later on;

- enhanced **Paste options**, including preview functionality;

- **Protected View**, which allows you to review documents you download from e-mail (or from the Internet) before saving or editing them; and

- **Web Applications**—free versions of Office 2010 programs that are stored on the Internet so that you can work on your documents even if you don't have access to a computer with MS Office loaded on it.

Also, Microsoft has made it possible to **customize the Ribbon** in several respects, a change that will cheer the many users who felt frustrated by the limited customization options available in Word 2007.

I will discuss each of these features in considerable detail in this section of the book.

<u>**An In-Depth Look at What Has Changed**</u>

<u>The Backstage View / File Drop-Down</u>

Word 2010 comes with a substantially reworked File drop-down, which Microsoft calls the "**Backstage View**."[1] This drop-down replaces Word 2007's Office button (the multicolored orb in the upper left-hand corner of the Word 2007 screen) as well as the traditional File menu found in older versions of the program. Both the appearance and the functionality of this feature have changed.

Like the Office button and the File menu in previous versions, the Backstage View gives you easy access to your recently used files; lets you open, save, and close files; helps you start a new document based on an existing template; displays print options and page setup options; allows you to send documents via e-mail and other means; offers information about the current document; and includes a button for exiting the program. The Backstage View also serves as the portal to most configuration options for Word (called "Word Options" in previous versions but simply "Options" in Word 2010).

So that you can grasp quickly the basic ways in which the feature has changed, here is an at-a-glance comparison (simplified) of the traditional file menu in older versions of Word with the Word 2007 Office button and the Word 2010 Backstage View (File drop-down):

Traditional File Menu (Prior to Word 2007)	Word 2007 Office Button	Word 2010 Backstage View
New	New	Save
Templates	Open	Save As
Open	Save	Open
Close	Save As	Close
Save	Print	Info
Save As	Prepare	Recent
***	Send	New
Page Setup	Publish	Print
Print Preview	Close	Save & Send
Print	Word Options	Help
***	Exit Word	Options
Recently Used File List		Exit
Exit	(Recent Documents List at right)	

---

[1] Throughout this book, I use the terms "**Backstage View**" and "**File drop-down**" more or less interchangeably. (People might find the new terminology confusing, whereas I suspect everyone will understand what "File drop-down" means.) I also refer to the "**File tab**," which is what you click to open the Backstage View.

Navigating the Backstage View

To open the Backstage View, *either* (1) click the dark blue **File tab** at the upper left-hand side of the Word 2010 screen *or* (2) press **Alt F**—the same keyboard shortcut that opens the File drop-down in all earlier versions of Word.[2] (To close the Backstage View, simply click the File tab again, or click any other tab.)

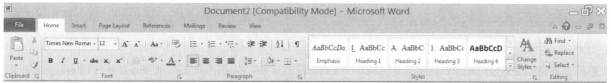

Click the File Tab (at Left) to Open the Backstage View

The first thing you'll notice is that the resulting drop-down (what I refer to throughout the book as a "**fly-out menu**" or simply a "**fly-out**") fills the entire screen.

Secondly, the familiar commands for working with documents are still present, albeit in an unfamiliar order: Save, Save As, Open, Close.

Thirdly, you'll see a different fly-out menu depending on whether or not you have a document open on screen. Specifically:

- When you first launch Word, before you open a file, the Backstage View displays the "**Recent**" fly-out.[3]

- When you already have a file open on your screen, the Backstage View opens to "**Info**."

In addition to Recent and Info, the Backstage View provides four other full-page fly-out menus: **New**, **Print**, **Save & Send**, and **Help**. Each fly-out groups a number of related commands that were somewhat scattered in prior versions of the program.

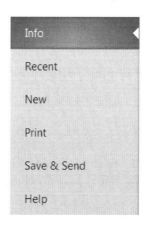

So, for example, the Print fly-out (now called "**Print Place**") includes not only all of the configuration options available in the standard Print dialog, but also a large print preview. Similarly, the Help fly-out lists information about the program, allows you to search online Help files, provides a link for contacting Microsoft directly, and also gives you ready access to the Word Options (available as well via the Options button at the bottom of the Backstage View).

---

[2] You might recall from Word 2007 that tapping **the Alt key alone** triggers "**mnemonics**" that are visible on the screen, making it easy to use keyboard shortcuts to carry out commands.

[3] At least, it does if you check the option to keep older versions of Word on your computer, rather than upgrading, when you install Office 2010.

In addition to the six fly-out menus, the Backstage View consists of commands for working with files (**Save**, **Save As**, **Open**, and **Close**) and for working with the program itself (**Options**—known as Word Options in previous versions—and **Exit**). The labels for the file and program commands appear in somewhat smaller text than the labels for the fly-outs, but they also are designated by icons, perhaps to make them easier to recognize at a glance.

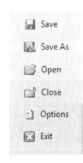

The "Recent" Fly-Out

As mentioned previously, the "Recent" fly-out menu appears when you first launch Word, before you have opened any documents. Also, you can produce this fly-out at any time by either clicking the **File tab**, **Recent** or pressing the key combination **Alt F, R**.

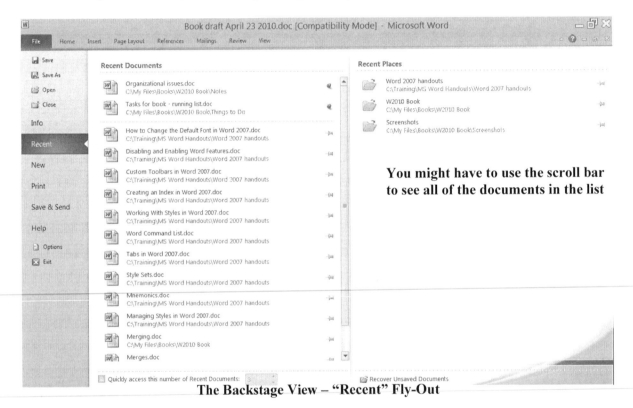

The Backstage View – "Recent" Fly-Out

The number of recent documents showing on the Recent fly-out is determined by a setting in the **Word Options**. To view or change this setting, press **Alt F, T**[4] or click the **File tab**, then click **Options**, **Advanced**, **Display**, "**Show this number of Recent Documents**." If you prefer not to show any recent documents, you can set the number to 0 (zero). Otherwise, you can set it to any integer between 1 and 50. (How many documents actually will display on your screen depends on the size of your screen as well as your screen resolution.)

If you choose to display a large number of recently opened documents, you'll probably have to scroll down to see all of the documents in the list. See the screenshot above.

---

[4] **NOTE**: In Word 2007, the keyboard shortcut for opening the Word Options is Alt F, I.

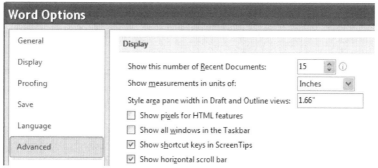

Show this number of Recent Documents
(Word Options, Advanced, Display)

Another Way to Display Recent Documents

In Word 2007, the Recent Documents List is an integral part of the File drop-down. As a result, it is visible most of the time (and appears, by default, at the right side of the drop-down). In Word 2010, by contrast, if a document is open on your screen, you'll see the Info fly-out rather than the Recent Documents List when you open the Backstage View. In other words, the Recent Documents List isn't visible unless/until you specifically click "**Recent.**"

However, there is a way to show your recent files whenever you open the File drop-down. Click the "Recent" command and then navigate to the very bottom of the fly-out. Note that there is an option labeled "**Quickly access this number of Recent Documents.**"

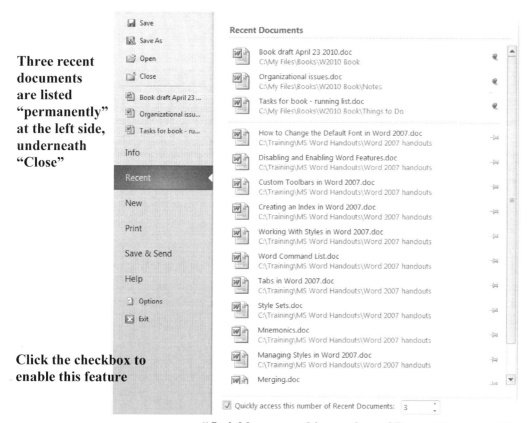

Three recent documents are listed "permanently" at the left side, underneath "Close"

Click the checkbox to enable this feature

"Quickly access this number of Recent Documents"

To activate the option, you must **click to put a check in the checkbox**, as in the screenshot immediately below this paragraph. You can set the number of documents to display at left by typing an integer or by using the up / down arrows ("spinners").

The number of files you choose to display on the left side of the File drop-down does not have to match the number you've set in Word Options.[5] For example, in Word Options, Advanced, Display, I've chosen to display 15 recent documents, but I have configured the "Quickly access" option to show only three recent documents "permanently." You'll see that there are, in fact, three documents listed at the left side of the screenshot (underneath the "Close" command). That list of recent documents will remain visible at the left even if / when I click another of the major / large commands (and another fly-out opens), such as Info, New, or Print.

NOTE: The "Quick Access" list puts pinned documents, if any, first and then lists the next items in the Recent Files list in sequence.

"Pinning" Documents

In both Word 2007 and Word 2010, you can "pin" one or more of your recent documents to the top of the Recent Documents list to prevent it / them from scrolling off the list as you open additional files. To pin a document, simply click the pin to the right of the document name in the list (see the screenshot on this page). (Alternatively, you can right-click a document and then choose the "Pin to list" option.) To unpin a pinned file, click the pin again.

Pinned and Unpinned Recent Documents   **Right-click a file in the list to see other options**

Recent Places

At the right side of the Recent fly-out menu, there is a "Recent Places" section. This portion of the fly-out keeps track of folders that you have opened recently. If you like, you can pin one or more of the folders to keep it handy.

---

[5] However, it must be smaller than or equal to the Word Options setting.

You can right-click an item in the "Recent Places" list in order to open a particular folder, pin it to the list, remove it from the list, or clear all of the unpinned folders from the list. The screenshot at right shows the context-sensitive menu that appears when you right-click one of the folders in the list.

Open
Pin to list
Remove from list
Clear unpinned Places

Working With Recent Documents: Right-Click Options

As with the "Recent Places" list, right-clicking any file in the "Recent Files" list produces a context menu. The menu offers the following options:

- Open
- Open a copy
- Pin to list
- Remove from list
- Clear unpinned documents

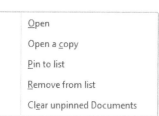

This convenient tool for working with recent documents is new in Word 2010. NOTE: The right-click menu does ***not*** appear if you right-click a file in the "menu" portion at the left side of the fly-out (i.e., documents you've placed there by clicking the "Quickly access this number of recent documents" link).

Recover Unsaved Documents

At the bottom right side of the "Recent" fly-out, there is an additional option: "**Recover Unsaved Documents**."

Recover Unsaved Documents

This option works in conjunction with a Save option new to this version of Word (see the section starting on page 65) that automatically creates a temporary backup file when you close a document without saving it. Word stores these temporary files (in .asd format[6]) in an "UnsavedFiles" folder.[7] It keeps them for four days, but will delete a draft sooner if you open one of the files and save it normally before four days have elapsed.

---

[6] Word also saves AutoRecover files, another type of temporary backup, in .asd format. I'll explain the differences between "Unsaved Documents" and AutoRecover files shortly.

[7] In Windows XP, copies of documents you close without saving are stored here: C:\Documents and Settings\User Name\Local Settings\Application Data\Microsoft\OFFICE\ UnsavedFiles

In Windows Vista and Windows 7, you can find them here: C:\Users\<UserName>\AppData\Local\Microsoft\Office\ UnsavedFiles

When you click the "Recover Unsaved Documents" link, Word opens your "UnsavedFiles" folder so that you can reopen one or more of the temporary files into Word if you so choose. Once you've done so, you can save them as a .docx or a .doc (or in one of the other formats Word 2010 supports).

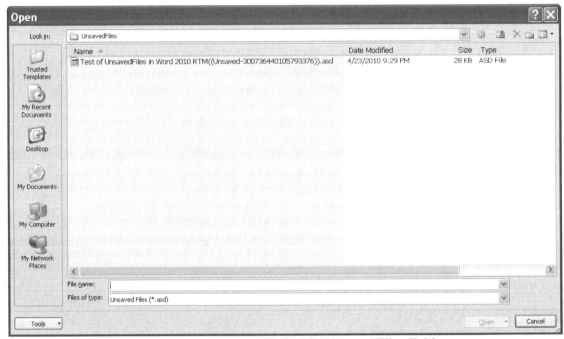

Temporary (Unsaved) File in My UnsavedFiles Folder

Upon opening an unsaved file, you'll see a message underneath the Ribbon alerting you to the fact that the document is a recovered unsaved file that is temporarily stored on your computer. (It will be deleted within four days unless you click the "Save As" button at the right side of the message.)

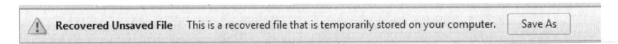

If you want to keep the file permanently, click the "Save As" button; when the Save As dialog opens, move the file to a different folder and, if necessary, give it a new name. If you don't care whether the file is deleted, click the "X" at the right side of the message to close the file.

Unsaved Documents Versus AutoRecover Files

These temporary files, which Microsoft calls "Unsaved Documents" (and which I will refer to as either the "**Unsaved Documents**" or the "**Closed Without Saving**" files)[8], are *not the same* as the temporary "**AutoRecover**" **files** (also called "**autosaved**" **file**s) that Word creates every few minutes while you are working on a document.

The AutoRecover files, which are stored in a different location from the "Unsaved Documents" ("Closed Without Saving") backups[9], are intended only as *emergency backup files*. Under normal circumstances, they are deleted when you exit from Word. However, if the program freezes or you experience a crash or other abnormal termination of Word, the AutoRecover files are preserved. They will appear in a pane at the left side of the screen the next time you open the program so that you can restore them (which you probably will want to do if they happen to be newer than the last draft you saved).

Unfortunately, Microsoft has blurred the lines between the AutoRecover files and the Unsaved Documents by including a somewhat misleadingly named "Versions" button in the Info fly-out alongside a list of the autosaved (AutoRecover) versions of the current document. Because of the proximity of two items, when you click the "Versions" button you expect to see a complete list of the autosaved (AutoRecover) drafts. *Instead, Word opens the folder where the Unsaved Documents are stored.* For more on this confusing issue, see the section about "Manage Versions," starting on page 21.

For more about the Unsaved Documents, as well as the new "Close" prompt, see the section starting on page 65.

---

[8] "Closed Without Saving" is a term that you will encounter from time to time if you are using the beta version of Word 2010. Microsoft appears to have abandoned this term in favor of "Unsaved Documents" in the official release.

[9] Specifically, the AutoRecover (.asd) files are stored in the following locations:

In Windows XP:
C:\Documents and Settings\<User Name>\Application Data\Microsoft\Word

In Vista and Windows 7:
C:\Users\<User Name>\AppData\Roaming\Microsoft\Word

The "Info" Fly-Out

When you have at least one document open (even a blank one), clicking the File drop-down produces the "Info" fly-out, which gives you easy access to in-depth information about the active document (the one currently in the document-editing screen).

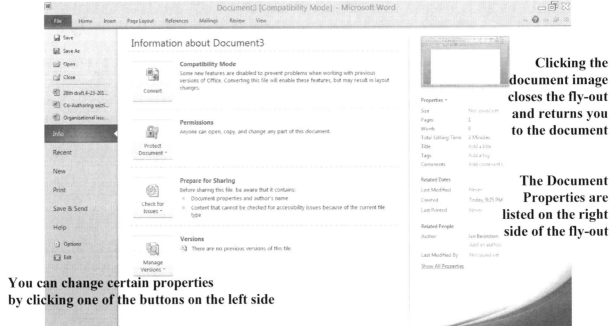

The Backstage View – "Info" Fly-Out

Similar to "**Properties**" in previous versions (found under the Office button, Prepare in Word 2007 and on the File menu in Word 2003), Word 2010's Info fly-out helps you keep track of a tremendous amount of information about the current document.

The Info fly-out consists of two portions. The left side, labeled "Information about [Document Name]," is a sort of "action" area, where you can do any of the following:

    (1)   convert the active document into a different format,

    (2)   change the permissions,

    (3)   check for metadata and other potential "issues" that might arise when you share the document with others, and/or

    (4)   open an earlier "autosaved" version of the current document, or

    (5)   open a draft of one of the documents that Word automatically backed up when you closed without saving.[10]

---

[10] The way numbers (4) and (5) work is somewhat confusing. See the discussions that start on page 22 and page 65.

The right side is a collection of statistics, divided into a few subcategories (Properties, Related Dates, Related People, and Related Documents). There's a truncated snapshot of your document just above the **Properties drop-down**; you can click the image to close the fly-out menu and return to the document editing screen.

Properties ▾	
Size	14.5MB
Pages	518
Words	128656
Total Editing Time	24 Minutes
Title	Add a title
Tags	Add a tag
Comments	Add comments

The **Properties** section of the flyout also provides information about various characteristics of your document: Size, Pages, Words, Total Editing Time, Title, Tags (if any), Comments (if any). You can add a title, tags, or comments if you like by clicking the "Add…" area ("Add a title," "Add a tag," "Add comments," etc.), then typing some text.

Under **Related Dates**, it shows the Last Modified date/time, the Created date/time, and the Last Printed date/time.

Related Dates	
Last Modified	Today, 10:24 PM
Created	Today, 10:11 PM
Last Printed	4/15/2010 5:21 PM

Under **Related People**, it shows the author and the person who last modified the document. Note that you can add other authors by clicking "Add…".

Related People	
Author	Jan Berinstein
	Add an author
Last Modified By	Jan Berinstein

Under **Related Documents**, there is a folder icon labeled "Open File Location." When you click that icon, Word will open Windows Explorer to the folder where the current file is stored so that you can view or work with other files in that folder.

Related Documents
📁 Open File Location
Show All Properties

The Properties Drop-Down

You can display still more characteristics of the document by clicking the **Properties drop-down** and selecting either **Show Document Panel** or **Advanced Properties**.

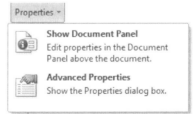

At the bottom of the Properties list, there is a link labeled "**Show All Properties**." When you click the link, Word displays additional document properties; the link label then changes to read "**Show Fewer Properties**."

Click the "Show Fewer Properties" link to collapse the properties list.

Show Document Panel

This command produces a so-called "**Document Panel**" (sometimes called the "Document Information Panel"), a sort of Properties Toolbar that appears between the Ribbon and the active document.

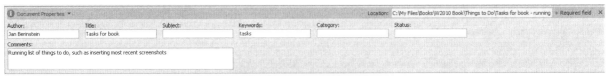

The Document Panel

Typically, the only fields that are filled in are the Author and Location fields. (You cannot delete the Location field from the Document Panel, although you can use the Metadata Inspector tool to remove the other information.[11]) In the screenshot above, there is text in the Title, Keywords, and Comments fields because I deliberately added a title, tags, and comments via the Properties portion of the Info fly-out.

Advanced Properties

Note the "Document Properties" drop-down at the top left side of the panel. When you click it, you will see a link to the Advanced Properties.

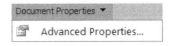

Clicking the link produces the standard **Properties dialog** that appears in older versions of Word (see the screenshots below), with the same set of tabs: General, Summary, Statistics, Contents, and Custom.

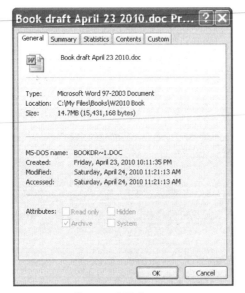

General Tab

Statistics Tab

---

[11] See the section on metadata, starting on page 555.

This dialog also opens if you click the Advanced Properties option directly from the Properties drop-down in the fly-out.

To close the Document Panel, click the "X" at the far right side (to the right of the words "Required Field").

Location: C:\My Files\Books\W2010 Book\Book draft April 23 2010.doc   * Required field   X

Show All Properties

When you click "**Show All Properties**," Word expands the list of properties, adding several fields under the main "Properties" heading: Template, Status, Categories, Subject, Hyperlink Base, and Company. All of those fields except "Template" are editable. In other words, you can add notes, comments, or other information. (The other fields are populated automatically.) Under "Related People," the expanded list shows one new item: "Manager."

The screenshot at right shows the expanded Properties for my book draft.

All of the editable fields display text in pale gray, indicating that you can add information. Just click in one of the fields and start typing. The text you type will remain with the document until and unless you delete it or type something else.

To compress the list, click the "**Show Fewer Properties**" link at the very bottom. (You might have to use the scroll bar in order to see that link.)

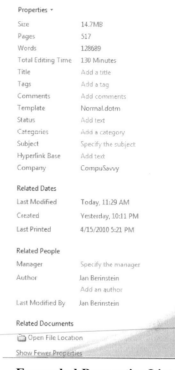

Expanded Properties List

Manipulating the Document Properties

The icons at the left side of the Information fly-out let you alter the properties of the current document in a number of ways. These icons allow you to configure the following items:

Compatibility Mode / Convert

When you are working in Compatibility Mode (i.e., using the .doc format), the fly-out displays an additional button, one labeled "Compatibility Mode."[12] Clicking the button produces a message box similar to the one depicted on the next page.

---

[12] Not surprisingly, the Convert icon isn't available when the current document is a .docx. It does appear, however, if you open a document that is in a different file format, such as a .wpd (WordPerfect document), a Rich Text Format file (.rtf), or an XML file (.xml).

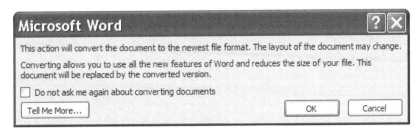

In other words, this option gives you a quick way to convert a .doc into a .docx. Note the warnings, however, about possible changes to the layout of the document upon conversion ("The layout of the document may change").

If you click OK, the program will convert your .doc into a .docx. You might not realize that the conversion has occurred, because the Title Bar likely will continue to show the file name followed by the .doc extension. Once you save the converted file, however, the Title Bar will show it as a .docx.

If you click "Tell Me More…," Word opens a Help article entitled "Use Word 2010 to open documents created in earlier versions of Word." The article explains that there actually are three different Word file types: .doc, which is Word 97-2003 "Compatibility Mode," as well as a Word 2007 version of the .docx and a Word 2010 version of the .docx. Apparently the original .docx format doesn't support certain new features of the program, including new shapes and text boxes, text effects, alternative text in tables, OpenType features, the ability to block authors (part of the innovative Co-Authoring function), new WordArt effects, and new content controls.

Note that when you click OK to convert the .doc to a .docx, Word doesn't ask which .docx format you wish to use. Presumably it converts the .doc to the newer .docx file format. That should suit most people's needs, but be aware that if you send the converted .docx file to someone who uses Word 2007 and doesn't have Office 2010 installed, the recipient won't have access to any newer features the document contains, and the layout might be different for that person as a result.

Permissions / Protect Document

The **Permissions** option encompasses several different methods for limiting access to the current document:

- Mark as Final

- Encrypt with Password

- Restrict Editing

- Add a Digital Signature

Mark as Final
Let readers know the document is final and make it read-only.

Encrypt with Password
Require a password to open this document.

Restrict Editing
Control what types of changes people can make to this document.

Add a Digital Signature
Ensure the integrity of the document by adding an invisible digital signature.

NOTE: Your ability to set these types of permissions might be limited by your organization's policies and procedures.

As discussed on page 518, the **Mark as Final** choice is not particularly restrictive (and it's less restrictive than Encrypt with Password). When you mark a document as final, Word applies the "Read-Only" attribute to it; anyone who opens the document will find editing options grayed out. However, it's a trivial matter to turn off the "Read-Only" attribute. By contrast, when you password-protect a document, no one can open it unless they know the password.

To apply a password to the current document, click the **Encrypt with Password** button.[13] An "**Encrypt Document**" **dialog** will open. **Type a password** into the box—make note of the password (mentally and/or in writing), keeping in mind that passwords are case-sensitive—and click "**OK**." Doing so will open a "**Confirm Password**" **dialog**; **type the password again** (with care to type it exactly as you did the first time), and then click "**OK**."

After you apply a password to your document, the Info fly-out will add this notification:

CAUTION: *You must save the document* in order for the password to take effect. If you close without saving, the password will not be applied, and anyone with access to your computer will be able to open the document.

If you are working in Compatibility Mode, you might see a message similar to the following when you first save the document after adding a password:

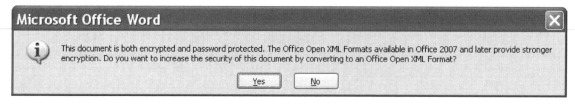

Essentially, the message is asking if you want to convert the file to the new .docx format. I didn't want to convert this particular document to a .docx file, so I clicked "No."

---

[13] Also, you can add a password the first time you save a document. After naming the document, click the **Tools button** at the lower left side of the **Save As dialog**, then click "**General Options**." When the **General Options dialog** opens, **type a new password**—be sure to make note of it—then click "**OK**." When prompted, type it again and click "**OK**," then click "**Save**."

Assuming that you have saved the document (and have succeeded in applying the password), the next time someone attempts to open the document, a **Password dialog** will appear and prompt the user to **type a password**. The password must match—exactly—the password you applied when you saved the document. If it does, clicking "**OK**" will open the file.

The **Restrict Editing** command effectively prevents certain types of editing and/or keeps certain individuals from working on the document.

When you click "**Restrict Editing**," the **Restrict Formatting and Editing Pane** opens at the right side of the screen (see the screenshot at right). You can change the settings in this pane to prevent people from altering the current document at all (by making it read-only). You can also limit other people's ability to create their own styles within the document or to turn off track changes, and you can allow them to insert comments only in certain "regions" of the document. In addition, you can control their ability to fill in form fields in the document.

To apply any restrictions that you have selected from the various drop-downs in the pane, you *must* click the "**Yes, Start Enforcing Protection**" **button**.

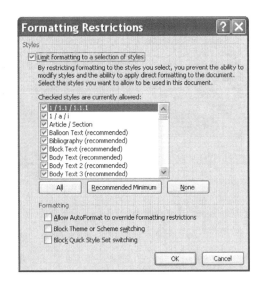

For more information about the Restrict Editing option, see page 518.

Finally, if your organization has purchased a digital signature, you can add one to a document by clicking the **Add a Digital Signature** button. (A digital signature can be a useful way of assuring the recipient of a document that it did, indeed, come from its purported—legitimate—source.) If neither you nor your organization has obtained / installed a digital signature, clicking the button will produce a message box similar to the one below.

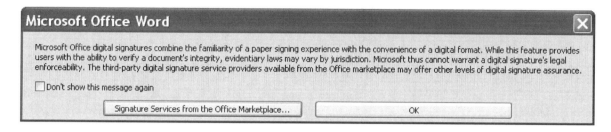

If you click "Signature Services from the Office Marketplace…," the Internet Explorer browser will open to a page where you can read more about several different types of digital signatures offered by various companies. The page contains links to those companies' web sites.

As with some of the other "permissions" options, your ability to use this feature could be limited by your organization's IT department or the company's management.

Prepare for Sharing / Check for Issues

The Prepare for Sharing option reminds you to review your document before sending it to someone else to make sure it doesn't contain sensitive, confidential, or otherwise problematic content. In particular, it is designed to prevent you from forwarding a document that includes "metadata"—identifying information about the document (dates created or modified, location in the computer, length, size, revision number, etc.), the computer(s) on which it was created and/or modified, the author(s), and so forth—as well as hidden text, comments, and revision marks (redlining and strikeout).

As soon as you open the Info. fly-out, Word starts searching the current document for any possible "issues."

Prepare for Sharing
Before sharing this file, be aware that it contains:
⠿ Searching for issues

It looks for document properties that you might not want others to see (author's name, printer path, related dates, etc.); headers and footers; hidden text; custom XML data; and so forth.

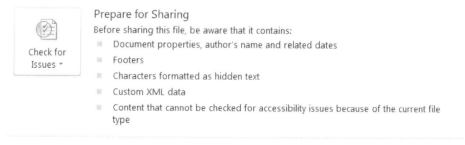

17

When you click the "Check for Issues" drop-down, Word offers three different ways of reviewing your document for potential problems: Inspect Document, Check Accessibility, and Check Compatibility.[14] The "Inspect Document" option is the same as that in Word 2007, except that the description of the feature in Word 2010 uses the phrase "hidden properties" instead of "hidden metadata."

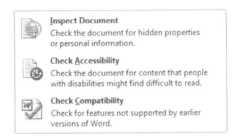

The Document Inspector

The Document Inspector, a built-in metadata removal utility, was introduced in Word 2007. I discuss this feature in detail later in the book. See the section starting on page 555.

The Accessibility Checker

The Accessibility Checker, which is new in Word 2010, works only in .docx files. When you click the "Check Accessibility" button, the utility examines your document, looking for various items that, according to Microsoft, can make a document harder to read, especially for a person with disabilities. These items have to do with the way that tables, headings, hyperlinks, images, and so forth are laid out and formatted in your document.

For instance, the Accessibility Checker will point out potential problems such as a table that lacks a header row, headings that are formatted as body text, and/or excessive white space. When the utility finds problems, it identifies the problems in an pane that opens at the right side of the screen. Clicking one of the items in the top portion of the pane produces an "Additional Information" box that explains why the item merits attention and provides information about how to fix it.

I ran a test with a .docx that included a table without a header row (among other accessibility issues), and the Accessibility Checker caught it. When I clicked the second item in the "Errors" box, Table (under "No Header Row Specified," the "Additional Information" box appeared at the bottom of the pane with "Why Fix" and "How To Fix" suggestions.

---

[14] In Word 2007, Inspect Document and Run Compatibility Checker were part of the Prepare fly-out from the Office button / File drop-down. There was no equivalent to the Accessibility Checker.

Similarly, when I typed some numbers in a table but (deliberately) left one row blank, the Accessibility Checker warned me that "Blank table cells can mislead a person with a vision disability into thinking there is nothing more in the table." The "Additional Information" section advised me to delete unnecessary blank cells or, alternatively, to clear all table styles from the table (and explained how to clear the styles).

In another test, I discovered that the Accessibility Checker also flags headings that are longer than one line.

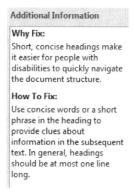

Obviously, you can choose to make the suggested changes or leave the document as is. Either way, it can be helpful to know how accessible the document is to people with disabilities.

For more about accessibility features in the Office 2010 suite, see:
http://blogs.technet.com/office2010/archive/2010/01/07/office-2010-accessibility-investments-document-accessibility.aspx

The Compatibility Checker

The compatibility checker is used primarily to let you know which of the newer features of Word won't translate well if someone opens your Word 2010 .docx file in an earlier version of the program.

For instance, if you have inserted SmartArt into a .docx, when you click the button to run the compatibility checker, a dialog box will open and advise you that the SmartArt "features may be lost or degraded when opening this document in an earlier version of Word or if you save this document in an earlier file format." (See the screenshot on the next page.)

The Compatibility Checker dialog box summarizes the feature(s) that are affected, what will happen on backwards conversion, and how many occurrences of the feature exist in the document.

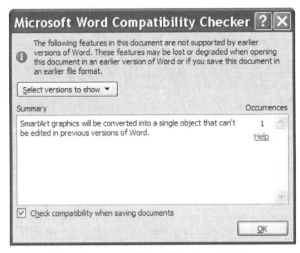

The Compatibility Checker Dialog

Some of the other features (besides Smart Art) that don't work in prior versions of Word, or that don't work the same way, include:

- Charts

- Images

- Equations

- Themes (will be converted permanently to *styles* in earlier versions of Word)

- Content Controls (will be converted permanently to *static text*)

- Bibliography and Citations (will be converted permanently to *static text*)

- Tracked Moves (will be converted permanently to **Insert** and **Delete**)

- Custom XML Datastore (will be lost permanently if the binary .doc is saved or edited in Word 97-2003)

- Text Boxes with Vertical Alignment (will be converted permanently to use ***Top vertical alignment***)

- Relative Positioned Text Boxes (will be converted permanently to ***absolute positioned*** text boxes)

If you attempt to save a .docx as a .doc, you'll see a slightly different version of the Compatibility Checker dialog, notifying you of the features that will be lost or degraded and prompting you to continue or cancel.

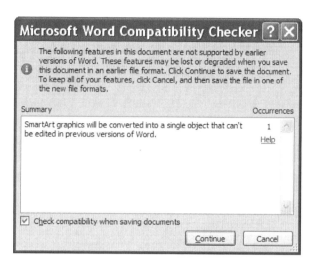

Clicking "Continue" will convert the file. Note that if you ever convert the .doc back to a .docx, some of the newer features that aren't functional in Compatibility Mode will work again. These features include SmartArt, Charts, Images, and Equations.

For more information about the Compatibility Checker, see this blog post by the Microsoft Developers' Team: http://blogs.msdn.com/microsoft_office_word/archive/2006/10/13/compatibility-in-word-2007-part-iv.aspx

Versions / Manage Versions

As discussed in the sections about the AutoRecover options and the new "Close / Save" options (see pages 9 and 65), Word periodically creates temporary backup copies of the current open document (i.e., the one that is active). By default, the program automatically saves these backup files every ten minutes, although you can change this interval if you so choose. This process is referred to as "**autosaving**," and each draft saved in this manner is referred to as an "**autosaved**" or "**autorecovered**" version.

Once Word has saved a draft, a list of the autosaved version(s)—if any—will appear at the bottom of the Info fly-out. For example, the next screenshot shows that Word has created autosaved versions of the draft of this book several times in the past hour-plus.[15]

---

[15] You might notice that the autosave intervals appear somewhat irregular. The reason is that the autosave function doesn't kick in at the normally scheduled time if you save a document yourself (by pressing Ctrl S, clicking the "Save" icon in the Quick Access Toolbar, or clicking the File tab, then clicking "Save") before the ten minute interval for automatic backups has elapsed. Apparently the clock starts ticking again after you manually save the document.

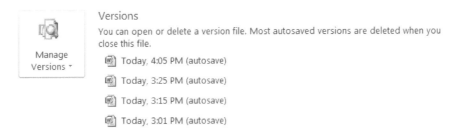

To restore one of the autosaved drafts, click it. The draft will open as a read-only .asd file with "(Autosaved Version)" appearing in the title bar. At that point, you can save it permanently (with a different name, in a different folder, and as either a .docx or a .doc).

The Title Bar, Indicating the File is a Read-Only AutoSaved Version

If you have manually saved the document more recently than Word's auto-save function kicked in, you'll see a warning above the document editing screen similar to the one below:

To see the differences between the autosaved version and the one you saved manually, click the "Compare" button. When you do, Word runs a Document Compare and opens a new window displaying the redlined (compared) document, the original document, the revised version of the document, and a summary of the additions, deletions, moves, and/or other changes (if any).

The "Manage Versions" Button

To the left of the list of autosaved versions at the bottom of the Info fly-out, there is a button labeled "Manage Versions." ***This label is misleading***.

Most people probably assume that "Manage Versions" refers to autosaved files (i.e., the temporary backups Word saves every ten minutes and, ordinarily, deletes when you exit from the program). That's a natural assumption because of the button's proximity to the list of autosaved files and because Microsoft uses the term "Versions" to describe the autosaved files. (Also, in the beta, there is text to the right of the button that reads, "You can open or delete a version file. Most autosaved versions are deleted when you close this file." This text has been removed.)

When you click the "Manage Versions" button, a drop-down opens. Under most circumstances, the drop-down offers one choice: **Recover Unsaved Documents**. (If you are working on a document that you ***have never saved***, another choice will be available: **Delete All Unsaved Documents**.)

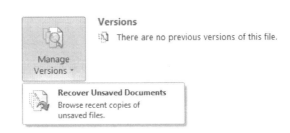

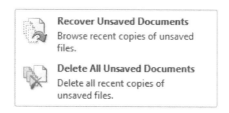

The first hint that this drop-down might not have anything to do with the autosaved files comes from a careful reading of the text underneath "**Recover Unsaved Documents**." That text reads: "Browse recent copies of unsaved files." The key phrase here is "*unsaved files*."

In fact, when you click "**Recover Unsaved Documents**," Word opens the UnsavedFiles folder and reveals the Unsaved ("closed without saving") Documents, *not* the temporary (AutoRecover) backups that Word saves every few minutes.

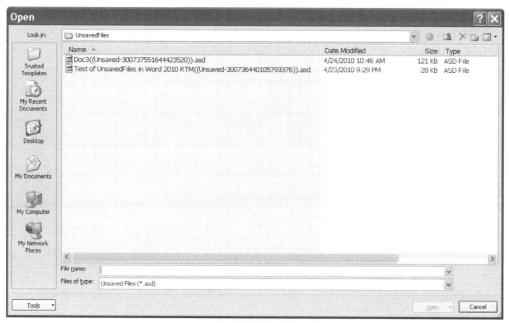

Clicking "Recover Unsaved Documents" Opens the UnsavedFiles Folder

It's helpful to have easy access to the Unsaved ("closed without saving") Documents, but I suspect most people will click the button in the mistaken belief that it will allow them to browse through the autosave files, rather than the Unsaved Documents. It might be less confusing if Microsoft moved, or at least re-labeled, this button.

As useful as this feature can be, there might be occasions when you don't want to retain Unsaved Documents—for instance, when you are using someone else's computer (or a computer in a public place, such as a library). What should you do in those circumstances?

First, click the Managed Versions button on the Info fly-out; you should see an option labeled "Delete All Unsaved Documents." If that doesn't work, you can try opening the UnsavedFiles folder and deleting your Unsaved Documents manually from there (but if you do so, be careful not to delete any Unsaved Documents that might have been created by another user).

The "New" Fly-Out

This fly-out menu is for creating a blank document or creating a document based on a built-in or customized template. It is divided into three sections: Available Templates, Office.com Templates, and Blank document / Create.

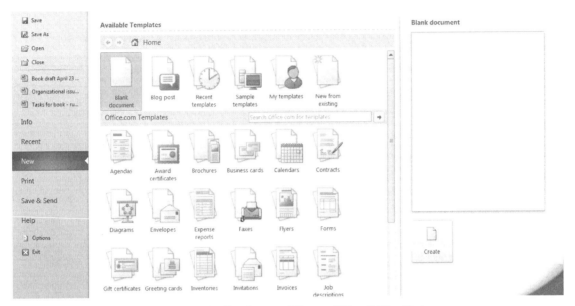

The Backstage View—"New" Fly-Out

Available Templates

The Available Templates section gives you easy access to your existing custom templates, as well as about three dozen built-in templates for letters, faxes, reports, resumes, and newsletters (which you can view by clicking "Samples"). It also allows you to create a new blank document, as well as to open a copy of an existing document, which you can then save as a different document or as a template (the "New from Existing" option).

Office.com Templates

The Office.com templates section provides links to a variety of forms available online from Microsoft. If you have just begun using Word and haven't made use of this option, you should see just a few categories, such as Budgets, Business cards, Calendars, Faxes, Forms, Gift certificates, Invoices, Minutes, Planners, Plans, and More Categories. If you click "More Categories," Word displays additional types of templates that you can download. (The screenshot above shows lots of categories because I've downloaded additional templates from Office.com.)

If you are connected to the Internet and you click an icon for a category of templates, such as calendars, Word displays various downloadable samples. When you click one, you can see a preview at the right side of the screen, along with a "Download" button. I experimented by downloading a simple 2010 calendar (one of several available styles) that I was able to start using right away.

CAUTION: After you download a template from the Office.com site, that portion of the "New" fly-out becomes pre-populated with numerous icons reflecting other types of categories you can obtain from the site. The resulting screen is somewhat cluttered visually (similar to the one shown in the previous screenshot), which can be a little overwhelming.

Another thing you can do while online is search for other categories of templates. Just type a word or phrase (such as "pleading") in the box to the right of the Office.com Templates label, then clicking the arrow. (Note that when my search with the word "pleading" returned only four pleading templates, none of which was entirely suitable for California. One of them did have 28 numbered lines, but in other respects it didn't conform to California rules.)

Once you have clicked any option other than "Blank Document," you can click the "Home" icon to return to the default view of the fly-out.

Blank Document

This aspect of the New fly-out is pretty self-explanatory. You can create a new blank document by clicking the "**Create**" **button** below the preview. (If for some reason you don't see the preview or the "Create" button, click the **Blank document icon** at the top left, in the "**Available Templates**" category.)

Or, if you prefer, you can create a new, blank document by pressing the key combination **Ctrl N** (for "New").

My Templates

When you click the "**My templates**" **button** in the "Available Templates" category, the "**New**" **dialog** will open. [16] (Yours might look different from the screenshot. I'm not using a network drive, so a "Personal Templates" tab is at the forefront. At work, you might see a "General" tab or something similar.) This dialog displays your customized templates (and those of your organization), as well as a template for creating a regular blank document and one for creating a blank XML document. Note that any templates you created in an older version of Word also should appear in this dialog.

---

[16] The "New" dialog should display both user templates and workgroup templates. When populating this dialog box, Word looks for both types of templates in the locations set in the Word Options (**File tab**, **Options**, **Advanced**, **File Locations**).

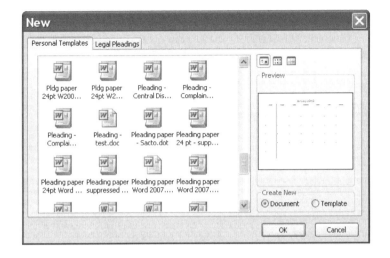

My templates

If you like, you can change how the templates in the dialog are displayed by clicking one of the "Preview" buttons at the top right side (the default is Large Icons; the other options are List and Details).

From this dialog, you can select a template and use it as the basis for either a new document or a new template. As shown in the screenshot (at the lower right side of the dialog), the default is to create a new document.

TIP: It's easy to add an icon to the Quick Access Toolbar (QAT) that lets you open a template with one click of the mouse. Simply do the following:

- **Right-click** within the QAT, then click "**Customize Quick Access Toolbar...**"

- When the Word Options screen opens, navigate to the top left side and change the "**Choose commands from:**" **drop-down** from "Popular Commands" to "**All Commands.**"

- In the commands area, scroll slightly more than halfway down until you see an icon labeled "**New Document or Template.**" Click to **select that icon**, then click the "**Add**" **button** at the center of the screen. That will add it to the right-hand side of the screen, and to the QAT.

- If you like, you can move the icon to the left or right by clicking the **Up button** (left) or the **Down button** (right).

- Be sure to click the "**OK**" **button** at the lower right-hand side of the Options screen in order to save your changes.

For more about using (and creating) templates, see the section starting on page 367.

Print ("Print Place")

In all Office 2010 applications, including Word, the traditional Print dialog has been replaced by "**Print Place**," a full page of print configuration options combined with a large print preview area. I'll discuss the print preview feature, which takes up the right side of the screen, before describing the print options.

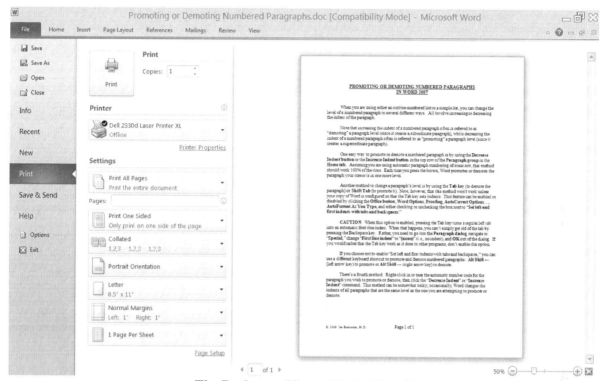

The Backstage View—"Print Place"

The Print Preview

There are a few important points to note about the way the print preview works in Print Place. First, the underlying document can't be edited from within the preview, which is a change from prior versions of Word. (You can retain the functionality of the older versions if you add a "Print Preview Edit Mode" icon to the Quick Access Toolbar, however. See the discussion on page 28.)

Normally, the print preview displays a single page at a reduced size (the exact magnification depends on the size of your screen and your screen resolution; on one of my laptops, the normal size is 59%; on another, it's 44%). You can use the slider at the bottom right to zoom in (increase the magnification) or out (decrease the magnification). In a multi-page document, zooming out allows you to view two or more pages at once. A "zoom to page" button to the right of the slider restores the normal full-page magnification.

To move to a different page from within the preview screen, you can either use the arrows at the bottom center (see the screenshot on the next page) or press Page Up / Pg Up or

Page Down / Pg Dn. (You might find that you have to click on the image of the document in the preview in order to get the Page Up and Page Dn keys to work properly—presumably because until you do so, another portion of Print Place has the focus.)

46 of 222

**Back / Forward Arrows to Change the Page
Displayed in the Preview in Print Place**

In Word 2007, most people preview the current document in one of two ways: (1) by clicking the Office button, Print, Print Preview; or (2) by pressing Ctrl F2. Both methods essentially display the document in a normal editing screen (with the Ribbon, the Quick Access Toolbar, and the Ruler showing), but at a reduced size.

Adding a Print Preview Icon to the QAT

In Word 2010, Print Preview has been incorporated into Print Place, and the keyboard shortcut Ctrl F2 merely opens Print Place. However, you can emulate the Print Preview functionality found in earlier versions of Word by adding an icon to the Quick Access Toolbar. In particular, the "**Print Preview Edit Mode**" icon produces a fully editable preview, separate from Print Place, that works the same way as in previous versions of Word.

To add the icon to the QAT:

1. Position the cursor anywhere within the QAT and **_right-click_**. You'll see a mini-menu like the one at right. (If you haven't moved your QAT, yours will read, "Show Quick Access Toolbar Below the Ribbon.")

2. Click "**Customize Quick Access Toolbar…**"

3. When the Word Options screen appears, change the "**Choose commands from:**" **drop-down** from "Popular" to "**All Commands**."

4. In the command list underneath the "Choose commands from:" drop-down, scroll down about 2/3 of the way until you locate the "Print Preview" commands. There are a few of them. The one you want is labeled "**Print Preview Edit Mode**."

5.   Click that command, then click the "**Add**" **button** in the middle of the screen.

6.   If you wish, click either the **up arrow** or the **down arrow** at the very right side of the screen (grayed out in the screenshot below) in order to move the "Print Preview Edit Mode" icon to the left (up) or to the right (down) on the QAT.

7.   Click "**OK**" to save your setting, close out of the Word Options, and return to the document editing screen.

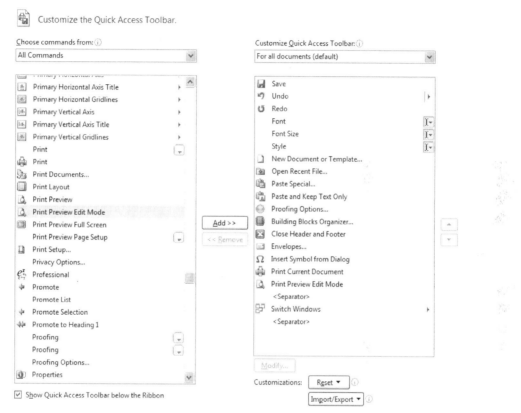

Customize the Quick Access Toolbar Screen

(NOTE: Your screen might look somewhat different because of the ways in which I've customized my QAT.)

    When you click the "Print Preview Edit Mode" button, you will see the current document in the traditional print preview mode, not within the framework of Print Place. A context-sensitive "Print Preview" tab will appear, offering pertinent commands (including a "Close Print Preview" button that returns you to the normal editing screen). **NOTE:** If you can't click in or edit the document in the preview screen (because the mouse pointer turns into a magnifying glass and clicking merely zooms in and out), click to uncheck "**Magnifier**" in the Ribbon.

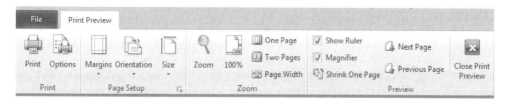

Print Settings

The entire left-hand side of the "Print Place" screen is devoted to various print settings. For the most part, the choices available are the same as those offered in the traditional Print dialog, but the graphical interface has changed. The drop-down lists, radio buttons, and checkboxes that appeared in the Print dialog have been replaced almost exclusively by drop-downs.

At the top, there is a large **Print button** with a printer icon, plus a box where you can set the number of copies (the default setting is one copy). Your active printer appears below that; if you click the drop-down, you can choose one of your other printers (if any), add a new printer, or print to a file. Note that there is a link labeled **"Printer Properties"** underneath the drop-down. This link lets you change your printer's configuration options—for example, in the case of my main printer (a Dell 2330d), I can specify automatic duplex (double-sided) printing from the Printer Properties dialog (even though the "Print One Sided" drop-down does not offer an automatic duplexing option). Another configuration option people commonly change from within the Printer Properties dialog relates to the active paper tray.

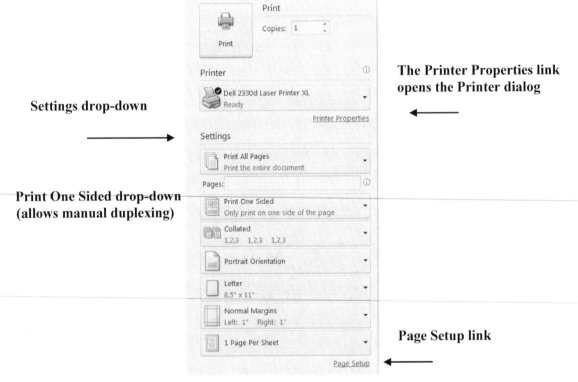

Print Settings

Underneath "**Settings**," there are several drop-downs. The first allows you to select the specific pages you wish to print: "Print All Pages," "Print Selection" (which is grayed out unless and until you select some text), "Print Current Page," and "Print Custom Range." Note that there's a "Pages" box underneath the drop-down, where you can type a custom page range (see the screenshot on the next page for examples of the syntax to use).

Print Selection

This option works as you might expect: After you have selected some text, the "Print Selection" option becomes available from the drop-down "Settings" menu. Click it, then click the Print button to print the selected text.

TIP: In Word 2010, as in Word 2007, it is possible to select non-contiguous portions of text. To do so, select the first portion, then press the Ctrl key, move the mouse pointer, select another portion, and so on.

Print Custom Range

Using "Print Custom Range," you can specify not merely a series of contiguous (1-3) or non-contiguous (2,5,11) pages, but also—if your document consists of multiple sections— a series of pages within a single section of the document. For example, you can print pages 1 through 12 of section 7 of a document by typing "p1s7-p12s7," without quotation marks, in the "Print Range" portion of the Print dialog. In fact, it is possible to print a few different portions of one section, and/or a few different portions of multiple sections, and/or one or more entire sections.

Indeed, if you position the mouse pointer over the "Information" button to the right of the "Pages:" field under "Settings," you'll see a pop-up that explains the syntax to use in order to print a custom page range. (Keep in mind that the examples are not exhaustive.)

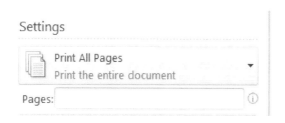
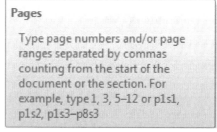

The Pages Box   **Syntax for Printing a Custom Range**

Only Print Odd Pages

At the bottom of the "Settings" drop-down, there is a command labeled "Only Print Odd Pages." You can use that command by itself to print all of the odd-numbered pages in your document, or you can use it in conjunction with the "Print Custom Range" command. If you apply both settings, Word will print only the odd pages within the page ranges that you've designated. As shown in the screenshot below left , I've entered a custom range: pages 1-31 (the hyphen character inserted before a number larger than 1 tells Word to start printing at the very beginning of the document) and pages 57-79. Because I've also clicked "Only Print Odd Pages," the print output will be the odd pages within those two page ranges.

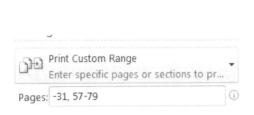

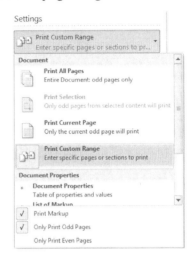

Only Print Even Pages

The "Only Print Even Pages" option works exactly the same way as "Only Print Odd Pages." Again, you can use the option by itself—and print all of the even-numbered pages in your document—or in conjunction with the "Print Custom Range" choice.

The Printing Specs

In addition to determining which pages to print, you can choose among various printing specifications available from drop-downs in the "Settings" section of Print Place. These options include:

- One sided or duplex

  Note that the duplex option says "Manually Print on Both Sides," which suggests that you have to remove the paper from the printer manually, turn it over, and replace it in order to print on the other side. If your printer allows automatic duplexing, you can set this option *via the Printer Properties link*.

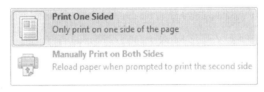

- Collated or uncollated

  This option is fairly straightforward.

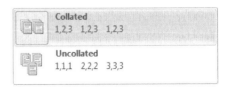

- Portrait or landscape orientation

  Also straightforward.

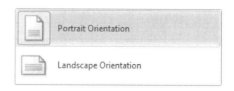

- Paper size

  The paper size choices include standard Letter and Legal sizes (which are common in the U.S.), A4 and A5 (common in Europe), a variety of envelopes, and more (you have to scroll down to see the entire list).

  Note that there is a "More Paper Sizes…" option at the bottom of the menu. Clicking that option opens the Page Setup dialog with the Paper tab at the forefront and allows you to scroll to find additional choices.

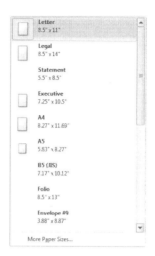

- Margins

  This menu offers assorted print margins, from whatever your normal page margins are (I've set mine to 1" all around; yours might be different, either because you are using the Word defaults of 1.25" left and right or because you have chosen custom settings) to mirrored margins (i.e., the left and right pages are mirror images, which is common in publishing but not in the legal profession).

  At the bottom of the menu there is a "Custom Margins" option. Clicking that option opens the Page Setup dialog with the Margins tab at the forefront so that you can configure custom margins.

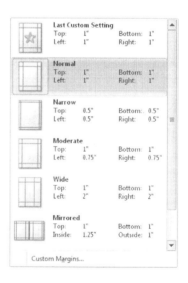

- Pages per sheet

  This option lets you print booklets, deposition summaries, and the like by subdividing a page into two or more virtual pages.

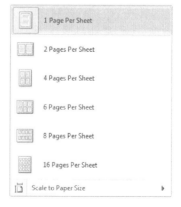

Page Setup

At the bottom right side of the Settings menu, there is a link labeled "Page Setup." Clicking the link opens the Page Setup dialog so that you can change the document's margins, the orientation, the paper type, the paper size, the paper source (i.e., which tray the printer pulls from), and so on directly from within that dialog.

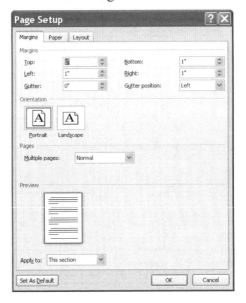

Print What / Document Properties

In earlier versions of Word, the Print dialog included a "Print what" option. This little known but handy feature made it simple to print objects other than the current document. The other "Print what" choices in the traditional Print dialog included the following:

- Document

- Document properties

- Document showing markup

- List of markup

- Styles

- Building Blocks entries

- Key assignments

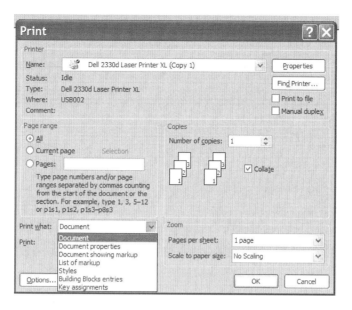

Traditional Print Dialog Showing "Print What" Drop-Down

If you chose "Document properties," a list of various properties of the current document (the one on the screen) printed. If you chose "Document showing markup," the document printed, with any revision marks therein (redlining, strikeout, comments, etc.) visible in the print-out. If you chose "List of markup," only a ***summary*** of the revision marks in the current document, rather than the document itself, printed.

If you chose "Styles" or "Key assignments," a list and description of any customized (user-created) styles or keyboard shortcuts used—or available for use—in the current document printed.

If you chose "Building Blocks entries" Word printed the customized (user-created) Building Blocks entries in the underlying template for the current document (usually the Normal template), as well as in any other templates attached to the document.

In Word 2010, the "Print what" drop-down has been replaced by a mini-menu in Print Place that is somewhat difficult to find. Indeed, it isn't visible in the main Print Place screen. Rather, it is tucked away in the drop-down under "**Settings**," "**Print All Pages**."

Click to Open the Drop-Down Menu

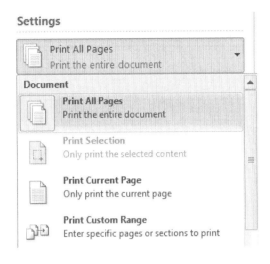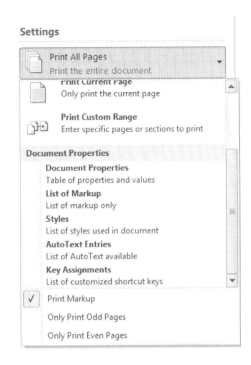

The Print All Pages drop-down menu is something of a hodgepodge. The top portion (shown above left) provides options for printing the document ("Print All Pages," "Print Selection," "Print Current Page," and "Print Custom Range"); the next portion (shown above right), which you have to scroll to see in its entirety, provides options for printing various attributes of a document and other types of objects.

The list of printable document attributes and objects appears below the somewhat confusing label "**Document Properties**." If you scroll through the items in the menu, you'll see almost the same list of printable items as in the "Print what" drop-down in the old Print dialog:

- Document Properties

- List of Markup

- Styles

- AutoText Entries (more or less comparable to Building Blocks Entries in the traditional Print dialog) [17]

- Key Assignments

When you select an object to print by clicking that object in the list, your choice will appear in the Settings area and the object (such as AutoText entries), shown in the screenshot at right) will print when you click the Print button.

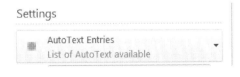

---

[17] The term "AutoText Entries" appears to mean only AutoText entries that have been imported from an earlier version or Word or new Quick Parts that you save to the AutoText gallery.

Document Properties

As in earlier versions of Word, choosing the "Document Properties" option will print an extensive list of the properties of the current document, including the filename, directory, template, title (if you've typed anything in the title field via the Info fly-out), subject (if you've typed anything in the subject field), author, keywords (if you've typed any), comments (if any), creation date, change number, last date saved, person who last saved the document, total editing time, last date printed, number of pages, number of words, and number of characters.

Styles, Key Assignments, and AutoText Entries

Choosing "Styles" will print a list and description of any built-in and customized (user-created) styles used—or available for use—in the current document.

Choosing "Key assignments" will print a list and description of customized (user-created) keyboard shortcuts used—or available for use—in the current document. As the next screenshot implies, the list does **not** include built-in shortcuts.

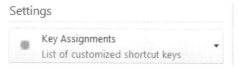

Choosing "AutoText entries" will print the Building Blocks (AutoText) entries used—or available for use—in the current document, including both built-in entries and customized (user-created) entries. However, in my tests, the list incorporated **only actual AutoText entries** contained in the Normal template and in a couple of attached (add-in) templates; it did not contain Quick Parts entries stored in either of the Building Blocks templates—not even one Quick Part entry I created from within one of the test documents.[18]

Print Markup

At the very bottom of the "Settings / Print All Pages" drop-down, there is an item labeled "Print Markup." It is enabled (checked) by default, but you can disable it by unchecking the checkbox. This last item is comparable to the old "Print what" option called "Document showing markup"; when the active document contains markup, the printout will display the markup unless you take the deliberate step of unchecking the box (by clicking it) before printing.

Print Markup Enabled   **Print Markup Disabled**
(the Default Setting)

The bottom section of the drop-down also proffers the options, discussed earlier in this section, for printing only odd pages or only even pages of your document.

---

[18] As mentioned elsewhere in the book, there is one Building Blocks template for built-in entries (entries that come with the program) and a separate one for custom (user-created) entries.

Configuring the Print Options

Although the Print Options in Word 2010 closely resemble those in Word 2007, it seems logical to discuss them here (briefly), despite the fact that this section of the book focuses mainly on new and modified features.

To view or change one or more of the default Print Options, click the **File tab**, **Options**, **Advanced**, and scroll a little more than halfway down to the **Print** category. It's unlikely that you'll have occasion to tweak most of these settings. However, a few of them might be useful on occasion. For example, if you are working on a very long document and you want to speed up the print process, you can try selecting the "Use draft quality" option. Just keep in mind that the quality of the printout might not be as sharp as normal.

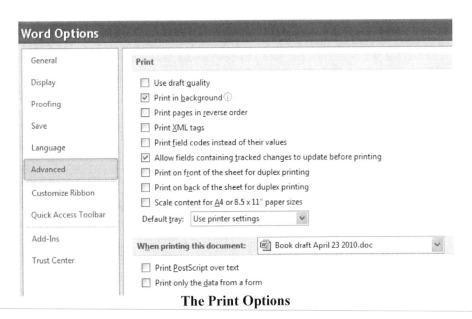

The Print Options

The "Print in background" option is enabled by default because it allows you to continue to work while a document is printing. If a particular print job seems to be exceptionally slow, you can try unchecking this option (which will allocate more memory to the printer), but you'll have to wait until the document finishes printing before you can edit another document.

"Print Postscript over text" is seldom used except with documents converted from Word for the Mac.

"Print only the data from a form" will print just the data you have input into a form, not the underlying form itself.

The "Print pages in reverse order" option might come in handy at some point.

You might want to *uncheck* "Allow fields containing tracked changes to update before printing" in certain circumstances (perhaps you inserted or deleted a code while tracking changes, but you don't want the code to update when you print a draft because the document hasn't been finalized yet).

The "Save & Send" Fly-Out

The "Save & Send" fly-out in Word 2010 incorporates many of the same commands found in the Save As, Send, and Publish fly-out menus in Word 2007.

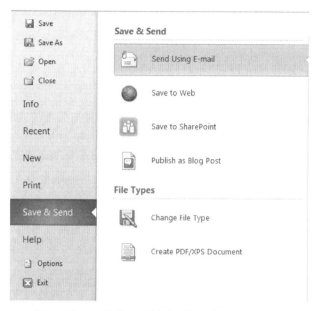

The "Save & Send" Fly-Out (Truncated)

In particular, "Save & Send" provides myriad ways of giving others access to your document: You can e-mail it, upload it to the Web via Microsoft's SkyDrive file storage / file-sharing service, put it on a shared network called SharePoint (another Microsoft service), publish it as a blog post, or change the file type to one that is compatible with software used by a client, a colleague, or opposing counsel.

When you click one of the "Save & Send" choices, a submenu opens, explaining (in general terms) what the choice involves and how it works.

Send Using E-Mail

The first Save & Send option, Send Using E-mail, offers a few different ways to forward a document: Send as attachment, Send a link, Send as PDF, Send as XPS, and Send as Internet fax (which requires you to have an Internet faxing service).

Send as Attachment

If you have Outlook installed on your computer, clicking the "Send as attachment " button opens a new mail message (i.e., a message composition screen) in Outlook, with the document already attached. See, for example, the next screenshot.

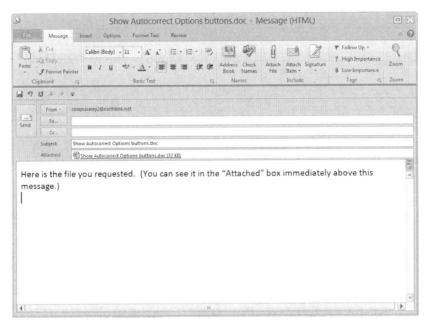

Send as Attachment Option – Opens a New Mail Message in Outlook

Send a Link

If your document is saved in a shared location (such as a SharePoint library or a network drive), you can use this option to send other users (typically other members of your organization) a link to the document via e-mail.

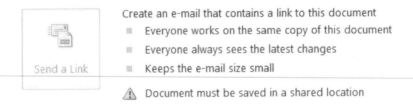

Create an e-mail that contains a link to this document
- Everyone works on the same copy of this document
- Everyone always sees the latest changes
- Keeps the e-mail size small

⚠ Document must be saved in a shared location

Send as PDF

If you click the "Send as PDF" icon, two things occur: Word makes a copy of the active file and converts it into a PDF, and Outlook opens a new mail message with the PDF attached. As far as I can tell, Word doesn't actually save the new PDF to your hard drive; if you wish to create and store a permanent copy, you'll need to right-click it from within Outlook and click "Save As."

Attach a PDF copy of this document to an e-mail
- Document looks the same on most computers
- Preserves fonts, formatting, and images
- Content cannot be easily changed

Send as XPS

The "Send as XPS" option lets you save a copy of the document in Microsoft's proprietary XPS format and send it to others who have an XPS reader.[19] Because XPS is a generic format, the document appears the same on most computers, and fonts, formatting, and images are preserved. However, it can be difficult to edit an XPS file.

Attach a XPS copy of this document to an e-mail
- Document looks the same on most computers
- Preserves fonts, formatting, and images
- Content cannot be easily changed

Most people who work in the legal field probably won't have much occasion to use this option.

Send as Internet Fax

You need a fax Internet service provider in order to use this option. If you haven't already signed up for such a service, clicking the "Send as Internet Fax" button produces a link to a web site where you can choose among various providers.

Send as Internet Fax
- Send a fax without using a fax machine
- Requires a fax service provider

<u>Save to Web</u>

The "Save to Web" option lets you upload files to SkyDrive, Microsoft's password-protected online file storage and sharing service, either for your own use or to share with others.[20] This feature has a number of advantages, including the following:

- It allows you to work on a file from any computer with Internet access, which means that you can edit documents from home or while traveling;

- It provides another means of backing up important files; and

- It lets two or more people edit the same file simultaneously with Office 2010's new Co-Authoring feature.

NOTE: To use SkyDrive, you must register for and sign into Windows Live, Microsoft's web portal. However, it is a free service.

---

[19] There is an XPS viewer built into Vista and Windows 7. For those who have Windows XP, Microsoft provides an XPS viewer for download, but you'll need .NET installed on your computer to make it work. See this link: http://www.microsoft.com/whdc/xps/viewxps.mspx

[20] Each SkyDrive account currently provides about 25 GB of file-storage space.

As illustrated in the next screenshot, when you click Save to Web, a "Save to Windows Live" submenu opens.

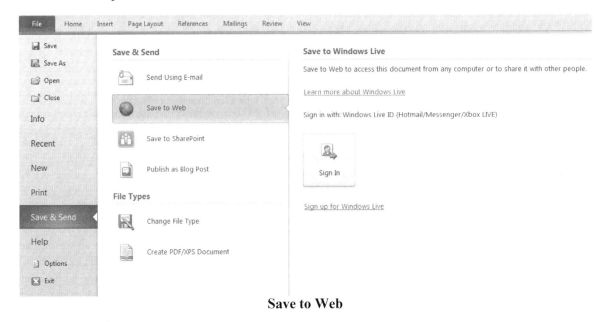

Save to Web

If you click the "**Sign In**" **button**, a .NET Passport Wizard opens. (At least, it does in Windows XP.) Essentially, the Passport service is another way of obtaining a Windows Live ID. It lets you sign in to a multitude of Microsoft web sites with one user ID.[21] However, you don't need to run the Wizard in order to sign up for Windows Live. See the discussion that follows.

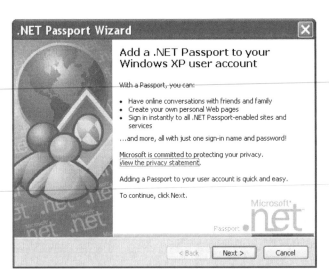

I already have a Windows Live ID (and I don't wish to add a .NET Password to my Windows XP user account), so I clicked "Cancel."

---

[21] For more information about this service, see this Wikipedia article:
http://en.wikipedia.org/wiki/Windows_Live_ID

as well as this Microsoft Knowledge Base article: http://support.microsoft.com/kb/309011

If you click the "**Sign up for Windows Live**" link, Internet Explorer opens and takes you to a page where you can sign up for a Windows Live account if you don't have one already. [22] See the next screenshot.

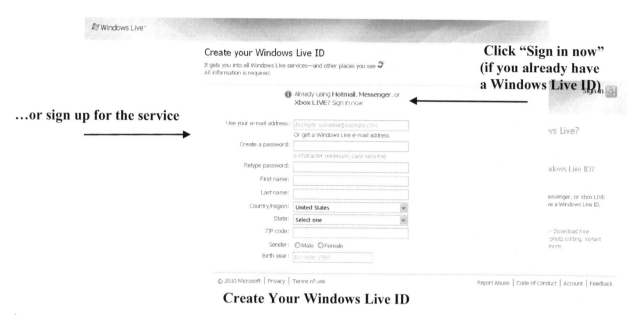

Create Your Windows Live ID

If you already have a Windows Live ID, you can click the "**Sign in now**" **link** toward the top of the page, which will take you to the Windows Live sign up / sign in page.

The Windows Live Portal

---

[22] If Internet Explorer (also known as "IE") is not your preferred browser, you can copy the URL from IE and paste it into the Address Bar of a different browser, such as Firefox, Safari, or Chrome. Although Microsoft says it doesn't recommend or support the use of Chrome with Windows Live, I have been using that browser for access to Windows Live without any evident problems.

Setting up a Windows Live account is fairly straightforward. Just follow the prompts. (You'll need to provide an e-mail address—for your user ID—and a password.)

Afterwards, you will see your SkyDrive home page with some built-in folders, including one labeled "My Documents" and one labeled "Public," plus a couple of "Favorites" folders and one set aside for photographs. By default, the "My Documents" folder is not shared; i.e., you are the only person with access to that folder (as indicated by the lock icon). However, you can share the entire folder—or any individual document it contains—with other people. You also have the option of creating additional folders and sharing those folders, or certain documents within the folders, with others. You have complete control over your online folders and files.

Creating a Folder

To create a new folder, click the "**Create folder**" **link** above your existing folders.

"Create folder"

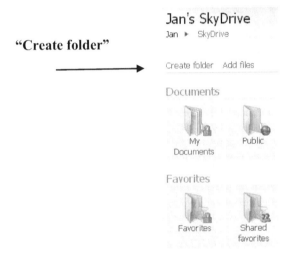

When you do, you'll see a "Create a folder" screen where you can type a name for your new folder and choose from several "Share with" options:

- Just me (the default)

- Everyone (public)

- My network

- Select people…

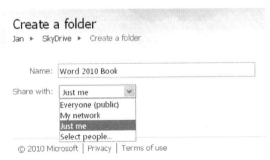

Create a Folder in SkyDrive

44

The first two options are fairly self-explanatory. The third option, "My network," encompasses people you add to your profile in SkyDrive (by clicking the "Profile" link at the top of your SkyDrive page and then navigating to "Network" and clicking "…add them to your profile").

Here are the people in your network who show up on your profile. What's your network? It's everyone you add to your profile or to Messenger-you get to see each other's recent photos, new personal messages, and more. But you control how much you want to share. ×

You don't have anyone in your network yet. To get started, invite some of your contacts.

Once you have added people to your network, you can decide whether to let them add, edit, and delete your shared files or merely view those files.

Public and networks

☐ Everyone (public)

☑ My network

☐ My extended network

Can view files ▼
Can view files
Can add, edit details, and delete files

As for the fourth option, clicking "Select people" produces a screen where you can type the names or e-mail addresses of individuals you want to have access to the folder.

Type a name or e-mail address →

After you enter the name or e-mail address of an individual and click "Next," you'll be given an opportunity to send that person a notification by e-mail. When the recipient clicks the link in the e-mail message, he or she will be taken directly into your folder on SkyDrive.

You can change the settings for access to any folder by clicking the "More" link within that folder, then clicking "Edit permissions."

Adding a File

You can add a file to any of your folders in one of two ways:

- by uploading a file from your computer; or

- by creating a file from scratch from within one of the Office Web Apps.

There are at least two different ways to upload a file. One way is by clicking the "Add files" link above your folders.

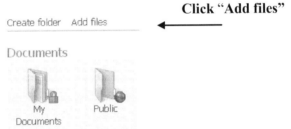

After you click the link, SkyDrive will open a screen where you can choose a folder in which to store your new file. The screen displays your existing folders as well as a button you can click to create a brand-new folder.

When I Clicked the My Documents Folder...   ..."Add files to My Documents" Appeared

When you click a folder, you'll be able to browse to one or more specific files on your computer and upload them to that folder. [23]

Alternatively, you can **click a folder** in order to open it and then click the "**Add files**" **link** (or, if the folder is empty, the "Why not add some files?" link), which also allows you to browse to a file on your computer.

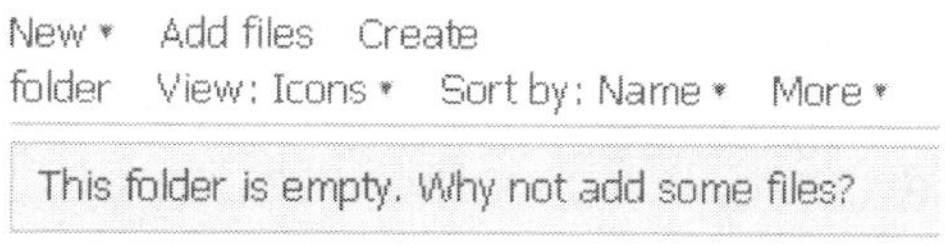

> New ▾ Add files Create
> folder View: Icons ▾ Sort by: Name ▾ More ▾
>
> This folder is empty. Why not add some files?

Click the Add Files Link or "Why Not Add Some Files?"

To create a new file from scratch from within the Web Apps, open a folder and, instead of clicking "Add files," click the "New" drop-down. You will see a menu similar to the one in the screenshot below.

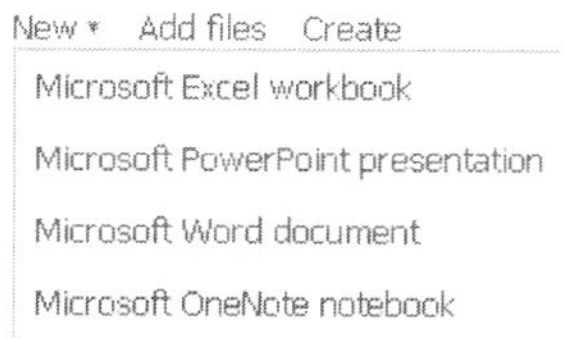

> New ▾ Add files Create
> Microsoft Excel workbook
> Microsoft PowerPoint presentation
> Microsoft Word document
> Microsoft OneNote notebook

As of early April, 2010, you can't create a Word document from scratch—if you do, you'll get an error message. However, you *can* create an Excel workbook or a PowerPoint presentation using the Web Apps. And, with luck, you will be able to create a Word document via the Web Apps soon after this book is published.[24]

Other File and Folder Options

SkyDrive makes it easy for you to rename files and folders as well as to move files from one folder to another. Without going into a lot of detail, when you click a file, you'll see a generic image of the file and, above it, a menu that lets you view, edit, download, delete, or move the file, plus a drop-down with more options. (As mentioned elsewhere, the editing function isn't available yet in Word or OneNote, but that should change in the second half of 2010.) The prompts are fairly self-explanatory.

---

[23] It's easy to move the files to another folder later on if you so choose.

[24] It is my understanding that Microsoft is planning to make the Web Apps available immediately to organizations that purchase Office 2010 after the software is officially released to businesses in May. However, consumers who wish to use the Web Apps will have to wait until sometime in the second half of 2010.

When You Click a File, You'll See a Menu of Options

File Sharing / Using the Co-Authoring Feature

One of the coolest things about using Save to Web that it lets you share files with other people. Even cooler, two or more people can edit a shared document simultaneously by dint of Office 2010's new Co-Authoring feature.

As discussed in more detail in the section about co-authoring with the Web Apps starting on page 120, after you give other people access to a particular Word file you've uploaded to SkyDrive, they can open the file into *the regular version of Word 2010* and edit it at the same time that you are working on it. (Co-authoring is not available in the Word Web App itself.)

For more about the way the Co-authoring feature works in general, see pages 115 and following.

Using SkyDrive to Back Up Files

One of the other benefits of using Save to Web is that it gives you an additional way to back up important files. Of course, you and/or the organization where you work should employ a couple of other, more traditional, methods for backing up files (you never know, for example, when Internet access might be unavailable because of a problem at your service provider's end or some other technical issue). Even so, uploading "mission critical" files can be a good idea—extra insurance in case of a computer glitch, a natural disaster, a fire, etc. In fact, I have stored a couple of drafts of this book online…just in case.

Save to SharePoint

SharePoint is a sort of network platform or intranet that enables members of a law firm, government agency, corporate legal department, or similar entity to collaborate on documents and to communicate via instant messaging. Many large organizations store documents in a "library" on a Microsoft SharePoint Server; users check documents out (and back in) much in the same way that library patrons check books out (and in). Also, it's very common for companies to run their intranets on SharePoint.

There are a couple of different SharePoint products available to large organizations: SharePoint Server and SharePoint Foundation.[25] Most individual users of Word 2010 don't need to know the difference(s) between these two products—or even know much about them, since they operate seamlessly in the background. (Your company's IT department handles the technical issues involved in setting up and maintaining a SharePoint server.)

What makes SharePoint noteworthy is its role in facilitating collaboration in Word 2010 and the other programs in the Office suite. For example, in order to use the new Co-Authoring feature, your company must have SharePoint Foundation 2010 installed or use a server running SharePoint Foundation 2010.[26]

Save to SharePoint

When you click the "Learn more about SharePoint" link, Internet Explorer opens and takes you to this page (http://www.microsoft.com/online/sharepoint-online.mspx):

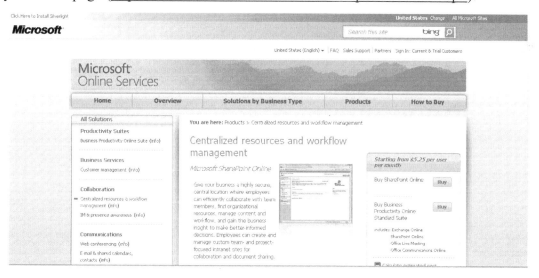

---

[25] There is also a product called SharePoint WorkSpace.

[26] Depending on how your IT department has configured the SharePoint Server, you might or might not be able to use the Co-authoring feature. See the section on Co-authoring, starting on page 115.

When you click the "Save As" button, a "Save As" dialog opens so that you can save the current document to the location where you normally store files in SharePoint.

For more information about SharePoint, see the following sites:

Microsoft's Discussion of SharePoint
http://sharepoint.microsoft.com/Pages/Default.aspx

Wikipedia's Discussion of SharePoint
http://en.wikipedia.org/wiki/Microsoft_SharePoint

Publish as Blog Post

The "Publish as Blog Post" option, albeit not something you're likely to use at work, nevertheless might come in handy if you have a copy of Word 2010 at home and wish to use it to create and format posts and upload them to an existing blog (web log).

Word 2010 supports several popular blogging sites / formats, including WordPress, Blogger, and TypePad. I have a blog on WordPress (CompuSavvy's Word & WordPerfect Tips), so for me, the ability to write and edit blog posts in Word 2010 could be very useful (particularly since the formatting options within WordPress are somewhat limited).

When you click "Publish as Blog Post," you'll see a fly-out similar to the one in the screenshot. Note the caution that you will need to register your blog account (i.e., within Word) before uploading a post from Word to your blog for the first time.

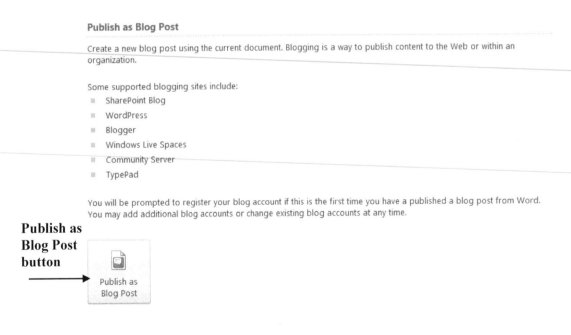

When I clicked the "Publish as Blog Post" button at the bottom of the fly-out, a pop-up message appeared, asking me to register my blog with Word, either now or later. I clicked the "Register Now" button.

Register a Blog Account

Word's blog registration wizard then prompted me for the name of my blog provider (WordPress), as well as the URL of my blog.

I chose WordPress from the drop-down, which activated the "Next" button. When I clicked "Next," a "New WordPress Account" dialog opened.

The "New WordPress Account" dialog contains a placeholder where you need to type the URL for your blog (in my case, compusavvy.wordpress.com). Be careful when filling in this information; don't delete anything other than *the portion between the chevrons* ("<" and ">"), as well as *the chevrons themselves*. (In other words, don't delete the "http://" at the beginning or the "/xmlrpc.php" at the end. Of course, if you are copying and pasting your blog's complete URL into the middle of the placeholder text, and you end up with two "http://" portions, then it's okay—in fact, necessary—to delete one of them.)

What you should end up with in that field is something like this (make adjustments as necessary for your own URL): http://compusavvy.wordpress.com/xmlrpc.php

Also enter your user name and password so that Word can open an Internet connection, locate your blog, and register it. There is a box labeled "Remember Password," but you don't need to check it, and I chose not to.

Word did register my blog, but for some reason it did so under the name of another of my blogs that is located at a different URL on WordPress. Although I tried registering it again, I couldn't get it to use the name of my CompuSavvy blog. However, I uploaded a test post—as a draft—and it went to the correct blog. So apparently providing an accurate URL is what counts.

Once you have registered your blog, you can start composing a post.[27] Note that when you are in Publish Blog Post mode, a context-sensitive Blog Post tab appears, with a few commands specific to the task, as well as various formatting options (font attributes, justification, bulleted and numbered lists, styles, spelling and proofing tools, etc.). Note, too, that all of the other tabs are hidden except the File tab and the Insert tab—presumably those remain visible because you might need to use commands on those tabs while working on your blog post.

The Context-Sensitive Blog Post Tab

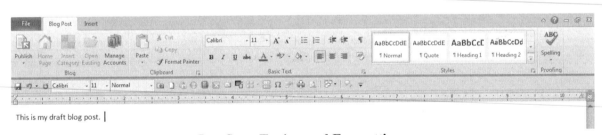

Just Start Typing and Formatting

---

[27] If you choose to register the blog later on (and dismiss the prompt), you can register at any point by clicking the "Manage Accounts" icon on the Blog Post tab. When the Blog Accounts dialog appears, click "New" to start the registration process.

After you write either a partial or a complete post, you can click the "Publish" drop-down at the left side of the tab in order to send the post to your blog. To be on the safe side, I would suggest using the "Publish as Draft" option until you have used this feature enough to feel comfortable publishing in final.

Change File Type

The "Change File Type" option allows you save the current document in several different formats. These include: the newer XML-based Word file format (.docx), the older Word 97-2003 file format (.doc), Open Document text—i.e., the file format used by the word processing program Open Office (.odt), Word template (.dotx), Plain Text (.txt), Rich Text Format (.rtf), a single-file web page (.mht or .mhtml), or "Another File Type."

If you click "Another File Type," the Save As dialog opens, offering all of the above file types, plus macro-enabled Word files (.docm), macro-enabled Word templates (.dotm), two different types of XML (.xml) files, two different types of Works (.wps) files, other types of web pages (.htm and .html), and XPS files (XPS is one of Microsoft's proprietary file formats; it isn't widely used except by IT people and other techies).

Note that you will not find WordPerfect files (.wpd) in the list; you can't save Word 2010 documents in WordPerfect format.

Change File Type

Create PDF/XPS Document

In addition to the ability to save documents in the file formats outlined in the previous section, you can save a document as a PDF (Portable Document File).

Word 2010's PDF capability is an improvement over Word 2007, which initially didn't include a built-in converter that allowed users to save .docx or .doc files in PDF format. Until 2009, when Microsoft released a patched version of Word 2007 that incorporated the PDF converter, anyone wishing to publish to PDF had to download a separate add-in. Happily, Word 2010 comes with a PDF conversion filter, so users no longer have to download an additional utility in order to turn a Word document into a PDF. And the quality of the converted file is, for the most part, very good.

To save a document as a PDF file, open the document and then click **File, Save & Send, Create PDF / XPS Document**, then click the "**Create a PDF/XPS" button**. A **Publish as PDF or XPS dialog** will open.

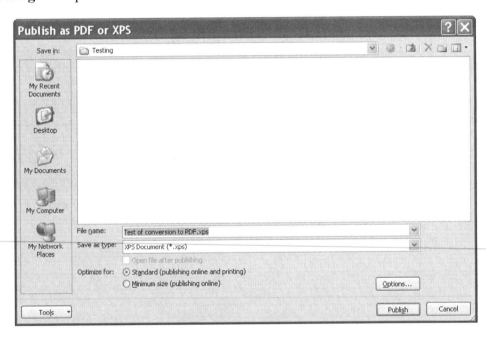

As you can see from the previous screenshot, the dialog box might open with the "Save as type" set to "XPS Document (*.xps)." If that's the case and you wish to create a PDF instead, click the "Save as type" drop-down and change it manually to PDF.

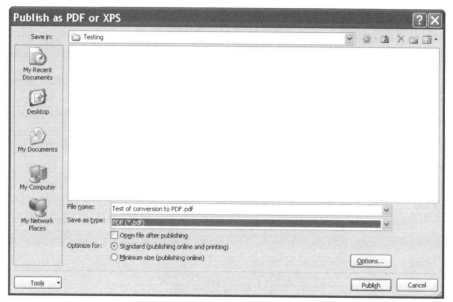

Publish as PDF or XPS

Before clicking "Publish," change the file name (and/or the "Save in" location) if you like, and then make note of the various configuration options at the bottom of the dialog. By default, Word uses "**Optimize for: Standard (publishing online and printing)**"; you can change this setting so that Word creates a smaller PDF file for publishing online (i.e., one that takes up less space in the computer, not one with smaller fonts).

If you check the "**Open file after publishing**" box, Word will open the PDF file in Adobe Acrobat after the conversion—assuming you have a version of Acrobat on your computer. (In my tests, this box was unchecked by default.) To see what other configuration options are available to you, click the "**Options**" button in the lower right-hand corner of the dialog.

PDF Options

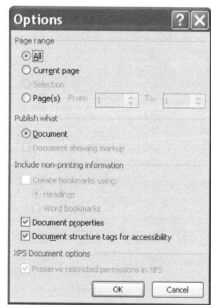

XPS Options

The main thing to be aware of—particularly if you are concerned about the possibility of including metadata in your documents—is that the Document Properties will be included in the PDF (and in the XPS) unless you specifically ***uncheck*** the "**Document properties**" **box** (in the section of the dialog labeled "**Include non-printing information**").

CAUTION: Don't assume that unchecking the "Document properties" box is sufficient to remove all metadata from the converted document. In fact, it might be a good idea to take additional steps to scrub the Word document prior to conversion. For more information, see the discussion of metadata starting on page 555.

ADDITIONAL CAUTION: If the document contains markup, the "**Document showing markup**" radio button, which normally is grayed out (as it is in the screenshots above), will be active. Unless you click the "**Document**" radio button instead, the PDF or XPS file will display the markup in the document.

You can convert the entire document, the page the cursor is on (Current page), or a range of pages. Note that the conversion utility automatically creates bookmarks in the PDF or XPS file using headings. (Unlike in Word 2007, the option to include bookmarks is grayed out; I'm not sure if there is a way to change this setting.)

Once you have set the configuration options the way you like, click "OK" to confirm your choices and close the **Options dialog**, and then click "**Publish.**" If you are converting to PDF, the PDF version of the file will open in Acrobat—assuming that (1) you have checked the "Open file after publishing" option and (2) you have a copy of Adobe Acrobat on your computer.

It's important to recognize that the converted file might not look exactly the way it would if you used Adobe Acrobat to perform the conversion. In my test files, the fonts appeared to be condensed and (perhaps as a result) the margins were wider than normal. However, the results were perfectly acceptable for my rather limited needs—and considering that the converter is available for free. Only you can determine whether the converted PDFs adequately suit your purposes.

Printing to a PDF Printer

As an alternative to saving a file as a PDF as outlined above, you should be able to print the document to a PDF printer. Just click the **File tab**, **Print** (or press **Ctrl P**), choose the **Adobe PDF** printer from the **Printer drop-down**, and click **OK**. (Your drop-down probably looks somewhat different from the screenshot; what appears in that menu depends on the specific printers and print drivers you are using.)

Adobe PDF Printer →

CAUTION: If you use the print-to-PDF option instead of the Save As option, *be sure to change back to your normal printer before attempting to print another document*. (Click the **File tab**, **Print** [or press **Ctrl P**], choose your regular printer from the **Printer Name drop-down**, and click **OK**.)

The "Help" Fly-Out

Although Word 2010 still has the small "Help" button—located at the top right side of the Ribbon—there's also an expanded Help function available from the Backstage View.

The Backstage View – Help Fly-Out

The Help fly-out is divided into three main sections: one labeled Support, one labeled Tools for Working With Office, and one that I'll call Product Info. (because it contains information about your copy of Word).

Support

The Support section of the Help fly-out provides a button that opens a help screen (and gives you access to both offline and online help), information about how to get started with Word, and a link that you can use to contact Microsoft directly.

Microsoft Office Help

When you click the Microsoft Office Help link, the Word Help dialog opens (see the screenshot on the next page). This dialog also appears if you click the Help button (the question mark) at the right side of the Ribbon.

You can type a search term, browse by topics, or look through the Table of Contents of the built-in help feature (by clicking the Book icon in the Word Help toolbar; see below).

The Word Help Toolbar (Magnified)

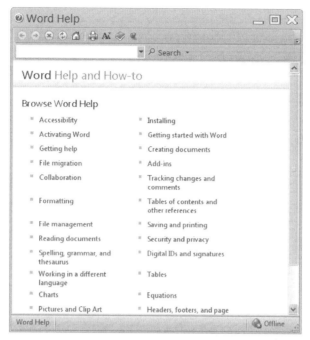

The Word Help Dialog

If you type a term in the search box at top left, then press Enter or click the magnifying glass, Word will search for that term either offline (i.e., using the help documentation that exists on your computer) or online, depending on what is checked in the "Search" drop-down to the right of the magnifying glass. The drop-down is divided into two main sections: **Content from Office.com** (i.e., online) and **Content from this computer** (i.e., offline).

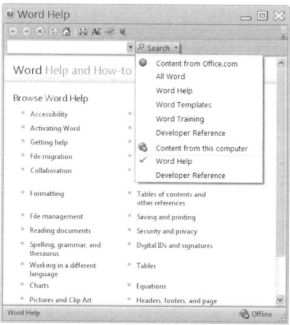

The Word Help Dialog With the Search Drop-Down Open

For example, when I typed the search term "table of contents" (without quotation marks) and pressed the "Enter" key, I got different results depending on which "Word Help" option was checked—the one in the "Content from Office.com" section or the one in the "Content on this computer" section.

Online Search Results   **Offine Search Results**

When you click the book icon in the Word Help toolbar, a "Table of Contents" pane opens at the left side of the Help dialog. Double-click a book to the left of any topic to read more about that topic. To close the Table of Contents pane, click the book icon in the toolbar again.

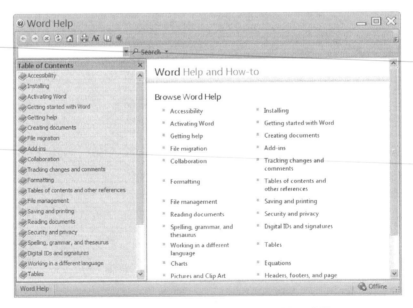

The Help Dialog Showing the (Help) Table of Contents

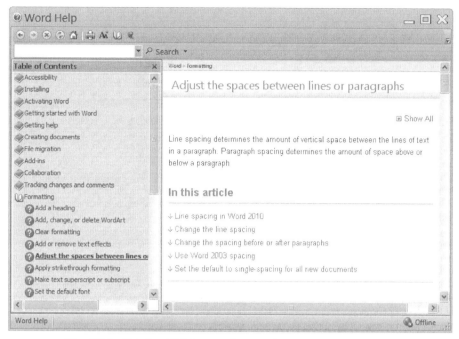

The Help Dialog With the Table of Contents Expanded
(to Show the Formatting Topic)

Getting Started

Getting Started
See what's new and find resources to help you
learn the basics quickly.

Clicking the "Getting Started" link in the Help fly-out menu launches the Internet Explorer browser and takes you to this web site:
http://office2010.microsoft.com/en-us/word-help/getting-started-with-word-2010-HA010370239.aspx

There are a couple of very useful links on that site. They include a downloadable Excel spreadsheet that shows where Word 2003 commands appear in the Word 2010 Ribbon. Note that there are similar workbooks available for Excel and PowerPoint. The "Word 2010: Menu to ribbon reference workbook" is available here: http://office2010.microsoft.com/en-us/templates/CL101817133.aspx?CTT=5&origin=HA101794130#ai:TC101817139|

(Or use this "**tiny URL**" that I created: http://tinyurl.com/W2010Menu2Ribbon)

The first "Getting Started" site mentioned above also links to interactive guides called "Learn Where Menu and Toolbar Commands Are." Only the interactive guides for Word, Excel, and PowerPoint are available at this time, but the others should be posted online soon. The URL for the interactive guides is:
http://office2010.microsoft.com/en-us/word-help/learn-where-menu-and-toolbar-commands-are-in-office-2010-HA101794130.aspx?CTT=5&origin=HA010370239

(Or use one of these "**tiny URLs**":
http://tinyurl.com/W2010WhereCommandsAre   *or*   http://tinyurl.com/W2010Interact)

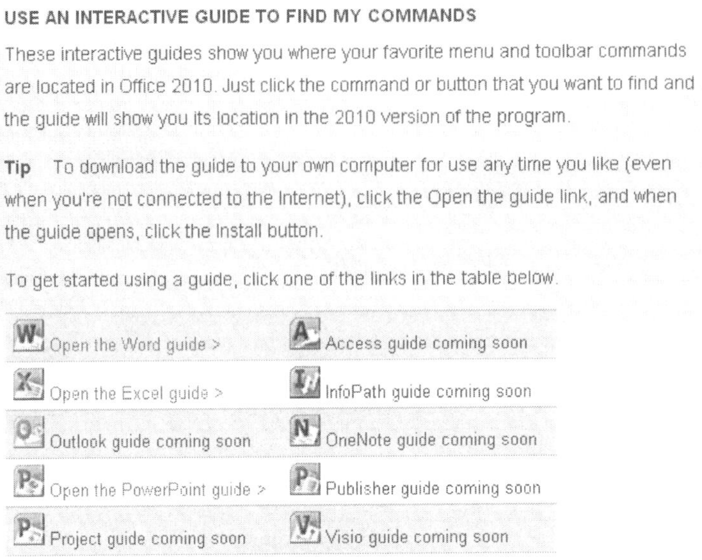

USE AN INTERACTIVE GUIDE TO FIND MY COMMANDS

These interactive guides show you where your favorite menu and toolbar commands are located in Office 2010. Just click the command or button that you want to find and the guide will show you its location in the 2010 version of the program.

Tip   To download the guide to your own computer for use any time you like (even when you're not connected to the Internet), click the Open the guide link, and when the guide opens, click the Install button.

To get started using a guide, click one of the links in the table below.

Open the Word guide >	Access guide coming soon
Open the Excel guide >	InfoPath guide coming soon
Outlook guide coming soon	OneNote guide coming soon
Open the PowerPoint guide >	Publisher guide coming soon
Project guide coming soon	Visio guide coming soon

Interactive Guides

When you click the "Open the Word guide" link, you will see a screen similar to the following:[28]

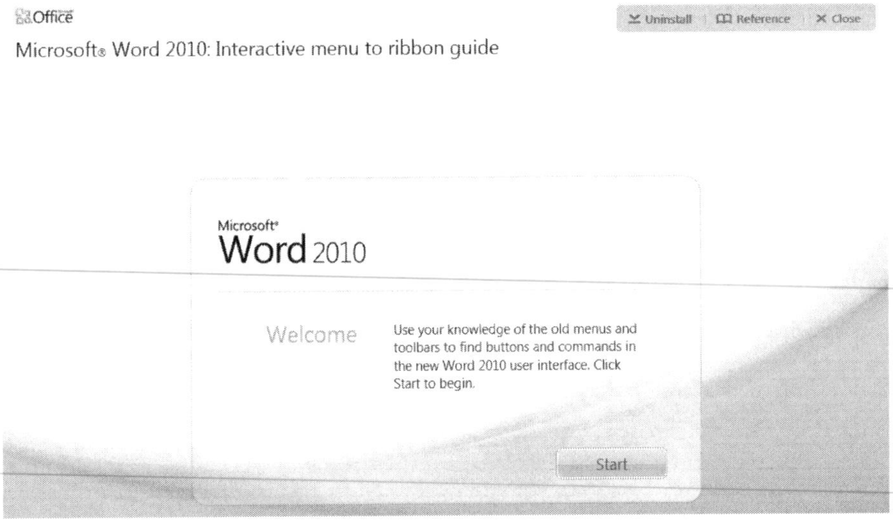

Office
⤓ Uninstall   Reference   ✕ Close

Microsoft® Word 2010: Interactive menu to ribbon guide

Microsoft®
Word 2010

Welcome   Use your knowledge of the old menus and toolbars to find buttons and commands in the new Word 2010 user interface. Click Start to begin.

Start

There are two links at the top right side of this page. One of them (labeled "Install") lets you install the Interactive Guide on your own computer (the link in the screenshot above says "Uninstall" because I went ahead and installed the guide); the other (labeled "Reference") takes you to Office.com, where there is a downloadable command reference.

To activate the Interactive Guide, click the "Start now" button. Then point to any icon or menu command in Word 2003 to see where it appears in Word 2010.

---

[28] **NOTE:** Your browser must work with Flash Player in order to use the Interactive Guides.

For example, the first screenshot below shows what happened when I pointed to the Spell-Check icon. The guide indicates—both via a pop-up near the mouse pointer and above the Word 2003 window—that this command can be found on the Review tab, then in the Proofing group Spelling & Grammar in Word 2010.

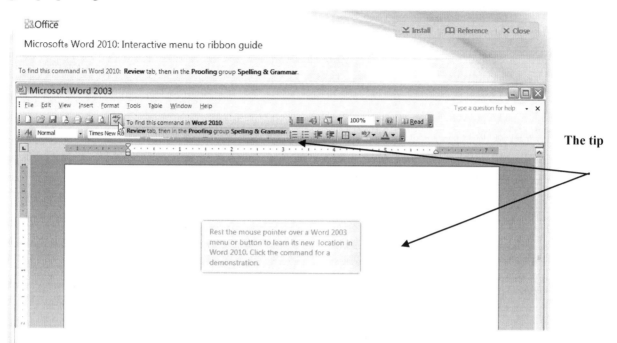

The second screenshot shows what happened when I clicked the Tools menu, then clicked the Word Count command.

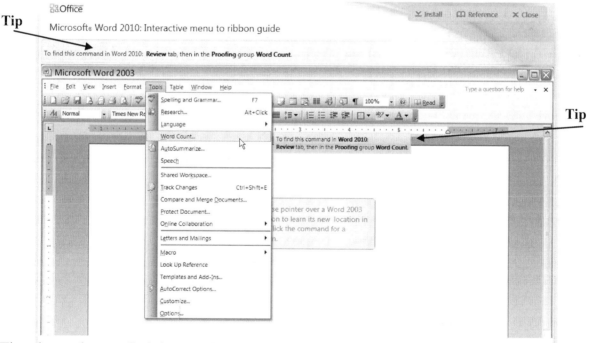

Tips about where to find the Word Count command in Word 2010 appeared in two places: (1) next to the command on the Word 2003 menu and (2) above the Word 2003 window. (The command is on the Review tab, in the Proofing group in Word 2010.)

Contact Us

Clicking the "Contact Us" link in the Help fly-out launches Internet Explorer and takes you to this Microsoft Support site: http://support.microsoft.com/contactus/?ws=support

From within this site, you can type a question and receive an "automated" answer; visit a Microsoft "product solution center"; transfer to a help site sponsored by the company that manufactured the computer you are using; get help from a "customer service center"; or buy Microsoft products.

Tools for Working With Office

Options

This link opens the Word Options so that you can view or change various configuration options.

Updates

Clicking the Updates link opens Internet Explorer and takes you to the Windows Update main page:
http://www.update.microsoft.com/windowsupdate/v6/default.aspx?ln=en-us

Note that the Windows Update site apparently doesn't work with browsers other than Internet Explorer (IE), and doesn't work with versions of IE earlier than IE 5.

Product Info.

The large portion of the Help fly-out at the right-hand side, which I have called the "Product Info." section, lets you view your product activation status, check which version of Word you're using, find Microsoft Customer Support contact information, and read the Microsoft software license terms.

Familiar Commands: Save, Save As, Open, and Close

The commands for working with files—Open, Close, Save, and Save As—have changed only minimally in Word 2010 (though they are listed in an untraditional order in the Backstage View). The notable exception is the "Close" command, which includes a significant new option.

Modified "Close / Save" Options

Microsoft has altered the "Close" command in Word 2010 to make it easier for you to recover documents you haven't saved to disk (as well as any unsaved edits to a document you've already saved).

To make sense of the new options, it might be helpful to understand how Word backs up files.

Two (Really Three!) Kinds of Temporary Backup Files

Like previous versions of Word, Word 2010 automatically creates a temporary backup copy of any document that has been open on your screen for at least ten minutes (the default autosave interval).[29] These traditional "**AutoRecover**" **files**, intended only as emergency backups that you can use to recover at least some of your work in the event of a computer crash or similar situation, *are deleted when you exit from Word*.

In Word 2010, there's a bit of a new twist. The program still creates traditional AutoRecover files, but in addition, it creates temporary backups of documents that you close without saving, and it *keeps them for four days*.[30] These backup files, called "**Unsaved Documents**," fall into two categories:

(a)   documents that you have worked on but then closed, either accidentally or deliberately, *without ever saving*; and

(b)   documents that you *have saved at least once* but have modified since your last save and closed without saving your changes.

The two types of Unsaved Documents are stored in different locations, and are opened in different ways. I will provide the details shortly.

The "Unsaved Documents" and the Modified "Close" Prompt

When you attempt to close a document that you haven't saved manually for several minutes, you'll note that the "**Close**" **prompt** differs from the standard prompt in previous versions of Word, which offered three seemingly straightforward choices: "Yes," "No," and

---

[29] As discussed later in this section, you can change this interval, or even disable the autosave feature altogether, in the "Save" category of the Word Options.

[30] That is, unless you open one of them and save it normally before four days have elapsed.

"Cancel." In Word 2010, the "Close" message also offers three choices, but they are have changed somewhat: "**Save**," "**Don't save**," and "**Cancel**."

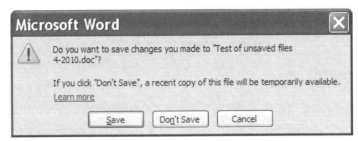

The New "Close" Prompt in Word 2010

Apart from a slight change in terminology—the "Yes" button has been renamed "Save"[31]—the first and third choices work the same way they worked in previous versions. However, the middle choice, "**Don't Save**," functions very differently from the old "No" option. In prior versions, when you clicked "No," Word discarded any unsaved edits and then closed the file. In Word 2010, when you click "Don't Save," the program *creates a temporary backup copy of the file, including any unsaved edits*, that you can restore later on if you wish. These temporary backups are the Unsaved Documents.

When Does the "Unsaved Documents" Backup Kick In?

The new "Unsaved Documents" backup works only under certain circumstances. The "**Keep the last autosaved version…**" **option** must be enabled (checked) in the **Word Options**, and a document must have been open on your screen for at least the minimum "**AutoRecover**" **interval** specified in your "**Save**" **options**. (See page 71 for more information.) If both of those conditions obtain, Word will warn you—and will give you an opportunity to save your work—when you attempt to close a document that you have created or modified without saving your changes.

If either condition is not met (i.e., if the "Keep the last autosaved version…" option isn't enabled *or* if the document hasn't been open for at least ten minutes—or whatever your minimum AutoRecover interval is), Word won't create a temporary backup copy of your unsaved document. Under those circumstances, when you close your document, you'll see a slightly different message:

The "Close" Prompt When AutoRecover Hasn't Kicked In

---

[31] Presumably Microsoft changed the label from "Yes" to "Save" solely for purposes of clarifying what that option does.

Since Word hasn't created a temporary backup—presumably because you have manually saved the file since the last autosave or because the document has been on screen for less time than the autosave interval—the prompt lacks the explanatory message, "If you choose 'Don't Save,' a draft of this file will be temporarily available." If you have made any edits that you haven't saved yet, be sure to click "**Save**," or those recent changes will be lost.

Recovering an Unsaved Document

The method for recovering an Unsaved Document depends on which type of Unsaved Document you are attempting to restore: (1) one that you closed without ever saving the document (let's call these the "**Never-Saved Documents**"); or (2) one that you saved at least once but then edited and closed without saving your edits (the "**Previously-Saved Documents**"[32]).

Never-Saved Documents can be opened and restored from two places in the Backstage View:

- from the **Manage Versions drop-down** on the **Info fly-out** (click the "**Recover Unsaved Documents**" button; and/or

- **from** the "**Recover Unsaved Documents**" **link** at the bottom of the **Recent fly-out**.

Alternatively, you can click **File, Open** (or press **Ctrl O**) and navigate to the location where the Never-Saved Documents are stored on your computer,[33] then open the file you want and save it permanently to a different folder. Remember that the Unsaved Documents (both types) are retained for only four days.

---

[32] I invented both terms for the sake of clarifying the differences between the two types of files.

[33] The "Never-Saved Documents" are stored in the following locations:

In Windows XP:
C:\Documents and Settings\<User Name>\Local Settings\Application Data\ Microsoft\ OFFICE\ UnsavedFiles

In Windows Vista and Windows 7:
C:\Documents and Settings\User Name\Local Settings\Application Data\Microsoft\OFFICE\ UnsavedFiles

CAUTION: If you open an Unsaved Document directly from the UnsavedFiles folder, it can be difficult to tell which "Unsaved Document" is which. Unless you already assigned a name to a file that you closed without saving (i.e., you hadn't saved the most recent edits), Word gives the "Closed Without Saving" files random names (sometimes, but seemingly not always, based on text at the beginning of the file).

When you open a Never-Saved Document, you will see a message bar above the document editing screen, indicating the status of the file and warning that it is "temporarily stored on your computer." (See the next screenshot.) To keep a copy permanently, click the "Save As" button, move the file to a different folder, and, if it doesn't have a meaningful name already, give it a new name.

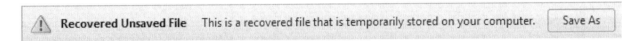

While the file is open on your screen, another warning message—this one with red text to flag your attention—will be displayed in the Backstage View (on the Info fly-out), letting you know that the file hasn't been saved permanently.

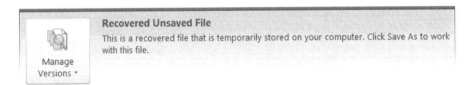

If you click the "**Manage Versions**" **button** while the file is on your screen, you'll see a new choice: "Save As."

You can use either the "**Save As**" **command** on this button or the one on the message bar above the document-editing screen to preserve a copy of the file.

To restore a Previously-Saved Document, use **File**, **Open** or **Ctrl O** to locate and open the version you last saved manually. After opening the file normally, click the **File tab**, **Info**, and look at the **Versions section** to the right of the **Manage Versions button** to see if there is a "closed without saving" version of the document.[34] See the screenshot below for an example.

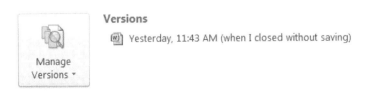

---

[34] The Never-Saved Documents do not appear in the Versions list.

If there is a "closed without saving" version, and you think it might be more recent than the version you last saved manually, click the icon. That version of the document will open, along with a message bar indicating that it is a recovered temporary file and giving you an opportunity to compare it to the version you last saved. To determine which version you want to keep, click the "**Compare**" button.

Word will perform a document comparison and will open the results in a new window. (To get a better understanding of what you're seeing on the document-comparison screen, see the tutorial about the document comparison feature, starting on page 519.)

If you decide to keep the backup version instead of the one you last saved manually, click the "**Restore**" button. A pop-up will appear, warning that you are about to overwrite the last-saved version with the temporary backup file.

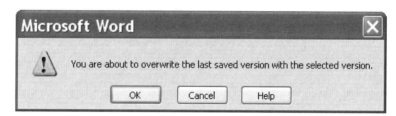

If you're sure you wish to do so, click "**OK**"; otherwise, click "**Cancel**."

The AutoRecover Files

Remember that the traditional AutoRecover files are temporary backups, intended only for emergencies, that normally are deleted when you exit from Word. Typically, you don't see such files unless you have experienced an abnormal event such as a power outage or a crash (in which case autosaved versions of any files that were open on your screen at the time of the outage or crash become available in an AutoRecover pane at the left side of the screen the next time you launch Word).

In Word 2010, you have access to these files from the Versions section of the Info fly-out during your work session. That is to say, assuming you have not changed the "Save" options, Word automatically saves a backup copy—also known as a "Version"—of each of your open documents every ten minutes. When you click File, Info, you can see all of the autosaved "Versions" of the current document.

If you want to recover an earlier "Version," you can click the link to that file; the autosaved draft will open in another window. You might see a warning message, indicating that there is a newer version of the document available and providing you with a way to compare the autosaved backup with the newer version so that you can decide which one to keep.

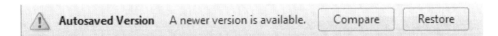

While the autosaved version is on your screen, the Info fly-out will display a message confirming that the file is not the newest version and that it has been opened in read-only mode.

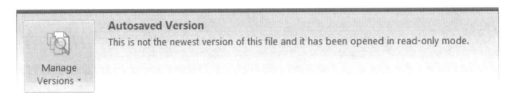

These reminders are intended to help you avoid losing critical data. If you restore an autosaved draft, it will replace the existing version unless you deliberately save the draft with a different name—a potential problem if indeed the autosaved draft *is not* the newest version of the file. And if you open an autosaved draft and then close it without saving, it will be deleted when you exit from Word—which could be a problem if the draft *is* the newest version.

The moral of the story is to try to get in the habit of manually saving documents often, especially those that are "mission critical." Although the AutoRecover function can be useful, it's best not to rely on automatic backups. They are not an adequate substitute for mindful, frequent, saves.

File Type and Storage Locations

Note that the AutoRecover Files and the Unsaved Documents both use the .asd extension (presumably "asd" stands for AutoSaved Document). The AutoRecover Files are stored in the same location as the Previously-Saved Documents; the Never-Saved Documents are stored in a different location.

Location of the AutoRecover Files and the Previously-Saved Documents:

In Windows XP:
C:\Documents and Settings\<User Name>\Application Data\Microsoft\Word

In Windows Vista and Windows 7:
C:\Users\<User Name>\AppData\Roaming\Microsoft\Word

Location of the Never-Saved Documents:

In Windows XP:
C:\Documents and Settings\<User Name>\Local Settings\Application Data\ Microsoft\ OFFICE\ UnsavedFiles

In Windows Vista and Windows 7:
C:\Users\<UserName>\AppData\Local\Microsoft\Office\ UnsavedFiles

Configuring Automatic Backups

The backup interval for both the AutoRecover files and the Unsaved Documents is determined by a setting in the **Word Options** (**File Drop-Down**, **Options**, **Save category**, **Save documents**), as shown in the next screenshot. The setting is labeled "**Save AutoRecover information every __ minutes**," and the default setting is ten minutes. [35]

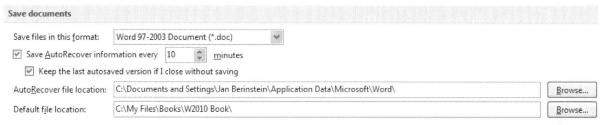

Word Options, Save Documents

Note as well the new option labeled "**Keep the last autosaved version if I close without saving**." This choice, which is the key to preserving the Unsaved Documents, is enabled by default. Unless you are working on a public computer (or a shared one), it is a good idea to leave the option checked.

Additionally, you can modify the AutoRecover file location and/or your default file location from this screen. (I have changed my default file location temporarily in order to have easy access to files related to this book project.)

Other Changes to Save, Save As, Open, and/or Close

Save As

When you first save a file in Word (.docx) format, you'll see a new option at the bottom of the "Save As" dialog that seemingly enables you to preserve the file's compatibility with earlier versions of Word.

---

[35] **CAUTION**: Although you can change the time interval at which "AutoRecover" drafts are saved, it's not a good idea to save more frequently than every 5 minutes. Doing so can tie up the computer's processor and prevent you from getting your work done normally.

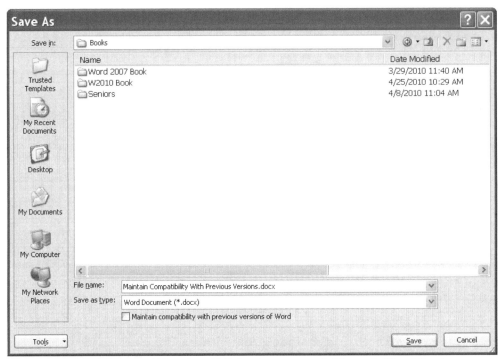

Save As Dialog (Showing "Maintain compatibility…" Checkbox)

Essentially, checking this option means only that some of the new features in Word 2010 will be disabled in the document. ***It doesn't actually make the file backwards compatible*** with Word 2003 or earlier because it remains a .docx, albeit not a full-fledged Word 2010 .docx. If you send the file to someone who uses Word 2002 or 2003, the recipient won't be able to open the file unless he or she has installed the Compatibility Pack.

Open

Microsoft has added a couple of new options to the "Open" button in the Open dialog. They are: **"Open in Protected View"** and **"Open with Transform."**

The latter, which ordinarily is grayed out, is pretty much for techies only (folks who work with XML files and, specifically, with .xsl or .xslt files); most people who work in the legal field won't ever need or use that option.

"Open in Protected View," however, is useful for opening a file you've downloaded from e-mail or or from the Internet or, for that matter, any other document you want to view but not edit. Protected View allows you to see the contents of the file while limiting your computer's exposure to any malicious code that might be embedded in the file. For more information, see the section about the Protected View on page 141.

Tips About Opening Files

While we're discussing the new options for opening files in Word 2010, it might be a good idea to review some of the other options available, even though you're probably aware of most of them. Knowing a few alternate methods for opening files can help you avoid accidentally overwriting an existing document and also can help you to minimize problems when working with a corrupted document or with a document that originated in another program (WordPerfect, Open Office, etc.)

Always try to follow "best practices" when you are creating a new document based on an existing one or creating a new draft (version) of a document. There are at least three methods that will preserve the original file:

(1)   Instead of using File, Open, use "**Open as Copy**" (see the screenshot at right), and then *immediately* use **File**, "**Save As**" (or press F12) to save the copy with a different name; or

| Open |
| Open Read-Only |
| Open as Copy |
| Open in Browser |
| Open with Transform |
| Open in Protected View |
| Open and Repair |

(2)   Use the "**Open Read-Only**" option and *immediately* use **File**, "**Save As**" (or press F12) to save the file with a different name; or

(3)   Open the existing document and then *immediately* use **File**, "**Save As**" (or press F12) and give the document on screen a different name from that of the original.[36]

"**Open as Copy**" and "**Open Read-Only**" work essentially the same way. Either of those options is a good choice if you want to ensure that the original file remains intact.

Yet another option for opening files into Word is to click the **Insert tab**, navigate to the **Text group**, click the **Object drop-down**, and click "**Text from File**." If you have a blank document open on the screen, Word will insert the text of the document you select into the blank screen, ready to rename. If you have a document on the screen that isn't blank, Word will insert the text of the selected document *at the cursor position* in the current document. This function comes in handy if, for example, you want to insert an existing, separate Proof of Service at the end of a pleading. It also can be useful for bringing the text from a WordPerfect document into a Word document, although the complex formatting in the WordPerfect file won't necessarily convert properly when you pull up the file in Word.

---

[36] This practice reduces the likelihood that you will accidentally overwrite the existing file or forget to save your changes—or that Word will save a backup copy of the original file that includes your edits, undermining your intention to leave the original file unchanged.

Note that this option will knock out some of the formatting and/or convert styles and automatic numbering schemes (and the like) from the original document into your default ("destination") styles.

"Open and Repair"

The "Open and Repair" command can be helpful if a document you're working on appears to be corrupted.[37] It is a method of last resort, to be used when nothing else you've tried works. And, to be on the safe side, make a copy of the document before using "Open and Repair."

To use the "Open and Repair" function, click File tab, Open or press Ctrl O, navigate to the document, click to select it, then *right-click* the "Open" button. When the menu appears, click "Open and Repair." Word will open the document and display a dialog box with a list of the items that were repaired (if any).

It's unnecessary (and usually an exercise in futility) to attempt to view the errors by clicking the "Go To" button. However, it's a good idea to close the "Show Repairs" dialog and then save the repaired file. If you close the file without saving, the repairs will be lost.

For more information about the "Open and Repair" feature, see this Microsoft Knowledge Base article: http://support.microsoft.com/kb/918429

For more information about document corruption, see the section starting on page 535.

---

[37] Symptoms of document corruption include, but are not limited to: sudden, unintended changes in formatting; inability to save a file; inability to open a file (or the program crashes when you do); unusual delays in opening or saving a file; uncontrollable movement of the cursor (and/or the cursor skips certain pages); constant repagination; and error messages about "insufficient memory."

SIDEBAR: Closing a Document Without Closing Word

Many people are accustomed to closing individual documents by clicking the "X" (the "Close" button) at the upper right-hand corner of the document window. That option has been available in Word (and in numerous other programs, including WordPerfect) through many, many versions.

Starting with Word 2007 and continuing in Word 2010, this setting has changed. By default, the program no longer displays a "Close" button for individual documents. Indeed, the "Minimize" and "Maximize/Restore" buttons for documents are missing, too. The only "Control buttons" visible in recent versions of Word are the ones at the right side of the Title bar—i.e., the ones that affect *the program*. Thus, when people click on the "X" in the upper right-hand corner of the screen, the program itself closes, to some people's surprise and consternation.

Fortunately, there is an easy way to change this setting and display a document window with the familiar trio of Control buttons (Minimize, Maximize/Restore, and Close). This sidebar also provides other tips for working with multiple document screens in Word 2010.

Adding a "Close Document" Button in Word 2010[38]

Click the **File tab**, click **Options**, and click **Advanced** (in the navigation bar on the left). Then, from within the Advanced options screen, scroll down to the **Display** category. Note whether "**Show all windows in the Taskbar**" is checked. If it is, click to *uncheck it* and then click **OK** to save your change.

Now you should see a second set of "Control buttons" at the upper right side of the screen — one for the program and one for the document. As in prior versions, the "X" on the lower rung is the one you should use to close the current document. (The "X" on the upper rung closes Word altogether.)[39]

There are other ways to close a document, of course. If you are a "mouse person," you can simply click the **File tab**, then click **Close**. If you are a "keyboard person," you can use one of the methods outlined below.

Keyboard Shortcuts to Close the Current Document

Ctrl F4 will close the current document, as will **Ctrl W**.

---

[38] Thanks to Herb Tyson, MS MVP and author of <u>The Word 2007 Bible</u>, for this first tip.

[39] Note that this choice involves a trade-off. If you decide to add the document Control buttons, you will lose some functionality, too—specifically, you won't be able to see individual documents listed in the Windows Taskbar.

My own preference is to use **Alt F, C**, the key combination I became accustomed to in earlier versions of Word (Alt F opens the File menu in previous versions and C executes the Close command). That key combo still works in Word 2010, and also works in WordPerfect.

Cycling Through Open Documents

Perhaps you just want to go back and forth among documents without closing any of them. It's relatively simple to move from one open document to another in Word 2010. As in previous versions of the program, the key combination **Ctrl F6** will cycle through all of your open documents. However, using that keystroke doesn't tell you which documents you have open, and you might have to cycle among several before you find the one you want.

Adding a "Switch Windows" Command to the QAT

In versions of Word prior to Word 2007, it was convenient to use the Window menu to see all open documents at a glance and switch back and forth between them. The menu bar was stationary, so the Window drop-down was available regardless of the task you were performing or the position of the cursor.

In Word 2010 (as in Word 2007), there is a **Switch Windows** command available in the **Window group** at the right side of the **View tab** (which certainly is a logical place for it). However, if you need to work with a command on a different tab or, perhaps, to edit a footer, you lose access to the Switch Windows command.

As a result, you might find it useful to add a Switch Windows button to the **Quick Access Toolbar**, also known as the QAT. To do so, either (1) click the **File tab, Options, Quick Access Toolbar**, or (2) *right*-click the QAT and click the **"Customize Quick Access Toolbar..." command**. When the Word Options screen appears, click to change the **Choose commands from: drop-down** to display "**All Commands**," then scroll down to **Switch Windows**, click the "**Add**" **button**, and click **OK**. That's all there is to it!

The Options (aka the Word Options)

Microsoft has made a few minor tweaks to the Word Options (besides reverting to the older term "Options" in the File drop-down). The most significant change since Word 2007 is a somewhat redesigned menu. Microsoft has renamed the top-level category ("General" instead of "Popular"), added a new "Language" category, replaced the "Customize" category with two separate categories (labeled "Customize Ribbon" and "Quick Access Toolbar," respectively), and removed the "Resources" category.

Apart from these cosmetic changes, there are some additional configuration options in Word 2010, all of them in the **Advanced category**. A few options have been removed, as well.

Most users won't use these new options, but I will mention them briefly just in case they prove helpful at some point.

Under **Display**, there is a new option to "Disable hardware graphics acceleration." This option, not available in Word 2007, is *off* (*unchecked*) by default. It can be turned on temporarily (meaning that hardware graphics acceleration will be *disabled*) if you are experiencing video issues or if you are working on an older computer with limited hardware graphics acceleration.

☐ Disable hardware graphics acceleration

Under **Image Size and Quality** (a new subcategory), there are some new choices: "Discard editing data" and "Do not compress images in file." Note that there is a small letter "i" in a circle next to each option. If you position the mouse pointer over the "i," an information pop-up appears.

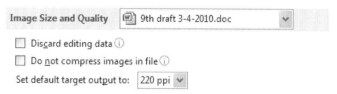

The pop-up for "Discard editing data" explains that the option deletes data used to restore edited pictures to their original state.

The pop-up for "Do not compress images in file" explains that this choice "provides maximum picture quality but may result in very large file sizes."

Exit (Close Word)

The Exit button at the bottom of the Backstage View / File Drop-Down works the same way as in previous versions: It closes the program. (If you like, you can use the familiar keyboard shortcut Alt F, X.) Of course, you also have the option of closing the program by clicking the large "X"—the Program Close button—at the top right side of the Word Title Bar. (For instructions on how to add a second, smaller "X" you can click to close a document without closing the entire program, see the sidebar on page 75.

Bypassing the Backstage View

Experienced users might find the Backstage View somewhat cumbersome. After all, it obscures the current document, and most of the fly-outs are somewhat cluttered. Fortunately, it's possible to use keyboard shortcuts—typically the same ones as in previous versions of Word—to bypass the Backstage View and go directly to many of the familiar dialog boxes.

As mentioned previously, you can use **F12** to open the **Save As** dialog. This keyboard shortcut is the same one used in prior versions of Word to invoke **Save As**. Here are a few other "bypass" key combinations:

Ctrl S for **Save**: This keystroke still saves the revisions you have made to the current document without the necessity of opening the Backstage View.

Ctrl O for **Open**: The familiar keystroke for opening documents still works as it did in previous versions and launches the Open dialog, allowing you to navigate directly to a file you want to open.

Ctrl F4 or **Ctrl W** ("W" as in "Window") for **Close**: Both of these shortcuts close the current document without going into the Bypass View. Note that **Alt F, C** also works, although you might see the Backstage View flash momentarily as the command is working.

I don't know of any built-in keyboard shortcut you can use to bypass "Print Place."

Closing the Backstage View

CAUTION: Because the Backstage View takes up an entire page, you might be tempted to click "Close" in order to return to the document editing screen. That would be a mistake. "Close," like the "Close" command in previous versions, closes *the active document*. To dismiss the Backstage View and resume work on your documents, do one of the following:

- Click the **File tab** or the **Home tab** (or, for that matter, any tab in the Ribbon); or

- Click the **document image** at the right side of the **Info fly-out menu**; or

- Press the **ESC key**.

Other New / Modified Features

The Navigation Pane / Enhanced "Find" Feature

The Navigation Pane is a new feature in Word 2010 that combines aspects of four different functions: Find, the Document Map, Browse Objects, and Thumbnails. Like the traditional "Find" dialog, it allows you search for text strings in your document. In addition, it provides an easy way for you to move quickly through a long document by jumping from one heading—or page—to another. And, like the Document Map, it serves as an organizational tool, letting you see the headings and subheadings in outline format, and even to move sections of the document around by dragging and dropping headings within the Navigation Pane.

There are three different ways to open the Navigation Pane:

1. by navigating to the **Editing group** at the right side of the **Home tab** and clicking **Find**; or

2. by pressing **Ctrl F** (the keyboard shortcut that opens the Find dialog in older versions of Word); or

3. by navigating to the **View tab, Show group** and clicking to check the **Navigation Pane checkbox** (if it isn't checked already; by default, it isn't).

Whichever method you use, the Navigation Pane typically opens at the left side of the screen (though you can move it), with the Browse Headings "tab" at the forefront. There are two other tabs: Browse Pages and Search. Clicking the top of a tab makes it the active one.

Search box →

Tabs →

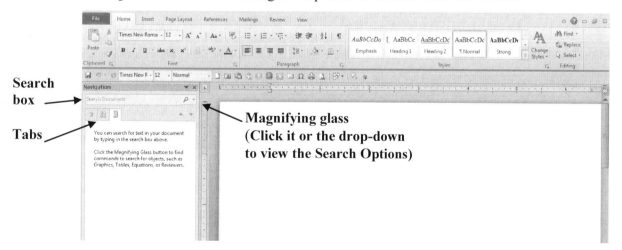

Magnifying glass
(Click it or the drop-down
to view the Search Options)

Navigation Pane at Left Side of Screen (With Headings Tab at the Forefront)

The screenshots below depict the three "tabs": Browse headings (the left-most tab), Browse pages (the center tab), and Browse search results (the right-most tab).

Browse Headings

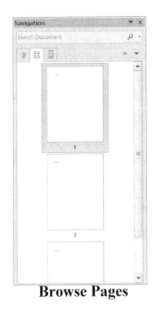

Browse Pages

Search

Searching

Always visible /available for use at the top of the Navigation Pane, regardless of which tab is at the forefront, there is a search box where you can type a word or phrase to find in your document. Word 2010 uses an "incremental find" function, which means that it looks for text, including partial words, *as you type* and displays matches within the Search tab. For example, if your document contains the words "page," "paperback," "apparent," and "pagination," Word shows instances of each of those words after you type the letters "pa." But as you continue and type a "g," for "pag," the words "paperback" and "apparent" drop out of the search results (the letter "g" serves as a filter). The final results depend on which character you type next.

Results for "pa"   **Results for "pag"**   **Results for "pagi"**

Alternatively, you can type a term in the search box and then press the Enter key. In either case, Word scrolls to a page containing your search term, shows the search results in the Search tab, and displays all instances of the term in yellow highlighting within the document so that you can see them more easily. The highlighting disappears when you stop the search—and clear the search box—by clicking the "X" to the right of the search box. (Be careful not to click the "X" at the very top of the Navigation Pane unless you want to close the pane itself.)

CAUTION: If you click the "X" to the right of the search box without first clicking to position the cursor in the page where the search took you, ***Word will return you to the page your cursor was on when you started the search***. This action is by design.[1] Indeed, if you position the mouse pointer over the "X" in the search box, you'll see a pop-up that says: "Click to end search ***and scroll back to your original place in the document***" (emphasis mine).

To avoid scrolling back to your last edit point, be sure to click somewhere within the search result page you intended as your destination before clicking the "X" to stop the search.

You can move to any other page that appears in the Search tab (i.e., the search results) by clicking on the text in the Search tab, or by using the up or down arrow above the tabs.

The screenshot below shows that, after typing the search term "page," I clicked the rectangle in the results area where it says "Second Page" (left side), which took me to the page where that text appears in the document (right side).

Clicking a Rectangle in the Search Results
Takes You to the Page Where the Text Appears

---

[1] Clicking the "X" that closes the Navigation Pane can have the same effect—that is, it sometimes scrolls back to the page your cursor was on when you began the search. This behavior doesn't appear to occur consistently, however.

Clearing the Search Box

As mentioned in the previous section, you can clear the search box (either to start a new search or simply to stop Word's incremental search feature from operating in the background) by clicking the "X" at the right side of the box.

When you click on a page to take a closer look at the search results, the search box often clears itself—even when you are not necessarily finished searching for a specific term. Sometimes pressing Ctrl F will cause the last search term you used to reappear in the search box. Also, you can copy your search term directly from the search box and then paste it back into the box (rather than having to retype it) if the box clears before you are finished searching.

Using the Traditional "Find" Dialog (or "Find and Replace")

Should you wish to use the traditional Find dialog, you can. There are two ways to invoke it:

- Press **Ctrl H** (a key combination that, as in previous versions of Word, opens the Find and Replace dialog, allowing you to click the "Find" tab); or

- Click either the **magnifying glass** at the top of the Search tab or **the arrow** to the right of it. Doing so produces a drop-down that offers various options, including "**Advanced Find**." Clicking "Advanced Find" produces the traditional Find dialog.

For more information, see the sidebar on page 96 about some of the advanced "Find" options.

Additional Search Commands

As mentioned previously, when you click either the magnifying glass or the arrow to the right of it, a menu with additional search commands appears. This menu is similar to the "Browse by Object" fly-out that appears (in all recent versions of Word) when you click the circle at the bottom of the vertical scroll-bar, except that it uses words, as well as icons, to label the commands. (Also, the drop-down menu contains fewer objects.) Both let you search for objects other than text in your document.

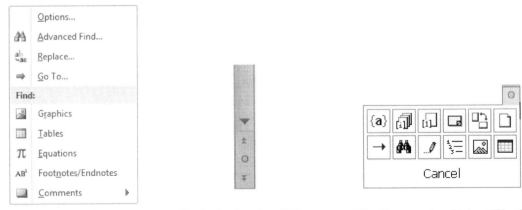

| Search Options | Circle in the Scroll Bar… | The Browse by Object Fly-Out |

The drop-down (much like the Browse by Objects fly-out) includes the following commands / selections:

- Options…
- Advanced Find…
- Replace…
- Go To…
- Graphics
- Tables
- Equations
- Footnotes/Endnotes
- Comments

I will discuss "Options" in the next section.

"Advanced Find" invokes the traditional Find dialog box, complete with tabs for Replace and Go To; "Replace" produces the same dialog, but with the Replace tab active (i.e., at the forefront); with Go To, you get the same dialog with the Go To tab active.

When you click the "Graphics" command, Word immediately searches the document for images. It stops at the first one it comes to (that is, the first one to appear in or after the page your cursor is in when you start the search). To see the next graphic in the document, click the Browse by Pages tab—the middle one—and then click the down arrow to the right of the tabs. (If you prefer, you can use the scroll bar to move more quickly through the Browse by Pages display.)

Note that searching for graphics (or other objects), like searching for text, serves as a filter on the Browse by Pages tab. In other words, if you click the Browse by Pages tab after searching for graphics in the document, you'll see that the tab displays **_only thumbnails of pages that contain graphics_**. That is apparent in the screenshot at right.

Searching for the other types of objects (tables, equations, footnotes / endnotes, or comments) works the same way. When you search for comments, however, you also have to click the fly-out and then select a particular reviewer or all reviewers.

After you have searched for a certain type of object, remember to click the "X" at the right side of the search box to clear it—and make the magnifying glass visible again—so that you can start a new search. You must do so regardless of whether the new search involves a different type of object or text.

The Find Options

The first command on the menu that appears when you click the magnifying glass (or the "Down" button to its right) is **Options…** Clicking **Options…** produces a dialog that displays several different "**Find Options**" you can use to delimit complex searches involving text.

You'll note that "Highlight all" and "Incremental find" already are checked. They are enabled because they are default settings. You can change them if you like. If you do uncheck "Incremental find," Word will stop searching for text strings as you type them in the search box. You will need to type the entire word or phrase and then either click the magnifying glass or press the Enter key to carry out the search.

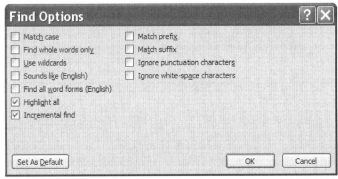

The Find Options

Once you have selected the options you wish to use, you can click the drop-down again, then click the binoculars to start a "Find" operation using the filters you've selected.

Here is a brief explanation of each option.

- Match case

  When this option is checked, Word will search for a word or phrase in the case that you use to type the word in the search box (or in the Find dialog): UPPER, lower, Initial Caps, etc. If the word or phrase occurs in the document in a different case from what you type in the search box (or Find dialog), those instances of the word or phrase will not appear in the search results.

- Find whole words only

  This option can be helpful if you are looking for a word (typically a short one) that can be subsumed within a longer word. For instance, let's say you want to find all occurrences of the word "he" in an estate plan so that you can replace the male gender with the female gender. Obviously, searching for the letters "he" without limiting the search to whole words will turn up all sorts of irrelevant results, such as "she," "whether," and "the." Applying the "whole words" filter will make the search results more meaningful.

- Use wildcards

   You might be familiar with wildcards from searches you've performed with Lexis or Westlaw or on the Internet. Wildcard characters such as the question mark (?), the asterisk (*), or the exclamation point (!) typically stand in for other characters, allowing you to find all forms of certain words in your document or to find a particular word even if you're not sure how it's spelled.

   In Word, some wildcards are fairly simple to use. For example, the question mark character (?) stands in for a single character. As an example, using the search term "f?rm" (without quotation marks) will produce results that include the words "farm," "firm," and "form" (if those words appear in your document).

   Some of the other wildcards work in a less straightforward manner. The asterisk (*), for example, stands in for multiple contiguous characters.[2] In theory, it lets you search for words when you're not certain of the spelling or when a word might appear in both American English ("color") and British English ("colour"). As in Internet searches, you would use the search term "col*r" (without quotation marks), whereby the asterisk would stand for multiple characters between the letter "l" and the letter "r." That would find both "color" and "colour."

   In Word, however, searches that use the asterisk character can lead to results that include *multiple consecutive words*. So, although such a search would turn up both "color" and "colour," Word might also highlight text in your document such as "column or"—because the asterisk wildcard apparently encompasses spaces (and punctuation marks), as well as alphabetical and numeric characters. Thus, it does not limit a search to individual words.

   You *can* perform wildcard searches and limit the results to individual words, but to do so requires the use of a more complex "expression."[3]

---

[2] This usage is somewhat different from what you might be used to if you perform searches in Lexis and/or Westlaw. In both of those legal-specific search engines, the asterisk wildcard stands in for a single character within a single word; you can use multiple asterisks to stand in for multiple characters within a single word. Thus in Lexis and/or Westlaw, "col**r" presumably finds both "color" and "colour." That search would not work the same way in Word, however.

[3] In place of the asterisk, you would use the expression "[a-z]@" (without quotation marks). The [a-z] tells Word to search for any character in the range from "a" to "z"; the "@" instructs the program to search for one or more such characters. In our example, you would check the "Wildcards" option and then type the following in the "Find" box (without quotation marks): "col[a-z]@r" (Word will look for "col" followed by any letter between "a" and "z," occurring one or more times, followed by the letter "r." Because the search restricts the characters between "col" and "r" to letters—excluding spaces and punctuation marks—the results will be limited to a single word.) **NOTE**: In my tests, this expression found lower-case letters only.

Advanced searches involving so-called regular expessions are beyond the scope of this book.[4]

- Sounds like

  You can use the "Sounds like" filter to search for words you're not sure how to spell. (For instance, suddenly you forget if it's "supercede" or "supersede," "admissible" or "admissable." "Sounds like" will find either.)

- Find all word forms

  This nifty option looks for all forms of a particular word. For example, you can search for the word "store," and the program will turn up results that include "store," "stored," and "stores." Similarly, "navigate" produces "navigate," "navigation," "navigated," and "navigating." Note that you can't use characters other than letters while searching in this mode.

- Match prefix

  This option looks for letters at the beginning of a word (or that form an entire word). As an example, if you click the "Match prefix" option and then search for the word "fix" (not within quotation marks), Word will find "fix" by itself, and also at the beginning of words (such as "fixed," "fixing," and "fixated") but not at the end of words ("prefix," "suffix," "affixed").

- Match suffix

  This option works like "Match prefix," but looks for words that appear at the end of a word rather than at the beginning. (It also finds whole words.) Hence, if this option is checked and you search for the word "fix," Word will not locate the words "fixed," "fixing," "fixated," "fixer," "fixed," and so on.

---

[4] For detailed instructions on using wildcards, as well as other complex expressions, see the Microsoft article: http://office.microsoft.com/en-us/word/HA012303921033.aspx, as well as Microsoft MVP Graham Mayor's article: http://www.gmayor.com/replace_using_wildcards.htm

- Ignore punctuation characters

  This option finds words regardless of whether they appear before a comma, a period, an exclamation point, a question mark, etcetera. But note that if you check this option and then specify a punctuation character as part of your search term, Word includes that character—and only that character—in the search results (if it finds any matches).

  For instance, if I enable the "Ignore punctuation characters" option and then search for "WordPerfect." (i.e., my search term is WordPerfect followed by a period, but without quotation marks), Word finds only those instances of "WordPerfect" that are followed by a period. It does not return instances of "WordPerfect" followed by a comma. If I use the "Ignore punctuation characters" filter and then remove the comma from the search term, Word finds all instances of "WordPerfect," whether in the middle of a sentence or followed by a comma or a period.

- Ignore white-space characters

  This option will find a search term regardless of whether it appears with or without white space incorporated into the term. For example, if you check this option and then search for "WordPerfect," Word will find both "WordPerfect" and "Word Perfect"; likewise, a search for "screenshot" will turn up both "screenshot" and "screen shot" (assuming your document contains both terms).

- Highlight all

  As mentioned previously, this option is enabled by default. It acts to highlight all instances of your search term in the document (in yellow) to help you locate them. The temporary highlighting disappears when you clear the search box by clicking the "X" to the right of your term.

- Incremental find

  Also mentioned previously, this default setting lets Word look for text strings, and filter the search results, in real time as you type characters in the search box. You don't have to press the "Enter" key to carry out the search.

CAUTION: After you have finished using one or more of these filters, remember to open the Find Options dialog and ***uncheck*** (clear) them. Otherwise, they will remain in place and, in future searches, will exclude certain results you probably did not intend to screen out. The same advice holds if you have used any other advanced search options available from the "Format" or "Special" buttons in the Find dialog. For more tips about using the Find feature, including a few of the advanced options, see the section starting on page 96.

Browse Pages / Thumbnail View

The Browse Pages tab, like the Thumbnail option on the View tab in Word 2007 and in the View menu in Word 2003, provides a "thumbnail" view of your document, with each page displayed individually within the Navigation Pane. The current page (the one your cursor is in) appears within a box, outlined in color. The display changes in real time—albeit sometimes with a slight lag—as you move around in your document while you are working.

The current page appears within a highlighted box

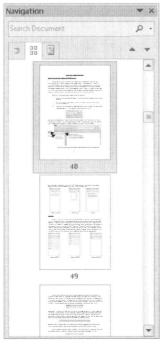

Use the Up and Down buttons or click on a thumbnail to move from page to page

The Browse Pages Tab

You can also use the Browse Pages tab to scroll through your document. To jump from one page to the previous or next page, just click one of the thumbnail images or click the "Up" and "Down" arrows at the top right of the tab. Alternatively, you can drag the scroll bar to move more quickly through the document.[5]

Note that you can't move pages around in your document via the Browse Pages tab (i.e., you can't drag and drop entire pages the way that you can drag and drop headings and subheadings via the Browse Headings tab).

Right-clicking the Navigation Pane scroll bar while the Browse Pages tab is at the forefront opens a context-sensitive menu that offers a few scrolling options. These options change what is displayed in the Browse Pages tab, but they don't actually move the cursor within the document or change what you see in the document editing screen.

---

[5] In my tests, clicking the thumbnail proved more reliable than using the arrows, which worked only intermittently. And both methods seem limited to moving only to the pages currently displayed in the Navigation Pane. To move to a page that is not displayed, you might have to scroll up or down and *then* click the thumbnail or use the up or down arrow.

Scroll Here

Top
Bottom

Page Up
Page Down

Scroll Up
Scroll Down

Which pages appear in the thumbnail view when you click the "Scroll Here" option depends on the position of your mouse pointer in the scroll bar. For instance, if the mouse pointer is about halfway down the scroll bar, clicking "Scroll Here" will present a thumbnail view of two or three pages located approximately in the middle of your document. If the mouse pointer is toward the top of the scroll bar, the command will result in the display of pages near the beginning of the document. And so forth.

The "Top" command displays the very first page of the document; the "Bottom" command displays the very last one. "Page Up" and "Page Down" show the page before or the page after whatever is currently displayed in the Browse Pages tab.

"Scroll Up" and "Scroll Down" move the thumbnails up or down incrementally.

TIP: If you like, you can widen the Navigation Pane by positioning the mouse pointer over the right border and, when the double-headed arrow appears, dragging the border farther to the right. That will allow you to see more pages, displayed in two or more columns, in thumbnail view. When you change the display to show thumbnails in multiple columns (as in the screenshot at right), the "Page Up" and "Page Down" commands on the context menu actually jump more than a single page at a time.

Using "Search" Filters the Browse Pages Display

It's worth pointing out that the "Search" function of the Navigation Pane acts as a filter on the Browse Pages tab. That is, if you have entered a word or phrase in the search box prior to clicking the Browse Pages tab in order to switch to a thumbnail view of your document, the Browse Pages tab will display *only those pages that contain your search term*. In order to see all pages, be sure to clear the search box by clicking the "X" at the right side of the box.[6]

---

[6] The "Find" function doesn't work quite the same way with respect to the Browse Headings tab. See page 94 for more information.

Browse Headings

The Browse Headings tab is very useful if you have used heading styles within your document. Any headings formatted with styles are automatically pulled into the Navigation Pane, where they are displayed in a condensed outline view.

The Browse Headings Tab

The Navigation Pane actually lets you move sections around in the document by dragging and dropping headings within the Headings tab. When you do so, the headings should renumber accordingly (assuming you have applied automatic numbering). Be sure to check. If they ***don't*** renumber properly (as in the screenshot below, where the paragraph I moved should have become paragraph 3.5 but the numbering didn't adjust), look at the document and locate the first heading that should have incremented but did not. **Right-click** in or near the paragraph number and, when the context-sensitive menu appears, choose the "**Continue Numbering**" command.

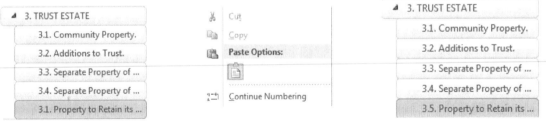

| **Number Didn't Adjust…** | **Right-Click Menu (Partial), Continue Numbering** | **…Updated Number** |

CAUTION: Consider making a backup copy of your document before experimenting with this feature, just in case you change your mind afterwards and have difficulty restoring the document's original organization.[7]

---

[7] You should be able to undo any moves by pressing Ctrl Z or clicking the Undo button on the Quick Access Toolbar, assuming you act quickly.

Right-clicking within the Headings tab lets you change how the headings are displayed there. A context-sensitive pop-up menu appears when you right-click and offers several helpful commands, including "**Expand All**" (show all of the heading levels in the document) and"**Collapse All**" (show only the level 1 headings).

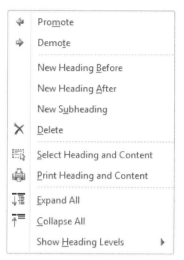

Right-Click Menu

The screenshots below show a sample contract as it was displayed in the Browse Headings pane after I clicked "Expand All" and after I clicked "Collapse All."

After Clicking "Expand All"   **After Clicking "Collapse All"**

The right-click menu also provides a "**Show Heading Levels**" command; when you click it, a sub-menu opens that lets you specify exactly how many levels to display in the Headings tab. (You can display any number of heading levels in your document from one to nine.) Note that choosing a particular level means displaying headings *up to and including* that level.

To display only certain levels of headings in the Navigation Pane, right-click within the Headings tab, then click "Show Heading Levels" and click a particular heading level to indicate how many levels of the outline to display. Remember that selecting a heading level will display headings **_up to and including_** that level. For instance, clicking "Show Heading 3" will show three levels of headings (i.e., all headings to which a Heading 1, a Heading 2, or a Heading 3 style has been applied). See the screenshots below.

Show Heading Levels   **Show Heading 3**   **Three Levels Are Displayed**
                                    (Up to and Including)

Note as well that individual headings that contain at least one section with a subheading can be expanded or collapsed. In the screenshots that follow, you'll notice a small triangle to the left of those headings that contain sections with subheadings. The dark triangles show headings that have been expanded; the light ones show headings that have been collapsed. Clicking a light triangle expands a heading "family"; clicking a dark one collapses it.

Expanded Heading Families;   **A Collapsed Heading Family;**
Click a Dark Triangle   **Click a Light Triangle**
to Collapse an Expanded Heading   **to Expand a Collapsed Heading**

In both of the above headings, Section 3 ("Contract Terms") has been expanded to show a single subheading (Section 3.1) below it. The screenshot at left shows Section 3.2 ("Scope of the Contract") expanded (revealing two subheadings, Sections 3.2.1 and 3.2.2, beneath it); the screenshot at right shows Section 3.2 collapsed (without the subheadings displayed). Note that the triangle is dark and points down at an angle—as if to say, "See the subheadings below"— when a heading family has been expanded, whereas it is white and points off to the right when the heading family has been collapsed.

Another very useful option available from the right-click menu lets you insert a new heading before or after an existing heading. Just click to select (highlight) the heading you want the new heading positioned before or after, right-click it, and, when the context menu appears, click to choose "New Heading Before" or "New Heading After" as appropriate.

Choose "New Heading Before" or "New Heading After"

The right-click menu also contains a "New Subheading" command It is somewhat quirky in that when you right-click a specific heading or subheading, then click the "New Subheading" command, Word does indeed create a new subheading, but places it ***after the last existing subheading*** at that level. (In other words, if you right-click a Level 2 subheading and click "New Subheading," Word will create a new Level 3 subheading and place it after any extant Level 3 subheadings, ***not necessarily*** after the Level 2 subheading itself.) However, if the new subheading doesn't appear where you want it, you can drag and drop it within the Headings tab to position it in the correct order.

For example, if Section 3.1 of my document already has two subheadings (Sections 3.1.1. and 3.1.2) and I right-click Section 3.1 and then click "New Subheading," Word puts the new subheading at the end and automatically numbers it Section 3.1.3.

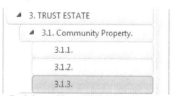

New Subheading Within Section 3.1

Similarly, if I right-click Section 3 itself (the major heading) and then click "New Subheading," Word adds a subheading after the existing Sections 3.1., 3.2., 3.3., 3.4., and 3.5.

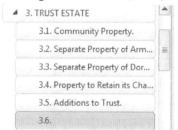

New Subheading Within Section 3

If that isn't where I want the new section, it's a trivial matter to drag and drop the new subheading within the Browse Headings pane, as shown in the next screenshot. (Moving the sections around within the Browse Headings pane also moves them around within the document.) As mentioned previously, Word automatically renumbers the paragraphs.

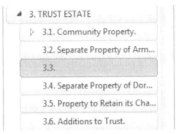

The Subheadings Automatically Renumber
After You Drag the New One to a Different Position

You can also use the right-click menu to promote or demote headings or subheadings (i.e., change their outline level); to delete them altogether; to print them (along with any text that follows); or to select them and then apply formatting. To do the latter, right-click a heading or subheading, choose "Select Heading and Content" (the content includes the heading family and associated text), and then apply character or paragraph formatting or a style.

A final word about the Browse Headings tab: If you recently used the "Find" feature to search for a word or phrase, your search term acts as a filter on what is displayed in the Browse Headings tab. That is, all of the headings and subheadings in your document to which styles have been applied will appear there, but you might notice that some of them—the ones that contain your search term—are highlighted.

The screenshot below shows headings and subheadings in my document after I have searched for the word "contract." To remove the highlighting (and clear the filter), just click the "X" at the right side of the search box.

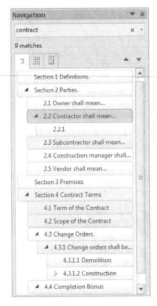

Moving the Navigation Pane

There are a couple of ways to move the Navigation Pane. You can drag it by its title bar and drop it in a new location. Or you can click the down-pointing triangle at the top right side of the Navigation Pane to open the drop-down (the "Control Menu"), then click Move, and then do a drag-and-drop operation. Note that after you drop the Nav Pane, you should ***click to anchor it in position***. Otherwise, it might continue to move when you reposition the mouse pointer.

The Navigation Pane's "Control Menu"

You also have the option of resizing the Navigation Pane, as mentioned previously, by dragging its right border ***or*** by clicking the Control Menu and clicking Size, then moving the mouse pointer. Again, be sure to click again when you're finished to stop the resizing operation.

Closing the Navigation Pane

You can close the Navigation Pane by doing one of the following:

- Clicking the "X" at the top right side of the Pane; or

- Pressing the Esc key; or

- Clicking the drop-down at the top of the Navigation Pane, then clicking "Close."

A "Sticky" Setting

The state of the Navigation Pane (i.e., whether it is on or off) is "sticky." In other words, if it's open when you close out of Word, it will be open when you re-launch the program and vice versa.

SIDEBAR: Exploring a Few Advanced "Find" Options

The Find feature was changed in some important respects in Word 2007. In particular, Microsoft added a couple of new advanced Find options that persist in Word 2010. One is the "**Reading Highlight**" option available in the "Find" dialog box. When you type a search term in the box and click the **Reading Highlight drop-down**, then click "**Highlight All**," Word goes through your document and highlights (normally in yellow) all instances of the term. When you want to turn the highlighting off again, just click "**Clear Highlighting**."

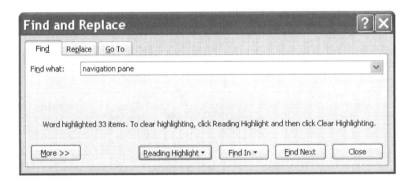

There is also a new "**Find in**" button that lets you specify which part of the document to search: the **Main Document, Headers and Footers, Footnotes, Text Boxes in Main Document** or, if you have text selected, **Current Selection**. Note that the options available from this drop-down vary depending on the types of formatting that exist in the current document.

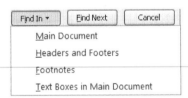

CAUTION: This feature occasionally goes awry, such that you might assume you are searching the entire document, but Word "gets stuck" searching only the footnotes. If you get an error message indicating that the program can't find any more instances of a particular word *in the footnotes*, be sure to click "**Find in**" and reset the search location to "**Main Document**," and then click "**Find Next**" to resume searching the document text.

Other Advanced "Find" Options

As you probably know, Word has the ability to search for formatted text. If you click the "**Format**" **button** in the Find dialog, then click "**Font**," you can check one or more of the font attribute boxes in order to search for a word or phrase that is in italics, bold, small caps, and so forth. You can also search for highlighting. After you run a search for formatted text, *be sure to clear the search criteria* by clicking the "**No Formatting**" button at the bottom of the Find dialog. If you don't clear the criteria, Word will continue looking for formatted text, and you might not realize that's why it doesn't find your search term.

If you apply a font attribute such as italics…

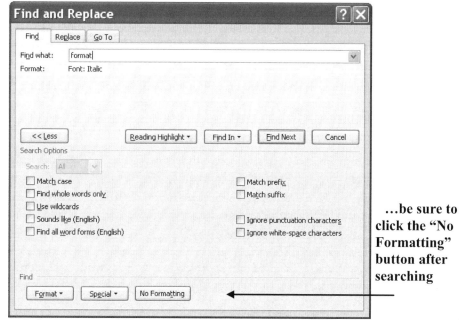

…be sure to click the "No Formatting" button after searching

Search for Formatted Text… Then Clear the Search Criteria

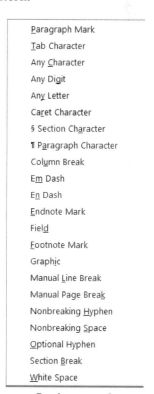

You also probably know that you can use the options available from the "**Format**" and "**Special**" buttons to search for specific styles, field codes, paragraph symbols, section breaks, line breaks, em dashes, nonbreaking spaces, footnote marks, highlighting, paragraph formatting such as line spacing and before and after spacing, and much more.

The screenshot at right shows the options available from the "Special" button; the screenshot below shows the commands available from the "Format" button (most of which provide multiple options).

Options Available From the "Format" Button

Options on the "Special" Button

For an extensive article that explains each of these options, see "Find and replace text or other items," located here: http://office.microsoft.com/en-us/word/HA012303921033.aspx The article deals with Word 2007, but applies to Word 2010 as well. (NOTE: Be sure to click "Show All" at the top of the article to display all of the content.)

Another very useful option in the Find dialog is the one to "**Find all word forms**." I used it just now to search through the book manuscript for all forms of the word "find" (without quotation marks). It turned up "find," "finding," and "found." **TIP/CAUTION**: You can perform a Find and Replace operation using "Find all word forms," but it's advisable to review each instance of the word or phrase rather than using "Replace All," since Word, while smart enough to *find* all of the forms of a particular word, isn't necessarily smart enough to *replace* with the correct word form.

As with most advanced find options, just remember to *clear the "Find all word forms" checkbox* when you have finished with the search. Note that you might have to run another (quick) search with the box unchecked in order to make sure Word doesn't turn the option back on when you close the Find dialog. This choice seems to be particularly "sticky."

For a discussion about the items in the "Search Options" portion of the Find dialog (Match case, Use wildcards, Find whole words only, Match prefix, Match suffix, etc.), see the section starting on page 84.

TROUBLESHOOTING TIP: "Find" Disables Page Up and Page Down

After you use "**Find**" (or "**Find and Replace**") to look for a word, phrase, or object, the keyboard shortcuts for Page Up (**Ctrl Page Up**) and Page Down (**Ctrl Page Dn**) stop working as navigation keys (and the Page Up and Page Down buttons in the scrollbar stop working as expected). This seemingly arbitrary change in functionality actually happens by design, but it can be disconcerting if you're not expecting it. It has to do with the "**Browse by Object**" feature and the fact that this feature is linked to "**Find**."

"**Browse by Object**," which is invoked by clicking a circular button at the bottom of the vertical scrollbar, can be quite useful. Related to "Go To," it allows you to search through your document according to any of the following criteria:

Browse By

- Go To   (opens the Go To dialog box[1])
- Find   (opens the Find dialog)
- Edits   (allows you to search by edits if you are using Track Changes)
- Heading
- Graphic
- Table
- Field
- Endnote
- Footnote
- Comment
- Section
- Page

Here's where things get tricky. For some reason—perhaps because the default search object is "Page"—Microsoft assigned the key combination for **Page Up (Ctrl Page Up)** and **Page Down (Ctrl Page Dn)** to the Browse by Object feature.

That fact, in and of itself, doesn't present a problem—unless and until you use "**Find**" or "**Find and Replace**." When you use Find or Find and Replace to search for text, the "Browse by" default search object *changes from "Page" to "Find."* Thus, when you try to go to the previous page or the next page by pressing Ctrl Page Up or Ctrl Page Dn—*or when you click the Page Up or Page Down arrows on the scrollbar*—Word stops browsing by page and instead browses by the word or phrase you last typed into the Find box![2]

---

[1] The "Go To" dialog, which you also can invoke by pressing Ctrl G, allows you to search for all of the above, as well as by Line, Bookmark, Equation, and Object. And, of course, the "Special" button in the Find dialog offers many additional searchable objects.

[2] In fact, the same problem occurs if you use the Browse by Object feature to search by anything other than Page—such as Comment.

If Word doesn't find any more instances of the word or phrase you last searched for, you might get a rather mystifying error message similar to the one in the screenshot below.

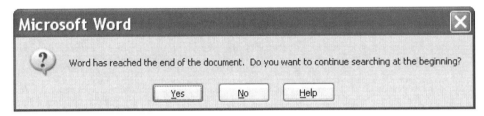

The thing to keep in mind is that whatever object you last used as your search criterion — whether you used one of the "Find" dialog boxes or "Browse by Object"—will become the new "Browse by Object" default. This new default will stick *until (1) you close out of and reopen Word* (the program restores the "Browse By Object" default settings when it reopens) *or (2) you specifically click the "Browse By" button and then click Page to reset the default object.*[3]

TIP / WORKAROUND: One workaround for the Browse By issue is to assign a different keyboard shortcut to the Page Up and Page Down commands and use that shortcut instead of Ctrl Page Up and Ctrl Page Dn .

To assign a new key combination to the Page Up and Page Down commands, click the **File tab, Options, Customize Ribbon**, then click the "**Keyboard shortcuts: Customize**" **button**. In the **Categories box**, scroll down to and click **All Commands**. In the **Commands** box, scroll down to and click **GoToNextPage**.

Next, click in the **Press new shortcut key:** box and press a new key combination, such as Ctrl Shift Page Dn. If that key combination isn't already assigned to another function in Word, click the **Assign** button.

Then, in the **Commands** box, scroll down to and click **GoToPreviousPage**. In the **Press new shortcut key:** box, press a different key combination, such as Ctrl Shift Page Up. If that key combination isn't already assigned to another function in Word, click the **Assign** button. When you've finished, click **Close**, and then be sure to click **OK** (not Cancel) to close out of Word Options.[4]

Now, when you wish to move up or down one full page, use your new keyboard shortcuts. They'll work regardless of whether you have recently used "Find," "Find and Replace," or "Browse by Object."

---

[3] Alternatively, you can open the **Go To dialog** by pressing Ctrl G, click **Page**, click **Next** (or **Previous**), then click **Close**. CAUTION: Simply clicking Page in the Go To dialog and then clicking Close without clicking Next or Previous *does not* re-set the default search object.

[4] If you prefer, you can remove the Ctrl Page Up and Ctrl Page Dn keystrokes from Browse Object and assign them, instead, to GoToPreviousPage and GoToNextPage, respectively. In some ways, that might be a better option because you won't have to memorize a new keyboard shortcut for those functions.

Web Apps

For the first time, users of MS Office have access to "lite" versions of a few of the applications in the suite—specifically, Word, Excel, PowerPoint, and OneNote—that reside online. These so-called Web Apps are free of charge to large businesses and individuals who already own Office 2010 and who meet certain specific criteria, as outlined below.[1]

The Web Apps serve much the same purpose, and work much the same way, as Google Docs. You can store documents online and use the Web Apps to view and edit those files from any computer that has Internet access. That gives you the flexibility to work at home, from a library, or even while you're traveling. You can share documents with other members of your organization and, via the new Co-authoring feature (discussed in the next section, starting on page 115), two or more people can edit the same document simultaneously.[2]

NOTE: Web Apps are not full-featured versions of the Office 2010 programs, and your editing options will be somewhat limited.

Eligibility Requirements

In order to qualify for the free Web Apps, you must meet the following eligibility requirements:

Businesses

Businesses that participate in Microsoft's Volume Licensing program are eligible for the Web Apps. If you fall into this category, you should be able to use the Web Apps on either Microsoft SharePoint Server 2010 or a server running Microsoft SharePoint Foundation 2010.

Individuals

Individuals can run the Web Apps via Windows Live.[3] It has been suggested that the versions available to consumers after the beta (trial) period ends will be a "free, ad-supported service," which means you will see ads while you are working online. As of this writing (in mid-May, 2010), I don't know whether that applies to everyone or only to people who don't own Office 2010.

---

[1] According to Microsoft, "Office 2010 is not required to work with Office Web Apps..." It is unclear, however, if people who don't own Office 2010 will be able to use the Web Apps *after the beta-testing period ends*. See this article: http://office2010.microsoft.com/en-us/web-apps-help/getting-started-with-office-web-apps-HA101785172.aspx?CTT=5&origin=HA101231889

[2] As with Google Docs, the documents are password-protected, but it is easy to give trusted individuals access to them.

[3] Office Watch says that people in the U.S. (and Japan) can try out the Web Apps even if they don't own Office 2010. See this article for more information, plus a link to SkyDrive: http://news.office-watch.com/t/n.aspx?articleid=1376&zoneid=24

Supported Browsers

Microsoft recommends that you use one of their "supported" browsers when working with the Web Apps: Internet Explorer (IE) (version 7 or later), Firefox (version 3.5 or later), or Safari (version 4 or later). In general, the most recent version of the browser will be better at rendering the images, although—as the saying goes—your mileage may vary. In my experience, Chrome (which is not among the supported browsers) did a superior job at displaying the images and also providing *all* of the menu options, whereas an older version of IE did not show all of the menu options and images were garbled in Firefox 2.X. I did not test with Safari.

Getting Started

You will need to create a Windows Live / SkyDrive account, if you don't have one already. You can sign up by going to this site: http://skydrive.live.com

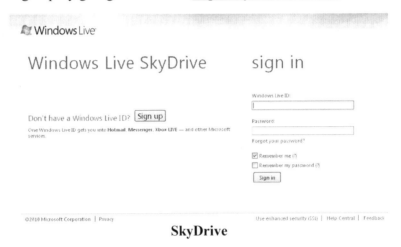

SkyDrive

As discussed in the section about saving to the Web (starting on page 41), it takes a few minutes to set up the SkyDrive account, but once you have done so, you can sign up for Microsoft's Preview Program and start using the Web Apps.

After you sign up, you might be taken to the Windows Live home page rather than SkyDrive (see the next screenshot). If so, click the "More" link at the top of the screen and, when the drop-down opens, click "SkyDrive."

The Windows Live Home Page

102

Uploading a File

Once you arrive at your SkyDrive page, the first step is to upload a file to one of your folders. Just click a folder icon, and then click either the "**Add files**" link or "**Why not add some files**?" I chose the "My Documents" folder, but you can select any existing folder (or even create and then click a new one, if you like).

Click a Folder Icon (Such as "My Documents")

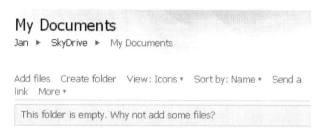

Then Click "Add files" or "Why not add some files?"

When you do so, you'll see a screen with "Choose File" buttons you can click to browse for files on your computer that you can upload to your SkyDrive folder. (The "Upload" button, grayed out in the screenshot below, becomes active once you select one or more files.) Note that large files, such as a complete book manuscript or several high-resolution photographs, can take some time to upload. **CAUTION**: Don't close the page during the upload process, or it might not complete.

Add Files to Your Folder (in This Case, "My Documents")

After you have uploaded at least one file, you will see another screen with a link labeled "**Join our preview program…**" Clicking that link will take you to a Microsoft Service Agreement (an end-user license) that you must accept in order to start using the Web Apps.

Join our preview program

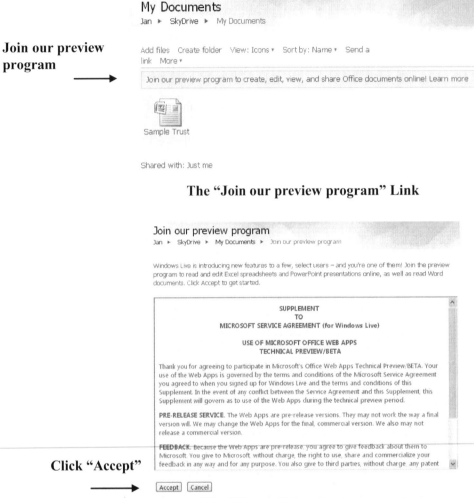

The "Join our preview program" Link

Click "Accept"

The Microsoft Service Agreement

Using the Web Apps

NOTE: Some of this information also appears in the section about Sharing to SkyDrive and the section about Co-authoring.

As of mid-April, 2010, the only fully functional Web Apps available are Excel and PowerPoint. You can use the Word Web App to view documents, but not to edit them. According to Microsoft, the editing capability of the Word Web App will be activated in the second half of 2010.

If you click a Word document that you have uploaded to SkyDrive, you will see an icon for the document and a few menu options above the document.

Menu Options for an Uploaded Word File

The menu options are: View, Edit, Download, Delete, Move, and More (a drop-down that offers two additional choices: Copy and Rename). The "Edit" option might lead you to believe that the Word Web App is fully functional, but when you click that choice, you will see a screen similar to the following:

Still to come...

Editing is not currently available. We are working on it though.

Check for updates.

There are a few things you *can* do with the Word Web App even at this point. You can view a document (and change its on-screen magnification), you can print a document, and you can even search for words and phrases within a document. (When you click "File," a drop-down menu appears.)

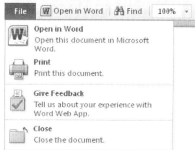

Some Currently Available Word Web App Options

Although Microsoft has indicated that the capacity to edit documents won't be available in the Word Web App until the second half of 2010, both the Excel Web App and the PowerPoint Web App, while perhaps not in their final incarnation, do allow for editing at present—as long as you are working on files in the new XML format (.xlsx for Excel workbooks and .pptx for PowerPoint presentations). [4]

Editing a File

After you have uploaded an Excel workbook, you can click the workbook icon, then choose the "Edit" option. Clicking that option opens your document into the Excel Web App.

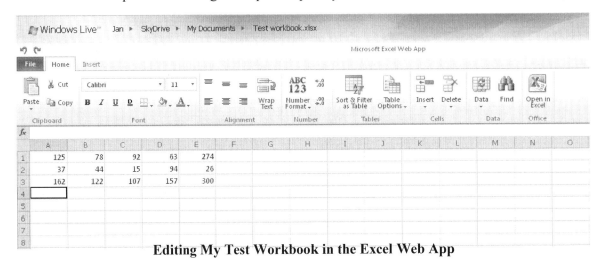

Editing My Test Workbook in the Excel Web App

Even though the online version of Excel doesn't offer as many choices as the regular version, you can enter data or text, format that data or text in different ways, type formulas, perform cut-copy-paste operations (including those that involve pasting formulas), calculate, and so forth.

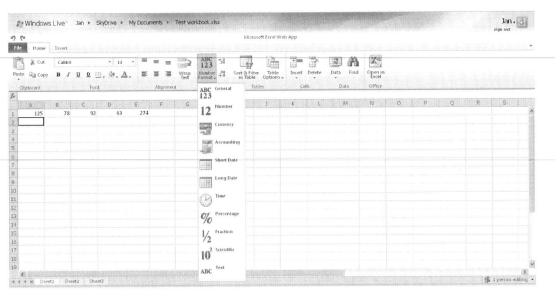

You Can Apply Different Number Formats

---

[4] Based upon my tests, if you attempt to edit an old-style Excel workbook (an .xls) or PowerPoint presentation (.ppt), you will get an error message. I was able to edit .xlsx and .pptx files in the Web Apps, though.

The next screenshot shows that I was able to enter a formula into cell A3 and then copy that formula to cells B3, C3, D3, and E3 (making use of relative addressing). As in the regular version of the program, when you insert your cursor into a cell that contains a formula, you can see the formula in a formula bar above the spreadsheet.

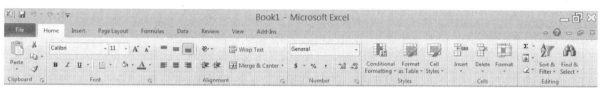

The Formula Bar in the Excel Web App

Although the screenshot below is somewhat difficult to see because it's very condensed in order to fit within the book's margins, it should give you some idea of the differences between the full version of Excel and the Web App. The Ribbon in the regular version has several tabs, each of which provides a vast range of options. By contrast, the Ribbon in the Web App offers significantly more limited choices.

The Ribbon in the Full Version of Excel

Saving and Downloading Files

You might notice while editing a document in the Web Apps that there is no "Save" button. Indeed, when you click the File drop-down in a Web App, you will see a menu similar to the screenshot at right.

If you click the "Where's the Save Button?" link, a pop-up appears that explains that there is no "Save" button because your document is being saved automatically—i.e., to SkyDrive. (The automatic backup of the file *does not* save it to your hard drive.)

The File drop-down in the Web App offers three additional "save" options:

(1)   You can click the "**Save As**" button and save a copy of your workbook with a different name; or

(2)   You can click "**Download a Snapshot**" to save a copy of the workbook that contains the values and formatting, but not the formulas; or

(3)   You can click "**Download a Copy**" to save the edited spreadsheet to your hard drive so that you can work on it offline.

Note that any changes you make offline are not automatically synched with the online version of the file. You would have to upload the draft you edited offline (possibly after deleting the online version, or else giving the newer draft a different name or adding the draft number to the file name).

Creating Files From Within the Web Apps

In addition to being able to upload files from your computer and use them in the Web Apps, you can create files from scratch from within one of the Web Apps. (Again, as of this writing, that ability is limited to the Excel and PowerPoint Web Apps.)

To create a new file from within a Web App, click to open a folder, then click the New link. A drop-down menu will open.

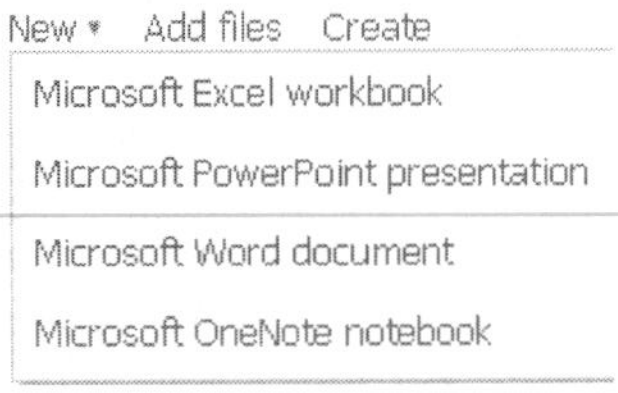

New ▾   Add files   Create

Microsoft Excel workbook

Microsoft PowerPoint presentation

Microsoft Word document

Microsoft OneNote notebook

The drop-down displays four choices: Microsoft Excel workbook, Microsoft PowerPoint presentation, Microsoft Word document, and Microsoft OneNote notebook. I clicked the PowerPoint option, and when I gave the new presentation a name and clicked OK, my new (blank) document in the PowerPoint Web App.

As you can see from the next screenshot, there aren't many design options available (yet) in the Web App. You probably have to apply designs from within the full version of the program.

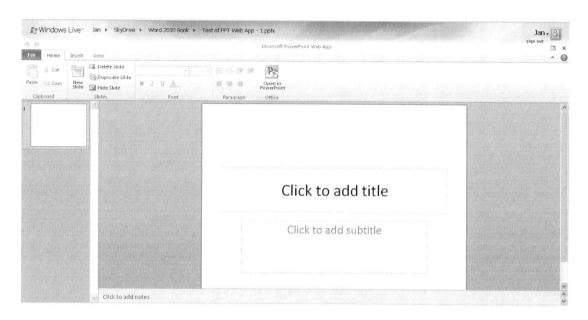

The PowerPoint Web App

Opening Files into the Full Version

The Web Apps ostensibly enable you to open a file you are viewing or editing within the Web App directly into the full version. However, whether you will be able to do so depends largely on the capabilities of your browser and whether a certain ActiveX control is installed and running.[5]

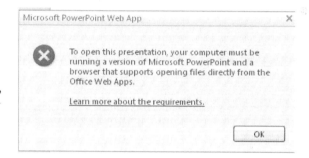

Using Chrome, I was not able to open files from the Excel Web App into the regular version of Excel or open files from the PowerPoint Web App into the regular version of PowerPoint. (In my older version of IE, I did not even have the option of opening the file—either in the Web App or in the full version.)

For the time being, you probably will have to click the File menu within the Web App, then click "Save As" and save a copy of the document to your hard drive in order to work on it in the full version of the program.

Sharing Files (Folders)

It is fairly simple to share files with someone else. At the outset, though, it is important to be aware that permissions on SkyDrive are attributes of ***folders***, not of individual files. If you wish to share a particular file with someone but you don't want that person to have access to your other files, make sure that the file you want to share is isolated in a separate folder.

---

[5] See this article for a fuller explanation: http://office2010.microsoft.com/en-us/web-apps-help/system-requirements-for-opening-files-from-office-web-apps-into-office-desktop-applications-HA010378334.aspx (or use the "tiny URL": http://tinyurl.com/WebApps2Desktop).

There are a couple of different ways you can share a folder. You can give access to a folder by changing its permissions, or you can send a link to the folder to someone else.

Changing the Folder Permissions

First, click the folder icon to open the folder. When the folder opens, you will see menu options; their exact appearance and location depends on which browser you are using. See the two screenshots below (the one on the left is from an older version of Internet Explorer and the one on the right is from Chrome).

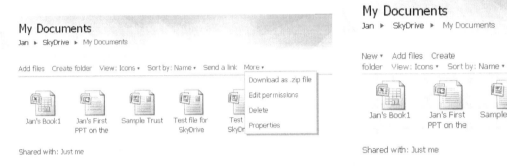

"My Documents" in Internet Explorer   **"My Documents" in Chrome**

When you click "**More**" (above the icons for the files in the folder), you will see an "**Edit permissions**" option. Click that command to change the folder permissions.

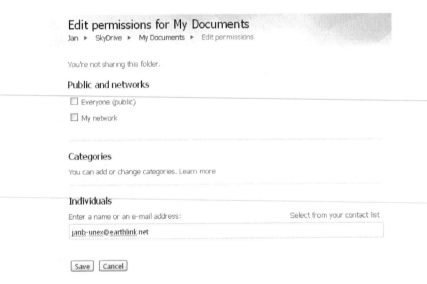

You can enter an e-mail address in the "Individuals" box to give someone access to your folder. Note that you will need to send the person your login information (user name and password) for SkyDrive in order for him or her to be able to open your folder.

110

Sending a Link

The other way to provide access to a folder is by sending someone a link. Again, note that the location of the "Send a link" option depends on which browser you are using. It might be in the menu bar above the files in your folder, or it might be on the "More" drop-down.

In either case, clicking the "Send a link" command takes you to a screen similar to the one below.

The "Send a link" Screen

Just enter the e-mail address of the person with whom you want to share the folder. Before you click the "Send" button, you can write a personal message, and you also have the option of checking a box so that the recipients can get into your folder without having to sign in to Windows Live / SkyDrive. The box, labeled "Don't require recipients to sign in with Windows Live ID," is located below the box where you can type a personal message. See the next screenshot, which shows that I am sharing the file with myself at my UCLA Extension e-mail address; I have included a personal message that explains how to gain access to my SkyDrive folder; and I have checked the "Don't require recipients to sign in with Windows Live ID" box.

.

Sending a Link With a Personal Message; Recipients Don't Have to Sign In

Creating a New Folder

At some point, you might decide to create a new folder so that you can share certain files while keeping others private. It's easy to do so, either from within an existing folder or from the main SkyDrive screen.

When you have opened a folder (by clicking its icon), you will see menu items that look something like the following:

The "Add files" menu option

You should see a "**Create folder**" command (depending on which browser you use, it might be scrunched onto two lines). Click that command, and a "**Create a new folder**" screen will appear.

Click the "Create folder" button

Create a New Folder

Type a name for your new folder and then click the "**Create folder**" button. SkyDrive will create the folder for you and open it so that you can add files to it if you so choose.

Alternatively, you can create a few folder from the main SkyDrive screen. To do so, click the "**Create folder**" link above your folder icons.

You will see a slightly different "**Create a folder**" screen from the one that appears when you use the "Create folder" link from within an existing folder, but it works more or less the same way. Just type a name for the new folder, change the permissions if you like (via the "Share with:" drop-down), and then click the "**Next**" button.

You can change permissions via the "Share with" drop-down

**Type a Name for Your Folder,
Then Change the "Share with" Options if You Like**

When you click "Next," you'll be taken to a screen where you can upload files to the new folder. If you choose not to add files at this point, you can click the "SkyDrive" link in the "breadcrumb trail" toward the top of the screen to go back to your main page in SkyDrive.

The "breadcrumb trail" will take you back to your main SkyDrive page

The "Add files" Screen

Resources

Here is a list of articles that provide more information about the Web Apps.

The Microsoft Web Apps support page:
http://office2010.microsoft.com/en-us/web-apps-help/?CTT=97

Getting Started With the Web Apps:
http://office2010.microsoft.com/en-us/web-apps-help/getting-started-with-office-web-apps-HA101785172.aspx

Using Office Web Apps in Windows Live:
http://office2010.microsoft.com/en-us/web-apps-help/using-office-web-apps-in-windows-live-HA101231889.aspx

The **Web Apps Product Guide** is available as a download (in PDF or XPS format) from the Office Product Guides page:
http://www.microsoft.com/downloads/details.aspx?FamilyID=e690baf0-9b9a-4c47-88da-3a84f3e9b247&displaylang=en

(Or use this **tiny URL**: http://tinyurl.com/Ofc2010Guides)

Co-Authoring

Word 2010 includes an innovative feature that makes it possible for two or more people edit a document simultaneously—without having to save and merge separate versions of the document. This new "co-authoring" capability also means that when you open a document that already is open on someone else's computer, you'll no longer see a warning that the document has been locked for editing. And you won't have to wait for the other person to finish editing (or to return from lunch) before jumping in and making changes of your own.

Prerequisites

There are a few significant prerequisites in order for you to use the co-authoring feature:

- Your organization must have Microsoft SharePoint Server 2010 or a server running SharePoint Foundation 2010.[1]

- Co-authoring works only with documents that are hosted on SharePoint Server 2010 or a server running SharePoint Foundation 2010 (or on Windows Live).

- Other authors must have access to the shared folder where your documents are stored, and also must have appropriate permissions for editing the files.

- Staff members wishing to use the co-authoring feature should avoid "checking out" documents from a SharePoint library. Checked-out documents will be locked for editing, and co-authoring will not be enabled.

- Co-authoring is available only with documents created / saved as a .docx (or one of the other Office Open XML file types—i.e., **.docm,** dotx, dotm, etc.).

- The feature doesn't work in Word 2007 (even in .docx files). In fact, if one member of your firm opens a document in Word 2007, that file will be locked to other users, ***including*** any users who have Word 2010 on their computers.

An Overview

As of this writing, I am unable to test the feature fully because (1) I don't have SharePoint Server 2010 or a server running SharePoint Foundation; and (2) co-authoring in Word is not yet enabled via SkyDrive / Windows Live.[2] I did do some testing in Excel Web App (which currently supports co-authoring), although it's important to point out that the experience isn't quite the same as co-authoring with the full version of Word.

---

[1] You also have the option of using Windows Live, a free online service, as a "host" for Word 2010 documents. Co-authoring is available in those documents ***if you open them in the full version of Word 2010*** (not in the Word Web App).

[2] It will available sometime in the second half of 2010, although you will not be able to use co-authoring while working in the Word Web App.

Despite those limitations, I can offer some insights into how the co-authoring feature works based on my experiments with ExcelWeb App, as well as on tutorials and screenshots provided by Microsoft.[3] Here's an overview:

User A—let's call him Jonathan—opens a Word 2010 document from a shared location as described in the "Prerequisites" section on the previous page (remember, it must be a .docx or one of the other Office Open XML file types). Jonathan starts editing the document.

User B—let's call him Sean—opens the same document on his own computer from the same shared location.

You also open the same document on your workstation from the same shared location. Note that you don't need to do anything special in order to activate the co-authoring feature. Assuming you have met all of the requirements spelled out in the "Prerequisites" section, each of you can just start editing the document. Word will lock the sections that the respective authors are working on and will show you— *in real time*—where other authors are active.

In the screenshot below, for instance, you can determine at a glance which portion of the document Sean is editing and which portion Jonathan is editing because you can see their names to the left of the sections they are working on.

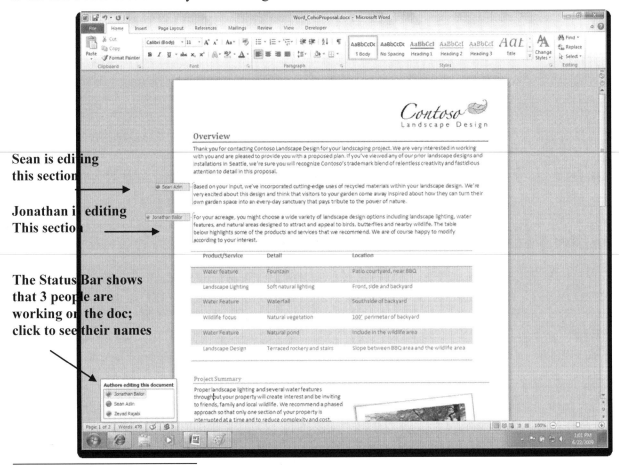

Sean is editing this section

Jonathan is editing This section

The Status Bar shows that 3 people are working on the doc; click to see their names

---

[3] Also, Beth Melton generously provided extensive assistance with this section of the book.

The Status Bar indicates that three people have the document open. If you click the "Number of Authors Editing" icon in the Status Bar, a pane will open, showing the names of all of the authors.[4] The screenshot shows that two people, Jonathan and Sean, are actively editing. (The other author, Zeyad, either has the document open and hasn't made a modification or he is editing another portion of the document that's not currently visible on the screen.)

Automatic Locking

Although multiple authors can work on a document, only one person can edit *a particular section* of the document during a co-authoring session.[5] That aspect of the feature—the automatic locking of a paragraph that is being edited—prevents potential conflicts should two (or more) people wish to make changes to the same content.

The Block Authors Command

In addition, there is a "Block Authors" function that lets you prevent other authors from modifying certain portions of a document that you intend to work on shortly but haven't actually changed yet. A new "Block Authors" command on the Review tab (in the Protect group) and also on the Developers tab (and in the Protect group) flags those additional areas of the document so that other authors don't start editing them and inadvertently lock you out.

Updates

During a co-authoring session, the other authors can tell which section(s) you're working on, but they can't see the exact changes you've made until you save the document. That gives you a chance to hone the wording of those sections before sharing them with others.

When you save, other authors receive a notification that updates are available. At that point, they can view your revisions. Likewise, when another author saves his or her changes, you should see an "Updates Available" message in the Status Bar, as shown below.[6] All you need to do in order to see the updates is save the document.[7]

---

[4] Alternatively, you can click the File tab to open the Backstage View; all of the authors will be listed on the Info fly-out.

[5] In other words, the *paragraph* that an author is working on is locked to other authors. (A paragraph is automatically locked as soon as someone makes a change to it.)

[6] This message appears if "Document Updates Available" is enabled in your Status Bar. (That option is enabled by default. However, if for some reason you don't see the "Updates Available" message, you can right-click the Status Bar to make sure the "Document Updates Available" option hasn't been turned off.)

[7] Remember to save frequently in order to see other people's changes. Saving also serves to unlock sections you are no longer editing so that other authors can work on them.

In addition, if another author has saved his or her edits and is no longer working in a section that previously was locked, you'll see an icon with two green arrows next to the modified portions of the document, as shown below.

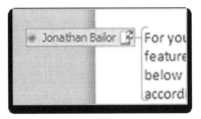

After you save the document, any content that has been revised by others since your last save will be displayed in the document with green highlighting (which appears as shading in the next screenshot). The green highlighting is helpful because it gives you an easy way to identify the most recent modifications. The next time you save the document (and retrieve any available updates), the green highlighting will disappear automatically.

Saving also makes it possible for you to determine which previously locked sections have become available for you to edit.

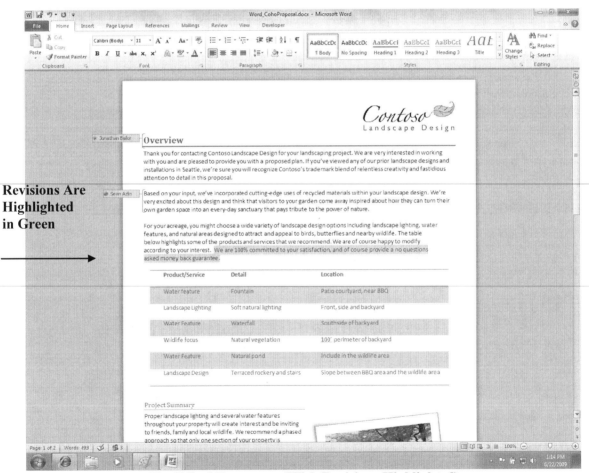

The Edited Document (With Revisions Highlighted)

Synchronization of Changes

According to Microsoft, while multiple users work on a document, SharePoint synchronizes the changes they make and keeps track of different versions of the document. The version-tracking process—which operates in the background—allows for synchronization and updating, but also allows companies to "roll back" edits and revert to a prior version of a document.

Communicating With Other Authors in Real Time

If your organization uses one of several compatible instant messaging applications,[8] you can initiate a real-time conversation with other authors during an editing session. This time-saving feature lets you ask another author a quick question about the document and get an equally quick answer, rather than sending an e-mail and having to wait for a reply.

To the left of an author's name you'll see a "presence icon" that indicates his or her availability while you are working on the document together. The next screenshot provides a close-up view of the presence icons (although you can't see them in color, unfortunately).

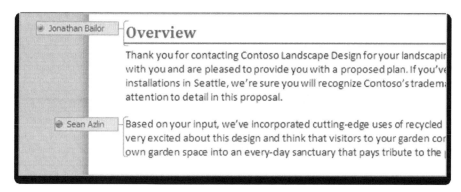

A green presence icon means that the person is available to chat; red means that the person is busy; yellow means that he or she is away. To initiate a conversation with another author, position your mouse pointer over a presence icon to display that individual's contact card (a new feature in Office 2010), as shown below.

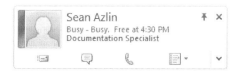

Icons displayed at the bottom of the card represent various communication options you can use. The colored "presence bar" to the left of the person's photo (or placeholder image)

---

[8] Namely, Microsoft Office Communicator 2007 R2 (which requires Microsoft Office Communicator Server 2007 R2), Windows Live Messenger, or another instant messaging application that supports Imessenger. If you are using Windows Live Messenger, the other authors must be using Windows Live Messenger as well, and you must add them to your contact list in order to view their presence information or to start an instant-message conversation.

indicates his or her availability. To start an instant message conversation, click the chat icon (the second from the left).[9]

Even if you don't use any type of instant messaging program, you can use the contact card to send an e-mail message to an author. Just click the e-mail icon (the first icon).

Using SkyDrive for Co-Authoring

As previously noted, you can use Windows Live / SkyDrive as a host for Word 2010 documents that you would like to work on simultaneously with other authors.[10] First, you need to upload a file (it must be a .docx or other Office Open XML file type) to one of your SkyDrive folders and share it with at least one other user.

A Sample Word Document Stored in My SkyDrive Folder

Next, click the document (or click "Edit"). It will open automatically in Word Web App. Since Word Web App *does not support co-authoring*, you (and the other author) need to take an additional step and open the document *in the regular version of Word*, which you can do from within SkyDrive.[11]

After the document displays in Word Web App, click the "**Open in Word**" **button** toward the left side of the mini-toolbar (see the screenshot on the next page) in order to open the doc in Word and start co-authoring.

---

[9] If you're using Office Communicator, you can start a voice call by clicking the phone icon. (Windows Live Messenger doesn't support voice calls; however, some other instant message programs do.)

[10] You can also utilize co-authoring on a server running SharePoint Foundation 2010. The commands to open the document in the offline version of Word should be similar to, if not exactly the same as, instructions provided in this section.

[11] Because Windows Live is based on SharePoint Foundation 2010, it supports the co-authoring feature *even though Word Web App does not*. Obviously you must have access to both the regular version of Word and Word Web App to use this functionality.

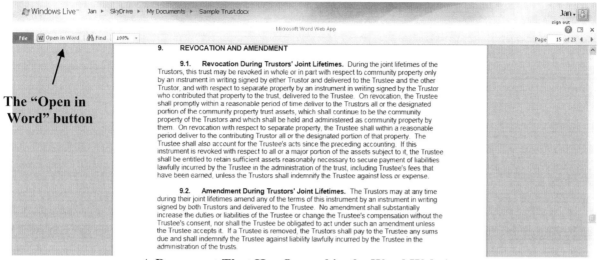

The "Open in Word" button

9.   REVOCATION AND AMENDMENT

    9.1.   **Revocation During Trustors' Joint Lifetimes.** During the joint lifetimes of the Trustors, this trust may be revoked in whole or in part with respect to community property only by an instrument in writing signed by either Trustor and delivered to the Trustee and the other Trustor, and with respect to separate property by an instrument in writing signed by the Trustor who contributed that property to the trust, delivered to the Trustee. On revocation, the Trustee shall promptly within a reasonable period of time deliver to the Trustors all or the designated portion of the community property trust assets, which shall continue to be the community property of the Trustors and which shall be held and administered as community property by them. On revocation with respect to separate property, the Trustee shall within a reasonable period deliver to the contributing Trustor all or the designated portion of that property. The Trustee shall also account for the Trustee's acts since the preceding accounting. If this instrument is revoked with respect to all or a major portion of the assets subject to it, the Trustee shall be entitled to retain sufficient assets reasonably necessary to secure payment of liabilities lawfully incurred by the Trustee in the administration of the trust, including Trustee's fees that have been earned, unless the Trustors shall indemnify the Trustee against loss or expense.

    9.2.   **Amendment During Trustors' Joint Lifetimes.** The Trustors may at any time during their joint lifetimes amend any of the terms of this instrument by an instrument in writing signed by both Trustors and delivered to the Trustee. No amendment shall substantially increase the duties or liabilities of the Trustee or change the Trustee's compensation without the Trustee's consent, nor shall the Trustee be obligated to act under such an amendment unless the Trustee accepts it. If a Trustee is removed, the Trustors shall pay to the Trustee any sums due and shall indemnify the Trustee against liability lawfully incurred by the Trustee in the administration of the trusts.

A Document That Has Opened in the Word Web App
(To Use Co-Authoring, You Must Open It in the Regular Version of Word)

WHERE DID IT GO? Dictionary

In Word 2010 (as in Word 2007), the dictionary feature is located at the left side of the **Review tab**, in the Proofing group, under "**Research**."

When you click the "**Research**" **button**, a Research Pane opens at the right side of the screen.

To look up the definition of **a single word** in your document, press the **Alt key** and **click the word**. To look up **a phrase**, such as "unlawful detainer," **select the phrase**, press the **Alt key**, and **click the selected text**.

Alternatively, you can **type a word or phrase** in the "**Search for**" **box** at the top of the Research Pane, then press the **green arrow key** to the right of the box.

Word will search through various online dictionaries and other reference materials and will display the results in the large area of the pane, as shown in the second screenshot at right. (In my tests, it started with Bing, Microsoft's proprietary search engine. Obviously, you must be online in order to use any of the online references.)

Note that you can instruct Word to use a different reference by clicking the drop-down below the "Search for" box and then clicking to select one of the reference books or research sites in the list. If you want to use a reference that isn't in the list, click the "**Check for more research sites...**" link (below the drop-down).

Click the "**Research options**" **link** at the bottom of the Research Pane to include more built-in references and/or to add your own Internet sites.

Paste Options

The Paste function has been revamped in a couple of significant respects in Word 2010.

For one thing, the program offers new and modified options for pasting text that you have copied or cut from another document (or from another location in the current document). For another thing, you can preview the way each option will affect the formatting of the text, which makes it easier for you to determine which one to use.

There are a few different ways to paste text in this version of Word. You can do any of the following:

- click the **Paste drop-down** in the **Clipboard group** at the left side of the **Home tab**, then choose one of the paste options; *or*

- **right-click** the location where you want the pasted text to go and then choose one of the options from the pop-up menu; *or*

- press the keyboard shortcut **Ctrl V**, then select an option from the **Paste Options button** that pops up after you paste the text.

Paste Preview

The most obvious manifestation of the enhanced functionality of the Paste feature in Word 2010 is the "live" Paste Preview aspect. The live Paste Preview (also available in Excel, PowerPoint, Outlook, and the rest of the Office 2010 suite) allows you to see what the text will look like—with different formatting applied—*before* you paste it. This feature is available when you cut or copy some text and then use either the Paste drop-down on the Home tab or the right-click menu. Whichever of the two methods you use, the menu displays various Paste Options icons; when you position the mouse pointer over an icon, you can see how the text would appear if you applied the formatting option that icon represents.

When you use the keyboard shortcut Ctrl V to paste, you don't get a *preview* of the different paste options, but the Paste Options button pops up with icons that let you see how each option would affect the formatting of the text. Then, if you like, you can change the formatting simply by clicking an icon *after* the text has been pasted. It's quick, easy, and fairly intuitive.

The Paste Drop-Down in the Home Tab

As a legal word processor, I am accustomed to using keyboard shortcuts (such as Ctrl V to paste) most of the time. However, there are many other methods for copying and pasting text. An easy "mouse" way to paste text is to click the **Paste drop-down** in the **Clipboard group** at the very left side of the **Home tab**. (Actually, you can paste just by clicking the Paste icon itself—the big clipboard—but the drop-down gives you more choices and also allows you to preview the various formatting options before you actually paste the text.[1])

Click Clipboard Icon to paste text immediately →

Click the drop-down to open a menu of formatting options →

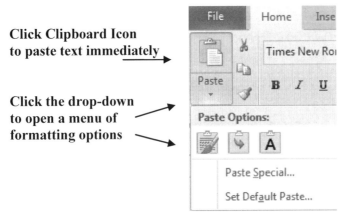

The Paste Drop-Down in the Home Tab (Word 2010)

If you have worked with Word 2007, you'll notice right away that the Paste drop-down in Word 2010 looks different. In Word 2007, the only choices on the menu are Paste, Paste Special…, and Paste as Hyperlink (which is grayed out in most circumstances).

The Paste Drop-Down in the Home Tab (Word 2007)

In Word 2010, the available choices—offered in the form of icons (each with a text label that pops up when you let the mouse hover over the icon)— include **Keep Source Formatting (K)**, **Merge Formatting (M)**, and **Keep Text Only (T)**. I will discuss the specific paste options in detail in the section about the Paste Options button.

When you position the mouse pointer over one of the Paste Options icons, you will see a preview of the text as it would look if you applied that option by clicking the icon. To apply a specific option, either (1) click the icon *or* (2) simply press the letter (i.e., the mnemonic) that appears in the pop-up label for the icon, as described in the previous paragraph.

---

[1] Clicking the Clipboard icon will paste the text immediately. However, the Paste Options will appear after you paste the text (unless you have disabled it), giving you a chance to apply a different formatting option after the fact. See the discussion, *infra*, about the Paste Options button. Note that when you click the Clipboard icon, Word pastes the text according to settings specified in the Word Options, as explained in detail later in this section.

In Word 2010, the Paste drop-down also includes a "Paste Special..." command, as well as a command to "Set Default Paste..." Clicking the "Paste Special..." command produces the Paste Special dialog, which offers additional formatting options depending on the type of item you are copying and pasting (text, images, etc.): Microsoft Word Document Object, Formatted Text (RTF) (Rich Text Format), Unformatted Text, Picture (Enhanced Metafile), HTML Format (for some reason, this choice is the default), and Unformatted Unicode Text, along with several other image formats. Because the new paste options are easy to find and use with a couple of mouse clicks or keystrokes, you probably won't need this dialog—which most people used in previous versions to apply the "Unformatted Text" option—very often.

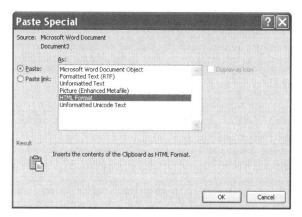

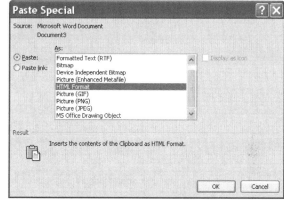

The "Normal" Paste Special Dialog

**The Dialog That Appears
When You Are Pasting an Image**

As for the "Set Default Paste..." option, see the discussion later in this section about configuring the Word Options for cut, copy, and paste.

The Right-Click Menu

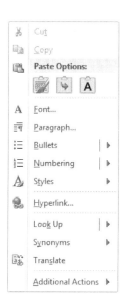

After you have cut or copied some text, you can right-click where you want to paste the text to open a context-sensitive menu that displays the new paste options buttons. The screenshot at right shows the right-click menu with the Paste Options displayed toward the top.

There's not very much to say about the right-click menu, other than to point out its existence and the fact that the available options are the same as those offered by the Paste Drop-Down in the Home tab and by the Paste Options button.

The Paste Options Button

The Paste Options button—the pop-up that appears when you paste some text—still bears certain similarities to the button in previous versions of Word, but it has been redesigned, both stylistically and functionally. It

125

typically proffers either three or four choices—in the form of large icons—for formatting pasted text and objects,[2] as well as a "Set Default Paste" option. Clicking the words "Set Default Paste" (or the mnemonic—i.e., the underlined letter "a") takes you directly into the Word Options, where you can configure the settings that control how text is pasted under various circumstances. See page 132 for more information about the Default Paste options.

If you are copying text to which no formatting has been applied—or to which only **direct** (font or paragraph) formatting, as opposed to a style, has been applied—the Paste Options button presents three different icons representing three different formatting choices. When you position the mouse pointer over an icon, a pop-up label appears, indicating what the icon does. From left to right, the options are: Keep Source Formatting (**K**) (depicted as a clipboard with a paintbrush in front of it), Merge Formatting (**M**) (a clipboard with text on it), and Keep Text Only (**T**, though a large letter "A" appears on the clipboard icon).

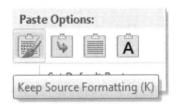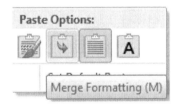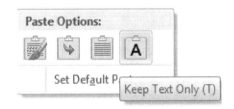

In some situations—such as pasting text into a document that makes heavy use of styles, pasting text to which a style has been applied, or (sometimes) pasting text from the Internet—a fourth option becomes available: Use Destination Styles (**S**) (a clipboard with an arrow pointing to the right).

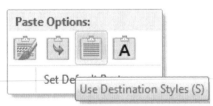

To apply one of the options, either (1) click the icon representing that option or (2) press the letter (mnemonic) associated with it (**K** for Keep Source Formatting, **M** for Merge Formatting, **T** for Keep Text Only, or **S** for Use Destination Styles).

---

[2] How many choices—and which ones—are available depends on **both** the formatting of the text you have cut or copied **and** the formatting of the text that already exists at the paste location. The available options also change depending on **what** you are pasting: ordinary text, an image, a list, and so forth. **NOTE**: the Paste Options button sometimes offers the Use Destination Styles (S) even when that choice is **not available** via the Paste Options drop-down and the right-click menu. I'm not sure why it doesn't appear consistently on all of the paste menus.

So how do these various paste options actually work? Not necessarily the way you might think. Let's do some experimenting.

I pasted a couple of paragraphs from a sample contract that uses *heading styles* based on the Arial font, 12 point type, bolded, with single spacing plus 12 points after the headings. (Note that all of those attributes are part of the styles.) The heading styles incorporate legal-style automatic numbering . The body text in the sample document uses the *Normal style* and the font is Arial, 12 points, not bolded, with single spacing and 0 points before, 0 points after. Here is the way the text I copied looks in the original document:

Section 4   Contract Terms

The following material terms shall apply:

4.1   Term of the Contract

The Contract shall be in effect for one (1) year from the date that the last party executes the Contract ("Effective Date").

Sample Text With Heading Styles and "Normal" Body Text

And here is what happened to the text when I pasted it into a blank document and then chose from among the four paste options.

Keep Source Formatting (K)

In theory, Keep Source Formatting should preserve both *styles* applied to text in the original document and *direct formatting* (font attributes applied via the Font dialog or paragraph formatting applied via the Paragraph dialog, rather than as part of a style).

In my tests, Keep Source Formatting worked more or less as expected in that the pasted text appeared with the same font formatting (the font face, the font size, bolding and italics) as in the source (originating) document. The single line spacing and 12 points after the heading paragraphs carried over in the pasted text. Keep Source Formatting also retained automatic numbering, although the pasted numbers did not use the same numbering *scheme* as in the original doc.

However, this option—significantly—*stripped out the heading styles*. In other words, the pasted headings display as "Normal" rather than as Heading 1 and Heading 2 styles, even though the Normal paragraph style of the destination document uses Times New Roman, no bolding, and no points after.

I.   Contract Terms

The following material terms shall apply:

A.   Term of the Contract

The Contract shall be in effect for one (1) year from the date that the last party executes the Contract ("Effective Date").

Pasted Text Using the "Keep Source Formatting" Option

In sum, Keep Source Formatting appears to **discard styles** but import most of the styles' attributes as **direct formatting**.

Merge Formatting (M)

The Merge Formatting option stripped out the heading styles and the font face (substituting the Times New Roman font that is the document default for the Arial font used in the original document), but preserved the bolding in the headings. It also retained automatic numbering (but did not use the same numbering scheme as in the source document). The font size and single spacing carried over, but the 12-points-after spacing of the heading paragraphs did not.

> **I.   Contract Terms**
> The following material terms shall apply:
>
> **A.   Term of the Contract**
> The Contract shall be in effect for one (1) year from the date that the last party executes the Contract ("Effective Date").

Pasted Text Using the "Merge Formatting" Option

In short, Merge Formatting appears to keep **certain font attributes** such as bolding, italics, underlining, and the like, as well as automatic numbering codes, but doesn't retain **styles**. In other tests I performed, it also removes any **directly applied font color** and **highlighting**. By contrast, both the "Keep Source Formatting" and "Use Destination Styles" options preserved the font color and highlighting from the source document.

Keep Text Only (T)

Keep Text Only is essentially the same as "Paste Unformatted Text." It pastes the text from the source document, but without any styles or direct formatting. This option comes in particularly handy when pasting from the Internet or when pasting text from a WordPerfect document into a Word doc.

> Contract Terms
> The following material terms shall apply:
>
> Term of the Contract
> The Contract shall be in effect for one (1) year from the date that the last party executes the Contract ("Effective Date").

Pasted Text Using the "Keep Text Only" Option

As you can see from the screenshot, the pasted text appears without any formatting (it uses the Normal style of the destination document). The tabs used to indent the body text in the source document carried over, but everything else was lost. I tested again after removing the tabs from the body text in the source doc and applying a half-inch first-line indent instead, and pasting the text using the Keep Text Only option knocked out the first-line indents, placing the body text at the left margin. So it appears that this paste option eliminates styles and most direct formatting.

Use Destination Styles (S)

Theoretically, the Use Destination Styles option should replace any styles and direct formatting that exist in the original document with the styles and direct formatting in the destination document.

However, in my tests, I was surprised to find that the Use Destination Styles option retained most of the formatting of the *source* document—rather than adopting the styles of the destination / target document. It retained *heading styles*, the same *numbering scheme* (legal style), the Arial *font*, the 12-point *font size*, and the 12-points-after *spacing* for the heading paragraphs (probably because that spacing was an attribute of the heading style, rather than direct formatting). However, it apparently did *not* retain direct formatting. At least, it substituted underlining for bolding (at least in the Level 1 heading).

Section 1　　Contract Terms

The following material terms shall apply:

1.1　　Term of the Contract

The Contract shall be in effect for one (1) year from the date that the last party executes the Contract ("Effective Date").

Pasted Text Using the "Use Destination Styles" Option

The lesson to take away from these experiments is that you will have to test each option for yourself to see how it works under various circumstances. I suspect that the options work more or less as expected if the formatting in both the source document and the destination document is relatively simple and straightforward. With more complex docs, you might get somewhat less predictable results.

Pasting an Object

As mentioned earlier (in a footnote), the available paste options also change depending on *what* you are pasting. For example, when you paste a graphic, you might see only one or two icons, as in the screenshot below. The options shown in the screenshot are **Keep Source Formatting (K)** and **Picture (U)**.

Although I'm not entirely sure of the difference, when I pasted a graphic as a picture, it seemed to lose some resolution (i.e., it pasted as a "second-generation" image), whereas when I pasted it using the "Keep Source Formatting" option, it remained relatively sharp.

Pasting a Numbered List

Other paste options appear in the menus when you are merging into an existing outline or list. If you copy a portion of an existing list and then paste somewhere within another list (either in the same document or in a different document), you will see paste options similar to the following:

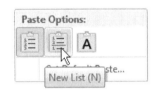

The option on the left is Continue List (**C**); the one in the middle is New List (**N**); the right-most option is Keep Text Only (**T**). Continue List renumbers the pasted portion of the list so that it continues the numbering of the existing list (based on the number of the preceding paragraph). New List, by contrast, restarts the numbering so that the pasted list (or partial list) begins at 1.

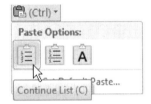

In my tests, there were no special options available for pasting into bulleted lists.

A Brief Review and Miscellaneous Pasting Tips

So to review:

You can apply different formatting options for text (as well as for lists and objects) by using (1) the Paste drop-down in the Home tab, (2) the right-click menu, or (3) the Paste Options button. The first two methods allow you to preview the formatting *before* pasting; the third method allows you to change the formatting ***after the fact*** by selecting a different choice from the drop-down. (As long as the Paste Options button remains visible on the screen, you can continue to choose from among the different formatting options. And once the Paste Options button appears, you can "preview" the various formatting options for text that you have pasted in case you change your mind about the way you want it to look.)

To apply an option, you can either (a) click the icon for that option or (b) press the letter of the alphabet (the mnemonic) associated with the option.

Here are a few tips about pasting in Word 2010, in no particular order:

To invoke the Paste Special dialog, you can press the key combination **Ctrl Alt V**.

If you like, you can add a command to the Quick Access Toolbar (QAT) that will paste text without formatting. This option is new in Word 2010.

To add the command, **right-click** the QAT and then click "**Customize Quick Access Toolbar...**" (or click the **File tab**, **Options**, **Quick Access Toolbar**). When the Word Options screen appears, change the "**Choose commands from:**" **drop-down** at the top left to "**All Commands**," then scroll about 2/3 of the way down in the commands box to "**Paste and Keep Text Only**." Click to **select** (highlight) **that command**, then click the "**Add**" **button** at the center of the screen. After doing so, you'll see the command on the right-hand side, in the large display area under "Customize Quick Access Toolbar." You can change its position in the QAT by clicking the Up Arrow (to move it to the left in the QAT) or the Down Arrow (to move it to the right). Be sure to click the "OK" button at the bottom right to save your changes.

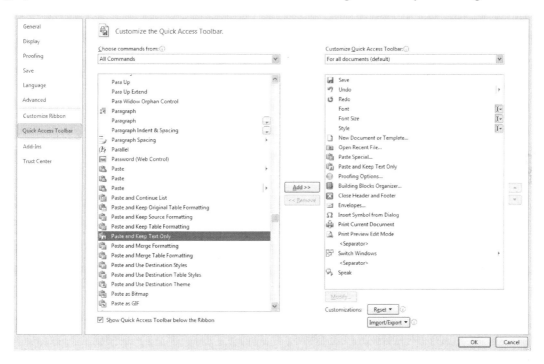

The new icon will appear in your QAT. It will be grayed out until you have cut or copied some text or an object in your document, at which point it will become active.

Also new in Word 2010 is the ability to add a keyboard shortcut for the **Keep Text Only** option (i.e., **Paste Special, Unformatted Text**). In previous versions of Word, there was no such command available.

To add a keyboard shortcut for the Keep Text Only option, either (1) **right-click** the **Ribbon** (or the Quick Access Toolbar), then click "**Customize the Ribbon...**," or (2) click the **File tab**, **Options**, **Customize Ribbon**. Then:

Navigate to the bottom of the Word Options screen and click the "**Keyboard shortcuts: Customize...**" button.

When the **Customize Keyboard dialog** appears, look at the left side, under "**Categories:**", and scroll all the way down. Click to select (highlight) "**All Commands**."

On the right side of the dialog, under "**Commands**," scroll down about 2/3 of the way until you see "**PasteTextOnly**." Click to select (highlight) that command.

Next, click in the "**Press new shortcut key:**" box. With the cursor in that box, press a **key combination** you would like to assign to the command, such as Alt V. If the key combination already has been assigned to another feature, you'll see a message to that effect in the "Currently assigned to:" area below the "Current keys" box. (At that point, you can assign the key combination to the PasteTextOnly command anyway, or you can type another keyboard shortcut in the "Press new shortcut key:" box.)

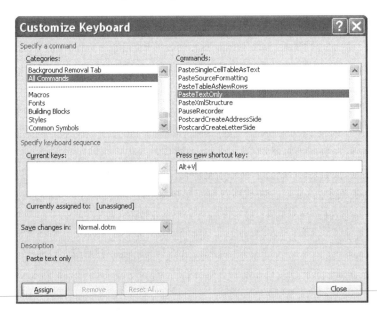

Customize Keyboard Dialog
With "All Commands" and "PasteTextOnly" Selected (Highlighted)

When you are ready, click the "**Assign**" **button** at the bottom left of the dialog, then close out. Be sure to click the "**OK**" **button** at the bottom right side of the Word Options screen in order to save your settings when you close out of the Options.

Configuring the Default Paste Options

Although configuring the default paste options works almost exactly the same way in Word 2010 as in Word 2007, I'm including a discussion on the topic in this section of the book because it seems like a logical place.

The default paste options settings are located in the Word Options (Click the **File tab**, **Options**, **Advanced** *or* press **Alt F**, **T**, click **Advanced**, then scroll down about ¼ of the way to **Cut, copy, and paste**).

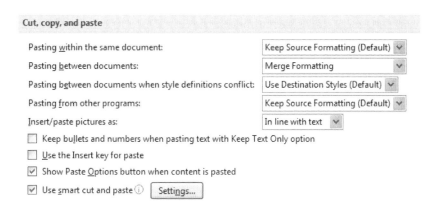

The Cut, Copy and Paste Options (in Word Options)

The options that control the way that pasted text appears in your document include various possible paste scenarios:

- Pasting within the same document

- Pasting between documents

- Pasting between documents when style definitions conflict

- Pasting from other programs

The first two are fairly self-explanatory. The third scenario, "Pasting between documents when style definitions conflict," envisions circumstances in which someone—either another member of your organization or someone from outside who sends you a Word document to edit—has created a style that has the same name as a style you use, but that is formatted differently.

This scenario occurs fairly frequently, particularly with respect to heading styles. You might find, for example, that associated counsel uses a Heading 1 style consisting of a 13-point font, Arial, bolded but without underlining, single-spaced but with 12 points after, whereas your firm uses a Heading 1 style with a 12-point font in Times New Roman, bolded and underlined, exactly 12 points but with 0 points after. When you paste a Heading 1 paragraph from your co-counsel's document into one of your firm's documents that contains differently formatted Heading 1 styles, would you prefer that the pasted Heading 1 paragraph retain the style used in the source document (i.e., the one created by co-counsel) or that it adopt the style used in the destination document (i.e., yours)? If you simply click the Clipboard icon or press Ctrl V, the formatting ***will be determined by the default setting in Word Options***.

You can change this setting on a case-by-case basis (applying one of the paste options described in the previous section), but if you find yourself having to perform this procedure often, you might want to change the setting in Word Options. That way, ***you can simply click the Paste icon in the Home tab or press Ctrl V***—i.e., without selecting a specific paste option each time—and Word will paste the Heading 1 paragraph ***based on your default settings***.

The "Pasting from other programs" scenario can mean a variety of things: pasting from WordPerfect or from Open Office, pasting from Excel, pasting from a legal-specific program such as Legal Solutions, etcetera. Take a look at the default setting and, if necessary, change it to suit your needs and preferences.

Other options that you can configure from this screen include:

- Insert/paste pictures as:
- Keep bullets and numbers when pasting text with Keep Text Only option
- Use the Insert key for paste
- Show Paste Options button when content is pasted
- Use smart cut and paste

These options are available in Word 2007, as well, except the wording of the fourth option is different (Word 2007 uses the label "Show Paste Options buttons").

The "Insert/paste pictures as" option lets you determine how pasted images are laid out and wrapped (in line, square, behind text, etc.) .

The "Keep bullets and numbers…" setting ensures that when you paste a list, the bullets or numbers used in the list are retained even when you choose to remove other formatting by using the "Keep Text Only" option. In my tests, this setting did, in fact, preserve the automatic numbering used in headings in the source document even when I chose to paste with the "Keep Text Only" option. See the screenshot below.

Section 4   Contract Terms
      The following material terms shall apply:

4.1   Term of the Contract
      The Contract shall be in effect for one (1) year from the date that the last party executes
the Contract ("Effective Date").

If you enable (check) "Use the Insert key for paste," pressing the Insert key pastes any text (or objects) that you have cut or copied. (By default, this option is disabled.)

The "Show Paste Options button…" option, enabled by default, is responsible for the button popping up whenever you paste text or objects. Many of my training clients complained about the persistence of this button in previous versions of Word, but as this section demonstrates, it can be very useful. If it annoys you, simply disable it by unchecking the box.

For information about "Use smart cut and paste," see the section starting on page 331.

Remember to click "OK" to save your settings when you close out of the Word Options.

Customizing the Ribbon

Many people who upgraded to Word 2007 from an earlier version of Word found the transition challenging at least partly because the familiar Standard and Formatting Toolbars were no longer available, and the Ribbon—which replaced the toolbars—couldn't be customized.

In Word 2010, however, users can customize the Ribbon in a number of respects. For example:

- You can create entire new tabs.

- You can create new groups within custom tabs and/or within built-in tabs.

- You can add commands to custom groups (but *not* to built-in groups).

- You can rename *any* tab, group, or command.

- You can change the icons for commands.

- You can move tabs around in the Ribbon.

- You can hide custom tabs and/or built-in tabs.

- You can remove groups from custom tabs and/or from built-in tabs.

- Once you have customized the Ribbon, you can export your customizations to a file and install them on another computer.

I provide detailed instructions for performing each of these tasks, as well as more information about the various options for customizing the Ribbon, in the portion of the book that deals with customizing the interface. See pages 191 and following.

QUICK TIP: Split Window, View Side by Side, and Arrange All

Most people know the basics of manipulating document windows: how to zoom in or out and how to switch from one open document to another. But you might not be familiar with the other options in the Window group on the View tab, which include View Side by Side, Arrange All, and Split. These options can come in handy, especially if you need to make a visual comparison of two documents or view two portions of the same document at once.

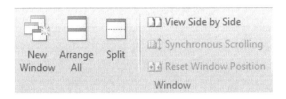

The Split Command

The Split command essentially enables you to look at different sections of the same document simultaneously. When you click the button, a horizontal line appears along with the mouse pointer. Position the mouse pointer where you want to split the document and then click. Word will divide the screen into two horizontally tiled windows, each with its own set of scrollbars, vertical ruler, and (if you choose to display it) horizontal ruler.

The screenshot below shows a document that I've split. The top window displays a portion of page 1, whereas the bottom window displays a portion of page 2. (The page indicator on the Status Bar changes depending on which window your cursor is in.)

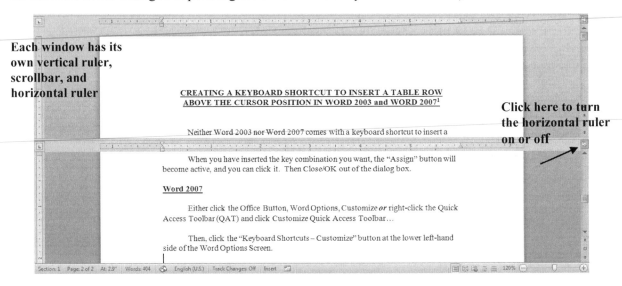

Any changes you make to the document will appear in both windows, assuming you are viewing the same portion of the document in each frame, in real time. (Keep in mind that you are viewing *the same copy of the document* in two different windows, *not* viewing two separate copies of the document.)

To return to a normal view of the document, click "Remove Split." (The "Split" command turns into "Remove Split" when you split a document.)

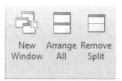

View Side by Side

By contrast, the View Side by Side command is used to compare two different documents. You must have at least two documents open in order to use this command. If you have more than two documents open when you click the button, a "Compare Side by Side" dialog will appear, prompting you to choose a document to compare with the current one.

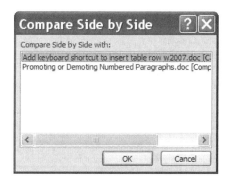

This feature can be useful for making a quick "at-a-glance" comparison of two drafts of the same document. (For a more detailed comparison, you also have the option of using the Compare Document feature. See the tutorial starting on page 519 for instructions.)

What you see when you view two documents side by side depends on whether "**Show all windows in the Taskbar**" is enabled in the **Word Options** (**File**, **Options**, **Advanced**, scroll down to the **Display section**).

☑ Show all windows in the Taskbar

If the option is enabled, as it is by default, each document appears in a separate window with vertical and horizontal rulers, vertical and horizontal scrollbars, its own complete Ribbon, its own complete Quick Access Toolbar, and its own complete set of program "control buttons" (to minimize, maximize, or close the window). In other words, there is no separate *program* window. You can determine which document window is active by the fact that its title bar is somewhat darker than that of the inactive document window.

If the option is disabled (unchecked), each document appears in a window with vertical and horizontal rulers and vertical and horizontal scrollbars. However, the windows are displayed within the program window—i.e., below, and separate from, a single Ribbon and a single Quick Access Toolbar. Moreover, only *the active window* (the one your cursor is in) has "control buttons" you can use to minimize, maximize, or close the window.

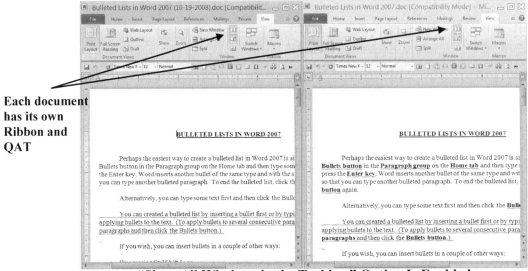

Each document has its own Ribbon and QAT

**"Show All Windows in the Taskbar" Option Is Enabled
Both Documents Appear in Full Program-Style Windows**

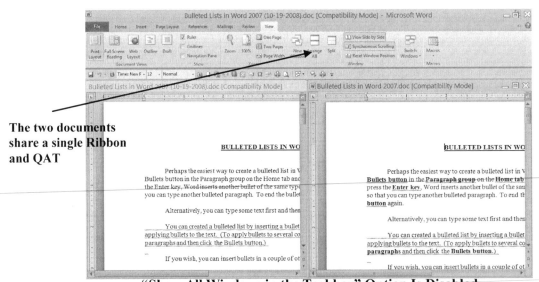

The two documents share a single Ribbon and QAT

**"Show All Windows in the Taskbar" Option Is Disabled
Documents Appear in Windows Within the Larger Program Window**

There is a **"Synchronous Scrolling" button** immediately below the "View Side by Side" button. If synchronous scrolling is enabled, both documents will scroll identically when you scroll through one of them. If it is disabled, scrolling through one of the documents will have no effect on the other one.

NOTE: If you have the "Show all Windows in the Taskbar" option enabled, the "View Side by Side" and "Synchronous Scrolling" icons might appear in condensed form, without labels (see the screenshot at right, which shows the "View Side by Side" icon on the top and the "Synchronous Scrolling" icon on the bottom).

You can drag the border of the active window to make the window larger (i.e., without maximizing the window, which would completely hide the other document window). See, for example, the next screenshot.

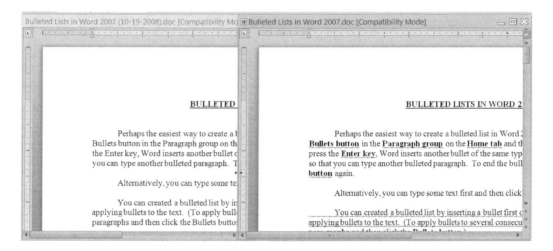

To restore the windows to their original (equal) size, click the "**Reset Window Position**" **button** (shown below as it appears when not condensed and as it appears when condensed).

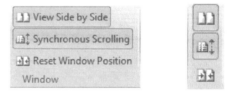

Arrange All

The "Arrange All" command appears to be less useful than the other two commands. Ostensibly, this feature places all open documents into tiled windows. However, in my tests with three documents open on my laptop, it didn't work very well, regardless of whether the "Show all windows in the Taskbar" option was enabled or disabled.

When the option was enabled, it was impossible to see anything other than the Ribbon (in part, this problem resulted from the fact that the documents were tiled horizontally, rather than vertically).

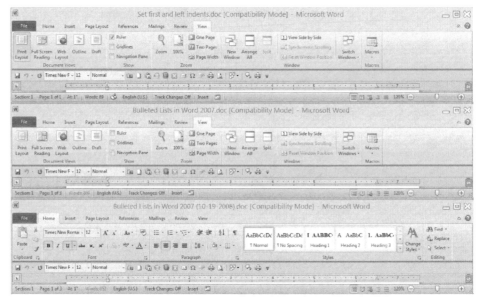

Arrange All ("Show All Windows…" Option Enabled)

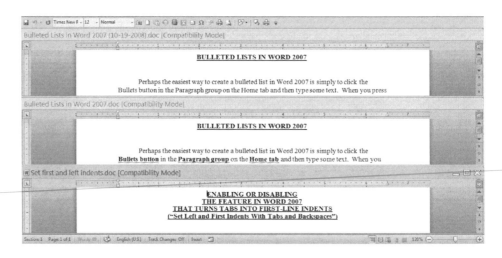

Arrange All ("Show All Windows…" Option Disabled

Presumably this option is more useful, and the tiled windows are easier to see, if you have a large computer monitor.

Protected View

Microsoft has added a new feature in Office 2010, Protected View, that is intended to help users avoid accidentally triggering a virus, worm, or other malicious content contained in documents they receive in e-mail messages or download from the Internet.

Protected View is enabled by default for all documents originating from those locations. Thus, when someone sends you a document via e-mail and you save it to your hard drive, then open it in Word, it will open in Protected View. That means that so-called active file content is disabled—including, among other things, add-ins, ActiveX controls, database connections, hyperlinks, and macros written with Visual Basic for Applications (VBA).[1]

You will see a message bar between the Ribbon and the document editing screen (Microsoft calls it the "Trust Bar") that warns that the document might be unsafe.

In Protected View mode, the document can't be edited or printed—or even saved from within Word. If you try to re-save a file that opens in Protected View, you will see an error message similar to the following:

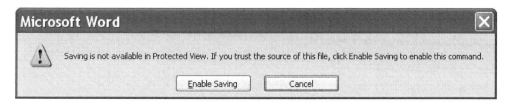

When a document opens in Protected View, all of the tabs of the Ribbon become minimized, and most of the commands that are still visible (for instance, on someone's customized Quick Access Toolbar) are grayed out, as shown in the next screenshot. (Note how the tabs are minimized—the groups and commands on the tabs aren't displayed—and all but a few of the commands on my personalized QAT are grayed out.)

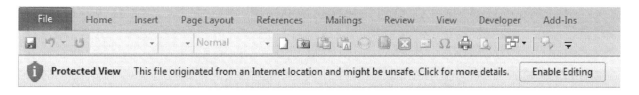

If you are certain the document comes from a trusted source and is free of malware, you can click the button marked "**Enable Editing**." That will allow you to edit and re-save the doc. (The Trust Bar will close, the Ribbon will become maximized, and commands that were grayed out will become available again.)

---

[1] For more, see this article: http://technet.microsoft.com/en-us/library/ee857087(office.14).aspx

NOTE: Once in a while, a file might open in protected view with a red message bar that lacks an "Enable Editing" button. The message warns that Office has detected a problem with the file and that editing it might harm your computer. If you are certain the file is safe, click the File tab; in the Backstage View, you'll see an "**Edit Anyway**" **button**. Clicking the button will activate the formatting commands so that you can work on the document.

There are two different places to configure the Protected View settings, both in the "**Trust Center**" in the Word Options: **Protected View** and **File Block Settings**. To view or change the settings, click the **File tab**, **Options**, then click **Trust Center** and click the "**Trust Center Settings**" **button** at the right side of the screen.

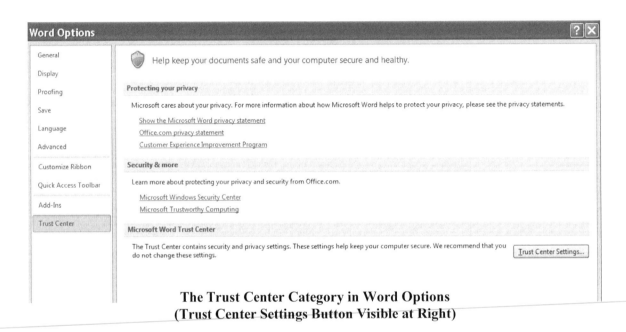

The Trust Center Category in Word Options
(Trust Center Settings Button Visible at Right)

From there, you can click the "**Protected View**" category / label at the left side of the screen. You'll see the Protected View settings for files originating from various locations (or files that fail the new Office File Validation process).

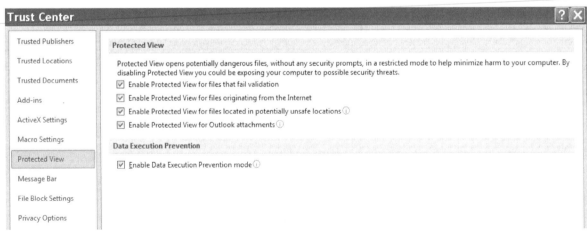

Protected View

142

By default, Word opens each of the following in Protected View:

- files that fail validation

- files originating from the Internet

- files located in potentially unsafe locations (such as your Temporary Internet folder or your Downloads folder)

- Outlook attachments

Although users can uncheck one or more of those options, it isn't advisable to do so. From the standpoint of computer security, it is far preferable to leave all of the options checked and then decide on a case-by-case basis which files Word flags as potentially harmful are safe to work on.

In addition to limiting access to files that are potentially unsafe because of their *origin*, you can restrict access to certain *file types*. To do so, from within the Trust Center, click the **File Block Settings** category (see the next screenshot). From this screen, you can pick and choose certain types of files to open in Protected View *without* the option to enable editing, to open in Protected View *with* the option to enable editing, or not to open at all.

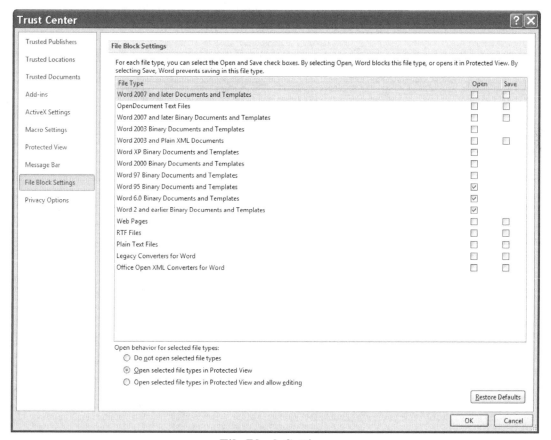

File Block Settings

When Files Fail Validation

When you open a document in Word 2010, the program performs a check in the background to ensure that the file meets certain technical criteria. This check is known as "file validation." If a file fails validation, you will see a message indicating that there is a problem with the file and that editing it could harm your computer. If you click the link, you will be taken to the Backstage View, where you can read more about the problem.

You'll also be prompted to send information about the problem to Microsoft. Depending on your organization's policies and the way it has configured Internet settings, you might or might not be able to forward the error log to Microsoft.

Note that the file validation process isn't foolproof. Every now and then, an innocuous file will be flagged for allegedly failing the validation process. If you believe a file that has failed validation is safe, you should be able to open it for editing by clicking the "Enable Editing" button. If you're not certain, check with your IT department just in case.

Inadvertent Disabling of Protected View

If you have a file open in Protected View and Word crashes and then restarts, the file could open in the Document Recovery Pane—without protection, and without an obvious way to save it. Click to select the file, then choose "Open." The file should re-open in Protected View.[2]

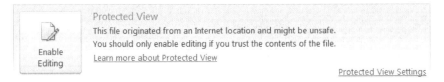

New Option in the "Open" dialog

As an aside, note that the **Open dialog** has a new option, namely "**Open in Protected View**." You can use it to open any Word file that you wish to view without triggering any malicious content it might contain. When you use this option, the file opens with a message bar across the top that says: "This file originated from an Internet location and might be unsafe."

If you are confident that the file is safe, click the "**Enable Editing" button**.

NOTE: Once in a while, a file might open in Protected View with a red message bar that lacks an "Enable Editing" button. The message warns that Office has detected a problem with the file and that editing it might harm your computer.

---

[2] This information is based on a tip in Word Help.

Mini-Translator

Word 2010 includes a Mini-Translator that you can use to translate words or phrases in your documents into any of several different languages. To use this feature, navigate to the **Review tab**, **Language group**, click the **Translate drop-down,** then click the "**Mini Translator**" command.

Note that when the Mini Translator is on / active, the command in the menu is highlighted (as in the screenshot above); when it is off / inactive, the command is not highlighted.

The first time you click the command, a Translation Language Options dialog will appear, allowing you can choose the language to which you want the text translated. As you can see in the next screenshot, I have selected French, but there are several languages available, from Arabic, Chinese, Dutch, Russian , and Swedish to Thai.

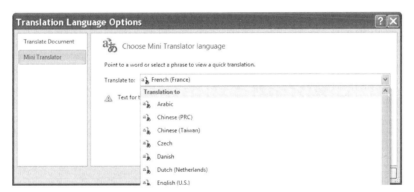

Translation Language Options (With Drop-Down Partially Displayed)

To perform the translation, you can do one of two things:

- To translate an individual word, point to the word long enough for a faint pop-up to appear above the word, then move the mouse pointer toward the pop-up (it will "solidify" so that you can read it); or

- To translate a block of text, select the text, then point to the selection and, when the pop-up appears, move the mouse toward it until it "solidifies."

The Mini-Translator

The screenshot above shows the French translation of the phrase, "This morning when I woke up."[1]

Note that the Mini-Translator has several buttons. The first, labeled "Expand," opens the Research Pane at the right side of the screen with additional translation options. (See the screenshot at right)

The second button can be used to copy and paste the translation (including the entire Mini-Translator) into another document or another program.

The third button lets you play back the selected phrase (i.e., hear it aloud). Note, however, that in order to get this feature to work properly, you need a text-to-speech engine for the language to which you are translating. I don't have a text-to-speech engine for French installed on any of my computers, so when I click the "Play" button, nothing happens.

The fourth button stops any ongoing playback.

The fifth button opens Word Help.

On subsequent use, simply navigate to the Review tab, click the Translate drop-down, and make sure that the "Mini Translator" command is active (highlighted). (If necessary, click it to activate it.) Then proceed as described on the previous page.

Alternatively, you can select some text and click the second command in the Translate drop-down ("Translate Selected Text"). The Research pane will open, with the translation appearing about halfway down, as shown in the screenshot.

---

[1] Note that in this example, Word is using the translation service WorldLingo. I don't know anything about that service, and I'm not fluent enough in French to know whether the translation is perfect—reflecting modern usage, idioms, and the like. To be on the safe side, it's probably best to keep in mind that the translation might or might not be 100% accurate.

For more about WorldLingo (and to use their free online translation service), see their web site: http://www.worldlingo.com/en/products_services/worldlingo_translator.html

Built-in Text-to-Speech

Another new feature, a built-in text-to-speech option, is mainly for fun, although it can be used by people who have some visual impairment, as well as by people with a speech impediment (such as a dysphonia). Hence, it can be thought of as an "accessibility" feature.

Text-to-speech makes use of the speech engine built into your version of Windows. The voice software it relies on is fairly crude, but it's more or less understandable.

The Speak command isn't built into the Ribbon, but you can add an icon to the Quick Access Toolbar. Just do the following:

- Right-click the QAT, then choose "Customize the Quick Access Toolbar..."

- When the Word Options screen appears, change the "Choose commands from:" drop-down to "Commands Not in the Ribbon" or "All Commands."

- Scroll down to the commands that start with the letter "S" and look for "Speak."

- Click to select "Speak," then click the "Add" button.

- Click the "OK" button to save your changes when you close out of the Word Options.

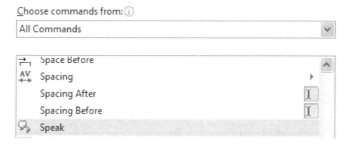

Once you have added a "Speak" icon to the QAT, simply click within a word or select some text, then click a "Speak" icon.

If you like, you can create a keyboard shortcut to trigger text-to-speech. To do so:

- Open the Word Options by clicking **File**, **Options** or by pressing **Alt F, T**, then click **Customize Ribbon**.

  o Alternatively, **right-click the Ribbon** (or the Quick Access Toolbar), then click "**Customize the Ribbon...**"

- Click the "**Keyboard shortcuts: Customize...**" **button** at the bottom left side of the screen.

Keyboard shortcuts: Customize...

- When the **Customize Keyboard dialog** appears, navigate to the **Categories box** on the left-hand side and scroll down to (and click to select) **All Commands**.

- In the **Commands box** on the right-hand side, scroll down to (and click to select) the **SpeakStopSpeaking command**.

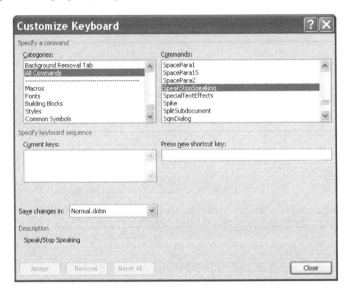

- Next, place the cursor in the "**Press new shortcut key**" **box** (if it isn't there already), and **press the key combination** you want to use to activate the text-to-speech feature. (I chose Alt 7.)

- If the key combination has been assigned to another feature, you will see a message to that effect under the "**Current keys" box**. If the message displays "unassigned," the key combination you chose has not been assigned to another feature, and it is safe to assign it to the text-to-speech function.

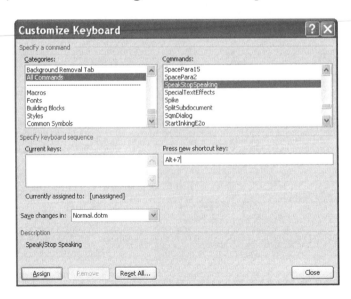

- If you wish to assign the keyboard shortcut even though it has been assigned to a different feature, you can proceed anyway.

- In either case, click the "**Assign**" **button** at the lower left-hand side of the dialog, then click "**Close**."

- Be sure to click the "**OK**" **button** at the right side of the Word Options screen in order to save your changes.

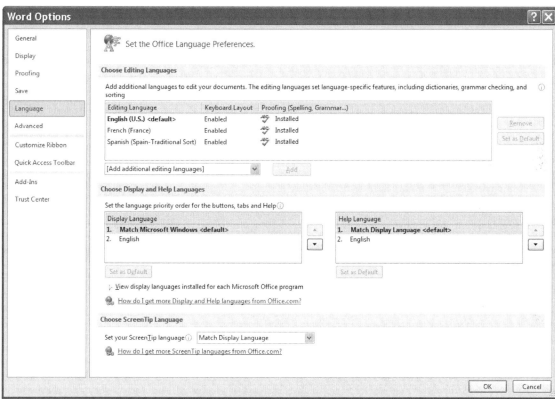

Word Options—Language

WHERE DID IT GO? AutoCorrect

AutoCorrect, formerly located on the Tools menu, is now found in the Word Options—specifically, by clicking the **File tab**, **Options**, **Proofing**, **AutoCorrect options**.

For information about where AutoCorrect files are stored, and a suggestion about making AutoCorrect entries from an earlier version of Word available in Word 2010, see the discussion starting on page 576.

Minor Tweaks to the Program

Microsoft has made a number of less apparent (and less radical) tweaks to this version of Word, as well. Those include:

Enhancements That Work Only With .Docx Files

A few of the enhancements to Word 2010 work only within .docx files. That is, they are not available in old-style .doc files (aka Word 97-2003 Compatibility Mode). Although most of these features aren't widely used in legal documents, they merit a brief mention here.

Text Effects

Some spiffy new Text Effects—outline, shadow, reflection, and glow—are available from an icon in the bottom row of the Font group on the Home tab (if you are working on a .docx).[1] The icon is grayed out if you are working in Compatibility Mode. Here is an example of the types of effects you can apply:

You can change the settings for each effect via a Format Text Effects dialog that opens when you click "Options" from a fly-out menu.

The "Reflection" Fly-Out Menu

The Format Text Effects Dialog

---

[1] The main difference between these effects and the ones available in prior versions of WordArt is that words to which the effects have been applied can be edited (and spell-checked) directly from within the program, without having to open the WordArt dialog.

Screenshot

Another new feature that is limited to .docx files is the ability to insert a screenshot directly into a Word document. You can insert either an image of any program that is open on another screen—as long as that program is not minimized—*or* a so-called "screen clipping" from one of the open programs.

The **Screenshot drop-down** is located on the **Insert tab**, in the **Illustrations group**. (If you are working in a .doc, the drop-down will be grayed out.) When you open the drop-down, Word shows you the available images from programs that are running in the background (but are not minimized), including browser windows if you are connected to the Internet. (See the screenshot below.) Clicking an icon inserts the image into your Word document at the cursor position. Alternatively, if you click the "**Screen Clipping**" **command** at the bottom of the drop-down, the mouse pointer turns into a crosshair, and you can drag to select a portion of the screen. That portion is inserted into your Word document at the cursor position.

In my tests, the Screen Clipping option took me out of Word, and I couldn't always predict which program it was going to take me into. The feature probably works best if you have only one other program window open in the background.

Background Removal

The new background removal tool is getting fairly favorable reviews from people who do work with photos in Word. And as you can see, it did a pretty good job of removing most of the background from a photo of some flowers that I took on an outing last year.

To use the tool, insert a photograph into your document. The **Picture Tools tab** will become active. When you click the **Background Removal button** at the left side of the tab, Word will remove a significant portion of the background. The tab then "morphs" and provides buttons you can click to mark (1) areas of the photo Word deleted that you want to keep or (2) additional areas you want to remove. (The mouse pointer turns into a pen that you click and drag; you don't need to be precise.) When you have finished, click a button to keep your changes or discard them.

152

Other Minor Changes

AutoComplete, a feature that exists in several older versions of Word but that was dropped in Word 2007, has been reinstated in Word 2010. When you create a Quick Part entry and give it a name (abbreviation) that consists of at least four characters, you can type the first four characters and an AutoComplete prompt will appear, at which point you can press the Enter key to insert the entire Quick Part entry. It's a convenience that many Word 2007 users missed.

In order to trigger the AutoComplete tip, a Quick Part entry must be stored in a template other than the BuildingBlocks.dotx template. For a fuller explanation, see the section about Quick Parts starting on page 339.

"Deprecated" Features: What's Gone (or Demoted)

Smart Tags

Smart Tags are no longer recognized automatically in Word 2010, although limited Smart Tag functionality remains available if you use Microsoft Office Communicator. (You must click to enable the "additional options" via File, Options, Proofing, AutoCorrect Options, "Actions" tab. Once you have done so, you can select some text in the document, right-click it, and choose the "Additional Actions" command—but again, only if you use Microsoft Office Communicator.)

Rich Text Format Compatibility With Open Office XML

Microsoft is no longer making enhancements to its proprietary Rich Text Format (RTF). You still can save a Word 2010 document in RTF format, but keep in mind that if you do so, the new features that are available in .docx files (and the other Open Office XML file types, i.e., .docm, .dotm, and .dotx) will be lost.

AutoSummary

The AutoSummary feature, found on the Tools menu in older versions of Word, was removed in Word 2007, and is not included in Word 2010. This feature was used to generate a list of document properties and/or an abstract of a document.

You can compensate for the loss of this feature, at least to some extent, by adding a "Summary Information" icon to the Quick Access Toolbar (QAT). That command makes it easy for you to insert a title, subject, keywords, comments, and similar information that will then appear in the Info fly-out menu of the Backstage View. (Of course, if you prefer you can insert that information directly in the Properties section of the Info fly-out menu.) For instructions about adding commands to the QAT, see the section starting on page 215.

This TechNet article contains more detailed information about the changes in Word 2010: http://technet.microsoft.com/en-us/library/cc179199(office.14).aspx

QUICK TIP: Striking Text (Without Using Track Changes)

To strike out text in your document without using the Track Changes feature, **select the text**, then do one of the following:

- navigate to the **Home tab** and click the **Strikethrough command** toward the bottom center of the **Font group**; or

- press **Ctrl D** (or click the dialog launcher in the Font group on the Home tab) to open the **Font dialog**, navigate to the **Effects section** and click the **Strikethrough checkbox**, and click "**OK**."

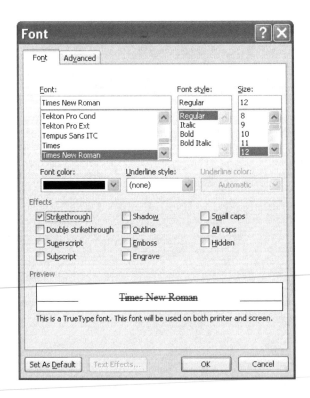

To remove strikethrough marks from text, select the text and use either of the above-described methods.

Note that you can strike out one word at a time by clicking within the word and then applying strikethrough. You can remove the strikethrough marks in the same way.

Changes Introduced in Word 2007 That Persist in Word 2010

Word 2007 constituted a rather radical departure from previous versions, at least in terms of the user interface. There were numerous other changes, too. What follows is a list, plus a brief discussion, of some of the most obvious / important changes introduced in Word 2007 that persist in Word 2010, albeit not always in exactly the same form. I go into considerably more detail about most of these features elsewhere in the book.

The New Interface

With the advent of Word 2007, the interface changed completely. A "Ribbon" (sort of a chunky toolbar) containing several "tabs" replaced the traditional menus and toolbars. In Word 2007, it was difficult and far from straightforward to customize the Ribbon (it involved XML coding); thankfully, it is much easier to customize the Ribbon in Word 2010. In addition, most of the keyboard shortcuts, including the ones that opened dialog boxes in earlier versions, still work in Word 2010, and there are other steps you can take to make the program more user-friendly, as described in the next section of the book.

The Ribbon, Tabs, and Groups

There are eight permanent "tabs" on the Ribbon (also sometimes referred to as the Main tabs): File, Home, Insert, Page Layout, References, Mailings, Review, and View. Each "tab" consists of "groups" of related commands (with command buttons). By default, the Home tab is at the forefront.

The Permanent Tabs

The Ribbon

Some additional context-sensitive tabs appear when you perform specific tasks (e.g., when you're working with tables, with headers and footers, or with images). For more information about the context-sensitive tabs, see the sidebar on page 159.

The Context-Sensitive Header & Footer Tools Tab

Word comes with a couple of optional tabs (the Developer tab and the Add-Ins tab) that can be added permanently to the Ribbon, as well. The Developer tab is particularly useful because it provides easy access to commands for working with macros.

The Developer Tab

Dialog Launchers

Some groups, such as the Font group and the Paragraph group on the Home tab, have a dialog launcher (an arrow pointing down and to the right) in the lower right-hand corner. The dialog launchers are small and unobtrusive, so people sometimes overlook them. That's unfortunate, because they come in handy at times. Clicking the arrow opens the dialog box.

Dialog Launcher

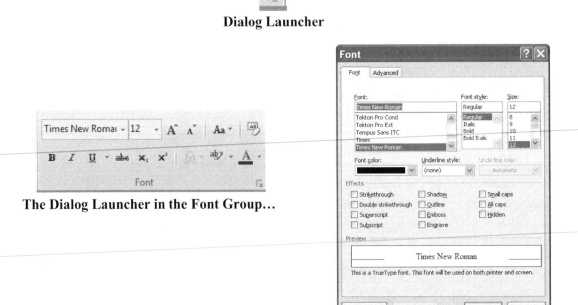

The Dialog Launcher in the Font Group…

…Opens the Font Dialog Box

The File Tab / Backstage View

As discussed in detail in the section starting on page 3, the **File tab** is a special tab at the left side of the screen. This tab has replaced Word 2007's Office button, as well as the traditional File menu. When you click the tab, you will see what Microsoft calls the **Backstage View**, which I also refer to at times as the **File Drop-Down**. In light of its greatly expanded functions in Word 2010 and throughout the Office 2010 suite of programs (including a full-page

156

Print fly-out), it can be thought of as a File menu on steroids. The tab stands out because it is colored dark blue regardless of which of Word's three available color schemes you are using.

Like the traditional File menu, the File tab includes the most common commands for working with files (Save, Save As, Open, and Close), as well as several detailed "fly-out menus" (my term): Info, Recent, New, Print, Save & Send, and Help. I have explored each of these commands and fly-out menus at length in the section about the Backstage View that starts on page 2.

The File tab also contains an "Options" button (i.e., options for configuring the program, formerly referred to as the "Word Options"). That crucial button is located toward the bottom of the drop-down. And there is an "Exit" button, too, for those of you who are accustomed to closing out of Word via the Exit button rather than the "X" in the upper right-hand corner of the program window.

Additional Tips for Working With the Ribbon

For additional tips about working with the Ribbon, see the lengthy section about customizing the Ribbon (starting on page 191), as well as the discussion about using mnemonics (keyboard shortcuts) to apply commands in the Ribbon (starting on page 319).

Finding Features That Have Been Moved

The redesigned interface can be somewhat intimidating, especially for long-time users of Word. One of the first (and most common) questions people who have migrated to Word 2010 from a pre-Word 2007 version ask is, "Where did it go?"—referring to a command or feature they use on a daily basis. Indeed, many familiar commands have been moved, and the tabs in Word 2010, like those in Word 2007, don't correspond to menus in prior versions.

For help in tracking down those essential features, take a look at "Locations of Word 2003 commands in Word 2007," which is available here: http://office.microsoft.com/en-us/word/HA100625841033.aspx

The article, which gives an overview of the Word 2007 interface, also contains a link to an extensive Excel spreadsheet that shows where various commands have moved in Word 2007. Although the article and accompanying spreadsheet deal with Word 2007, most of the information applies to Word 2010 as well.

For a Word 2010-specific reference, see Microsoft's video, "Acquaint Yourself With the Ribbon," located here: http://office2010.microsoft.com/en-us/word-help/acquaint-yourself-with-the-ribbon-RZ101816356.aspx?lc=en-us&section=2

Or use this "**tiny URL**": http://tinyurl.com/AcqRibbon

In addition, I've sprinkled a few tips for finding everyday features (labeled "Where Did It Go?") throughout the book.

SIDEBAR: Minimizing the Ribbon

The Ribbon can be "minimized" to save screen space. When you minimize the Ribbon, everything disappears except the tab labels (names).

The Minimized Ribbon

There are a few different ways to accomplish this task. For one, in this version of Word, there's actually a special "**Minimize Ribbon**" **button**. It takes the form of a carat that appears at the far right side of the Ribbon, underneath the Minimize, Maximize / Restore and Close buttons (to the left of the "Help" button). Ordinarily, the carat points up. To minimize the Ribbon, simply click the carat, which will cause it to point down. To restore the Ribbon to its full size, click the carat a second time.

The Minimize Ribbon Button

The Minimize Button—"Before"   **The Minimize Button—"After"**

Another way to minimize the Ribbon is by double-clicking any tab label. To maximize the Ribbon, double-click a tab label again (doing so will bring that tab to the forefront). **NOTE**: If you minimize the Ribbon and then *single*-click a tab heading, the Ribbon expands, but the Quick Access Toolbar disappears (if you normally display your QAT below the ribbon).

Perhaps the fastest way to minimize and maximize the Ribbon is by pressing the keyboard shortcut Ctrl F1. (It's a toggle; simply press it again to alternate between minimizing and maximizing.)

And finally, you can *right-click* somewhere within the tab headings, the Ribbon, or the QAT, and select "**Minimize the Ribbon**" from the context-sensitive menu. When you have minimized the Ribbon, a checkmark appears next to the "Minimize the Ribbon" command to show that the Ribbon has been hidden. (There is no "Maximize the Ribbon" command.) Just click the command again to uncheck it, and the Ribbon will reopen at full size.

SIDEBAR: The Context-Sensitive Tabs

As you probably have noticed if you have worked with headers and/or footers, with tables, or with images—or if you have experimented with customizing the Ribbon—Word 2010 comes with a variety of context-sensitive tabs. The context-sensitive tabs appear only when you are performing a specific task or using a certain feature, such as when your cursor is in a header or footer editing screen or within a table or when you have clicked an image.

Sometimes, the tabs disappear when you perform a different task. For example, if you are setting up a header or footer and you click the Home tab in order to change a font setting or adjust paragraph formatting, the Header & Footer Tools tab vanishes, taking with it some icons you might wish to use—including the all-important Close Header and Footer button.

Never fear! The tab is still there, though it has faded into the background. You should see the tab toward the top of the screen. Just click it to bring it to the forefront again. The same is true with the Picture Tools tab and many of the other context-sensitive tabs. (In the case of the Table Tools tabs, you need to click somewhere within the table to make the tabs visible.)

Note that if you work in Compatibility Mode—that is, if you use the .doc format (compatible with Word 97-2003) rather than the .docx format or one of the other Open Office XML file types—some of the context-sensitive tabs will not be available, or they will work differently from the way they work in the newer format (because the feature is either unavailable or somewhat limited in Compatibility Mode). The Smart Art feature, for example, doesn't work the same way in Word 2010 as in earlier versions, including Word 2007. When you insert Smart Art into a .doc in Word 2010, you have access to only the diagrams, and after you insert a diagram, you will see the Diagram context-sensitive tab. In Word 2007, by contrast, you can insert Smart Art into a .doc—as well as into a .docx—and you will have access to the full range of Smart Art options (and will see the Smart Art context-sensitive tab).

Here is a complete list of the context-sensitive tabs and commands in Word 2010. (You can display the full list by **right-clicking the Ribbon** (or the QAT) and clicking "**Customize the Ribbon…**," then navigating to the right-hand side of the Word Options screen and changing the "**Customize the Ribbon**" **drop-down** from "Main Tabs" to "**All Tabs**." You'll probably have to scroll to see everything.)

Most of the items are self-explanatory.

- Blog Post
- Insert (Blog Post)
- Outlining
- Background Removal

(The Background Removal command, part of the Picture Tools tab, appears when you are working with photographs. It provides a method for removing the background from your images. Note that it does not appear unless your document is a .docx or one of the other Open Office XML file formats.)

- Smart Art Tools
  - Design
  - Format
- Chart Tools
  - Design
  - Layout
  - Format
- Drawing Tools
  - Format
- Picture Tools
  - Format
- Table Tools
  - Design
  - Layout
- Header & Footer Tools
  - Design
- Equation Tools
  - Design
- Ink Tools
  - Pens
- Text Box Tools (Compatibility Mode)
  - Format
- Drawing Tools (Compatibility Mode)
  - Format
- WordArt Tools (Compatibility Mode)
- Diagram Tools (Compatibility Mode)
- Organization Chart Tools (Compatibility Mode)
- Picture Tools (Compatibility Mode)

Main Tabs
- ☑ Home
- ☑ Insert
- ☑ Page Layout
- ☑ References
- ☑ Mailings
- ☑ Review
- ☑ View
- ☐ Developer
- ☐ Add-Ins
- ☑ Blog Post
- ☑ Insert (Blog Post)
- ☑ Outlining
- ☑ Background Removal

SmartArt Tools
- ☑ Design
- ☑ Format

Chart Tools
- ☑ Design
- ☑ Layout
- ☑ Format

Drawing Tools
- ☑ Format

Picture Tools
- ☑ Format

Table Tools
- ☑ Design
- ☑ Layout

Header & Footer Tools
- ☑ Design

Equation Tools
- ☑ Design

Ink Tools
- ☑ Pens

Text Box Tools (Compatibility Mode)
- ☑ Format

Drawing Tools (Compatibility Mode)
- ☑ Format

WordArt Tools (Compatibility Mode)
- ☑ Format

Diagram Tools (Compatibility Mode)
- ☑ Format

Organization Chart Tools (Compatibility Mode)
- ☑ Format

Picture Tools (Compatibility Mode)
- ☑ Format

The Quick Access Toolbar ("QAT")

Part of the new interface, the Quick Access Toolbar (also known as the "QAT") is the sole functional toolbar in both Word 2007 and Word 2010. Like the dialog launchers, it is sometimes overlooked because when you first start using Word, it is small—consisting of a few icons—and scrunched into a tiny portion of the upper left-hand corner of the screen.

The QAT in Its Default State

However, the QAT is exceptionally useful. You can move it below the Ribbon so that it expands into a full-sized toolbar, then add icons for the features you use most often.

Because the QAT is stationary, it's a good place to add items that you want visible at all times, regardless of which tab is active. (It's also convenient because it makes it easy to find commands, even if you can't remember where they're located in the Ribbon.) For example, if you want to keep track of the font face, the font size, and the styles at various places in your document, you can add a font face box, a font size box, and a style box to the QAT, as I've done.

My Customized QAT

For instructions on customizing the QAT (including how to move it), see the section that starts on page 215.

View Mini-Toolbar / Zoom Controls

Both Word 2007 and Word 2010 prominently feature a View Mini-Toolbar and Zoom Controls at the right side of the Status Bar.

The View Mini-Toolbar

When you position the mouse pointer over the icons on the View Mini-Toolbar, a pop-up tells you which one it is. From left to right, the buttons represent Print Layout, Full Screen Reading, Web Layout, Outline, and Draft (called "Normal" in versions of Word prior to Word 2007). You can use the buttons interchangeably with the commands at the left side of the **View tab**, in the **Document Views group**. Or you can use keystrokes:

- Print Layout—Alt Ctrl P

- Full Screen Reading— Alt W, H

- Web Layout—Alt W, L

- Outline—Alt Ctrl O

- Draft (Normal)—Alt Ctrl N

The Zoom Controls on the Status Bar give you a quick way of changing the document magnification. To make the document bigger on screen (zoom in), click the plus sign; to make it smaller (zoom out), click the minus sign. You can also use the slider, although it can be difficult to get a precise magnification that way, even if you're good with the mouse.

Zoom Controls

Of course, you can use the Zoom command on the View tab if you prefer. (I typically use that because I like to work at 125% on my laptop, and the Zoom Controls typically increment and decrement by tens.)

The Default Font and the Default Line Spacing

Starting with Word 2007, Microsoft changed the default settings for some of the most fundamental aspects of the program. It changed the **default fonts** for ordinary text (from Times New Roman to Calibri) and for headings (from Arial to Cambria), and it changed the **default font size** (from 12 points to 11 points).

In addition, Microsoft changed the **default line spacing** (from single to 1.15) and the **spacing between paragraphs** (from none to 10 points after).

It's possible to change these defaults in a couple of different ways. The easiest method is via the Font dialog and the Paragraph dialog, as explained in the section starting on page 236, but certain caveats apply.

The New File Format (.docx)

Word 2007 introduced, and Word 2010 refined, a new **default file format** (**.docx** rather than .doc), based on Extensible Markup Language (XML) coding.

Backwards Compatibility

The new .docx format is ***not backwards-compatible with older versions of Word*** (i.e., prior to Word 2007). Those versions use the .doc format and do not have a built-in converter that is capable of reading XML coding.

In order to open native Word 2010 and Word 2007 (.docx) files into older versions of Word, your contacts who own an earlier version of Word will need to install a special converter (also called a ***compatibility pack***)—unless you specifically re-save the files in the older (.doc) format.[1] The latest version of this converter (Version 4) is available as a free download from Microsoft at the following site:

---

[1] To save a file in .doc format, click the File tab, Save As, and when the Save As dialog opens, click the "Save as type" drop-down and change it to Word 97-2003 Document (*.doc). Or click the File tab, Save & Send, Change File Type, Word 97-2003 Document (*.doc).

Compatibility Pack for Word, Excel, and PowerPoint (dated January 10, 2010): www.microsoft.com/downloads/details.aspx?FamilyID=941b3470-3ae9-4aee-8f43-c6bb74cd1466&displaylang=en

I've created a "**tiny URL**" for that site: http://tinyurl.com/CompatPack

Before installing the Compatibility Pack, it's essential for your contacts to read the Overview and System Requirements information and, if necessary, update / patch their version of Windows. Also, they might want to take a look at this Microsoft Knowledge Base article, which was written about Office 2007 programs but also applies to the Office 2010 apps:

"How to open and save Word 2007, Excel 2007, and PowerPoint 2007 files in earlier versions of Office programs": http://support.microsoft.com/kb/924074

Forward Compatibility

You *can* open documents created in older versions directly into Word 2010. They will open in so-called Compatibility Mode—as .doc files. As a result, some of the new features that are enabled only in Open Office XML file types won't be available.

Other Open Office XML Formats Used in Word

If you don't do anything to change the default file format, your regular documents will be saved as **.docx files**. These files are not *macro-enabled*; that is, they cannot contain macros written in Visual Basic for Applications, or VBA.

There are at least three other new XML-based file formats available in Word 2010 (and Word 2007). They are:

- **.docm files**—regular Word documents that (unlike .docx files) *are* macro-enabled;

- **.dotx files**—Word templates that are *not* macro-enabled (this is the default format for Word 2010 and Word 2007 templates); and

- **.dotm files**—Word templates that *are* macro-enabled.

For instance, the NORMAL template on which most new documents are based is a .dotm file, which means that it is macro-enabled. The BuildingBlocks.dotx template, by contrast, is a .dotx file, which means that it is *not* macro-enabled.

Together, these four file formats comprise **Open Office XML** files (sometimes known as Open XML or OOXML).[2]

---

[2] Recent versions of Excel and PowerPoint (the Office 2010 and Office 2007 versions) use additional Open Office XML file types.

Note that the Open Office XML formats have changed somewhat between Word 2007 and Word 2010. In particular, the Word 2010 Open Office XML file types have a few capabilities not found in their Word 2007 counterparts—for example, co-authoring and the ability to share files on the Web (via Windows Live). Although Word 2007 can read all four types of files (.docx, .docm, .dotx, and .dotm), those newer capabilities won't work, or won't work the same way, if you open native Word documents into Word 2007. Examples include, among other things, text effects, the Block Authors feature, certain new shapes and text boxes, and certain new WordArt effects.

According to Microsoft, the the Open Office XML file formats have a number of advantages over the "binary" file formats used in pre-Office 2007 applications, including but not limited to the following:

- XML files are "zipped" (compressed), which means they are significantly smaller than their binary counterparts;

- because the individual components of XML files are isolated from one another, it's often possible to continue to work with a document even if a portion of the document (such as a table) becomes damaged or corrupted;

- the default file formats can't contain macros, which makes them less vulnerable to macro viruses (a fact that should be reassuring to people who send and receive .docx files via e-mail).

Style Sets

Built-in "**Style Sets**" determine a number of default settings in your document that in previous versions of Word were configured mainly via the Normal paragraph style. For this reason, changing the defaults isn't entirely straightforward. (You *can* create your own Style Set or even replace the default Style Set, although that isn't a complete solution.) I provide details and workarounds in the section that starts on page 222.

Themes

Beginning with Word 2007, built-in "**Themes**" now determine the default font face and color for text as well as for built-in heading styles. Together with Style Sets, they operate in the background, and most new users have no idea how to disable them. (One way is by creating your own "Theme" that applies your preferred fonts for text and headings, then setting that theme as the default for use with a particular template.[3])

---

[3] For a full discussion of these issues and instructions for changing the defaults, see the next section, starting on page 221.

Galleries

Word 2010, like Word 2007, provides several "Galleries" that consist of built-in styles or formats—for headings, headers and footers, page numbering, a Table of Contents, numbered lists, watermarks, and other commonly used document elements. You can select one of the built-in styles or, if you prefer, simply create your own.

For example, when you want to change the page margins in your document, you can use the old-fashioned method of launching the Page Setup dialog (by clicking the **dialog launcher** in the lower right-hand corner of the **Page Layout tab**, **Page Setup group**) *or* you can click the **Margins drop-down** in the **Page Setup group** and choose one of the options in the gallery. (Clicking the "Custom Margins" command opens the Page Setup dialog.)

Similarly, there is a **Footer drop-down** on the **Insert tab** (in the **Header & Footer group**) that offers various pre-configured footers, including one with three columns (so that you can type some text at the left, in the center, and at the right side of the footer.)

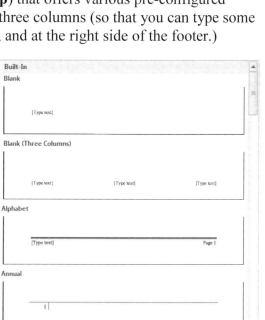

The Footer Gallery

The gallery contains several other sample footers; you need to scroll down in order to see them.

The Watermark gallery (Page Layout tab, Page Background group) incorporates several different built-in watermarks; you have to scroll down to see all of them. The next screenshot shows about 2/3 of the items in the gallery.

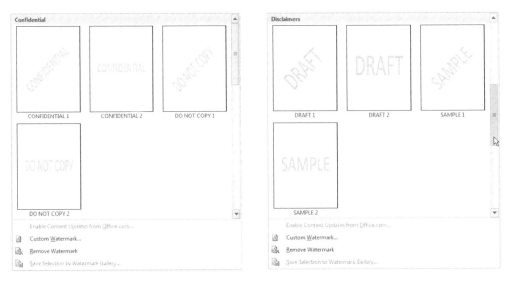

And the Table of Contents drop-down on the References tab provides two different built-in TOC styles that use automatic page numbering, as well as one that is static (it just inserts placeholders so that you can type headings and page numbers manually).

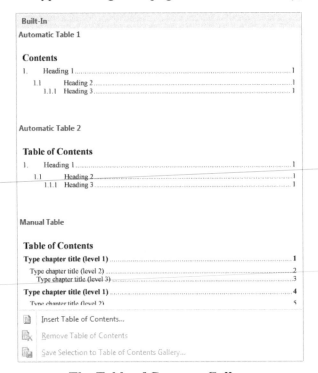

The Table of Contents Gallery

Of course, you don't have to use any of the built-in styles in any of the galleries, but they give you some additional choices. You might want to experiment at some point and see how you like them.

The Quick Style Gallery

The Quick Style Gallery, situated on the Home tab, was introduced in Word 2007. It puts some of the most commonly used built-in styles, as well as the other styles in your document (if any), within easy reach. Moreover, the icons in the gallery feature mini-samples of the styles, so you can see at a glance what each style will look like.

The Quick Style Gallery

To apply a Quick Style to a paragraph, place the cursor within the paragraph and then click the icon for the style in the gallery. (To apply a character style rather than a paragraph style, select the text you want to reformat before clicking the icon.)

Note that when you position the mouse pointer over a style (either deliberately or accidentally), Word displays the text in your document at the cursor position as if you had applied the style. That's because of a new feature called **Live Preview** (see the next section). It's a useful feature, but can be disconcerting if it happens unexpectedly. Watch out for it, and don't panic! The style won't be applied unless and until you actually click it.

For more details about Quick Styles and the Quick Style Gallery, see the section starting on page 357.

Live Preview

Because of a feature called **Live Preview** (introduced in Word 2007), you can see what your document would look like before you actually apply a particular style or font attribute. To preview a paragraph style, simply click within some text and then position your mouse pointer over a style icon in the **Quick Styles gallery;** to preview a character style, select the text and then hold the mouse pointer over a style icon.

To preview a font attribute, select some text and then click one of the drop-downs in the **Font group** on the **Home tab**. In addition to font faces, you can preview font sizes, underlining styles, highlighter colors, font colors, and text effects. (You can also preview paragraph background colors with the shading drop-down in the **Paragraph group** on the **Home tab**, and you can preview page colors by using the page color drop-down in the **Page Background group** on the **Page Layout tab**.)

Building Blocks / Quick Parts

In the newer versions of Word, AutoText has been replaced by "**Building Blocks**" (also known as "**Quick Parts**"—in fact, that is the term I use throughout the book—and located on the **Insert tab**, **Text group**, **Quick Parts**). The Quick Parts feature works more or less the same way as AutoText, except that the new Building Blocks Organizer (the gallery where the Quick

Parts entries reside) is somewhat unwieldy. But compensating for that unwieldiness, at least to some degree, the AutoComplete feature has been reinstated in Word 2010.

AutoComplete is a handy feature that recognizes Quick Parts entries by the first four characters of their names as you are typing and prompts you with a pop-up that shows the full entry. If you wish, you can insert the entry at the cursor position simply by pressing the Enter key, or you can keep typing. For a fuller discussion of AutoComplete, see the section about Quick Parts starting on page 339.

Floating MiniToolbar

Word 2007 was the first version to make use of a floating Mini Toolbar that appears nearby when you select text. The Mini Toolbar also appears—above a context-sensitive menu—when you right-click selected text.

The Mini Toolbar includes commands for working with fonts (font face, font size, size up, size down, bold, italics, underlining, highlighting, font color), as well as for changing justification and copying paragraph formatting via the Format Paintbrush.

Additional commands become available depending on the context (for example, if you select text within a table, commands for borders and shading appear along with the other commands).

When you select text, the Mini Toolbar first appears as a sort of hazy apparition. It solidifies when you move the mouse closer to it.

Word Counter

In Word 2007 and Word 2010, there is a **Word Counter** on the Status Bar that keeps track of the number of words in your document (including footnotes) as you type.[4] When you click it, a pop-up displays the number of pages, lines, characters, and paragraphs as well as words.

The Word Counter is displayed by default on the Status Bar in Word 2010.

Words: 914

---

[4] As in Word 2007, there is also a Word Count icon on the Review tab (in the Proofing Group).

Color Schemes

You can apply any of three different **color schemes**: silver, blue, and black. To change the color scheme, click the **File Tab**, **Options**; the color scheme option is about halfway down the main Options page. Be sure to click "**OK**" to save your changes when you close the Options screen.

I normally use blue, which is one reason objects in the screenshots for this book might look somewhat different from the way they appear on your screen.

Text Selection

Regardless of which color scheme you are using, **text selection** is blue-gray, rather than the traditional color (black). Most other programs still use black.

* * * * *

In the next section of the book, before I move on to tips about customizing and automating Word, I provide an analysis of the program's "logic." This discussion is intended to help both experienced users and newbies (typically, people who are moving from WordPerfect to Word) understand what is going on "under the hood." Fundamental knowledge about the way that Word works is essential because: (1) it enables you to produce the results you desire and expect, and (2) it helps you to troubleshoot problems effectively. Even if you consider yourself well versed in the program, you'll likely find this information useful—particularly when (note that I didn't say "if"!) something goes wrong.

SIDEBAR: Unraveling the Ribbon

Don't let the new interface intimidate you. There are multiple ways to master its mysteries. Keep in mind that all of the following tools are available to you, and don't hesitate to use them.

Tool	Description	Pages in Book
Mnemonics	When you press the Alt key, alone or in combination with other keys, the program shows keys to press in order to use commands on the Ribbon and on the QAT	See the section starting on page 319.
Keyboard Shortcuts	Most KB shortcuts from earlier versions of Word still work in Word 2010	See, *inter alia*, the section starting on page 307.
Interactive Guides	Show you where the commands you're familiar with from Word 2003 have been moved in Word 2010	See pages 566 and following
Customization of the Ribbon	Add your own custom tabs, groups, and/or commands; hide tabs; etc.	See the sections starting on pages 135 and 191
Customization of the Quick Access Toolbar (QAT)	Move below Ribbon so that it expands into a full-sized toolbar; add icons for your commonly used commands	The full discussion starts on page 215.
Pop-Up Tips	Appear when you hold the mouse pointer over most commands and/or icons	(Throughout)
Right-Clicking	Produces different context-sensitive menus depending on where the cursor is	(Throughout)
Third-Party Tools for Customizing the Ribbon	Some of these tools allow you to emulate the traditional menus and toolbars from earlier versions of Word	See the sidebar starting on page 214

Word's "Logic"
(and How It Compares With WordPerfect's)

WordPerfect vs. Word—Some Fundamental Differences in "Logic"

The following chart makes it easy to compare the essential differences between WordPerfect's "logic" and that of Word. Understanding how the two programs work "under the hood" gives you more control over document formatting in at least two significant ways: (1) it makes the behavior of the software less mysterious / easier to predict; and (2) it provides clues about how to troubleshoot problematic formatting.

TIP: The information in this chart, together with the explanations that follow about paragraph and section formatting, is the key to mastering Word.

WordPerfect's Logic	Word's Logic
Based on ***text-stream formatting***:	Based on ***paragraph formatting***:
You insert a code at the cursor position, and everything that follows—i.e., in the stream of text—is governed by that code (until you insert a new code that supersedes the first one).	The paragraph is the basic formatting unit in Word. (***Section formatting*** is used for features like page orientation, margins, and headers/footers; ***character formatting*** is used for attributes like bold and italics that can be applied to individual characters).

Examples:
    Font face / size
    Text alignment (left, center, right)
    Line spacing
	Examples:
	    Justification (left, center, right)
	    Indentation

Implications:	Implications:
Easy to format small bits of text—e.g., you can indent or center <u>part</u> of a line	Harder to format individual pieces of text, because Word sees everything as a paragraph
Formatting codes are visible with Reveal Codes (and many codes can be expanded)	Formatting codes are contained in the paragraph symbol (¶); they're not directly visible[1]
Formatting you apply to a specific paragraph usually ***does not*** carry over to the next paragraph	Formatting you apply to an entire paragraph ***carries over to the next paragraph*** when you press the Enter key

---

[1] This aspect of paragraph formatting in Word is critical to understand because it means, among other things, that you can modify the formatting of one paragraph by copying and pasting the pilcrow from the end of another paragraph—an extremely handy "fix-it" tool.

WordPerfect's Logic	**Word's Logic**
Uses "*select, then do*" to some extent, but generally more stream-based than Word	Much formatting requires "*select, then do*" (example: changing fonts in the document)
Extensive use of function keys, both alone and in combination with Alt, Ctrl, and/or Shift key	Extensive use of Ctrl key + letter
Reveal Codes simplifies troubleshooting because 90% of problems with the document can be diagnosed and fixed by using Reveal Codes. (It's very easy to delete offending codes, move codes around, and/or double-click codes, thereby opening dialog boxes so you can change configuration settings.)	Word has no single feature comparable to Reveal Codes, but there are at least four different ways you can get information about document formatting:
	1. **Reveal Formatting** (Select text, then press **Shift F1** *or* launch the **Style pane** and press **Style Inspector / Reveal Formatting**)—somewhat useful
	2. **Paragraph dialog** (available from the Home tab and also from the Page Layout tab)—very useful!
	3. **Page Setup dialog** (available from the Page Layout tab)—also quite useful
	4. **Show/Hide Non-Printing Characters**—helpful in a variety of circumstances
"*Plain vanilla*" unless you apply formatting (but is becoming more like Word—using more automatic formatting features)	*Automatic formatting* (which can be great if it's what you want, but can be annoying if it isn't)

The Key to How Word Works: Paragraph Formatting

KEY CONCEPT 1: Word, unlike WordPerfect, interprets all text as part of a paragraph[1].

KEY CONCEPT 2: When you type a document from scratch, paragraph formatting normally carries over from one paragraph to the next. The formatting instructions (codes) are contained within the paragraph symbol (¶) at the end of the paragraph, which is copied to the next paragraph when you press the Enter key.

Obviously, paragraph formatting is an important concept in Word. What exactly *is* paragraph formatting?

Basically, the term refers to any attribute of paragraphs that you can change through the **Paragraph dialog box** (**Home tab, Paragraph group**, click the dialog-launcher arrow at the bottom right to display the dialog, *or* **Page Layout tab, Paragraph** group, click the arrow to display the dialog, *or* click **Alt O, P**). In other words, it includes **alignment** (justification), **indentation** (which means not only the left and right margins of the paragraph, but also the first line thereof), **spacing before and after the paragraph**, **line spacing**, and **tabs**.

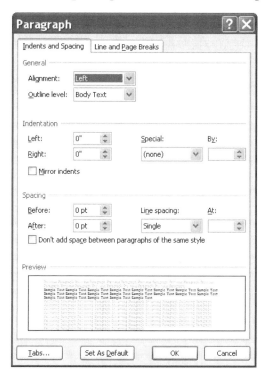

Indents and Spacing tab

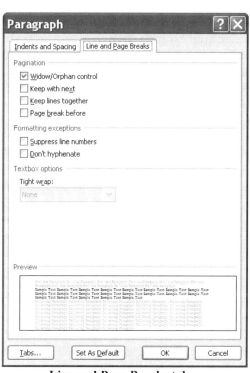

Line and Page Breaks tab

---

[1] In Word, the paragraph is the basic unit to which you apply most types of formatting. In WordPerfect, formatting such as alignment and indents can be applied separately to smaller units (text strings or streams).

It also includes **outline numbering** (where applicable). In addition, paragraph formatting encompasses **line breaks** and **page breaks** (whether you allow lines or paragraphs to break across pages).

The dialog box pictured on the previous page shows my default or "normal" paragraph settings in Word 2010. (I've modified the settings because the defaults that came with the program—1.15 line spacing and 10 points after each paragraph—didn't suit my needs.)

If you use either the configuration options in the Paragraph dialog box or the equivalent keyboard shortcuts to change the formatting of a few paragraphs (e.g., the line spacing) and then want to resume "normal" formatting, you can either (1) restore the default settings through the **Paragraph dialog box** *or* (2) press the **Enter key** to start a new paragraph and then press **Ctrl Q** to remove all "manually applied" paragraph formatting and restore the default settings.

NOTE: Ctrl Q will remove paragraph formatting in most instances. There is one important exception to this rule, however. If you (or someone else) used a *STYLE* to format a paragraph (or series of paragraphs), Ctrl Q won't work because *it won't remove the style* that is affecting the paragraph formatting. Instead, with the cursor within the paragraph you want to change back to the default settings, press **Ctrl Shift N**. That key combination is the keyboard shortcut for the **Normal paragraph style**; use it to replace any existing paragraph style with the Normal (default) style. Or, if you are a "mouse person," click the "**Normal**" icon in the **Quick Style gallery** (in the **Styles group** on the **Home tab**). You might have to scroll to see it, using the up arrow or the down arrow at the right side of the gallery.

The "Normal" Icon in the Quick Style Gallery

Indentation

You can use the **Paragraph dialog box** to set the left and/or right indentation of one or more paragraphs. This feature can be useful for (among other things) indented quotations in pleadings. You can apply the indentation either before or after you type the quotation; just make sure that your cursor is positioned where you want the indented text to go. Then open the **Paragraph dialog box** and set both the **Left** indentation and **Right** indentation to 1" (or whatever measurement you prefer).

If you also want the first line of each paragraph to be indented (half an inch is standard in legal documents, but you can choose almost any setting you like), navigate to the "Special" box and select "**First line**" from the drop-down list. If 0.5" is not displayed in the "**By**" box, you can simply delete the number in the box and type .5 (no need to insert the quotation marks) *or* you can use the **spinners (arrows)** to set the number.

The "**Special**" box determines the indentation of the first line of the paragraph. Note that there are two other options under "**Special**" besides **First line: (none)** and **Hanging**. The "(none)" option means that the first line of the paragraph will not be indented beyond the indent you've set for the paragraph as a whole; the "Hanging" option means that every line of the paragraph *except the first* will be by indented an additional amount beyond the Left indent you've set for the entire paragraph. The default setting in Word is half an inch, but you can change this setting to suit your needs.

Understanding Paragraph Spacing ("Spacing Before" and "Spacing After")

"**Spacing Before**" and "**Spacing After**" refer to the amount of space—usually measured in points—that Word will insert automatically before and after a paragraph. If you want Word to insert one blank line between paragraphs, you can set the "Spacing After" to 12 points, the equivalent of a standard single-spaced line. (Remember that "points" refers to the *height* of the characters.) Or you can set both the "Spacing Before" and the "Spacing After" to 6 points (half a line).

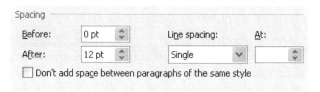

Spacing Before and Spacing After are commonly used with styles to achieve uniform spacing between paragraphs in a document. **CAUTION**: People who use this feature have to get into the habit of not pressing the Enter key twice after typing a paragraph.

NOTE: In Word 2010 (as in Word 2007), there is an additional item in the Paragraph dialog labeled "**Don't add space between paragraphs of the same style.**" This option is disabled by default for the Normal paragraph style, which means you can increase the "Before" and/or "After" paragraph spacing for this style and your changes will go into effect as expected. However, if the option is enabled, Word *will ignore* the "Before" and/or "After" settings. (Even with the box checked, you'll be able to add space between paragraphs manually—i.e., by pressing the Enter key.)

Note that Microsoft *applies this setting differently to different built-in styles*.[2] By default, it *enables* the setting for bulleted and numbered lists (especially those that are created by applying a List Bullet or List Number style)—depriving you of the ability to determine the amount of white space between items in those lists via Before or After Spacing.

---

[2] **NOTE**: Any style you create that is based on a built-in style will inherit the settings of the underlying style.

If you find that you can't add white space by changing the settings in the Before and/or After Spacing boxes, note whether "Don't add space between paragraphs of the same style" is checked. Close the Paragraph dialog, then make sure to select the list (or other text to which you wish to add more white space), reopen the Paragraph dialog, **_uncheck_** the option, and click **OK**.

In the event that you wish to make "Don't add space between paragraphs of the same style" the default for the Normal paragraph style, **_check_** the checkbox for the option, click the "**Set As Default**" button at the bottom of the dialog, and then when prompted about having the change affect all new documents based on the NORMAL template, click "**Yes**."

Understanding How Word Handles Line Spacing

In Word, the **Line Spacing drop-down** provides some unusual configuration options, including "**Exactly**," "**At Least**," and "**Multiple**."

"Exactly" allows you to set custom line spacing that remains fixed, whereas "At Least" gives you the option of specifying a minimum line spacing and letting Word adjust the spacing if, and as, necessary to accommodate graphics (or other characters) that wouldn't otherwise fit. (This option probably is used widely in desktop publishing but, for obvious reasons, isn't suitable for pleadings or any similar type of document that is subject to strict formatting rules.)

The "Multiple" option is for setting line spacing at an interval other than single, double, or 1.5. For example, if you wanted triple spacing, you would use the "Multiple" option and type "3" in the "At" box.

"Exactly" can be important when you are working on pleadings. The process of generating pleading paper usually results in line numbering that does not use true double-spacing. True double-spacing is approximately 240% of the size of your chosen font; with a 12-point font—standard for most pleadings in California—true double-spacing is roughly the equivalent of 28.8 points. But for technical reasons, the line numbers on pleading paper often are spaced **_22.75 points_** apart (or some other fraction). In order to get the text of the pleading to align properly with the line numbers, you have to make sure the line spacing of the text matches that of the line numbers (which you can determine by going into the document's header, clicking somewhere within the line numbering, and then launching the Paragraph dialog by clicking the **dialog launcher** in the **Paragraph group** on the **Home tab** or by pressing **Alt O, P**). If it doesn't, you'll have to select the text and change the setting via the "Exactly" option.

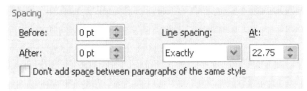

Understanding Line and Page Breaks in Word

Always keep in mind that this feature is found in the **Paragraph** dialog box. That means that each option under "**Line and Page Breaks**" applies to **_an entire paragraph_**.

Thus, "**Keep lines together**" means keep the entire paragraph—all of its lines—on one page. In other words, don't split a paragraph across pages. When this option is checked (enabled), if the entire paragraph won't fit at the bottom of one page, Word bumps the paragraph to the next page.

Note that this feature is different from Widow/Orphan Control. With "**Widow/Orphan Control**" checked (enabled), Word does allow paragraphs to split across pages, but won't allow *a single line of a paragraph* to dangle by itself at the top or bottom of a page.

"**Keep with next**" also differs from "Keep lines together." Whereas "Keep lines together" refers to the lines of a single paragraph, "Keep with next" refers to more than one paragraph. That is, when "Keep with next" is checked (enabled), Word will attempt to keep the paragraph that contains this setting with the following paragraph, and if the following paragraph is on the next page, Word will bump the current paragraph to the next page, as well.

One common use of this feature is to keep a heading on the same page as the body text that follows the heading (but **NOTE**: you usually have to apply the "Keep with next" setting to *both the heading and the blank line below the heading*, because Word considers the blank line a separate paragraph that requires its own formatting. If you apply the setting only to the heading, it will keep the heading together with the blank line but it won't keep the blank line together with the text immediately below).

CAUTION: This feature sometimes causes text to move around within your document for no apparent reason! If text won't stay where you type it, put the cursor into one of the meandering paragraphs, open the **Paragraph dialog**, and look to see whether "Keep with next" is checked. If it is, uncheck it. You might have to select the entire document, or several paragraphs, and then uncheck that option.

"**Page break before**" means exactly what it sounds like. When this option is checked, Word will insert a page break before the paragraph that contains that setting. This result also can be achieved by pressing **Ctrl Enter** (the keyboard shortcut for page break).

Other Paragraph Formatting Options

There are three additional paragraph formatting options -- **Outline level, Suppress line numbers**, and **Don't hyphenate**. Of the three, you probably will find the "Outline level" option the most useful.

In Word 2002, Microsoft introduced the ability to mark any text (i.e., text *not already formatted with a heading style*) for inclusion in the Table of Contents simply by applying a particular outline level to that text. This method is much easier than marking text the old way — using the Mark Table of Contents Entry dialog box. With the cursor positioned within some text you wish to mark for inclusion in the TOC, open the Paragraph dialog and select the appropriate level in the "Outline level" drop-down. When you generate the TOC, the text should appear automatically (with the correct indentation). If you select the wrong level, simply start over, select a different level from the drop-down, and regenerate or update the TOC.

In truth, I never use Suppress line numbers or Don't hyphenate. As for the former, it's difficult to imagine a situation where you would want to suppress line numbering in a legal document. As for the latter, hyphenation options in Word are set from the **Page Layout tab**, **Hyphenation drop-down**, **Hyphenation Options**. By default, hyphenation is turned off. If you enable automatic hyphenation, you can use the **Paragraph dialog** to exclude certain paragraphs from automatic hyphenation.

The Default Button

There is a **"Set As Default" button** at the bottom of the Indents and Spacing tab of the Paragraph dialog. This relatively new feature, first introduced in Word 2007 (but with a button labeled simply "Default" in that version), allows you to change the default paragraph settings for the existing document *and all future documents* with a couple of clicks.[3]

Simply go through the dialog and modify any settings you wish. Then, before closing the dialog, click the **"Set As Default" button**. A message box will open, prompting you to confirm that you wish to change the underlying template so that the default paragraph style in future documents will reflect the changes you are making now. If you want to do so, click **"Yes."** Otherwise, click "No" or "Cancel." ("No" closes both the message box and the Paragraph dialog; "Cancel" closes only the message box, leaving the Paragraph dialog open on your screen.)

Another enhancement first introduced in Word 2007 is the **"Mirror Indents"** command on the **Indents and Spacing tab**. Essentially, that command allows you to set either a left or right indent for a paragraph that goes into effect on even pages only and is indented (usually by the same amount) from the other margin on odd pages only. For example, you might set a 2" **left indent** that goes into effect on even pages and then becomes a 2" **right indent** on odd pages. Note that when you use this feature (by checking the "Mirror Indents" box), the labels in the Indentation section of the dialog change from "Left" and "Right" to "Inside" and "Outside."

---

[3] **CAUTION**: In versions of Word prior to Word 2007, you could set defaults for the Normal paragraph style and they would remain in place unless and until you deliberately changed them. In Word 2010 (and Word 2007), the Normal paragraph style *can be overwritten by Style Sets*, template-like objects that use XML coding to determine most of the basic formatting of your documents.

Paragraph Formatting vs. Section Formatting

Unlike in WordPerfect, formatting in Word is applied mainly to ***paragraphs*** or to ***sections*** of a document. The types of formatting you can apply to paragraphs (usually via the **Paragraph dialog box**) are listed in the left-hand column of the chart below. For more detailed information, see the discussion of paragraph formatting in the preceding section.

Page layout actually is applied section by section in a document in Word. When you need to ***change*** page layout, you must insert a ***section break (next page)*** in order to apply different formatting. The break goes ***on the page before*** any formatting change.[1] (If you don't want to change the page layout anywhere in your document, you don't need a section break. You simply apply the formatting to the entire document or to one or more paragraphs.) The types of page formatting that are applied section by section—and for which a section break is needed if you wish to make a change—are listed in the right-hand column of the chart.

Paragraph Formatting	Section Formatting (Page Layout)
Alignment (Justification)	Margins (page margins)
Indentation—Left and Right	Headers and footers (especially multiple headers and footers)
Indentation—First Line, subsequent lines (hanging indent)	Page orientation—portrait vs. landscape
Spacing before / Spacing after	Columns (i.e., mixed with regular text on the same page)
Line spacing	Page numbering
Tabs	Footnotes
Widow and orphan	Page borders
Keep with next (paragraph)	
Keep together (i.e., keep entire paragraph together on one page)	
Page break before	

---

[1] In Word 2010, you add a section break by clicking the **Page Layout tab**, **Breaks (Alt P, B)**.

Practical Implications

What does the chart on page 181 mean in practical terms?

It means that if you want to change the page margins somewhere in your document (as opposed to the margins of one or two isolated paragraphs), you need to insert a section break on the page before the page where the change is to go into effect.

It means that if you need to format one page of a document so that it has a "landscape" (sideways) orientation, you have to insert a section break on the last "portrait"-oriented page before the landscape-formatted material (and, if you're changing back to portrait orientation afterwards, you need a second section break on the page before the formatting reverts to portrait).

It means that if you are writing a book or other material where footnotes in the various chapters or sections need to start over with the number 1, you need to insert a section break on the page before the renumbering is to start.

It means that if you are working on a pleading that includes a Table of Contents and a Table of Authorities and you need the page numbering to restart—and/or you need to switch from Arabic numerals to roman numerals and back again—you must insert section breaks ahead of the page(s) where the value and/or style of the page numbering will be different.

And it means that if you want to use more than one header or footer in your document, you need to insert a section break on the page before any page where a new/different header or footer is to begin (or, if appropriate, use the Different First Page option, which automatically sets up a first-page header or footer that is distinct from any header or footer that follows).

Keep these general rules in mind when you are working with page formatting, and eventually they will become second nature.

Help! Word Doesn't Have Reveal Codes!

Part of what can make the transition from WordPerfect to Word formidable is the fact that Word doesn't have any single feature comparable to WordPerfect's Reveal Codes, which means troubleshooting can be tricky at times. Word does, however, have several other features that can help you troubleshoot problems.

Reveal Formatting

One of these is **Reveal Formatting**. Reveal Formatting gives you some information about paragraph formatting in your document, such as indentation and alignment, and about character formatting, such as the font and whether the text is bolded or italicized.

To use Reveal Formatting, press **Shift F1** and then click some text (or select some text and then press Shift F1).[1] NOTE: This feature has been significantly "jazzed up" in recent versions of Word. It now appears in a Task Pane that opens at the right-hand side of the screen (see below).

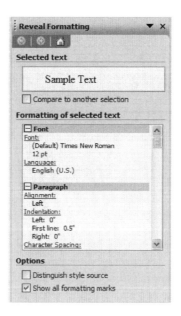

The Reveal Formatting Task Pane also can be used to compare the formatting of selected text with other text in the document, or to determine whether a style has been applied. In addition, if you position the mouse pointer over the "**Selected text**" box, an arrow appears that allows you to select all text with formatting similar to the text you've selected, apply the formatting of the surrounding text, or clear the formatting altogether.

---

[1]In some old versions of Word, you can click the Help Button (question mark in the upper right corner of the standard toolbar) and then click the text.

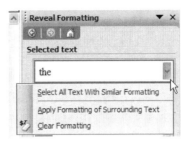

The Style Inspector

A new feature called the **Style Inspector**, introduced in Word 2007, allows you to see—and clear (remove)—certain paragraph formatting that has been applied via a style or directly (manually). Position your cursor in the paragraph you want to "inspect," click the **Styles dialog launcher** (**Home tab**, **Styles group**) and click the **Style Inspector button** at the bottom of the **Styles pane**.

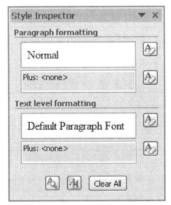

The Style Inspector actually doesn't provide as much information as Reveal Formatting, but it does allow you to clear either paragraph formatting or style formatting, or both, with the click of a couple of buttons. For more information, see the sidebar on page 364.

The Paragraph Dialog

Another way to try to figure out what is causing a problem is to open the **Paragraph dialog box** (**Home tab**, **Paragraph group**, **dialog launcher** *or* press **Alt O, P**). Check both the Indents and Spacing tab and the Line and Page Breaks tab (called Text Flow in some earlier versions of Word) to see if any of the settings need to be changed.

The Page Setup Dialog

Also, check margin settings and other formatting information by opening the **Page Setup dialog** (**Page Layout tab**, Page **Setup group**, **dialog launcher** *or* press the **Alt key**, then **P, S, P** *or* press **Alt, P, M, A**). In particular, make sure to check the Margins and Layout tabs. (The Paper tab is less important unless you are experiencing printing problems that could be affected by the paper format or paper source.) The Layout tab contains information about headers and footers.

TIP: Be sure to look at the "**Apply to:**" box on both tabs, since occasionally you will find that formatting that should have been applied to the whole document has been applied to just one section.

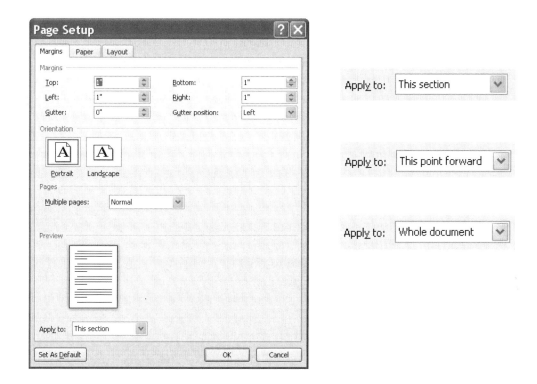

Show Non-Printing Characters

When you are having problems, it can be helpful to display **non-printing characters**, such as paragraph symbols, tab marks, and spaces. Remember that the paragraph symbols contain the formatting codes—affecting justification, indentation, line spacing, before and after spacing, line and page breaks, and automatic numbering—*for the immediately preceding paragraph*.

Sometimes you can fix a problem by deleting a paragraph symbol, or by copying a symbol from a correctly formatted paragraph to the end of a paragraph that isn't formatted the way you want it to be. To display the paragraph symbol in order to delete or copy it, click the **paragraph icon (Home tab, Paragraph group)** or press **Ctrl Shift * (asterisk)**. Click again to hide the non-printing characters (it's a toggle).

Select, Then Do

There are a couple of other things to keep in mind that can help you with troubleshooting. Remember that Word is based on the concept, "Select, Then Do." Occasionally you will try to apply paragraph formatting, such as a first-line indent, and it won't "take." If that happens, *select* the paragraph you want to apply the formatting to, and *then* perform the steps to apply the formatting.

Remove (or Apply) Paragraph Formatting

Other times, paragraph formatting carries over to the next paragraph when you don't want it to. This characteristic of Word is something that WordPerfect users have a little trouble getting used to. To prevent paragraph formatting from carrying over to the next paragraph, you can do one of several things, including the following:

(a)   Press Enter to start the next paragraph, and then press **Ctrl Shift N** or **Ctrl Q** (depending on whether the formatting was applied *via the Paragraph dialog* or *via a style*) to remove the formatting that carried over from the previous paragraph; *or*

(b)   Start the next paragraph, select the paragraph, and apply the formatting you want; *or*

(c)   Start the next paragraph, then insert the cursor into a paragraph that contains the formatting you want to apply. Click the **Format Painter** icon in the **Clipboard Group** on the **Home tab**, then click the new paragraph; *or*

(d)   Start the next paragraph, then select the paragraph symbol at the end of a paragraph that contains the formatting you want to apply, copy the paragraph symbol (Ctrl C) and paste it at the end of the new paragraph (Ctrl V); *or*

(e)   Start the next paragraph, then click within a paragraph that contains the formatting you want to apply, press **Ctrl Shift C** to copy the formatting, then click somewhere within the new paragraph and press **Ctrl Shift V** to paste the formatting; *or*

(f)   Create a paragraph style (open the **Styles Pane** and click the **New Style button**) that specifies *different* formatting (i.e., a different style) for the following paragraph. See the section on Styles, starting on page 347, for more detailed instructions.

When All Else Fails…Try "Undo"

Also, don't forget that you can undo actions (up to the last 300 actions, in fact!) with the **Undo icon** on the **Quick Access Toolbar** (or **Ctrl Z**). Occasionally something as simple as using the Undo command will fix your problem.

More About the Non-Printing Characters

There are several non-printing characters that ordinarily are not displayed on the screen. These include the paragraph symbol (pilcrow), tabs, spaces between words or letters (created by pressing the spacebar), end-of-cell markers in tables, hidden text, and more.

Tab characters	→
Spaces	···
Paragraph marks	¶
Hidden text	a̲b̲c̲
Optional hyphens	¬
Object anchors	⚓

The Non-Printing Characters
(End-of-Cell Markers Not Shown)

End·of·cell·markers·(they·look· somewhat·like·little·suns)¤	¤	¤
¤	¤	¤

Displaying those characters can be useful for troubleshooting purposes (e.g., to determine if you really did press the spacebar twice between two words, when you meant to press it once). Also, it's useful when you want to copy one paragraph's formatting to another paragraph—remember that the formatting codes for any given paragraph are contained within the paragraph symbol at the end of that paragraph.

You might want to hide the non-printing characters in certain circumstances, too. When you mark headings for inclusion in a Table of Contents or citations for inclusion in a Table of Authorities, Word displays the non-printing characters and TOC/TOA field codes. Those characters and codes actually take up space in the document, such that they can bump headings or citations down to the next page. As a result, when you generate the TOC and TOA, the generated page numbers will be incorrect. In order to avoid that problem, you need to hide the non-printing characters before generating a TOC or TOA.

To display the non-printing characters, either

(1)   click the **paragraph symbol** in the **Paragraph group** on the **Home tab** *or*

(2)   press **Ctrl Shift * (asterisk)**.

Repeat either of those steps to hide the non-printing characters again (it's a toggle).

Getting Word to Work
the Way <u>You</u> Want

Customizing the Word 2010 Interface to Make It More User-Friendly

For long-time Word users, the new graphical interface that first appeared in Word 2007 can be disorienting. It's a bit like coming home from work to find that all of your furniture has been moved around, and in addition, entire rooms have been remodeled—reconfigured, resized, even removed. Oh, and by the way, eight dinner guests are on their way over. (At least in this scenario, you'd have the option of taking the entire group out to a restaurant.)

Don't let the interface intimidate you. As a matter of fact, there are lots of steps you can take to get up to speed quickly despite the unfamiliar interface—for one thing, you can use keyboard shortcuts for many everyday tasks—and you can customize the interface in several ways that make it much easier to use.

One of the most common complaints from people who upgraded from an older version of Word to Word 2007 was that it wasn't nearly as easily customizable as older versions. Indeed, users who wished to modify the Ribbon or any of its tabs soon found that they couldn't do so themselves without mastering XML coding.[1]

Thankfully, Microsoft responded to this feedback by giving Word 2010 users the ability to add their own custom tabs and groups and make other tweaks to the Ribbon, as described in the section immediately below this introduction.

Also, there are a couple of additional customizable elements of the interface: the **Quick Access Toolbar** (the "**QAT**") and the **Status Bar**. The Quick Access Toolbar comes in very handy because you can move it below the Ribbon, where it expands into a full-length toolbar, and then add icons for the commands you use most often. And the Status Bar can be modified to show assorted information you might find useful.

In this section of the book, I explain how to make Word more user-friendly by tweaking each of these all-important elements of the interface.

Customizing the Ribbon

As first mentioned on page 135, it is possible to customize the Word 2010 Ribbon in a number of ways. This capability, which was not available in Word 2007, makes the program significantly easier to use. It compensates to a great extent for the absence of customizable toolbars in the new graphical interface.

---

[1]**NOTE**: There are several third-party tools available that allow you to customize the Ribbon; some of these utilities emulate the traditional interface, with old-style menus and toolbars. For specific information, see the sidebar on page 214.

In particular, you can make any or all of the following changes to the Ribbon in Word 2010:

- You can create entire new tabs.

- You can create new groups within custom tabs and/or within built-in tabs.

- You can add commands to custom groups (but *not* to built-in groups).

- You can rename *any* tab, group, or command.

- You can change the icons for commands.

- You can move tabs around in the Ribbon.

- You can hide custom tabs and/or built-in tabs.

- You can remove groups from custom tabs and/or from built-in tabs.

- Once you have customized the Ribbon, you can export your customizations to a file and install them on another computer.

This section provides detailed instructions for performing each of these tasks, as well as more information about the various options for—and limitations on—customizing the Ribbon.

Creating a Custom Tab Plus a Custom Group

To create a new tab plus a new group, do one of the following:

- **Right-click** the **Ribbon** (or the **Quick Access Toolbar**) and click the new "**Customize the Ribbon…**" option (see the screenshot at right); *or*

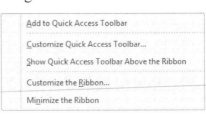

- Click the **File tab**, **Options**, then click the "**Customize Ribbon**" category at the left side of the Options window (as in the screenshot on the next page).

Either of those methods will take you to the Customize Ribbon screen within Word Options.[2]

---

[2] As an aside: It is from this section of the Word Options, not from the Customize the Quick Access Toolbar section, that you create **customized keyboard shortcuts**. Take a look at the very bottom of the screen, where it says "**Keyboard shortcuts:**," followed by a "**Customize**" button. I will reiterate and expand on this point later on.

192

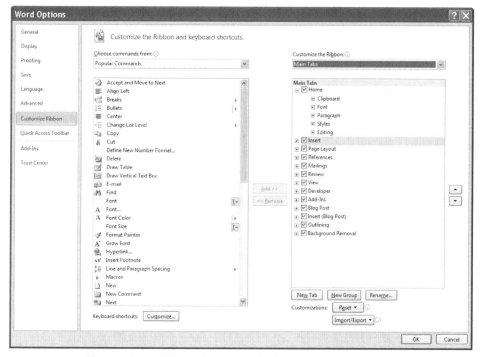

Customize Ribbon Screen Within the Word Options

To add your own tab, do as follows:

1. First, **decide where** you want the new tab to appear in the Ribbon.[3]

2. Next, click to **select (highlight) the built-in tab** that you want displayed in the Ribbon *to the left of* your new custom tab.

3. Navigate to the **right-hand side** of the screen. You should see the "New Tab" button at the bottom, below the diagram of the Main Tabs.

4. Click the "**New Tab**" **button**.

    Word creates both a new tab and, within the tab, a new group. The new tab appears below the tab you selected (highlighted) in step 1, as illustrated in the screenshot on the next page. (**NOTE**: Because I selected the Home tab in step 1, my new tab appears below that tab, which means it will appear to its right in the Ribbon.)

---

[3] Don't worry about the placement of the new tab at this point. You can always move it later.

New Tab (Custom) and New Group (Custom)

5.   You'll might want to change the generic names that Word assigns to the new tab and the new group. Let's rename the new tab first.[4] Before proceeding, make sure *New Tab* rather than *New Group* is selected. If it isn't, click it. (Otherwise, clicking the "Rename" button as in step 6 will rename the *group*, not the *tab*.)

6.   Next, locate the "**Rename" button** (toward the bottom right) and **click it**.

7.   When the **Rename dialog box** opens, **type a name** for the new tab, then click **OK**. (I typed "Jan's Stuff," as you can see in the screenshot on the next page.)

Rename Your Custom Tab

---

[4] You can rename the new group first if you prefer.

8. Now, let's rename your custom group. To do so, **select (highlight) it** and then **repeat steps 6 and 7**. (If you don't see the group, click the **plus sign (+)** to the left of the label for your custom tab. That will expand the tab and show the custom group underneath it.) **NOTE:** this time, when the Rename dialog opens, it displays dozens of icons.[5]

Rename Dialog for a Custom Group

9. **Type a name** for the new group—I chose "Legal Tools," but you could use a name like "Numbering," "Everyday Features," "My Goodies," or anything that makes sense to you—and then **click OK**.

You should see your new tab, and your new group within the custom tab, in the Ribbon.

Adding Commands to a Custom Group

To add commands to your new group, return to the Customize Ribbon screen in the Word Options and do the following:[6]

1. First, **select (highlight) the group**. (Again, if you don't see the group, click the plus sign to the left of the custom tab to expand the tab and display the group.)

2. Next, navigate to the top left side of the screen and change the **"Choose Commands From:" drop-down** from "Popular Commands" to "**All Commands**."

---

[5] There is one dialog for renaming tabs and a different one for renaming groups. The inclusion of icons in the latter is misleading because it isn't possible to apply an icon to a group. Rather, they are used to designate *individual commands within a group*.

[6] You can add (or remove) commands—or make other changes, such as moving your custom tab(s) to a different location in the Ribbon—at any time.

NOTE: There are other choices besides "All commands": "Commands Not in the Ribbon," "Macros," "File Tab," "All Tabs," "Main Tabs," "Tool Tabs," and "Custom Tabs and Groups." I prefer "All Commands" because that option makes it easy for me to find every available command without needing to know which command belongs on which tab. However, the other lists let you narrow the available choices, which can make the process somewhat less overwhelming.

3.   Once you have selected a "Choose commands from:" option, **scroll down** to locate the commands you wish to add to your new group. The commands are listed in numeric order and then in alphabetical order.

TIP: To find a command quickly, place your cursor within the command list and press the letter the command starts with. For example, to find the "Overtype" command, press the letter "O." That will take you to the first command in the list that begins with that letter. Keep pressing the letter until the cursor lands on the command you want, or use the scroll bar to move down faster.

4.   **Click to select (highlight) a command**, then click the "**Add**" **button** at the center of the screen. In the next screenshot, you can see that I've selected Table of Contents, so that I can add that command / icon to my new "Legal Tools" group.

5.   If you prefer, you can **drag a command** to your new group.[7]

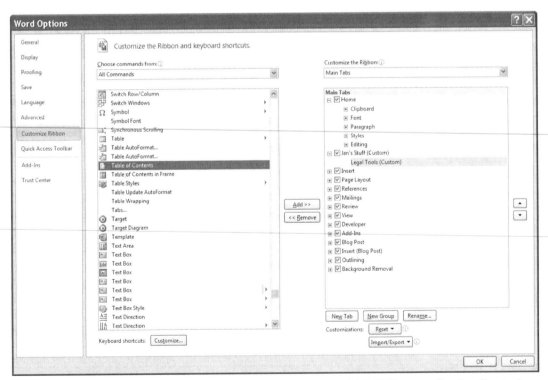

Click to Select a Command (at Left), Then Click the "Add" Button (in the Center)

---

[7] You can drag commands to custom groups (but **not** to built-in groups), and you can even drag entire groups to custom tabs (I was able to drag the whole Font group to my "Jan's Stuff" tab).

The new command should appear below your custom group.

My New Tab, New Group, and New Command

6.   You can add more commands at this point, but let's stop here so we can to save your new stuff and see what it looks like in the ribbon. To do so, click "**OK**" at the bottom right side of the Options screen. (**CAUTION**: Always be sure to click "OK" after you add, rename, or otherwise modify a custom tab, or your changes won't be preserved when you close out of the Word Options.)

7.   After you click OK, you should see your new tab in the Ribbon.

Success!
(My New Tab, Group, and Command Appear in the Ribbon)

You can see from the (truncated) screenshot above that I have successfully added a new tab called "Jan's Stuff," which appears between the Home Tab and the Insert Tab, as well as a new group labeled "Legal Tools" and a Table of Contents command (with a drop-down).

Now that you've added a new tab and a new group, let's return to the Customization Screen in the Word options and experiment some more. We can do any or all of the following:

- Add another custom tab;

- Add another group to your custom tab (or add a group to a built-in tab);

- Add more commands to your new group;

- Change the icons for commands you've placed in a custom group;

- Rename a custom or built-in tab or group;

- Move a tab or group to a different location in the Ribbon;

- Hide a tab;

- Delete commands from a custom group;

- Remove built-in or custom groups or custom tabs;

- Reset all customizations to the factory default settings; or

- Export your customizations to a file in order to use them on another computer.

Remember that there are two different ways to get to the Customize Ribbon screen in the Word Options. Either:

1. **Right-click the Ribbon** (or the **Quick Access Toolbar**) and click **Customize the Ribbon...** *or*

2. Click the **File tab**, **Options**, **Customize Ribbon**.

The following sections provide instructions for all of the additional customization options outlined above.

Adding Another Tab, Group, or Command

Adding a new tab should be fairly self-explanatory at this point. It's pretty simple to add more groups, too. Just keep in mind that you need to click to select (highlight) the tab you want to contain your group. Also, note that you can add groups to both custom tabs and built-in tabs.

Commands, however, can be added only to custom groups. There are two methods for adding commands: You can click a command and then click the "Add" button or you can click, drag, and drop a command.

To add another tab to the Ribbon:

1. Select (highlight) an existing tab (the one you want to appear in the Ribbon to the left of your new tab).

2. Click the New Tab button.

3. If necessary, click to select (highlight) the new tab in the diagram of tabs and groups, then click the Rename button.

4. Type a name for your new tab and click OK.

5. Select (highlight) the new group that Word created within your new tab.

6. Click the Rename button.

7. Type a name for your new group and click OK.

8. Click the OK button at the bottom right side of the Word Options screen to save your changes.

To add a group (to either a custom tab or a built-in tab):

1. Click the tab you want to contain your new group.

2. Click the New Group button.

3. Click the Rename button.

4. Type a name for your new group.

5. Click the OK button at the bottom right side of the Word Options screen to save your changes.

To add another command (to a custom group only):

1. First, **click the group** where you want to insert the command. Before moving on to step 2, note the following:

    (a) If you plan to use the "drag-and-drop" method to add a command, you *must* expand the group by clicking the plus sign (+) to the left of the group's name. Otherwise, Word won't let you drop the command.

    (b) If you plan to use the "click 'Add' button" method, you don't need to expand the group.

2. Navigate to the left side of the screen and click to change the "Choose commands from:" drop-down to "All Commands" (or any other list you prefer).

3. Next, locate the command you wish to add by using the scroll bar or by clicking within the command list and pressing the letter of the alphabet that matches the first letter of the command name, then scrolling down.

4. Do one of the following:

    (a) Click to select (highlight) the command, then click the "Add" button; *or*

    (b) Click the command, keep the left mouse button depressed and drag the command to your group, then position the mouse pointer where you want the command to go and release the mouse button to drop the command.

5. If necessary, click the "Up" arrow or the "Down" arrow to reposition the command.

6. Continue adding commands in this fashion if you like. (Remember that you can add more commands later on.)

7. When you're finished, be sure to click the OK button at the bottom right side of the Word Options screen to save your changes.

CAUTION: Remember that you can't add commands to built-in groups. If you try to do so, you will get a warning prompt, as follows:

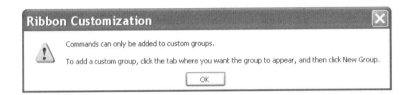

Ribbon Customization

Commands can only be added to custom groups.

To add a custom group, click the tab where you want the group to appear, and then click New Group.

OK

Renaming a Custom Group or Tab

From within the Customize Ribbon screen in the Word Options:

1. Click the group or tab you want to rename.

2. Click the "Rename" button.

3. Type a new name and click OK.

4. Click OK to save your changes when you exit from the Word Options.

Moving a Tab or Group

It's easy to move a tab or group within the Ribbon. Navigate to the right-hand side of the Customize Ribbon screen in the Word Options and do the following:

1. First, **locate the tab or group** you wish to move.

2. Click to **select (highlight) the tab or group**.

3. Next, click the "**Up**" **arrow** or the "**Down**" **arrow** at the right side of the screen. The "**Up**" arrow repositions the tab or group to the left in the Ribbon; the "**Down**" arrow moves it to the right.

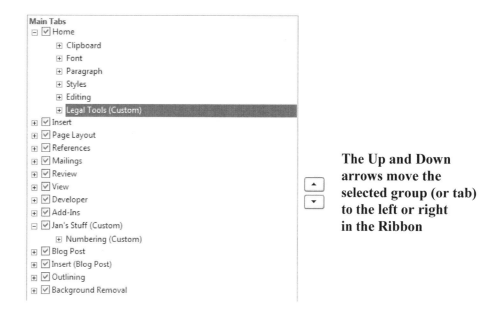

The Up and Down
arrows move the
selected group (or tab)
to the left or right
in the Ribbon

4.	Click the **OK** button at the bottom right side of the Word Options screen to save your changes.

In the next screenshot, you can see that I moved my custom tab ahead of (to the left of) the Home tab. To do so, I simply clicked my custom tab and then clicked the "Up" arrow at the right side of the screen.

CAUTION: If you choose to place your custom tab first, ahead of the Home tab, the custom tab will appear at the forefront when you launch Word. That might or might not be desirable; you'll have to experiment and decide what you prefer.

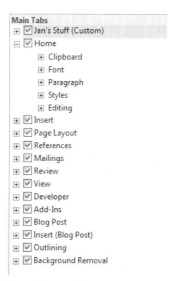

**You Can Move Your Custom Group Anywhere,
Even Ahead of the Home Tab…**

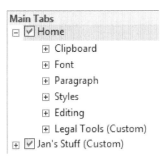

…Or Add a Custom Group (Here, "Legal Tools") to an Existing Tab

The screenshot above shows that I've moved my custom group ("Legal Tools") onto the Home Tab. To do so, I clicked the Legal Tools group, then clicked the "Up" arrow. I took this shot before I moved my custom tab ("Jan's Stuff") ahead of the Home Tab.

The screenshot below shows the modified Ribbon, with my custom "Jan's Stuff" tab ahead of the Home tab and my custom "Legal Tools" group at the right side of the Home Tab. (I could have moved the new group farther to the left in the Home Tab, or added it to any of the other existing Tabs, by using the "Up" or "Down" arrow.)

Modified Ribbon With My Legal Tools Group at the Right of the Home Tab

Hiding a Tab

You can't hide a group, but you *can* hide an entire tab (even a built-in tab). To do so, return to the Customize Ribbon screen in the Word Options and do as follows:

1. **Click** to **uncheck the checkbox** to the left of the tab name.

   In the screenshot at right, I have unchecked the box next to my "Jan's Stuff (Custom)" Tab.

2. **Click OK** at the bottom right side of the Word Options screen to save your changes.

3. To un-hide a tab, **click the checkbox again** in order to put a check back in the checkbox, then **OK** out.

Ribbon With "Jan's Stuff" Tab Hidden

Removing Groups

You can remove custom groups and/or built-in groups. To do so from within the Customization Screen of the Word Options:

1. First, if you can't see the group you want to remove, expand the tab the group is in by **clicking the plus sign (+)** to the left of the tab name.

2. **Click to select (highlight) the group** you want to delete.

    In the screenshot at right, I've clicked the Themes group, a built-in group that is part of the Page Layout tab.

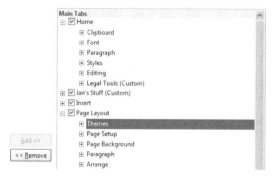

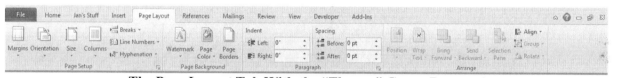

Click the Group, Then Click "Remove"

3. **Click** the "**Remove**" **button.**[8]

4. Remember to **click "OK"** to save your changes when you exit from the Word Options.

After you close the Word Options, the group you removed will not appear in the Ribbon.

The Page Layout Tab With the "Themes" Group Removed

Restoring a Removed Group

If you change your mind after removing a group or deleting a command, not to worry—you can restore it. To do so, return to the Customization Screen in the Word Options and do the following:

1. Change the "**Choose commands from:**" **drop-down** to "**All Tabs.**"[9]

2. **Locate the tab** where the group you deleted normally resides (in the example below, the Page Layout tab) and **click the plus sign (+)** to the left of the tab name in order to expand it and display the groups contained in that tab.

---

[8] You can restore the removed group later on if you so choose, as explained on the next page.

[9] If you are restoring a group that belongs to a Main Tab, you could choose "Main Tabs" instead.

3.   Click to **select (highlight) the group** you want to restore.

Click the Group You Want to Restore

4.   Click the "**Add**" **button**.

5.   Look at the right side of the screen and, if necessary, click the "**Up**" or **Down**" **arrow** to move the group back to the location in the Ribbon where you want it.

6.   Remember to **click** "**OK**" to save your changes when you exit from the Word Options.

The Page Layout Tab With the "Themes" Group Restored

Deleting Commands

You can delete a command from a custom group, but not from a built-in group. When you try to select a command in a built-in group in order to remove it, you'll see that the commands are grayed out, as are the "Add" and "Remove" buttons in the Customize Ribbon screen of the Word Options.

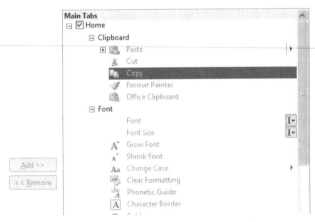

**Commands in Built-In Groups Are Grayed Out,
As Are the Add and Remove Buttons**

To delete a command from a custom group:

1. First, expand the group if necessary (in order to show the commands) by **clicking the plus sign (+)** to the left of the group name.

2. **Click the command** you want to delete.

Click to Select (Highlight) the Command You Want to Remove

3. **Click** the "**Remove**" **button.**[10]

4. Remember to **click "OK"** to **save** your changes when you exit from the Word Options.

Restoring a Deleted Command

Perhaps the most difficult aspect of restoring a deleted command is locating it in the command list at the left side of the Customize Ribbon screen in the Word Options. Again, I find it easiest to change the "Choose commands from:" drop-down to "All Commands," but if you know where the command is located, you might prefer to choose a different drop-down, such as "Main Tabs."

Remember that you can move quickly through the command list by positioning your cursor in the list and then pressing the letter of the alphabet that is the first letter of the name of the command you seek.

Once you have chosen a drop-down command list and have located the command you want to restore, just do the following:

1. **Click the command,**

2. **Click** the "**Add**" button,

---

[10] You can add the command back later on if you so choose.

3. Remember to **click "OK"** to save your changes when you exit from the Word Options.

Renaming Commands or Changing an Icon

From within the Customize Ribbon screen in the Word Options:

1. Expand the tab and/or the group that the command is in if necessary. Then **click the command or icon** you want to change or rename.

2. To rename a command, click the "**Rename**" **button**, then **type a new name** for the command and click **OK**.

3. To change a command's icon, click the "**Rename**" **button**, then locate an icon you prefer in the "**Rename**" **dialog box**, **click it**, and click **OK**.[11]

4. Remember to **click "OK"** to save your changes.

Hiding Command Labels in a Custom Group

You can hide the icon labels for the commands in a custom group—in effect, leaving only the icons, and no text, by doing the following:

1. From within the Customize Ribbon screen in the Word Options, first make sure you can **see the group** with the commands whose labels you want to hide (if necessary, **click the plus sign [+]** to the left of the name of the tab containing the group in order to expand the tab).

2. Next, *right-click* the group and, when the pop-up menu appears, click "**Hide Command Labels.**"[12]

3. Remember to **click "OK"** to save your changes when you exit from the Word Options.

| Add New Tab |
| Add New Group |
| Rename |
| Remove |
| Hide Command Labels |
| Move Up |
| Move Down |

In the next screenshot, you can see that I've added two groups ("Numbering" and "Miscellany") to my "Jan's Stuff" tab and have hidden

---

[11] It's possible to create custom icons, although it sounds more complicated than in older versions. See Word MVP Greg Maxey's tips for creating custom icons in Word 2007, which likely work the same way in Word 2010: gregmaxey.mvps.org/Ribbon_Custom_Icons.htm

For more help with custom icons, you could post a question in the Word Processing forum of the Windows Secrets Lounge (formerly Woody's Lounge) at www.lounge.windowssecrets.com or www.wopr.com. You'll have to register before you can post.

[12] This option applies to all commands within a custom group. In other words, you can't hide the label for one or more individual commands; it's an all-or-nothing proposition.

the command labels for all of the commands in both groups. All you can see is the icons (buttons) for the commands.

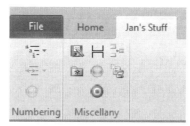

Custom Tabs With Hidden Command Labels

To restore the command labels, just repeat the steps you took to hide the labels. (Clicking "Hide Command Labels" a second time toggles the labels back on.) In other words:

1.   From within the Customize Ribbon screen in the Word Options, first make sure you can **see the group** with the commands whose labels you want to restore (if necessary, **click the plus sign [+]** to the left of the name of the tab containing the group in order to expand the tab).

2.   Next, *right-click* the group and, when the pop-up menu opens, click "**Hide Command Labels**" again.

3.   Remember to **click "OK"** to save your changes when you exit from the Word Options.

The next screenshot shows what my custom tab looks like with the command labels restored in both groups (I've hidden the other tabs, except for the Home tab, to make the image less distracting).

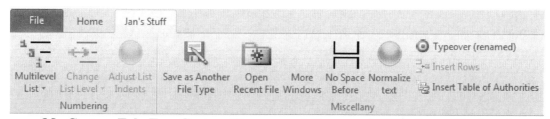

My Custom Tab, Two Custom Groups, and Commands With Icons Displayed

Resetting Customizations to the Factory Defaults

You can restore the default "factory" settings for an individual tab or for the entire Ribbon. From within the Customize Ribbon screen in the Word Options:

1.　To restore the default settings for one tab, **locate the tab** and **click it**.

2.　Click the "**Reset**" **button**, which opens a drop-down.

3.　From the drop-down, click the "**Reset only selected Ribbon tab**" button.

　　Word immediately resets the tab, removing any new group / commands you added to that tab.

4.　When you have finished resetting tabs, **OK out** of the Word Options.

Let's say you decide to restore everything—both the Ribbon and the Quick Access Toolbar—to the factory defaults.[13] Reopen the Word Options and do as follows:

1.　Click the "**Reset**" **button**, then click "**Reset all customizations**."

2.　A warning message will appear, asking if you're sure you want to delete all of the customizations for the ribbon and the QAT.

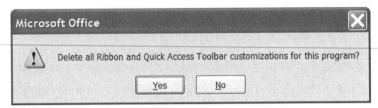

3.　If you aren't sure you want to delete all of the customizations, click "**No**."[14]

---

[13] **CAUTION:** You can't reset the Ribbon without also resetting the QAT. If you don't want to lose the customizations you've made to your QAT, ***don't use this option***! Instead, try making incremental changes to individual tabs and groups to restore the defaults.

Note that it ***is*** possible to reset the QAT without resetting the Ribbon. To do so, you must be in the Quick Access Toolbar portion of the Word Options. From that screen, you can click the "Reset" button, which will display two choices: "Reset only Quick Access Toolbar" and "Reset all customizations." (If you see only one choice, exit from the Options and then go back in.)

[14] To be on the safe side, consider using the "Export" option to save a backup copy of your customizations prior to experimenting with the "Reset" button. That way, you can use "Import"

4.	If you do wish to proceed, click "**Yes**."

Word immediately reverts to the factory default settings, removing all custom tabs, groups, and commands from the Ribbon and all custom commands from the QAT. (It doesn't move the QAT back above the Ribbon if you have placed it below the Ribbon, however.)

5.	At this point, you can click "**OK**" to close out of Word Options. (Note that clicking the "Cancel" button *does not* restore the customizations.)

Importing / Exporting Your Customizations

Word 2010 allows you to save the customizations that you have made to the Ribbon (and to the Quick Access Toolbar) and copy those settings to another computer. To do so, *either* **right-click the Ribbon** (or the **Quick Access Toolbar**) and click **Customize the Ribbon...** *or* click the **File tab**, **Options**, **Customize Ribbon**.

1.	When the Customize Ribbon screen appears, navigate to the lower right-hand side and locate the **Import/Export button**.

2.	Click the button to open the drop-down list. You'll see two choices: **Import customization file** and **Export all customizations**.

3.	To save your Ribbon configurations to a file, click **Export all customizations**.

4.	Word will open a "File Save" dialog similar to the one in the screenshot at the top of the next page.[15]

As you can see, the program automatically assigns the name "Word Customization" to the configuration file, but you can rename it. (Just be sure to use a name that clearly describes the file's contents).

---

later on to restore any changes you previously made to the Ribbon and the QAT that are discarded when you revert to the factory defaults.

[15] By default, Word will save the configuration file in your "My Documents" folder, but you can use the drop-down at the top of the dialog to save it to a different folder.

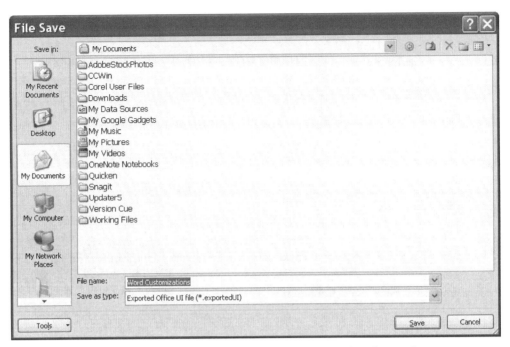

File Save Dialog for Exporting Your Ribbon Configurations

5.   Optional step: Use the drop-down to **change the location** if you wish.

6.   Optional step: **Rename the file** if you wish.

7.   **Click "Save."**[16]

Once you have saved this file to your hard drive, you can copy it to a USB drive, an external drive, a CD, or some similar medium, paste the copy into another computer, and then import the configuration file via the Word Options on the additional computer.

1.   To import the file, go into the Customize Ribbon screen of the Word Options and click the **"Import / Export" button**, then click **"Import Customization File."**

2.   **Browse** to the location of the file.

3.   Click to select (highlight) the file, then click the "Open" button.

4.   A warning message will appear, prompting you in case you're not sure you wish to proceed.

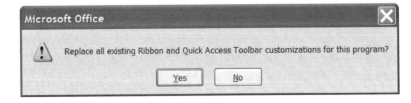

---

[16] Word saves the file as an "Exported Office UI file" ("UI" stands for "User Interface").

5. If you are unsure whether you wish to replace all customizations to the Ribbon and the Quick Access Toolbar, click "**No**."

6. If you are sure you want to proceed, click "**Yes**."

The changes will go into effect regardless of whether you click "OK" or "Cancel" when you close out of the Word Options.

CAUTION: When you import the configuration file to another computer, you will overwrite not only any customizations the user has made to the Ribbon on that machine, but also any customizations he or she has made to the Quick Access Toolbar. As with the "Reset" option, it's a good idea to export the configuration file on the "destination" machine (as well as on the "source" machine, the one you're copying from) *before* installing and importing the configuration file to the other machine. That way, you have a backup copy you can use to restore the original settings if need be.

Right-Click Options for Working With Tabs, Groups, and Commands

Word 2010 provides helpful context-sensitive menus when you right-click a group or tab from within the Customize Ribbon screen within the Word Options. The right-click options make it easy for you to add a new tab, add a new group, rename an existing tab or group, show or hide a tab, show or hide command labels, remove a tab or group, and/or move a tab or group up or down (left or right in the Ribbon).

The options available in the pop-up menus vary depending on *what type of object* you right-click (for instance, a built-in tab versus a custom tab) and *whether you have modified it* in any way. As an example, right-clicking **a custom tab** produces the pop-up menu you see on the left, and right-clicking **a custom group** produces the pop-up menu you see on the right:

A Custom Tab   **A Custom Group**

The difference between the two is that—logically enough—the menu for the custom tab includes the "Show Tab" option but not the "Hide Command Labels" option, whereas the menu for the custom group has the "Hide Command Labels" option but not the "Show Tab" option. (If you have hidden a custom tab, the "Show Tab" command appears in the menu without a check mark next to it. Click that command to un-hide the tab.)

NOTE: The "Hide Command Labels" option appears *only* when you right-click on the name of a custom group (*not* a custom tab, a built-in group, or a built-in tab—or on an individual command).

Right-clicking a command that you have added to a custom group produces a pop-up menu similar to the one that follows:

Right-Clicking a Command in a Custom Group

Whether both the "Move Up" and "Move Down" options are available depends on where the command is located in your group (i.e., whether there are other commands above it [to the left of it in the Ribbon] or below it [to the right of it in the Ribbon]). No pop-up menu appears when you right-click a built-in command because you can't modify built-in commands.

Right-clicking a **built-in tab** produces one of the following pop-up menus. The difference between the two has to do with whether or not you have modified the tab (i.e., by adding a custom group to it). If you've modified the tab, the "Reset Tab" option that is normally grayed out becomes available.

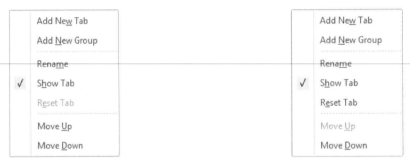

Right-Clicking an Unmodified Built-in Tab   **Right-Clicking a Modified Built-In Tab**

Right-clicking a **built-in group** produces the following pop-up menu:

Right-Clicking a Built-In Group

Note that it lacks a "Show Tab" option and a "Reset Tab" option, but it includes a "Remove" option. (You can remove, rename, or relocate a built-in group, but you can't add any commands to it.)

Limitations on Customizing the Ribbon

The main limitations on customizing the Ribbon at this point are that you can't add commands to built-in groups, and you can't hide groups. Also, it is difficult to create custom icons, though it can be done (if you are adventurous, very computer-literate, and patient, and if you have the appropriate permissions).

SIDEBAR: Third-Party Tools for Customizing the Ribbon

After Word 2007 was released, a few third-party companies developed tools for customizing the Ribbon, including a couple that let you use the classic menus and toolbars from prior versions of Word. I haven't tested these add-ons, but am providing a short list in case you wish to investigate further. Be sure to do your due diligence before purchasing / installing any of them, and be cautious about applying a utility intended for Word 2007 to Word 2010.

Classic Menu and Ribbon Customizer

http://www.addintools.com/digital-river/customize_ribbon/default.htm

A company called "Addintools" (add-in tools) offers a utility for Word 2007 that supposedly emulates the classic menus. See the company's web site for more information. Note that toward the bottom of the page for the Classic Menu for Office 2007, there is a blurb that states: "Get FREE upgrade to Classic Menu for Office Professional 2010, if you purchase Classic Menu for Office 2007 after Jan 1, 2010." However, there is no product page for any Classic Menu for Office 2010 or Word 2010. The company also advertises a Ribbon Customizer for Word 2010, but the links to that product don't work. Addintools also makes a Ribbon Customizer for Word 2007; the links for that version do work.

Ribbon Customizer

There is another "Ribbon Customizer" add-in for Word 2007 available here:
http://pschmid.net/office2007/ribboncustomizer/index.php

The Customizer has received favorable mention on the Word MVPs site, which means it's a legitimate and well-designed utility. (Word MVPs are highly skilled experts who volunteer to provide assistance to other users via various online newsgroups. They work *with* Microsoft to some extent but are *not* employed by the company.) At this writing, it appears that the Ribbon Customizer, which was designed for use with Word 2007, has not been updated for Word 2010. I am not certain whether it works in Word 2010.

Toolbar Toggle

The MVPs page also mentions an add-in for Word 2007 called "Toolbar Toggle." See the MVPs discussion of various Ribbon Customizers here:
http://word.mvps.org/FAQs/Customization/CustomizeRibbon.htm

http://www.toolbartoggle.com/

The Toolbar Toggle site says, among other things: "ToolbarToggle is an exact replica of Office 2003 classic menus and toolbars for use with Office 2007 and 2010." There is also a "lite" version available. You can see a comparison of the two versions, and watch a demo, on this site, download a five-day free trial, and/or purchase the utility. The full version currently costs $19.95.

Customizing the Quick Access Toolbar

Some people who have adopted Word 2010 miss the customizable toolbars available in earlier versions of Word (and in WordPerfect). Happily, Word 2010 still has one versatile toolbar, the **Quick Access Toolbar** (sometimes referred to as the **QAT**). And happier still, it can be customized in a couple of ways that make Word 2010 significantly more functional.

First, you can move the QAT below the Ribbon, where it expands to fill the entire width of the screen. (In its original form, the QAT is teeny-tiny and it contains only a few icons.) That makes it easier to see, and it gives you extra room to add icons and drop-down lists so you have ready access to the features and commands you use most often.

My Customized QAT (Below the Ribbon)

Moreover, the QAT remains stationary—which means your frequently used icons are always available, regardless of which tab of the Ribbon is active at any given time. That fact can be a tremendous boon. For instance, you can attach boxes that display the font face, the font size, and the style of the paragraph your cursor is in (items that were available at all times on the Formatting toolbar in previous versions of Word). I've provided basic instructions on the following pages.

There are lots of other possibilities. As you can see from the screenshots below this paragraph, I have added icons for the following tasks (moving from left to right): opening a recently used file; starting a new blank document or opening a template; pasting cut or copied text only (i.e., with no formatting); gaining access to Proofing Options (so that I can make changes to my AutoCorrect options); opening the Building Blocks Organizer; closing the header or footer editing screen when the Header and Footer Tools tab isn't at the forefront; addressing an envelope; inserting a symbol; deleting a row; using Quick Print (printing the entire document without invoking "Print Place,"); opening Print Preview in edit mode; switching windows (so that I can see at a glance which documents I have open); invoking the new "text-to-speech" feature; and running a macro I created to print the current page.

My Customized QAT in Word 2010

Closeup View of the Buttons I Added

You can add icons to run macros, and you can add whole "groups" (such as the Header & Footer group from the Insert tab or the Table of Contents and/or Table of Authorities group from the References tab). One secretary I know put a button for inserting a section break on her QAT. The possibilities, while not endless, are vast.

To move the QAT below the Ribbon, **right-click** anywhere within it and choose **Show Quick Access Toolbar Below the Ribbon**. (To put it back above the Ribbon, **right-click** it and choose **Show Quick Access Toolbar Above the Ribbon**.)

To add icons or drop-down boxes to the QAT, **right-click it** and choose **Customize Quick Access Toolbar**. When the Word Options screen opens, click *the drop-down list at the top left side* and change the selection from Popular Commands (the default) to **All Commands** (so that you can see all of your choices). In the command list immediately below the drop-down, the icons and drop-down boxes are listed in name (alphabetical) order. After scrolling down and locating one that you wish to add, **click it** and click the **Add button**.

To add boxes for the font face and font size, use the scrollbar in the command list to locate the icon labeled "Font" that displays both an arrow pointing down and what looks like an I-beam pointer (see the screenshot at right).   Font   I▾

Click the icon in the command list, then click the **Add button**. You can add a Font Size and Style box in the same manner (you can't select more than one icon at a time, however; you must add each icon separately).

The Font Icon

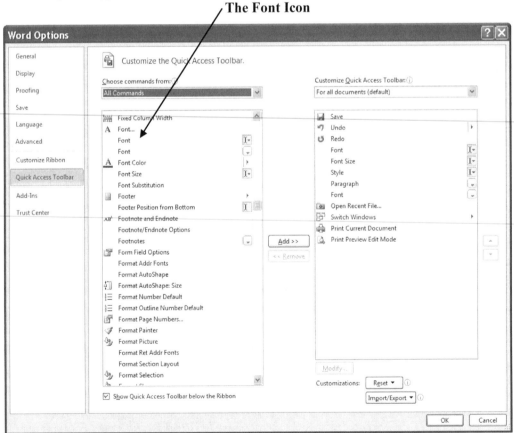

Click to select an icon from the "Command List" on the left, then click "Add"

After you've added an icon, you can move it up or down (i.e., left or right on the QAT) by clicking one of the arrow buttons to the right of the "Customize Quick Access Toolbar" box (they become active when you click one of the icons).

When you have finished customizing the QAT, click **OK**.

You can remove icons and drop-downs from the QAT by following the same steps, except that you'll select an item from *the box on the right* and then click **Remove**. Or you can simply **right-click** a button on the QAT, then click **Remove from Quick Access Toolbar**.

You might have noticed an arrow at the right side of the QAT.

It opens a drop-down that gives you an easy way to add several commonly used commands to the QAT: New, Open, Save, E-mail, Quick Print (which sends the document directly to the printer without going through Print Place), Print Preview and Print, Spelling & Grammar, Undo, Redo, Draw Table, and Open Recent File.

Simply click to put a checkmark next to the one(s) you want to add to the QAT. (Save, Undo, and Redo are checked—i.e., placed on the QAT—by default.) To remove one or more of the commands in this list from the QAT, click to uncheck it.

The drop-down also provides a link to "More Commands"; clicking that item opens the "Customize Quick Access Toolbar" screen in the Word Options.

Additionally, there's an option on the drop-down to change the position of the QAT (to show it above the Ribbon if you've moved it down, or show it below the Ribbon if you haven't).

The QAT has a couple of built-in limitations:

(1)   There is no way to display more than one row, no matter how many icons you add (you can view any "excess" icons by clicking the double arrows at the right side of the QAT); and

(2)   You can't change the size of the buttons without tinkering with your screen resolution, which usually isn't advisable for the uninitiated because, done incorrectly, it can cause display problems.

Customizing the Status Bar

You can customize the Status Bar by adding such useful information as Section number (which, in a departure from all previous versions of Word, is ***not*** displayed by default), Overtype mode, Track Changes, and—perhaps a nod to WordPerfect users—Vertical Page Position. The full range of options, and the status of each item (On or Off, etc.) is shown in the screenshot below.

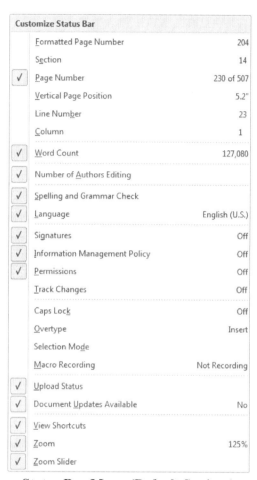

Status Bar Menu (Default Settings)

To add or remove Status Bar icons/text, ***right***-click within the Status Bar, then **click** to check or uncheck individual items.

Just press the **Esc key** or click somewhere outside the menu in order to close it.

Default Settings

By default, the following items are ***not enabled or displayed*** in the Status Bar in Word 2010:

- Formatted Page Number
- Section
- Vertical Page Position
- Line Number
- Column
- Track Changes
- Caps Lock
- Overtype
- Selection Mode
- Macro Recording.

The items that ***are enabled*** by default (and are displayed if the feature they relate to is in use) are:

- Page Number
- Word Count
- Number of Authors Editing
- Spelling and Grammar Check
- Language
- Signatures
- Information Management Policy
- Permissions
- Upload Status
- Document Updates Available
- View Shortcuts
- Zoom
- Zoom Slider.

There are a few new Status Bar options in Word 2010: "Number of Authors Editing," "Upload Status," and "Document Updates Available." The "Number of Authors Editing" and "Document Updates Available" items are related to the co-authoring feature (see the section about co-authoring that starts on page 115).

Making Word 2010 Work Like Older Versions of Word

Starting with Word 2007, Microsoft made three major changes to Word's default formatting:

1. It changed the default font for regular (body) text to **Calibri** (and changed the default font for heading styles to **Cambria**[1]);

2. It changed the default line spacing to **1.15**; and

3. It changed the default "spacing after" paragraphs to **10 points**.

Microsoft says it increased the line spacing and "spacing after" paragraphs in order to improve readability (I'm not sure why the company changed the default font). However, the modifications pose problems for those of us who work in the legal field because of the strict formatting rules in effect for litigation-related documents that have to be submitted to a court or other judicial body. Hence, one of the first things you'll probably want to do after installing Word 2010 is to *restore the default formatting you used in prior versions*.

In the past, restoring the default formatting was a relatively simple matter of changing the **Normal paragraph style** and the **default font** and saving those changes in the **NORMAL template**—the template that is the basis for all new documents on each user's machine. The Normal paragraph style is what traditionally determined the characteristics of such key elements as the default font face, font size, font color, line spacing, paragraph justification, first-line indent (if any), left and right indentation (if any), before and/or after spacing (if any), and tab settings.

However, the "architecture" underlying Word 2010 (and Word 2007) is fundamentally different from that of pre-Word 2007 versions. The default settings actually derive from a "**Style Set**" that is applied behind the scenes *to the document as a whole* ("**Document Defaults**"). Complicating the picture even more, Word 2010 also applies "**Themes**" that can change the font attributes for headings and body text—in effect, overriding your customized defaults. Style Sets work in conjunction with Themes, and these two obscure but critically important features must be addressed if you are to gain control over your document formatting.

Of course, if you just need to get up and running in a hurry, you can simply change the paragraph and font settings, but *those changes won't necessarily persist*, even if you make them the defaults. The most lasting, and perhaps the easiest, method of replacing the built-in settings with your own preferences is to edit the default Style Set. That will ensure that new documents you create on your computer reflect your chosen font attributes, line spacing, indents, before and after spacing, tab settings, and so forth.[2]

---

[1] Also, the default font color for at least some of the heading styles is blue rather than black.

[2] For more about how the newer versions of Word determine so-called "Document Defaults," see http://blogs.msdn.com/microsoft_office_word/archive/2008/10/28/behind-the-curtain-styles-doc-

In this section, I will explain how to modify the default Style Set, as well as how to create a new Style Set and a new set of Theme Fonts; change the default font; alter the Normal paragraph style; and edit certain other styles, including heading styles.[3]

The Role of "Style Sets" and "Themes" in Determining Default Settings

You probably don't realize it, but right out of the box, Word 2010 applies a Style Set and a Theme to your documents. That initial Style Set, working together with its companion Theme, is what sets most of the default paragraph and font formatting in your documents. You can take back control of that formatting, but first you have to understand what is going on under the hood.

The program comes with a number of different Style Sets and Themes. You can switch Style Sets and/or Themes (they can be mixed and matched) whenever you want to change the appearance of a document without actually using another template. In theory, that sounds appealing. However, put into practice in a law office, corporate legal department, or government agency, it can lead to frustration because it's hard to trace the cause of sudden formatting changes, especially if you're accustomed to how defaults worked in earlier versions of Word.

In Word 2010 (as in Word 2007), the so-called Document Defaults are based on an XML-coded **Style Set** that determines the font size, line spacing, "after" spacing, and certain other formatting. In particular, it is the "**Word 2010**" Style Set, operating unobtrusively in the background, that imposes the 11-point font size, the 1.15 line spacing, and the 10 points "after" spacing in effect in every new document.[4] A **Theme** called "**Office**," also operating in the background when you first start using Word 2010, is what produces the Calibri font face for regular (body) text and Cambria for built-in heading styles and tints the heading fonts blue.

In general, Style Sets establish a document's *paragraph formatting*: the indents (including first-line indent), the line spacing, the before and/or after spacing, and tab settings. Style Sets also can dictate *font attributes* such as font size, boldface, italics, and the like.

---

defaults-style-sets-and-themes.aspx. I have borrowed the term "Document Defaults" from this blog article because it strikes me as particularly clear and succinct.

[3] I strongly advise you to make a backup copy of your NORMAL template (normal.dotm), which is where many of your customizations are stored, right after you complete the modifications described in this section. Otherwise, you might have to start over from scratch if Word crashes, because when it does it usually creates a new—generic—normal.dotm. If you have a backup normal.dotm, it is easy to restore your customizations after a crash: With Word closed, launch Windows Explorer or My Computer (or a similar file management utility) and locate the backup. *Make a copy of it*, then rename either the original backup or the copy "normal.dotm" (without quotation marks). When you reopen Word, all of the customizations that were stored in your NORMAL template prior to the crash should be available, and you'll still have a backup copy.

[4] This Style Set resides in a file called **Default.dotx**. You can edit this file directly, but you'll probably need to create a new set of Theme Fonts and make it the default, as well. Read on for an explanation, as well as for instructions on editing the file.

Typically, however, it is a companion Theme that determines the ***font face and color*** of regular (body) text and headings.

Themes, which can be thought of as a layer placed on top of an underlying Style Set, consist of three main elements:

(1)   a set of **font faces** for regular (body) text and headings;

(2)   a **color scheme** similar to those found in PowerPoint presentations (matching various colors with various design elements, namely text, background, and "accents"); and

(3)   styles for "**effects**" like graphic lines and fill.

For our purposes, the only aspect of Themes you really need to understand is how Themes affect font faces, though basic knowledge about the relationship between Themes and font color will help you prevent unexpected color changes.

Each Theme has its own distinct fonts for body text and headings, as explained in more detail later in this section. When a particular Theme is in effect, its font attributes (font face and color) are applied by default to regular (body) text and heading styles.[5] Thus, if the Office Theme is active, body text will appear in the Calibri font and headings will appear in Cambria. Heading fonts will be blue. It doesn't matter which Style Set you're using. If you superimpose the Office Theme on any of various built-in Style Sets, the font faces and colors for body text and headings change accordingly.

As noted above, you can switch Themes or—more importantly for our purposes—you can switch ***Theme Fonts*** (without changing the Theme colors or effects). Better yet, ***you can change which Theme or set of Theme Fonts is the default for all new documents***.

None of the built-in Themes or sets of Theme Fonts is well-suited for legal documents (at least, not according to the state and local formatting rules here in California), but it's possible to create your own customized Theme Fonts for body text and headings and then make them the default. Doing so will ensure that your preferred font settings take precedence. Instructions follow on page 229.

---

[5] **CAUTION**: In Word 2010, Themes work only in .docx files and are disabled when you are working on a .doc file (i.e., a file saved in Compatibility Mode). However, that is not necessarily the case in Word 2007. Although the Themes buttons are grayed out in both versions of the program when you open or save an existing file in .doc format, you can in fact apply a Theme to ***a blank document*** in Word 2007, and the Theme settings ***will persist even after you save the file as a .doc***. (Based on my tests, it appears that this issue does not exist in Word 2010; in other words, Themes are ***not*** available in blank .doc files.)

Working With Style Sets

You might not be able to get rid of Style Sets (or Themes) entirely (even if you work in Compatibility Mode), but you can customize Style Sets in a couple of different ways. You can create your own Style Set and make it the default, or you can edit the default Style Set directly.[6] I provide instructions herein for both options, starting with the more drastic one.

The "Nuclear" Option: Editing the Default Style Set

The most effective way to change the Document Defaults is to edit the default Style Set. As discussed above, that Style Set, which is stored in a file called "Default.dotx" but actually appears in the Style Set menu as "Word 2010," is responsible for the basic paragraph formatting of your documents. That is to say, it controls all of the aspects of formatting that can be set from within the Paragraph dialog: alignment (justification), indentation, first-line indent, before and after spacing, line spacing, tabs, and so on. By editing the Default.dotx file, you can modify a number of those settings in one fell swoop.

At first blush, that might not seem necessary: Word 2010 actually comes with a number of different Style Sets, any of which you can make the default. (To see the built-in Style Sets, locate the **Styles group** on the **Home tab**, click "**Change Styles**," then position your mouse pointer over "**Style Set**." A fly-out menu displays the various Style Sets that are available. If you have some text on your screen, moving the mouse pointer over a Style Set name provides a preview of how the text formatting would change if you selected that particular Style Set.) In fact, there's even a "**Word 2003**" Style Set that looks perfectly serviceable. (It applies single-spacing and zero spacing after the paragraph.) Why not simply use that?

You can, but the Word 2003 Style Set ordinarily works together with the Office Theme, which means that unless you also create and apply your own Theme Fonts, you'll still end up with Calibri as your default font for regular (body) text (and Cambria as your default font for heading styles).

To modify the default Style Set, just open the Default.dotx file as if it were a regular document.[7] (It's actually a template, as you might have figured out from the file extension.) Click the **File tab**, **Open** or press **Ctrl O**, then navigate to the following location (it should be the same regardless of whether you have Windows XP, Vista, or Windows 7):

C:\Program Files\Microsoft Office\Office 14\1033\QuickStyles

---

[6] **NOTE** for IT people and Firm Administrators: There is a setting that allows you to prevent users from changing Style Sets. See the sidebar that follows this section.

[7] Ordinarily I avoid modifying built-in files, for two reasons: (1) doing so could cause the program to work abnormally; and (2) I might decide at some point that I want to use them. Rather than overwriting the existing Default.dotx, it might be wise to open the file and save a backup copy with a different name, such as DefaultOriginal.dotx (so that you can restore the original later on if necessary), then close the copy and reopen the Default.dotx for editing.

Locate Default.dotx and open it. With the blank file on your screen, do the following:

Open the Paragraph dialog, either by clicking the dialog launcher in the **Paragraph group** in the **Home tab** (or the one in the Page Layout tab) or by pressing **Alt O, P**. When the dialog appears, make any changes you desire (you'll probably want to reset the "after" spacing and the line spacing). Then click the "**Set As Default**" **button** at the bottom of the dialog to save your settings. Word will prompt you to choose between applying your changes to "this document only" or to "All documents based on the Default.dotx template." To ensure that your modifications become the default settings—i.e., that they are applied to all new documents—be sure to click the radio button to the left of the "**All documents based on the Default.dotx template**" choice, and then click "**OK**."[8] **CAUTION**: By default, the message box will apply your changes only to the current document *unless you specifically click the other radio button before clicking "OK."*

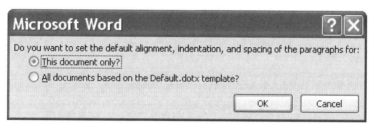

Watch out: "This document only" is the default!

Next, open the Fonts dialog by either clicking the **dialog launcher** in the **Font group** on the **Home tab** or pressing **Ctrl D**.

Note the "+ Body" font

and the "Automatic" color

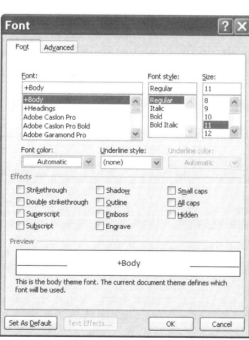

---

[8] This prompt differs from the prompt in Word 2007, which asked, "Do you want this change to affect all new documents based on the Default template?" and offered three choices: "Yes," "No," and "Cancel."

You might notice that instead of a definite font face such as Times New Roman or Arial, the Font box shows "**+Body**." This designation is a placeholder or variable; when it is specified, the font for regular (body) text will change ***depending on which Theme is applied to your document*** (a more detailed explanation follows). It is important that you choose a particular font instead of the +Body placeholder, especially since you are about to set the default font. Note also that you probably need to change the font size (from 11 to 12). Also make sure to change the Font color from "Automatic" to **black** by clicking one of the black squares (preferably one where a pop-up label displays "**Black, Text 1**" when you position the mouse pointer over it).

Make the changes you wish, then click the "**Set As Default**" button. Word will prompt you to choose between applying your changes to "this document only" or to "All documents based on the Default.dotx template." To do the latter—i.e., to ensure that your modifications become the default settings and are applied to all new documents—be sure to click the radio button to the left of the "**All documents based on the Default.dotx template**" choice, and then click "**OK**."[9] **CAUTION**: By default, the message box will apply your changes only to the current document ***unless you specifically click the other radio button before clicking "OK."***

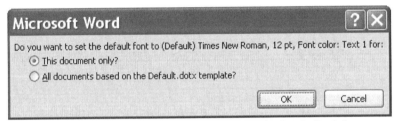

Watch out: "This document only" is the default!

Finally, click the "**Save**" **icon** or press **Ctrl S**—it's always a good idea to save your changes before closing—and then **close** the Default.dotx file. (If you forget to save the file and Word prompts you to save your changes, ***be sure to click "Yes."***)

These modifications should produce regular (body) text that reflects your preferred font and paragraph format settings.[10]

---

[9] Like the prompt when you change the default paragraph style, this message box has changed since Word 2007 and now offers you a choice between applying your modified settings to the current document only or to all future documents based on the Normal.dotm.

[10] Note that these changes constitute a good start, but they might not be sufficient. One reason is that many built-in styles, including heading styles, specify a particular font size and/or apply font attributes such as bolding, italics, and/or underlining. As a result, although those styles might make use of the font ***face*** you selected as the default, they might need further tweaking. And keep in mind that any style that uses the +Body or +Heading designation instead of a definite font will "morph" if a Theme is applied that is based on fonts other than your default.

Creating and Applying Your Own Style Set

If you prefer, you can build your own Style Set and then make it the default. Here's how:

In a blank document to which you haven't applied any Style Set or Theme, launch the **Paragraph dialog** (either by clicking the **dialog launcher** in the **Paragraph group** on the **Home tab** or by pressing **Alt O, P**), and change the settings to match your preferences. Most likely you will want to put everything back to "neutral": No indents, single-spacing, no before or after spacing.

Next, launch the **Font dialog** (either by clicking the **dialog launcher** in the **Font group** on the **Home tab** or by pressing **Ctrl D**). Scroll through the Font list until you locate the font face you want to use for regular (body) text, such as Times New Roman or Arial. **CAUTION**: *Do not use the +Body font or select a font that is followed by a parenthetical stating (Heading) or (Body)!* The reason should be clear from the foregoing discussion about the default Style Set; it will become even clearer as we progress.

Leave the Font style set to **Regular** and pick a **size** (probably 12 points) that you want to use as your default for regular (body) text. Before you OK out of the dialog, change the **Font color** from Automatic to **black** by clicking to open the drop-down list and then clicking a black square (preferably "Black, Text 1" rather than one of the "lighter" blacks) in the color palette. When you've finished, click **OK** to save your font settings.

Locate the **Change Styles drop-down** at the right side of the **Styles group** in the **Home tab** and position the cursor over **Style Set** to open the menu. Click "**Save as Quick Style Set...**" When the "**Save Quick Style Set**" **dialog** opens, navigate to the **File name:** box at the bottom and type a descriptive name, such as TNR12 (for Times New Roman 12). You don't have to add an extension; Word automatically affixes the .dotx extension (it saves the Style Set as a template). Then click the "**Save**" button.

Save as Quick Style Set

Save Quick Style Set dialog

Default (Black and White)
Distinctive
Elegant
Fancy
Formal
Manuscript
Modern
Newsprint
Perspective
Simple
Thatch
TNR 12
Traditional
Word 2003
Word 2010

Reset to Quick Styles from Template

Reset Document Quick Styles

Save as Quick Style Set...

The Styles Set Menu Showing the New Custom Style Set

Now click **Change Styles** again and open the **Style Set menu**. Your new custom Style Set should appear in the drop-down (see the screenshot above).

To apply your new Style Set, simply click it. Finally, click **Change Styles**, and this time click the **Set as Default** command. That will make your custom Style Set the default for all future documents. (You still have the option of applying a different Style Set to a particular document if you wish.)

Applying Themes / Creating Your Own Theme Fonts

Changing the default Style Set will go a long way toward giving you back control over your document formatting. However, so far we haven't changed the default Theme (or the Theme Fonts). As a result, you still could end up with a font setting you don't want, depending on the situation. (If, for example, you apply a Style Set that uses a specific font for regular [body] text, such as Times New Roman, and then apply a Theme that uses a different font for regular [body] text, such as Calibri, *the Theme font will govern*.)

The solution is to set up a customized Theme (or set of Theme Fonts) and make it the default.

You can tell which Theme is active in the current document by navigating to the **Page Layout tab** and holding the mouse pointer over the **Themes drop-down** in the **Themes group**.[11]

---

[11] The *current* Theme might or might not be the same as the *default* theme, but if you haven't deliberately applied a specific Theme, chances are that it is.

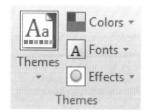 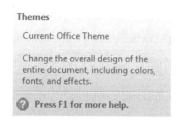 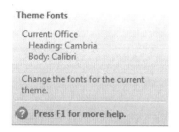

When you position the mouse pointer over the Themes drop-down in the Themes group…	…a pop-up shows the Current Theme (in this case, Office)	Pointing to the "A" icon (Fonts) in the Themes group shows the Current Theme Fonts (in this case, Office)[12]

As noted above, each Theme employs distinct fonts for headings and regular (body) text. When a Theme is applied, its fonts affect ***all body text and heading styles that do not have a predefined font***, such as Arial or Helvetica. That matters because, to reiterate an important point, many built-in paragraph styles in Word 2010—including all of the Heading styles—are set up with *variables* or *placeholders* in lieu of specific fonts. These variables or placeholders use the designation **+Body** (for regular body text) or **+Headings** (for heading styles).

Keep in mind that any time there is a +Body or +Headings designation associated with a style, the font for that style ***will change depending on which Theme is applied***. Obviously, that can present problems when it comes to formatting legal documents, many of which must conform to strict requirements regarding the font face, size, and color.

There are a couple of possible workarounds (you might want to employ both):

(1)   You can create a new Theme (or set of Theme Fonts) and set it as the default; and/or

(2)   You can modify any "variable" styles you wish to use so that they are based on a particular font rather than a +Body or +Headings placeholder font.[13]

To create your own Theme Fonts, you must be working with a .docx or other Open Office XML file type. If you normally work in Compatibility Mode, open a blank document and save it as a Word document (*.docx). If Word displays a warning similar to the one shown below, click "**OK.**"

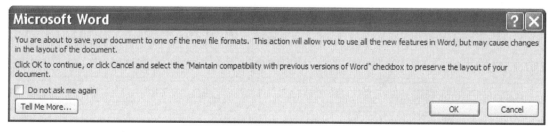

---

[12] Note that you can have one Theme active and a different set of Theme Fonts active.

[13]**CAUTION**: When you modify styles, always make sure to save the modified styles to the underlying template.

229

Next, navigate to the **Page Layout tab**, **Themes group**. Click the **Fonts drop-down**, then click **Create new theme fonts**. You'll see a **Create New Theme Fonts dialog** like the one shown below.

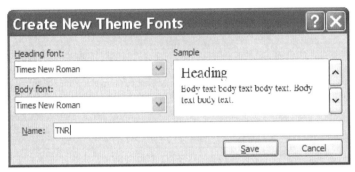

Using the drop-downs at the left side of the dialog, select a **Heading font**, select a **Body font**, type a succinct and descriptive **name** for the new Theme (I've chosen "TNR" for mine), then click **Save**.

If you want the Theme to appear in the Themes "menu," click the **Themes drop-down** and then click the "**Save Current Theme…**" command at the bottom. A "**Save Current Theme**" **dialog** opens, where you can type a name for the theme and save it permanently to your Document Themes folder. (The dialog uses a generic name such as Theme1.thmx; be sure to change it to something more descriptive. I changed mine to TNR, for Times New Roman.)

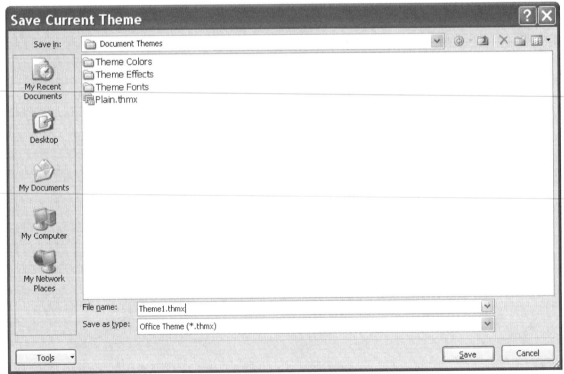

Save Current Theme Dialog

230

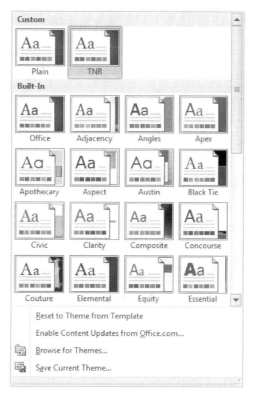

After you save your theme, you should see it in the "**Custom**" section at the top of the **Themes drop-down** on the **Page Layout tab**. (I have created two custom themes, which is why there are two displayed in the screenshot.)

With the Theme applied, navigate to the **Styles group** in the **Home tab**, click the **Change Styles drop-down**, then click the **Set as Default command** at the bottom of the menu, as in the screenshot below.

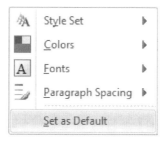

Afterwards, your new Theme, as well as your new Style Set, will be applied automatically to all new .docx files.

SIDEBAR: Block Quick Style Set and/or Theme Switching

IT people and firm administrators might be interested in using the "**Block Quick Style Set Switching**" and/or the "**Block Theme or Scheme Switching**" options in the **Manage Styles dialog box**. If you have distributed to all users a new Default.dotx or other Style Set that contains your preferred paragraph settings, along with a new set of Theme Fonts, and have made those the defaults, you can prevent users from switching to a different Style Set or Theme.

To open the **Manage Styles dialog**, click the **dialog launcher** in the **Styles group** on the **Home tab** (or press **Ctrl Alt Shift S**). When the **Styles Pane** opens, click the "**Manage Styles**" **button** (the right-most button at the bottom, to the left of "**Options**…").

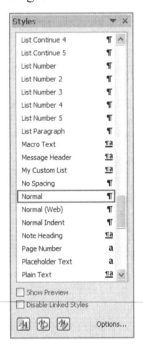

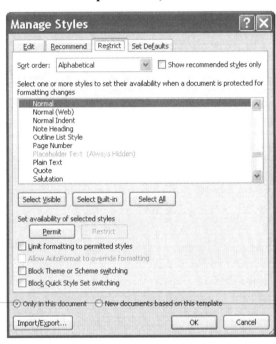

The right-most button at the bottom…   **…opens the Manage Styles dialog**

Navigate to the **Restrict tab**, and at the bottom left you'll see checkboxes labeled "**Block Theme or Scheme switching**" and "**Block Quick Style Set switching**." If you want to keep users from switching the Document Defaults for both paragraph settings and font settings, check both boxes. (Note that doing so will *not* prevent users from applying different fonts manually or changing the fonts in various styles.) It's important to keep in mind that if you check only the first option, users will be able to apply different Style Sets, and if you check only the second option, users will be able to switch Themes and Theme Fonts.

Be sure to click the "**New documents based on this template**" radio button before **OK**-ing out of the dialog.

Needless to say, savvy users (including those who read this book!) will be able to circumvent these restrictions. Even so, blocking Style Set and/or Theme switching might prove useful in certain circumstances.

Changing the Default Font

If you modify the Document Defaults by editing the default Style Set as well as creating and applying your own set of Theme Fonts, you might never need to change the default font—at least, the one associated with the NORMAL template. I'm providing instructions regardless, in part so that you'll know how to set a new default font in any custom templates that you create, such as templates for pleadings, estate documents, letterhead, faxes, and the like.

The default font is the one that works with the **Normal paragraph style** in a particular template. Changes you make to the default font will affect *only* that one paragraph style (as well as any others that are *based on* the Normal paragraph style) in *only* that one template.

To change the default font for a given template, open either the template itself or a document based on the template and invoke the **Font dialog**, using either of the following methods:

(1)   Make sure the **Home tab** is active and locate the **Font group**, then click the **dialog launcher** (the arrow at the bottom right side of the group); *or*

(2)   Press **Ctrl D**.

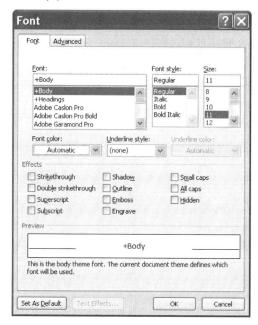

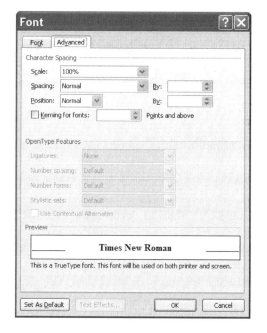

Font Dialog—Font Tab
(Note the +Body designation under "Font" and the Automatic designation under "Font color")

Font Dialog—Advanced Tab

Depending on which Style Set is active, you might notice a +Body designation at the top of the Font list. As noted throughout this section, you definitely should *avoid using the +Body placeholder* for your default font.

Instead, select a specific font, such as Times New Roman, Courier New, or Helvetica. Make sure that it is set to use the Regular style (as opposed to Italic, Bold, or Bold Italic) and that the font size is set appropriately for your default regular (body) text (12 points?).

CAUTION: Again, you might not think to do so, but you also need to check the font color settings. Locate the **Font color drop-down** underneath the font list and, if it says "**Automatic**," click the drop-down and then click one of the black squares ("Black, Text 1") to ensure that the default color will be black. Otherwise, the font color could change depending on which Theme is applied to a particular document.

When everything looks correct, click the **Default button** at the bottom of the dialog box. Word should prompt you to confirm that change, asking whether you want to change the default font to a certain typeface, size, and color, and if so, for "This document only?" or for "All documents based on the Normal.dotm template?"

If in fact you want all new documents based on the template to use the font face, size, and color you've just selected, ***make sure to click the radio button to the left of "All documents…"*** —ordinarily, the other button ("This document only") is selected—and then click the **"OK" button**. Otherwise, Word will change the font ***only in the current document***, which probably is not your intention.

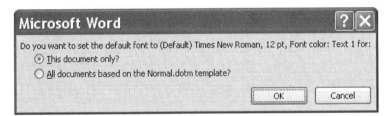

To Change the Default Font, Be Sure to Click "All documents…" and Then Click OK

It is important to recognize that modifying the default font in a particular template will not have an effect on the default font in your other templates. You might need to repeat the above steps for other templates you use.

Changing the Default Font for Headings (and Other Styles)

Even after you have made the changes described in this section—creating a new Style Set and a new set of Theme Fonts and making them the defaults, as well as changing the default font for regular (body) text—you might find that certain styles, including heading styles, continue to use a font you don't want. If that is the case, you'll have to modify those styles manually (to change the font from a +Headings or +Body font to whichever specific font you wish to use). For instructions on how to modify a style, see the tutorial immediately below, as well as the section starting on page 352.

Modifying the Normal Paragraph Style

You might want to modify the **Normal paragraph style**, as well. As noted throughout this portion of the book, in most versions of Word, the Normal paragraph style controls the default line spacing, justification, first-line indent (if any), left and right indentation (if any), before and/or after spacing (if any), and tab settings for regular (body) text, as well as for all styles that are based on the Normal style. In Word 2010, the Normal paragraph style performs a similar role—when all other things are equal.[14] Keep in mind that you can have different Normal paragraph styles for different templates.

To modify the Normal paragraph style, navigate to the **Home tab**, **Styles group** and click the **dialog launcher** to open the **Styles pane** (or press **Ctrl Alt Shift S**). Scroll down to the "**Normal**" style and right-click it.

When the **Modify Style dialog** appears, *immediately* click the "**New documents based on this template**" **radio button** at the bottom. Otherwise, any changes you make to the Normal paragraph style will be saved *only in the current document*, not in the template itself.

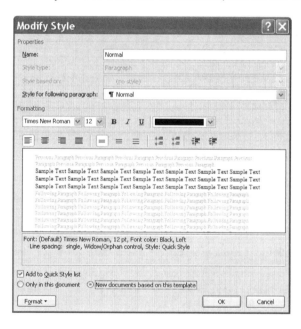

Next, click the "**Format**" **button** in the lower left-hand corner of the dialog. Then click "**Font**." When the **Font dialog** appears, choose a specific font face (*don't use the +Body setting*, or Word will select the font for body text based on the Theme that is in effect in a given document), a specific font size, *and* a specific font color. Again, *don't leave the color set to*

---

[14] At times, Style Sets and Themes seem to "hijack" the settings in the Normal paragraph style and/or the default font, a fact that underscores the importance of changing the default Style Set and Theme in addition to changing the Normal paragraph style, the default font, and other settings. The Word developers have described the Normal paragraph style in Word 2007 (and, by extension, in Word 2010) as "**empty**," which might explain its chameleon-like behavior.

Automatic unless you want Word to choose a color for you based on Themes. Click **OK** to save your Font settings.

Before OK-ing out of the dialog, click the **Format button** again, and this time click "**Paragraph**." Go through every setting in the **Paragraph dialog**—both tabs—to make sure that alignment, indentation, spacing (including line spacing and before and after spacing), and pagination are configured to your liking. Click **OK** to save your Paragraph settings, then click **OK** to save the modified Normal Paragraph style.

Changing the Default Formatting Via the Paragraph and Font Dialogs

Of course, you also have the option of changing individual settings such as line spacing or before and after spacing from within the **Paragraph dialog** and then clicking the "**Set As Default**" button at the bottom of the dialog. Likewise, you can adjust the font properties in the **Font dialog** and then click the "**Set As Default**" button. However, the method described in the previous section is a handy way to modify several aspects of the Normal paragraph style (paragraph formatting, font attributes, and so on) all at once.

Modifying the NORMAL Template

One final item you might wish to change is the NORMAL template.[15]

As you probably know, each user has his or her own NORMAL template. It is located on the user's hard drive, not on a shared drive.[16] Under most circumstances, this template is the basis for all new documents. It stores **page formatting** settings—default margins, margins for headers and footers, paper orientation (portrait versus landscape), and so forth.

In addition, the normal.dotm stores a number of user customizations, including **formatted AutoCorrect entries** (unformatted AutoCorrect entries are located in each user's application data folder in Windows); **styles; keyboard shortcuts;** and **macros**. In Word 2010, unlike in Word 2007, the normal.dotm also stores AutoText entries.

Should you wish to make "permanent" changes to page formatting or any of these other items, you can do so by editing the NORMAL template directly.

To open an individual's NORMAL template, simply click the **File tab, Open**.[17] In the **Open dialog**, click "**Trusted Templates**" at the top of the navigation bar on the left side of the

---

[15] **NOTE:** the NORMAL template and the default Style Set are not the same thing, although they appear to work in concert. Among other differences, the latter does not hold customized styles, macros, or keyboard shortcuts.

[16] Many organizations also make use of shared templates located on a network drive. You might or might not be able to modify any such shared templates.

[17] **CAUTION:** You should *close all other documents* prior to opening the default template for editing.

dialog.[18] You should see a file called "**normal.dotm**."[19] (If you have upgraded from a pre-Word 2007 version, you might see a file called "normal.dot," too. The one you want to edit is normal.dotm.)

Just open the normal.dotm template, modify it as you wish, and save it as you would save any other document.

Although ordinarily you wouldn't insert text in the NORMAL template—remember that this template is the basis for all new documents—some people like to add a code for the file name and path, often in a footer (which means it will appear on every page). For detailed instructions, see the section starting on page 323. Here are the basic steps:

- Position the cursor where you want the code to appear—perhaps at the end of the document or in a footer (**Insert tab**, **Header & Footer group**, **Footer**, **Blank**).

- Click the **Insert tab**, **Quick Parts drop-down**, **Field** *or* press **Alt I**, **F**.

- When the **Field dialog** appears, press the letter "**F**" to move to the first Field code that starts with that letter; if it's anything other than **FileName**, scroll to the FileName code and click to select it.

- To add the path as well as the file name, click the "**Add path to filename**" checkbox.

- Click "**OK**."

If you want to change the font face or size, select the code and change the font attributes via the **Font Dialog (Ctrl D)** or via one of the **font drop-down menus** in the **Font group** on the **Home tab**. Then **save and close** the template.

CAUTION: Before you save the NORMAL template, be very careful to delete any text that you have inserted while you are making your changes (such as expanded Quick Parts), unless you want all new documents to contain that text.

FURTHER CAUTION: If you create or modify any styles from within the NORMAL template, it's a good idea to go through the template methodically before saving it to make sure you haven't inadvertently applied any of those new or modified styles to blank paragraphs, which could wreak havoc with your future documents. An easy way to check is to switch to **Draft view** (**View tab**, **Document Views**, **Draft** or click the **Draft icon** at the right side of the

_____

[18] These instructions are based on Windows XP. For the exact location of the NORMAL template in Windows Vista and in Windows 7 (as well as XP), see page 573.

[19] The "m" at the end of the file extension means that the template is macro-enabled—i.e., it can contain macros created with Visual Basic for Applications, or VBA. Word templates that end with .dotx *cannot* contain VBA macros.

Status Bar) and look in the **Style Area** at the left margin. (**NOTE**: If you don't see anything in the left margin when you switch views, you'll need to configure Word to show the Style Area in Draft view. To do so, click the **File Tab, Options, Advanced**, scroll down to **Display**, and make sure the **Style Area Pane width in Draft and Outline views** is set to a minimum of 1". Then **OK** out of Word options.)

Draft View Showing Style Area Pane in Margin (Document is at Right)

If any style name other than Normal is displayed in the Style Area Pane, double-click it. A **Style dialog** will open.

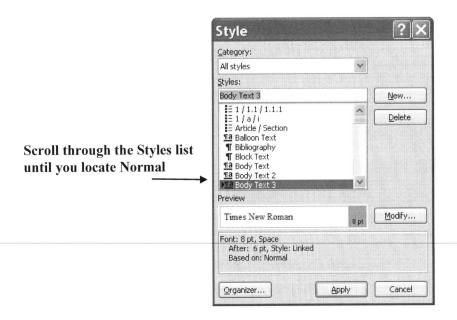

Style Dialog

You'll see a truncated style list in the center of the dialog. Scroll down to **Normal, click** to select it, and click the **Apply button**. Repeat these steps for every style you see in the Style Area Pane. When you have finished, **save and close** the modified NORMAL template.

There are other ways to clear styles, of course. One simple method is to select the entire template by pressing **Ctrl A**, then press **Ctrl Shift N** to impose the **Normal paragraph style**. But the Style Area Pane comes in handy from time to time—it's a great way to see at a glance which styles have been applied in your document—and now you know how to use it!

Taming the New Default File Format

As you know, Word 2010's default file format, .docx, is not backwards compatible with earlier versions of Word, and it isn't readable in versions of WordPerfect prior to X4 (14). So how do you share files with clients, co-counsel, and others who don't have Word 2010? Here are a couple of suggestions.

Saving in Compatibility Mode

You can save individual documents in "Compatibility Mode"— i.e., in .doc format, also known as Word 97-Word 2003 format—so that you can share them easily with others. When you save a document, just change the "**Save as type**" to **Word 97-2003 Document (*.doc)**.

Alternatively, you can configure Word 2010 to save *all* new documents in Compatibility Mode. To do the latter, click the **File tab**, **Options**, **Save**, click the "**Save files in this format:**" **drop-down**, and choose **Word 97-2003 Document (*.doc).** Be sure to click "**OK**" to save your changes.

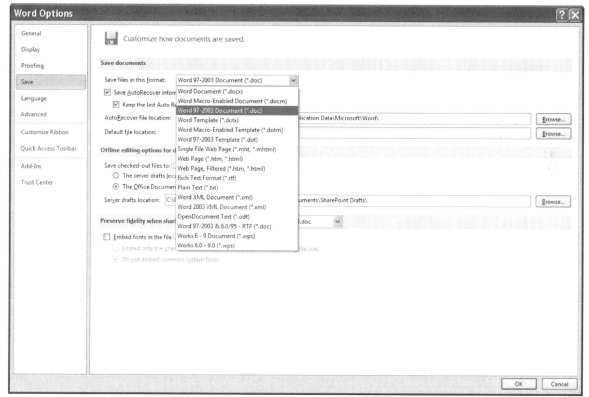

Changing the Default File Format Via Options, Save

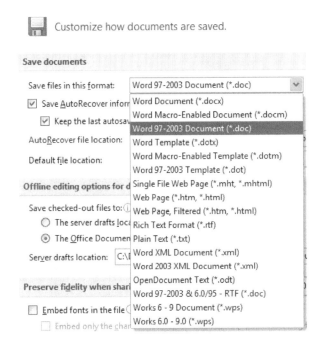

Close-Up of Default File Format Options

Should you choose to work in .doc format, just be aware that certain features that were introduced in Word 2007 and/or in Word 2010—Themes, screenshots, Text Effects, the background removal tool, and the image selection pane (among others)—either won't work at all in your documents or will work with somewhat limited functionality.

Sharing .docx Files With Others

Creating a PDF

If you regularly share documents with others who might not have Word 2010, consider saving those documents in .doc format.

For contacts who don't need to edit the documents, you can use the "Create PDF" option to create a PDF copy, which the recipients can open with Adobe Reader—a free, downloadable program available at www.adobe.com. See the instructions starting on page 54 for converting Word files to PDF. (It's easy!)

Using the Compatibility Pack

Alternatively, you might point them to a utility they can download that will allow them to read native Word 2010 documents (i.e., .docx files). You can even send them a link.

To read more about this utility, called a "Compatibility Pack," see the following MS Knowledge Base article:

"How to use earlier versions of Excel, PowerPoint, and Word to open and save files from 2007 Office programs": http://support.microsoft.com/kb/924074

Even though the article refers to Office 2007, the instructions also apply (with minor modifications) to Office 2010.

The most recent compatibility pack for Word, Excel, and PowerPoint (at least, the most recent as of April, 2010) is located here: www.microsoft.com/downloads/details.aspx?FamilyID=941b3470-3ae9-4aee-8f43-c6bb74cd1466&displaylang=en

Or you can use this "tiny URL": http://tinyurl.com/CompatPack

QUICK TIP: Enable "Use the Insert Key to Control Overtype Mode"

Hiding demurely in the middle of the "Editing options" subcategory of the Advanced Word Options is an option labeled "**Use the Insert key to control overtype mode.**"

You might be surprised to find that this setting is turned off by default. That is a change from pre-Word 2007 versions of Word—and from nearly all other Windows programs—in which the Insert key toggles between Insert mode (where new typing bumps existing text over to the right, rather than replacing it) and Typeover or Overtype mode (where new typing actually erases existing text).

Upon reflection, it makes sense that Microsoft chose to disable this feature by default, considering how commonly people press the Insert key and end up overwriting existing text by accident. Still, considering what a radical departure this change represents, many people are caught off guard by it.

If you want to enable the option, making Word 2010 behave more like traditional Windows programs, click the **File tab**, **Options**, **Advanced**, locate the settings in the "**Editing options**" section, and just click the first checkbox ("**Use the Insert key to control overtype mode**"). Watch out, though: The *second* checkbox (labeled "Use overtype mode") makes Typeover / Overtype the default, which is neither the norm nor the mode that most people prefer.

Disabling or Enabling Certain Features in Word

Microsoft has chosen to enable (or disable) certain features by default that you might prefer to turn off (or on). These features include the new paragraph option, "Don't add space between paragraphs of the same style," which is turned *off* by default in the Normal paragraph style but turned *on* by default in numbered and bulleted lists and certain other styles—meaning that Word might prevent you from adding space between paragraphs of the same style by changing Before and/or After spacing. Also, if you use the new .docx format rather than the older (.doc) file format, you might find your settings for the font face, font size, and font color of body text and headings hijacked by Word 2010's built-in "Themes." This behavior can be unsettling, mystifying, and frustrating—and can have a negative impact on productivity.

The following chart provides some tips about changing the default settings of a few features operating in the background that might make it more difficult for you to format your document to your (or your firm's) specifications.[1]

Feature	Comments	How to Disable (or Enable)
Don't add space between paragraphs of the same style (Paragraph dialog)	This new Paragraph formatting option is *unchecked* (*disabled*) by default in the Normal paragraph style and *checked* (*enabled*) by default in list styles and certain other styles. That means that Word might prevent you from adding space between paragraphs by using the Before and/or After setting(s) in the Paragraph dialog unless you specifically turn this option off.	If necessary, *select the affected paragraphs*, then launch the **Paragraph dialog** and click to check or uncheck the "Don't add space between paragraphs of the same style" option (depending on whether you want to enable or disable it) and click **OK**. You can change the default settings for this option (as it affects the Normal paragraph style) in at least two different ways: (1) by turning it on or off, clicking the "**Set As Default**" button at the bottom of the Paragraph dialog, then clicking **OK**; or (2) by opening your **NORMAL template** for editing, enabling or disabling the option, clicking **OK**, and then **saving** the revised NORMAL template. **CAUTION**: You probably will need to disable this setting on *a style-by-style basis*.

---

[1] Thankfully, the ubiquitous Clippy was removed in Word 2007, so it is no longer necessary to include instructions for disabling him.

Feature	Comments	How to Disable (or Enable)
Themes	By default, Word applies a Theme to every new .docx. Each Theme uses a certain font face, size, and color for body text and for heading styles. These choices are predetermined for you and, if you're not well versed on Themes and how they behave, it can be frustrating to try to work around them.	The only sure-fire way to disable Themes altogether is to work in Compatibility Mode (i.e., use the .doc format rather than .docx). If you need to use the .docx format, a reasonably good workaround is to create a custom Theme that uses your preferred fonts (making sure to configure the specific font face, size, *and* color you want) for body text and for heading styles, and then make that Theme the default. Or you can create a custom Theme Fonts set and make that set the default. See the instructions on page 229.
Paste Options Button	On by default in Word 2010 Some people find this pop-up distracting. Note that the functionality of this button has changed in Word 2010. See the section starting on page 125 for more details.	Click the **File tab, Options, Advanced,** navigate to the **Cut, copy and paste** section, and *un*check "**Show Paste Options button when content is pasted.**"
Set Left- and First-Indent With Tabs and Backspaces	This option is on by default in Word 2010. With this setting enabled, pressing the Tab key results in a first-line indent and or a left indent rather than a simple tab. Pressing the Enter key copies the first-line indent or left indent to the following paragraph. This setting also enables you to promote or demote outline levels by pressing the Tab key or Shift Tab.	**File tab, Options, Proofing, AutoCorrect Options…, AutoFormat As You Type tab,** *un*check Set left- and first-indent with tabs and backspaces.

Feature	Comments	How to Disable (or Enable)
White Space Between Pages	This feature is turned on by default in Word 2010. When white space is hidden, *headers and footers also are hidden* (though footnotes and endnotes are not).	**File tab, Options, Display, Show white space between pages in Print Layout view,** *check* to enable. You also can this setting turn on and off (temporarily) by double-clicking the gray area or hairline division between pages.
Reviewing toolbar—Final Showing Markup	With this feature enabled, revision marks, comments, and other interlineations inserted in a document via "Track Changes" or "Compare Documents" are visible. Note that Microsoft has chosen to make this setting the default so that you are less likely to send a document containing metadata to people who are not supposed to see such information.	I don't know how to change this setting so that Final Showing Markup isn't the default, but you *can* change the Tracking Options so that revisions aren't displayed in balloons in the document margins. See the next item. If you are sending the document to outside counsel or anyone else you don't want to see the markup, you should make a copy of the document and *accept or reject each (all) of the changes* before forwarding that copy of the doc. That is the *only* sure way to keep others from seeing the revisions.
Use Balloons	"Balloons" are used for revision marks (Track Changes) and comments. They appear in the margins and *they print with the document* (unless you remember to change the **Balloons** setting in the **Tracking Options**, as described at right.	To configure balloons, go to the **Review tab, Tracking group**, and click the **Track Changes drop-down, Change Tracking Options**, and navigate to the **Balloons section**. There are three choices for displaying balloons: • Always • Never • Only for comments / formatting

Demystifying Everyday Features

Adjusting Line Spacing

Remember that line spacing in Word is considered an attribute of a paragraph. Therefore, the line-spacing controls are located in the Paragraph dialog. (See the left-hand screenshot on page 175.)

If you haven't started typing your document, you can set line spacing at the beginning and the spacing will continue from paragraph to paragraph until you change to a different setting. If you need to change the line spacing of existing text, *you have to select the text first*.

For simple single- or double-spacing, you can use the keyboard shortcuts **Ctrl 1** (single spacing) and **Ctrl 2** (double spacing). For 1.5 spacing, you can press **Ctrl 5**.

There's also a **drop-down** toward the middle of the **Paragraph group** in the **Home tab** that provides several different choices, including "Add Space Before Paragraph" and "Add Space After Paragraph" (both of which add 12 points). If you've added space before and/or after a paragraph, the drop-down includes choices for removing that extra spacing.

The Line Spacing Button in the Paragraph Group

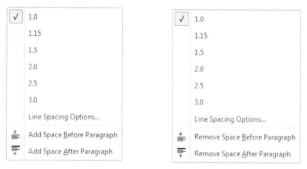

The Line Spacing Menus

For anything more complex, you need to use the **Paragraph dialog** and choose one of the other options. (Clicking "**Line Spacing Options…**" in the drop-down launches the Paragraph dialog.) If you need triple spacing, for example, click **Multiple** and then enter the number 3 and OK out of the dialog.

Line spacing in pleadings can be complex because of the way that the line numbers in the pleading paper are generated. If necessary, you can specify an exact number of "points" for single and double spacing in pleadings. ("Points" has to do with the height of the characters you type.) Normal single spacing with a standard 12-point font is 12 points; normal double spacing with a standard 12-point font is 24 points. However, in pleadings you might need to set single spacing at a fraction such as 11.375 points and double spacing at an Exact fraction such as 22.75 points. To do so, use the "**Exactly**" setting in the Paragraph dialog.

This issue is discussed in more detail in other sections of the book, including "Aligning Text With Pleading Line Numbers" (see pages 429 and following). If you don't work with pleadings or if your pleading template is set up in such a way that you're able to use standard single and double spacing, you might never encounter this situation.

NOTE: "**Before**" and "**After**" spacing control the amount of spacing that is inserted automatically before and/or after a paragraph. Many people use these controls to put 12 points of space between paragraphs—eliminating the need to press the Enter key twice after typing a paragraph. (To do so, you can set both "Before" and "After" to 6 points *or* simply set "After" to 12 points.) Some users—particularly people who have worked with WordPerfect for many years—dislike "Before" and "After" paragraph spacing and prefer to keep both settings at 0 (zero). You will develop your own preferences as you work more regularly with Word.

Either way, it is important to understand these options for troubleshooting purposes—i.e., in case you encounter paragraph spacing that appears to be "off" in some way and you're not sure why, or if a certain section of your document requires more or less space between paragraphs. For more about this aspect of paragraph formatting, see the "Paragraph Formatting" section of the book (pages 175 and following).

QUICK TIP: Setting Line Height

In Word, you can approximate the "Line Height" feature found in WordPerfect in a couple of ways.

One way is to use "**Exactly**" line spacing. As noted in the previous section, as well as in the discussion about line spacing starting on page 178, this option—found in the **Paragraph dialog** on the **Line spacing drop-down**—lets you fine-tune character height down to fractions of a point. (For what it's worth, there are 72 points per inch; one point is one-twelfth of a pica.) You might have to experiment somewhat to get the precise measurement you want; if you normally use 12-point spacing, try 11 or 11.5 (unless, of course, you are formatting a pleading or other type of document that requires you to use a 12-point or larger font).

Another way is to use "**Multiple**" line spacing and set the spacing to a number less than 1—for example, .97 or .94. Again, you might have to experiment to get the setting just right.

TROUBLESHOOTING TIP: Where'd That Line Come From?

If the automatic borders feature is turned on—which it appears to be by default in Word 2010—pressing the hyphen key three times, then pressing Enter, produces a horizontal line. That's great if you intended to create a line, but it can be disquieting if you didn't! How do you get rid of it?

If you're quick enough, you can undo the line by clicking the **Undo button**, by pressing **Ctrl Z**, or by clicking the **AutoCorrect Options button** that pops up when you insert an automatic border. Clicking the AutoCorrect Options button opens a drop-down that offers three choices: **Undo Border Line**, **Stop Automatically Creating Border Lines** (which turns off the automatic borders), and **Control AutoFormat Options** (which takes you into Word Options so that you can configure the AutoCorrect options to your liking).

If you don't notice the line immediately or you notice it but don't take action right away to remove the line, you can delete it later on. To do so, display the non-printing characters by clicking the **paragraph symbol (¶)** in the **Paragraph group** in the **Home tab** (*or* by pressing **Ctrl Shift * [asterisk]**). Locate and delete the paragraph symbol just *above* the line. (That almost always works, but if it doesn't, try deleting the paragraph symbol *below* the line.)

To turn off automatic borders altogether, click the **File tab**, **Options**, **Proofing**, **AutoCorrect Options**, **AutoFormat As You Type tab**, and *uncheck* **Border lines**.

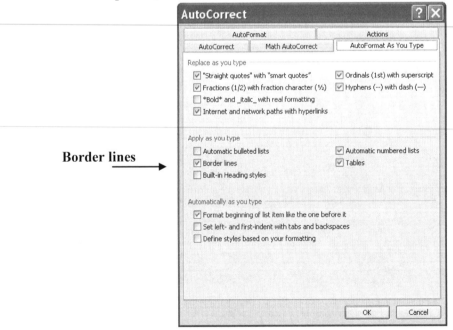

AutoCorrect Dialog, AutoFormat As You Type Tab

NOTE: Be sure to explore the AutoCorrect Options on the AutoFormat As You Type tab and uncheck any that you don't want (note that some options appear on both that tab and the AutoFormat tab; however, the options on the AutoFormat tab don't go into effect automatically, so you don't need to uncheck any of them).

If you're unsure what a particular option does, click the question mark in the upper right-hand corner of the AutoCorrect dialog. That will open Word Help, where you can research the various options. (Note that you will find a greater range of articles if you click the "Search" drop-down in the Help dialog and choose "All Word," which will broaden your search to include online references. Obviously, you must be online in order to gain access to the reference materials available on the Internet.)

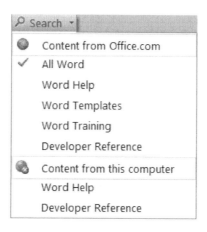

QUICK TIP: Contextual Spelling

Contextual spelling, first introduced in Word 2007, is a nifty feature, albeit one with definite limitations.

When the "**Use contextual spelling**" **option** is enabled, Word flags not only misspelled words, but also words that are spelled correctly but aren't appropriate in the context in which you use them. For instance, if you type "Their are many reasons…," Word will either change "Their" to "There" automatically or mark the word with a blue squiggly underline—even if you do not have the grammar checker enabled.

<u>Their are</u> many reasons

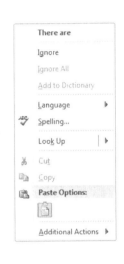

Right-clicking an item that the contextual spell-checker flags will produce a pop-up menu with some suggested alternatives.

To enable or disable the option, click **File, Options, Proofing,** and navigate to the section labeled "**When correcting spelling and grammar in Word.**" Click to check (enable) or uncheck (disable) the "**Use contextual spelling**" **option,** then be sure to click "**OK**" to save your settings when you exit from the Word Options.

When correcting spelling and grammar in Word

☑ Check spelling as you type
☑ Use contextual spelling
☐ Mark grammar errors as you type
☐ Check grammar with spelling

A few caveats about this feature:

- It doesn't always catch contextual spelling errors, so you still need to proofread your documents;

- It occasionally produces "false positives";

- If you have less than 1 GB of RAM on your computer, the option will be automatically disabled to save memory; and

- If your computer seems unusually slow or your system resources appear to be low, try disabling the option. According to Microsoft, the option consumes a fair amount of memory.

Changing Margins

Changing Margins for the Entire Document

The first thing to keep in mind about margins is that in Word, document margins are considered an attribute of *page layout*. That means that you set margins for the entire document—as opposed to only a few paragraphs—via **Page Setup** on the **Page Layout tab**.

From the **Page Layout tab**, you can either (1) click the "**Margins**" drop-down, then click the **Custom Margins** command at the bottom of the menu, which will open the **Page Setup dialog**; or (2) open the **Page Setup dialog** directly by clicking the **dialog launcher** at the lower right-hand side of the **Page Setup group**. (Or, as a quick alternative, you can open the **Page Setup dialog** from anywhere within Word by using the keyboard shortcut **Alt P, S, P** *or* **Alt P, M, A**.)

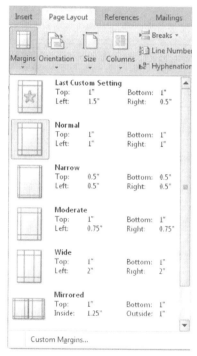

Page Layout, Custom Margins...

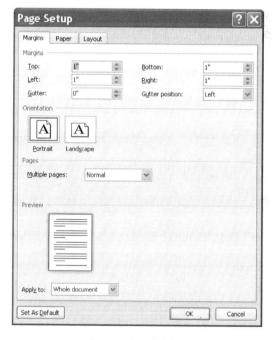

Page Setup Dialog

Once the **Page Setup dialog** is open, you can simply type numbers for the Top, Bottom, Left, and/or Right margins directly in the respective boxes. (Some people click the up/down arrows—known as "spinners"—but I find it faster to type the numbers in the boxes.) Note that you don't need to add quotation marks for inches after the digits; Word automatically inserts those for you. To save your settings, be sure to click **OK** rather than pressing Cancel or Esc.

If you want your new settings to apply to all future documents—i.e., to become the default settings—click the "**Set As Default**" button at the bottom of the dialog before OK-ing out.

To display page margin borders, click the **File tab, Options, Advanced,** and under **Show document content**, click to check **Show text boundaries**, then click **OK**. (**CAUTION:** This setting will not affect other documents you have open on your screen, but will affect documents you open in the future.) These guidelines will not print with the document.

Changing Margins for Only Certain Paragraphs

Should you wish to change margins for only a few paragraphs—without changing the margins for the entire document, or for a section—just select the paragraphs and use the Paragraph dialog to change the left and/or right indent. (If the paragraphs are not contiguous, you will have to select them separately, rather than as a group.)

Alternatively, if the paragraphs are contiguous, you can do the following: **Select the text**, launch the **Page setup dialog**, and **change the margin settings**. *Before clicking OK,* navigate to the **"Apply to:" drop-down** at the lower left-hand side of the dialog box and make sure it is set to "**Selected Text**." Then **OK** out of the dialog.

Because Word applies page margins on a section-by-section basis, the program automatically inserts section breaks before and after the text you selected in order to set that portion of the document off from other portions that use different margin settings.

Indenting Paragraphs

The previous section explains how to set page margins in your document (as well as margins for individual paragraphs). This section covers a related topic: how to configure paragraph indentation. You can do so via the **Indents and Spacing tab** of the **Paragraph dialog box** (which you can launch from the **Home tab**, **Paragraph group**, **dialog launcher** *or* simply by pressing **Alt O, P**). By default, the dialog box opens with the Indents and Spacing tab active (as opposed to the Line and Page Breaks tab). For more details, see the screenshot below; both tabs of the Paragraph dialog are shown on page 175.

You can, for example, set the Left indent of a paragraph and/or the Right indent of a paragraph. Doing so is particularly useful for block quotes in a pleading.

Left indent
Right Indent

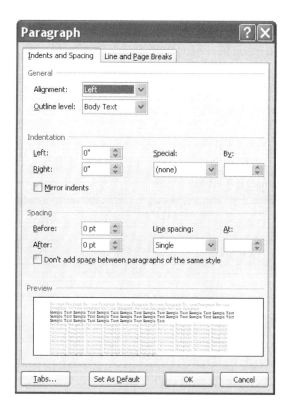

"**Special**" controls the indentation of the first line (none, First line, Hanging)

Before spacing
After spacing

Line spacing

There is no single key combination in Word for setting a left and right indent, as there is in WordPerfect. However, you can create *a style* to set a left and right indent and then assign a keyboard shortcut to that style. See the section entitled "Setting Up a Simple Style (and Keyboard Shortcut) for Indented Quotes," starting on page 459.

To indent *from the left only*, you can use the Paragraph dialog *or* the keyboard shortcut **Ctrl M**. Each time you press Ctrl M, the left indent increases by one tab stop. (This function is similar to using the F7 key in WordPerfect—or F4 if you use WP's DOS-compatible keyboard.) To reverse the indent by one tab stop, press **Ctrl Shift M**.

The Paragraph dialog also has a drop-down under "Special" where you can choose to format a paragraph so that the first line automatically indents by half an inch (or .25 inches or one inch or some other amount). This is the "**First line**" option.

The other choice you have under "Special" is **Hanging Indent**. With a hanging indent, the first line is "outdented"[1]—i.e., it begins one tab stop or more to the left of the rest of the paragraph. This paragraph style is commonly used in bibliographies. It is seldom used in legal document formatting, but be on the alert for it because *it is the default setting for numbered lists* and certain other items in Word. When you encounter it, you might have to change the setting, which you can do either from within the Paragraph dialog or from the Ruler.

You might find that you prefer using the Paragraph dialog to adjust indents because it is somewhat more precise than using the Ruler. With the Ruler, you position your cursor in the paragraph you want to adjust and drag one or more of the **Indent Markers**.

First Line Indent Marker

Hanging Indent Marker (triangle)

Left Indent Marker (rectangle)

The down-pointing triangle at the left side of the Ruler (but shown at the 1" mark in the screenshot above) controls the first line of the paragraph your cursor is in. You can drag that triangle—called the **First Line Indent Marker**—to indent the first line of the paragraph by as much as you like. At the 1" position as in the screenshot, it would create a first-line indent of one inch. (If I had left it at its default position, there would be no first-line indent—i.e., the first line would begin flush with the left margin.)

The up-pointing triangle at the left side of the Ruler controls the indentation of the remainder of the paragraph—i.e., every line except the first. It is the **Hanging Indent Marker**. You can drag it by itself (leaving the First Line Indent Marker where it is) when you want the second line of a paragraph to indent an inch more than the first line, for example.

By contrast, the rectangle at the bottom left of the Ruler (the **Left Indent Marker**) controls the indentation of the entire paragraph. When you drag it, the First Line Indent and the Hanging Indent markers move accordingly, but they retain the same relationship with each other.

CAUTION: It is easy to click and drag the Left Indent Marker by accident when you are trying to drag the Hanging Indent marker. It takes a certain amount of practice to get it right.

To see how these indent markers work in practice, experiment with them. You'll quickly see their utility.

---

[1] I don't like that term—it strikes me as "technobabble"—but it gets the point across.

Setting and Deleting Tabs

There are a couple of ways to set tabs in Word 2010. You can set them directly on the **horizontal Ruler**, or you can use the **Tabs dialog box**.

By default, the horizontal Ruler is not displayed in Word 2010. To show it, click the **View tab** and make sure there is a check in the **Ruler** checkbox in the **Show group**.

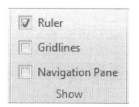

You can open the **Tabs dialog** in at least three different ways. Perhaps the most common method is via the **Paragraph dialog**, which in turn can be opened by clicking the dialog launcher in the **Paragraph group** on the **Home tab** *or* clicking the dialog launcher in the **Paragraph group** on the **Page Layout tab**. (Or you can use a keyboard shortcut—specifically, **Alt O, P**—to open the Paragraph dialog, regardless of which tab is active). After the Paragraph dialog appears, click the "**Tabs**" **button** at the lower left-hand side to launch the Tabs dialog.

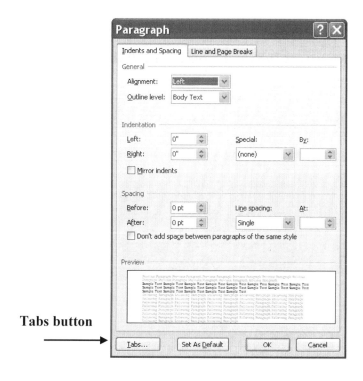

Tabs button

Note as well that you can open the Tabs dialog directly by double-clicking a tab stop on the Ruler (**CAUTION**: if you click the top border of the Ruler or a portion of the Ruler that is within the margins, the Page Setup dialog opens instead). Or you can use the keyboard shortcut **Alt O, T**.

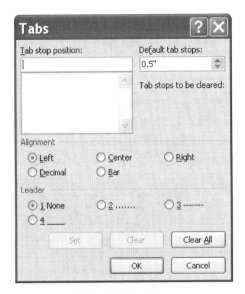

Tabs Dialog Box

Note the Default tab stops field in the upper right-hand corner of the Tabs dialog box. By default, tabs are set every half inch in Word. (The default tab stops appear as short vertical marks in the gray area below the Ruler.) To change the default tab setting, just type a new setting in the Default tab stops field or use the up and down arrows to adjust the setting.

To set custom tabs by using the Tabs Dialog Box, type a setting in the **Tab stop position box**, set the **alignment** if necessary (Left, Center, Right, Decimal, or Bar[1]), set any desired **Leader**, then click **Set**. When you're finished, be sure to click **OK**.

CAUTION: Be aware that when you set individual tabs, ***any existing tabs to the left of your custom settings will be cleared***. In other words, if you type 1.75 in the Tab stop position box, Word will delete the tabs set at .5, 1, and 1.5! (Word also clears tabs to the left of your first custom tab if you set tabs directly on the Ruler.)

Another way to clear individual tabs from within the dialog box is by **clicking the setting** in the **Tab stop position box** and then clicking the **Clear** button.

To insert custom tab settings directly on the Ruler, first click the **Tab type button** at the far left of the Ruler to change to the appropriate tab type. The "L" symbol sets Left tabs; the upside-down "T" symbol (⊥) sets Center tabs; the backwards "L" symbol sets Right tabs; and the inverted "T" with a period to the right of the bar of the "T" sets Decimal Tabs. Once you have the Tab type button set the way you want, just left-click at the point on the Ruler where you want to insert a tab stop. (To clear tab settings, just drag the tab symbols off the Ruler.)

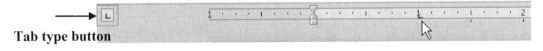

Tab type button

---

[1]Definitions of Left, Center, Right, Decimal, and Bar tabs follow below.

Keep in mind that in Word, tab formatting is associated with ***paragraphs***. Thus, if you change tab settings before you start typing or while you are typing, the new settings will be copied to successive paragraphs when you press the Enter key. However, if you need to adjust tab settings in a portion of the document you have already typed, ***you must select the paragraph(s) you want the new settings to affect.***

TYPES OF TABS

(NOTE: In the following examples, **X** marks the location of the tab stop.)

Left tabs (the most commonly used type): Text moves *to the right* from the tab stop.
    X
This is an example of a Left tab.

Right tabs: Text moves *to the left* from the tab stop.
                                X
This is an example of a Right tab.

Center tabs: Text *centers around* the tab stop.
                    X
This is an example of a Center tab.

Decimal tabs: Text (consisting of numbers) *aligns at a decimal point.*
                               .**X**
This is an example of a Decimal tab   1,279,567.85
                                    734.27

Bar tabs[2]: Word inserts *a vertical line* at the tab stop.

This is an example of a Bar tab. | You can type text on either side of the "bar."
Note: Word extends the bar when you
press Enter (which copies the paragraph
formatting containing the bar tab
to the next paragraph) or if you press
the Tab key continuously.

TYPES OF LEADERS

NOTE: Leaders work with **Right tabs**. They move *to the left* from the leader tab stop to the previous tab stop.

Dot..**X**
Dash ---**X**
Underline   **X**

---

[2] Not to be confused with your running account for drinks you've bought at the local tavern.

SIDEBAR: Alignment Tabs

In Word 2007, Microsoft introduced a new form of tabs called "Alignment Tabs." Similar to WordPerfect's longstanding Relative Tabs feature, alignment tabs are useful because they readjust automatically if you change the page margins in a way that alters the location of the left, right, and/or center point of the document. **NOTE:** Alignment tabs work only in .docx files (and other Open Office XML file types). They are not available in .doc files.

These new tabs are something of a "stealth" feature because there's no reference to them anywhere on the Ribbon (or in any dialog boxes) unless you happen to be working with headers or footers. When your cursor is in a header or footer editing screen, you will see an "**Insert Alignment Tab**" command in the **Position group** on the **Header & Footer Tools tab**.

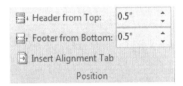

Clicking the command opens a dialog that lets you set a left, center, or right tab—with or without a leader—in the header or footer (and align it relative to either the margin or an indent).

Remember that tabs are an element of paragraph formatting. That means that when you insert an alignment tab on one line of a header or footer, the setting will apply *only to the paragraph your cursor is in*. However, if you press the Enter key after inserting an alignment tab, the tab setting will carry over to the next paragraph. As you know, that is the way paragraph formatting works in general.

Unlike the left, center, and right tabs built into headers and footers, alignment tabs do not appear on the Ruler. (In fact, Microsoft recommends that you remove any pre-existing tabs from the Ruler when you use alignment tabs—which you can do by dragging the tabs off the Ruler—so as to avoid any unwanted profusion of tabs or confusion about where the tabs exist in your headers and footers.)

Although the "Alignment Tab" command appears only on the Header & Footer Tools tab, you can add it to the Quick Access Toolbar so that you can use alignment tabs in the body of your document. To do so, either (1) go into a header or footer editing screen, **right-click** the "**Insert Alignment Tab**" icon, and then click "**Add to Quick Access Toolbar**" *or* (2) **right-click** the QAT, click "**Customize the Quick Access Toolbar...**," change the "Popular Commands" drop-down at the top left side of the Word Options screen to "**All Commands**," scroll to the "**Insert Alignment Tab**" **command**, click the "**Add**" **button**, and then click "**OK**" to save your settings.

A Few Tips About Fonts

This section offers selected tips for working with fonts and font-related features. It is not meant to be an exhaustive discussion of fonts.

Applying Fonts to an Entire Document

Under most circumstances, new documents automatically use the default font that you have selected *or* the font that is applied by default as a result of a Style Set and Theme. (For more about the role of Style Sets and Themes in determining default settings for your documents, see the section starting on page 222; see also the section starting on page 233 about changing the default font.)

If you want to use a different font in a particular document, you can change fonts (via the Font dialog or the font drop-down in the Home tab) before you start typing, and the font should go into effect immediately. Or you can select the entire document (by pressing Ctrl A or clicking the Select drop-down at the right side of the Home tab, then clicking "Select All") and then apply the font you wish to use. But note that (1) changing the font, even before you start typing, affects only the text in the body of the document, *not* in "substructures" such as headers and footers or footnotes. The formatting of those items is determined by pre-existing header, footer, and footnote *styles*. Also, (2) even after you change the font, you might find that certain items revert to the original default font.

In order to apply your custom font throughout the document, you can make the font the default *for the document*. Just click the dialog launcher at the bottom right side of the Font group in the Home tab or press Ctrl D, select the font face, style, and size (plus the color and any other attributes you want to use), and then click the "**Set as Default**" button at the bottom left side of the dialog.

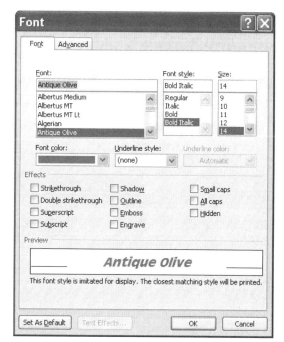

A message box will appear, asking if you want to set the default font for:

- **This document only?** or

- **All documents based on the Normal.dotm template** (or whichever template the current document is based on)

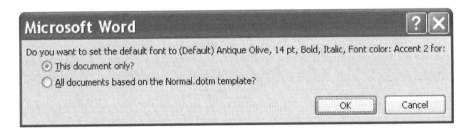

The first option, "This document only?" is automatically selected. To apply the font throughout the entire document, click "**OK**" (**CAUTION**: Do *not* click the "All documents based on the XX template?" choice unless you are absolutely certain you want to apply the font to all new documents!).

After you change the default font for the document, the font you have chosen will be used in the body of the document as well as in headers, footers, footnotes, and similar document "substructures."

Applying Fonts to Certain Portions of a Document

To apply a font only to certain portions of a document that you have typed already, select those portions before applying the font.

TIP: In Word 2010, it is possible to select non-continuous areas of text by pressing and holding the **Ctrl key** while selecting the text.

You also have the option of applying a font at the cursor position (before you have typed any text), in which case it will affect all text you type from that point forward—until you change the font again. (Even though font attributes are considered *character* formatting rather than *paragraph* formatting, they are copied to the next paragraph when you press the Enter key.)

Font Attributes

Font Color

As mentioned previously, it's a good idea to choose a specific font color, rather than using the "Automatic" setting, which actually is the default in this version of Word (and in Word 2007). When the "Automatic" setting is in effect, Word determines the font color based on the Style Set and Theme, if any, that currently are in effect. If your fonts appear in a color you don't like, check the font dialog to make sure that the "Font color" drop-down shows your preferred color, rather than "Automatic."

Underline Style

By default, the underline style in Word is set to "(none)" (i.e., the program doesn't apply underlining unless you choose to underline certain text).

When you select contiguous words and apply underlining, Word automatically underlines both the text and the spaces between words. You can, however, change this setting via the **Underline style drop-down** in the **Font dialog** so that the program underlines only the words, not the spaces between words. Note that if you have typed and underlined some text already, you must select that text to change the underline style applied to that text. (Otherwise, the new underline style will go into effect from the cursor position forward.)

The drop-down also offers options for double underlining, as well as a variety of line styles.

Remember, too, that you can toggle underlining on and off by pressing **Ctrl U** (or clicking the Underline button in the Font group on the Home tab); you can apply double underlining by pressing the key combination **Ctrl Shift D** (for **D**ouble?), and you can apply underlining to words but not spaces by pressing **Ctrl Shift W** (for **W**ords?).

All Caps and Small Caps

You can apply the "All Caps" attribute to text by checking that option in the Font dialog; you can do the same with respect to the "Small Caps" attribute (remember to click "OK" to save your settings when you close the dialog). Or you can use keyboard shortcuts. For All Caps, press the key combination **Ctrl Shift A**; for Small Caps, press the key combination **Ctrl Shift K**.

As with other font attributes, these formatting options can be applied to selected text or turned on and applied from the cursor position forward.

The Advanced Tab

The Advanced tab of the Font dialog, formerly called the "Character Spacing" tab, provides options for changing the **scale** of certain characters (i.e., you can make them a certain percentage larger or smaller than "normal," where normal is defined as 100%); the spacing **between characters** (which can be expanded or condensed); the **vertical position** relative to a line of text (in other words, you can raise or lower characters relative to the normal line position, somewhat like superscripting or subscripting), and **kerning** (which has to do with the distance between pairs of fonts). Use these options with care.

Changing Case

To change case in Word 2010, **select** the text and press **Shift F3**. If you press Shift F3 repeatedly, the text will alternate among **UPPER CASE, lower case,** and either **Initial Caps** (which Microsoft refers to as "**Capitalize Each Word**") or **Sentence case** (depending on the context—i.e., whether the selected text includes a period, which will trigger Sentence case).

Note, as well, that there is **a Change Case drop-down** in the top row (toward the right) of the **Font group** on the **Home tab**.

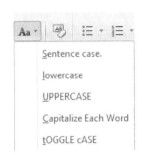

The drop-down includes Sentence case and tOGGLE cASE; the latter is not available via the Shift F3 keystroke.

Inserting Symbols

In Word 2010, the **Symbol dialog** is available from the **Insert tab, Symbols group**. Clicking the **Symbol drop-down** opens the **Most Recently Used (MRU) list**, giving you easy access to the last 20 symbols you used. (When you first install the program, you'll see an MRU list that contains 20 symbols chosen by Microsoft, but the list changes to reflect your personal choices as you insert different symbols.) To open the **Symbol dialog**, click the **More Symbols** label at the bottom of the **MRU list**.

When the dialog opens, you can choose symbol sets by selecting a Font (at the upper left) and/or a sub-set of symbols for that font (at the upper left). To insert a symbol, either double-click it or click once, then click the **Insert button**. After you've done so, the label on the **Cancel** button changes to **Close** so that you can close the dialog box if you wish. The dialog box also has buttons that make it easy to set up a keyboard shortcut for any of the symbols.

Note that there is a second tab to the dialog box (labeled "**Special Characters**") that displays commonly used symbols, such as the paragraph mark (pilcrow) (¶), the section sign (§), the copyright symbol (©), non-breaking hyphens, and em-dashes (among others). Most of those symbols already have keyboard shortcuts assigned to them, but you can add or change the assignments by using the **Shortcut Key…** button at the bottom of the dialog (on both tabs).

There is also an **AutoCorrect** button that allows you to create AutoCorrect entries. For example, when you click on the symbol for ½ and click the AutoCorrect button, Word opens the AutoCorrect dialog with the cursor positioned in the "Replace" box so that when you type 1/2 and press the Spacebar, Word automatically converts the numbers-plus-forward-slash into the smaller fraction. This feature can come in very handy and is worth exploring.

Inserting Footnotes

To create a footnote in Word 2010, do the following:

1.   First, position the cursor in the document where you want to insert a footnote and *either* click the **References tab**, **Footnote group**, **Insert Footnote** (toward the left side of the Ribbon) *or* press **Alt I**, **N**, **N** (think of "N" for "Note").

Word inserts a footnote number code in both the body of the document (the footnote reference number) and the footnote area, and places the cursor in a special footnote editing screen so you can begin typing the note.

2.   To move the cursor back to the document at the point where you left off, *either* double-click the footnote number *or* click the "**Show Notes**" button.

(This button acts as a toggle that moves the cursor between the footnote reference in the document text and the footnote text itself.) **CAUTION:** Whichever method you use, Word normally puts the cursor *to the left of* the footnote number, not to the right of it. Be sure to move the cursor past the footnote number before you continue typing.

3.   Note that you can see the text of the footnote without scrolling down to the footnote screen. Just position the mouse pointer over the footnote reference number in the document and Word will display a pop-up box containing the text of the footnote.

4.   Should you wish to change any of the footnote options, click the arrow in the lower right-hand corner of the Footnotes group (the dialog launcher) to launch the **Footnote and Endnote dialog**.

5.   When the Footnote and Endnote dialog box appears, you can change the placement of the footnotes, the number format, the starting number, and whether numbering is continuous (the norm in legal documents) or restarts on every page or in every section of the document.

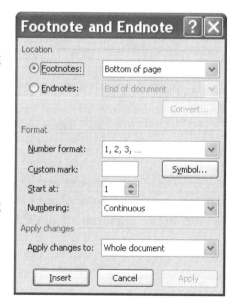

NOTE ALSO: If you switch to **Draft View** (by clicking the **View tab**, **Draft View** or clicking the **Draft View button** in the **Status Bar**), then click the **Show Notes button** in the **References tab**, a footnote bar appears that splits the screen so that you can see both the footnote editing area (sometimes called the **note pane**) and the document at the same time. Switching back to Print Layout view closes the note pane. (There's also an **X** at the far-right side of the note pane that you can click to close it.)

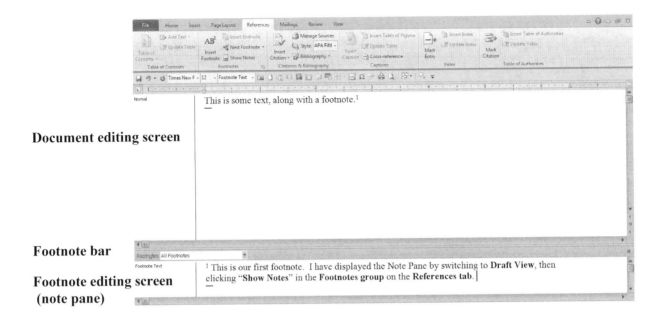

Document editing screen

Footnote bar

Footnote editing screen
(note pane)

Note that you can drag the footnote bar up or down in order to view more or less of the footnote text / document text.

6. To **delete** a footnote, simply select the footnote number *in the text* and press the **Delete key** (or cut it using **Ctrl X** or any method for cutting text that you prefer).

7. To **move** a footnote, simply select the footnote reference number in the text and cut it (with **Ctrl X** or any method you prefer), then position the cursor where you want the number to be and paste it (with **Ctrl V** or any method you prefer). Alternatively, if you are good at using the mouse, you can drag the reference number to a different position.

8. To **edit** a footnote, simply go into the footnote (by clicking in the footnote editing screen *or* by double-clicking the footnote reference number in the document) and make your changes.

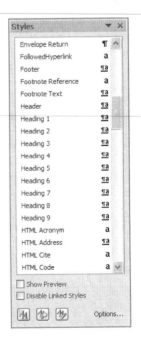

9. If you like, you can **change the appearance** of the footnote (such as the font face or size or the line spacing) by modifying the Footnote Text style. Navigate to the **Home** tab, **Styles** group and click the dialog launcher to open the **Styles Pane**.

10. When the Styles Pane appears, scroll down to **Footnote Text** and **right-click** it. Click **Modify** and, when the **Modify Style dialog** opens, make any changes you desire.

If you want your changes to take effect in all new documents, be sure to follow Step 11 (on the next page).

11.   Before closing the dialog box, click the "**New Documents based on this template**" radio button. That will ensure that the modifications you have made will apply to footnotes in future documents. (If you don't click that radio button, the changes will apply only in the current document.

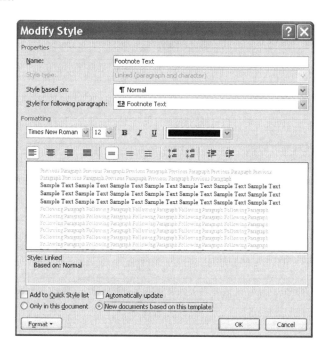

12.   Once you have finished, **OK** out of the dialog and then click the **X** at the upper right-hand side of the Styles Pane to close it.

NOTE: If for some reason you need footnotes to start re-numbering with the value of 1 at some point in your document, you *must insert a section break (next page)* on the page before the page where you want the numbering to re-start. Otherwise, the note numbers will be continuous throughout your document.

SIDEBAR: Changing the Footnote Separator

If you have attempted to change the footnote separator line in Word 2010, you might have noticed that you can't select the line with the mouse. Left-clicking, right-clicking, and double-clicking are exercises in frustration; they move you between the note text and the note reference or they offer a command for opening the footnote options dialog, but they don't let you anywhere near the line itself.

To delete or change the separator line, you need to do the following:

1.   Switch to **Draft view**. (**View tab, Document Views, Draft** or click the **Draft icon** in the **View Mini-Toolbar** in the Status Bar.)

2.   Click the **References tab, Footnotes group, Show Notes**.

3.   In the **Note Pane**, locate the **drop-down** and change it to display "**Footnote Separator**."

Now you can delete the separator if you like and replace it with a different line.

Working With Headers and Footers

As you might know already, headers and footers work very differently in Word from the way they work in WordPerfect. In WordPerfect, it is relatively easy to insert two separate headers and two separate footers (actually, more than two); each can be formatted independently of the other(s).

In Word, although you can create multiple headers and footers, there is a bit of a trick to doing so. First, you have to break the document into *sections*. After you do so, all headers and footers in the various sections are *linked together*, such that if you change one, the others change as well. In order to insert a different header (or footer), you must navigate to the document section where you want to create a new header (or footer) and *break the link* to the header (or footer) in the previous section. I'll provide step-by-step instructions below.

In Word, headers and footers are considered "hidden text" or a separate "layer" of the document. (You'll notice that they appear grayed out when you are working in the document editing screen.) That "hidden" attribute might explain why the Headers and Footers command was found on the View menu in pre-Word 2007 versions of Word.

To insert a header or footer, click the **Insert tab**, **Header & Footer** group, and click either **Header** or **Footer** (as appropriate). A drop-down opens. You can select one of the pre-formatted header or footer styles from the gallery *or* simply click "**Edit Header**" (or "**Edit Footer**") at the bottom of the drop-down. When you do so, Word puts you in the header or footer editing screen, and the Ribbon morphs into a context-sensitive **Header & Footer Tools Design tab** (shown below).

Note that this tab makes it easy to change the header or footer margins (see the **Position group**) and to choose various formatting options.

> **TIP:** There are a couple of quick and easy ways to open a header or footer editing screen. One way is to right-click within the header or footer area of the document—that is, the white space between the text and the top or bottom edge of the page—and click the "Edit Header" or "Edit Footer" pop-up. Another way is to double-click in the header or footer area.

In the screenshot above, in the **Navigation group**, "Go to Footer" is active and "Go to Header" is grayed out because my cursor was in the header editing screen when I took the screenshot. If I had moved my cursor to the footer editing screen, the reverse would be true.

You can move between the header and footer editing screens by either (1) clicking "Go to Header" (or "Go to Footer") in the **Navigation group**, *or* (2) pressing the down arrow or the up arrow on the keyboard as appropriate (down arrow to move from the Header screen to the Footer screen, up arrow to move from the Footer screen to the Header screen).

Headers and footers in Word are pre-configured with a center tab at the 3" mark and a right tab at the 6" mark. That makes it easy to insert a centered page number and a right-aligned file name and path code. However, be aware that if you use L/R margins that differ from the default margins in Word (1.25"), 3" will not be true center and 6" will not be the true right margin. In order to compensate, you'll have to drag the tab markers on the ruler bar in both the header and the footer editing screens.[1]

If all you want to do is insert one header and/or one footer, just type the text you want (and/or insert the codes you want) and click the **Close** button, and you're done.

Using the "Different First Page" Option

But let's say you want to do something more complex. For example, you plan to type a multi-page letter that will go on your firm's letterhead, and you want to insert a header on every page except the first. Word provides a couple of fairly easy ways to accomplish this task.

Method 1:

Assuming you have created at least one page break in your document, click the **Insert tab**, **Header & Footer**, click **Header**, then click **Edit Header** and click to put a check in the "**Different First Page**" box.[2]

---

[1] To change the tab settings in the underlying default template, see the instructions for modifying the default template at page 236.

[2] One caution about using the "Different First Page" option: If you decide to use it to "suppress" page numbering on the first page of pleadings, the page number won't appear, *but neither will the pleading paper*. The reason is that headers and footers are linked together, so using a different first-page footer also wipes out the first-page header. Thankfully, however, there is a workaround for the vanishing pleading-paper problem (see the sidebar on page 276).

Another caution: If you decide to use the "Different First Page" option, be sure to *turn that option off* (i.e., uncheck it) in the other sections of the document. (Make sure your cursor is in the correct header or footer when you disable the option.) Otherwise, *each section* will have both a regular Header/Footer *and* a First Page Header/Footer—which can be very confusing.

Look at the header editing screen and note whether your cursor is in the **First Page Header** or the main **Header**. If necessary, move the cursor from the First Page Header to the Header by clicking the **Next button** in the Navigation group of the Header & Footer Tools tab. To move back to the First Page Header, click the **Previous button**.

If in fact you are working on a multi-page letter, remember to leave the First Page Header blank if the first page will be printed on store-bought paper with pre-printed letterhead.

<u>Method 2</u>:

With your cursor somewhere in the first page of the letter, click the **Page Layout tab** and launch the **Page Setup** dialog. Click the **Layout tab** of the dialog box, then click to check the "**Different First Page**" option and click **OK**. Note that you can select this option even if you haven't yet typed more than one page of text (or created a hard page break in the document by pressing Ctrl Enter), but you must insert at least one additional page before setting up the main header (the one that will go on all pages but page 1).

Once you have done so, click the **Insert tab, Header & Footer group**, and click **Header, Edit Header**. Look at the lower left side of the header editing screen to see if it is labeled **First Page Header** or simply **Header**. If the former, be sure to click the "**Next**" **button** in order to move the cursor to the editing screen for the main **Header**. Then type the text of the header and click the **Close Header and Footer** button.

TIP: An easy way to make space for the letterhead—and ensure that the text on page 1 starts in the right place—is to insert the cursor into the First Page Header and press the Enter key several times. You might have to experiment to get the right amount of space (if necessary, you can measure the letterhead with a ruler and adjust the margin accordingly).

NOTE: If you are creating a more complex document that requires multiple headers and footers, check the Status Bar to see which section your cursor is located in before launching the **Page Setup dialog**.[3] Either enable or disable the "**Different First Page**" option as appropriate, making sure that the "**Apply to:**" **drop-down** at the bottom of the dialog is displaying "**This section.**" Then **OK** out of the dialog and repeat these steps, if necessary, for the other sections of the document.

---

[3] In previous versions of Word, "**Display Section**" was enabled on the Status Bar, making it easy to see which section your cursor was in. (Every blank Word document already comprises one section.) However, Display Section is disabled by default in Word 2010. You can change this setting easily by right-clicking within the Status Bar and clicking to put a checkmark next to "Section," then clicking anywhere outside the pop-up menu to close it.

Creating Multiple Headers and/or Footers

If you want to create more than one header or footer, things become a little more complicated. In Word, in order to have different headers and footers, you must create—and put the separate headers or footers in—different *sections*.

Let's assume you want to create two different footers. First, you need to insert a section break, which will split the document into two sections. Position the cursor at the bottom of the page *immediately before* the page where you want the new footer to go into effect. Then click the **Page Layout tab, Breaks, Section Break, Next Page**.[4]

Next, click the **Insert tab, Header & Footer group, Footer, Edit Footer**. Note which footer editing screen you're in (it should say **Footer -Section 2-** or **Footer -Section 1-**). Note as well whether the words "Same as Previous" appear at the right-hand side of the footer editing screen (just below it).

Make sure your cursor is in the Section 2 footer editing screen and, if the words "Same as Previous" do appear, click the **Link to Previous** button (labeled "Same as Previous" in some earlier versions of Word). Doing so will *UNLINK* the Section 2 footer from the Section 1 footer—allowing you to create two different footers. After breaking the link, you can type the text for the Section 2 footer.

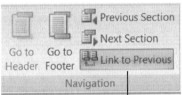

Link to Previous button

NOTE: *This is a critical step*. If you don't turn off "Link to Previous," whatever you type in the Section 1 footer will replace what you have typed in the Section 2 footer—and vice versa.

When you have finished typing the text in the Section 2 footer (and the Section 1 footer), click the **Close Header and Footer** button.

If you want to create another (different) footer, you need to insert another "Next Page" section break on the page before the page where you want the new footer to start. Before you start typing the text for the additional footer, be sure to position your cursor in the footer editing screen for the new section, and then turn off "Link to Previous" by clicking the Link to Previous button.

The same general steps, and precautions, apply to the creation of multiple headers.

---

[4] Assuming you have enabled "Display Section" per the instructions in footnote 3, the Status Bar should indicate that your cursor is in Section 2.

CAUTION: Sometimes Word will change a "Next Page" section break into a "Continuous" section break with no warning and for no apparent reason. If that happens, it can cause problems with your document. (To see which type of section breaks exist in your document, switch from Print Layout view to Draft view by clicking the **View tab, Draft**.[5]) For a solution, see the Sidebar on page 279.

ANOTHER CAUTION: Formatting for each section of your document is contained in the section breaks. (Each section break stores the formatting codes *for the section preceding the break*.) If you accidentally delete a section break, the text will take on the formatting of the *following* section (i.e., it will be affected by the codes within the next section break). So be sure to click the **Undo button** on the **Quick Access Toolbar** (or press **Ctrl Z**) as soon as you realize what happened.

---

[5] **TIP**: You might find it helpful to switch to Draft view whenever you are working with section breaks. In Draft view, section breaks are graphically represented as double lines that extend across the page.

SIDEBAR: Using the "Different First Page" Option

Creating and Editing a Second-Page Header (or Footer) in a Template

Many people use the "Different First Page" option to set up a letterhead template. It's an ideal method because it allows you to have a blank header on the first page (a placeholder for the firm's printed letterhead) and a header starting on page two and continuing on all subsequent pages (if any) that contains the recipient's name, the date of the letter, and a page number code.

In order to create a header for the second section, you'll need to insert a page break in the body of the letter. However, you should delete the page break (and any extra hard returns) in the final draft of the template, since many, if not most, letters are limited to a single page. But what if you need to edit the second header in the template at some later point? Is there an easier way to do so than to create another hard page break that you'll have to remove?

Indeed there is. Just go into the header editing screen (**Insert tab, Header, Edit Header**) and click to *uncheck* "**Different First Page**." When you do, Word should put the cursor in the main (second-page) Header editing screen, as opposed to the First Page Header editing screen. Make any desired changes, then click to *check* "Different First Page," close out of the Header editing screen, save the template, and close it.[1]

Note that this principle works exactly the same way with respect to setting up and editing a pleading footer where the page number is "suppressed" on (or deleted from) the caption page but not on the other pages of the document.

How to Prevent the Pleading Paper Lines From Disappearing

As discussed in footnote 2 on page 272, using the "Different First Page" option in a pleading can cause the pleading lines and numbers to disappear. If you're concerned about that possibility, go into the header editing screen on the first page of the document, display the non-printing characters (by pressing Ctrl Shift * [asterisk] or clicking the paragraph symbol at the top center of the Home tab), and copy the very first paragraph symbol. That symbol contains the formatting codes for the header, including the graphics (pleading lines and numbering).

Next, click the "Different First Page" option. Don't panic if the pleading paper disappears. Instead, simply paste the paragraph symbol at the top of the first-page header. The pleading paper should come back. Once it does, you should be able to create a first-page footer with a "suppressed" page number (i.e., a placeholder instead of a page number code) and a different footer for the second and following pages that has a page number code above the horizontal line.

---

[1] **CAUTION:** When "Different First Page" is checked, sometimes the main header or footer editing screen becomes hidden. This behavior can be confusing. If you are having trouble finding the main header or footer editing screen, try *unchecking* "Different First Page"—if only temporarily. The hidden header or footer editing screen should reappear.

SIDEBAR: Modifying the Footer Style

To modify the Footer style in order to change the built-in tab stops so that they will work with pleadings, as suggested elsewhere (see page 282), locate the **Styles group** on the **Home tab** and **click the dialog launcher**. The **Styles Pane** should open.

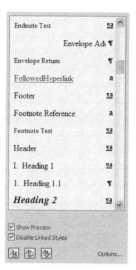

Find and select the **Footer style** in the Styles list, then either (1) position the cursor within the name of the style, *right*-click and click the "**Modify**" button, *or* (2) click the **drop-down arrow** —the paragraph symbol and letter "a" turn into a drop-down when you hold the mouse over the style name—and then click "**Modify**." The **Modify Style dialog** should open.

Click the **"Format" button** in the lower left corner of the **Modify Style dialog**, then click **"Tabs."** When the Tabs dialog appears, type the desired number for a center tab (probably 3.25") in the "**Tab stop position**" **box**, make sure the **Alignment** is set to Center and **Leader** is set to None, and click **"Set."** Then click the 6" setting, type 6.5 in the Tab stop position box, and click **"Set."** Finally, click the 3" setting (if any) and click **"Clear,"** click the 6" setting (if any) and click **"Clear,"** then click **"OK."**

Before clicking "OK" a second time, be sure to click the **"New documents based on this template"** radio button, or the changes will take effect *only* in the current document.

WHERE DID IT GO? Section Breaks

Section breaks, located on the Insert menu in versions of Word prior to Word 2007, have been moved to the **Page Layout tab.** Specifically, they are available from the **Breaks drop-down** at the top right-hand corner of the **Page Setup group**.

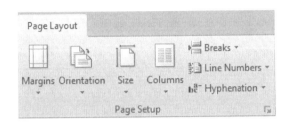
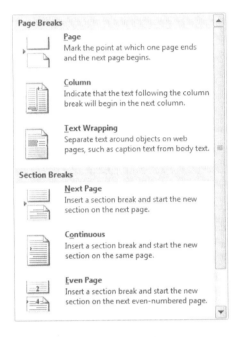

You can add a page break from the Breaks drop-down in the Page Setup group, too. In addition, there is a **Page Break** command on the **Insert tab**, under **Pages**.

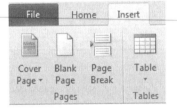

Alternatively, you can insert a page break ahead of the paragraph your cursor is in (effectively bumping the paragraph to the next page) by launching the **Paragraph dialog**, clicking the **Line and Page Breaks tab**, and clicking the "**Page break before**" **checkbox**. Or you can simply press **Ctrl Enter** to insert a page break at the cursor position.

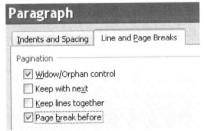

SIDEBAR: The Curious Case of the Mutating Section Breaks

Perhaps the most confounding aspect of working with section breaks is their tendency to mutate spontaneously from one type of break to another (for instance, from a "next page" break to a "continuous" break), which can create all sorts of headaches. Trying to delete the offending section break often makes things worse; you might find that section breaks that had been formatted correctly suddenly go bad, too.

::::::::::::::::::Section Break (Next Page)::::::::::::::::::

::::::::::::::::::Section Break (Next Page)::::::::::::::::::

::::::::::::::::::Section Break (Continuous)::::::::::::::::::

::::::::::::::::::Section Break (Next Page)::::::::::::::::::

What makes things particularly confusing is that each section break stores the formatting for the document section that *precedes* it. So when you delete a section break, the text ahead of it takes on the formatting of the section that comes immediately *after*.[1]

But, complicating the situation further, the information that determines each section break's *type*—that is, whether an individual section break is a "Next Page" or "Continuous" break—actually is stored in the section *after* that specific break. (***Huh?***)

What that means is that when you delete a section break, the prior section break takes on the characteristics of the one you deleted. (In other words, although it is completely counter-intuitive, deleting a rogue "Continuous" section break doesn't help matters because it ***turns the previous break into a "Continuous" section break***.) Are you tearing your hair out yet?

Not to worry. Here's a workaround:

- First, switch to **Draft view** so that the section breaks in the document are easier to see / identify.

- Suppress your impulse to delete the misbehaving section break. Instead, put your cursor on—or, better yet, select—the ***next*** section break.[2]

---

[1] In this regard, section breaks are similar to paragraph marks, which store the formatting information for the preceding text.

[2] Alternatively, you can double-click the section break, which will open the Page Setup dialog.

- Open the **Page** Setup **dialog**, click the **Layout tab**, and click to open the **Section start drop-down**.

Page Setup dialog

- Select the type of section break you want, which probably is "**New page**."

- Make sure that choice is displayed, then click **OK**.

The "bad" section break should change to reflect your "Section start" choice. Problem solved!

Using Left, Center, and Right Alignment on One Line

WordPerfect's text-stream formatting makes it easy to put left-aligned, centered, and right-aligned text on the same line. In Word, this task is complicated by the fact that Word considers all text part of a paragraph—and, not surprisingly, the program can't figure out how to format one paragraph so that it uses three different types of justification.

Fortunately, there are a few reasonably good workarounds available. To left-justify, center-justify, and right-justify text on the same line in Word, do one of the following:

1. Use Word's "**Click and Type**" feature (similar to the Shadow Cursor in WordPerfect): Type some text at the left margin, then slide the mouse pointer to the right until you see an I-beam with a "shadow" that looks like several centered lines. **Double-click** to position the cursor, and then type the text you want centered.

    Then slide the mouse pointer farther to the right until you see an I-beam with a "shadow" that consists of lines at the left side of the I-beam. **Double-click**, then type the text you want right-justified.[1]

2. Alternatively, use the Tab dialog or the horizontal Ruler to set a center tab and a right tab at appropriate intervals. If you are using 1" left and right margins, the center tab should be at approximately 3.25" and the right tab at approximately 6.5". If you are using the Ruler, you might have to position the right tab shy of the 6.5" mark and then drag it over. (**NOTE**: It's best to set the tabs *before* you begin typing; that way, your settings will apply to the entire document.)

    A corollary to this tip: Headers and footers in Word are automatically configured with a center tab and a right tab, so all you need to do to center and/or right-align text in a header or footer is press the Tab key the appropriate number of times.

    CAUTION: The header/footer tab settings are based on Word's default margin settings of 1.25" left and 1.25" right. If you change the L/R margin settings (for a pleading) to 1.5" and .5", the header/footer tab settings will **not** adjust automatically—even if you make the new L/R margin settings the default for new documents. Thus, you could end up with a situation in which text in the document uses a center point of (approximately) 3.25", whereas text in the footer (incorrectly) uses a center point of 3".

---

[1] This feature must be enabled in the Word Options. It is enabled by default, but if it doesn't appear to be working, click the **File tab, Options, Advanced**, and click to check "**Enable click and type**." Note that when you double-click to position the cursor at the center , Word inserts a center tab at that position; when you do the same at the right margin, Word inserts a right tab.

One possible workaround is to use alignment tabs, which are positioned relative to the page margins (and automatically adjust if you change the margins). For an extended discussion of this feature, see the section starting on page 262. Remember that alignment tabs work only in .docx files (and other Open Office XML file types).

It's easy to change the tab settings within headers and footers by turning on the Ruler and dragging the tab markers—if you do, be sure to change the settings in both the header(s) and the footer(s)—but if you want to use the new tab settings in all future documents, you must either (1) modify the Footer style and save the modified style to the template or (2) modify the default template.

3.   Create a three-column table and use different justification in the three cells. (**NOTE**: You will have to turn off the table border to prevent it from printing along with the text. To do so, insert your cursor into a table, then click the **Borders drop-down arrow** at the right side of the **Table Styles group** and click **No Borders**.)

Creating Bulleted Lists

You can created a bulleted list in Word 2010 by inserting a bullet first or by typing text first and then applying bullets to the text.

Perhaps the easiest way is simply to click the **Bullets button** in the **Paragraph group** on the **Home tab** and then type some text. When you press the **Enter key**, Word inserts another bullet of the same type and with the same indentation so that you can type another bulleted paragraph. To end the bulleted list, click the **Bullets button** again.

Alternatively, you can type some text first and then click the **Bullets button**. To apply bullets to several consecutive paragraphs, **select the paragraphs** and then click the **Bullets button**.

If you wish, you can insert bullets in a couple of other ways:

- By pressing **Ctrl Shift L**; or
- If Automatic Bulleted Lists has been enabled, by **typing an asterisk** and pressing either the **Spacebar** *or* the **Tab key**

To enable or disable Automatic Bulleted Lists, click the **File tab**, **Options**, **Proofing**, **AutoCorrect Options**, and click the **AutoFormat As You Type tab**.

Creating a Multilevel Bulleted List

After you have inserted a bullet and typed some text (or applied a bullet to existing text), you can change the level of the bulleted paragraph by doing any of the following:

- pressing **Alt Shift** → (to "demote" the list level of the paragraph)[1]; or
- **right-clicking** within the paragraph, clicking **Numbering**, **Change List Level**, and clicking on one of the **list level icons**; or
- opening the **Bullets drop-down**, choosing **Change List Level**, and clicking on one of the **list level icons**.

Changing the Indentation of the Bulleted List

By default, the first level of Word's built-in bulleted lists indents the bullet by .25" and begins the text at .5". You can change the indentation of any list level by **right-clicking**

---

[1] For any level of the list other than the first one, you can press **Alt Shift** ← to "promote" the paragraph to a higher level. Note that if "**Set left- and first-indent with tabs and backspaces**" is enabled, you can use the **Tab key** to demote a level and **Shift Tab** to promote a level. To check or change this setting, click the **File tab**, **Options**, **Proofing**, **AutoCorrect Options**, **AutoFormat As You Type tab**.

somewhere within a paragraph, choosing **Adjust List Indents**, changing the indentation of the bullet and/or the text, then clicking **OK**. Note that doing so will change the indentation of all paragraphs in the current list that are at that level, but will not affect other bulleted lists in your document.

One way to change the indentation of those lists is to use the **Format Painter** (the **paintbrush icon** in the **Clipboard group** on the **Home tab**). With your cursor somewhere within one of the paragraphs whose indentation you wish to copy, **double-click the Format Painter**, then click on **every bulleted paragraph** that you want to adopt the indentation of the "model" paragraph. Be sure to click the Format Painter again to turn it off.

Changing the Bullet Size

It can be somewhat tricky to change the bullet size without also changing the size of the text in a bulleted paragraph.

The trick is to turn on **Show Nonprinting Characters** (by clicking the **paragraph symbol**/pilcrow [¶] in the **Paragraph group** or by pressing **Ctrl Shift *** (asterisk—the asterisk is above the number 8 at the top of the keyboard), then **select the paragraph symbol** at the end of the paragraph and use any method you like to decrease or increase the font size. (You might find it helpful to insert a space between the last character in the paragraph and the paragraph symbol at the end.) **NOTE:** *Changing the size of the paragraph symbol changes the size of the bullet but not the size of the text*.

After you change the size of the bullet in one paragraph, you should be able to copy the formatting by using the Format Painter. However, in my tests I was unable to get that to work. What *did* work was **copying the paragraph symbol** from a "successful" paragraph and **pasting it** at the end of a paragraph whose formatting I wanted to change.

Changing the Bullet Character

To change the appearance of a bullet, insert the cursor into a paragraph whose bullet you wish to modify, then open the **Bullets drop-down** and select a bullet from the gallery.

If none of the existing choices appeals to you, click **Define New Bullet**. The **Define New Bullet dialog** will enable you to browse through various font sets to locate another symbol or to browse through a picture gallery and find an image that you can use for your bullet.

Multiple Bulleted Lists and Nested Lists

Word allows you to insert different bulleted lists in different parts of your document *and/or* to nest various types of lists (up to nine separate lists) inside one another.

Probably the easiest way to create nested lists is to type the text, select one section at a time, and then apply bullet and/or numbering formatting to that section. You can then format the remaining sections of the nested list in similar fashion.

WHERE DID IT GO? Watermark

The Watermark feature is now found on the **Page Layout tab** in the **Page Background group**. When you click the drop-down, you have the option of using one of the built-in watermarks available in the gallery (be sure to scroll down to see all of them) or creating your own customized watermark.

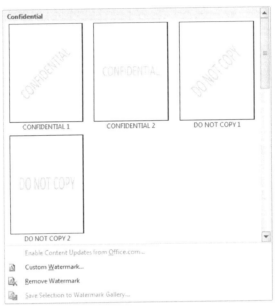

If you choose to create a custom watermark, a dialog opens that allows you to insert text or a picture. The Text watermark drop-down is pre-populated with some slogans you can use, but you can type your own words (as I've done in the example below). You can set the font, size, color, and layout (diagonal or horizontal) from the dialog. You might have to change the color—by default, it's set to a very light shade of gray—in order to see the watermark.

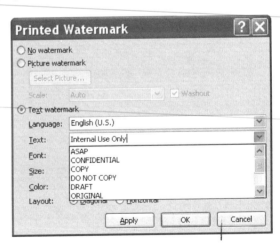

Note that the Watermark drop-down features a "**Remove Watermark**" option. It also has an option to save your custom watermark to the gallery. (That option is grayed out until you go into the Header editing screen and use Crtl A to select the watermark.)

Outlining

Getting Started

To start an outline from scratch or apply an outline to an existing document in Word 2010, you need to switch to **Outline view**. You can do so either from the **View tab** or from the **View buttons** toward the right side of the Status Bar. As soon as you switch to Outline view, the context-sensitive **Outlining tab** appears, allowing you to apply the Outline Tools as you work.

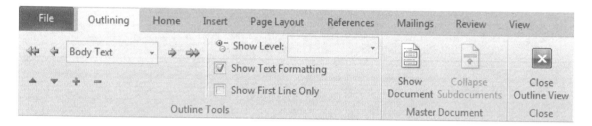

In Outline view, all paragraphs are assigned an outline level. There are nine levels, plus "body text" (for simple text that is not intended to be part of a heading).[1] First-level paragraphs appear at the left margin, and each lower or subordinate level is indented one additional tab stop.

Gray circles appear next to each paragraph you type, including body text. If you like, you can move a paragraph up or down in the outline by dragging the gray circle, or you can use normal cut-and-paste operations.

Word's Heading Styles

When you start typing an outline from scratch, Word automatically applies a Heading 1 style to the text. Unless you have customized the heading styles to conform to your firm's standards, Word uses built-in heading styles based on its default "Theme." There are nine built-in heading levels in all.

Because the built-in styles aren't terribly useful as Microsoft has formatted them, you can —and probably should—modify them. (As noted throughout the book, you must take special steps to ensure that the changes you make to styles of any kind are available for all future documents, and not merely in the document that is on your screen when you modify the styles. By default, changes to styles are saved *only* in the document where you make the changes.) You can modify them before you begin working on an outline or at a later time. (To modify a style, see the instructions starting on page 352.)

---

[1] In my tests with a blank document, Word automatically inserted a Heading 1 style when I switched to Outline View, which is logical behavior under the circumstances.

Changing the Heading Levels

When you finish typing one paragraph and press the Enter key to begin another one, the following paragraph inherits the heading level of the previous one. To change the heading level, you can do any of the following:

- Press the **Tab key** to "demote" a paragraph (i.e., make it a lower or subordinate level) or press **Shift Tab** to "promote" a paragraph (make it a higher level)[2]

- Press **Alt Shift** → to demote a paragraph or **Alt Shift** ← to promote a paragraph

- Press the "**demote**" or "**promote**" button (represented by single green arrows) in the Outline Tools group

- Press the **demote** or **promote** button in the Paragraph group

- Grab a paragraph by the **gray circle** to its left and drag it to the left or right

Needless to say, you will want some of the paragraphs you type to appear as plain text rather than as headings. To designate paragraphs as "body text" rather than as headings, just click the right-pointing **double green arrow** at the top of the Outline tools ("Demote to body text") *or*, with your cursor somewhere within the paragraph, use the drop-down and select "**Body Text**."

Showing Levels

On the right side of the Outline Tools group, there is a drop-down list that allows you to show only certain levels of the outline (i.e., collapse the outline) or show all levels (expand the outline). If your outline consists of, say, seven levels but you wish to display only the first three levels, select Level 3 in the drop-down.

Relationships Among Outline Level Paragraphs; Collapsing and Expanding Selected Paragraph Groups Within the Outline

A plus in the gray circle next to a paragraph in an outline indicates that it has sub-paragraphs. The sub-paragraphs can consist of lower-level outline paragraphs or of body text.

---

[2] Note that the Tab key and Shift Tab work in Outline view to demote and promote paragraphs, even if you have not enabled the "set left- and first-indent with tabs and backspaces" function in the Word Options (**File tab**, **Options**, **Proofing**, **AutoCorrect Options**, **AutoFormat as You Type**). Note also that if you wish to insert an actual Tab while you are working in Outline view, you need to use *Ctrl Tab* (the key combination in Word for a "hard tab").

A minus in the gray circle next to a paragraph in an outline indicates that it does not have any sub-paragraphs. In other words, it stands alone.

In the "Showing Levels" section, you learned how to display only certain outline level paragraphs, such as the first three levels. You also have the option of collapsing or expanding only certain paragraph groups within the outline. For example, let's say one section of your outline contains a level 3 paragraph followed by four level 4 paragraphs, and you want to see only the level 3 paragraph in that particular section. To collapse that group (sometimes called an "outline family") so that you see only the level 3 paragraph, click the gray circle to the left of the level 3 paragraph, then click the minus sign in the Outline Tools group. That section should collapse so that only the higher-level paragraph is displayed. To expand a group or family of paragraphs again, click the plus sign in the Outline Tools group.

The plus and minus signs expand or collapse paragraph groups ("families")

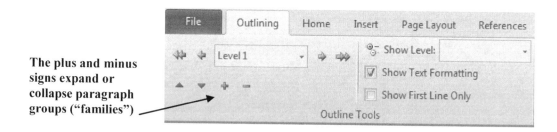

Show First Line Only

This option is similar to the option to collapse the outline (or to collapse certain paragraph groups or families within the outline), except that it displays only the first *line* of each paragraph in the outline, as opposed to only certain paragraphs.

Show Text Formatting

If this option is checked—which it is by default—Word will show the character formatting that has been applied to the paragraphs (font face, font size, bolding, underlining, etc.). If you want to see plain text only, uncheck that option. **CAUTION**: With the option unchecked, you might not realize that incorrect formatting has been applied to one or more headings in your document.

Applying a Multilevel List to an Outline

Should you wish to apply a multilevel list to an outline, rather than using numbering linked to headings, just select the entire outline, then switch to the **Home tab**, click the **Multilevel list button**, and click the image of a list in the library that contains the number scheme you want to use.

A Few Tips About Outlines

1. There is a relatively easy way to display the paragraph styles while in Outline view. Click the **File tab**, **Options**, then click **Advanced**. Scroll down about halfway to **Display**, and look for "**Style area pane width in Draft and Outline views**." Type a number in the box that is **at least 1"**, then **OK** out of the Word Options dialog.

2. In Word 2007, there was a glitch that made it impossible to print a condensed outline. If you attempted to do so, Word printed the outline in its expanded form. I have tested printing a condensed outline in Word 2010 and, although the print preview does display the expanded outline, the print output is condensed. So the bug appears to have been fixed.

3. You can apply an outline level to *any* paragraph, whether the paragraph consists of plain text or has had a style (other than one of the nine heading styles) applied to it. Doing so will ensure that the paragraph appears in the Table of Contents at the outline level you designate. To apply an outline level, (a) when your document is displayed in Outline View, insert your cursor anywhere within the paragraph and then either use the **level drop-down** in the **Outline Tools group**; *or* (b) when the document is displayed in any view other than Outline View, open the **Paragraph dialog** and select a level from the **Outline level drop-down** on the **Indents and Spacing tab**. Then **OK** out of the dialog. (**NOTE**: You can't open the Paragraph dialog while you are in Outline view.)

The Navigation Pane

On the **View tab**, in the **Show group**, there is a checkbox for the **Navigation Pane**. As discussed in detail in the section starting on page 79, when you click to put a check in the box, Word displays a pane at the left side of the screen where you can view an outline of your document (assuming that you have applied headings or outline levels to one or more paragraphs in the document). If you like, you can reorganize your document by moving headings around directly from within the Navigation Pane. This feature can be useful in any document that uses heading styles, not merely in outlines.

Clicking a particular heading in the Navigation Pane moves the cursor to that heading within the document.

To close the Navigation Pane, just click the "X" in the upper right-hand corner of the pane or press the Esc key.

Using Paste Special

When you need to move or copy text but you don't want to retain its formatting, use Paste Special, Unformatted Text rather than the regular Paste command. In Word 2010, you can find the Paste Special command at the left side of the **Home tab** in the **Clipboard group**. (Alternatively, **Ctrl Alt V** opens the Paste Special dialog.) In most instances, you'll choose Unformatted Text so that whatever you are pasting takes on the formatting of the destination document (or portion of a document). Note that this feature is particularly useful if you need to copy and paste text from a WordPerfect document or from the Internet into a Word doc.

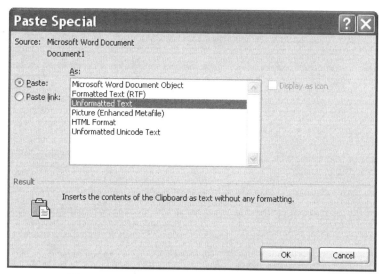

Choose the "Unformatted Text" Option

A couple of other pasting tips:

In recent versions of Word, when you paste text that you have copied or cut, a **Paste Options button** pops up.  Clicking the arrow opens a drop-down menu where you can choose among different options for how the text will be pasted, as shown in the screenshot below this paragraph.

The exact drop-down you will see depends on the type of object you have copied—plain text, images, part of a list, and so forth. For a detailed discussion of the different options available, see the lengthy section about the new paste options in Word 2010 starting on page 123.

Note that clicking "**Set Default Paste…**" opens the **Word Options** to the **Advanced** category.   Under **Cut, copy, and paste**, you can change the way that pasting operations work in various situations: when you paste within the same document, when you paste between documents, when you paste between two documents containing a style that has the same name but applies different formatting, when you paste from other programs (such as WordPerfect or the Internet), and so on.

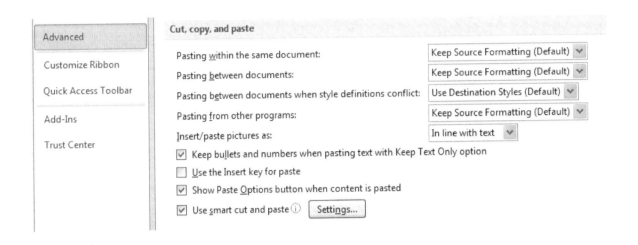

Of course, you can modify these settings at any time (by clicking the **File tab**, **Options**, **Advanced**, **Cut, copy and paste**), not only when the Paste Options button appears.

One of the nicest enhancements to Word 2010 is that you can create a keyboard shortcut for Paste Special, Unformatted (called "**Paste and Keep Text Only**"). For instructions, see the section starting on page 131.

Creating a Custom Dictionary

When Word's spell-checker stumbles on a word that it doesn't recognize—such as parol, interpleader, or Trustor—you can click the **"Add to Dictionary" button**, and the word will be incorporated into the program's built-in dictionary, a file called "Custom.dic."

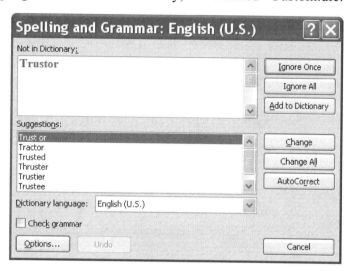

While it can be useful to add words to the dictionary "on the fly," you also have the option of creating one or more custom dictionaries—a legal dictionary, a medical dictionary, an architectural dictionary, or even a client-specific dictionary—and adding words without running a spell-check.

There are a couple of ways to create a custom dictionary. You can do so from within the Speller (by clicking the **Options** button) or by clicking the **File tab**, **Options**, **Proofing**. Either method will take you into the Proofing category of the Word Options. Once there, navigate to the section labeled "**When correcting spelling in Microsoft Office programs**."

Before proceeding, make sure the "Suggest from main dictionary only" option is **not** checked. Otherwise, the Speller will suggest alternative words based only on the contents of the main dictionary, not on any custom dictionaries you set up. Next, click the "**Custom Dictionaries...**" button.

A **Custom Dictionaries dialog** will open (see the screenshot on the next page).

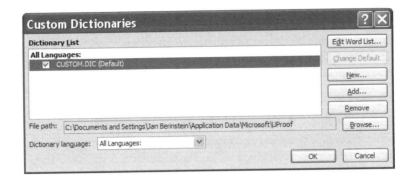

From this very handy dialog, you can edit the existing word list (to add words, delete and retype misspelled words that have been added accidentally, and/or delete words that don't belong in the dictionary). Alternatively, you can create a new dictionary by clicking the "**New…**" **button**.

When you click "New," a "**Create Custom Dictionary**" **dialog** opens. Type a name for your dictionary, such as "Legal" or "Engineering" (or some other concise description), then click "**Save**." Word automatically adds the ".dic" extension to the file name.

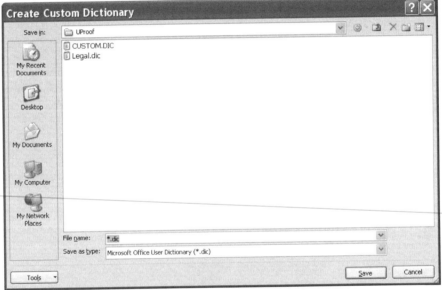

Create Custom Dictionary Dialog

The new dictionary will be added to the dictionary list.

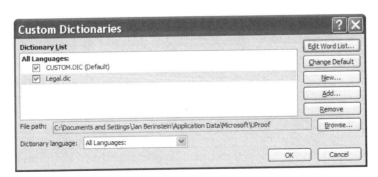

The "Checked" Dictionaries and the Default Dictionary

You will note that some dictionaries in the list are checked, and one is marked as the default. What is the significance of those designations?

Think of the "*checked*" dictionaries as *active*. What that means is that the Spell-Checker compares the words in your document against the content of all of the dictionaries that are checked. (You can uncheck one or more dictionaries if you don't want the Speller to look there).

The *default* dictionary is the one to which the Speller adds words when you click the "**Add**" **button** during a spell-check. If you wish, you can change the default dictionary from the "Custom Dictionaries" dialog. To do so, click the dictionary you want to use as the default, then click the "**Change Default**" **button**. The dictionary will move to the top of the list, with "**(Default)**" after its name. (The "Change Default button" then becomes inactive until you click a dictionary name again.)

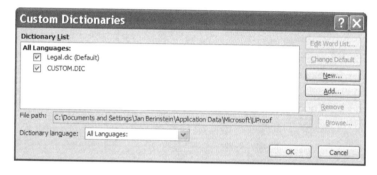

Adding or Deleting Words

It's easy to edit a custom dictionary from this dialog. First, click to select the dictionary, then click "**Edit Word List.**" When the dictionary dialog opens, you can click in the "Word(s):" box and type a new word, then click "**Add**" (the "Add" button is grayed out until you type a word). You also have the option of deleting one word, or even all of the words in the dictionary (but be careful not to click the "Delete all" button unless that's your intention). Be sure to click "**OK**" to save your changes.

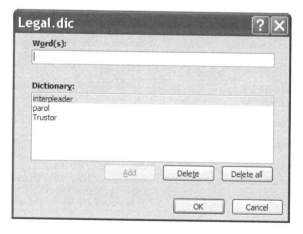
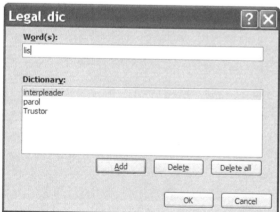

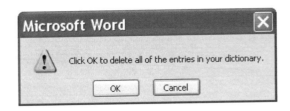

This Warning Appears if You Click "Delete All Entries"

Note that it can be advantageous to add one word at a time, rather than an entire phrase, such as "lis pendens." If you add a phrase, the Spell-Checker will recognize the phrase but not the individual words that comprise the phrase—unless you add them separately. (If the words are always used as part of the phrase, that shouldn't be problematic, but if any of the words ever appear alone, the speller will flag them.)

You can add up to 5,000 words to each custom dictionary. Individual words can consist of one to 64 characters.

Editing the Word List Directly

It is possible to edit the word list for a particular dictionary directly, since word lists are plain-text files. Exit from Word and launch **Windows Explorer**, navigate to the folder where the custom dictionaries are stored,[1] and **right-click the dictionary** you want to edit.

When the pop-up menu appears, choose "**Open with...**" and select **Notepad**. When the dictionary opens, type one word per line, then click the **File menu**, **Save**. (You don't need to use "Save As" to give the file a new name; in fact, it's probably best not to.)

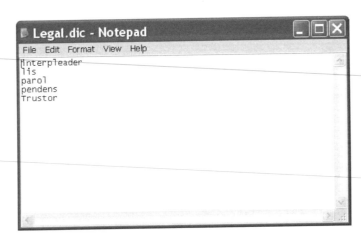

---

[1] In Windows XP, the location is:
C:\Documents and Settings\<User Name>\Application Data\Microsoft\UProof

In Windows Vista and Windows 7, the location is:
C:\Users\<User Name>\AppData\Roaming\Microsoft\UProof

Close the edited dictionary file either by clicking the red "**X**" in the upper right-hand corner or by clicking the **File menu**, **Exit**.

Running the Spell-Checker

To run the Spell-Checker, either:

- Click the "**Spelling & Grammar**" **button** in the **Proofing group** at the left side of the **Review tab**; or

- Press **F7**.

To add a word to the default dictionary while using the Speller, click the "**Add to Dictionary**" button.

WHERE DID IT GO? Spell-Checker

The **Spelling & Grammar** command has been moved to the left-hand side of the **Review tab,** in the **Proofing group**.

Note that you still can use the **F7** keystroke to start the **Spell-Checker**, as in previous versions of Word.

QUICK TIP: Using the Grammar Checker
to Change Spaces Between Sentences

A useful but little-known feature of Word is that the Grammar Checker can be configured to change the number of spaces between sentences (from two to one, if you are an old-school journalist like me, or from one to two, if you subscribe to a more modern theory about typography).

To adjust this setting, click the **File tab, Options, Proofing**. In the section labeled **"When correcting spelling and grammar in Word,"** click the **"Settings..." button**. (It doesn't matter whether the "Writing Style" drop-down is set to "Grammar & Style" or "Grammar Only." If the former is selected, the grammar-checker will flag stylistic errors in your document—or, at least, items that conflict with certain rules you apply—whereas if the latter is selected, the utility will look only for grammatical mistakes.)

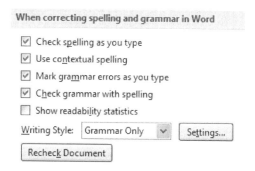

When you click the "Settings" button, a **"Grammar Settings" dialog** will open. In the top portion, under "Grammar and style options," there is a section labeled "Require" where you can configure the utility to review your document to make sure that (1) a comma has been inserted before the last item in a list, (2) punctuation for a quote has been placed within quotation marks, and/or (3) the number of spaces between sentences matches your preference (whether two spaces or one). (If you are indifferent about one or more of those items, you can instruct the utility not to check it.)

NOTE: The "**Check Grammar with spelling**" option must be enabled (checked) in order for this aspect of the feature to work. As long as that option is enabled, the Grammar Checker will run when you perform a spell check.

To run a grammar / spelling check, either (1) click the **Review tab**, then click the **Spell Check button** in the **Proofing group** at the left side of the Ribbon or (2) press **F7**. The utility will go through the document, looking for misspelled words and also for items that violate the grammatical and stylistic rules you've checked in the Word Options.

When it encounters an ostensible violation, a **Spelling and Grammar dialog** will pop up, identifying the problem (in the screenshot below, a label toward the top of the dialog indicates that the issue is "**Spaces between Sentences**") and prompting you to choose a course of action. You can ignore the rule once, ignore the rule throughout the document, change the item to conform with the rule, or click an "**Explain**" button to find out why the utility singled out that particular item.

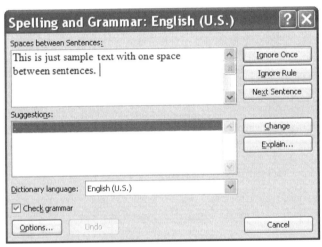

Clicking "Explain" opens Word Help to a page with more information about the rule.

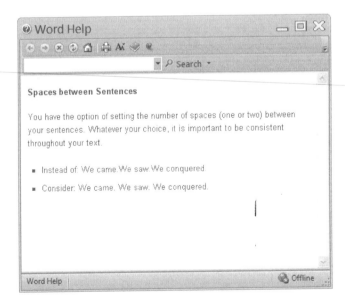

300

Note that the Grammar Checker will stop and prompt you each time it encounters what it considers to be a rule violation (unless you click "Ignore rule," in which case it won't give you the opportunity to correct any remaining errors).

Working Smarter and Faster / Automating Word

Saving Time by Using Keyboard Shortcuts

This section of the book deals with features that can help you get your work done, and out the door, more efficiently and with fewer hassles. In particular, it covers keyboard shortcuts—which not only save time because you don't have to keep reaching for the mouse to perform common tasks, but also make it easier to find features that were moved when Microsoft introduced the new interface. It also explains how to automate your documents with field codes, simple macros, Quick Parts, and styles.

Keyboard Shortcuts

As a legal word processor (and a fast typist—I can bang out documents at 85-95 wpm when I'm really cranking), I rely heavily on keyboard shortcuts. They allow me to work much more quickly and efficiently than if I were using the mouse to click my way around the Ribbon, tabs, groups, icons, and dialog boxes. Every time I take my hands off the keyboard, my productivity drops. I couldn't tell you precisely how much, though I remember reading efficiency studies years ago that suggested that people who use keyboard shortcuts shave 20% to 40% off their time. That sounds about right to me.

In any case, fast typists will be pleased to know that Word offers lots of built-in keyboard shortcuts. And it's easy to set up additional shortcuts of your own.

For Users of Prior Versions of Word

Keyboard shortcuts also come in handy because the interface has changed so drastically in Word 2010. Without the familiar menus and toolbars, you might feel a little lost trying to determine where a particular feature went. Luckily, one of the best ways to invoke dialog boxes and carry out commands in Word is with keystrokes. Most of the shortcuts you learned for prior versions of Word still work in Word 2010 (and if you never learned them, you'll be glad to learn of them now).

Note, too, that you can use most of the familiar keyboard shortcuts to work with "File" commands (now accessible from the **File tab**). So, for example, **Alt F** opens the drop-down equivalent of the File menu; **Alt F, S** is Save; **Alt F, A** is Save As; **Alt F, C** is Close; **Alt F, O** is Open (as is **Ctrl O**); **Alt F, P** is Print, as is **Ctrl P** (both key combinations open Print Place); **Alt F, X** is Exit (i.e., from Word).

And the Paragraph dialog, which will come to be an old friend, can be opened from just about anywhere in the program by pressing **Alt O, P**. Who needs to remember which tab(s) it's on?

For WordPerfect Users

For the most part, Word's standard keyboard shortcuts differ from those you might be accustomed to in WordPerfect. The good news is that many of them are simple to remember because they are mnemonic (i.e., they use the Ctrl key plus a letter of the alphabet that is the first letter of the command, such as Ctrl P for Print). Others will become second nature because you will use them every day.

Should you wish to assign familiar WordPerfect keyboard shortcuts to Word functions, be sure to read the next section, "Creating Your Own Keyboard Shortcuts."

All Manner of Shortcuts

I have provided lists of keyboard shortcuts that are organized in a few different ways. The first list represents many commands that make use of the Ctrl key plus a letter or number; the second offers keyboard commands that use various function keys; the third is organized by feature or function; and the fourth contains keyboard shortcuts for access to tabs of the Ribbon and to dialog boxes. The lists aren't exhaustive, and there is some overlap. My intention and hope in including these lists is that they will familiarize you with the keyboard shortcuts you will use most often.

Document Automation

It's surprising to me how many people still type every element of their documents from scratch: date codes, paragraph numbers, the file name and path, and so on. One of the benefits of using a sophisticated word processing program such as Word 2010 is that it allows you to automate these rather tedious tasks, which means (1) you don't have to put in as much time; and (2) you don't have to remember to update various parts of the document (dates, paragraph numbers) manually during each work session. In addition, if everyone in your firm has had at least a modicum of training in basic document automation, you're less likely to experience problems such as duplicate paragraph numbers (something I used to see at various law firms where some of the secretaries were using automatic numbering and some were not).

Some people who hear the word "macro" might be intimidated by the thought that they have to create, or figure out how to use, complicated scripts and subroutines. In reality, while many brave souls do venture into sophisticated macro coding that involves Visual Basic for Applications (VBA), it's not necessary to do so.[1] For one thing, it's easy to create simple macros by recording keystrokes. I've provided an example to get you started. For another thing, you can set up boilerplate, such as signature blocks, by using a feature formerly known as AutoText and now called Quick Parts. Essentially, you copy some boilerplate text and assign a short name (abbreviation), then invoke the boilerplate by typing the name and pressing F3. What could be easier?

Likewise, field codes and styles are not as daunting as you might think. As with macros and Quick Parts, I will introduce you gently to those forms of document automation. You can start with the basics and then explore more advanced functionality as your time and temperament permit.

Once you start using these time-saving features, you'll probably wonder how you managed without them.

---

[1] I admire, but am not among, those VBA wizards.

Creating Your Own Keyboard Shortcuts

Setting up your own keyboard shortcuts for nearly any function is a relatively simple matter.

First, do one of the following:

(1)   click the **File tab**, **Options**, **Customize Ribbon**; or

(2)   right-click the **Quick Access Toolbar** (or the **Ribbon**), then click **Customize the Ribbon**.

Next, scroll to the bottom of the **Word Options dialog** and click the **Keyboard Shortcuts: Customize button**. You'll see the **Customize Keyboard dialog** (screenshot below).

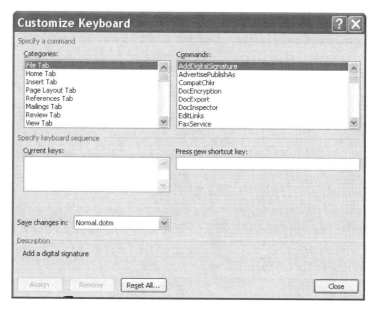

Customize Keyboard dialog

Note the **Categories list** on the left and the **Commands list** on the right. What you highlight in the **Categories list** determines the commands that are displayed in the **Commands list**. (In the screenshot, the File tab is highlighted on the left, which means that all of the commands displayed on the right are items accessible from the File drop-down.)

The Categories are organized roughly by tabs of the Ribbon (the first item in the box is the File tab). As you scroll down, you'll see as well the context-sensitive tabs, and then, toward the bottom, **All Commands**. Below **All Commands** there are a few other miscellaneous categories, including **Fonts**, **Macros**, **Styles**, and **Common Symbols**.

Depending on which feature(s) to which you wish to assign a keyboard shortcut, scroll down to the appropriate category in the **Categories box**.

TIP: If you're not sure which tab a particular feature is associated with, scroll down to the **All Commands** category. That category can be somewhat overwhelming, but it's probably your best bet for finding a specific item. Keep in mind as you scroll through the commands that they are listed in alphabetical order. Also keep in mind that Microsoft often uses a verb—and not necessarily the verb that first comes to mind—where you might assume a noun as the name of a command. So, for example, GrowFont and ShrinkFont are the commands to increase and decrease font size, respectively.

ANOTHER TIP: You can search through the commands by pressing a letter of the alphabet, such as "S," to see all of the commands that begin with that letter. That may or may not speed up the process of looking for a particular command. Be sure to click in the Command list first.

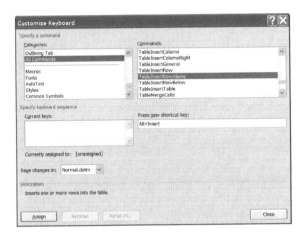

Once you have located the command you want, click to highlight it. Then position your cursor in the **Press new shortcut key** box (refer to the screenshot above) and press the keys you wish to use. For example, if you want to create a shortcut key to insert a table row above the cursor position using the Alt key plus the Insert key, press Alt Ins. If you want to create a shortcut key for the section sign (§) using the Alt key plus the letter "S," press Alt S. If you want to use the key combination Alt Ctrl F1, press those keys in sequence.

If the keyboard shortcut you type in the **Press new shortcut key** box is already assigned to a Word feature or function, you'll see "**Currently assigned to:**" underneath the **Current keys:** box on the left side of the dialog. (See screenshot below for an example.)

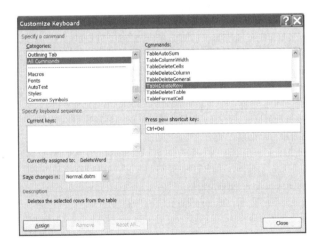

If you want to use a keyboard shortcut that is assigned to another feature, just click the "**Assign**" button in the lower left-hand corner of the dialog. That will remove the key assignment from the feature it was associated with previously and associate it with the feature you have highlighted instead. **CAUTION**: Word will make this change without warning you, so don't click the Assign button unless you're certain you want to reassign the key combination. Should you wish to remove a key assignment, **select** the keys in the "**Current keys**" box, then click the "**Remove**" button.

If you don't want to use keystrokes that have been assigned to a different function, simply type another key combination in the **Press a new shortcut key** box. If that combination isn't already assigned to a feature, click **Assign**.

Once you have finished setting up your own keyboard shortcuts, simply **Close** the dialog box and **OK** out of **Word Options** (don't click the Cancel button).

It's always a good idea to test your keyboard shortcuts to make sure they work as you intended. Also, keep in mind that by default, you are saving your customized keystrokes in your **Normal template (Normal.dotm)**.

SIDEBAR: Some Cool Built-In Keyboard Shortcuts

Here are a few keyboard shortcuts you might not know about—but you'll definitely appreciate. I've chosen them somewhat randomly. To me they're cool because they make it easy to perform tasks I actually use in my legal word processing work.

Did you know that Word 2010 comes with a keyboard shortcut you can use to apply highlighting? It's Ctrl Alt H (or Alt Ctrl H). Just be sure to select the text first. (After applying highlighting, you can turn it off by selecting the text and pressing Ctrl Alt H again.)

Ctrl Alt C inserts the copyright symbol (©); Ctrl Alt R inserts the registered symbol (®); and Ctrl Alt T inserts the Trademark symbol (™).

Ctrl Alt F inserts a footnote reference in the text and positions the cursor in the footnote pane. Alt I, N, N does the same thing.

Ctrl Shift A applies the ALL CAPS attribute to text (if subsequent text takes on all caps formatting, select the text and use Shift F3 to change case *or* press Ctrl D to open the Font dialog and deselect All Caps, then OK out of the dialog, to change back to lower case). To remove the attribute, press Ctrl Shift A again (the following three keyboard shortcuts also work as toggles).

Ctrl Shift K applies the SMALL CAPS font attribute.

Ctrl Shift W underlines words (but not spaces or tabs).

Ctrl Shift D applies double underline.

Ctrl Spacebar removes *character formatting* (such as the font attributes applied by the four previous keyboard shortcuts).

Ctrl Alt P switches to Print Layout view; Ctrl Alt N switches to Draft view (formerly called "Normal" view, which explains the mnemonic); and Ctrl Alt O switches to Outline view.

F7 starts the Spell-Checker and Shift F7 opens the Thesaurus, while Alt Shift F7 opens the Dictionary / Translator.

Shift F5 moves the cursor to the previous editing position. Very useful!

There is no built-in keyboard shortcut for the section sign (§), but it's easy to create one. Open the Symbols dialog (Insert tab, Symbols group, Symbol drop-down, More Symbols), then click the Special Characters tab. Click the symbol and then click the Shortcut Key button and proceed as described in the section above. See also the discussion about symbols on page 266.

Keyboard Shortcuts That Use the Control ("Ctrl") Key

Keystrokes	Function	Comments
Ctrl A	Select All (i.e., the entire document *or* an entire header or footer *or* an entire table)	
Ctrl B	Bold	
Ctrl C	Copy	
Ctrl D	Font dialog	
Ctrl E	Center	In Word 2010, toggles Center Justification on and off
Ctrl F	Find	
Ctrl G	Go To	
Ctrl H	Replace	
Ctrl I	Italics	
Ctrl J	Justify (Full Justification)	In Word 2010, toggles between Full Justification and Left Justification
Ctrl K	Insert Hyperlink	
Ctrl L	Left Align (Left Justification)	In Word 2010, toggles between Left Justification and Full Justification
Ctrl M	Indent Paragraph (i.e., indent entire paragraph from the left) Each time you press Ctrl M, it indents by one additional tab stop	Ctrl Shift M = Decrease Indent
Ctrl N	New Document (blank screen)	
Ctrl O	Open Document	
Ctrl P	Print	
Ctrl Q	Remove Paragraph Formatting (i.e., formatting applied through the Paragraph dialog)	

Keystrokes	Function	Comments
Ctrl R	Right Align (Right Justification)	In Word 2010, toggles between Right Justification and Left Justification
Ctrl S	Save	
Ctrl T	Hanging Indent Each time you press Ctrl T, it increases the hanging indent by one additional tab stop	Ctrl Shift T = Decrease Hanging Indent
Ctrl U	Underline	
Ctrl V	Paste	
Ctrl W	Close (Document Window)	
Ctrl X	Cut	
Ctrl Y	Repeat Action	
Ctrl Z	Undo	
Ctrl 0 (Zero)	Add/Close Space Before Paragraph	Adds or removes extra points before a paragraph.
Ctrl 1	Single Spacing	
Ctrl 2	Double Spacing	
Ctrl 5	One-and-One-Half Spacing	
Ctrl Alt V	Paste Special dialog	
Ctrl Alt Enter	Style Separator	Used to prevent the text of a paragraph from being inserted into a generated TOC along with the paragraph heading.
Ctrl Shift * (asterisk)	Display (or hide) Non-Printing Characters (Hidden Text)—a toggle	
Ctrl Shift D	Double Underline Words	
Ctrl Shift A	All Caps	
Ctrl Shift K	Small Caps	

Keystrokes	Function	Comments
Ctrl Shift N	Applies the Normal paragraph style for the template you're using	
Ctrl Shift C	Copy paragraph formatting (not text)	The Ctrl Shift C and Ctrl Shift V keystrokes work like the Format Painter in that you can use them to copy formatting from one paragraph to another
Ctrl Shift V	Paste paragraph formatting (not text)	Note that these keystrokes are used for copying and pasting *formatting only*, not text
Ctrl Shift = (equal sign)	Superscript	
Ctrl = (equal sign)	Subscript	
Ctrl - (hyphen)	Soft Hyphen	
Ctrl Shift - (hyphen)	Hard (Non-Breaking) Hyphen	
Ctrl Shift Spacebar	Hard (Non-Breaking) Space	
Ctrl Delete	Deletes the word to the right of the cursor	Cursor must be on the first letter of the word
Ctrl Backspace	Deletes the word to the left of the cursor	Cursor must be to the right of the last letter of the word
Ctrl] (close bracket)	Increase font size by 1 point	Select text first
Ctrl [(open bracket)	Decrease font size by 1 point	Select text first
Ctrl Shift > (greater than / close chevron)	Increase font size by 2 points	Select text first
Ctrl Shift < (less than / open chevron)	Decrease font size by 2 points	Select text first

Favorite Ctrl Key Tips

Everyone—or nearly everyone—knows that Ctrl B applies boldface, Ctrl I applies italics, Ctrl U applies underlining, and Ctrl A selects the entire document. But not everyone knows about the following Ctrl key shortcuts, which come in very handy. I use them almost every day!

Applying the Normal Paragraph Style

The key combination **Ctrl Shift N** applies the Normal paragraph style (for whichever template your document is based on; different templates can have different Normal styles). It wipes out any formatting that has been applied manually via the Paragraph dialog: justification, line spacing, indentation, first-line indent, before and/or after spacing, line and page breaks, tab settings. It also restores the default font face and size (and color) for the Normal style.

Just insert your cursor within a paragraph that you want to strip of formatting, press **Ctrl Shift N**, and the paragraph should go from fancy to plain vanilla.

NOTE: Ctrl Q also removes paragraph formatting, ***with the exception of formatting that has been applied via a style***. If you attempt to use Ctrl Q to strip a paragraph's formatting and it doesn't work, try Ctrl Shift N instead.

Using Keystrokes for Indent and Hanging Indent

In Word, **Ctrl M** (M for Margin?) is like Indent in WordPerfect (F7 or, for those of you who still use the DOS-compatible keyboard, F4). **Ctrl T**, on the other hand, creates a hanging indent (T for indenT?). Each time you press Ctrl M or Ctrl T, you increase the indentation by one tab stop. To reverse the amount of indentation, press **Ctrl Shift M** or **Ctrl Shift T**.

Increasing or Decreasing Font Size on the Fly

A quick way to increase or decrease font size by **1 point** is to select the text and press **Ctrl]** (close bracket—increase) or **Ctrl [** (open bracket—decrease). While the text is selected, you can continue pressing Ctrl] or Ctrl [until the text attains the desired size.

To increase or decrease font size by **2 points**, select the text and press **Ctrl Shift >** (increase) or **Ctrl Shift <** (decrease). **NOTE:** In both Word 2010 and Word 2007, this shortcut increments or decrements font sizes below 12 points by 1 point, and increments or decrements fonts that are 12 points and above by 2 points.

Other Faves

I also regularly use **Ctrl D** to open the Font dialog and **Ctrl H** for Find and Replace. And I often insert non-breaking spaces with **Ctrl Shift Spacebar**, as well as non-breaking hyphens with **Ctrl Shift -** (hyphen).

Selected Function Key Shortcuts
(Listed by Keystrokes)

Keystrokes	Function	Comments
F1	Help	
Shift F1	Reveal Formatting	
Ctrl F2	Print Preview / Print Place	In previous versions, toggled between Print Preview and regular view; in Word 2010, takes you to the print preview within the Print Place screen (but does not act like a toggle and move between Print Place and the normal document editing screen).
Shift F3	Change Case (of selected text)	Toggles among ALL CAPS, lower case, and Initial Caps or Sentence Case (depending on context)
Alt F3	Opens Quick Parts / Building Blocks dialog	Must select text first
F4	Repeat Previous Command	
Ctrl F4	Close Document Window	
Alt F4	Exit Word	
F5	Go To (page, section, line, footnote, comment, etc.)	Ctrl G performs the same function
Shift F5	Go To Previous Cursor Position	
Ctrl F6	Next Document Window	Like F3 (Switch Screen) in WordPerfect
F7	Spell-Check	
Shift F7	Thesaurus/Research	

Keystrokes	Function	Comments
F9	Update Field Codes	(To update an individual field, put the cursor into the field and press F9; to update all fields in document, select the entire document with Ctrl A and press F9)
Alt F9	Toggle Between Field Codes and Field Results in Document	
Shift F10	Display Shortcut Menu	
F12	Save As	
Shift F12	Save	
Ctrl Shift * (asterisk)	Display (or hide) Non-Printing Characters, including Hidden Text	This is a toggle; press once to display and a second time to hide
Ctrl Shift D	Double Underline Words	
Ctrl Shift A	All Caps	
Ctrl Shift K	Small Caps	
Ctrl Shift N	Applies the Normal paragraph style for the template you're using	
Ctrl Shift = (equal sign)	Superscript	
Ctrl = (equal sign)	Subscript	
Ctrl - (hyphen)	Soft Hyphen	
Ctrl Shift - (hyphen)	Hard (Non-Breaking) Hyphen	
Ctrl Shift Spacebar	Hard (Non-Breaking) Space	

Selected Function Key and Ctrl Key Shortcuts
(Listed by Feature)

Feature	Keystrokes	Comments
Help	F1	
Reveal Formatting	Shift F1	
Change Case (selected text)	Shift F3	
Close Document Window	Ctrl F4 *or* Ctrl W	
Go To	F5 *or* Ctrl G	
Go To Previous Cursor Position	Shift F5	
Next Document (Switch Screen)	Ctrl F6	
Previous Document	Shift Ctrl F6	
Spell-Check	F7	
Thesaurus	Shift F7	
Update Field Codes	F9	
Toggle Between Codes and Results	Alt F9	
All Caps	Ctrl Shift A	
Small Caps	Ctrl Shift K	
Double Underline	Ctrl Shift D	
Normal Paragraph Style	Ctrl Shift N	
Display Non-Printing Characters	Ctrl Shift * (asterisk)	
Soft Hyphen	Ctrl - (hyphen)	
Hard (Non-Breaking) Hyphen	Ctrl Shift - (hyphen)	
Hard (Non-Breaking) Space	Ctrl Shift Spacebar	
Superscript	Ctrl Shift = (equal sign)	

Feature	Keystrokes	Comments
Subscript	Ctrl = (equal sign)	
Increase Font Size by 1 Point	Ctrl] (close bracket)	See * below.
Decrease Font Size by 1 Point*	Ctrl [(open bracket)	See * below.
Increase Font Size by 2 Points*	Ctrl Shift > (greater than / close chevron)	See * below.
Decrease Font Size by 2 Points*	Ctrl Shift < (less than / open chevron)	See * below.
Style Separator	Ctrl Alt Enter	Used to prevent the text of a paragraph from being inserted into a generated TOC along with the paragraph heading.

*Be sure to select the text first. Note that Ctrl Shift > (greater than / close chevron) and Ctrl Shift < (less than / open chevron) change the text size by 2 points only for font sizes from 12 points and up; below 12 points, they change the text size by 1 point.

Mnemonics and Keyboard Shortcuts for Tabs and Dialog Boxes

In Word 2010 (as in Word 2007), tapping the **Alt key** displays **mnemonics** (shortcut keys) that you can use to open the File Drop-Down and the other tabs on the Ribbon, as well as icons/drop-downs and commands on the Quick Access Toolbar (QAT).[1] Some people refer to these mnemonics as "**badges**." You might see them referred to elsewhere as **KeyTips**. They can be very useful. If you haven't tried working with them, give them a whirl and see what you think.

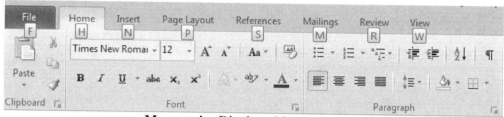

Mnemonics Displayed in the Ribbon

Mnemonics Displayed in the QAT

Once you have tapped the Alt key, you can open a tab by pressing the mnemonic for that tab (such as **F** to open the File drop-down, **N** to open the Insert tab, or **W** to open the View tab). After you press one of the mnemonics to open a tab—as shown in the screenshot below, I pressed "N" to open the Insert tab—you'll see mnemonics for the commands on that tab.

Mnemonics on the Insert Tab

To use a command on a tab or on the QAT, press the mnemonic for that command. If more than one letter or number is displayed, press all of the letters or numbers in sequence, such as **Alt P, S, P** or **Alt 09**.

Alternatively, after you have pressed the Alt key, you can press the **Tab key** to move the cursor in sequence from icon to icon on the Ribbon and then from icon to icon on the QAT. To use a highlighted icon, simply press the **Enter key**.

---

[1] To stop the mnemonics from displaying, either press the Alt key again or press the Esc key.

The following keyboard shortcuts provide quick access to tabs on the Word 2010 Ribbon and to certain dialog boxes. (This list is not intended to be comprehensive.)

Displaying the Mnemonics (Badges) on the Various Tabs

Alt F—Opens the Backstage View and displays mnemonics (badges) for commands therein.

Alt F, S = Save

Alt F, A = Save As

Alt F, O = Open

Alt F, C = Close

Alt F, I = Info (in Word 2007, Alt F, I opens the Options)

Alt F, R = Recent

Alt F, N = New

Alt F, P = Print

Alt F, D = Save & Send

Alt F, H = Help

Alt F, T = Options (Word Options)

Alt F, X = Exit from Word

Alt H—Displays mnemonics (badges) for commands on the Home tab

Alt N—Displays mnemonics (badges) for commands on the Insert tab

Alt P—Displays mnemonics (badges) for commands on the Page Layout tab

Alt S—Displays mnemonics (badges) for commands on the References tab

Alt M—Displays mnemonics (badges) for commands on the Mailings tab

Alt R—Displays mnemonics (badges) for commands on the Review tab

Alt W—Displays mnemonics (badges) for commands on the View tab

Alt L—Displays mnemonics (badges) for commands on the Developer tab (if displayed)

Alt X—Displays mnemonics (badges) for commands on the Add-Ins tab (if displayed)

Using Keyboard Shortcuts to Open Various Dialog Boxes and Panes

Alt O, P—opens the Paragraph dialog (works regardless of which tab is active)

Alt P, M, A *or* Alt P, S, P—opens the Page Setup dialog

Alt Ctrl Shift S—opens the Styles Pane (you can press the first three keys in any sequence; just keep them depressed and then tap "S")

Ctrl D—opens the Font dialog

Alt I, T *or* Alt N, D—opens the Date and Time dialog

Alt I, S—opens the Symbols dialog

Alt I, N, N *or* Alt S, Q—opens the Footnote dialog

Alt O, T—opens the Tabs dialog

Alt V, Z—opens the Zoom dialog (for changing magnification of the document on the screen)

Alt V, Z, E—opens the Zoom dialog and positions the cursor in the Percent box so you can change the magnification easily

Alt H, F, O—opens the Clipboard

Shift F1—opens the Reveal Formatting pane

Miscellaneous

Alt N, H, E—puts the cursor in the Header editing screen

Alt N, O, E—puts the cursor in the Footer editing screen

Keyboard Shortcuts—Miscellaneous Tips

Moving Up or Down One Page

Microsoft keeps changing the keyboard shortcut for moving up or down one page at a time. In some versions of Word, they used Ctrl Alt Page Up and Ctrl Alt Page Down; in other versions, they used Ctrl Page Up and Ctrl Page down.

In Word 2010, as in Word 2007, you can move up or down one full page at a time by pressing **Ctrl Page Up** or **Ctrl Page Down**. (Page Up and Page Down move you up or down one *screen* at a time.) Of course, you can also click the Page Up / Page Down arrows toward the bottom of the vertical scrollbar, assuming you have "Browse By Object" set to "page."[1]

Incidentally, the keyboard shortcut to open "Browse by Object" is **Alt Ctrl Home**.

Copying and Pasting Paragraph Formatting

I recently learned about two highly useful keyboard shortcuts that allow you to copy and paste paragraph formatting. **Ctrl Shift C** copies the formatting of the paragraph your cursor is in; to apply that formatting to another paragraph, position the cursor within the "target" paragraph and press **Ctrl Shift V**.

Exactly what are you pasting when you use Ctrl Shift V?

If your cursor is at the beginning or end of the target paragraph, or within white space, Ctrl Shift V will paste only *paragraph formatting* (the types of formatting that can be applied from the Paragraph dialog): justification, indentation, line spacing, before and after spacing, widow and orphan control settings, etc. If your cursor is within text, Ctrl Shift V will apply paragraph formatting and also will apply *direct character formatting*—such as bolding, italics, and/or font face/size—to *the word the cursor is in*. To apply character formatting to the entire paragraph, along with paragraph formatting, select the text of the target paragraph before pressing Ctrl Shift V.

In any case, Ctrl Shift C / Ctrl Shift V copy and paste only formatting, not text.

---

[1] **Watch out!** If the "**Browse by Object**" feature is active, it will attempt to perform a Find when you press the Page Up/Page Down keystrokes or click the Page Up/Page Down arrows. To disable it, click the round **"Browse by" button** near the bottom of the vertical scrollbar (between the Page Up and Page Down arrows), then click the Page icon. See "'Find' Disables Page Up and Page Down," page 99.

Using Field Codes

This section provides a few tips for automating your documents with field codes. These tips, which I present in no particular order, are among the most frequently asked questions I get from clients.

Inserting a Date Code

Word's default date format is MM/DD/YYYY, so before inserting a date code, you'll probably want to select a different format. Click the **Insert tab**, **Text group**, **Date and Time** (or press **Alt I, T**), select a format you like, and click the "**Set As Default**" button. That format will be used as the default from now on.

Once you have chosen a default format, it's easy to insert a date code by using the keyboard shortcut **Alt Shift D**. This code will update automatically whenever you open or print the document. (However, codes can be locked or unlinked; see page 326 for instructions.)

Note that you can insert the date (or date and time) as text rather than a code by *unchecking* the "**Update Automatically**" checkbox in the lower right-hand corner of the **Date and Time dialog**. Also, it's easy to open the **Date and Time dialog** by using the keyboard shortcut **Alt I, T**. This key combination works regardless of which tab of the Ribbon is active.

Another alternative is to insert a **CREATEDATE** field (**Insert tab**, **Text group**, **Quick Parts drop-down**, **Field**, then scroll to **CREATEDATE**, select the date format you want, and click **OK**). The CREATEDATE field reflects the date a particular document was created; it won't update automatically every time you open or print the file. **CAUTION:** You do need to be careful not to re-save a file containing the CREATEDATE field if you open it after the original creation date, or the field *will* update, which likely is not your intention.

NOTE: If Word inserts a leading zero before dates, you need to edit Regional Settings in Windows. To do so in Windows XP, click the **Windows Start menu** > **Settings** > **Control Panel**, and double-click **Regional and Language Options**. Click the **Customize** button, then click the **Date** tab. Navigate to the **Long date format** drop-down at the bottom of the tab, and select the option you want (**MMMM dd, yyyy**). Since "dd" produces the leading zero, click directly in the box and *delete one of the d's*, then click "**Apply**" and **OK** out of the dialog box.

Inserting the File Name and Path

In versions of Word prior to Word 2007, it was simple to insert a code for the **file name** or for the **file name and path** because both codes were included in the program as built-in AutoText entries. To insert a code for the file name, you would position the cursor where you wanted the file name to appear, type "**filename**" (as a single word and without quotation marks), and press **F3**. To insert a code for the file name and path, position the cursor, you would type "**filename and path**" (without quotation marks), and press **F3**.

However, Microsoft did not incorporate those entries into Building Blocks, the new incarnation of the AutoText feature, in Word 2007 (they're not built into Word 2010, either). The file name and file name and path AutoText entries will work in Word 2010 (and Word 2007), but (1) they aren't imported automatically when you upgrade, so you must take active steps to import your AutoText entries from an older version of the program into Word 2010 (or Word 2007); and (2) many people move straight from WordPerfect to Word 2010 (or Word 2007), and as a result they do not have access to the AutoText entries available in older versions of Word.

Thankfully, there is another way to insert a code for the file name or a code for the file name and path.

First, position the cursor where you want the code to appear. Most people insert the code into the document footer. As you know, you can open the footer editing screen by doing any of the following:

- double-clicking in the footer area; *or*

- right-clicking in the footer area and then clicking "Edit Footer"; *or*

- clicking the Footer drop-down on the Insert tab, then clicking "Edit Footer."

In the footer editing screen, place the cursor where you want the code to go. Then either click the **Insert tab**, **Quick Parts drop-down**, **Field** *or* press **Alt I, F**. The **Field dialog** will open.

Insert, Quick Parts, Field

When the **Field dialog** appears, scroll through the Field names box until you come to the **FileName field**. Click to **select it**, then—if you want to include the path as well as the file name in the code—click to put a check in the "**Add path to filename**" box at the upper right side of the Field dialog. This step is optional, of course.

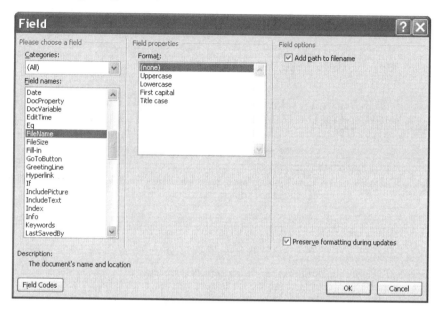

Next, look at the "**Field properties**" box at the center of the dialog and, if you wish, click to select a particular format for the code. You can choose uppercase, lowercase, first capital (sentence case), or title case (initial caps). When you are ready to insert the code, click "**OK**."

If you haven't saved the document yet, the code will display a generic name, such as Document2. After you save / name the document, you still might have to update the code manually by **clicking in (or selecting) the code** and pressing **F9**.

The code will update automatically when you print the document—*if* "**Update fields before printing**" is enabled in the Word Options. To enable that option, click the **File tab**, **Options**, then click the **Display category** and review the **Printing options**. If "**Update fields before printing**" is unchecked, **click to put a checkmark in the box**, then be sure to click "**OK**" to save your settings.

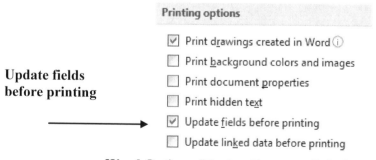

Update fields before printing

Word Options, Display Category, Printing Options

Note that you can change the font size, the font face, or other formatting simply by selecting the code and applying various attributes. Be sure to save your changes before closing the document.

Updating Field Codes

Some field codes update automatically; others update automatically when you print or reopen a document; still others require manual updating. Note, too, that you can configure Word Options to update fields when you print; this option is *disabled* by default. To change the setting, click the **File tab**, **Options**, **Display**; **Printing Options** (including "**Update fields before printing**") are at the bottom of the screen.

Printing options

☑ Print drawings created in Word ⓘ
☐ Print background colors and images
☐ Print document properties
☐ Print hidden text
☐ Update fields before printing
☐ Update linked data before printing

You can update an individual code by placing the cursor within the code and pressing the **F9** key. To update all of the manually updatable field codes in your document (date code, file name/path, Page X of Y, Table of Contents, SEQ codes and other automatic numbers, etc.), select the entire document by pressing **Ctrl A**, then press **F9**.

NOTE: Codes within headers and footers usually do not update unless you go into the editing screen for the header or footer (right-click the header or footer area, then click "Edit Header" or "Edit Footer"; alternatively, click the **Insert tab**, **Header & Footer group**, **Header drop-down** or **Footer drop-down**, and then click "**Edit Header**" or "**Edit Footer**"), select the header or footer by pressing **Ctrl A**, and finally press **F9**.

Locking, Unlocking, and Unlinking Field Codes

It is possible to lock codes (for example, a date code) so that they don't update unless they're unlocked. To lock a field code, click the code and press the key combination **Ctrl F11**. To unlock a field code (assuming it's actually locked), click the code and press **Ctrl Shift F11**.

Also, you can convert certain codes into plain text by *unlinking* them. To unlink a code, select it (or insert the cursor into the code), then press **Ctrl Shift F9**.

Using Fill-in Fields

Field codes have many uses in MS Word. For example, as shown in the section that starts on page 489, you can insert **SEQ codes** from the Fields dialog box to produce automatic numbers such as those used in headings for discovery and discovery responses (e.g., Interrogatories and Responses to Interrogatories, or Requests for Production of Documents and Responses to Requests for Production of Documents).

Another example is **Fill-In fields**, which you typically embed in templates to prompt the person working on the document to enter variable information at certain points in the document. (Fill-In fields are somewhat akin to variables in keyboard merges in WordPerfect.)

The Fields Dialog Box

Most people insert field codes via the **Fields dialog box**. Because the user interface has changed dramatically, perhaps the easiest way to open the **Fields dialog box** in Word 2010 is by using the key combination **Alt I, F**.

In this version of Word, the Fields command—which used to be on the Insert menu—has been moved and renamed. It now appears in a couple of places: (1) on the **Insert tab**, on the **Text Group**, under **Quick Parts** (toward the bottom of the drop-down), and (2) on the **Mailings tab**, on the **Write & Insert Fields group**, under **Rules**.

As for option (2), specific Field codes are available from Rules (which opens the Fields dialog), but note that Rules is grayed out—i.e., not activated—unless you are in a merge document (a document that contains merge codes)! So if you want to use a Field code without beginning a merge or opening a merge document, you should use the keyboard shortcut.

Using Fill-In fields

As mentioned above, Fill-In fields in Word are somewhat comparable to keyboard merges in WordPerfect.

In order for Fill-In fields to work properly, you need to do the following:

(1)   embed them in a template;

(2)   put the template in the default template location in Word (note that you might have to copy the templates to each staff member's computer or put them in a shared network location); and

(3)   open a new document based on the template by clicking the **File tab**, **New**.

Note that after clicking the File tab, New, users might have to click "**My templates….**" in order to locate the template that contains the Fill-In fields (depending on where you've stored the template).

Creating a Template With Embedded Fill-In fields

You can start with a blank document or with a form you're already using. In either case, position the cursor at the first point where you want variable information to be inserted. Then open the **Fields dialog** (again, an easy way is by using the keyboard shortcut **Alt I, F**) and locate the **Fill-In fields** command. One quick way to get to that command is by pressing the letter "F" as many times as necessary to move the cursor down through the Field names. In this case, pressing "F" three times took me to the Fill-In field.

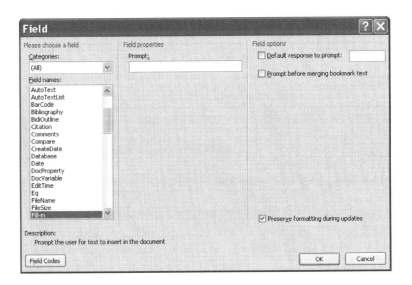

At this point, you have the option of **adding a specific prompt** to help guide the users (see the top center of the dialog box). You also have the option of setting up a **default response** (see the upper right-hand corner of the dialog box), which will be inserted automatically into the document if the person filling in the fields in response to the prompts leaves that field blank.

When you are ready to insert the field code into the document, click **OK** *or* press the **Enter key**.

A **prompt box** will appear. Since you are still in the process of creating the template, don't type anything in the box. (If you like, you can type a placeholder such as an "X," which users will be able to type over when they are prompted to enter text in the box.) Simply click "**OK**," and the code will be inserted at the cursor position.

Note that unless you specifically choose to display the codes while creating the template, you won't be able to see them, which can make things somewhat challenging. In order to display the codes, press **Alt F9**. To hide the codes, simply press Alt F9 again (it's a toggle).

Continue inserting fill-in field codes at appropriate places in the document. Then, when everything is to your liking, save it as a template.

To save the template, click the **File tab** (*or* press Alt F), then click **Save As** (*or* press the letter A). Navigate to the folder where templates are stored. If you are using Windows XP, it is likely to be the following:

C:\Documents and Settings\<User Name>\Application Data\Microsoft\Templates

In Windows Vista, the templates folder usually is located here:

C:\Users\<UserName>\AppData\Roaming\Microsoft\Templates

Be sure to save the document as a template. Note that you have a choice of saving the template as a **Word 2010 template (*.dotx)** or as a **Word 97-2003 template (*.dot)**. If you think you might also use the template in an earlier version of Word, you should save it as the latter, since the dotx format isn't backwards compatible.

Using a Document Based on the Template

After you've saved the template, users will be able to create a new document based on the template by clicking the **File tab, New, My templates**. (If the template doesn't appear in the tab that is at the forefront of the **New dialog**, they will have to click a different tab to locate it.) To create a document based on the template, either **double-click the icon** for the template *or* **click "OK."**

Alternatively, if you have created a macro to open the template and have added an icon for the macro to each user's Quick Access Toolbar, as discussed in the section starting on page 374, users can click that icon rather than clicking **File**, **New**, **My templates**.

When the doc opens, the first prompt will pop up. **Type the information** and click **OK**. (**NOTE**: pressing Enter won't dismiss the prompt. Rather, it will merely move the insertion point down to the next line within the prompt.)

The next prompt (if any) will pop up. Continue as in the previous paragraph.

When you have filled in the last prompt, you'll be returned to the document, where you can make any necessary changes.

Note that if you close the document and reopen it, you won't be prompted to fill in the fields. *Prompting occurs only when you open a new document based on a template that was created with Fill-In fields embedded in it.* However, you can press **F11** to move your cursor to the first field in the document, then press **F9** to open the pop-up for that field, type any text you want, and click **OK** to dismiss the pop-up. To continue, repeat the F11, F9 sequence.

Also note: If "Update fields before printing" is enabled in the Word Options, fill-in fields will pop up every time you print a document containing the fields. That can become burdensome. To prevent this behavior, you can turn off the "Update fields before printing" option (**File tab**, **Options**, **Display**, **Printing options**, and *uncheck* "**Update fields before printing**"), *or* you can **select the fill-in fields** and convert the codes to text before you print by pressing **Ctrl Shift F9**.

CAUTION: If there are fields in the document that you want to update, such as a date code, don't select the entire document before pressing Ctrl Shift F9.

Get Smart: Understanding Word 2010's "Smart" Features

Smart Cursoring

When you scroll through a document, you might find that the cursor doesn't follow you. Instead, it remains in the original position, where you can't see it. Of course you can reposition it by clicking at the new location, but Word offers you another option, as well. That option is called **Smart Cursoring**. When that option is enabled, pressing any of the arrow keys brings the cursor to your current position (unless you have selected some text at the prior position).

Smart Cursoring should be turned on by default in Word 2010, but if for some reason it isn't, you can enable it by clicking the **File tab**, **Options**, **Advanced**, **Editing options**, **Use smart cursoring**.

For more information, see the following article. It deals with Word 2003, but the general principles also apply to Word 2010.

http://office.microsoft.com/en-us/word/HP051893871033.aspx

Smart Paragraph Selection

When the **Smart Paragraph Selection** option is enabled, Word automatically includes the paragraph symbol when you select a paragraph by using keystrokes, by dragging with the mouse, by double-clicking in the margin to the left of the paragraph, or by triple-clicking within the paragraph. The assumption is that you wish to include the formatting instructions for the paragraph when you move or copy the text to another location in the document. (Remember that formatting codes are contained within the paragraph symbol, also known as a pilcrow.)

To turn Smart Paragraph Selection off (it's enabled by default), click the **File tab**, **Options**, **Advanced**, **Editing options**, and uncheck **Use smart paragraph selection**.[1]

Smart Cut and Paste

The **Smart Cut and Paste** options control the appearance and formatting of sentences, words, paragraphs, bulleted and/or numbered list items, tables, as well as content from a PowerPoint presentation or from an Excel spreadsheet, that you cut (or copy) and paste into a Word 2010 document.

---

[1] There is a similar feature called "**When selecting, automatically select entire word**." With this option turned on (as it is by default), double-clicking a word selects both the word itself and the space after the word, something you may or may not intend to do. To disable the option, click the **File tab**, **Options**, **Advanced**, **Editing options**, and uncheck the **When selecting, automatically select entire word** checkbox.

Smart cut and paste options are set by clicking the **File tab, Options, Advanced, Cut, copy, and paste** and clicking the **Settings button** to the right of the **Use smart cut and paste** checkbox. Make any changes you like in the **Settings dialog**, shown below, and **OK** out.

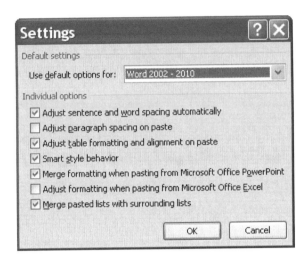

The setting for sentence and word spacing is intended to ensure that there is adequate—but not excessive—white space between pasted text and any surrounding text into which it is inserted. (This setting also controls the amount of space left between words and sentences when you **delete** text.)

The setting for paragraph spacing is intended to avoid inconsistently formatted paragraphs and/or empty paragraphs when you cut (or copy) paragraphs.

According to Microsoft, when the table adjustment option is enabled, "single cells are pasted as text, table portions are pasted as rows into an existing table (rather than as a nested table), and tables added to an existing table are adjusted to match the existing table."

Microsoft says that the Smart Styles option "has no effect." Rather, it is the "**Pasting between documents when style definitions conflict**" option (also under the **File tab, Options, Advanced, Cut, copy, and paste**) that determines which style takes precedence—the one in the source document or the one in the destination document—when the styles have the same name but are formatted differently.

For more information on **Smart Cut and Paste** options, see Microsoft's online article, "Control the formatting when you paste text," available here:

http://office.microsoft.com/en-us/help/HA102157081033.aspx#6

The article deals with Word 2007 but the concepts apply to Word 2010, as well.

Smart Tags

The Smart Tags feature has been "deprecated" in Word 2010. Essentially, that means that Word won't automatically recognize names, addresses, and similar items or link them to Outlook. It's still possible to perform certain actions by right-clicking these former Smart Tag items, but you need to purchase additional software in order to do so.

As Microsoft explains:

> "Smart tags are deprecated in Excel 2010 and Word 2010. Although you can still use the related APIs in projects for Excel 2010 and Word 2010, these applications do not automatically recognize terms, and recognized terms are no longer underlined. Users must trigger recognition and view custom actions associated with text by right-clicking the text and clicking the Additional Actions on the context menu. For more information about this change in Word 2010, see http://go.microsoft.com/fwlink/?LinkId=178847."

Source: msdn.microsoft.com/en-us/library/ms178786.aspx

Here is another Microsoft article that details the types of actions you can perform with the former Smart Tags, and a brief description of the software you need for each action: http://office2010.microsoft.com/en-us/providers/available-actions-HA001050482.aspx

WHERE DID IT GO? Macros

If you've scoured the Ribbon for a Macros command, you're probably completely at a loss. Where the heck did it go?

For some reason, Microsoft moved the Macros command(s) to the **View tab**. There's a **Macros group**, with a **Macros drop-down** that you can use to record macros (or to view the built-in macros), at the far-right side of the tab.

In addition, Microsoft added icons for Macros, Record Macro, and Macro Security to the **Developer tab** (in the **Code group**), which by default doesn't display in the Ribbon. However, it's easy to add the Developer tab to the Ribbon. Just right-click the **Ribbon**, click **Customize the Ribbon...**, navigate to the right side of the screen (the large area underneath "Customize the Ribbon"), and click to put a check in the **checkbox** to the left of "**Developer tab**." Then **OK** out of Word Options.

<u>Creating a Simple Macro to Print the Current Page</u>[1]

In Word 2010, there are three different ways to start recording macros:

1.   Click the **Macro icon** on the **Status Bar**; *or*

2.   Navigate to the **View tab**, **Macros group**, click the **Macros drop-down** and then click **Record Macro…**; *or*

3.   Display the **Developer tab**, an optional tab that ordinarily is hidden,[2] then click the **Record Macro** button on that tab.

Whichever method you choose, you will see the **Record Macro dialog box**.

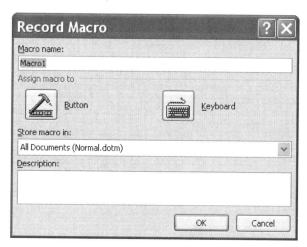

Record Macro dialog box

In the **Macro name** box, type a short, memorable name for the macro that identifies what it does, such as PrintCurrentPage. **NOTE**: Spaces are not allowed in macro names.

You can type a description of the macro in the **Description** box. This is an optional step, but it has two advantages: (1) It permits other users who open the Macros dialog box to figure out what the macro does; and (2) if you assign the macro to a toolbar, the description you type will appear on the toolbar button that runs the macro. A good description for our sample macro might be "Prints the current page."

---

[1]This section of the book is intended to introduce you to the process of writing (recording) macros in MS Word. I've deliberately chosen a very simple macro to get you started.

[2] To display the Developer tab, **right-click** the **Ribbon** or the Quick Access Toolbar and click "**Customize the Ribbon…**" When the Word Options screen appears, navigate to the right-hand side. Locate and **click** to put a checkmark in the box to the left of "**Developer**," then **OK out** of the Options.

NOTE: By default, the macro will be stored in your NORMAL template. If you prefer, you can use the **Store macro in:** drop-down and choose to store it in the current document.

At this point, you can either create a **button** so that you can run the macro from the Quick Access Toolbar or designate a **keyboard shortcut** for the macro. Let's start by assigning a keyboard shortcut; later on, we'll also put a button to run the macro on the QAT.

First, click the **Keyboard** button in the section of the dialog box labeled "**Assign macro to:**" You will see a **Customize Keyboard** dialog similar to the following:

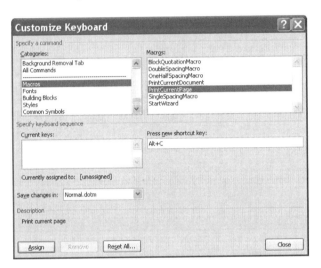

Type a key combination in the "**Press new shortcut key:**" box. In the example above, I used Alt C. The main thing is to be sure to choose a key combination that hasn't already been assigned to another function. If the key combo you type is in use, you'll see "Currently assigned to:" and the function below the "Press new shortcut key"; otherwise, you'll see "Currently assigned to: [unassigned]." If the key combination is available, click the **Assign** button to assign that shortcut to your macro. Then click **Close**.

Now create your macro by using the keyboard and/or the mouse as if you were going to print the current page. In other words, press **Ctrl P** (or click the **File tab, Print**), then click the **Current Page radio button**, then click **OK**. (The page your cursor is in should print, unless you don't have a printer attached or running.)

Next, stop recording the macro by clicking the **Macros drop-down** in the **Macros group** on the **View tab**, then clicking the "**Stop Recording**" icon (or clicking the "**Stop Recording**" icon in the **Code group** of the **Developer tab**.) Alternatively, you can click the **Macro Recorder** icon in the Status Bar.

To run (play) the macro, you can simply press the key combination you assigned to the macro—*or* you can open the Macros dialog by pressing **Alt F8** (or clicking the **Macros button** in the **Macros group** on the **View tab** *or* the **Macros icon** in the **Developer tab**), scrolling to the PrintCurrentPage macro, and either clicking **Run** *or* **double-clicking** the macro name.

You can assign the macro to the Quick Access Toolbar after you have recorded the macro. To do so, click the **File tab**, **Options**, **Customize Quick Access Toolbar…** (or right-click the **QAT** (or the **Ribbon**) and click **Customize Quick Access Toolbar…**), then click the **Choose commands from: drop-down** and select **Macros**.

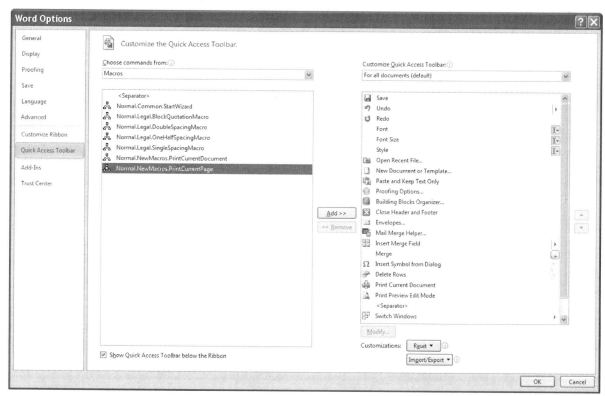

The macro will appear with the name you chose for it, preceded by something like "Normal.NewMacros." **Click to select** the macro (I've already created several macros, which is why there are so many of them visible in the screenshot) and then click the **Add button** in the middle column to add the macro to the Quick Access Toolbar. Once you've done so, a grayed-out "**Modify**" button underneath the **Customize Quick Access Toolbar box** will become active. **Click** the "**Modify**" button. A dialog similar to the one shown below will open.

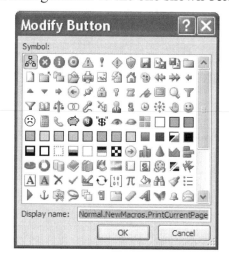

Note that this dialog allows you to type a "**Display name**" for the macro—one that is more user-friendly than the VBA-coded name Microsoft assigns when you record the macro. For example, I've chosen to use the display name "**Print Current Page**" (without the quotation marks). (Display names can have blank spaces between letters.) You can simply put your cursor in the "**Display name**" box and delete or type over the existing name.

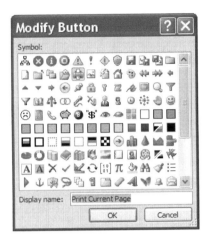

Before OK-ing out of the Modify Button dialog, you can select an icon for the macro by double-clicking it. I've chosen one that looks like a printer.

Now I have an icon on the Quick Access Toolbar that I can click to print whatever page my cursor is in.

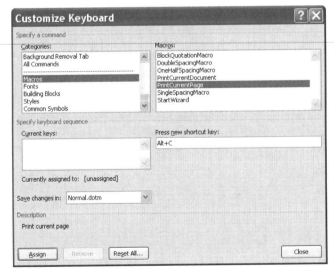

Note that if you choose to run the macro via a button rather than a keyboard shortcut when you first create your macro, you can go back later and add a keyboard shortcut to the macro. To do so, right-click the **Ribbon**, click "**Customize the Ribbon...**," then click the **Keyboard shortcuts: Customize button** (or click the **File tab**, **Options**, **Customize Ribbon**, and then click the **Keyboard shortcuts: Customize button**).

When the dialog opens, navigate to **Categories** on the left side, then scroll down to and click **Macros**. Next, navigate to **Macros** on the right side and scroll down to and **click the name of your macro**. Position your cursor in the **Press new keyboard key:** box and press a key combination. If the keyboard shortcut you wish to use isn't assigned to another function—or if you're willing to reassign that shortcut to your macro—click the "**Assign**" button. Finally, click **Close** and then **OK** out of the Word Options dialog.

Creating and Using "Quick Parts" (Formerly Called AutoText)

Word's Quick Parts feature allows you to insert commonly used phrases, boilerplate paragraphs, signature blocks, and other frequently used text and graphics into your documents with just a few keystrokes. Note that Quick Parts are referred to at times as Building Blocks.

To create a Quick Parts entry, first type and format some text, along with any graphics you wish to use. Then select everything—including any tabs or other formatting you want to incorporate.[1] (If you want a blank line inserted below the entry, select the next line, too.)

Next, do one of the following:

- click the **Insert tab**, **Text group**, **Quick Parts drop-down**, **Save Selection to Quick Part Gallery…**; or

- click the **Insert tab**, **Text group**, **Quick Parts drop-down**, scroll down to **AutoText**, slide the mouse pointer to the left, and click **Save Selection to AutoText Gallery** (a new option in Word 2010); or

- simply press **Alt F3**.

All three methods launch the **Create New Building Block dialog**. However, note that the first method by default saves Quick Parts entries in the BuildingBlocks.dotx template, whereas the other two methods by default save Quick Parts entries in the Normal.dotm template. That difference has important consequences, as I will explain momentarily.

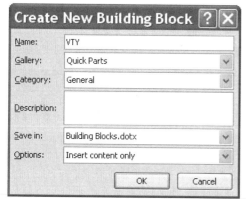

Create New Building Block Dialog
Using "Save Selection to Quick Part Gallery"

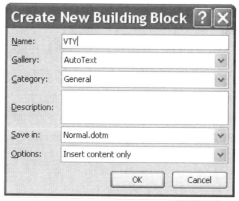

Create New Building Block Dialog
Using Alt F3 or "Save Selection to AutoText Gallery"

---

[1] Also, if you wish to preserve any paragraph formatting, be sure to select the paragraph symbol at the end of the paragraph along with any text and graphics. To ensure that you select the paragraph symbol (as well as tabs), turn on Show Non-Printing Characters by clicking the **paragraph icon** on the **Home tab**, **Paragraph group** (or pressing **Ctrl Shift ***) before selecting the text (and graphics).

At this point, type an abbreviation in the "**Name**" **field**. This abbreviation, plus the F3 key, is what you will use to insert the Quick Parts entry into your document. (If you want Word to prompt you when you type the abbreviation so that you can insert the entry simply by pressing the Enter key—using a feature known as **AutoComplete**—make sure the abbreviation is at least four characters long.)

Note that the Quick Parts feature *is NOT case-sensitive*. In other words, the abbreviation VTY is the same, in effect, as vty, and Vty (and all other permutations).

You can add a brief description in the "**Description**" **field** if it will help you remember what your abbreviation does, but that step is optional.

The default "**Save in**" **location** is the **BuildingBlocks.dotx template**. Each user has one.[2] Storing Quick Parts in that template makes them available globally, i.e., regardless of which template you are using at any given time (such as a pleading template or letterhead). However, there are two possible reasons why you might want to change the "Save in" location. For one thing, you might wish to create certain entries for use only with one specific template, in which case, you should change the "Save in" location to that template.

For another thing, as of this writing the AutoComplete feature, described below, *doesn't work with Quick Parts entries that are stored in the BuildingBlocks.dotx template*. If you change the "Save in" location to any other template, AutoComplete should work (as long as the abbreviations you assign to your entries are at least four characters long).

To change the "Save in" location, just click the drop-down and select a different template. (The screenshot at right shows three different templates, including my old Normal.dot from Word 2003.)

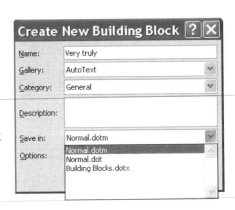

Remember, too, that *the method you use to create the Quick Part* determines the template where the Quick Part will be stored. If you use Alt F3, it will be stored in your normal.dotm template by default; otherwise, it will go into the BuildingBlocks.dotx template. (Fortunately, Quick Parts stored in the normal.dotm template will be available globally.)

---

[2]Actually, there are two different Building Blocks templates on each machine. One, located under C:\Program Files\Microsoft Office\Office14\Document Parts\1033\14 and called Built-In Building Blocks.dotx, includes dozens of pre-formatted cover pages, footers, headers, page numbers, tables, text boxes, watermarks, and similar items; the other, located in the individual user's application data folder under Microsoft\Document Building Blocks, is the "working" copy. The latter is the one where the user's customized entries are stored. **NOTE**: It is a good idea to back up this customized template from time to time (and save it to another location such as an external drive) because it occasionally gets corrupted.

If you like, you can change the gallery where your Quick Parts entry will appear, as well. For example, if you move a Quick Part to the new AutoText gallery (located toward the bottom of the Quick Parts drop-down), it will display in that gallery. The next screenshot provides a partial view of the AutoText gallery, where I stored a Quick Part that expands into my signature block.

My New Quick Parts Entry in the AutoText Gallery
(Truncated View)

After creating your Quick Parts entry, click **OK**.

To insert your Quick Part at the cursor position, do one of the following:

(1)   simply **type the abbreviation** (assuming you remember it!) and press **F3**; *or*

(2)   if the abbreviation is four characters or longer (and if you've stored the entry in a template other than BuildingBlocks.dotx), **type those characters** and, when the **AutoComplete prompt** appears, press the **Enter key**; *or*

(3)   click the **Insert tab**, navigate to the **Text group**, click the **Quick Parts drop-down**, click "**Building Blocks Organizer**," **locate your entry** in the list, click to **select it**, and click **Insert**.

AutoComplete

As mentioned elsewhere in the book, the AutoComplete feature, which was discontinued in Word 2007, has been reinstated in Word 2010. Essentially, it's a quick method of inserting a Quick Parts entry into your document. It works only if:

•   your Quick Parts entry has a name / abbreviation that is at least four characters long; and

•   the entry is stored in a template *other than* the default template, BuildingBlocks.dotx.

If the Quick Parts entry satisfies those criteria, you'll see an AutoComplete prompt (sometimes referred to as a "tip") after you type the fourth character of the name / abbreviation. When the prompt appears, you can either press the Enter key to insert the Quick Parts entry into the document or keep typing (if the name / abbreviation you've assigned is a real word and you want to use the word, rather than the full Quick Parts entry, in this specific situation). Of course, you also have the option of expanding your Quick Parts entry by pressing the F3 key.

So, for example, let's say that I create an interrogatory heading—as described in the section about SEQ codes that starts on page 489—and give it the name / abbreviation "ROGG." (Ordinarily, I'd call it "ROG," but the name has to be four characters long to trigger the AutoComplete prompt. Remember, too, that Quick Parts aren't case sensitive, so I could call the entry "rogg" or "Rogg" and it would work the same way.) When I set up the entry, I make sure to store it in the normal.dotm template rather than in BuildingBlocks.dotx.

Now, when I type "ROGG" (or "rogg" or "Rogg," etcetera), I see an AutoComplete prompt, as follows:

ROGG (Press ENTER to Insert)
rogg

The prompt merely shows me the name of the entry, followed by the parenthetical instruction, "(Press ENTER to Insert)." If I press the Enter key, my Quick Part is inserted at the cursor position. (See the next screenshot.)

INTERROGATORY NO. 1:

Sometimes, the AutoCorrect prompt shows what the entry will look like when expanded, as with a simple Quick Part I set up (using the abbreviation "janb") to insert my name:

Jan Berinstein (Press ENTER to Insert)
janb

Managing / Deleting Quick Parts Entries

When you click **Insert**, **Quick Parts**, then click **Building Block Organizer**, you will see that there are already a number of Quick Parts entries that come with the program. They appear in various drop-down galleries throughout the program, such as the Page Numbers gallery, the Headers gallery, the Footers gallery, and the Watermarks gallery. Within each gallery, Quick Parts are assigned to, and divided into, certain categories (Built-In, General, Simple, etc.). The categories are used mainly as a way of organizing the drop-downs.

By default, your new entries go in the Quick Parts gallery, but you can create your own custom galleries and assign existing or new Quick Parts to one of those galleries if you like.

Note that clicking the Gallery heading in the Organizer sorts the entries alphabetically by gallery name; clicking the Category heading sorts the entries alphabetically by category name; and clicking the Name heading sorts the entries alphabetically by name (abbreviation). You might have to click a heading twice; one click sorts in descending order and another click sorts in ascending order (or vice versa).

Because there are so many entries in the Organizer, you might want to create, and assign your entries to, a new gallery called AAA (or that starts with an underscore character), then sort by gallery. That way, your most frequently used entries will be easier to locate in the Organizer.

Of course, if you remember the abbreviations, you can insert entries simply by typing the abbreviation and pressing the F3 key.

And you can delete entries that you are unlikely to use. Doing so has the added benefit of making it easier to find your own entries in the list. Just go into the **Building Blocks Organizer**, click to select an entry, and click the "**Delete**" **button**. Word will prompt you to make sure you wish to delete the entry. If you're sure, click "**Yes**." Unfortunately, you can't select multiple entries; you have to select and delete one at a time.

Sharing Quick Parts

To share Quick Parts with other users, create a new blank template, preferably in a shared folder on a network drive. Then create Quick Parts from within that template, making sure the "Save in" field displays the name of the new template rather than the Building Blocks template or any other default. Continue creating your entries in and saving them to the new template.

Before distributing the template to others in the firm, delete any content (i.e., the "expanded" Quick Parts) and save the blank template. Even though you have deleted the content, the Quick Parts remain stored in the template.

When you give others access to the template, instruct them to *make a copy* and *store the copy in their Building Blocks folder*.

In Windows XP, the path is:
C:\Documents and Settings\<User Name>\Application Data\Microsoft\Document Building Blocks

In Vista and Windows 7, the path is:
C:\Users\<User Name>\AppData\Roaming\Microsoft\Document Building Blocks.

Note that they might have to close and reopen Word before the entries will appear in the Building Blocks Organizer.

To share *existing* Quick Parts, create a new template and then, one by one, edit the properties of the Quick Parts entries to change the "Save in" location to the new template. (From the Building Blocks Organizer, click to select an entry, click the "Edit Properties" button, and click the "Save in" drop-down. Select the new template. Repeat those steps for each Quick Parts entry you wish to distribute to other users.)

Note that you are *moving*, *not copying*, the Quick Parts entries to the new template, which means they might not be globally available to you (if you are working on a document created with a different template).

Importing Your Existing AutoText Entries into Word 2010

If you are upgrading from Word 2007, your Building Blocks / Quick Parts entries will be imported into Word 2010 automatically. However, upgrading doesn't automatically import the AutoText entries from an earlier version of Word, such as Word 2002 or Word 2003. You must import them manually.

Most of your AutoText entries from a previous version of Word are stored in your NORMAL template from that version (although you might also have created AutoText entries within one or more customized templates).[3] To import them into Word 2010, you'll need to copy your old NORMAL template into either (1) the same folder where your personalized Building Blocks template (Building Blocks.dotx) is located *or* (2) the Word Startup folder. That way, the AutoText entries from your earlier version of Word will load when you open the Building Blocks Organizer.

First, **locate the NORMAL template** from your prior version of Word. (If you previously used Word 2003, the installation process for Word 2010 changed the name of your original Word 2003 NORMAL template from **normal.dot** to "**Normal11.dot**." That is the one you want. Otherwise, look for normal.dot.) **Make a copy** of the old template and **rename the copy** "AutoText.dot." You can open the AutoText.dot template into Word 2010 and then save it as a .dotx template (the new Open Office XML template format), but it isn't necessary to do so.

Next, **paste** the renamed template into the **Document Building Blocks folder**, which contains your user-specific Building Blocks template. It is located here in Windows XP: C:\Documents and Settings\<User Name>\Application Data\Microsoft\Document Building Blocks.

And located here in Vista and Windows 7: C:\Users\<User Name>\AppData\Roaming\Microsoft\Document Building Blocks.

Alternatively, paste the template into the **Word Startup folder**, located here in Windows XP: C:\Documents and Settings\<User Name>\Application Data\Microsoft\Word\STARTUP

And located here in Vista and Windows 7: C:\Users\<User Name>\AppData\Roaming\Microsoft\Word\STARTUP.

The next time you open the Building Blocks Organizer, you should see your AutoText entries, shown as being stored in an AutoText Gallery. (Clicking the "Gallery" heading in the Organizer will sort the entries alphabetically by gallery, and all of the AutoText entries will be displayed together.)

You might have to exit from Word and then re-launch the program before the AutoText entries will appear in the Building Blocks Organizer.

---

[3] Copying other templates in which you have stored AutoText entries to the Document Building Blocks folder or the Word Startup folder will make those entries globally available, too.

The New AutoText Gallery

In Word 2010, there is a new AutoText gallery that appears as a fly-out from the Quick Parts drop-down. You can insert AutoText entries into your document from the gallery, and you also have the option of saving selected text and/or graphics directly to the AutoText gallery (note the "**Save Selection to AutoText Gallery**" command at the bottom of the fly-out menu).

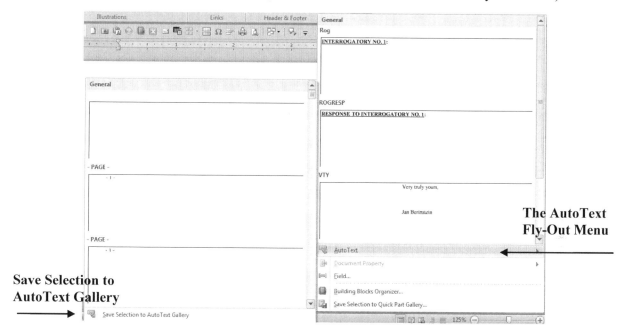

Save Selection to
AutoText Gallery

The AutoText
Fly-Out Menu

The AutoText Fly-Out Menu in the Quick Parts Gallery

To move an entry manually to the AutoText gallery (or any other gallery), **select the entry** in the Organizer, then click the "**Edit Properties**" **button**. When the "**Modify Building Block**" **dialog** appears, simply click the "**Gallery**" **drop-down** and click "**AutoText**" (or any other gallery in the list).

Click "**OK**" to save your change. A prompt will appear, asking "Do you want to redefine the building block entry?" Unless you have changed your mind for some reason, click "**Yes**."

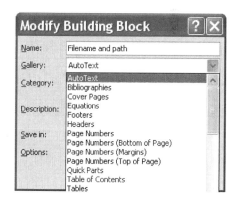

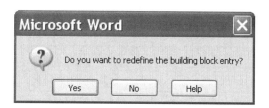

Finally, click "**Close**" to close the Building Blocks Organizer.

345

SIDEBAR: Creating a Page X of Y Quick Part

In a blank document, type "Page" (without quotation marks) and press the Spacebar.

Next, press **Alt Shift P** (which will insert a page number code for the current page) and press the Spacebar.

Type "of" (without quotation marks) and press the Spacebar.

Press **Alt I, F**, and when the **Field dialog** opens, press the letter **"N"** as many times as necessary to move the cursor to "**NumPages**" (the code for the total number of pages in the document), and then click **OK**.

You should see "Page X of Y," where X represents the page number of the current page and Y represents the total number of pages in your document. Select the text (and codes) and press **Alt F3**. (Alternatively, you can click the **Insert tab, Quick Parts, Save Selection to Quick Part Gallery**, but this method will place the new Quick Part in the BuildingBlocks.dotx template, you won't be able to use AutoComplete to expand the entry. See the discussion on page 340.)

When the **Create New Building Block dialog** appears, type an abbreviation such as PXOY, then click **OK**.

To insert the Page X of Y entry, position the cursor where you want the text and codes to appear, then **type your abbreviation** and **press F3** (or, when the **AutoComplete prompt** appears, press the **Enter key**).

Working With Styles

What Are Styles?

Styles are merely groups of formatting codes that can be applied all at once to a paragraph or series of paragraphs.[1] For example, you could create a style called "Block Quote" that indents a paragraph 1" from the left and 1" from the right and has a first-line indent of .5". Then you could turn on that style before typing a block quotation in a pleading (or apply the style after typing the text of the quotation), rather than applying the various indents separately.

You can configure a particular style so that it is always followed by another particular style. To use a typical example, many people create heading styles that are followed by a text style that indents the first line by half an inch or an inch, so that when they type a heading and press the Enter key, the cursor moves to the next line (or two lines down) and is indented the appropriate amount.

What Are the Advantages of Using Styles?

One advantage of using styles is that they provide a certain uniformity of appearance throughout your documents. If you don't use styles, you might inadvertently indent outline-numbered paragraphs differently; if you use styles, the numbered paragraphs always will be indented the same amount of space.

Styles save you time because you can apply multiple formatting codes all at once, rather than individually.

Also, it's easy to modify a particular style—let's say you have set up a heading style that uses boldface type, but you want underlining instead—and when you do, all of the paragraphs to which you have applied that style will reflect the change automatically, without your having to go through the document and reformat individual paragraphs.[2] Very convenient!

And if you use Word's built-in heading or outline numbered styles (even after you modify them to suit your needs), Word will pull your headings into a Table of Contents automatically—without your having to mark the headings for inclusion in the TOC.

---

[1] Actually, Word uses both paragraph styles and character styles, but paragraph styles are the ones most people are referring to when they use the term "styles." Generally speaking, character styles involve formatting attributes such as font face, font size, bolding, italics, small caps, etc., and paragraph styles involve formatting attributes such as alignment (justification), indentation, first-line indent (if any), hanging indent (if any), line spacing, space before, space after, and tabs.

[2] That phenomenon is not the same as the "Automatically Update" option. Rather, "Automatically Update" actually *redefines a style* when you make *a manual formatting change* to any paragraph to which that style has been applied. As you might imagine, that can be highly problematic, so use the option sparingly, if at all. See the sidebar on page 366.

What Are the Potential "Gotchas" of Using Styles?

1.   For one thing, you have to remember that when you create or modify a style, you are creating or modifying a style *ONLY* in the current document. This very important point is simply the way styles work in both MS Word and WordPerfect. In order to ensure that your customizations are available in new documents, ***you must check the "New documents based on this template" radio button*** at the bottom of the Create New Style From Formatting dialog box or the Modify Style dialog box (i.e., before you close the dialog after creating or modifying a style).

2.   Styles can change unexpectedly. There are a few possible reasons why:

(a)   You previously checked the "**Automatically update**" box in the Create New Style from Formatting dialog box or the Modify Formatting dialog box and have **manually reformatted** a paragraph to which that style has been applied in a document you are working on.

(b)   You have (or someone else has) modified **an underlying style** that is the basis for your style.

(c)   You have (or someone else has) modified **the template** in which your style is stored.

(d)   You are working on a different computer, and there is a style in the NORMAL template (normal.dotm) on that machine that has ***the same name*** as your style but ***is formatted differently***. (A document you create from scratch will reflect the formatting of the style in the normal.dotm of the machine you are working on.)

What Is the "Normal" Style?

The "Normal" style is the ***default paragraph style***—i.e., it uses the default settings in the **Paragraph dialog box (Home tab, Paragraph group, dialog launcher**; alternatively, press the keystrokes **Alt O, P**). The "Normal" style typically inherits the default font face and size specified in your underlying template (usually meaning the **NORMAL template**). So, for example, if your Normal.dotm uses a 10-point Times New Roman font, that is the font you'll get when you apply the "Normal" style to a paragraph.[3] When you do so, you'll also strip out any and all indentation, alignment, space before and after, etc. that you have applied to the paragraph manually via the Paragraph dialog.

CAUTION: In Word 2010, the Normal paragraph style ***does not*** determine the font settings for built-in Heading styles. Those settings are determined by "Themes." For

---

[3] **NOTE**: Different templates can—but do not necessarily— have different Normal paragraph styles.

348

instructions on creating a new "Theme" that uses your preferred font for Heading styles, see the "Making Word 2010 Work Like Older Versions" section of the book starting on page 221.

How Do I Use Word's Built-In Styles?

Word comes with a number of built-in styles, including nine heading styles (corresponding to various "levels" of headings). Note that built-in styles are responsible for the appearance of various features of your documents, including footnotes and footers. You can use any of the existing styles as is, or you can modify them to suit your needs.

To use a built-in style, click somewhere within the paragraph to which you want to apply the style (or select contiguous paragraphs), then use one of the following methods:

1.   On the **Home tab**, locate the **Styles group** and click the **dialog launcher** (or press **Ctrl Alt Shift S**). When the **Styles Pane** opens, select the style from the Styles list, and click it. Word will apply the style to the paragraph your cursor is in.

Styles Pane

NOTE: By default, Word 2010 displays only some of the built-in styles. In order to change which styles are displayed, click the **Options button** at the lower right-hand side of the Styles pane and select **All Styles**. If you like, change the order in which the styles are displayed (from Recommended to Alphabetical, for example). Then **OK** out of the Style Pane Options dialog.

2.   Alternatively, you can position your cursor to the right of the **Quick Styles Gallery** at the right side of the **Home tab**, click the **up arrow** or **down arrow** to scroll through the gallery row by row and, if you see an icon for the style you want to use, click that icon.

3.   You can click the "**More**" button (underneath the up and down arrows) to open the gallery and click "**Apply Styles**" (at the bottom of the gallery), then type a name of the style you want to use—or click the drop-down and choose a style from the list—and finally click "**Reapply**."

4.   If you click "**Change Styles**," you will open a drop-down with a "**Style Set**" option. This option provides a gallery of predefined "Style Sets" that you can apply to your document as a whole (as opposed to a paragraph style).[4] *Use this option with some caution*, for obvious reasons. For more about Style Sets, see the section starting on page 222.

5.   There is a "mini" style pane called the **Apply Styles dialog** that you can open by pressing the key combination **Ctrl Shift S**. When it opens, you can select a style from the drop-down list (or type the name of an existing style) and apply the style by clicking the somewhat confusingly labeled "**Reapply**" **button** or you can modify the style by clicking the **Modify button**. (The Apply Styles dialog also features a button that opens the full Styles Pane.)

6.   If you have assigned a **keyboard combination** to a style, just press that key combination.

How Do I Create My Own Custom Styles?

There are two different ways to create a custom style:

1.   **By Example**:

    (a)   You can create a style from a paragraph that is already formatted a certain way by placing the cursor within the paragraph, pressing **Ctrl Shift S** to open the **Apply Styles dialog**, typing a name in the **Style Name** box, then clicking **New** and closing the Apply Styles dialog. **NOTE:** Styles created in this manner *are not added to the underlying template*, which means they are available only in the current document.

    (b)   You can select some text, **right-click**, click "Styles," then click "**Save selection as a New Quick Style**." When the **Create New Style from Formatting** dialog opens, type a **unique name** for the style. To add the new style to the underlying template, click the "**Modify**" **button**, click the "**New documents based on this template**" **radio button**, and **OK** out.

2.   **From Scratch**:

    (a)   On the **Home tab**, locate the **Styles group** and click the **dialog launcher**. When the Styles Pane opens, click the "**New Style**" button in the lower left-hand corner. That will open an expanded version of the **Create New Style from Formatting dialog box** (see the screenshot on the next page).

---

[4] The Style Sets include one that Microsoft has labeled "Word 2003." As mentioned on page 224, this label is somewhat misleading because when you apply the Word 2003 Style Set, you still get the Calibri font, which was not the default font in Word 2003.

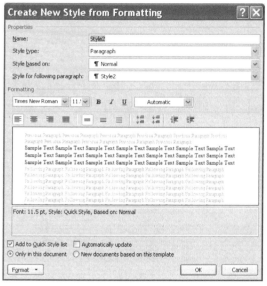

Create New Style from Formatting dialog

(b)   When the dialog appears, **type a name** for the style (it must be unique, and it should describe what the style does). Ignore the style type; Word assumes that you're creating a paragraph style, which you are. Therefore, you don't want to change the style type.

(c)   You can base the style on an existing style. If you wish to do so, type the name of the base style in the "**Style based on**" field. (**CAUTION**: When you use this option, it's important to remember that *any modification to the base style will affect your new style as well*.)

(d)   Also, you can specify a style for the following paragraph by typing a style name in the "**Style for Following Paragraph**" field. If you don't specify a style, the following paragraph will use the same style.

(e)   To specify formatting details, such as font, tabs, numbering, and so forth, click the "**Format**" **button** and choose the appropriate options.

(f)   When you have finished, click the "**New documents based on this template**" radio button, then **OK** out of the dialog. (If you don't click the "New documents based on this template" radio button, the style will be available *only in the current document*.)

(g)   Note that if you check "**Automatically update**," any *manual formatting changes* you make to one paragraph to which that style has been applied will redefine the style and, as a result, will be reflected in *all* paragraphs to which that style has been applied. That option can be useful, but, as mentioned previously, it can produce unexpected results, so *use it with caution, if at all*.

How Do I Modify Styles?

There are a couple of ways to modify a style:

1.   Click within a paragraph to which that style has been applied. Make any formatting changes you like, then **right-click** and select **Styles, Update <style name> to match selection**.

> The modifications you just made will be incorporated into the style. Note that this method *does not add your modifications to the underlying template* (i.e., it will modify the style only in the current document).

2.   Alternatively, from the **Home tab**, click the **Styles Pane launcher**. When the Styles Pane appears, *right*-click the style name, then click "**Modify**." Make any changes you like. If you want the modifications to go into effect in all new documents based on the underlying template, be sure to click the "**New documents based on this template**" radio button before OK-ing out of the dialog.

Can I Copy a Style From Another Document (or Template) into This One?

Yes! Just copy the paragraph symbol at the end of a "styled" paragraph in your "source" document (which can be a regular document or a template) and paste it into your "destination" document (which also can be either a regular document or a template). You can copy some text, too, if you like, but *the key is to copy the paragraph symbol* because—as you know—it contains the formatting codes for that paragraph, including the information about the style.

If necessary, turn on **Show Non-Printing Characters** (press **Ctrl Shift * [asterisk]**, or click the **¶ button** in the **Paragraph group** on the **Home tab**) so that you can see the paragraph symbol.

Copying Styles With the Organizer

In addition to the method described above, you can copy styles between documents and/or templates by using the **Organizer**.

There are at least three different ways to open the Organizer in Word 2010:

(1)   Launch the **Styles Pane**, click the **Manage Styles button**, then click the **Import/Export button** at the bottom of the **Manage Styles dialog**; *or*

(2)   If you have displayed the **Developer tab**, click it, then navigate to the **Templates group** and click the **Document Template icon**, then click "**Organizer**"; *or*

(3)   Click the **File tab, Options, Add-Ins**, then click the "**Manage**" drop-down and change it to **Templates**, and finally click "**Go**." When the **Templates and Add-Ins dialog** opens, click "**Organizer**."

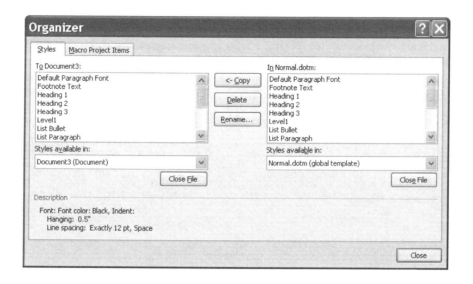

The Organizer

When the Organizer opens, you'll see a box on the left and a box on the right. The left-hand box typically shows the styles available in the document on your screen; the right-hand box typically shows the styles available in your NORMAL template (normal.dotm). To copy a style from one to the other, click the style in the "**source**" document (the one you want to copy *from*). The "**Copy**" **button** will become active, and will display an arrow pointing left or right, depending on which box you're copying into (the arrow points to the "**destination**" document or template—the one you're copying *to*). Click the button to copy a style from one document or template to the other. Note that you can select and copy multiple styles all at once (by pressing the **Ctrl key** before clicking the styles you wish to copy).

CAUTION: If a style in the source document or template has the same name as a style in the destination document or template, Word will warn you and ask if you want to overwrite the style in the destination document. Pay attention to this warning; it is designed to prevent you from accidentally overwriting *a custom style* that you might have assigned the same name as a style that actually is formatted differently. Styles with the same name *are not necessarily the same style*!

You can delete or rename styles in documents and templates via the Organizer, as well. Again, use caution before deleting or renaming a style, especially from within a template. (On the other hand, people sometimes clutter their documents and templates with lots of styles they never use; if you're sure you don't need particular styles, it's not a bad idea to delete them, since a profusion of styles can lead to document corruption.)

Although the Organizer opens with items in the current document displayed on the left and items in the NORMAL template displayed on the right, you can display a different document or template on either side simply by clicking the "**Close File**" button underneath one of the boxes, which then becomes an "**Open File**" button. Click the "Open File" button and navigate to the document or template you wish to use instead, then click the "**Open**" button. (If you like, you can repeat the process for the other document or template.)

When you have finished copying, renaming, and/or deleting styles, just click "**Close**" to close the Organizer. (At that point, Word might prompt you to save any changes you've made.) If you're through with the Styles Pane, click the **X** at the upper right-hand side of the Styles Pane to close it.

How Do I Assign a Keyboard Shortcut to a Style?

As you can see from the screenshot on page 351, the **Create New Style from Formatting** dialog box has a **Format button** at the bottom left. Clicking the button opens a menu that has a "**Shortcut key**" command (at the end). If you click the Shortcut key command, the "Customize Keyboard" dialog appears.

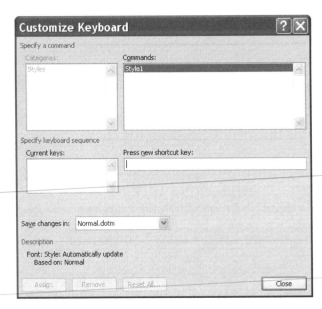

Customize Keyboard dialog

To assign a keyboard shortcut, type the shortcut you wish to use in the "**Press new shortcut key**" box. (For keyboard combinations that use function keys or the Alt key, the Ctrl key, and/or the Shift key, simply press the keys in the sequence you desire.) If that shortcut already has been assigned to another function, you'll see the words "**Currently assigned to**," followed by the function. If you wish to use the keyboard shortcut (even if it is currently assigned to another function), just click the "**Assign**" button (it is grayed out until you insert a key combination in the "Press new shortcut key" box), then **close** the dialog.

As mentioned toward the beginning of the book in the section on keyboard shortcuts, there are a few predefined keystrokes in Word that will apply (or remove) styles. These shortcuts include the following:

Ctrl Q   – removes paragraph formatting (unless applied via a style)

Ctrl Shift N   – applies the Normal paragraph style

Ctrl Shift L   – applies the bulleted list style

Ctrl Alt 1   – applies the Heading 1 style

Ctrl Alt 2   – applies the Heading 2 style

Ctrl Alt 3   – applies the Heading 3 style

How Can I View the Styles in a Document?

First, click the **File tab**, **Options**, click **Advanced**, then scroll down to **Display**. In the box labeled **Style area pane width in Draft and Outline views**, set a width larger than 0" (1" is usually sufficient), and **OK** out of the dialog box.

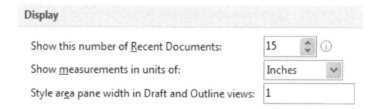

Then switch to **Draft view** (by clicking the **View tab**, **Draft** or clicking the **Draft View icon** on the Status Bar). You should see a **Style Area** at the left-hand side of your document that shows the styles (if any) that have been applied to the various paragraphs in the document.

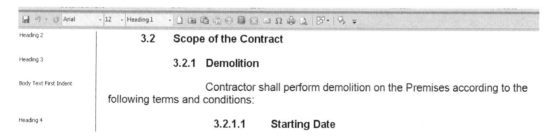

What Are Those Weird-Looking Styles in the Style Pane?

If a somewhat obscure feature called **Keep track of formatting** is enabled, the Styles pane will display the name of the style in use in a particular paragraph, *plus* any formatting you've applied directly, such as bold, underlining, a first-line indent, or a custom font size (or, as in the example below, only the font attributes, without a style name). This feature can be both confusing and distracting.

To turn it off, click the **File tab**, **Options**, **Advanced**, **Editing**, uncheck **Keep track of formatting**, and **OK** out.

CAUTION: There's another place you might inadvertently turn on this feature. If you click **Options** in the **Style pane**, you'll see an option to "**Select formatting to show as styles**," with checkboxes for Paragraph level formatting, Font formatting, and bullet and numbering formatting. (See the screenshot below.)

If you check one or more of those boxes and OK out of the dialog, you will in effect enable the Keep track of formatting feature.

For a fuller discussion of "Keep track of formatting," including its benefits, see the section starting on page 530.

The Quick Style Gallery

The Quick Style Gallery, a prominent part of the Home tab (at the right side, in the Styles group), made its debut in Word 2007. Although there are other ways of finding and applying styles, the Quick Style Gallery is particularly convenient because it provides easy access to—and a visual representation of—some of the most commonly used built-in styles (heading styles, the Normal paragraph style, and so on). It also displays the other styles (built-in or custom) that exist in the current document.

The Quick Style Gallery

Applying a Quick Style

To apply one of the styles in the gallery, simply click the icon for that style. In order to see all the available Quick Styles, you might have to scroll up or down, or pull down the entire menu of styles, by using one of the arrows at the right side of the gallery. The single up and down arrows are for scrolling one row at a time; the down arrow with the line above it is for opening the drop-down menu of styles.

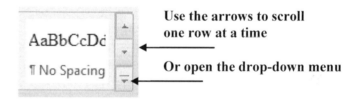

My Default Quick Styles Gallery (the Drop-Down Menu)

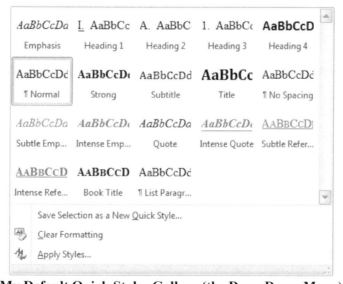

Live Preview

The Quick Styles Gallery makes use of another feature introduced in Word 2007, **Live Preview**. Live Preview means that when you position the mouse pointer over a style in the gallery (either deliberately or accidentally), Word **changes the appearance of the text** at the cursor position in your document, showing what it would look like with that style applied.

The Quick Styles Gallery makes use of another feature introduced in Word 2007, Live Preview. Live Preview means that when you position the mouse pointer over a style in the gallery (either deliberately or accidentally), Word changes the appearance of the text at the cursor position in your document, showing what it would look like with that style applied.

A Preview of the "Intense Quote" Style Applied to the Previous Paragraph

(The screenshot immediately above shows what happened when I moved my mouse pointer over the "Intense Quote" style in the gallery while my cursor was inserted in the previous paragraph.)

The sudden change can be disconcerting if you don't realize what's going on. Don't panic! It's just a preview, and it's temporary. If you don't click the icon representing that style, the style will **not** be applied to the text. As soon as you move your mouse, the appearance of the text will return to normal.

What the Gallery Contains

Which styles are displayed in the gallery? And what determines the order in which they're shown?

When you first start using Word, the gallery is already populated with certain frequently used styles, including heading styles, the Normal style, and a few other paragraph and character styles.[1] In addition, it will display any styles that exist in the current document. (An important point about Quick Styles is that Quick Styles are document-specific; that is, they are stored in individual documents. In other words, with the exception of the "canned" Quick Styles that Microsoft has added to the gallery by default, what you see in the gallery depends on which document you have on your screen.)

Adding and Removing Styles

It is very easy to add styles to, and remove styles from, the gallery. To remove a style, simply **right-click** it and, when the context-sensitive menu opens, click "**Remove from Quick Style Gallery.**"

---

[1] I don't know for certain, but it seems likely that Microsoft has chosen those styles based on user feedback.

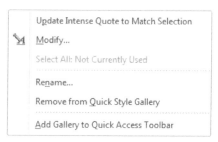

Right-Click a Style to Remove It From the Gallery

To add an existing style to the gallery, open the **Styles Pane** (so that you can see all available styles) by either (1) clicking the **dialog launcher** at the bottom right side of the Styles group or (2) pressing the key combination **Alt Ctrl Shift S**. Next, locate the style you want to add to the gallery, **right-click** it, and choose "**Add to Quick Style Gallery.**"

There are a couple of other ways that styles are added to the Quick Style Gallery. For one thing, when you create a new (custom) style, it's automatically added to the Quick Style Gallery. You might notice an additional checkbox at the bottom of the "Create New Style from Formatting" dialog that is labeled "Add to Quick Style list"; the box is checked by default. Unless you deliberately *uncheck* it, your new style will appear in the Quick Style Gallery.

For another thing, it's easy to create Quick Styles "on the fly" from formatted text. To do so, select the text, then right-click it.[2] One of the options on the context-sensitive menu is "Styles"; position the mouse over that command, then click "Save Selection as a new Quick Style…"

When you do so, a dialog opens where you can type a descriptive name for the new Quick Style, then click OK to save the style to the gallery. (But before you click OK, note the cautionary paragraph below.)

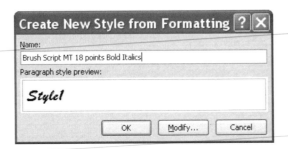

CAUTION: By default, your new Quick Style will be available *only in the current document* unless you take steps to add it to the underlying template. You can do so in a couple of different ways. The easiest way is to click the "**Modify**" **button** in the small dialog box before clicking "**OK**" and, when the large dialog appears, click the "**New documents based on this template**" **radio button**, and *then* click "**OK**." See the screenshot on the next page.

---

[2] With paragraph styles, you shouldn't have to select the text first. Positioning your cursor somewhere within the formatted text should be sufficient.

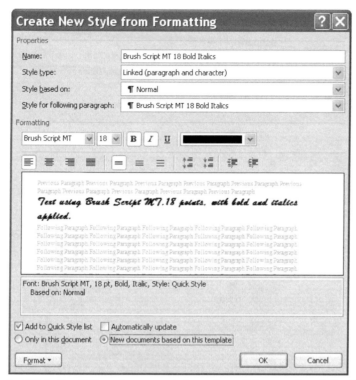

Be Sure to Click the "New documents based on this template" Radio Button

Alternatively, if you forget this step when you first set up the style, you can right-click the style in either the Quick Styles Gallery or the Styles Pane, and when the dialog opens, click "**Modify**," click the "**New documents based on this template" radio button**, then click "**OK**."

Right-Click the Style in the Gallery, then click "Modify…"

What Determines the Order of Styles in the Gallery?

The order of the styles in the Quick Style Gallery is based on each style's "priority" setting, which in turn is set by Microsoft. You can find, and change, a style's priority by opening the Styles Pane (again, either by clicking the dialog launcher at the bottom right side of the Styles group or pressing the key combination Alt Ctrl Shift S), and then clicking the right-most button at the bottom of the pane, which will open the **Manage Styles dialog**.

The Right-Most Button Opens the Manage Styles Dialog

When the Manage Styles dialog appears, click the "Recommend" tab. In that tab, styles appear with their pre-assigned priority to the left. To change a style's priority, click it in the list and, when it is selected (highlighted), click the "Assign Value" button (in the section of the dialog labeled "Set priority to use when sorting in recommended order").

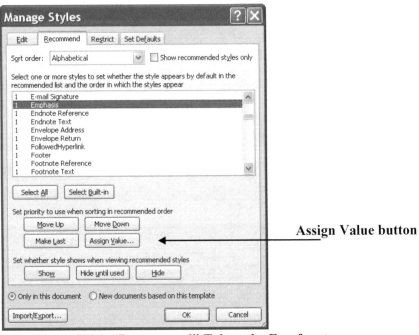

Manage Styles Dialog With "Recommend" Tab at the Forefront

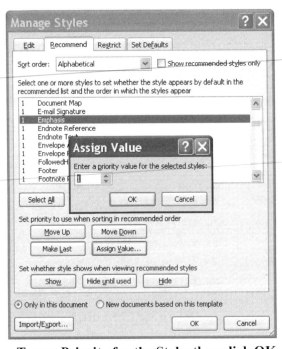

Type a Priority for the Style, then click OK

Type a new priority in the box, then click OK. The style should appear in a different position in the Quick Styles Gallery, based on the priority that you assigned.

Other Options

When you right-click a style in the gallery, you'll see a context-sensitive menu similar to the following:

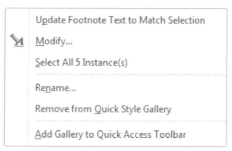

The menu offers several options, including:

- **"Update [Style Name] to Match Selection"** (this option provides an easy way to modify a style on the fly so that the style will match the formatting of selected text);

- **"Modify"** (which opens the "Modify Style" dialog and allows you to make various changes);

- **"Select All [Number of] Instance(s)"** (i.e., to select all instances of the style existing in the current document so that you can change the formatting, delete them, etc.);

- **"Rename..."**;

- **"Remove from Quick Style Gallery"**; and

- **"Add Gallery to Quick Access Toolbar"** (this last command lets you put a drop-down for the Quick Styles Gallery on the QAT so that it is readily available even if the Home tab isn't at the forefront).

Quick Styles Gallery Drop-Down Button on QAT

SIDEBAR: The Style Inspector

The Style Inspector

Word 2010 contains a tool called the "**Style Inspector**," first introduced in Word 2007, that lets you see—and remove—paragraph formatting and character formatting (the latter is referred to in the Style Inspector as Text-level formatting) in a paragraph.

For the example shown below, I typed some text and applied the Body Text Indent 3 style (a paragraph style) to it. Then I went into the Paragraph dialog and manually set the Before Spacing—in this one paragraph only—to 12 points (I did ***not*** modify the style so that it always uses Before Spacing of 12 points).

After that, I selected certain portions of the text and changed the font size to 9 points (the default font size for that style is 8 points), bolded and italicized other portions, and used strikeout (there's a strikeout button in the **Font group** on the **Home tab**, though I could have applied the strikeout attribute from the **Font dialog**).

I clicked in the portion of the text with the various font changes, then launched the Style Pane and clicked the Style Inspector button (the one in the middle at the bottom of the Pane). The result is shown below.

Note that the top portion of the dialog box deals with Paragraph formatting and the bottom with character or Text-level formatting. Under Paragraph formatting, the top box shows any style that has been applied to the paragraph and the bottom box shows any formatting you've applied manually via the Paragraph dialog. In this case, it displays the 12-point Before Spacing that I added.

Under Text level formatting, the top box shows the font face that is in use in the paragraph, while the bottom box shows any character or font attributes you've applied to the text. In this case, it displays the change in the size of the text (to 9 points), as well as the Bold Italic, and Strikethrough attributes.

You can clear paragraph or character formatting by clicking one or more of the button(s) at the right side of the dialog—the ones with the eraser on them. Note that if you wish to clear either type of paragraph formatting, it doesn't matter where your cursor is as long as it's somewhere within the affected paragraph. However, if you wish to clear Text-level formatting, you need to select the text before stripping the formatting. (As far as I know, if you've applied several different font attributes, you can't clear only one via the Style Inspector; the "Clear" buttons wipe out all attributes at once. Of course, you always have the option of opening the Font dialog and unchecking one or more individual attributes, leaving the others intact.)

You don't need to select text to use the "Clear All" option. That option works on the entire paragraph.

Note, incidentally, that there is a button in the Font group on the Home tab that will clear the formatting of selected text.

Clear Formatting Button

SIDEBAR: Why the "Automatically Update" Option Is a Bad Idea

If you enable the "Automatically Update" option when you create or modify a style, any manual formatting changes you make in a paragraph to which the style has been applied *will redefine the style itself.*[1]

For example, let's say you create a style for indented quotes (per the instructions starting on page 459). You use Exactly 12 point line spacing, a left indent of 1" and a right indent of 1", no "Special" formatting for the first line of a paragraph, and no spacing after. You check the "Automatically update" option, as well as the "New documents based on this template" option, before saving the style. Afterwards, you apply the style to several paragraphs in your document. Everything works fine, but then you decide to apply a First-line indent to one of the paragraphs. You click in that paragraph, open the Paragraph dialog, change the "Special" drop-down to "First line" and accept the default of .5", then click "OK."

As you scroll through your document, you notice that the first line of *all* of the paragraphs to which you applied the indented quotes style has been indented half an inch. You remove the indent on one of the paragraphs that should not be indented, and all of the other paragraphs to which the style has been applied also change. The same type of thing happens if you apply italics or boldface to one paragraph within a lengthy indented quote. Every other paragraph in the indented quote also becomes italicized or bold. Argh!

You can see why the "Automatically update" option is a bad idea.

But what if you truly do want to modify a style to match formatting changes you have made manually in a paragraph to which the style has been applied?

Not to worry. There are other ways of updating a style to match selected text. You can (1) right-click the icon for the style in the Quick Styles gallery, then click "Update [Style Name] to Match Selection"; or (2) right-click the style name in the Styles Pane, then click "Update [Style Name] to Match Selection." Also, you can select a paragraph to which a style has been applied and right-click the selected text, slide the mouse over the "Styles" option, and click "Update [Style Name] to Match Selection."

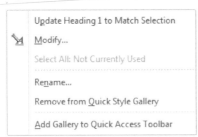

Right-click the icon in the Quick Styles gallery, or…

Right-click the style name in the Styles Pane, or…

Select the paragraph, then right-click, and choose Styles

---

[1] For other ways to modify a style, see the section starting on page 352.

Creating Your Own Templates

Templates are form documents that you can use over and over.[1] Common examples include letterhead, a fax cover sheet, a proof of service, or a generic pleading that consists mainly of a caption, a footer, and a signature block (with placeholders in lieu of specific information).

It's fairly easy to create a template. In this tutorial, I will provide the basic steps for creating and saving simple templates and using documents based thereon.

Creating a Template From an Existing Document

You can create a template from scratch—starting with a blank document and then adding any text, field codes, graphics, and/or formatting you want—or you can turn an existing document into a template. To turn an existing document into a template, locate the document and, in order to avoid overwriting it, open it as a copy. (Just click to select the document, then instead of clicking the "Open" button in the Open dialog, click the arrow at the right side of the button and, when the menu appears, click either "**Open as Copy**" or "**Open Read-Only**." The two commands work more or less the same way.)

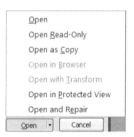

When the file opens, delete any specific information that you don't want to appear in new documents based on the template. (For obvious reasons, templates need to be as generic as possible, although the specific situation will determine which information remains in the template. As an example, one of my Word 2007 training clients recently asked me to help them set up a letterhead template that any member of the firm could use, plus individual templates for all of the attorneys. The communal letterhead template used a generic signature block; the other templates contained contact information and signature blocks for the individual lawyers.)

Go ahead and make any changes you desire. You might need to change some of the formatting, too.

When you have finished, you will need to take two important steps in order to use the document as a template: (1) change the file format to one of Word's template formats, as explained in the following sections; and (2) save it in the specific location where Word will look for your templates.

---

[1] All documents, including blank ones, are based on a template. Under most circumstances, the NORMAL template (normal.dotm)—each user has one—is the basis for new documents.

Word Template File Formats

In Word 2010, templates take the form of **.dotx files** and **.dotm files**. The difference is that .dotx files (like .docx files), can't contain macros created in Visual Basic for Applications (VBA). By contrast, .dotm files (like .docm files) can contain VBA macros. If you are a macro whiz and you want to incorporate VBA macros in your templates, be sure to save them as .dotm files rather than .dotx. Otherwise, you can save your templates in the more common .dotx file format.[2]

If you are planning to share a template with other people and you're not sure if they have Word 2010 (or Word 2007), or if they have a converter that will enable them to open Word templates saved in one of the Open Office XML file formats, consider saving the file as an old-fashioned **.dot file**—i.e., a Word 97-2003 compatible template.

To turn your document into a template, click the **File tab**, **Save As**, and when the **Save As dialog** appears, click the "**Save as type**" **drop-down** and change the document type to "**Word Template (*.dotx)**"—or, if you intend to create macros within the template, to "**Word Macro-Enabled Template (*.dotm)**."

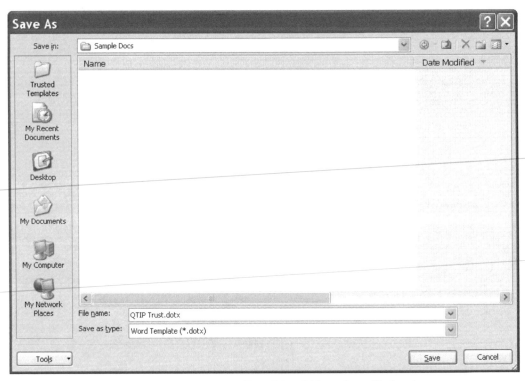

Change the "Save as type" to Word Template (*.dotx)

---

[2] **NOTE**: Although .dotx templates are not macro-enabled (they can't contain VBA-coded macros), you can create documents based on those templates that *are* macro-enabled. However, you must save those documents in the .docm format (or the old .doc format) rather than the standard Word 2010 .docx format. None of the Open Office XML file formats that end with "x" can store macros. (Think of the "x" as meaning "no.")

Next, give the document a **descriptive name**. In the examples, I have named the template QTIP Trust (where QTIP stands for Qualified Terminable Interest Property).

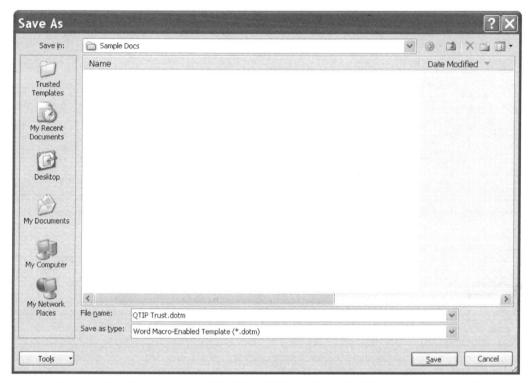

Change the "Save as type" to Word Macro-Enabled Template (*.dotm)

After changing the file type and giving the template a descriptive name, you'll need to click the "**Save in" drop-down** and store the template in a folder where Word ordinarily looks for templates. This step is critical. (As you can see from the screenshots above, I haven't saved the template to the correct location yet.)

Where Word Templates Are Stored

By default, Word stores each individual's customized templates in a so-called "**User templates**" folder. Ordinarily that folder is located in your user data folder, as follows:

If you are using Windows XP:
C:\Documents and Settings\<User Name>\Application Data\Microsoft\Templates

If you are using Windows Vista or Windows 7:
C:\Users\<User Name>\AppData\Roaming\Microsoft\Templates

Word stores shared templates in a so-called "**Workgroup templates**" folder, which usually is on a network drive. If you are creating a template that will be used by other members of your organization, make sure (1) that you save it in the location where other shared templates normally are stored (if you don't know where that is, check with your office administrator or your IT department); and (2) that each person's computer points to that location.

To set up individual workstations so that they point to the correct template folders, click the **File tab**, **Options**, and click the **Advanced category**. Then scroll all the way to the bottom and click the "**File Locations**" button.

Click the File Locations button →

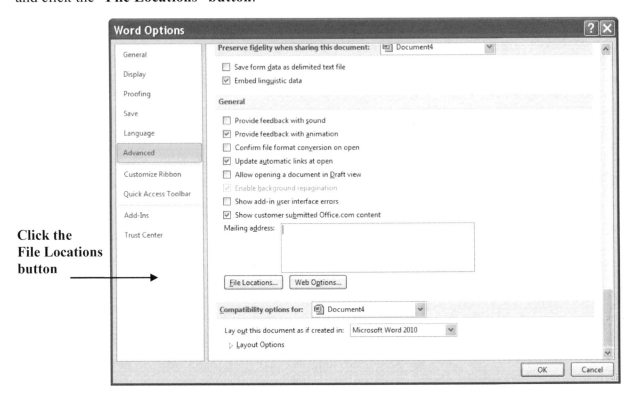

A **File Locations dialog** will open, showing the default locations for the various types of documents.

In the screenshot at right, you can see that the location for the Workgroup templates—i.e., the shared templates—is blank, meaning it hasn't been set up.

To tell Word where to look for any Workgroup templates, **click "Workgroup templates**," then click the "**Modify…**" **button**. **Browse** to the folder where your organization stores its shared templates, then click "**OK**."

Afterwards, the new location will appear in the File Locations dialog. Be sure to click "**OK**" to save your settings when you close the dialog.

File Locations Dialog

370

Creating a Document Based on Your Custom Template

To create a document based on your template, click the **File tab**, **New**, then click "**My templates**." The **New dialog** will open. It will display your personal templates, as well as certain other built-in templates and templates shared among members of your organization.

Note that the dialog you see probably will look somewhat different from the one in the screenshot (in part because I'm not on a network and in part because I've created a number of customized templates as well as a "Custom Templates" folder—a subfolder of my User templates folder in Windows XP—in which to store them).

New Dialog Showing My Personal Templates

As an aside, note that there is a Blank Document template showing in the Personal Templates area, which is my NORMAL template (normal.dotm). Note, too, that the icons for the macro-enabled dotm. templates (including normal.dotm) look slightly different from the regular Word templates icon; they have an exclamation point in the lower right-hand corner.

Creating Another Template Based on Your Custom Template

Take a look at the lower right-hand side of the dialog. Under "**Create New**," the "**Document**" **radio button** is enabled by default. That means that when you either (1) **double-click an icon** for one of the templates *or* (2) **single-click an icon** and click "**OK**," Word will create a brand-new document based on the template. Microsoft made that behavior the default so that the underlying template will remain intact and you can use it again and again to create individual documents.

The other radio button, labeled "**Template**," is used to create *another template* that is based on the existing one. For instance, let's say you already set up a generic letterhead template that can be used by any employee of your organization. You can open the New dialog, click to select that template, click the "Template" radio button, and start working on and customizing a letterhead template for a particular attorney. (The template opens with a name like "Template1," "Template2," etcetera.) When you finish working on the attorney's letterhead template, click the **File tab**, "**Save As**." The **Save As dialog** opens to the same location where you stored the underlying template, so all you need to do is give the new template a different name, such as the attorney's initials followed by the word "Letterhead." Because you opened the file as a template, the "Save as type" drop-down already indicates that the template will be saved as a .dotx (or a .dotm, depending on the file format of the underlying template).

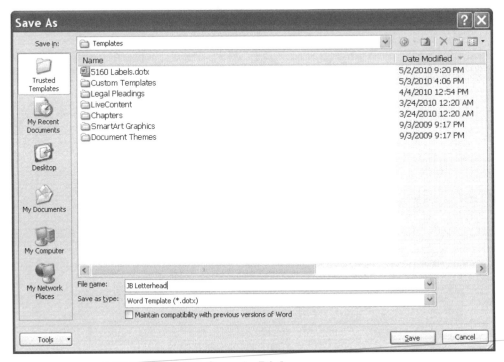

Save As Dialog

Editing a Template

If at some point you want to revise an existing template, you will have to open the template in the same way you open regular documents for editing. In other words, be sure to click the **File tab**, **Open** *or* press **Ctrl O** (and then **select the template** and click the "**Open**" **button**), rather than clicking the File tab, New. It's easy to get confused and click File, New, but if you do so, you will end up editing either a new document based on the template or a new template based thereon—***not*** the template itself.

Miscellaneous Tips About Templates

Many organizations incorporate a code for the file name and path into templates, typically in the footer. The code will update automatically when you save a new document based on the template, making it easy to locate. Although I have provided instructions elsewhere in the book for inserting a code for the file name or for the file name and path (see the section starting on page 323), I thought it might be helpful to repeat those steps in this section.

To insert a code for the file name and path in the footer while you are creating or revising a template, go into the footer editing screen by doing any of the following:

- double-clicking in the footer area; or

- right-clicking in the footer area and then clicking "Edit Footer"; or

- clicking the Footer drop-down on the Insert tab, then clicking "Edit Footer."

Position your cursor where you want the code to go. Then click the **Insert tab**, **Quick Parts**, **Field** *or* press **Alt I, F**. When the **Field dialog** appears, scroll through the Field names box until you come to the **FileName field**. Click to **select it**, then—if you want to include the path as well as the file name in the code—click to put a check in the "**Add path to filename**" **box** at the upper right side of the Field dialog. This step is optional, of course.

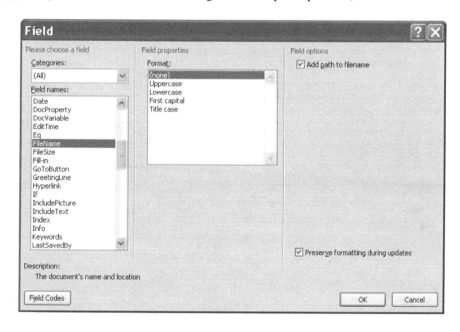

Before clicking "OK," look at the "**Field properties**" **box** at the center of the dialog and, if you wish, click to select a particular format for the code. You can choose among uppercase, lowercase, first capital (sentence case), and title case (initial caps). When you are ready to insert the code, click "**OK**."

If you haven't saved the template yet, the code will display a generic name, such as Document2. After you save the template and give it a name, the code still might not update until and unless you update it manually by **clicking in (or selecting)** the code and pressing **F9**. (The code will update automatically when you print the template, or a document based on the template, but only if "**Update fields before printing**" is enabled in the Word Options. To enable that option, click the **File tab**, **Options**, then click the **Display category** and look at the **Printing options**, about a third of the way down the page. If "**Update fields before printing**" is unchecked, **click to put a checkmark in the box**, then be sure to click "**OK**" to save your settings.)

General

Display

Proofing

Save

Language

Advanced

Customize Ribbon

Quick Access Toolbar

Add-Ins

Trust Center

Change how document content is displayed on the screen and when printed.

Page display options

☑ Show white space between pages in Print Layout view ⓘ
☑ Show highlighter marks ⓘ
☑ Show document tooltips on hover

Always show these formatting marks on the screen

☐ Tab characters   →
☐ Spaces   ...
☐ Paragraph marks   ¶
☐ Hidden text   a̶b̶c̶
☐ Optional hyphens   ¬
☐ Object anchors   ⚓
☐ Show all formatting marks

Printing options

☑ Print drawings created in Word ⓘ
☐ Print background colors and images
☐ Print document properties
☐ Print hidden text
☑ Update fields before printing
☐ Update linked data before printing

Update fields before printing ⟶

Word Options, Display Category, Printing Options

If the code appears in a font size or font face other than what you want, just select the code and apply any font formatting you like. (You can make the code smaller or larger, change the font face, apply bolding or italics, and so forth.)

Be sure to save your changes before closing the template.

Using Fill-In Fields

As mentioned in the section starting on page 96, you can add fill-in fields to a template to prompt users to enter specific information. For example, you can set up an envelope template that prompts users to type contact names and addresses or a pleading template that prompts users for the names of plaintiffs and defendants.

Because this feature is covered in detail elsewhere, I won't repeat the steps here.

Adding Template Icons to the QAT

An easy way to open a new document based on one of your custom templates is by creating a macro to open the template and then adding an icon for the macro to your QAT. Here's how to do so:

- Either click the **Macro icon** on the **Status Bar** *or* click the **View tab**, **Macros drop-down**, and click "**Record Macro**."

- When the **Record Macro dialog** appears, give the macro **a name** such as "OpenLetterhead" (remember that macro names can't have spaces between words).

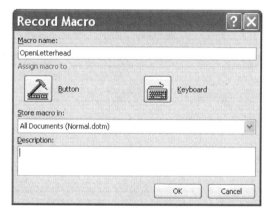

- If you like, add **a description** in the "Description" box.

- Click "**OK**" to start recording the macro. (Essentially, you're going to record your keystrokes while you open a document based on your template.)

- Next, click the **File tab**, **New**.

- Click "**My templates**."

- When the **New dialog** opens, navigate to the icon for your letterhead template and either double-click it *or* click it once and then click "**OK**."

- When the letterhead opens, either click the **Macro icon** on the **Status Bar** again *or* click the **Macros drop-down** on the **View tab** and click "**Stop Recording**."

To add an icon to the Quick Access Toolbar (QAT) that will open a document based on the template, do the following:

- **Right-click** the **QAT**.

- Click "**Customize the Quick Access Toolbar...**"

- Change the "**Choose commands from:**" **drop-down** to "**Macros.**"

- Locate your macro in the list and **click to select it**. It might look something like the following:

  Normal.NewMacros.OpenLetterhead

- Click the "**Add**" button.

- Navigate to the **right side** of the Options screen, **click the macro** there, and then click the "**Modify**" button.

- Give the macro **a meaningful name**, such as "Letterhead."

- Select **an icon** for the macro (I chose a white rectangle with a big letter "A" on it, representing text).

- Click "**OK.**"

- If you like, move the macro to the left or right in the QAT by clicking the "**Up**" button or the "**Down**" button.

- Be sure to click the "**OK**" button at the lower right side of the Options screen to save your settings.

The icon for the letterhead should appear in your QAT (see the screenshot below). When you click the icon, a blank document containing the letterhead will open so that you can type a new letter.

Working With Mailings and Forms

Merges (Mail Merges)

There are three different ways to perform a mail merge in Word 2010:

(1)   You can use the **Wizard**, which will walk you through the steps; or

(2)   You can set up the necessary files and perform the merge **manually** (without the Wizard); or

(3)   You can use the **Mail Merge Helper**, the method used in legacy versions of Word (some users prefer it because it is somewhat quicker than the Wizard).

In this section, I will provide tutorials for the first two methods. (The second method is pretty easy, obviating the need to use the Mail Merge Helper.) Before jumping in, I offer a quick explanation of how the mail merge process works in general.

Overview

Mail merges involve two different files: **a form file**, such as a form letter you intend to send to multiple people, envelopes, or a fax cover sheet, and a **data file** that contains specific information, such as the names, addresses, and phone or fax numbers of the people to whom you want to send the letter or a fax. You insert **merge fields**—which act as placeholders or variables for each bit of information —into the form file, and during the merge process, information from the data file is pulled into those fields.

Data files typically store information in table form, for reasons outlined later in this section.

The term "mail merge" is somewhat misleading because you can merge information into *any type of document*—not just letters, envelopes, and other mail-related files. For instance, you can merge names of the parties into a pleading caption, or you can merge case or client information into various types of court or in-house forms. Keep those broader uses in mind and don't be deterred by the fact that Word's Mail Merge Wizard uses terminology that refers to mailings.

Using the Mail Merge Wizard

To use the Wizard, navigate to the **Mailings tab**, **Start Mail Merge group**, and click the **Start Mail Merge drop-down**.

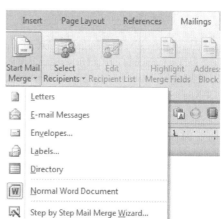

The drop-down includes commands for working with letters, e-mail messages, envelopes, labels, and more. For now, however, we'll use the last command: **Step by Step Mail Merge Wizard…**.

When you click that command, Word opens a **Mail Merge pane** at the right side of the screen that walks you through the six steps involved in setting up a form file and a data file and then merging the data into the form. **NOTE:** At every stage in the process, you will be able to go back to a prior step by clicking the "**Previous**" **button** at the bottom of the Mail Merge pane.

In Step 1, you select from a list of **document types**. Because Word doesn't provide a generic "Form" option, choose "Letters" if you are creating any type of form (e.g., a fax cover sheet, a pleading caption, or a court form) that doesn't fit into any of the other categories. Once you have chosen a document type, click the "**Next**" **button** at the bottom of the pane.

In Step 2, you indicate whether you want to use the **current document** (typically, but not necessarily, a new, blank document); start from **an existing template**; or start from **an existing document**. Click to make your selection (or leave the default set at "current document" if you like), then click the "**Next**" **button** at the bottom of the pane.

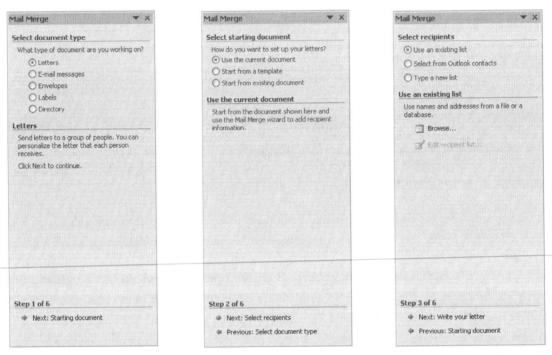

In Step 3, you choose the **recipients** (assuming that you are creating an actual letter or envelope). You can use an existing mailing list, use your Outlook contacts, or start a new list.

Again, although the Wizard is based on mailings, it can be used for other types of form documents. If you are working on a court form, for example, you would use not a *mailing list* but a *list of information* about the court case—for instance, the names of the plaintiffs and defendants, the type of case, the courthouse, the hearing date(s), the trial date, and so forth. It might make the process clearer if you mentally substitute the term "**data file**" for "recipient list." (Instead of *recipients*, you are inserting *data*.) So in Step 3, you would either (1) use an existing data file containing data (information) about cases, clients, etc., or (2) create a data file from scratch. In either case, the data file becomes *associated with* the form file you are using, though you can use a different data file with the form file if you like.

Data Files

As mentioned previously, data files typically are set up as tables.[1] Although it isn't necessary, tables are useful because they make it easy to store the pertinent information in discrete pieces—such as an individual's first name, last name, street address, city, state, zip, and so on. The main advantage is that those discrete pieces can be pulled into your form file individually, as appropriate.

So, for example, if you *are* creating a form letter, you can create a contact list as a table that uses separate columns for each person's first name and last name (essentially setting up a first name *field* and a last name *field*). That gives you the option of addressing the individuals by either their first names ("Dear Jan") or their last names ("Dear Ms. Berinstein" or "Dear Dr. Berinstein").

Another advantage of storing data in table form, with separate columns for each bit of information, is that you can sort based on different types of information, such as last name or zip code.

In tables, each column represents a **field**, and each row represents a complete **record** (the full information about an individual, such as title, first name, last name, company, street address, city, state, zip, home phone, work phone, e-mail address, and so on; or the full information about a court case, a client, or the like).

If you create a new "recipient list" (data file), Word presents you with a blank table (with a header row consisting of labels for the columns / fields). You will have the opportunity to delete, rename, and/or add columns / fields that suit your needs.

TIP: When you are planning a merge, give some thought beforehand to the exact information you will want to include in the data file. Will you want a title field so that you can address people as "Mr.," "Ms.", "Doctor," etc.? Will you want a job title field, too? Will you need to break addresses down so that you can sort records later on by city or zip code? Will you need to include a fax number so that you can pull that into a fax cover sheet? The more thought you give to the project beforehand, the less editing of the data file you'll have to do in the long run.

Using an Existing Data File / Mailing List

Continuing with the mail merge: If you have created a mailing list or other data file, **click** the "**Browse**" **button** about one-third of the way down the Mail Merge pane (see the third screenshot on the previous page). A **Select Data Source dialog** will open to the location where you have stored any database files (when you create one from scratch, Word automatically places it in a specific location on your computer—typically, a subfolder within your "My

---

[1] That is the case in WordPerfect—and, for that matter, most other programs that make use of merges—as well.

Documents" folder—and adds the extension ".mdb," which stands for Microsoft database).[2] However, you might have created a list in Excel, or even in Word, and stored it in another location. If necessary, browse to a different folder, click to select the file you wish to use, then click the "**Open**" **button**. (See the screenshots that follow.)

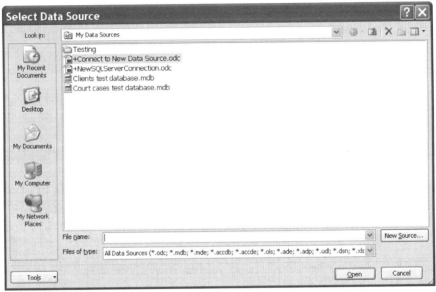

Select Data Source Dialog

When you open an existing file, you should see something like the next screenshot (a fictitious court cases database that I created for testing purposes). Note that the entries are arranged in table form, with each case in a separate row and each type of information about cases (case name, type of case, the names of the plaintiffs, etc.) in a separate column.

To edit the file, click the file name in the "Data Source" box

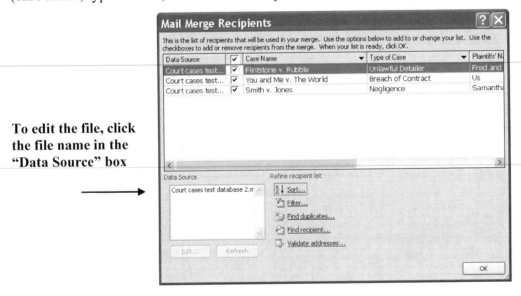

---

[2] You can use many different file types as your data file, including an Excel spreadsheet, an Outlook contact list, and a regular Word file (but it must be in the form of a table, with a header row that consists of the field names), among others.

NOTE: To add to or edit the list, click the file name in the lower left-hand corner (under "**Data Source**"). That will activate the "**Edit**" **button**; click the button to enter more information and/or modify existing information. (You will be able to change the names of the columns—i.e., the field names—as well as to edit any specific information that you entered previously.)

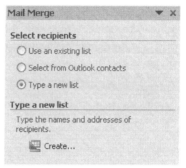

Creating a New Data File / Mailing List

If you click the "**Type a New List**" **radio button**, the "Browse" command changes to "**Create…**" Clicking the "**Create…**" **button** produces a "**New Address List**" **dialog**—again, think of it as a "New Data File" dialog—where you can set up the fields and records that will make up your data file.

When the "**New Address List**" **dialog** opens, it already consists of one blank row (record), plus several columns (fields) with labels assigned by Microsoft.

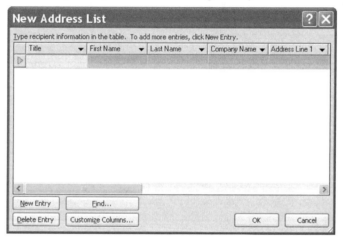

New Address List Dialog

To change the column labels, click the "**Customize Columns…**" **button**. Doing so will open a "**Customize Address List**" **dialog** where you can delete, rename, and/or add fields.

Customize Address List Dialog

383

As noted on page 381, it's important to figure out in advance which fields to include in your data file. Once you have decided on the fields, editing the fields in the list is fairly straightforward. Just click to select a field, then click "**Delete**," "**Rename**," "**Move Down**," or "**Move Up**," as appropriate. To add a field, click the "**Add**" **button**. (Word will insert the new field below the highlighted field, but you can move it up or down later on.) When you click "Add," a small "**Add Field**" **dialog** appears where you can type a name for your new field. Afterwards, click "**OK**", and the new field name will be inserted into the **Field Names list**.

Add Field Dialog

Continue in this manner until you are satisfied with the Field Names list. Then click "**OK**" to save your customized list. Word will prompt you to save the list.

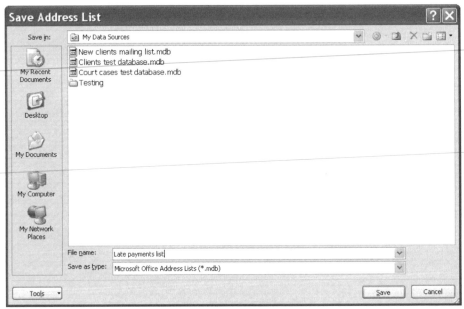

Save Address List

Give the list an easily identifiable descriptive name (and, if you like, change the folder where the list will be stored—but ***be sure to make note of the new location*** if you do so, because you'll have to browse to that location when you want to use the list) and then click "**Save**."

To start adding information to the list, you need to **click the file name** in the "**Data Source**" area at the lower left-hand side of the **Mail Merge Recipients dialog** (i.e., the data file).

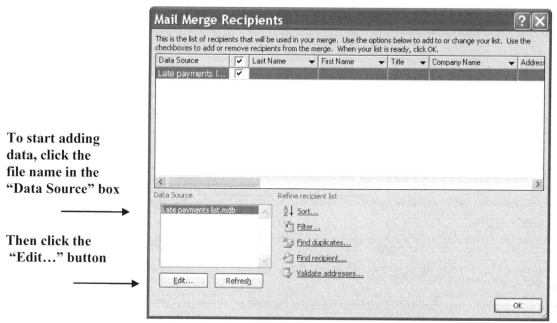

To start adding data, click the file name in the "Data Source" box

Then click the "Edit..." button

Mail Merge Recipients Dialog

As soon as you click the file name, the "**Edit...**" button will become active. Click the "**Edit...**" **button** in order to open an "**Edit Data Source**" dialog where you can start entering information into the list. (Just click in any field and start typing.)

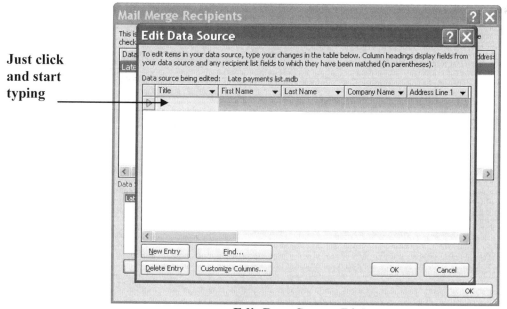

Just click and start typing

Edit Data Source Dialog

When you have entered information in the first row and you're ready to create another "record," click the "**New Entry**" **button**. A second blank row will appear.

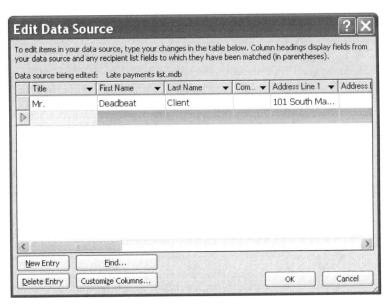

Note that you can change the field headings even after you have started entering information, although obviously it's preferable to make the changes beforehand, especially if you need to delete a field. If you click the "Customize Columns" button after you've inserted information into the list, Word will warn you that you need to save or discard your changes. To save them, be sure to click "Yes." If you click "No," your changes will be lost; if you click "Cancel," you won't be given a chance to edit the field headings (customize the columns).

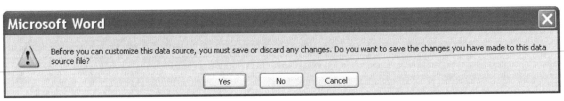

The screenshot at right shows that I am adding a "Middle Name or Initial" field. Because I have selected the "First Name" field, the new field will be inserted between the "First Name" field and the "Last Name" field. (But if it appeared in the wrong spot, I could reposition it by clicking the "Move Up" button or the "Move Down" button.)

Adding a field after you have started setting up the list is easier than deleting a field, for obvious reasons.

CAUTION: If you delete a field, you might lose critical information.

Keep going until you have finished setting up the data file. (If you don't finish, you can add more information at a later date.) Then click "OK" to save your changes. If Word prompts you to update the list and save the changes, click "Yes." If you click "No," your edits will be lost.

After you save the list, click the "**Next**" **button** at the bottom of the Mail Merge pane to move on from Step 3—where we are now—to Step 4 (see the screenshot at right) and set up the form file ("Write your letter") (see the screenshot below).

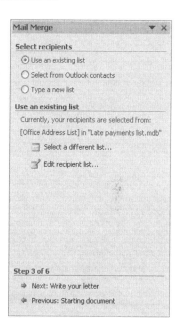

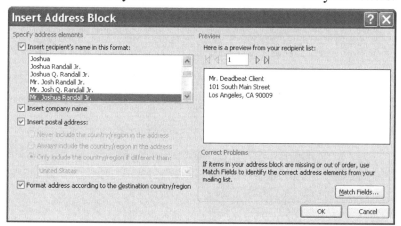

Step 4: Write your letter

Setting Up the Form File

In Step 4, you set up the form file, referred to in Word merge terminology as the "letter." As discussed previously, the form file might be a letter, but it could be any number of other document types: an envelope, a fax cover sheet, a pleading, a court form, and so forth.

If the file *is* a letter, you can insert codes for the address at the cursor position by clicking the "**Address block…**" **link** in the Mail Merge pane. That will open an **Insert Address Block dialog**, where you can review the way addresses will be inserted into your letters.

NOTE: If you have customized the fields (columns) in your data file, some fields might be missing or out of order in the preview area. In that case, click the "**Match Fields**" button at the lower right side of the dialog and use the drop-downs, if necessary, to ensure that the field names on the right (which are pulled from your data file) side match those on the left, which Word "requires" or "expects" when you use the built-in Address Block field.

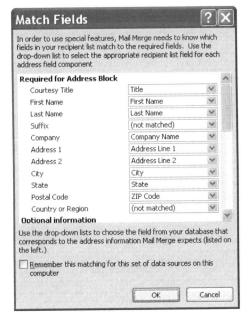

When you finish matching the fields, click "**OK**," then click "**OK**" in the **Insert Address Block dialog**. Word will insert an Address Block field, bracketed by double chevrons, at the cursor position. (The double chevrons indicate that it is a code.) You can move it if you like, but be careful not to delete the chevrons.

«AddressBlock»

If you like, you can insert a preformatted greeting line, too. Just click the "**Greeting line…**" **link** in the Mail Merge pane, which will launch an **Insert Greeting Line dialog box**. You can review the way the greeting will appear in your letter and make any changes you want.

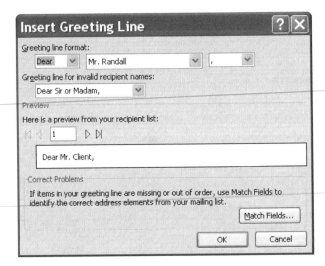

When you click **OK**, Word will insert a **Greeting Line code** at the cursor position. Again, you can reposition the code if you like, taking care not to delete the double chevrons.

«GreetingLine»

You don't have to use either the Address Block field or the Greeting Line field. If you prefer, you can insert individual merge codes for portions of the address and the greeting at appropriate places in the form file, as described below.

Inserting Individual Address Fields

If you prefer—and if you want more control over the merge process—you can insert individual address fields (and a code for the greeting) into your form file. To do so, position the cursor where the address will go, and then, instead of clicking the "Address block…" link in the Mail Merge pane, click "**More items…**" An **Insert Merge Field dialog**, displaying fields you can insert into the form file, will open.

Insert Merge Field Dialog

To insert a field at the cursor position, click the **field name**, then click the "**Insert**" **button**. Unfortunately, you have to click to close the dialog box after inserting each merge field code (the "Cancel" button turns into a "**Close**" **button** that you can click).

Keep in mind that you need to lay out the field codes using spaces, commas, and other punctuation you normally would use in your form document. So, for instance, if you insert a First Name field, you need to press the space bar before inserting a Last Name field. Otherwise, when you perform the merge, the first and last names will run into each other. The same is true with field codes for city, state, and zip code: You need to press the space bar and/or commas between the codes.

Also, if you want to use titles (Mr., Ms., Dr., etc.) for the recipients of the letter, be sure to insert a Title field before the First Name field. See the examples below.

«First_Name» «Last_Name» «Title» «First_Name» «Last_Name»
«Address_Line_1»   «Address_Line_1»
«Address_Line_2»   «Address_Line_2»
«City», «State» «ZIP_Code» «City», «State» «ZIP_Code»

With respect to the greeting line, you can type a greeting yourself and just insert a Title Field, a space, and a Last Name field followed by a colon. See the sample below.

Dear «Title» «Last_Name»:

The advantage of inserting individual fields, as opposed to using the built-in Address Block and Greeting fields, will become apparent later in this section.

Typing the Form and Inserting Merge Codes

Go ahead and begin typing the text of the letter, stopping where the merge fields will go. Stop when you reach a point where you want to insert a placeholder for certain variable information—in the case of our sample collection letter, that includes the past-due amount, the amount last paid, the date of last payment, and the payment deadline.

At the first point where you want to insert a merge field, click the **"More items…" link** in the **Mail Merge pane**. The **Insert Merge Field dialog** will open.

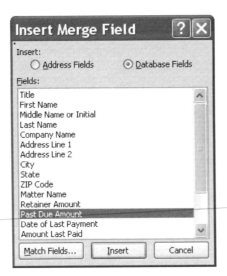

Insert Merge Field Dialog

Click the field you wish to insert (you might have to scroll through the field list to find the one you want), then click the **"Insert" button**. Note that you can choose to insert individual codes for the first name, last name, address, city, state, and zip rather than using the Address Block code. In any case, Word will insert the merge code at the cursor position. Like the codes you inserted previously, the merge code will be enclosed in double chevrons.

It has come to our attention that your account is past due in the amount of «Past_Due_Amount».

Continue typing and inserting merge codes until the form letter looks the way you want. The completed collection letter, using the Address Block and Greeting Line codes, is shown on the next page.

May 3, 2010

«AddressBlock»

Re: Your Past-Due Balance

«GreetingLine»

It has come to our attention that your account is past due in the amount of «Past_Due_Amount». We note that you have not made a payment since you paid the sum of «Amount_Last_Paid» on «Date_of_Last_Payment».

We recognize that people are experiencing financial hardships as a result of the economic downturn. However, in order to pursue the aggressive litigation strategy you have approved, we need to be able to pay filing fees and other costs on your behalf. Those costs add up quickly.

Kindly remit payment by «Payment_Deadline», or give us a call to make other arrangements. We will do what we can to help.

Very truly yours,

Click the "Next" button at the bottom of the Mail Merge pane to preview the merge.

Previewing the Merge

In Step 5, you can preview the merge. This step is critical because it gives you a chance to pinpoint, and correct, any existing problems with the merge setup before you perform the merge.

In fact, in my test merge, I did encounter some problems that were not apparent to me before I clicked the "Next" button to move on to Step 5. The screenshot on the following page shows those problems in graphic form.

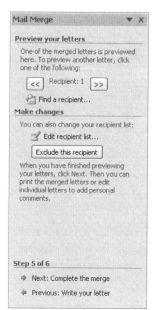

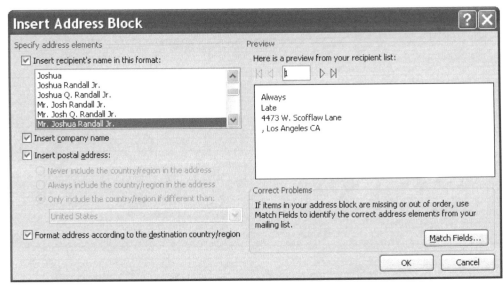

The Preview Reveals Some Serious Problems

As discussed earlier, when items in the address block are missing or out of order, you need to click the "**Match Fields**" **button** to make sure that your custom fields align with the address codes Word requires in order to perform the merge correctly using the Address Block code. To get a clearer idea of what can go wrong and how to fix it, I've provided side-by-side comparisons of the Match Fields dialog before and after I made the fields correspond.

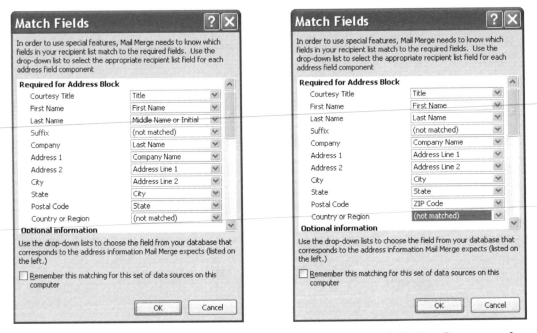

Before: The Fields Don't Correspond   **After: The Fields Do Correspond**

Note that in the dialog box on the left, several of the fields don't match. For instance, where Word requires a Last Name field, the drop-down shows my custom Middle Name or Initial field. I used the drop-down to find and select a corresponding Last Name field. I had to do the same with the Company, Address 1, Address 2, City, State, and Postal Code fields.

After I made sure that all of the fields corresponded, I clicked "**OK**." The preview in the Insert Address Block dialog then showed the information laid out correctly.

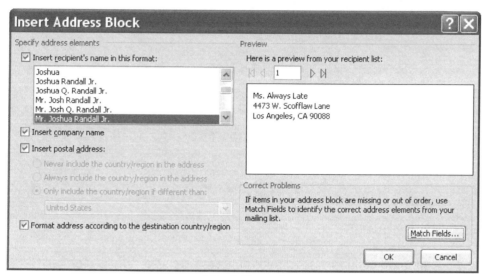

Much Better!

And when I clicked "**OK**," the preview of the letter looked fine (see below).

May 3, 2010

Ms. Always Late
4473 W. Scofflaw Lane
Los Angeles, CA 90088

     Re: Your Past-Due Balance

Dear Ms. Late,

It has come to our attention that your account is past due in the amount of $225.00. We note that you have not made a payment since you paid the sum of $125.00 on February 4, 2010.

We recognize that people are experiencing financial hardships as a result of the economic downturn. However, in order to pursue the aggressive litigation strategy you have approved, we need to be able to pay filing fees and other costs on your behalf. Those costs add up quickly.

Kindly remit payment by May 15, 2010, or give us a call to make other arrangements. We will do what we can to help.

Very truly yours,

Note that the preview by default displays only one of the letters. You can click the "back" or "forward" arrow toward the top of the Mail Merge pane to see another letter.

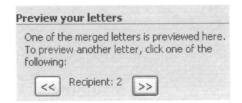

Click the Back or Forward Arrow to Preview Another Letter

Be sure to scroll up and down to make sure the entire letter (or other form file) is formatted to your liking before you move on to Step 6.

Excluding Certain Recipients

You can choose to exclude a particular recipient / record from the merge. While you are previewing a specific letter, click the "**Exclude Recipient**" button, and that letter will not be included in the final merge. (If you click the "**Edit list**" link, you can see that the record has been unchecked in the **Mail Merge Recipients dialog**, as shown below. If you change your mind and decide to include the record, simply click to check the box again. Also, you can click to exclude other records from this dialog box if you like. Just be sure to click "**OK**" to save your changes.)

This record is unchecked, so it won't be included in the merge →

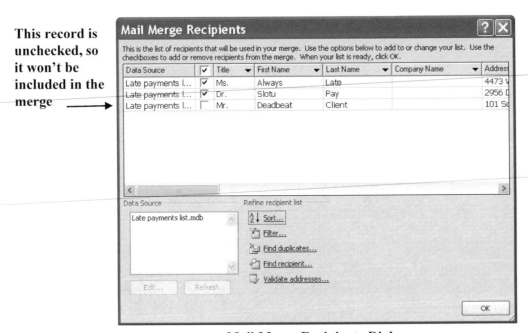

Mail Merge Recipients Dialog

Performing the Merge

In Step 6, you'll complete the merge process. When you are ready to perform the merge, click the "**Next**" **button** at the bottom of the **Mail Merge pane**.

The options in the pane are "**Print…**" and "**Edit individual letters…**"

Note that if you hold the mouse pointer over the "**Edit individual letters…**" **link** , you'll see a pop-up message with the words, "**Merge to new document**."

Clicking that link opens a "**Merge to New Document**" **dialog** that lets you choose which records to include. The default is "All," but you can click the "Current record" option or specify a range of records (the records must be concurrent, such as 2 to 7 or 14 to 33).

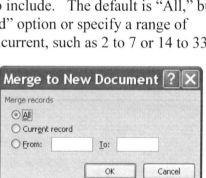

Select the records you want to merge (or leave the default set to "All"), and then click the "**OK**" button to perform the merge.

Once the merge is complete, you can revise individual letters if you so choose.

Printing the Merged Letters / Forms

If you click "**Print…**," a **Merge to Printer dialog** opens. Similar to the "Merge to New Document" dialog, it lets you print all of the records, the current record only, or a range of records.

When you are ready, click "OK" to print the records.

Setting Up the Files and Performing the Merge "Manually"

If you prefer, you can set up the data file and the form file and perform the merge without using the Mail Merge Wizard.

The essential point to keep in mind is that the commands for inserting merge fields into your form document will be grayed out until you click the "**Select Recipients**" **button** and set up a **data file** (whether the data consist of contact information for a mailing or other types of information). Once you set up a data file—by typing one from scratch, by selecting an existing file, or by using Outlook contacts—you will be able to work with merge fields. That makes sense if you think about it, because *the specific merge fields that you will insert into your form file are based on the fields you set up in your data file*.

Creating the Form File

To get started, navigate to the **Mailings tab** and click the **Start Mail Merge button**. This time, instead of choosing "Start Mail Merge Wizard," click the type of document you want to create. If you want to set up a letter, click "**Letter**." If you want to set up any type of form that doesn't fall neatly into one of the other categories (e-mails, envelopes, labels, directory), click "**Normal Word Document**."

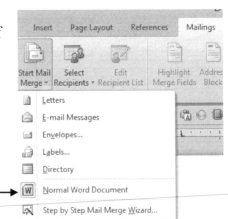

You can begin typing the form document at this point or type it later on.

Note the "Normal Word Document" option

Creating the Data File

Next, click the "**Select Recipients**" **button** and choose from among the three options (Type New List, Use Existing List, or Select from Outlook Contacts). This is a critical step; until you start creating the data file, the commands in the Write & Insert Fields group—including the commands to insert merge fields—are grayed out, indicating that they are unavailable.)

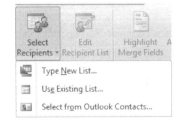

If you decide to type a new list, remember that you can customize the field names to suit the circumstances. For step-by-step instructions on setting up a new list and customizing the field names, see the tutorial that starts on page 383.

To demonstrate how the process works, I have used the Normal Word Document option to create (and save) a sample form document, and I have started typing a new list (data file). Before I enter any specific information (records) into the list, I have customized the field names. The next screenshot shows that the dialog is labeled "**Customize Address List**" even though the data file isn't an address list per se.

My Customized Data File

After you finish setting up your list, click the "**OK**" button. A "**New Address List**" **dialog** will appear (it's formatted as a table) so that you can start typing the information (individual records) into the list. When you have finished typing one complete record, either press the **Tab key** or click the "**New Entry**" button toward the bottom left side of the dialog to start a new row (record).

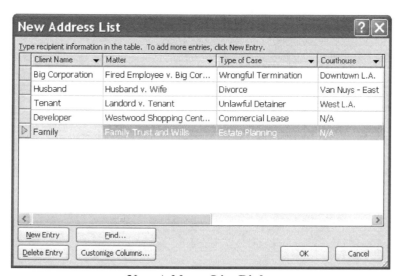

New Address List Dialog

397

When you finish entering data, click "**OK**." Word will open a "**Save Address List**" **dialog** so you can save the form file. If necessary, browse to a different folder, give the file a name, make note of where you are storing it, and click "**Save**."

Once you have saved the data file, the commands in the **Write & Insert Fields group** on the **Mailings tab** will become available, and you will be able to insert merge fields into your form file.

The Write & Insert Fields Become Available
When You Save Your Data File

Inserting Merge Fields into Your Form File

To insert a merge field, position your cursor at the exact point in your form file where you want the field to go, then click the "Insert Merge Field" drop-down and click the field you want to use.

Alternatively, if you click the "Insert Merge Field" button, an Insert Field dialog will appear. You can add fields to your form document from this dialog if you like (just click a field and then click the "Insert" button). However, you'll have to close the dialog (and reopen it) if you want to tweak the formatting between adding fields.

Insert Merge Field Dialog

NOTE: The merge fields that appear on the "Insert Merge Field" drop-down are derived from your data file.

Continue to insert fields into your form file. Then finish typing and formatting the document. When everything looks the way you want, you are ready to preview the merge and then merge the data into the form file.

Previewing the Merge

To preview the merge, click the "**Preview Results**" button in the **Preview Results group** toward the right side of the **Mailings tab**. Doing so will preview one merged document; to see the rest, click the "forward" arrow or the "back" arrow at the top of the Preview Results group. (The single arrows move one record at a time; the arrows with a vertical line next to them move either to the beginning of the data file, i.e., the first record, or to the end of the data file, i.e., the last record.)

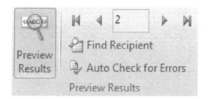

Preview Results Group

Performing the Merge

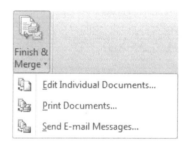

If you are satisfied with the way things look in the preview, click the "**Finish & Merge**" **drop-down** in the **Finish group** on the **Mailings tab**. The drop-down offers three choices: **Edit Individual Documents**; **Print Documents**; and **Send E-mail Messages**.

The first option, "Edit Individual Documents," essentially means that the merge will proceed and you can modify one or more of the merged documents afterwards. If you click that command, a "**Merge to New Document**" dialog will open, giving you the opportunity to include all of the records in the merge (which is the default), to merge only the current record (i.e., the one on the screen), or to specify a range of consecutive records to merge.

Merge to New Document Dialog

After you choose which records to merge, click "**OK**." The merged documents will open in a new document.

TIP / CAUTION: After the merge completes, the form file remains open on another screen.[3] If you haven't saved the final version of that file, be sure to save it at this point for future use. It's easy to forget to take this crucial step.

Also, if you want, you can save the merged documents and print them later on. To do so, be sure to save the file containing the merged documents.

Printing Merged Documents

To send one or more of the merged documents to the printer, click the "Print Documents" command. A "Merge to Printer" dialog will open. Like the "Merge to New Document" dialog, it allows you to include all of the records (the default), only the current record (the one on your screen), or a range of consecutive records.

Make your choice, then click "OK" to send the merged document(s) to the printer.

This discussion of the Mail Merge feature barely scratches the surface of what you can do with merges. If you're interested in learning more, you can take this Microsoft online training course that covers complex merges in Word 2007:
http://office.microsoft.com/training/Training.aspx?AssetID=RC102798041033&CTT=6&Origin=RC102798041033

Or use this "**tiny URL**": http://tinyurl.com/ComplexMerge

See also this Microsoft Knowledge Base article: "Use mail merge to create and print letters and other documents": http://office.microsoft.com/en-us/word/HA100819761033.aspx

Both tutorials deal specifically with Word 2007, but the steps described therein are essentially the same in Word 2010.

---

[3] When you switch screens and return to that file, you might see the Mail Merge pane at the right side, even though you didn't specifically invoke it.

Creating a Sheet of Different Labels
Using Mail Merge in Word 2010

Unlike WordPerfect, Word doesn't provide an easy way to create a sheet of labels and populate the labels with different names and addresses. Word's default options for labels consist solely of the option to create and print one label at a time *or* the option to populate a sheet of labels with *the same name and address*. To assemble a sheet of labels addressed to different people or entities, you have to perform a mail merge. (Note that the basic instructions for performing a mail merge with labels are almost the same as performing a mail merge with letters and/or envelopes.)

As in WordPerfect, a mail merge in Word involves two separate documents: (1) a *form* of some type (in this case, a sheet of labels) into which you will insert merge codes; and (2) a *data file* that includes the information that will get pulled into the form when you merge the two documents (here, the names and addresses).

Setting Up the Form File

With labels, you'll format the labels first, then insert merge codes, then replicate the merge codes throughout the sheet of labels.[1]

To get started, navigate to the **Mailings tab**, **Start Mail Merge group**, and click the **Start Mail Merge** button, then click **Labels**. The **Label Options dialog** will open.

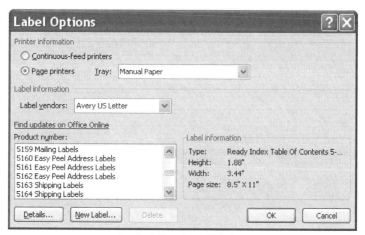

Label Options Dialog

About halfway down the dialog, you'll see "**Label vendors**." If you are using a standard Avery label, click the drop-down and select **Avery US letter**.[2] Then in the **Product number**

---

[1] You might consider creating a separate template for each type of labels you use (such as Avery 5160 or 5162 labels).

[2] There are additional Avery labels available for those who reside outside the United States.

box, scroll down until you locate the label you wish to use. Click to **select (highlight) it**, then click **OK**. Word might prompt you that it needs to "delete" the content of the document (even if you are using a blank document) in order to set up the label form. Assuming that's what you intended to do—i.e., that it's safe to delete the contents of the document currently on your screen—click **OK**. Word should format the page as a sheet of labels of the type you selected.

Setting Up the Data File (Recipient List)

Before you can insert merge fields, you have to click the "**Select Recipients**" button in the Start Mail Merge group.

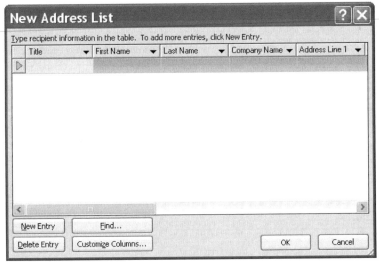

When you do, Word offers you three choices:

(1) **Type New List**;

(2) **Use Existing List**; or

(3) **Select from Outlook Contacts**.

When you choose the first or second option, Word expects you to insert the contact information in table form, with each discrete piece of information (First Name, Last Name, Company, Address, City, State, Zip, etc.) in a separate cell and each complete contact record in a separate row of the table.

Type New List

If you choose to type a new list, Word provides you with a form in which to enter the information.

Once you have added contacts, click "**OK**." Word will prompt you to save the list as a database file (automatically adding the .mdb extension) and will place the file by default in your "My Data Sources" folder, typically located in the following path (if you are using Windows XP):

C:\Documents and Settings\<User Name>\My Documents\My Data Sources

It's okay to leave the file there, since Word will look for the file in that location when you perform a merge using that mailing list.

Use an Existing List

If you choose to use an existing list, Word opens a window where you can browse for any mailing list you have set up previously (as mentioned above, the list needs to be in table form, rather than in regular paragraph form).

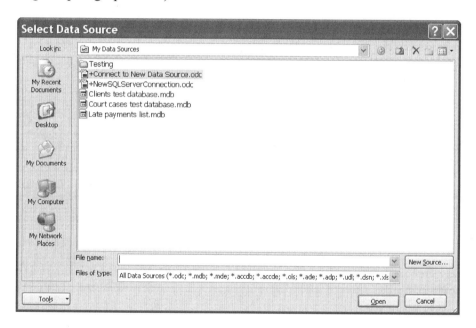

To use an existing list (a data file), click to select it, then click "**Open**."

At that point, Word will insert the records from the data file into the sheet of labels. You will see something like the following:

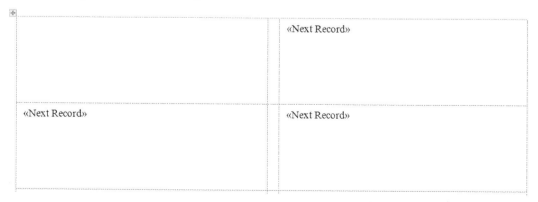

Whether you type a new list or use an existing list, you'll be able to insert merge fields into the label form after you have the names and addresses set up in table format in Word (the Insert Merge Field button is grayed out before / until you select the recipients). Then, when you perform the merge, Word will pull the specific contact information into those fields.

Select From Outlook Contacts

If you maintain all of your contact information in Outlook, the third option is a good choice. When you click that option, Word opens a list of your Outlook contacts—already set up in table format—and you can pick and choose which of those contacts to use in the merge.

When the Outlook contact list opens, check to make sure it looks okay. Next, click to **uncheck** any contacts you don't want to include in the merge, then click "**OK**" to dismiss the dialog box.

Inserting Merge Fields

At this point, you can insert merge fields into the first label in the sheet. You can either (1) click the **"Insert Merge Field" button** (located in the **Write and Insert Fields** group) and insert individual fields (laying them out the way you want them to appear in the merged labels) **or** (2) simply click the **"Address Block" button**. The second option is particularly easy.

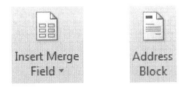

When you first click the "Address Block" button, the **Insert Address Block dialog** appears, allowing you to double-check the information that will be included and the layout of that information.

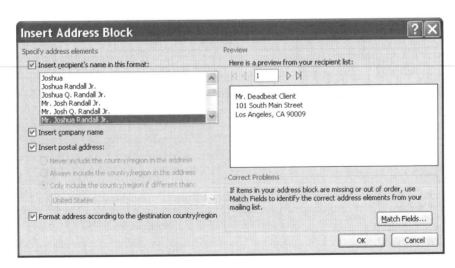

Make any changes you like, then click **OK**. Word will insert an <<**Address Block**>> **code** in the label.

«AddressBlock»	«Next Record»

Remember that unless you specifically ***uncheck*** the first item in the dialog box ("Insert recipient's name in this format"), the Address Block code ***includes the contact's name***. So if you use the Address Block code, don't also insert codes for the contact's first and last names, or you'll end up with the individual's name appearing in the label twice.

After you have set up the first label, just click the **"Update Labels" button**, which will copy the information from Label 1 into all of the other labels in the sheet.[3]

Update Labels

«AddressBlock»	«Next Record»«AddressBlock»
«Next Record»«AddressBlock»	«Next Record»«AddressBlock»

You're almost ready to start the merge!

Before Proceeding With the Merge

CAUTION: By default, Word inserts extra space between the lines when it merges contact information into a form. Therefore, be sure to launch the **Paragraph dialog** before starting the merge and change **Before spacing** to **0 (zero)**; change **After spacing** to **0 (zero)**; and change **Line spacing** to **Single**.

---

[3] If you know in advance that you will need more than one full sheet (page) of labels, navigate to the last label on the sheet and press the Tab key—several times, if necessary—to create as many additional rows as you need (labels are set up as tables in Word). It's a good idea to do so at the outset so that when you duplicate labels, Word inserts the information in each label, including any beyond the first full sheet / page.

Performing the Merge

When everything is set up the way you want, you're ready to perform the merge. Note that Word will merge the information into a new document, which is ideal because it allows you to keep your label form document and reuse it every time you want to print labels. (You'll simply open the form, select the recipients, and merge.)

Unfortunately, the button you need to click to execute the merge is confusingly labeled. The command you want is under **Finish**, at the far right side of the **Mailings tab**. Click the **Finish & Merge drop-down**. The available commands are (1) **Edit Individual Documents**; (2) **Print Documents**; and (3) **Send E-mail Messages**.

Most people perform the merge first and then, if everything looks okay, print the labels. To start the merge, click **Edit Individual Documents**, an option that actually doesn't involve "editing" documents (except that it prompts you to select certain records to include in the merge). Doing so will open a **Merge to New Document dialog**, where you can choose to merge all of the records in your recipient list (the default setting), merge only the Current Record (presumably the first one in the list), or select several consecutive records.

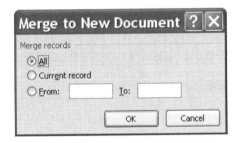

When you are ready, click **OK**, and the merged information will appear in a new document.

Mr. Deadbeat Client	Ms. Always Late	Dr. Slotu Pay
101 South Main Street	4473 W. Scofflaw Lane	2956 DeLay Place
Los Angeles, CA 90009	Los Angeles, CA 90088	Beverly Hills, CA 90212

If you are likely to send mail on a regular basis to the recipients whose contact information you've inserted into this sheet of labels, save the sheet as a separate file for future mailings. Be sure to save the form document, too (make a note—mental or otherwise—of the location where you store it).

Reusing an Existing Form Document

It's fairly simple to reuse an existing form document to perform a merge. Just navigate to and open the form. When you do so, Word might prompt you to make sure you want to run an SQL command (essentially acknowledging that there are merge codes in the file); if it does, click "**Yes**" to continue.

The document will open, along with a **Mail Merge pane** at the right side of the screen.

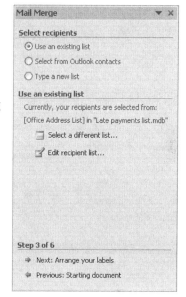

You can follow the prompts in the pane—they are more or less self-explanatory, and are similar to those outlined in the Mail Merge tutorial starting on page 379.

Or, if you prefer, you can click the **Select Recipients drop-down** in the **Start Mail Merge group** in order to choose an existing mailing list or start a new one.

From this point on, just repeat the steps described earlier in this lesson, starting with the "Setting Up the Data File (Recipient List)" section that begins on page 402.

QUICK TIP: Make the Mail Merge Pane Go Away

   If the Mail Merge pane keeps popping up when you don't want to see it, try the following:

   Navigate to the **Mailings tab**, **Start Mail Merge group**, click the **Start Mail Merge drop-down**, and then click "**Normal Word Document**."

CAUTION: The Write & Insert fields might become inactive (grayed out) after you click "Normal Word Document." To reactivate the fields, click "**Select Recipients**," choose the "**Use Existing List**" **command**, and locate and **open the data file** that you have associated with the current document. That should do the trick!

Quick 'n' Dirty Address Labels

If you already have a list of names and addresses set up in WordPerfect—let's say, a lengthy service list—and you want to insert those address labels into a Word document without going through the hassle of a full-fledged merge, you can, in fact, simply copy and paste from your WordPerfect document into a sheet of labels in Word. Unfortunately, you have to copy and paste one "record" (name and address) at a time.

To get started, navigate to the **Create group** on the left side of the **Mailings tab** and click the "**Labels**" **icon**.

When the **Envelopes and Labels dialog** opens, click the "**Options…**" **button** at the bottom to display the available labels.

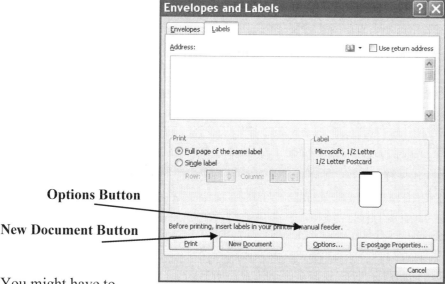

Options Button

New Document Button

You might have to change the label vendor. In the screenshot below, the vendor displayed is Microsoft. To change vendors, click the drop-down toward the middle of the dialog.

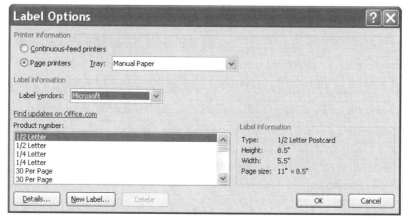

Label Options Dialog

If your organization uses Avery labels, choose "**Avery US Letter**." Then scroll through the product list at the bottom left side of the Label Options dialog and, when you locate the specific label that you want to use, click to **select it**, then click the "**OK**" **button**. The following screenshot shows that I have chosen the 5160 Address Labels.

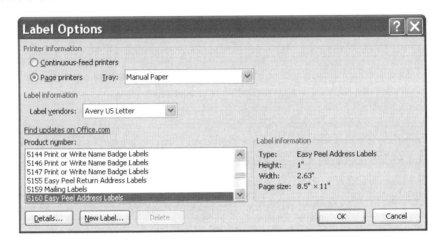

Next, click the "**New Document**" button at the bottom of the Envelopes and Labels dialog.

A sheet of labels will open in a separate window.

Before doing anything else, click in a label and open the Paragraph dialog so that you can check the line spacing and spacing-after settings. If the line spacing and spacing after—or any other aspects of paragraph formatting—are not to your liking, close the Paragraph dialog, select the entire sheet of labels by pressing Ctrl A, reopen the Paragraph dialog, change the line spacing and spacing after, then click "OK."

Next, save the labels so that you can use them again. To save them as a regular document, click **File**, **Save As** and navigate to a folder where you are likely to look for the document the next time you need to print labels—whether a personal folder or a shared folder on your firm's network drive. Give the document a logical name, such as "5160 Labels," then click "Save."

CAUTION: To avoid overwriting the original document the next time you use it, open it as a copy. That is, instead of clicking the "Open" button in the Open dialog, click the arrow on the

"Open" button and, when the pop-up menu opens, choose "**Open as Copy**" or "**Open Read-Only**." Then, as soon as the document appears on your screen, save it with a new name.

If you prefer, you can save the blank sheet of labels as a template. Before proceeding, decide where to save the template. You might want to store it in a shared folder on a network drive or in your personal "Trusted Templates" folder on your hard drive. (If you save a template in your Trusted Templates folder, it will be available only to you.)

Next, review the information in the section that starts on page 369, which explains where personal templates and shared templates typically are stored and how to ensure that your computer is pointing to the correct location.

When you have chosen a location for the labels template, click the **File tab**, **Save As**, and navigate to the appropriate folder. Change the "**Save as type**" to **Word Template (*.dotx)** and give the template **a descriptive name**, such as "5160 Labels." Finally, click "**OK**" to save the new template.

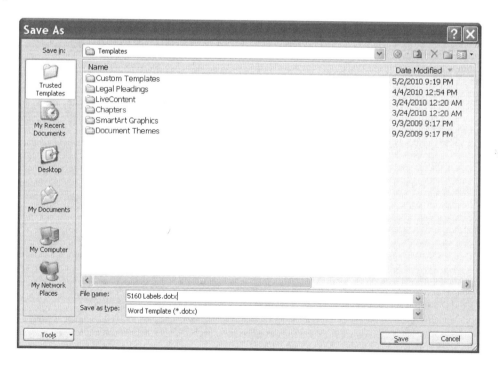

To open a document based on the labels template, click the **File tab**, **New**, and click "**My templates**."

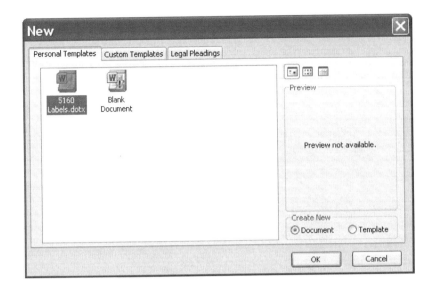

When the **New dialog** appears, you should see your new template (you might have to click a tab other than the one at the forefront in order to locate the template). Either **double-click it** or **click it once** and then click the "**OK**" **button**. A new document consisting of a sheet of labels should open.

At this point, you can simply copy and paste the names and addresses from your WordPerfect mailing list into the labels in Word. (For best results, you probably should use either the "**Merge Formatting**" paste option or the "**Keep Text Only**" paste option. Remember that you can preview how a paste option would look simply by clicking to open the drop-down from the **Paste Options button** and positioning your mouse pointer over an option.)

"Encino" should not be indented;
clicking the "Merge Formatting"
option or the "Keep Text Only"
option fixed the problem ⎯⎯⎯⎯→

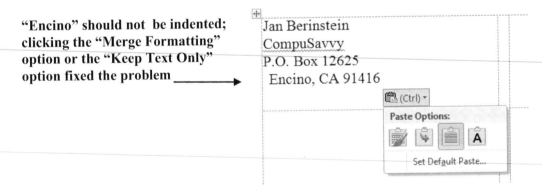

CAUTION: If you configured the labels to use your preferred line spacing and spacing-after settings, they should be formatted correctly after you paste. However, it's a good idea to check to make sure before sending the labels to the printer.

<u>Setting Up and Printing Envelopes in Word 2010</u>

To create an envelope, navigate to the **Mailings tab**, **Create group**.

To set up envelopes from scratch, simply (1) click the **Envelopes button**, which will open the **Envelope and Labels dialog** with the Envelopes tab at the forefront, and then (2) type the recipient's name and address in the **Delivery address** area.

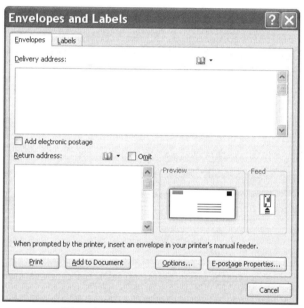

Envelopes and Labels Dialog

Alternatively, position your cursor immediately ahead of—or somewhere within—a name and address in an existing letter and then click the **Envelopes button**. When you do so, Word should pull the name and address into the **Delivery address** area of the dialog. *You do not have to select (highlight) the name and address*, although you can do so if you like.

In either case, when the dialog is open, you can type a return address in the area located below the "Delivery address" field if you wish. (If at some point later on—after you've set up a return address in the dialog—you want to print one or more envelopes *without* a return address, you can simply click to check the "**Omit**" **checkbox** in that specific instance, rather than deleting what you've typed.)

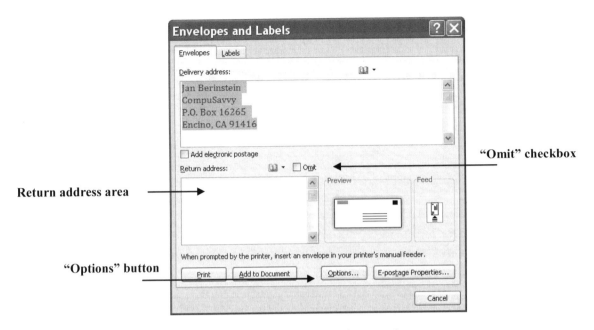

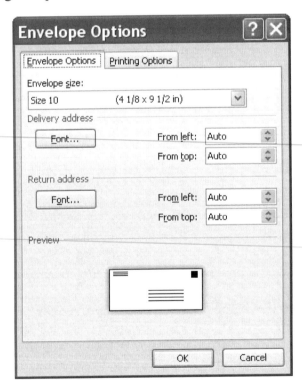

At this point, you can set various options for the envelope.

Clicking the **Options button** toward the bottom center of the dialog allows you to select a different envelope type, change the font face and/or size for the return address and/or the delivery address, or change the placement of the return address and/or the delivery address.

To change the font for the delivery address and/or the return address, click the appropriate "**Font" button**. Depending on which one you click, either an "**Envelope Address**" **dialog** or an "**Envelope Return Address**" **dialog** will open.

Note that both addresses are configured to use the **+Headings font**, which is a placeholder. The specific font that is applied is determined by the preexisting **Envelope Address** and **Envelope Return styles**, plus **the active "Theme"** in your document. All other things being equal, the Cambria font is used by default, with font size for the envelope address set at 12 points and the font size for the return address set at 10 points.

To specify a different font face or font size, you can either (1) change the settings in the **Envelope Address dialog**, which will affect only the current envelope, or (2) modify the **Envelope Address style** and/or **Envelope Return style**, which will affect all future envelopes.[1]

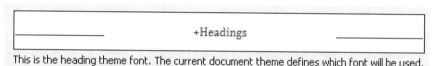

Another option is to create a custom Theme and make it the default. For instructions on creating your own theme and setting it as the default, see the section starting on page 228.

If you wish, you can change the placement of the addresses on the envelope, as well.

Once you have tweaked the options to your satisfaction, you can do one of two things: (1) append the envelope to a document for printing later or, (2) if you have a blank envelope in the printer tray, click the Print button, which will send it straight to the printer.

If you append the envelope to your document, be sure to do one of the following when you are ready to print:

(1)   **click somewhere within the envelope** before opening Print Place, then choose **"Print Current Page"** from the **Settings**); *or*

(2)   open **Print Place**, choose **"Print Custom Range,"** and **specify the page number** where the envelope is situated.

Otherwise, the entire document will be sent to the printer.

---

[1] To modify one or both of the styles, press **Ctrl Alt Shift S** to display the **Styles Pane**, click **Options** and make sure **All Styles** are showing, navigate to the **Envelope Address** and/or **Envelope Return style** in the list, **right-click, Modify...**, click **"New documents based on this template"** (to ensure that the modifications you're making apply to all envelopes you create in the future), make changes to the font face and/or size, and click **"OK"** to save your changes.

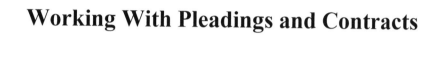

Working With Pleadings and Contracts

Creating Your Own Pleading Paper

The Pleading Wizard was discontinued in Word 2007. Presumably Microsoft took that step in the belief that most people who purchased that version of the program were upgrading from an earlier version that included the Pleading Wizard and therefore already had access to the utility. However, based on exchanges I've seen on the Internet and on comments from a few of my clients, it seems clear to me that many companies and individuals who adopted Word 2007 migrated not from a prior version of Word but from WordPerfect. Because complex documents don't always convert well between the two programs—and pleading paper by definition is complex because of the vertical lines in the margins and the line numbers—these folks often were at a loss about how to create their own pleading paper in Word.

As far as I know, there still isn't a particularly good solution for people in that situation. Through the Office.com site, Microsoft does offer a couple of pleading templates, but they aren't very well suited for California (as mentioned on page 25).

If you are ambitious, patient, and willing to do some experimentation, you can create your own pleading paper from scratch. I will provide the instructions, with the proviso that any time you "roll your own," you might not be completely satisfied with the results—and you can expect to have to do some tweaking down the line.

Creating Your Own Pleading Paper

Start with a blank document. Click the **Page Layout tab** and click the **dialog launcher** at the lower right side of the **Page Setup group** or press **Alt P, S, P**. When the **Page Setup dialog** opens, set the left margin to 1.5" and the right margin to .5". (**NOTE:** This is a critical step, and it's best to do it at the beginning of the process.) Click **OK** to save your settings.

Next, go into the header editing screen by using any of the following methods:

- **Right-click** in the blank header area at the top of the page, then click "**Edit Header**"; or

- **Double-click** in the header area; or

- Click the **Insert tab, Header drop-down, Edit Header**.

Next, click the **Insert tab, Shapes**, locate the "**Lines**" **category**, and click the **basic line shape** at the left side.

Your cursor will turn into a sort of cross-hair. Position the cursor at the very top of the page, about 1.5 inches in from the left margin, and **left-click**.

Next, quickly **drag straight down** and **release the left mouse button**. The line doesn't have to be very long; you can adjust the length of the line later on. Just try to keep it straight.

When you insert the line, a context-sensitive **Drawing Tools tab** will appear. (The tab will look somewhat different depending on whether you are working with a .docx or a .doc file.) Navigate to the right-hand side, locate the **Size group**, and type the number 11 in the box representing the height.

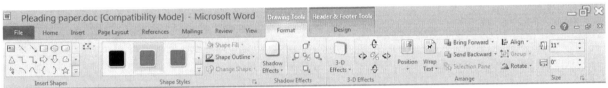

Drawing Tab—Compatibility Mode (.doc Files)

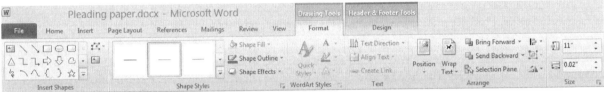

Drawing Tab—Word Mode (.docx Files)

Alternatively, you can click the **dialog launcher** at the lower right-hand corner of the **Size group** to launch a **Format AutoShape dialog** or, if you are working with a .docx or other Open Office XML file format, a **Layout dialog**. When the dialog opens, you can set the height there. (Although the two dialog boxes look slightly different, they both have a **Size tab.** Also, you can manipulate the position of the line by using the **Layout tab** in the Format AutoShape dialog and the **Position tab** in the Layout dialog.) Be sure to click "OK" to save your settings.

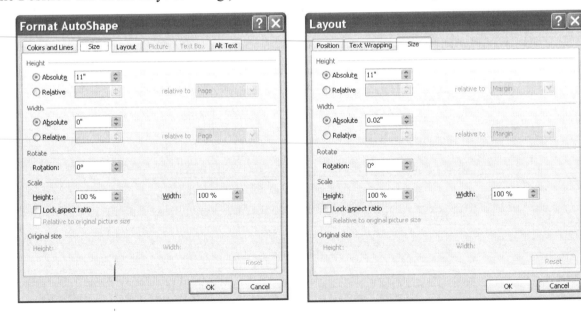

Format AutoShape Dialog (.doc Files)   **Layout Dialog (.docx Files)**

If the line doesn't quite reach the top or bottom of the page, click the end that is too short—when you do, you should see a circle you can use as a handle—then drag it as far as necessary. See the screenshot at right for an example (note the circle at the top of the line, which is the "handle").

Next, **right-click** the line and click the "**Copy**" command. Then press **Ctrl V** or use any other method you like to **paste a copy** of the line. **Drag the line** and drop it where you want it to be (either next to the first line or .5" from the right edge of the page).

TIP: You might find it helpful to turn on the horizontal Ruler, if it isn't visible already. To do so, click the View tab, and click to check "Ruler" in the Show group.

ANOTHER TIP: You can click a line and then move it incrementally to the left or right by using the left / right arrow keys.

Repeat this process to create the third vertical line in the pleading paper. You should see something like the screenshot below.

Now you need to insert a text box to the left of the double vertical lines to hold the line numbers. Click the **Insert tab**, navigate to the **Text group** and click the **Text Box drop-down**, and then click **Draw Text Box**.

This time, position your cursor below the header margin, as indicated by the dotted blue guideline. Drag down and slightly to the right. You don't have to drag all the way to the bottom or make the text box any wider at this point; you can do both of those things later, using the sizing handles.

Note that what you see might look somewhat different from the image at right.

If you don't like the way the text box looks, click the **Undo button** on the QAT or press **Ctrl Z**, then start over.

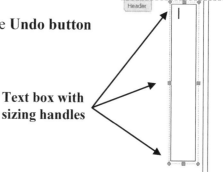

Text box with sizing handles

When you are satisfied with the appearance of the text box, **click the bottom border** (you should see a square "sizing handle" in the middle) and **drag it down**, stopping at or just below the blue footer guideline.

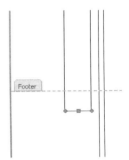

Note that if you extend the text box below the footer margin, some of the line numbers might appear in the footer area. However, you can fix that later on by adjusting the bottom margin of the pleading paper.

Next, right-click one of the text-box borders. If you are working with a .doc file, click the "Format Text Box" command and, when the Format Text Box dialog appears, click the Line Color drop-down and select "No Color." Then click "OK" to save your changes.

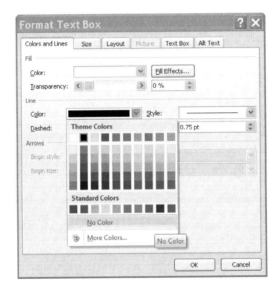

If you are working with a .docx file, right-click a text-box border and then click "Format Shape." When the Format Shape dialog opens, click "Line Color," click the "No line" radio button, and then click "Close."

In either case, the black borders will disappear, but you still should see dashed blue "gridlines" when you click within the text box.

Click within the text box, then press **Ctrl R** to turn on right justification so that the line numbers you type will be aligned correctly. Before moving on, check to make sure that the font face and the font size conform to state and local requirements.[1]

Next, *either*

- navigate to the **Home tab** click the dialog launcher at the bottom right side of the **Paragraph group** to open the **Paragraph dialog**; *or*

- press **Alt O, P**.

When the **Paragraph dialog** opens, change the **Line spacing** to **Exactly 12 pt** and change the **Spacing After to 12 pt**.

CAUTION: Be sure to use Exactly 12 pt line spacing, *not* Single spacing. If you use Single, the line numbers will be too far apart.

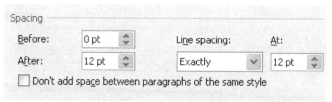

When you have finished, click **OK** to save your settings.

Next, simply start typing line numbers from 1 to 28, pressing "Enter" after each number.

You might find that the double-digit numbers are "squished," such that one of the digits gets bumped to the next line.

8

9

1

0

---

[1] As of this writing, the California Rules of Court specify a font face equivalent to Courier, Times New Roman, or Arial, and a font size in the body of the pleading no smaller than 12 points. (Text within footers must be at least 10 points.) Times New Roman, 12 points, is standard. In order to match up with the pleading text, the line numbers should use the same font face and size as the body of the pleading.

If that happens, position the mouse pointer at the top left side of the text box guideline—the trick is to use the "handle," as shown in the screenshot at right—and drag it slightly to the left (just until the double-digit numbers line up properly).

Note that numbers might not adjust until you release the left mouse button.

If you reach the bottom of the text box and can't type (or see) 28 numbers, click the bottom "handle" and drag it down somewhat. Don't worry if the line numbers spill into the footer area. Changing the footer margin and the bottom page margin, as described below. will help.

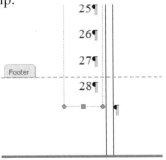

Next, click the Header & Footer Tools tab to bring it to the forefront, and, if necessary, change the "Header from Top" setting to .5" and the "Footer from Bottom" setting to .3".

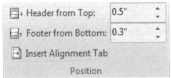

Those tweaks might or might not prevent the line numbers from intruding into the footer area. You'll probably need to adjust the bottom page margin—which is *not* the same thing as changing the distance of the footer from the bottom of the text. To do so, close out of the header editing screen (by clicking the **Close Header and Footer button**), then open the **Page Setup dialog** by either (1) navigating to the **Page Layout tab** and clicking the **dialog launcher** at the bottom right side of the **Page Setup group** *or* (2) pressing **Alt P, S, P**.

When the dialog appears, change the bottom margin to a smaller figure, such as .7" or .5". (You might have to experiment with this setting to get it right.) That should bump the footer editing screen down below the last line number.

Making Adjustments

You might find that the first line number isn't perfectly aligned with the first line of the document. If not, you can move the text box containing the line numbers up slightly (assuming you have a steady hand and a certain amount of patience). Just drag it by the top sizing handle. (Also, see the section on the next page about the "Don't center 'exact line height' lines" option.)

As you test the pleading, you'll probably discover additional items that need some adjustment.

For example, if you've created the line numbers with a 12-point font, have set the line spacing to Exactly 12 points, and have added 12 points afterwards, you will likely need to use Exactly 12 point line spacing for single spacing in the document and Exactly 24 point line spacing for double spacing.

Be sure to let other people in your firm who work on documents based on your custom pleading paper know about that requirement. Make sure they understand that the "single" and "double" line spacing designations in the Paragraph dialog, and the "1.0" and "2.0" options on the line spacing drop-down in the Paragraph group on the Home tab, are ***not*** the same as Exactly 12 points and Exactly 24 points.

Changing the "Don't Center 'Exact Line Height' Lines" Option

If you are working with a .docx, you might find that you need to change one specific setting in the Word Options in order to get the line numbers and the text to align perfectly on each page of your pleading. (You probably don't have to take this step if you are using a .doc file.)

To adjust this setting, click the File tab, Options, then click the Advanced category. Scroll all the way down to, and click, "Layout Options." Scroll down again, and click to put a check in the box to the left of the "Don't center 'exact line height' lines" option. Be sure to click the "OK" button at the lower right side of the Word Options screen to save your settings.

Inserting a Footer

At this point, you can insert a generic footer if you like. Here are some quick instructions:[2]

- Right-click within the footer area, then click "Edit Footer."

- With your cursor in the footer editing screen, right-click again and select "Paragraph" from the pop-up menu. Make sure the line spacing is set to Exactly 12 and, if necessary, click OK to save your settings.

- Press Ctrl E to turn on center justification and move the cursor to the center of the screen. To insert a page number code, simply press the key combination Alt Shift P. If necessary, select the code and adjust the font size.

---

[2] These instructions will place a page number code on every page of the pleading. To "suppress" the page number on the caption page, see the tutorial that starts on page 451, and in particular Step 11, which starts on page 453.

- Press the Enter key to move the cursor to the next line. Then, type three hyphens and press Enter again. The hyphens should expand into a full-length horizontal line.

- Press Enter again, then type a placeholder for the short document title. In my sample, I've typed two "X's." (See the next screenshot.)

- When you've finished, click the "Close Header and Footer" button.

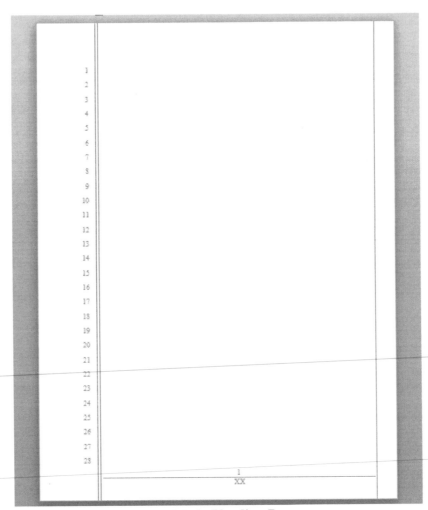

Home-Made Pleading Paper

Saving the File as a Template

If everything looks the way you want it to, you can go ahead and save the pleading paper either as a regular document or as a template. It probably makes more sense to save it as a template so that you can reuse it.

To do so, follow these steps:

- Click the **File tab**, **Save As**.

- Navigate to the location where you will store the template. That might be a shared network drive or your "Trusted Templates" location on your own workstation. If the former, click the "**Save in**" **drop-down** and **browse** to the folder where your firm keeps its templates. If the latter, click the "**Trusted Templates**" **icon** at the left side of the Save As dialog (in Windows XP).

- **Type a name** for the template, such as "Pleading paper."

- Next, be sure to **change the "Save as type:"** to **Word Template (*.dotx)**.

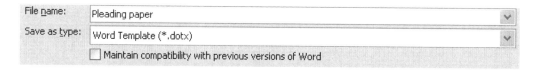

- Finally, **click** the "**Save**" **button**.

Creating a Document Based on the Template

To create a new document based on the template, click the **File tab**, **New**, then click "**My templates**" and **double-click the icon** for the template (or **left-click** it and then click "**OK**").

To edit the template, click the **File tab**, **Open**, navigate to the folder where you have stored the template, click to **select it**, and click the "**Open**" **button**.

CAUTION: It is essential to keep in mind that in order to modify the template, you need to open it the same way you would open any other file for editing. If you use the "File tab, New" method, *you will be editing a document based on the template, not the template itself.*

Adding a Firm Logo in the Left Margin

Adding a firm logo in the left margin usually is a simple matter of inserting another text box. As with the text box that contains the line numbers, you'll need to remove the border lines.

If you are typing the firm's name and contact information, you will want to change the text direction. Fortunately, the **Drawing Tools tab** makes that a simple matter. There is a **Text Direction icon** in the **Text group**; its appearance and its location on the tab varies slightly depending on whether you are working with a .docx or a .doc, but the feature works more or less the same way.

If you are using a .docx, the icon produces a drop-down with different choices; if you are using a .doc, the text changes direction each time you click the icon.

 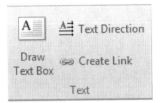

Text Direction Drop-Down (.docx)   **Text Direction Icon (.doc)**

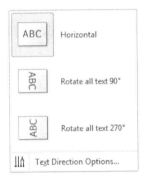

Text Direction Drop-Down Menu (.docx)

One of the trickiest aspects of inserting a logo in the margin is getting the text box positioned exactly right. Vertical positioning can be especially difficult. Remember, though, that clicking a border of the text box enables you to move the box incrementally by using the arrow keys.

With a certain amount of trial and error—and an abundance of patience— you should be able to produce customized pleading paper even without a Pleading Wizard.

Aligning Text With Pleading Line Numbers

One of the most common problems people in the legal profession encounter with pleadings created in or converted to MS Word is that the text doesn't align with the pleading line numbers. This problem arises most frequently with documents originally created in WordPerfect (or some other word processing program) *and* documents originally created in an earlier version of Word.

The discrepancy usually results from an error in the configuration settings described below—and can be fixed by adjusting one or more of those settings. Note, however, that there can be other, less obvious, factors that affect the alignment of text. If the "typical" fixes don't work, try the workarounds suggested toward the end of this section.

The Usual Suspects

1.   Line Spacing.

The line spacing of the text might be different from the line spacing of the pleading line numbers. If that's the case, you can change the line spacing of the text to match that of the pleading line numbers. To determine the line spacing of the numbers, go into the header editing screen (by clicking the **Insert tab**, **Header**, **Edit Header** *or* by **right-clicking** in the **header area** of the page, then clicking "**Edit Header**" *or* by **double-clicking** in the header area) and click somewhere within the line numbers at the left side of the header; then press **Alt O, P** to open the **Paragraph dialog** and note the setting in the **Line spacing** box. Close the Paragraph dialog box, close out of the Header editing screen, and check the line spacing of one or more "double-spaced" paragraphs. If in fact there is a disparity, **select** the relevant portions of the text, press **Alt O, P** (or click the Paragraph dialog launcher), configure the **Line spacing** to match (using **Exactly**—e.g., Exactly 22.75 pt, or whatever matches the pleading line numbers), and **OK** out of the dialog. **NOTE**: You will have to change the spacing of all single-spaced portions of text to be half that of the double-spaced portions (e.g., Exactly 11.375 pt, if the pleading line number spacing is set at 22.75 pt). Don't worry if Word adjusts the single spacing slightly.

2.   "Before" or "After" Spacing.

If any paragraphs have been configured to use "Before" or "After" spacing (for example, 6 pt before the paragraph or 3 pt after the paragraph), that could throw off the alignment of the text. Click in some paragraphs randomly and check for "Before" and/or "After" spacing (launch the **Paragraph dialog box** and look at the **Spacing** section of the dialog box, about halfway down the Indents and Spacing tab). It's especially important to check paragraphs to which a style has been applied. If necessary, reset the "Before" and "After" boxes to zero (0) and OK out of the dialog. ***NOTE: In some situations, adding space before or after can help.*** In one sample pleading, going into the Header editing screen and adding 10 points before the first pleading line number (via the **Paragraph dialog**, Spacing Before) actually fixed the problem. But watch out! Pressing the Enter key will copy that additional spacing to the next paragraph.

3. **Different Fonts That Handle "Leading" Differently**.

If the document uses one font for the pleading line numbers and a different font for the text, that can cause problems if the two fonts handle "leading" differently. ("Leading" has to do with the amount of white space inserted between lines of text). Sometimes you can fix things simply by changing either the font used in the pleading line numbers *or* the font used in the document. (To change the font, select the text—you can use **Ctrl A** to select the entire document—and use the **Font dialog launcher** in the **Font group** on the **Home tab** *or* click **Ctrl D** to open the font dialog. To change the font used for the pleading line numbers, click the **Insert tab**, **Header**, **Edit Header**, and click within the numbers, press **Ctrl A**, use the **Font dialog launcher** *or* press **Ctrl D**, make any changes, **OK** out, and close the Header editing screen.)

4. **Unexpected or Seemingly Random Font Size Changes**.

Check the document for unexpected font size changes, especially with respect to blank lines between paragraphs. For this task, it can be helpful to turn on Show Non-Printing Characters (click the paragraph icon in the **Paragraph group** of the **Home tab** *or* press **Ctrl Shift * [asterisk]**). Look for any paragraph symbols that seem larger than the rest. If you find any, select the paragraph symbol itself and change the font size via the font dialog box.

5. **Section Breaks**.

If the document contains section breaks, it's possible the sections are formatted differently. Take a look and make any necessary changes. (You can tell which section the cursor is in by looking at the left-hand side of the Status Bar, assuming you have enabled Display Section by right-clicking the Status Bar and checking Section.)

6. **Widows and Orphans**.

Sometimes having Widow/Orphan control enabled can cause problems with text alignment. This feature ordinarily shouldn't be enabled in pleadings because in general you want text going all the way to the bottom of the page, even if it means one line dangling by itself at the top or bottom of a page. However, *it is enabled by default*, and because many people aren't aware of that fact, they don't think to turn it off. (It's also difficult to turn off in an entire document, even when you select the document, then launch the **Paragraph dialog**, click the **Line and Page Breaks tab**, and *uncheck* **Widow/Orphan control**.)

7. **Footers, Footnotes, etc.**

It can be worthwhile to check existing footers and footnotes to see if line spacing, "Before" and/or "After" spacing, or other configuration settings for those specific features could be causing problems with the alignment of the text in the body of the document.

Also Notorious

If the factors mentioned above aren't at fault, here are some additional things to investigate:

8. Compatibility Settings.

These settings, found under the **File tab**, **Options**, **Advanced** (scroll all the way down to the bottom of the screen and click the triangle next to **Layout Options**), can have a significant impact on document formatting. It's not necessary to be familiar with all of the options; just be aware that there are several—including "**Don't add extra space for raised / lowered characters**," "**Don't add leading (extra space) between rows of text**," and "**Don't center 'exact line height' lines**"[1]—that can change the appearance of your document. Selecting Microsoft Office Word 2003 from the drop-down list (so that your files will be compatible with that version of Word) can help in certain instances, but you will have to experiment (preferably using *copies* of your documents, not originals).

9. "At Least" vs. "Exactly" Line Spacing.

"At Least" line spacing can be useful in desktop publishing, where there might be dropped caps, graphics in line with text, and other special effects. The "At Least" option ensures a minimum height (point size) for text but allows text to expand to accommodate such special effects. Pleadings, however, often need to use "Exactly" line spacing. When the "At Least" option is used in pleadings, it can create havoc. For example, in a sample pleading with no section breaks, the text on most pages started at 1" from the top of the page, but started at 0.8" on a couple of pages. Eventually I determined that the line spacing for one or more paragraphs on the problematic pages had been set using the "At Least" option. As soon as I changed to "Exactly," the misbehaving pages adjusted and the text moved down to the 1" point.

When All Else Fails

10. Page Setup/Margins and Layout for Headers and Footers.

As a very last resort, you can try fiddling with the top margin of the document and/or the header and footer margins. Note that Word uses negative top and bottom margins in pleadings *by design* in order to prevent the header and footer area from expanding (which could cause the body text and the pleading line numbers to become misaligned). See, for example, MS Knowledge Base Article #211611 (found here: http://support.microsoft.com/kb/211611). You

---

[1] Recently I attempted to save as a .docx file a pleading template I originally created in .doc format. The text alignment changed unexpectedly, such that the first line of the text (which had been aligned perfectly in the .doc version) began slightly above the first line number. I investigated all of the usual suspects listed above, to no avail. Finally, I unchecked the "Don't center 'exact line height' lines" option under Compatibility Settings, which fixed the problem. As you can imagine, troubleshooting this type of problem can be very difficult unless you are aware of obscure settings such as the ones I've mentioned here.

might be able to adjust the margins—for instance, you could change the top margin and/or the header margin from -1.19" to -1"—but just be aware that doing so could make matters worse. Make a note of the existing margins before changing them, and be prepared to undo if necessary.

Miscellaneous Tips

Always try the least drastic—and most obvious—solutions first. (Sometimes simply bumping text down a "single-spaced" line—which might mean a line that is 11.375 points or some other odd fraction—will solve the problem.)

Remember that more than one setting might need to be adjusted.

Check the options in the Paragraph dialog (both tabs) early in the process. It's possible there's an easy fix (for instance, "Before" and/or "After" spacing might be the culprit).

Never assume that fixing the formatting of one paragraph will fix the formatting of the other paragraphs in the document—or that selecting the entire document and then changing the paragraph formatting options will succeed. Word can be quirky, and sometimes you have to go back in and change the formatting of individual paragraphs. If necessary, check a few paragraphs at random to see if your new settings have, in fact, taken effect.

Working With Tables to Create Case Captions

Tables have many uses in the legal field. For instance, you can use them for case captions in pleadings, for exhibit lists, and even for lengthy service lists. I'm sure you can think of other applications for tables.

As it turns out, tables are fairly easy to use in Word (and actually more intuitive than WordPerfect's column feature). This section explains how to use tables to format a case caption and offers additional tips for working with tables in Word.

If for some reason you need to set up your own case caption, or you have to set up a Separate Statement of Disputed and Undisputed Material Facts, it's a good idea to use tables rather than columns. Word's column feature uses *newspaper*-style columns (the kind that go all the way to the bottom of the page and then wrap around), not the *parallel* columns needed for legal documents. In addition, if you use columns, you can't set a middle column narrow enough for just one character, as you can in WordPerfect.

SUPERIOR COURT OF THE STATE OF CALIFORNIA

FOR THE COUNTY OF LOS ANGELES

PAPA DOE, MAMA DOE, and BABY DOE,	)))	**CASE NO. LC 12345678**
Plaintiffs,	)))	**NOTICE OF MOTION AND MOTION TO COMPEL DEPOSITION TESTIMONY; MEMORANDUM OF POINTS AND AUTHORITIES IN SUPPORT THEREOF**
vs.	))	
DO RE MI , SOL LA TI DO, and DOES 1 to 20, inclusive,	)))	Hearing Date:　May 12, 2010 Time:　9:00 A.M. Dept.:　"Z"
Defendants.	))))	Discovery Cutoff:　None Motion Cutoff:　None Trial Date:　None

To set up a caption, go to the **Insert tab** and click the **Table** drop-down in the **Tables group**.

When the drop-down appears, either:

(1) **click and drag the mouse over the table graphic** to designate the number of rows and columns you want; *or*

(2) **click Insert Table…** and, when the **Insert Table dialog** appears, **set the number of rows and columns** (by typing the numbers or using the "spinner" arrows).

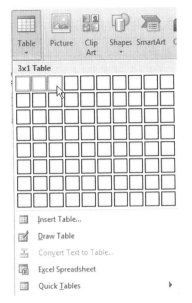

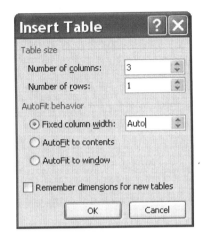

The Click and Drag Method...   **The "Insert Table" Dialog Method**

For the case caption, you'll likely want to create a table with three columns and one row—one column for the parties box, one (very narrow) column for the end parentheses, and another column for the case number, document title, hearing and trial dates, and other information. Some people like to set up captions with four columns, using an "empty" column as a buffer between the end parentheses and the document title (as I did on the prior page).

For a Separate Statement, you can use two columns (one for the facts and one for the supporting evidence), or perhaps even four (one each for the facts and supporting evidence, plus two small columns for the numbering).

Setting the Column Widths

There are a few different ways to set the width of the columns in your table. One way is by **dragging the column margin markers on the ruler** until the columns are formatted to your liking. (The column margin markers appear when your cursor is within a table cell.)

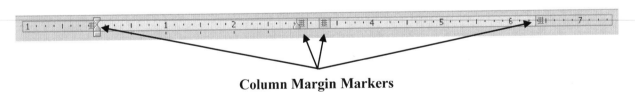

Column Margin Markers

Or you can move the mouse pointer over a table margin and, when the pointer turns into a double-headed arrow, click and drag the margin to the left or right. (See the screenshot below.)

Of course, both of those methods work best for people who are highly skilled at using the mouse. Even so, they can be tricky because sometimes the outer margins move when you're adjusting an inner margin (i.e., the entire table shrinks).

Thankfully for those of us who are not terribly dexterous, there are other ways to adjust the column margins. For example, you can click within the table, then click the **Table Tools Layout tab** and set the width of each column manually, either by typing a number in the "**Width**" **box** or by using the up or down **arrows** ("**spinners**"). In the screenshot below, the width appears in the second box from the top in the **Cell Size group** (where it displays 2.22").

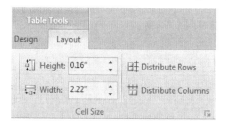

Or you can launch the **Table Properties dialog box** by clicking the arrow at the lower right-hand corner of the **Cell Size group**, click the **Column** tab, and set the column widths from there. (Note the "**Previous Column**" and "**Next Column**" buttons, which you can use to set the widths of the other columns.)

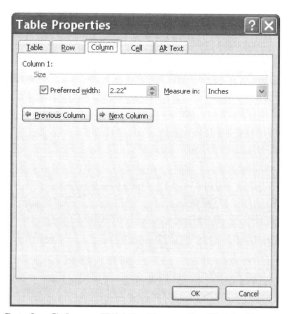

You Can Set the Column Widths From the Table Properties Dialog

Table Borders and Gridlines

When you first insert a table in Word, the table ordinarily appears with borders around each cell. These borders normally print with the document. For purposes of a pleading caption, you will want to remove the borders, except for the bottom border of the left-hand column (i.e., the parties box portion of the caption).

There are a few different ways you can remove the table borders. I will outline a couple of methods below.

1.　First, **position your cursor somewhere within the table**. When your cursor is within a table, the context-sensitive **Table Tools tab** (consisting of a **Design tab** and a **Layout tab**) appears in the Ribbon.

2.　Click the **Design tab** and launch the **Borders and Shading** dialog by clicking the dialog launcher in the lower right-hand corner of the **Draw Borders** group.

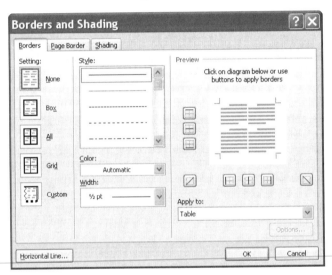

Borders and Shading Dialog

3.　Make sure that the **Apply to:** drop-down in the lower right-hand side of the dialog displays "**Table**" (as opposed to "Cell" or "Paragraph"), and then click the "**None**" icon at the top of the left-hand column.

4.　Finally, **OK** out.

Alternatively, you can do the following:

1.　*Right*-click somewhere within the table, then click the **Borders and Shading** command;

2.　Make sure that the **Apply to:** drop-down in the lower right-hand side of the dialog displays "**Table**" (as opposed to "Cell" or "Paragraph"), and then click the "**None**" icon at the top of the left-hand column.

3.   **OK** out of the dialog.

Or you can use this method:

1.   Click the **Home tab**, **Paragraph group**, click the drop-down **Borders icon**, and click the "**Borders and Shading**" **command** at the bottom of the list.[1]

2.   Make sure that the **Apply to: drop-down** in the lower right-hand side of the dialog displays "**Table**" (as opposed to "Cell" or "Paragraph"), and then click the "**None**" icon at the top of the left-hand column.

3.   **OK** out of the dialog.

When you remove the table borders, you may or may not see a pale blue or gray outline around the table and all table cells. This outline is called a "**gridline**." It is a non-printing border provided to help you navigate within the table. If you prefer not to see the gridlines, click inside the table, then click the **Table Tools Layout tab**, navigate to the **Table group** at the left side of the Ribbon, and click **View Gridlines**.

The View Gridlines button is a toggle; it alternates between turning gridlines on and off (depending on the state of the gridlines—i.e., whether they are visible or hidden—when you click the button).

Gridlines can be turned on or off, as well, from the **Borders** button on the **Table Tools Design tab**. That button opens a drop-down list; the second command from the bottom is **View Gridlines**.

Remember that gridlines do not print. If you ever create a table and you want the borders to print, you need to use one of the above methods to create or restore missing table borders.

CAUTION! There is a "Gridlines" command on the **View tab** that has *absolutely nothing to do with Table Gridlines*. Rather, it has to do with hidden *drawing gridlines* in the NORMAL template that comes with the program and that most users never see or need to see.

---

[1] Note that if you select the "**No Border**" command from the Borders drop-down instead of the Borders and Shading command, Word will remove the borders *only* from the cell your cursor is in, *not* from the entire table.

Creating the Line at the Bottom of Column 1

Once you have removed the table borders, you'll need to create a horizontal line at the bottom of the first column. There are several ways to accomplish this task. One particularly easy way is to click anywhere within the first column, then locate the **Borders icon** on the **Table Tools Design tab**, click the down-pointing arrow to the right of the icon, locate the icon with the bottom border, and click it. Note that you also can launch the **Borders and Shading** dialog by clicking the arrow in the lower right-hand side of the **Draw Borders** group, the right-most group in the **Table Tools Design tab**.

Another easy way to create the line is to **right-click** within the cell, click **Borders and Shading**, click the **Bottom Border** button (or click the bottom of the diagram), then make sure "**Apply to**" displays **Cell** (rather than Table or Paragraph) and click **OK**.

Entering Text and Moving Around Within a Table

To set up your caption, start typing the text in column 1 normally. It will wrap around when it reaches the right-hand margin of the column.

When you need to tab over *within the cell* to type the word "Plaintiffs," press **Ctrl Tab** rather than **Tab**. *Pressing the Tab key by itself will move the cursor to the next cell (column).* (Pressing **Shift Tab** moves the cursor to the previous column.)

Once you have finished typing the text in the first column, press the **Tab key** to move the cursor to the next column. To insert the end parentheses, you'll probably have to type one at a time, followed by the **Enter key**. (In Word, unlike in WordPerfect, the column will expand if you continue typing end parentheses without pressing the Enter key after each one.)

Continue setting up the other columns as you would in WordPerfect. You don't have to turn off the columns when you're finished, but **don't press Tab when you reach the end of Column 3**, or you'll inadvertently create a new row! **Instead, use the down arrow to move the cursor out of the table.**

Watch Out for "Typing Replaces Selected Text"

There is a configuration option in Word (**File tab**, **Options**, **Advanced**, **Editing options**) called "**Typing Replaces Selected Text**" (formerly called "Typing Replaces Selection") that you should be aware of. If this option has been checked, when you press Tab to move to the next column, Word highlights the text in that column—and overwrites the text when you press any key to insert a letter or number. In other words, the highlighted text is deleted and replaced by whatever character(s) you type. (Pressing the cursor movement keys does not delete the highlighted text, but pressing the Spacebar does.)

If you accidentally delete highlighted text, press **Ctrl Z** or click the **Undo button** on the Quick Access Toolbar. If you like, you can turn off the "Typing Replaces Selected Text" option by clicking the **File tab**, **Options**, **Advanced**, **Editing options**, and unchecking the box next to that option.

Some Additional Tips About Working With Tables

Inserting and Deleting Rows (and Columns)

An easy way to insert a row is to right-click within a row, then click the "Insert" command and, when the context menu opens, choose either the "Insert Rows Above" command or the "Insert Rows Below" command (where "above" and "below" refer to the row your cursor is in), as appropriate. Clicking either command inserts one additional row.

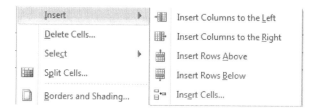

Also, there are buttons in the Rows & Columns group on the Table Tools Layout tab that you can use to insert rows (or columns). The buttons are useful if you need to insert multiple rows (or columns). Although one row is inserted per click, you can click repeatedly, which you can't do if you use the right-click menu.[2]

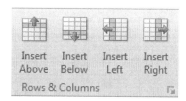

And, if you click the dialog launcher in the Rows & Columns group, a tiny "Insert Cells" dialog appears, offering more specific choices.

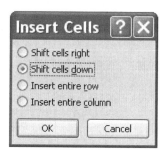

---

[2] However, you might recall that there is a keyboard shortcut that makes it easy to repeat an action: **Ctrl Y**. So after you insert one row above or below the current row, you can press Ctrl Y to continue inserting rows.

To delete a row, you can use any of the methods discussed above. While your cursor is within a table cell, **right-clicking** presents a "Delete Cells" option. When you click that option, a small **Delete Cells dialog** appears so that you can choose to delete an entire row or an entire column or, if you wish to delete only a single cell, shift the remaining cells to the left or upward.

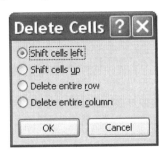

The "**Delete**" drop-down at the left side of the **Table group** in the **Table Tools Layout tab** includes commands to delete individual cells, columns, and rows, as well as a command to delete the whole table.

NOTE: There is no built-in keyboard shortcut to insert or delete a table row, but it's easy to create your own. For instructions, see the sidebar starting on page 444.

Adding a Row at the End of a Table

As in WordPerfect, you can add one or more rows easily by positioning the cursor in the last cell of the table and pressing the **Tab key** (keep pressing Tab to add more than one row).

Header Rows

If you are using a table that spans multiple pages (for instance, in a Separate Statement), you might want to create a header row that repeats at the top of each page. With the cursor in the row you wish to use as the header row, click the **Table Tools Layout tab**, **Table Properties**, click the **Row tab**, and check the "**Repeat as header row at the top of each page**" box.

CAUTION: There is a **Header Row** option in the **Table Tools Design tab**, **Table Style Options group** (the left-most group). By default, it is checked (enabled).

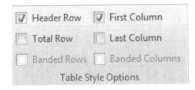

This feature has to do with the ***design*** of tables that have alternating shaded rows; it determines whether the top row of the table is or is not shaded. Obviously, therefore, it has ***nothing to do with*** creating repetitive content at the top of each page of a table.

Merging Cells or Splitting the Table

If you need to insert regular text in a row between rows that contain multiple columns, you can either merge the cells in one row or split the table. To merge cells, first select the cells, then click **Merge Cells** on the **Table Tools Layout tab**. To split a table, position the cursor in the row where you want to insert text and click **Split Table**, also found on the **Table Tools Layout tab**.

Allowing Rows to Break Across Pages

Note that you can choose to allow rows to split across pages or configure them not to do so. With your cursor in the row, click the **Table Tools Layout tab**, **Table Properties**, click the **Row tab**, and either check or uncheck the "**Allow row to break across pages**" box.

Setting the Table Alignment and Size

If your table appears to you to be off center, click the **Table Tools Layout tab**, **Table Properties** (or **right-click** within the table and then click "**Table Properties**"), click the **Table tab**, and make sure the alignment is set to **Center**. (For some reason, the default is **Left**.)

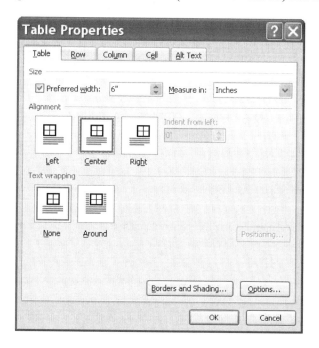

You can set the table width from this dialog, as well.

Selecting the Table (or Table Components)

One more quick tip: At the left end of the **Table Tools Layout tab** (in the **Table group**), there is a **Select drop-down** that enables you to select a cell, a column, a row, or an entire table.

Another way to do the same thing is by right-clicking within a table cell; the "Select" command offers the same four choices (shown in the truncated image below).

Also, there is a keyboard shortcut for selecting a table: **Alt Num 5** (i.e., the number 5 on the Numeric Keypad). If you are working on a laptop, you might need to press **Alt Fn 5** (where "Fn" is "Function" and the "5" is not the one on the row of numbers at the top but the one in a different color somewhere within the keyboard. On my main laptop, it is on the same key as the letter "I," and it is a sort of periwinkle blue color).

QUICK TIPS: Tabbing Within a Table Cell / Adding a Row at the End of a Table

Although I mention both of these tips in passing in the long section about working with tables, I decided to reiterate them in a separate sidebar because they involve two aspects of tables that my clients ask about most frequently: how to insert a tab in a table cell and how to create an additional row at the end of a table using only keystrokes.

In both Word and WordPerfect, ordinary tabbing within a table cell moves the cursor into the next cell. To insert a "hard tab" within a table cell, press **Ctrl Tab** instead of the Tab key alone.

Both programs also allow you to add another row at the end of a table simply by positioning the cursor in the **last (bottom right-most) cell** of the table and pressing **Tab**. This feature can be useful, but if you didn't intend to add another row, you can just click the **Undo** icon, which is located on the **Quick Access Toolbar** (or press **Ctrl Z**, the keyboard shortcut for Undo) immediately after pressing Tab.

SIDEBAR: Creating a Keyboard Shortcut to Insert a Table Row

There is no built-in keyboard shortcut in Word 2010 to insert a table row above (or below) an existing row. However, you can create your own keyboard shortcut for this function. To set up a key combination that will insert a table row above the current cursor position, do one of the following:

- Click the **File tab, Options, Customize Ribbon**; or

- **Right-click** the **Quick Access Toolbar** (QAT) and click **Customize the Ribbon**.

Then, navigate to the "**Keyboard Shortcuts**" button at the lower left-hand side of the Word Options screen and click the "**Customize" button**.

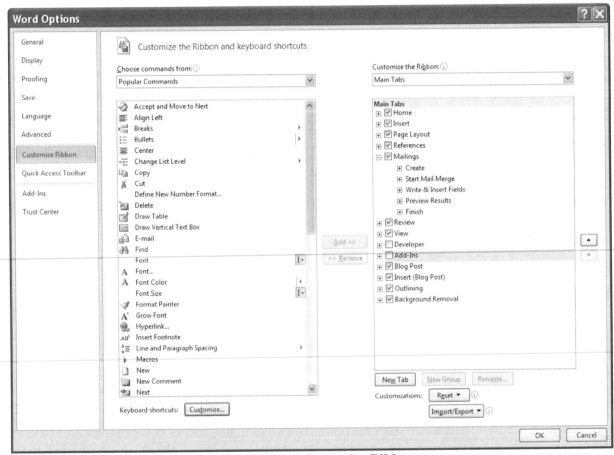

Word Options, Customize Ribbon
Keyboard Shortcuts "Customize" Button at Bottom Left

When the **Customize Keyboard dialog** appears, locate "**Categories:**" on the left-hand side of the dialog, scroll down if necessary, and click to select "**Table Tools, Layout Tab.**" Then on the right-hand side, under "**Commands,**" scroll down and click to select **TableInsertRowAbove.**[1]

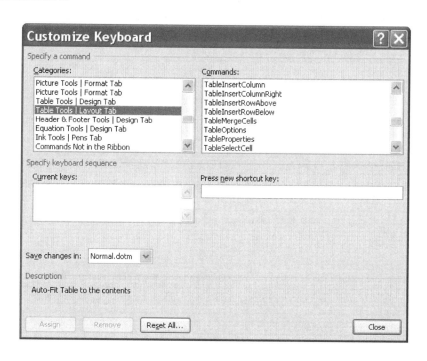

Click to position the cursor in the "**Press new shortcut key**" box and then press any key combination you like, such as **Alt Insert**, the key combination that inserts a table row above the current row in WordPerfect. If the key combination is already assigned to another feature or function, Word will so indicate (see "**Currently assigned to,**" a little more than halfway down the dialog box). You can choose to override the existing assignment or select a different key combination.

When you have inserted the key combination you want, the "**Assign**" button will become active. Click it to assign the key combination to the function. Then click "**Close**" and **OK** out of the dialog box.

Now you can insert a new table row with just a couple of keystrokes!

---

[1] To insert a table row below the cursor position, use the **TableInsertRowBelow** command instead. To **delete** a table row at the cursor position, use **TableDeleteRow** (perhaps assigning the keyboard shortcut Alt Del, the key combination to delete a table row in WordPerfect).

WHERE DID IT GO? Sort

The **Sort command** is now available via a button in the **Paragraph group** on the **Home tab**. (It's located immediately to the left of the paragraph symbol or pilcrow.)   The button looks like this:

A↓
Z

There's another **Sort command** on the context-sensitive **Table Tools Layout tab** (in the **Data group**), which becomes available when your cursor is positioned within a table.

Basic Sorting: A Brief Review

If you wish to perform a simple sort and there's no other text on the page, you don't even have to select the text; just click the **Sort button** (in the **Paragraph group** on the **Home tab**) and the **Sort Text dialog** will open. If there's any other text on the page, be sure to select the text first.

The default sort type is Paragraph. You can sort alphabetically by text (in either ascending or descending order) or, if the items to be sorted include numbers, you can sort numerically (in ascending or descending order).

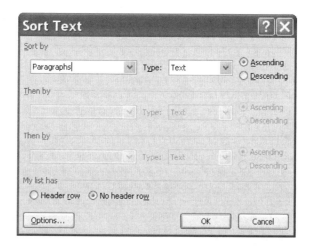

Depending on the items to be sorted, you might need to do some tweaking to the "Sort by" settings. If the information includes "fields" separated by tabs or commas, click the "Options" button and, if necessary, click to change the field separator type.

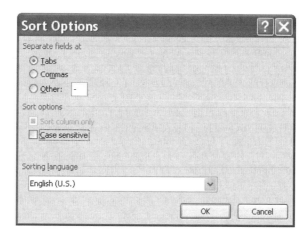

If you select Tabs or Commas, the "Sort by" options will change so that you can sort by field. For example, if Field 1 is the first name and Field 2 is the last name, you can sort by Field 2, then by Field1 (so that names are alphabetized primarily by last name and secondarily by first name, in case there are two or more people with the same last name).

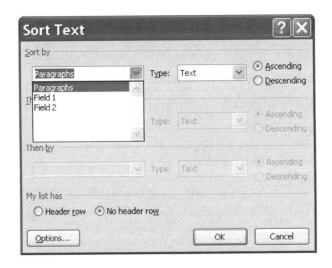

Note that you can sort by word, which is a convenient option if, for example, you are sorting a list of people's names and the first name and last name are separated by a space rather than by a tab or a comma. To do so, click the "Other" option, then click in the box to the right, delete the character in the box and press the Spacebar instead, then click "OK." The "Sort by" drop-down changes to allow you to sort by word, rather than by field.

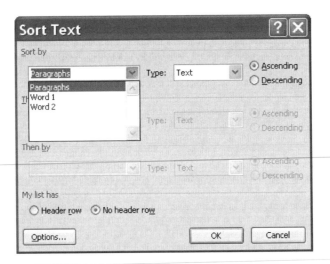

TIP: If you are sorting a list of names and some of the people use their middle initials or middle names or have compound first names, insert a hard space (Ctrl Shift Spacebar) between the first name and the middle initial (or second name) before sorting.

When you initiate a sort with your cursor within a table, the Sort dialog provides different options. It defaults to sorting by column, as opposed to by paragraph. You still have the option of sorting text, as well as by number or by date.

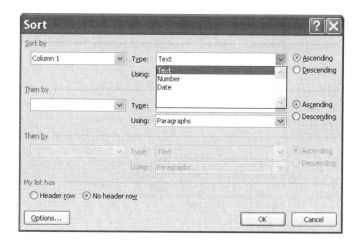

QUICK TIP: Easy Access to Indent and Spacing Options

In addition to the paragraph formatting tools that are available from the Paragraph group in the Home tab, Word provides easy access to paragraph indent and spacing options via the **Paragraph group** in the **Page Layout tab**. Specifically, there are boxes where you can set left and right indents, as well as before and after paragraph spacing. You can type the exact measurements in the boxes or use the "spinner" arrows, as you prefer.

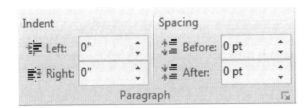

Note that the Paragraph group on the Page Layout tab, like its counterpart on the Home tab, features a dialog launcher that you can click to open the full Paragraph dialog.

Creating a California Rules of Court ("CRC") Rule 2.110[1]-Compliant Footer

1. With your pleading on the screen, click the **Insert** tab, then navigate to the **Header & Footer** group and click **Footer, Edit Footer**. Word puts you in a special footer editing screen.[2]

2. Once in the footer editing screen, open the **Paragraph dialog** by pressing **Alt O, P**, then click the **Line spacing drop-down** and choose "**Exactly.**" Enter an appropriate figure in the "**At**" **box** to make sure the footer will be single-spaced and click "**OK**" to save your settings.[3] If you forget to change the line spacing at this point, you can change it later on by selecting the entire footer (by pressing Ctrl A while in the footer editing screen), opening the Paragraph dialog, and then setting an appropriate "Exactly" figure from the Line spacing drop-down.

3. If you haven't already inserted page numbers in your document, position the cursor at the center of the footer (which is also the center of the page). There are two ways to do so:

    (a)   by pressing **Ctrl E**; or

    (b)   by clicking the **Home** tab, then clicking the **Center Justification** button in the **Paragraph** group.[4]

4. Next, insert a page number code by either (a) clicking the **Page Number** icon in the **Header & Footer group** on the **Header & Footer Tools Design tab**, **Current Position, Simple**[5] *or* (b) simply pressing **Alt Shift P**.

---

[1] Formerly numbered 201(g).

[2] Note: To move between the footer editing screen and the header editing screen, you can either (a) click the **Go to Header button** on the **Design tab** (or the **Go to Footer button** if your cursor is in the header screen) or (b) press the **up or down arrow** as appropriate.

[3] Although you can use Ctrl 1 to apply standard single spacing, it's preferable to use an "Exact" measure in the footer if your pleading text is based on "Exact" line spacing. Remember that the "double" line spacing should match the spacing of the pleading line numbers and the "single" line spacing should be exactly half that figure.

[4] Pressing the **Tab key** once will move the cursor to the 3" mark, which isn't true center because our pleading uses margins of 1.5" on the left and .5" on the right. Note that although there is a *center tab stop* at 3" (which means any text you type will be centered around the 3" mark), this method does not use *center justification*. In other words, when you press the Enter key to move the cursor to the next line, the cursor will go back to the left margin.

[5] **CAUTION:** If you use any of the other built-in options besides Current Position, Word will overwrite any text you've already inserted into your footer.

5.	If you <u>have</u> already inserted page numbers in your document, press the **End** key to move the cursor to the end of the line.

6.	Next, press the **Enter** key to move the cursor to the next line so that you can insert a horizontal line below the page number. There are at least three ways to insert the horizontal line. The first one is particularly easy.

(1)	**Automatic Borders**. If you have automatic formatting of borders turned on, just type **three hyphens** and press the **Enter** key. (If that doesn't work, automatic formatting of borders is turned off. To turn it on, click the **File tab, Options, Proofing, AutoCorrect, AutoFormat As You Type**, click the **Border lines** checkbox, and click **OK**.) When you have finished, Word will automatically bump the cursor to the next line.

(2)	**The Border Button**. Using the **up arrow key** (not the Backspace key), move the cursor back up a line so that it is just past the number code and ahead of the paragraph symbol. Then locate the **Border button** on the **Home tab** (at the bottom right side of the **Paragraph group**), click the down-pointing triangle to the right of the button, and click the **Bottom Border icon**.[6] Next, press the **down arrow key** to move the cursor to the next line.

(3)	**Shift + Underscore**. Alternatively, hold down the **Shift key** and press the **underscore key** (the key to the right of the zero/close parenthesis key) until the line stretches across the footer editing screen. (If you go too far, just press the Backspace key and delete any excess.) When you have finished, press the Enter key to move the cursor to the next line. **NOTE**: This is *the least elegant method*, but it works.

7.	For the short document title, you'll probably want to use a smaller font than what you're using in the body of the pleading. Remember that California Rules of Court mandates that pleadings for the Superior Court use a footer font no smaller than 10 points. To change to a smaller font, do one of the following:

(a)	Navigate to the **Home** tab, **Font** group, and make a selection from the drop-down font size list; *or*

(b)	Open the Font dialog box (by pressing **Ctrl D**) and change the size from there; *or*

(c)	Simply press **Ctrl [** (open bracket) once or twice. (Each time you press **Ctrl [**, the font size decreases by one point.)

---

[6] Paragraph borders come in handy in certain situations, but keep in mind that they apply to the entire paragraph, so they aren't always appropriate.

8.   To center the document title,[7] just start typing (assuming you turned center justification on in step 3).

9.   When you're finished, just click the **Close Header and Footer** button.

10.   You may need to adjust the bottom margin of the pleading so that you're able to type on all 28 lines. To do so, click the **Page Layout** tab and launch the **Page Setup dialog** (or click **Alt P, M, A** or **Alt P, S, P**). Change the bottom margin setting as necessary. You might have to experiment with this setting.

11.   If you want to "suppress" the page number on the caption page, you will have to divide the document into two *sections* (one consisting of the first page and the other consisting of the rest of the document); *unlink* the Section 2 footer from the Section 1 footer; then modify the footer in Section 1 by deleting the page number code.

        (a)   To divide the document into sections:

                (1)   First, switch to **Draft View** (use the icons at the right-side of the Status Bar or click the **View tab, Draft**) so you can see the section breaks and page breaks more easily.

                (2)   Position the cursor at the bottom of the first page and click the **Page Layout** tab, **Page Setup** group, **Breaks, Next Page**.

                (3)   The section break should replace the existing page break. If it doesn't, delete the page break.

        (b)   To unlink the Section 2 footer from the Section 1 footer:

                (1)   Change back to **Print Layout** view.

                (2)   Click the **Insert** tab, **Footer, Edit Footer** and navigate to the Section 2 footer by clicking **Next**. Note the words "Same as Previous" at the right-hand side of the footer editing screen for Section 2.

---

[7] If you prefer (and if it is your firm's standard), you can right align the title. To do so, press Ctrl R and start typing. To indent the title from the left, press Ctrl M a few times and start typing. (To decrease the indent, either press Ctrl Shift M or click the Decrease Indent button on the formatting toolbar.)

(3)   Locate the **Link to Previous button** in the Header & Footer Tools tab and click it to turn it *off*. The words "Same as Previous" in the footer editing screen should disappear.

(c)   To modify the Section 1 footer:

(1)   Now click the "**Previous**" button to move to the Section 1 footer editing screen.

(2)   Select the page number code in the Section 1 footer—being careful not to select the paragraph symbol immediately to the right of the number code—and press **Delete** (or cut using Ctrl X or any method you prefer).

(3)   Click **Close Header and Footer**. Scroll through the document to make sure the Section 1 and Section 2 footers are in fact different.

<u>Creating a CRC Rule 2.110 Compliant Footer
Using the "Different First Page" Option
To "Suppress" the Page Number on the Caption Page</u>

This tutorial has been revised significantly to allow for "suppressing" the page number on the caption page of pleadings. In MS Word, when you want to have more than one header or footer—for example, a footer *without* a page number and a second footer *with* a page number—you must divide the document.

Word has a "Different First Page" option that lets you create a footer without a page number on the caption page, as well as footers on the remaining pages that have page number codes. But there is a very important "gotcha" to be aware of when you use the "Different First Page" option: Headers are linked to footers in Word, and the pleading paper is part of a header. As a result, when you first apply "Different First Page," *the pleading paper will disappear!* We can get it back, but we have to remember to follow all the steps outlined below.

1. With your pleading on the screen, click the **Insert tab**, **Header**, **Edit Header**. Word puts you in a special header editing screen. The first thing you need to do is press **Ctrl Shift * (asterisk)** (or click the paragraph symbol in the **Paragraph group** on the **Home tab**) to turn on Show Nonprinting Characters.

2. When Show Nonprinting Characters is turned on, you should see (among other things) paragraph symbols. Remember that the paragraph symbols contain formatting codes. The very first paragraph symbol at the top of the header editing screen contains codes that configure the pleading paper. We will need to reinsert this code in a few minutes, so **select (highlight) that paragraph symbol** and either press **Ctrl C** to copy or use any other method you prefer to copy selected characters.

3. Next, click the **Header and Footer Tools Design tab**, **Options group**, and check the "**Different First Page**" option.

4. The pleading paper disappears! Eek! But not to worry: Just press **Ctrl V** or use any other method you like to paste the paragraph symbol you copied in step 2 above in place of the paragraph symbol at the top of the header editing screen. The pleading paper should reappear.

5. With the pleading paper back, we will create a footer with no page number for the first page (caption page) of the pleading. To do so, you need to move the cursor to the footer editing screen by either (a) clicking the **Go to Footer button** *or* (b) pressing the **down arrow**.

6. Once in the footer editing screen, we need to make sure the footer will be single-spaced. Because of the way we generated our pleading, the line numbers do not use standard double-spacing, so we will have to use "Exact" line spacing. First, select the entire footer by pressing **Ctrl A**. Then press **Alt O, P** to open the **Paragraph dialog**, and under **Line spacing**, select **Exactly** from the drop-down and type **11.375** (or whatever is exactly half the figure for the spacing of the line numbers in your pleading), and click **OK**.

7. We are not going to insert a page number code in the first-page footer, but we want to leave a blank space—a sort of placeholder—where the page number ordinarily would go. Doing so ensures that the footers on the caption page and the succeeding pages all line up correctly.

8. Press the **Enter** key to move the cursor to the next line so that you can insert a horizontal line below the space where the page number ordinarily would go. There are at least three ways to insert the horizontal line. The first one is particularly easy.

   (1) **Automatic Borders**. If you have automatic formatting of borders turned on, just type **three hyphens** and press the **Enter** key. (If that doesn't work, automatic formatting of borders is turned off. To turn it on, click the **File tab**, **Options**, **Proofing**, **AutoCorrect**, **AutoFormat As You Type**, click the **Border lines** checkbox, and click **OK**.) When you have finished, Word will automatically bump the cursor to the next line.

   (2) **The Border Button**. Using the **up arrow key** (not the Backspace key), move the cursor back up a line so that it is just past the number code and ahead of the paragraph symbol. Then locate the **Border button** on the **Home tab** (at the bottom right side of the **Paragraph group**), click the down-pointing triangle to the right of the button, and click the **Bottom Border icon**. Next, press the **down arrow key** to move the cursor to the next line.

   (3) **Shift + Underscore**. Alternatively, hold down the **Shift key** and press the **underscore key** (the key to the right of the zero/close parenthesis key) until the line stretches across the footer editing screen. (If you go too far, just press the Backspace key and delete any excess.) When you have finished, press the Enter key to move the cursor to the next line. NOTE: This is *the least elegant method*, but it works.

9. For the short document title, you'll probably want to use a smaller font than what you're using in the body of the pleading. Remember that California Rules of Court mandates that pleadings for the Superior Court use a footer font no smaller than10 points. To change to a smaller font, do one of the following:

(a)   Navigate to the **Home tab**, **Font group**, and make a selection from the drop-down font size list; *or*

(b)   Open the **Font dialog box** (by pressing **Ctrl D**) and change the size from there; *or*

(c)   Simply press **Ctrl [** (open bracket) once or twice. (Each time you press Ctrl [, the font size decreases by one point.)

10.   To center the document title,[1] turn on center justification by pressing **Ctrl E**, and then just start typing.[2]

11.   Next, we will create a footer with a page number code. That footer will appear on every page of the pleading except the caption page. (Later on, we will need to insert section breaks so that we can change the page number to start at 1 on the first page of the Memorandum of Points and Authorities and to start at 1 and use small Roman numerals, rather than Arabic numerals, on the first page of the Table of Contents.) First, let's copy the existing footer by pressing **Ctrl A** (to select the entire footer), then pressing **Ctrl C** (or using any other method you prefer to copy selected text).

12.   Then, let's move to the next footer editing screen by clicking the "**Next**" **button** in the **Header & Footer Tools Design tab**. (We automatically divided the document so that there is a first-page footer and a main footer when we applied the "Different First Page" option. Note that using "Different First Page" does not create a new section; it splits an existing section so that the first page can be formatted separately from the rest of the section.)

13.   With your cursor in the next footer editing screen, press **Ctrl V** or use any other method you like to paste the first-page footer we copied in step 11 above. Once you've done so, position the cursor above the horizontal line, press **Ctrl E**, and insert a page number code by either (a) clicking the **Page Number** icon on the Design tab, **Current Position**, **Simple**[3] *or* (b) simply pressing **Alt Shift P**.

---

[1] If you prefer (and if it is your firm's standard), you can right align the title. To do so, press Ctrl R and start typing. To indent the title from the left, press Ctrl M a few times and start typing. (To decrease the indent, either press Ctrl Shift M or click the Decrease Indent button on the formatting toolbar.)

[2] Pressing the Tab key once will move the cursor to the 3" mark, which isn't true center because our pleading uses margins of 1.5" on the left and .5" on the right. Note that although there is a *center tab stop* at 3" (which means any text you type will be centered around the 3" mark), this method does not use *center justification*. In other words, when you press the Enter key to move the cursor to the next line, the cursor will go back to the left margin.

[3] **CAUTION**: If you use any of the other built-in options besides Current Position, Word will overwrite any text you've already inserted into your footer.

14.   When you're finished, just click the **Close Header and Footer** button. You may need to adjust the bottom margin of the pleading so that you're able to type on all 28 lines. To do so, click the **Page Layout** tab and launch the **Page Setup dialog** (or press **Alt P, M, A** *or* **Alt P, S, P**). Change the bottom margin setting as necessary. You might have to experiment with this setting.

Setting Up a Style (and Keyboard Shortcut)
for Indented Quotes

1.   Start typing the text for your indented quote.

2.   With the cursor somewhere within the text, launch the **Paragraph dialog** by clicking the **dialog launcher** in the lower right-hand corner of the **Paragraph group** on the **Home tab** *or* by pressing **Alt O, P**.

3.   Navigate to the **Indentation** box and set both the **Left indent** and the **Right indent** to 1". Make sure the **Special** box is set to **(none)**, unless you want the first line of the quote to be indented an additional half-inch, in which case click the drop down list in the **Special** box, select **First line** and set **By** to .5". Click **OK**.

4.   With the cursor still within the text, launch the **Styles Pane** by clicking the dialog launcher in the lower right-hand corner of the **Styles group** on the **Home tab** *or* by pressing the key combination **Ctrl Alt Shift S**.

5.   When the Style Pane opens, navigate to the very bottom and click the **New Style** button—the first one from the left. A **Create New Style from Formatting** dialog box appears. In the **Name** box at the top of the dialog, **type a name** for the style you are creating (for example, Double Indent, Indented Quote, or Block Quote).

6.   In the box labeled **Style for following paragraph**, click the drop-down list and scroll until you find **Normal**. (**NOTE**: Setting the style for the following paragraph as Normal means that when you finish typing one paragraph of an indented quote and you press the Enter key, the cursor will go back to the left margin and you will be able to type a paragraph that has no special formatting. You might prefer to set up your new style so that when you press Enter, that style's formatting carries over to the next paragraph. If you do so, you can turn off the style at any point by pressing **Ctrl Shift N** or by clicking the **Normal icon** in the **Quick Style Gallery** in the **Styles group** on the **Home tab**, which applies the Normal paragraph style to the paragraph containing the cursor.)

7.   Depending on how your firm formats indented quotes, you also might want to change the line spacing and/or the font in your style. To do so, click the **Format** button at the bottom of the dialog box, then click **Paragraph** (and/or **Font**), and change the settings to suit your preferences.

8.   To set up a keyboard shortcut for your new style, click the **Format** button again, then click **Shortcut key**. Another dialog box appears with the cursor already in the **Press new shortcut key** box. Press the key combination you wish to assign to your style, such as Ctrl Shift F7 or Shift F4 (the WordPerfect keyboard shortcuts for Double Indent). If your preferred key combination already has been assigned

to another feature, Word displays a message to that effect. If the key combination is available or if you wish to override the existing assignment, click the **Assign** button to assign the keystrokes to your style, and click Close.

9. **IMPORTANT**: Before OK-ing out of the Create New Style from Formatting dialog box, be sure to click the **New documents based on this template** radio button at the bottom center. Otherwise, the style will be available *only in the specific document in which you have created the style*. After you have clicked this radio button, click **OK** to save your new style and close the dialog box, and click the X in the upper right-hand corner of the Styles Pane to close it.

Type a **name** here

Set the style for the **following paragraph**

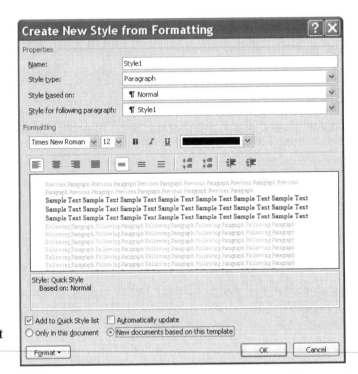

Format button—to set the font, indents, and so on

Be sure to click "**New documents based on this template**" to make the style available in all new documents

10. To use the style, just press the key combination you assigned and start typing. Alternatively, you can apply the style by using the keyboard shortcut after you have typed some text, so long as the cursor is somewhere within the paragraph or you have selected the text. Or you can click somewhere within the paragraph (or select some text), then press **Ctrl Shift S** to open the **Apply Styles** dialog, pull down the Style list, and click to apply a particular style.

11. Note that you can print a list of Styles (and/or a list of Key assignments) from Print Place. When you press **Ctrl P** (or click the **File tab**, **Print**), then click the **Print All Pages drop-down** toward the top left side of Print Place, you'll see a list of various items that you can print (besides the current document or certain pages thereof), beginning with "**Document Properties**." That list includes options to print Styles and Key assignments, among other things.

Inserting Automatic Paragraph Numbers
With the Numbering Button

When you use the Numbering button in Word 2010 (found on the **Home tab**, in the **Paragraph group**), Word begins a *single-level list.* The program normally inserts the number code at the left margin and formats the text as a *hanging indent*, like so:

1. This is the default formatting of numbered lists inserted via the Numbering button in Word. Word indents the first line of the paragraph (i.e., starts the number) at .25" and indents the remainder of the paragraph at .5".

Obviously, this isn't the right format for numbering in a complaint or cross-complaint, or even in a standard agreement.

There are a few workarounds for this problem. All involve tinkering with the formatting so that the number you insert with the Numbering button is indented half an inch (the standard indention for pleadings and most legal documents) and the text wraps around to the left margin.

Method 1:

This method is probably the best one to use, because it will retain your modified formatting even if you end your numbered list and then restart numbering later in the document.

1. **Right-click** somewhere near or within the paragraph number. (Right-clicking is one of the best ways to modify numbered lists in Word 2010; you can't modify a list directly from the list gallery). When the shortcut menu appears, click **Adjust List Indents**. The **Adjust List Indents dialog** will open.

2. If you want to use standard numbering for complaints and such, set the **Number position** at .5" and the **Text indent** at 0 (zero)—so that the text will wrap to the left margin. You don't need to check the "Add tab stop at:" box.

3. Click **OK** (or press **Enter**) to confirm your settings.

4.   Type enough text to make sure the second line of the paragraph wraps to the left margin, and then press the **Enter key**. Word should insert another numbered paragraph with the same settings.[1]

5.   In order to save this modified list style so that you can use it in future documents, *right*-click near or within the number. When the shortcut menu appears, click **Styles, Save Selection as a New Quick Style…**

Type a name here

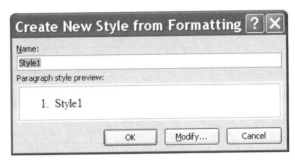

Modify Button

6.   When the condensed **Create New Style from Formatting** box appears, type a short descriptive **name** for the style (such as Numbered Paragraph).

7.   ***Before OK-ing out of the dialog***, click the **Modify** button, which will open the full **Create New Style from Formatting dialog**. The reason for doing so is to allow you to save the new numbering style to the underlying template so that it is available in future documents. If you don't specify otherwise, the numbering style (with your modified indents) will be available only in the current document.

8.   When the expanded **Create New Style from Formatting dialog** appears, make any further changes you want. Be sure to review the "Style for following paragraph" option (as discussed on page 459) and, if necessary, modify it to reflect your wishes.

9.   Next, navigate to the bottom of the dialog and click to mark the "**New documents based on this template**" **radio button**. (See the screenshot on the next page.) **NOTE**: This is a critical step!

10.   Click **OK** to save your changes.

---

[1] **NOTE:** When you use the Numbering button, Word inserts a number code both when you first press the button and when you press Enter after typing a numbered paragraph. To *turn off numbering*, click the Numbering button again. Alternatively, you can press the Enter key a second time, but doing so might bump the next paragraph down a line, which may or may not be your intention. (If you wish to retain numbering but also want a blank line between numbered paragraphs, either (1) press **Shift Enter** rather than Enter, which inserts a **Line Break**, *or* (2) open the Paragraph dialog and navigate to the **Spacing After** box, type **12** [to insert 12 points of blank space after each numbered paragraph], then click **OK**.)

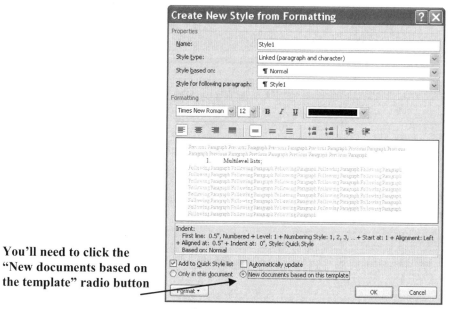

You'll need to click the "New documents based on the template" radio button

Create New Style from Formatting dialog

11.   The new list style should now appear in the Quick Styles gallery on the Home tab as well as in the Styles pane.[2]

Method 2:

This method works, but if you have to restart numbering later in the document, the formatting (i.e., the indents) reverts to Word's defaults, which can be frustrating. You can, however, save the modified list as a Quick Style by following steps 5-10 above. That way, you'll be able to apply the style to a new list in any document by clicking within the first paragraph and then clicking the style name in the gallery or in the Style pane.

1.   **Click the Numbering button** and type some text.

2.   With the cursor somewhere within the paragraph, **drag the First Line Indent marker on the Ruler** (the downward-pointing triangle) so that the number is indented ½ inch.[3]

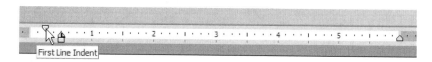

First Line Indent

3.   Next, **drag the Left Indent marker** (the upward-pointing triangle labeled Hanging Indent in the screenshot on the next page) to the left so that all subsequent lines of the paragraph will wrap to the left margin.

---

[2] In case you have difficulty creating—and saving to your NORMAL template—a style that retains the indents you specify, I've provided a workaround in the sidebar following this section.

[3] If the Ruler is not visible, click the **View tab**, **Show group** and check the **Ruler box**.

463

Hanging Indent

Be careful to drag by the triangle rather than by the rectangle. If you drag by the rectangle, you'll reset **both** the First Line Indent and the indentation of subsequent lines. (You might have to delete the "L," which is a left tab marker, in order to drag the Left Indent marker. To delete the "L," simply drag it down into the document editing screen and release the mouse button.)

4.   Position the cursor at the end of the paragraph and **press the Enter key**. Word should insert the next number in sequence, and the paragraph should retain the formatting you just configured (i.e., the indents).

Method 3:

You can tell Word to indent the first line of every paragraph .5", but you have to do this *after* you click the Numbering button and start typing the numbered paragraph. (If you try to set up a first line indent beforehand, Word will undo the indentation as soon as you click the Numbering button.) Note that this method is subject to the same problem as Method 2—i.e., if you restart numbering, you might lose your formatting.

1.   To indent the first line, *either* (a) make sure the insertion point (cursor) is somewhere within the paragraph *or* (b) select (block, highlight) the paragraph.

2.   Next, click the **Paragraph dialog launcher**. When the dialog opens, navigate to **Special**, and choose **First Line Indent**. Make sure the indent is set for .5". Also make sure that the Left Indent is set to 0 (zero) (so that the text wraps to the left margin). Click **OK**.

3.   When you finish typing the first numbered paragraph and press Enter, Word should retain the first-line indent. Again, unless you save this modified list as a style that is available for future documents, it will be available only in the current document.

To Stop/Skip or Restart Numbering:

To stop numbering, press the Enter key twice *or* put the cursor between the number and the text and press Backspace. (To remove the indent, press Backspace again.) Of course you also can stop numbering simply by clicking the numbering button again, but that method often leaves text indented incorrectly. Also keep in mind that when you click the button to restart numbering, Word typically reverts to the original indentation (i.e., a hanging indent, with the number at .25 rather than at .5).

To skip numbering one or more paragraphs, press **Shift Enter** (to insert a manual **line break**) rather than Enter. The next number in sequence will be inserted when you press Enter again. **CAUTION**: Because text that follows a manual line break retains the formatting of the previous paragraph (other than the number)—in fact, technically it's part of the same paragraph—this method isn't always appropriate.

To Resume Numbering in Sequence:

There are several different ways to resume numbering:

1.   Simply click within the first paragraph where you want the numbering to resume (continue from the previous list) and click the **Numbering button**; *or*

2.   Right-click within a numbered paragraph and select "**Continue Numbering**" (**WATCH OUT**: Doing so might cause the indents to revert to Word's defaults); *or*

3.   Click the drop-down next to the numbering button, click "**Set numbering value**," make sure "**Continue from previous list**" has been marked, change the value as you wish, then click **OK**. (**CAUTION**: This method sometimes causes Word to use the original (problematic) indentation.)

If the paragraph number doesn't change appropriately, you might have to reopen the **Set Numbering Value** box and, in addition to clicking "**Continue from previous list**," click "**Advance value**" and manually set the number value for the paragraph before clicking **OK** (see screenshot).

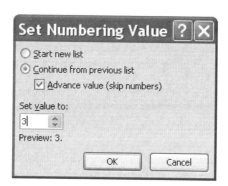

4.   **TIP:** An exceptionally easy way to resume numbering is simply to copy the paragraph symbol from the end of the previous numbered paragraph and paste it where you want to begin numbering again. The advantage of this method is that Word will restart numbering consecutively *and* will retain the indentation of the previous numbered paragraph, as well.

To copy the paragraph symbol, turn on Show Non-Printing Characters by clicking the paragraph symbol (pilcrow = ¶) in the Paragraph group, select the symbol, copy it, and paste it *at the very end* of the paragraph whose formatting you want to conform to the "good" paragraphs.

Note that copying and pasting the paragraph symbol also works well to insert a new paragraph 1 at the beginning of your list. Just insert the cursor *ahead of* any text in the first numbered paragraph before pasting the paragraph symbol.

5.   A similar (and easy) method is to copy and paste formatting via keyboard shortcuts. To copy the formatting of the paragraph your cursor is in, press **Ctrl Shift C**. To paste the formatting, click within the "destination" paragraph and then press **Ctrl Shift V**.

SIDEBAR: Troubleshooting a Single-Level List Style

Creating a "global" style for a single-level list—i.e., one that is saved in the NORMAL template so that you can use it in all future documents—can be tricky. Sometimes it works fine, but other times you might attempt to apply the style in a new document, only to find that your indent settings have changed.

Without fully understanding the reasons why settings in list styles don't always stick, or why the fixes outlined below seem to work, I offer a few troubleshooting tips (based on my extended experiments with this feature) that should help you resolve the problem.

First, you are likely to have better luck if you base your new list style on the **Normal** style, on one of the **List Number** styles, or on "**(no style)**," rather than on the List Paragraph style. In my various tests, the List Paragraph style appeared to be somewhat quirky and unreliable. Avoid it.

Secondly, make sure you configure the indents for your list (the first-line indent and the text indent) via the **Adjust List Indents dialog** rather than the Paragraph dialog. The settings in the former seem to be "stickier" than the ones in the latter, at least when it comes to numbered lists.[1]

Thirdly, you might find that your new style doesn't "take" even though you are careful to click the "New documents based on this template" radio button in the Create New Style from Formatting dialog. In other words, it works as expected in the current document but apparently isn't being saved to the NORMAL template.

To correct that situation, position your cursor in a paragraph to which the style has been applied, *right*-**click** one of the numbers, click **Adjust List Indents**, make your changes to the **Number position** and the **Text indent**, and **OK** out. Then, use the **Style Organizer** to copy the style from the current document into the NORMAL template (normal.dotm). (For help using the Organizer, see page 352 and following.) For unknown reasons, that procedure sometimes works better than saving the list style to the template from within the Create New Style…dialog.

---

[1] **NOTE**: You can set up a keyboard shortcut to open the Adjust List Indents dialog. Just follow the instructions that start on page 307, making sure that "All Commands" is showing in the Categories list, and then scrolling down to AdjustListIndents in the Commands list.

QUICK TIP: Using the ListNum Field

A lesser-known form of automatic numbering in Word, the ListNum field can be very useful. It allows you to insert numbers in sequence *within* a paragraph, using numbering such as (i), (ii), (iii) or (a), (b), (c).

There are three main numbering schemes available with the ListNum field, each of which has nine levels: LegalDefault, NumberDefault, and OutlineDefault. The schemes work pretty much the way their names suggest. The Legal scheme uses typical legal-style numbering (1., 1.1., 1.1.1., etc.); the Outline scheme uses typical outline numbering (I., A., 1., etc.); and the Number scheme uses a mix of number and letter formats for its nine levels, as follows: 1), a), i), (1), (a), (i), 1., a., i.

One of the advantages of using the ListNum field is that—as in WordPerfect—the list levels are not tied to tab stops, so you can insert a number code for any level at any cursor position. As mentioned above, people often use ListNum codes to insert subparagraph numbers like (a) and (b) within the text of a numbered paragraph. And as with SEQ codes, you can have more than one type of ListNum code in the same document—and even within the same paragraph.

To insert a ListNum field code, click the **Insert tab**, **Quick Parts**, **Field** or press **Alt I**, **F**, then press the letter "L" a few times until the cursor lands on the **ListNum field**. (Alternatively, change the category to Numbering, then choose ListNum.)[1]

Click to select one of the three numbering schemes. Then, if you like, you can click to check one or both of the checkboxes to the right to select a particular level in the list and/or a default start-at value (the default level and start-at value are both 1).

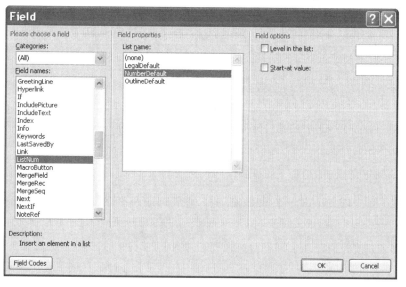

Level in the list

Start-at value

---

[1] Also, the keyboard shortcut **Alt Ctrl L** inserts a ListNum field (in the NumberDefault style).

After you have inserted a ListNum code into your document, you can change the level or the start value by pressing **Alt F9** to display the code itself (rather than the code results) and then inserting the appropriate "switch." The switch for the list level is \l, so to change to a level 4 paragraph you would type "\l 4" (without quotation marks) within the French braces after the LISTNUM designation.

{ LISTNUM NumberDefault \l4 }

Press Alt F9 again to switch back to the code results. A level 4 code using the NumberDefault style produces the number (1).

The switch for the start-at value is \s, so to change to start at 6, you would insert "\s 6" (without quotation marks).

{ LISTNUM NumberDefault \l4 \s 6}

Press Alt F9 again to switch back to the code results. These particular switches produce the following number: (6).

If you **don't** set a specific level, you can change the level of a ListNum code by selecting the code and then clicking the **Increase Indent** or **Decrease Indent** button in the **Paragraph group** on the **Home tab**. (Note that this action changes only the *level* of the code; the *indentation* of the code actually remains the same.) Or, after selecting a code, press the key combination **Alt Shift** → (right arrow key) or **Alt Shift** ← (left arrow key).

Creating Multilevel Lists

In Word 2010, multilevel lists (formerly called outline numbered lists) work differently from the way they worked in versions older than Word 2007. There are a few critical points to keep in mind as you are creating and applying multilevel lists in Word 2010:

1. You should avoid using the "Define New Multilevel List" option in the drop-down, because *you can't edit lists that you create using that option*. Instead, use the "**Define New List Style**" option to create an editable list *style*.

2. When you define a new list style, consider **linking each level of the list with a heading style**. You can set up a list without linking to heading styles, but if you use multilevel lists mainly in connection with headings, linking your list style to heading styles accomplishes two important tasks at once.

3. If you are going to create a list style and link it to heading styles, it helps to define the list style first, then modify the heading styles as necessary.

4. Unlike in prior versions of Word, you will *not* be able to tinker with the numbering in a heading style from within the Modify Style dialog; attempting to do so will lead to a dead end—a dialog that contains only single-level lists and doesn't let you format those lists. When you need to tweak the number formatting, you *must* do it *from within the list style itself* (and specifically, by right-clicking its image in the gallery)!

5. Be sure to **save your new list style to the underlying template**. Otherwise, it will be available only in the current document.

The Multilevel List Gallery

Microsoft has provided a number of "canned" multilevel lists, each with nine different "levels" of numbering. They are available via the **Multilevel List button** in the **Paragraph group** on the **Home tab** (top row, toward the center).

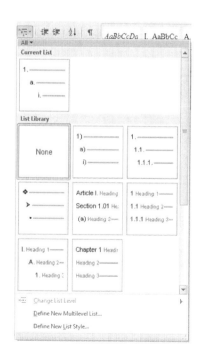

The Multilevel List gallery is divided into several parts: The top shows you the **current list** in effect in your document (if any); the second level shows you a "**library**" of built-in lists; the third level shows you the **existing list styles** (if any); and, if you have inserted several different lists in your document, the bottom level shows you those lists.

Unfortunately, there is no way to modify any of the pre-defined Multilevel lists from within the library, but not to worry. What you will do, instead, is *create your own list styles* for each type of numbered list you use (outlines, legal numbering, and the like) and perhaps link those list styles with heading styles. You can use an existing list as a model for your new style, or you can start from scratch.

When you set up a customized list style, you need to format **each level** of the list style. For each level, you will select the *type* (style) of number (Arabic, upper-case roman, lowercase roman, letters, etc.), any surrounding *punctuation* (periods or parentheses), how far the *paragraph number* is *indented* from the left margin, how far the *text* is indented from the left margin and whether the *next line* wraps to the margin or is set up as a *hanging indent*, the *font*, and several other attributes. If you like, you can add text (such as the word "Section") before a number code, as well.

Getting Started: Creating a New List Style

When you use the Multilevel list drop-down, you will see two options at the bottom:

1. Define New Multilevel List; and

2. Define New List Style.

Intuitively, you might think the best option is Define New Multilevel List. However, as mentioned previously, in Word 2010, you can't modify lists created with that option. If you try, what you'll end up doing is defining several new lists within the same document or template, which can lead to document corruption or other problems.

What you should do instead is use **Define New List Style**. That option allows you to set up and customize an editable multilevel list, save it as a **Quick Style** (and also save it to the NORMAL template) so that you can use it in future documents. You can even set up a keyboard shortcut so that you can apply the list with a couple of keystrokes.

Basing a New List Style on an Existing List

If you like, you can select a list from the gallery and use it as the basis for a new customized list style. Should you wish to do so, be sure to choose a list that already has heading styles associated with it (i.e., the image in the gallery displays text—Heading 1, Heading 2, Heading 3—next to the level numbers).[1]

Creating the List Style

Open the **Multilevel List drop-down**, navigate to the **List Library** section, and click one of the lists associated with heading styles. Word will insert a number. Ignore it.

Next, click the **MultiLevel List drop-down** again and click **Define New List Style**. The **Define New List Style dialog** will open.

---

[1] Thanks to Eva Eilenberg for suggesting this option.

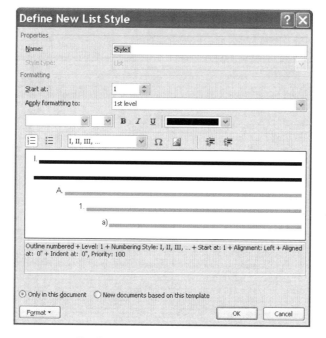

Format button

Define New List Style dialog

At this point, start creating your customized list style. I would suggest that you go through this process step by step, formatting each of the nine list levels from the same dialog. *Do not click OK to save the style* until *after* you have everything set up.

First, give the style a unique, descriptive name, such as **Outline Numbering** or **Legal Numbering**. Note that this name will apply to *the entire multilevel list*, not merely to one of the levels within the list.

Second, navigate to the bottom of the dialog and click the "**New documents based on the template**" button so that when you save the list, you will be able to use it in future documents based on the template currently in use.

CAUTION: Unless you take this step, your customized list will be saved *only in the document in which you are creating it.* (Technically, you'll be able to save the list as a Quick Style Set after you create it, but for a number of reasons it's better to get in the habit of saving new lists to the template as you create them.)

Third, *do not click OK yet*. Instead, click "**Format**," then click "**Numbering**." You should see a **Modify Multilevel List dialog** similar to the one in the screenshot on the next page. Don't be concerned if yours differs in some respects from the screenshot.

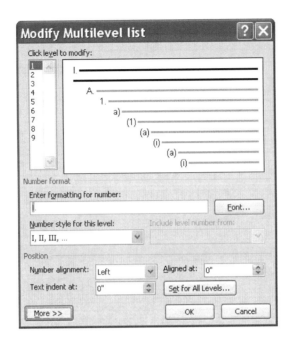

Modify Multilevel List Dialog

Click the "**More**" **button** in the lower left-hand corner of the dialog. The dialog will expand and provide additional options for setting up the list style.

Take a few minutes to acquaint yourself with the expanded dialog and its options.

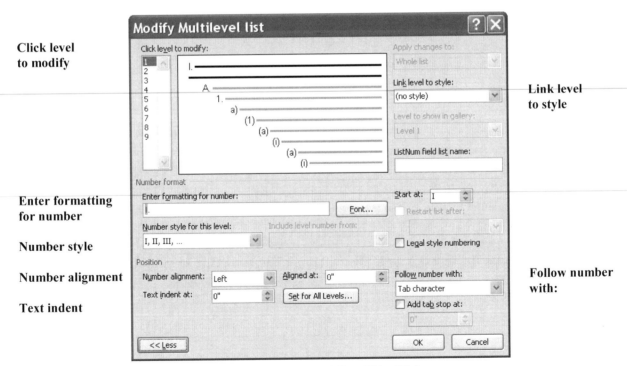

Expanded Modify Multilevel List Dialog

472

The "**Click level to modify**" box on the left side of the dialog provides an easy way to modify each level of the list individually (simply click the level you wish to edit; the level number will be highlighted in blue).

TIP: Glance at it from time to time as you work to keep track of which level you're modifying (it's easy to get confused).

Note the "**Link level to style**" drop-down on the right. This option allows you to link each list level to a specific heading style (whether a built-in heading style or one that you have created), which is a good idea. I will walk you through this process, and after we set up the list style, we'll modify the heading styles as well.

Underneath the preview windows, you'll see a field labeled "**Enter formatting for number**." There should be a number in the field, highlighted in gray. The gray portion *is a code* and is based on the "**Number style for this level**" **drop-down** immediately below the field. If you wish to change the type of number or letter for a particular level, use the drop-down. Then, *being careful not to delete the gray number or letter code*, you can edit the characters or text before or after the number or letter. For example, there might be an end parenthesis after the gray number code. You could delete the end paren and replace it with a period if you like. Alternatively, you could add an open paren before the number code, or you could delete the end paren and add the word "Chapter" or "Section" plus a space before the number code. It's up to you; just be careful not to delete the code itself.

Toward the bottom of the dialog, you can set the number and text positions. The **Number alignment** field is somewhat confusing. Essentially it determines whether numbers align on the first digit, even when the numbers increment above 9, or whether they align on any punctuation that follows (typically a period/decimal point or an end paren). The difference is exemplified by the following series, with the former pair of numbers left aligned and the latter pair right-aligned (aligned on the decimal point):

> 9.
> 10.
>
> 9.
> 10.

Although right alignment seems preferable, it can result in heading numbers being outside the left margin, so you'll probably want to use left alignment. Remember that you can modify the list style later on if you decide you prefer to right-align the numbers.

"**Aligned at**" sets the left indent *for the number itself*: i.e., how far over from the left margin the number starts. For instance, if you are creating a list level to be used in standard paragraphs in a Complaint, you'll probably use .5" for the "Aligned at" setting. Note that in Word 2010, you have the option of setting the indent for all levels at once, which can be very useful—particularly if your firm typically indents each outline level an additional .5" from the previous level.

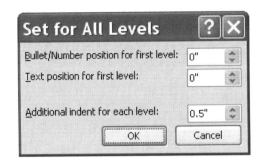

By contrast, "***Text indent at***" sets the left indent for every line of text following the number ***except*** for the first line. (The first-line indent is governed by the "Aligned at" setting.) So, again using the example of a numbered paragraph in a Complaint, you would set the text indent at 0"—because you want the text of the paragraph to wrap to the left margin.

Note that Word provides an option to follow the paragraph number with a Tab (the default setting), a space, or nothing (the "nothing" option is useful when you want a centered number with text centered **below** the number). It also allows you to add an extra tab stop, which can come in handy in certain situations.

When you start formatting a level other than level 1, you'll see an additional button: "**Restart list after [current level number]**." Ordinarily you will leave this option, which is the default, checked. When it is checked, each sublevel starts numbering anew (beginning with "1" or "a" as appropriate), rather than continuing the numbering from the previous level. That is desirable in most circumstances, because otherwise you could end up with a situation where you want the first sublevel after paragraph 6 to appear as 6.1 but, because the last subparagraph in the previous section was 5.6, it appears as 6.7 instead.

Once you are familiar with the various options, go ahead and ***set up each of the nine levels of the list*** (or fewer, if you're absolutely certain you won't use all nine levels). Click the representation of the level you want to format (modify) in either the narrow list of levels at the top of the dialog or the full preview window. Start with level 1. Just keep track of which level you're modifying by glancing periodically at the highlighted level on the left as you are working.

Checklist for Formatting Each Level of the List Style

For each level, do the following:

✓ Choose a number style from the drop-down.

✓ Format the number (delete and/or add punctuation, such as an open paren, a close paren, and/or a period).

✓ Decide on a number alignment (you can leave it set at Left, which is the default, or experiment with Right or Centered).

✓ Set the "Aligned at" (if you want level 1 to be aligned at the left margin, leave it set to zero; if you want it aligned at the first tab stop, set it to .5"—it's up to you).

✓ Set the "Text indent at" and, if you want all levels indented by the same amount, click the "Set for All Levels…" button (you won't need to do the latter after you create the first level of the list style).

✓ Assuming you want to link the list style with heading styles, click the **Link level to style drop-down** and scroll to **Heading 1**. Click to select it.

This is an important step. If you are associating the list style with heading styles, you need to make sure that *each list level* is linked to *a corresponding heading style level*, as shown in the screenshot below.

After you have set up each of the nine levels, click **OK**, then click **OK** again.

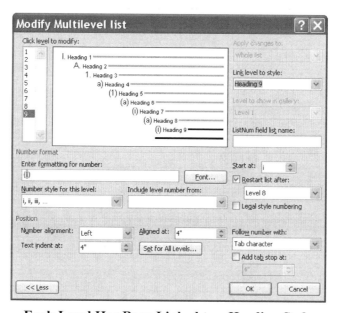

Each Level Has Been Linked to a Heading Style

Modifying the Built-In Heading Styles

The next step, if you are linking the list style to heading styles, is to edit each of the nine heading styles to ensure that they use the font face, font size, and font color you want and that the paragraph formatting (indents, line spacing, and so forth) is set up to your liking.[2]

You can edit a heading style from the **Styles Pane** or from the **Quick Styles Gallery**. Because it's slightly less error-prone, let's use the Styles Pane. Either click the **dialog launcher** in the **Styles group** on the **Home tab** or press **Ctrl Alt Shift S**. Then scroll down to the Heading 1 style, *right*-click it, and click **Modify**.

---

[2] If you plan to set up other list styles and associate them with heading styles, you should create additional heading styles and give them new names—such as Legal Heading 1 (through Legal Heading 9) or Outline Heading 1 (through Outline Heading 9).

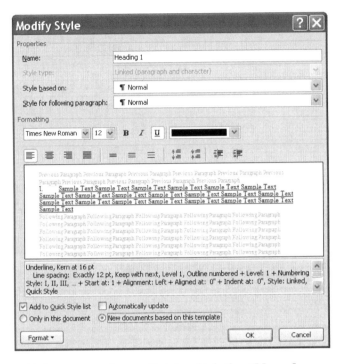

When the **Modify Style dialog** opens, immediately click the "**New documents based on this template**" radio button.

Before doing anything else, look at the "**Style for following paragraph**" option toward the top of the dialog. Ordinarily heading styles will be set up so that a heading is followed by the Normal style (or the Body Text) style, which makes sense when you think about it. If for some reason you want to change the style for the following paragraph, use the drop-down list to select the style you want to use.

Next, click the "**Format**" **button** and click the **Font button**. Make sure the font face, font style, and size are set to your satisfaction.[3] Before clicking OK, also check to make sure that the font color is set to ***black***, rather than to ***Automatic***. If necessary, click the drop-down and click one of the black squares, preferably one that displays a pop-up that says "Black, Text 1" when you hold the mouse pointer over it. Once you've finished, click **OK**—*but only once*.

Click the **Format button** again, and this time click the **Paragraph button**. When the **Paragraph dialog** opens, check the following settings to make sure they conform to your specifications:

- Indentation
- Special (first-line indent or hanging indent)

---

[3] You also have the option of choosing to apply font formatting such as underlining and all caps to the heading text, although sometimes Word gets confused and continues to apply all caps or other font attributes to the text of the paragraph that follows.

- Before spacing

- After spacing

- Line spacing

The indents should be set up correctly, assuming you were successful in setting the indents from the **Modify Multilevel List dialog**, but it's a good idea to check them to make sure.

The line spacing is a tough call; you might want headings set double-spaced or single-spaced, but if you are going to apply the heading styles in a pleading, you might need to apply "Exactly" spacing. For a more complete discussion of this issue, see pages 178, 250, and 429.

I have chosen to use Exactly 24 point spacing for my outline-style headings because I will be using them mainly in pleadings where single spacing is set to Exactly 12 points and double spacing is set to Exactly 24 points.

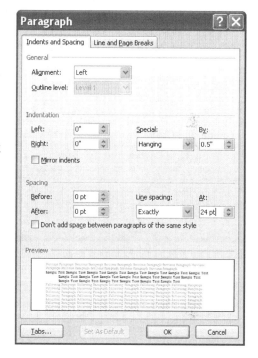

Note that I've also set up my headings to use a hanging indent of half an inch, so that if any heading text wraps to the next line, it will be indented in a way that aligns with the first line of heading text.

Take care to ensure that all of the paragraph formatting options are set the way you want, then click **OK**. The Paragraph dialog will close, returning you to the Modify Style dialog so that you can finalize the heading style.

If you want to create a keyboard shortcut, you can click the **Format button** again and then click **Shortcut key…**, but keep in mind that Word already has built-in shortcuts for the first three heading level styles (Ctrl Alt 1, Ctrl Alt 2, and Ctrl Alt 3).

When you have finished modifying the heading style, click **OK** to save your changes and close the **Modify Style dialog**.

Repeat the above steps for each of the nine paragraph levels.

Double-Checking to Make Sure Everything Works

To double-check to make sure the list style is set up correctly, open the **Multilevel List drop-down** and scroll down to the **List Styles section**. You can determine which style is which by positioning the mouse pointer over an icon, which will produce a pop-up with the style name.

Take a look at the image of your list style to see if the levels are linked to heading styles. (Sometimes even though you have linked all of the list levels to heading styles, the links do not "take.") If they're not, *right*-click the style, click "**Modify**," and when the **Modify Styles dialog** appears, do the following: (1) click the "**New documents based on this template**" radio button, (2) click **Format**, (3) click **Numbering**, and (4) for each level of the list that isn't associated with a heading style, **link it to the appropriate style**. When you have finished, click "**OK**" to save your changes and close the dialog..

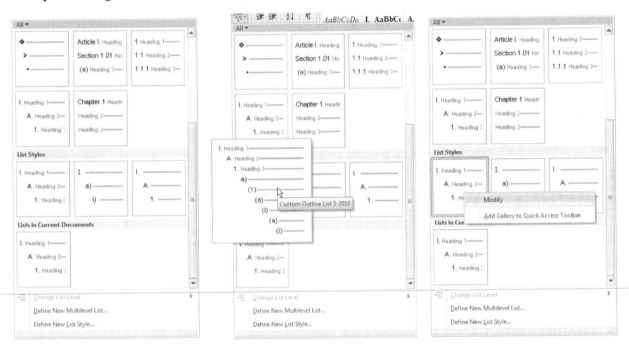

Scroll to the List Styles Section   **The List Name Appears When You Hover the Mouse Pointer**   **To Modify the List, Right-Click the Icon in the Gallery**

TIP: Remember that if you need to modify the numbering in a heading style that is associated with a list style, you need to do it by modifying the list style itself, *not* by modifying the heading style. The numbering options available when you modify the heading style are very limited.

Applying Your List Style

Once you have set up a list style that is linked to heading styles, you can apply it in two different ways: (1) by applying *a heading level style* to text (from either the **Styles Pane** or the **Quick Styles Gallery**); *or* (2) by inserting *the list style* from the Multilevel List gallery.

Changing List Levels

You can change levels of an existing list paragraph by clicking the **Increase Indent** (Demote) **button** or **Decrease Indent** (Promote) **button** in the **Paragraph group** on the **Home tab** or by pressing **Alt Shift →** (right arrow) or **Alt Shift ←** (left arrow). If "Set left- and first-indent with tabs and backspaces" is enabled in Word Options (File tab, Options, Proofing, AutoCorrect Options, Format as You Go tab), you can use **Tab** (Demote) and **Shift Tab** (Promote), too.

Modifying a Multilevel List: Tips and Caveats

The Right-Click Options

Note that icons in the different sections of the gallery offer different right-click options. In particular, when you right-click an icon for one of the lists in the **List Styles section,** the resulting context-sensitive menu provides a "**Modify**" option. When you right-click an icon for one of the lists in the **Library section** or in the **Lists in Current Document section**, the context-menu won't provide that option.

Icons in the **Current List** section offer a "**Modify**" option *if you have applied the list in the current document*. Otherwise, right-clicking the icon does *not* produce that option.

Changing the Numeric Formatting

This point is so important—and so confusing to people who are familiar with the way this feature worked in pre-Word 2007 versions of the program—that it bears repeating several times.

You can't modify the *numeric* formatting of any level of your multilevel list by right-clicking within the list (or by right-clicking a heading style and then clicking "Modify").

When you right-click in or near a paragraph number in your list, then click the "Numbering" command, a "Numbering Library" fly-out menu appears. However, as you can see, the options are very limited: You can change the number style of the level your cursor is in, the list level (i.e., to promote or demote the current paragraph); or the value of the number of the paragraph your cursor is in. Also, you can define a new number format—for a single list level.

You'll encounter the same problem if you attempt to change the numbering style by modifying a heading style. When you right-click a heading style and click "Modify," a Modify Style dialog opens. Clicking the "Format" button at the lower left side of the dialog seems to give you lots of formatting choices; both the "Numbering" command and the "Paragraph" command are active (i.e., not grayed out). But when you click the "Numbering" command, the resulting dialog offers the same limited options available from the right-click fly-out menu.

The upshot is that if you want to modify the numbering of one or more levels of your custom list, *you must do so via the Multilevel List gallery*. In particular, take the following steps:

If you have applied the list in the document on your screen, *navigate to a Level 1 paragraph*—regardless of which level you want to modify—before proceeding. The best way to ensure the integrity of a multilevel list style in Word is to begin the editing process *for any level of the list* from within a Level 1 paragraph. That is true for earlier versions of Word, as well.

If you haven't applied the list in the current document, simply proceed to the next step.

Open the Multilevel List Gallery, locate the image of the list **in the List Styles section** at the bottom of the gallery, *right*-click it and then click "**Modify**."

Immediately click the "**New documents based on this template**" radio button—something you will need to do every single time you modify the style—so that your modifications will take effect in all new documents, rather than only in the current document.

Next, click the **Format button**, click **Numbering**, and after the **Modify Multilevel List dialog** opens, **click the level you wish to modify**, and make any adjustments.

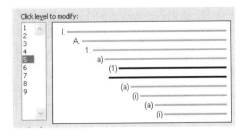

If you want to modify additional levels, just make sure you click the correct level before making your changes.

When you have finished, click "**OK**" to save your changes.

Changing the Paragraph Formatting

This advice is somewhat counterintuitive, as well, which is why I'm emphasizing it by putting it in a separate section.

An easy way to modify paragraph formatting for any level of your list style is by positioning the cursor within any paragraph at that level, and then *right-clicking* in or near the paragraph number. When the **pop-up menu** appears, click the "**Paragraph**" **command**.

Then make any changes you want to the indents, line spacing, spacing after, and so forth, and click "**OK**" to save your formatting changes.

To ensure that the changes will take effect the next time you apply your list, right-click in or near the paragraph number. When the pop-up menu opens, position the mouse over the **Styles command** to produce the fly-out menu. Choose the "**Update Heading XX to Match Selection**" command (where "XX" represents the heading level).

Alternatively, you can **right-click** the icon for the **heading style** in the **Quick Styles gallery**, then click "**Update Heading XX to Match Selection**" (where "XX" represents the heading level). See the screenshot at right.

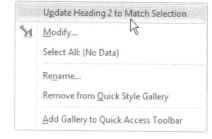

Saving the List as a Quick Style

If you save the list as a Quick Style, it will be readily available from the Quick Style gallery.

The first step is to **apply the list** in the current document. Just **click the Multilevel List drop-down**, navigate to the **List Styles section** at the bottom, and **click the image of your list**. Word will insert a number.

Right-click in or near the number, and when the pop-up menu appears, point to "**Styles,**" then, when the fly-out opens, click "**Save Selection as a New Quick Style.**" A small "**Create New Style from Formatting**" **dialog** will open.

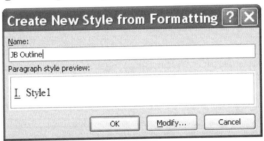

Type a **descriptive name** for the Quick Style, and then immediately click the "**Modify**" **button**. This step is important because it will enable you to save the Quick Style to the underlying template so that it is available in all new documents.

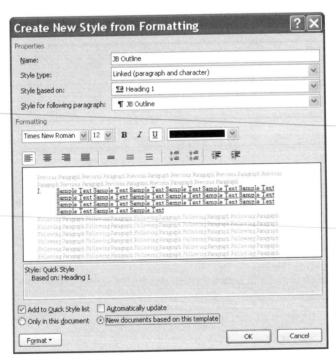

Indeed, as soon as the full-sized "**Create New Style from Formatting**" **dialog** opens, navigate to the bottom and click the "**New documents based on this template**" **radio button**. Don't click "OK" just yet.

Adding a Keyboard Shortcut to Apply the List

If you'd like to add a keyboard shortcut for the list, click the "**Format**" **button** at the lower left side of the dialog, then click the "**Shortcut Key**" **command**. When the "**Customize Keyboard**" **dialog** appears, click in the "**Press new shortcut key**" **box** (if the cursor isn't there already), then **press the key combination** you would like to use to apply the list. If the key combo is already in use, you will see a message to that effect below the "Current keys" box (where it says "**Currently assigned to:**"). You can override that assignment if you like, or you can choose another series of keystrokes.

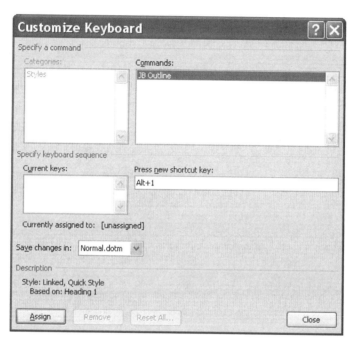

As you can see from the screenshot, I have chosen the key combination Alt 1 (i.e., using the number one, not the letter "L").

Be sure to click the "**Assign**" **button**, then click "**Close.**" Finally, click "**OK**" to save your settings.

It's a good idea to test both the keyboard shortcut and the icon in the Quick Styles gallery to make sure everything is working to your satisfaction. Note that although you can right-click the icon in the Quick Styles gallery, then click "Modify," you will encounter the same limitations as to the numbering formats that I discussed earlier in this section. To tweak the numbering of the list, you have to go into the Multilevel List gallery, locate the icon for the list in the List Styles area, right-click it, and click "Modify."

Remember that you must click the "New documents based on this template" radio button *every time you modify the list style* if you want your changes to be available in all future documents based on the template.

483

QUICK TIP: Setting Up a "Simple" Multilevel List
and Saving It as a Quick Style

This Quick Tip provides somewhat simplified instructions for creating a "simple" multilevel list—that is, one that isn't linked to heading styles—and saving it as a Quick Style.

Navigate to the **Home tab**, **Paragraph group**, and click the **Multilevel List drop-down**.

Click "**Define New List Style…**" and immediately click the "**New documents based on this template**" radio button. Then give the style a **descriptive name**.

Next, click the "**Format**" **button**, "**Numbering**." Go through level by level, selecting the number and letter types you want to use for each level and inserting any punctuation you like, always being careful not to delete the gray number code.

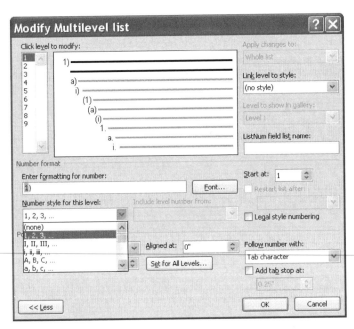

Make sure to set the **indents** for each level. You'll probably want each level indented one additional half inch (with a tab half an inch after the letter or number); the easiest method to do so is by clicking the "**Set for All Levels…**" button.

Note that you won't be able to alter the paragraph formatting from this dialog; when you click the "Format" button, you'll notice that the "Paragraph" command is unavailable (grayed out). Rather, you'll have to save the list as a Quick Style and then modify the Quick Style from either the Quick Style gallery or the Styles Pane. I will provide instructions momentarily.

Once the list is set up—before OK-ing out of the dialog—you can click the "**Format**" **button**, "**Shortcut**" **key**, and assign a keyboard shortcut. Finally, be sure to click "**OK**" to save your settings.

Saving the List as a Quick Style

To change the paragraph formatting—for example, to add 12 points after spacing to each level of the list, you'll need to save the list as a Quick Style. If you haven't done so already, apply the list in a blank document, right-click in or near a paragraph number, point to "Styles," and then click "**Save Selection as a Quick Style**."

A "**Create New Style from Formatting**" **dialog** will open. Type a **descriptive name** for the Quick Style, such as Outline List or Legal List (as appropriate), and then click the "**Modify**" button.

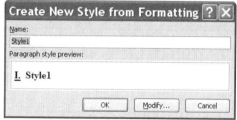

CAUTION: If you click "OK" instead of "Modify," the Quick Style will be available only in the current document, not in all future documents.

After you click "**Modify**," an expanded "**Create New Style from Formatting**" **dialog** will open. Immediately click the "**New documents based on this template**" **radio button** at the bottom of the dialog to ensure that the Quick Style will be available in all new documents.

Then click the "**Format**" **button**, click the "**Paragraph**" **command**, and make any changes you like. When you have finished, click "OK" to save the Quick Style.

After you save the list as a Quick Style, you should see it in the Quick Style gallery. (It also should appear in the Styles Pane, depending on how the pane is configured—i.e., whether it is set to show all styles.)

If you need to make any further changes to the paragraph formatting, **right-click** the list either in the Quick Style gallery or in the Styles Pane and click "**Modify**." When the "**Modify Style**" **dialog** appears, click the "**New documents based on this template**" radio button, click the "**Format**" button, click "**Paragraph**," make your changes, and click "**OK**."

QUICK TIP: Sharing Your Custom List Style

To share your custom list style with other members of your organization, apply the list in a blank document and save the document to a shared folder on the network drive. Then ask each user to do the following:

1. Open the document containing the list style. With the document open, open the **Styles Pane**. You can either:

   a. Click the **dialog launcher** in the lower right-hand corner of the **Styles group** in the **Home tab**; or

   b. Press **Ctrl Alt Shift S**.

2. **Locate the style** in the pane. (You'll need to tell everyone the name of the style.)

   a. If the style isn't visible in the Styles Pane, click the **Options button** at the lower right-hand side of the pane and, when the dialog opens, (1) make sure "**All styles**" is displayed in the first drop-down and (2) select "**Alphabetical**" in the second drop-down.

   b. Optional: Click the "**New documents based on this template**" button in order to display all styles in alphabetical order whenever you start a new document.

   c. **OK** out.

3. Next, click the **Manage Styles button** at the bottom of the Styles Pane. It is the third button from the left (immediately to the left of Options).

4. Click the **Import/Export button** at the bottom left side of the Manage Styles dialog. The Organizer will appear.

   a. In the box at the left, you'll see the styles in the current document.

   b. In the box at the right, you'll see the styles in your normal.dotm (your NORMAL template).

5. **Locate the style** in the box on the left, click to **select it**, then click **Copy** to copy it to your normal.dotm and click Close.

6. If you wish to set up a keyboard shortcut to invoke the style, **locate the style in the Styles Pane** and **right-click** it, then click **Modify**.

7. Immediately click the "**New documents based on this template button**" so that the keyboard shortcut will work in all future documents. If you don't click this button, any changes you make to the style will go into effect only in the current document.

8. Click the **Format button** at the lower left-hand side of the Modify Style dialog, then click **Shortcut key**.

9. Position your cursor in the **Press new shortcut key** box, and then press the **key combination** you want to use, such as Alt L (for List). If your key combo has been assigned to another function, you'll see a message to that effect. You can override the assignment or choose a different keyboard shortcut.

10. After you've entered the keystrokes, click the **Assign button**, then click **Close**. Click the "**X**" at the upper right-hand side of the Styles Pane to close it.

11. **NOTE:** When you close Word, the program might prompt you to save changes you have made to the normal.dotm template. *Be sure to click OK or Yes to save your changes*, or the modifications you've made—including adding the custom list style to your NORMAL template—will be lost.

Once they have followed these steps, your co-workers should be able to start using your custom list style. (They can apply the style by pressing the key combination they assigned to the style, if any, *or* by clicking the icon for the style in the Quick Styles gallery on the Home tab, *or* by opening the Styles Pane and clicking the name of the style from there.)

Using the "SEQ" Field for Automatic Numbering in Discovery Headings

The "SEQ" (sequence) field is extremely useful. What makes it particularly well-suited for legal documents is that it allows you to apply automatic numbering to different types of discovery headings in the same document (such as Interrogatories and Interrogatory Responses) and have the numbers in each type of heading increment properly. Essentially the way it works is that it uses a different identifier for each numbered list—for example, one identifier for the Interrogatories and another one for the Responses to Interrogatories.[1]

In this section, you'll learn how to use the SEQ field to set up headings for Interrogatories and Rog Responses, and then how to create a Quick Part so you can insert the headings with just a few keystrokes.

1. Let's start with the Interrogatories. Begin typing the heading as you normally would. For example, for an Interrogatory, you would turn on underlining (and perhaps also bold) and CAPS Lock, and type **INTERROGATORY NO.**

2. Press the Spacebar and then click the **Insert tab**, **Quick Parts**, **Field...** *or* press **Alt I, F**. When the **Field dialog** opens, locate the **Field Names box** and scroll down until you find "Seq" *or* (this method is faster) simply press the "S" key until "Seq" appears in the list of field codes. You should also see "SEQ" in the "**Field codes**" **box** under "**Advanced field properties**" (toward the right side of the screen).

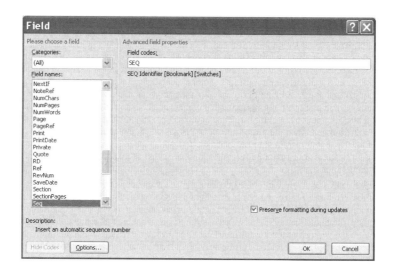

---

[1] It's similar to the Counters feature in WordPerfect.

3.   You're not done yet! The SEQ code requires an "**identifier**." If you click OK before typing an identifier, you'll see the following message: "**ERROR! No sequence specified**."[2] To avoid that problem, position the cursor after "SEQ" in the Field codes box, and type a unique word such as "Rog," or "Int," or "Interrogatory"—some label that will tell Word, and you, exactly what this SEQ code does.

The identifier can be up to 40 characters long, though shorter generally is better. Note that you should have a unique identifier for each type of SEQ code you use in your document; e.g., if you have a document that contains both Interrogatories and Interrogatory Responses, you *must* create one distinctive identifier for the SEQ codes you use in the Interrogatories and a different identifier for the SEQ codes you use in the Rog Responses.

4.   You might notice that there is an **Options button** at the bottom left side of the Field dialog box. If you click the Options button, a **Field Options dialog** opens. In the "**Formatting**" **box** on the "**General Switches**" **tab** of the dialog there are several different types of numbering and lettering you can use with SEQ fields. The default is Arabic numerals, so you don't need to do anything special to format the numbering in your discovery headings. However, if you ever need to use SEQ fields for other types of automatic numbering or lettering—for example, to insert Exhibit letters (as in the section on Cross-Referencing that follows this section)—you would **click that format in the list**, then click the **Add to Field button**, then click **OK** to add a "switch" for the "ALPHABETIC" letter format to the SEQ code before proceeding.

[2] If you accidentally click "OK" before typing an identifier, you can fix the problem without deleting the error message and starting over. All you need to do is press Alt F9 to display the code itself (as in paragraph 6 on the next page), then type an identifier after the word SEQ. Press Alt F9 to display the results of the code. If you still get an error message, make sure your cursor is somewhere within the error message and press F9 to update the code.

5.   When you have created an identifier, click **OK**. You should see something like this:

INTERROGATORY NO. 1

6.   If instead you see something like the following, simply press Alt F9 (the keystroke to toggle between displaying the field codes themselves and the field code results).

INTERROGATORY NO. {SEQ Rog * MERGEFORMAT }

Either way, continue to format your heading.

7.   When you have finished, you can set up the heading as a "Quick Part" (formerly known as AutoText) so that you can insert it into *any document* you create or work on in the future (and have it automatically number correctly) with just a couple of keystrokes.[3] Select the heading (*be sure to include the paragraph symbol at the end of the heading* so that Word inserts a new blank line underneath the heading when you expand the Quick Part) and then press **Alt F3** (or click **Insert tab**, **Text group**, **Quick Parts**, **Save Selection to Quick Part Gallery**). Next, type an abbreviation for the heading (such as "Int" or "Rog"), type a description if you like (optional), and click **OK**.

8.   Now, when you want to insert a heading, just type the abbreviation you assigned to it—or the first few letters, if none of your other Quick Parts start with those letters—and **press F3** to expand the abbreviation.

      NOTE: The "AutoComplete" feature has been reinstated in Word 2010. Thus, if you have assigned a name to your Quick Part that is at least four characters long (and you've used the Alt F3 method in Step 7, thereby saving the Quick Part to your NORMAL template), you can type the first four characters and, when the prompt appears, press Enter to insert the Quick Part.

9.   Remember that the heading contains an automatic numbering code. If you need to delete or move a heading (for example, if you need to move a series of interrogatories within the document, and move the headings with them), you don't have to do anything to change the numbering sequence. If the numbers don't change automatically when you move the text, just select the document by pressing **Ctrl A** and then press **F9** to "update" the codes.

10.   To create headings for the Rog Responses, repeat the above steps, but be sure to use a different identifier—perhaps something like RogResp.

---

[3] By default, user-created Quick Parts are stored in a template called "BuildingBlocks.dotx" unless you use the Alt F3 method to create your entries. See the section that starts on page 339.

Once you have set up both types of headings using SEQ codes, you'll find that the numbering for the two separate types of headings remains distinct and increments appropriately, even when you alternate Interrogatories and Interrogatory Responses.

11.   It is possible (and relatively simple) to insert a code that starts numbering with a number other than 1. To do so, press **Alt F9** to display the field codes. Position the cursor in the heading where you want to start renumbering, immediately following the backslash after your identifier (in the screenshot below, "Rog" is the identifier.) Then type the letter "r" (without quotation marks) followed by a space and the number you want to start with. Then type a space followed by another backslash. So, for example, if you want to start with the number 20, you'll insert "r 20 \" and the heading with the edited code will look something like the following:

INTERROGATORY NO. {SEQ Rog \r 20 * MERGEFORMAT }

12.   Press **Alt F9** again to display the field code results. If for some reason you get an error message, insert your cursor within the code (or press Ctrl A to select the entire document) and press F9 to update the code(s). The code results should display properly, and the Interrogatory number should be 20.

Cross-Referencing Exhibit Letters (or Numbers) and Automatic Paragraph Numbers

Word's Cross-Reference feature can be very useful in formatting legal documents. Many people use the feature to refer back to specific exhibits in a pleading or a contract. It also comes in handy when you need to refer to a particular numbered paragraph. I'll provide instructions for both types of cross-referencing below.

Cross-Referencing Document Exhibits and Similar Items[1]

1.   **Select** the item to be cross-referenced, in this case an exhibit letter or number. (Note that you can select just the letter or number *or* the entire exhibit title, such as Exhibit A or Exhibit 1. Whichever you choose to do, just be consistent throughout your document.)

2.   Next, you need to create a bookmark. (You will create a unique bookmark for each exhibit to the document.) To do so, click the **Insert tab**, **Bookmark** (in the **Links group**).

3.   **Type a name** for the bookmark you are creating. **NOTE**: The name cannot contain spaces, cannot begin with a number, and cannot contain non-alphanumeric characters (other than an underscore character at the beginning of the name, which will turn the bookmark into a hidden bookmark). The name should be descriptive, so that you remember what it does. A good name might be ExhibitA or ExhibitB or Exhibit1 or Exhibit2 (whichever is appropriate).

4.   Click **Add**.

5.   Next, position the cursor at the point in the document where you want to refer to the bookmarked item, and locate and click **Cross-Reference** (also on the **Insert tab**, in the **Links group**)[2]. The Cross-Reference dialog will open.

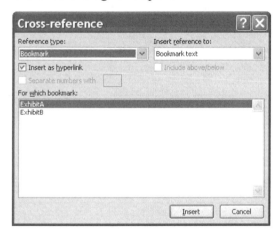

---

[1] This feature works whether you create the exhibit letter manually or with SEQ codes, as in the previous section.

[2] There is also a Cross-Reference button in the **Captions** group on the **References tab**.

6.   From the **Reference type** drop-down list on the left-side of the dialog, select **Bookmark**.[3] Make sure that the **Insert reference to:** drop-down is pointing to **Bookmark text**.

7.   Click the appropriate bookmark name in the list, click the **Insert** button, then click the **Close** button.

8.   Continue setting up Bookmarks and Cross-References for each exhibit (or other item) you wish to refer back to.

9.   **NOTE**: If, later on, you add an exhibit to your document in a way that causes the existing exhibit numbers or letters to change, select the entire document (by clicking **Ctrl A**) and then press **F9** to update the bookmark and cross-reference codes.

Cross-Referencing Numbered Paragraphs

You can use the Cross-Reference feature to refer to any numbered paragraphs in your document. Assuming you are using automatic paragraph numbering, you don't need to create bookmarks for the numbered paragraphs; Word recognizes the number codes.

1.   Simply position the cursor where you want to insert a cross-reference (for instance, "as mentioned in paragraph XX above," but without the XX placeholder), and click the **References tab, Cross-Reference**.

2.   From the **Reference type:** drop-down list on the left-side of the dialog, click to select **Numbered item**.[4]

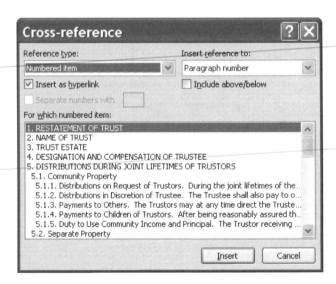

---

[3] The other available reference types include Numbered item, Heading, Footnote, Endnote, Equation, Figure, and Table.

[4] Alternatively, "Heading" can be a good choice, especially if you use style separators. For an explanation, see the discussion in the sidebar that follows.

3.   Click the **Insert reference to:** drop-down and point to **Paragraph number**, **Paragraph number (full context),** or **Paragraph number (no context).**[5]

NOTE: The different options for displaying a paragraph number are available only when a subparagraph is on a separate line from the "parent" paragraph.

In that event, the "Paragraph" option uses a partial number for a subparagraph if you're referring to it from within the parent paragraph (because the full paragraph number is obvious from the context), whereas it uses a full number if you're referring to it from elsewhere in the document; the "Full Context" option uses the complete number (parent and child paragraphs); and the "No Context" option uses only the level of the selected paragraph.

4.   Navigate to the "**For which numbered item**" section of the dialog and scroll down to locate the paragraph in question. Click to select it, then click the **Insert button.**

5.   Finally, click **Close**. (The label on the Cancel button changes to "Close" when you click the Insert button.)

---

[5] The other available "Insert reference to:" objects include Page number and Above/below (the latter inserts the word "above" or the word "below" instead of a specific page number reference).

SIDEBAR: Cross-Reference Tips

A Workaround for Cross-References Not Displaying When "Style Separators" Are Used[1]

At the end of 2009, I received an inquiry from a lawyer who said his firm was experiencing a perplexing issue with Word 2007. The firm uses **numbered heading styles** plus **style separators** for "run-in" paragraphs—paragraphs where a heading is followed by text on the same line, rather than the heading and the text being in different paragraphs.

A style separator is a sort of "hidden" paragraph symbol that tells Word to treat the text that follows as if it were in fact part of a different paragraph. That makes it possible, in effect, to apply two distinct paragraph styles to the same paragraph. For example, you can format the beginning of a paragraph with the Heading 1 (or Heading 2, etc.) style, while applying Normal or Body Text to the remainder of the paragraph.[2]

The main advantage of using a style separator is that the text following the heading isn't automatically pulled into the Table of Contents, a common problem with documents that contain run-in paragraphs. However, there is a sort of glitch in Word 2007 (and Word 2010) whereby paragraphs that employ both numbered headings and a style separator seemingly *aren't displayed in the Cross-Reference dialog*, preventing users from inserting a cross-reference to one of the numbered paragraphs.[3]

After a little research, I discovered a workaround (suggested by Word MVP Suzanne Barnhill). When you are working with numbered paragraphs, by default the Cross-Reference dialog opens with the "**Reference type**" **drop-down** (on the left side of the dialog) showing "Numbered Item." However, when you click the drop-down, you'll see additional reference types; the second one is "**Heading**." If you choose that option, the numbered paragraphs that use style separators magically appear. Now you can use the "**Insert reference to**" **drop-down** on the right side of the dialog to choose the appropriate option—"**Heading number**" if you wish to

---

[1] This section first appeared, in slightly different form, as a post in my blog (see the following URL): http://compusavvy.wordpress.com .

[2] To insert a style separator at the cursor position (you normally place it immediately after a heading), press **Ctrl Alt Enter**. Alternatively, you can add a style separator icon to the Quick Access Toolbar (QAT) by doing the following: **Right-click the QAT** and click "**Customize Quick Access Toolbar...**," then use the "**Choose commands from**" **drop-down** toward the top left of the Word Options screen to select either "**Commands Not in the Ribbon**" or "**All Commands**." In the box below the "Choose commands from" drop-down, scroll about 7/8 of the way down and look for "**Style Separator**." Click to **select it**, click the "**Add**" **button**, use the "**Move Up**" or "**Move Down**" **buttons** at the right side of the screen to move the icon to the left or right on the QAT if you wish, then click "**OK**" to save your settings.

[3] You can open the **Cross-Reference dialog** from either the **Insert tab**, **Links group** or the **References tab**, **Captions group**.

refer to the paragraph number or "**Page number**" if you wish to refer to the page on which the paragraph appears. (**Watch out**: The default is "Heading text," which may or may not be the choice you want. Presumably most people intend to insert the heading number / paragraph number.)

Reference type is Numbered item

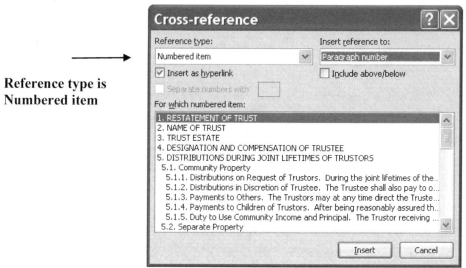

Note that in the screenshot above, the subparagraphs for Sections 3 and 4 are not visible (because style separators have been used). However, when the "Reference type:" is changed to "Heading" (and the "Insert reference to:" is changed to "Heading number"—though "Heading text" or "Page number" also would work), the subparagraphs are displayed despite the existence of style separators, as shown in the screenshot below.

Reference type is Heading (and the Insert reference to: drop-down has been changed to show the Heading Number

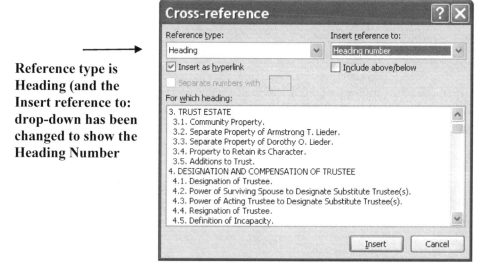

Note that when you change the "Reference type" to "Heading," the Cross-Reference dialog won't display numbered paragraphs that do not have heading styles applied to them. That shouldn't be a major issue, though. You can switch back and forth between or among "Reference types" while inserting cross-references. The result will be the same as if all of the numbered paragraphs—including those using a style separator—appeared together in the dialog box without your having to change the "Reference type."

This workaround seems like a simple and elegant solution to the problem. Thanks to Suzanne Barnhill for the tip, which she proffered in an exchange in one of the Office KB Community forums (www.officekb.com).

Another workaround is to bookmark the headings that use style separators and then select "Bookmark" as the "Reference type." But this solution is somewhat more complicated and time-consuming than the first one. Also, because you can't use punctuation (including periods) in bookmark names, you don't have the option of using a logical name such as "Par2.3" (though you could substitute something such as "Par2point3"). Still, the bookmark workaround does work and is worth keeping in mind should the "switch reference type" solution not be suitable in certain circumstances.

To create a bookmark, select the heading *or* insert the cursor between the paragraph number and the style separator—not *after* the style separator!—and click **Insert**, **Bookmark**, then give the bookmark a name and click "**Add**."

When you go to insert a cross-reference to a bookmarked paragraph, click the "**Reference type**" **drop-down**, select "**Bookmark**," **click the bookmark** you want to use, make sure "**Insert reference to**" is showing the appropriate option (probably "Paragraph number"), and then click the "**Insert**" button.

Caveats About the Cross-Reference Feature

It is very easy to "break" cross-references because they make use of hidden "target" codes that can be deleted, moved, or otherwise changed accidentally (and without your knowledge). Thus, you need to be extra-careful when *attempting to insert a new paragraph between existing numbered paragraphs* as well as when *adding*, *deleting*, *cutting and pasting*, or *copying and pasting text* to or from a portion of your document that contains bookmarks or cross-references.[4]

In particular, never start a new paragraph by pressing the Enter key from within a paragraph that contains a cross-reference (*especially not* when the cursor is between the paragraph number and the text). This very common practice is almost guaranteed to sever the link between the paragraph and the hidden target code.

If you need to insert a new paragraph, make sure your cursor is *at the end of the previous paragraph—i.e., ahead of where you want the new paragraph to go*—before you press the Enter key.

Let's say you want to insert a new numbered paragraph between section 4.2 and section 4.3 (at the same heading / outline level). The new paragraph would become paragraph 4.3 and the existing section 4.3 ("Power of Acting Trustee to Designate Substitute Trustee(s)") would become paragraph 4.4. See the screenshots on the next page.

---

[4] I am indebted to Linda Hopkins and Eva Eilenberg for these tips about methods for avoiding broken cross-references.

Don't place the
cursor after a
paragraph number
and press Enter

4.2. **Power of Surviving Spouse to Designate Substitute Trustee(s).** After the death of one Trustor, the Surviving Spouse shall have the power to designate one or more individuals or corporate fiduciaries as Trustee of any trust created hereunder, to serve concurrently with him or her or to serve serially upon Surviving Spouse's death, resignation or incapacity, and any such designation by the Surviving Spouse shall supersede any designation of successor trustees made by Trustors elsewhere in this document.

4.3. XX Power of Acting Trustee to Designate Substitute Trustee(s). The acting Trustee shall have the power to designate one or more individuals or corporate fiduciaries as Trustee of any trust created hereunder, to serve concurrently with him or her or to serve serially upon acting Trustee's death, resignation or incapacity, and any such designation by the acting Trustee shall supersede any designation of successor trustees made by Trustors elsewhere in this document. The acting Trustee may from time to time revoke or amend any such designation of a successor Trustee. All such designations shall be exercised in writing and shall be effective upon delivery to the beneficiaries of the Trust.

Incorrect Way to Start a New Numbered Paragraph

The screenshot above shows what *not* to do.

Although you might be tempted to position the cursor before the heading text in section 4.3—that is, between the paragraph number and the heading text (I've inserted two X's to make it easier to see the cursor)—and then press the Enter key, doing so almost certainly would break the existing cross-reference. Any places in the document where you use cross-references to point to the paragraph entitled "Power of Acting Trustee to Designate Substitute Trustee(s)" (which becomes section 4.4 after you insert the new paragraph) probably will not update correctly, or at all.

Here's a better way to insert the new paragraph.

Do place the
cursor at the
end of the previous
paragraph and
press Enter

4.2. **Power of Surviving Spouse to Designate Substitute Trustee(s).** After the death of one Trustor, the Surviving Spouse shall have the power to designate one or more individuals or corporate fiduciaries as Trustee of any trust created hereunder, to serve concurrently with him or her or to serve serially upon Surviving Spouse's death, resignation or incapacity, and any such designation by the Surviving Spouse shall supersede any designation of successor trustees made by Trustors elsewhere in this document. XX

4.3. **Power of Acting Trustee to Designate Substitute Trustee(s).** The acting Trustee shall have the power to designate one or more individuals or corporate fiduciaries as Trustee of any trust created hereunder, to serve concurrently with him or her or to serve serially upon acting Trustee's death, resignation or incapacity, and any such designation by the acting Trustee shall supersede any designation of successor trustees made by Trustors elsewhere in this document. The acting Trustee may from time to time revoke or amend any such designation of a successor Trustee. All such designations shall be exercised in writing and shall be effective upon delivery to the beneficiaries of the Trust.

Correct Way to Start a New Numbered Paragraph

Instead of putting your cursor at the beginning of the heading text for the existing paragraph 4.3, position it at the end of paragraph 4.2, as in the screenshot above. Now, when you press the Enter key, you get a new paragraph 4.3 *without breaking any existing cross-references*.

In the case of the sample document I used to illustrate this procedure, the situation was a little more complicated than usual because the numbered paragraphs make use of style separators to keep the "run-in" text (text on the same line as the headings) from being pulled into the Table of Contents. The headings are formatted with heading styles, and the run-in text is formatted with a body text style. So positioning the cursor at the end of a numbered paragraph and pressing the Enter key *does* create a new paragraph, but it lacks a paragraph number because pressing Enter copies the body text style contained in the paragraph symbol at the end of the paragraph.

As a workaround, after I pressed the Enter key, I inserted the cursor back into the heading for paragraph 4.2, clicked the Format Painter (Home tab, Clipboard group), and then clicked in the new empty paragraph (to copy the heading style to the new paragraph). My second step was to copy and paste the style separator from paragraph 4.2 into the new paragraph. And finally, I clicked within the text of paragraph 4.2, clicked the Format painter, and clicked after the style separator in the new paragraph (to copy the body text style into the new paragraph).

Despite how complicated that might sound, it actually works fairly well. And the advantage is that you can insert new numbered paragraphs without severing the cross-references.

Another possible workaround is to copy and paste an entire paragraph, making sure to position the cursor ahead of the paragraph you wish to copy before selecting that paragraph and then being careful to put the cursor at the end of the paragraph ahead of where you want to paste. The numbering in the new (pasted) paragraph might not increment automatically, but it's a trivial matter to right-click in or near the paragraph number, then click "Continue Numbering." That should fix the numbering of the new paragraph and any paragraphs that follow. You can type over the existing heading and text; just take care not to backspace or otherwise delete anything between the paragraph number and the heading text.

Additional Cautions

Another caution: Be careful not to paste text at the beginning of a paragraph that contains a cross-reference. Doing so could damage or delete the hidden target code. Instead, paste into an "empty" paragraph.

Also note that there is a bug in Word 2007—I'm not sure if the bug also exists in Word 2010—whereby if you update a cross-reference, it might not print correctly. For a description of the problem and a fix (which involves editing the Registry—something that should not be attempted by novices, and in any event not without first backing up the Registry in case of a problem), see Microsoft Knowledge Base Article No. 954541:

"The Ref field is updated incorrectly when you print a Word 2007 document"
http://support.microsoft.com/kb/954541

Creating and Generating a Table of Contents (TOC) and a Table of Authorities (TOA)

There are four basic steps involved in creating and generating a Table of Contents and a Table of Authorities in Word. These are:

- Changing the page numbers / inserting section breaks
- Marking the headings (TOC) and/or authorities (TOA)
- Generating the tables
- Editing the TOC/TOA.

1. Changing the Page Numbers / Inserting Section Breaks.

In my on-site training sessions, we typically use as a sample document a Notice of Motion and Motion for Summary Judgment that I provide. As you probably know, in a Motion, the Notice pages use Arabic numerals, starting with 1; the Motion itself (the Points and Authorities) uses Arabic numerals, starting with 1; and the TOC and TOA use small roman numerals, starting with i on the first page of the TOC and continuing consecutively through the last page of the TOA. (Do not start over with i on the first page of the TOA.)

To ensure that Word inserts the correct page numbers for all three parts of the document, we have to divide the document into three "*sections*." (Remember, to apply different page formatting options within a document in Word, you must divide the document into sections and format each section separately. For example, you must insert section breaks when you want to change the page numbering format, use multiple headers and footers, change page margins, switch from portrait to landscape orientation, or insert columns in the middle of a page that also contains regular text.) Our three sections will consist of the Notice pages (Section 1), the Motion (Points and Authorities) (Section 2), and the TOC / TOA (Section 3). In a hard copy of the document the TOC and TOA follow the Notice pages, but it's easiest to create them at the end of the Motion and then simply collate the pages by hand after printing.

Let's assume we've already inserted CRC Rule 2.110 compliant footers containing page numbers into our document.[1] Now we need to create section breaks. Because Word assumes that every new document already comprises one section, we'll actually insert only two section breaks: one between the Notice pages and the Motion and one at the end of the Motion, where we're going to insert our Table of Contents and Table of Authorities. We'll insert the section breaks first and then go back and format the page numbering in each section.

TIP: You might want to switch from Print Layout View to Draft View while working with section breaks, because it's easier to see the section breaks (and delete them if necessary) in Draft View. To do so, click the **View tab**, **Draft**, or click the **Draft View button** on the Status Bar.

---

[1] See pages 451 and 455.

First, we'll create a section break after the Notice of Motion.

(a)   Put the cursor at the bottom of the second page of the Notice and click the **Page Layout tab**, **Page Setup group**, **Breaks**, **Section breaks**, **Next page**.

(b)   If inserting the section break bumps the heading for the Memorandum of Points and Authorities down, simply press the Delete key to bring it back to the top of the page.

As mentioned above, the easiest way to set up a TOC and TOA in Word is to put it at the end of the document (and simply collate the pages after printing). So we'll create another section break at the end of the document, then set up a rudimentary TOC and TOA.

(a)   Press **Ctrl End** to move the cursor to the very end of the document.

(b)   Click **Page Layout tab**, **Page Setup group**, **Breaks**, **Section breaks**, **Next page**.

While we're here, let's create simple headings for the TOC and the TOA (unless the sample document already contains headings, in which case let's skip steps (a) through (e) below and move to the top of the next page). This exercise is for practice only. Don't worry about making the headings look perfect.

(a)   At the top of the new page, press Ctrl E to center the cursor, press Ctrl U to turn on underlining, press Caps Lock, and type TABLE OF CONTENTS.

(b)   Press Ctrl U to turn off underlining, press the Enter key twice, press Ctrl R to put the cursor at the right margin and turn on right alignment, press Ctrl U to turn underlining on again, and type PAGE.

(c)   Press Ctrl U to turn off underlining, press the Enter key twice, and press Ctrl L to put the cursor at the left margin. Then press the Enter key and keep it depressed until you create a soft page break.

(d)   Repeat steps (a) and (b) immediately above, except type TABLE OF AUTHORITIES instead of TABLE OF CONTENTS.

(e)   Press Ctrl U to turn off underlining, press the Enter key twice, and press Ctrl L to put the cursor at the left margin. Then press the Enter key two or three times.

Now we've created two section breaks, which has divided the document into three sections. Section 1 is the Notice pages, Section 2 is the Motion (the Memorandum of Points and Authorities), and Section 3 is the Table of Contents and Table of Authorities. We've also created simple headings for the TOC and TOA.

Next, we need to format the page numbering in the two new sections.

(a)   First, press Ctrl Home to move the cursor back to the very top of the document. Click the **Insert tab**, **Header & Footer**, **Footer**, and either click "**Blank**" or click "**Edit footer**." Word will put you in the footer editing screen for Section 1.

(b)   Next, go to the footer editing screen *for Section 2* by clicking the "**Next**" button.

(c)   At this point, click **Page Number**, **Format Page Numbers**. Make sure the Number format field is set for Arabic numerals (1, 2, 3) and that the "Start at" radio button is checked and the box shows the number 1. Click OK.

(d)   When the footer for Section 2 is correct, click "**Next**" to move to the footer editing screen for Section 3. Click **Page Number, Format Page Numbers**, but this time change the Number format to small roman (i, ii, iii). Make sure that the "Start at" button is checked and the box shows the number i. Click OK.

(e)   Click **Close Header and Footer** to close the Header and Footer editing screen.

2.   <u>Marking the Headings (TOC) and/or the Authorities (TOA)</u>.

<u>Table of Contents</u>

If you have used built-in or custom styles to create the headings, ***you don't have to do anything special (e.g., manually mark them) in order to have them appear in the TOC***. When you generate the TOC, Word automatically pulls headings created with styles into the TOC.

Prior to Word 2002, if you created the headings "manually" (i.e., simply typed the headings, without using *styles*), you had to use the "Mark Table of Contents Entry" dialog box to mark them for inclusion in the TOC. Word 2002 introduced a somewhat simpler way of marking manually created headings in the TOC. I will provide the steps below, while still providing instructions on marking headings with the "Mark Table of Contents Entry dialog in case you ever need to use that method.

<u>Marking "Manual" Headings by Applying Outline Levels</u>

In Word 2010, you can mark a manually created heading simply by doing the following:

- Place the cursor within the heading.

- Click the **Paragraph dialog launcher** *or* press **Alt O, P**.

- Locate the Outline level drop-down toward the top of the dialog box.

- Select the appropriate heading level (from 1 to 9) and OK out.

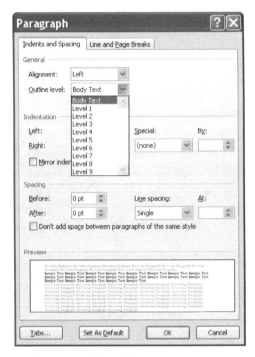

- Repeat for each manually created heading.

Here's an alternate way to do the same thing:

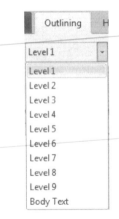

- Place the cursor within the heading and switch to Outline view.

- Use the drop-down to select a heading level (from 1 to 9).

- Continue marking manually created headings in this fashion.

- After you have marked all the headings, change back to Print Layout view by clicking the View tab, Print Layout or pressing Alt V, P.

Generating the TOC (See Also: Generating the Tables)

When you have finished, position your cursor where you want the TOC to appear and click the **References tab**, **Table of Contents**.

At this point, you have the option of simply clicking one of the first two built-in "automatic" TOC schemes, which will generate the TOC and also inserts a heading at the top left margin of the page (either "Contents" or "Table of Contents"). There's one additional option: You can insert a "Manual Table," which simply sets up *a TOC format* with placeholders for text and page numbering that you need to type yourself. Note that this option *does not allow for automatic updating of text or page numbers*; therefore, it is of somewhat limited utility. It is useful mainly for setting up a skeletal TOC *format*, complete with dot leaders.

Rather than using any of the built-in schemes (automatic or manual), you might find it preferable to click "**Insert Table of Contents**" at the bottom of the TOC menu, which launches the TOC dialog box. This method gives you more control over the process by allowing you to check—and change—various settings before generating the TOC. **NOTE:** This method also is somewhat more reliable than using the built-in schemes.

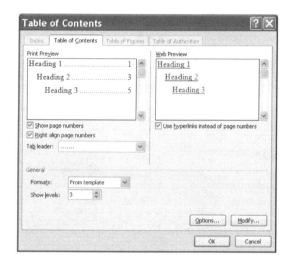

One of the settings you should examine is the "**Show levels**" field toward the bottom of the dialog box. Make sure that it is set to show as many heading levels as you wish to display in the TOC. In the screenshot above, the field shows the number 3, which means *only the first three heading levels* will appear in the generated TOC, regardless of the number of levels in the doc.

Also click the **Options button** so that you can review the checkboxes under "Build table of contents from" and make sure that the boxes for both "**Styles**" and "**Outline levels**" are checked, then click **OK**. (See the screenshot that follows.)

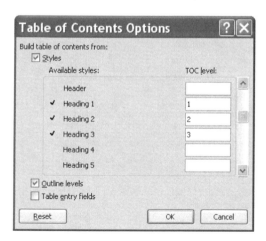

Once everything is set to your satisfaction, click **OK** to generate the TOC. Word will incorporate into the TOC the headings you have marked, and will apply the appropriate indentation for the outline level you selected. Note that generating the TOC from the dialog box rather than from one of the automatic TOC schemes in the drop-down will ***not*** insert a heading (i.e., a page title) at the top of the Table of Contents; you'll have to type that yourself.

After you generate the TOC, you can update it by **right-clicking** somewhere within the TOC, clicking **Update field**, clicking **Update entire table**, **OK**.

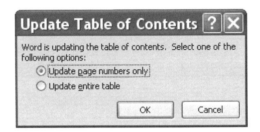

CAUTION: If you have marked headings by applying outline levels to them, right-clicking and using "Update Table of Contents" doesn't always work properly. You might find that you have to regenerate the TOC directly from the Table of Contents dialog box instead.

The Old Method of Marking "Manual" Headings

This method is somewhat more time-consuming than the method explained immediately above, but it still works. It is also useful for pulling headings for "run-in" style paragraphs into the TOC without also pulling in any of the text of the paragraph. For more information on "run-in" paragraphs, see the section on page 507 about using the Style Separator.)

To mark "manual" headings for inclusion in the TOC, do the following:

(a)   **Select** (block, highlight) the heading.

(b)   While text is selected, press **Alt Shift O**, which brings up the "Mark Table of Contents Entry" dialog box.

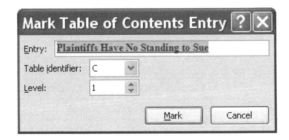

(c)   For TOC entries, make sure the table identifier says "C" (for Table of Contents) and that the "level" field is set correctly (i.e., 1 for a level 1 heading, 2 for a level 2 heading, etc.) When everything looks okay, click "**Mark**."

NOTE: When Word marks the entries, it automatically switches to "Show Non-Printing Characters" mode. If you find this distracting, click the Paragraph symbol (¶) in the Paragraph group (on the Home tab) *or* just press Ctrl Shift * (asterisk) to turn "Show Non-Printing Characters" off.

Continue marking headings in this fashion.

Tip: Using the Style Separator in Word

Occasionally, you will work on a document in which the paragraph heading is in the same line as the text of the paragraph (a "run-in" paragraph). That can cause problems because when you apply a heading style, Word doesn't differentiate between the heading itself and the text of the paragraph. It pulls everything—text and all—into the TOC.

In order to prevent that from happening, you can insert a "Style Separator" between the heading and the text of the paragraph.[2] The easiest way to insert a Style Separator is by using a keyboard shortcut: **Ctrl Alt Enter**. Note that because the symbol for the Style Separator (a special paragraph symbol) is inserted as "hidden text," you should turn on Show Non-Printing Characters and reposition your cursor if necessary before inserting the Style Separator.

CAUTION: If you have already applied a style to the paragraph, make sure the Style Separator is positioned between the heading and the paragraph text. If necessary, you can cut and paste the Style Separator. After inserting the Style Separator, you might have to select the paragraph text and either apply the Normal paragraph style to it or apply some other style (such as Body Text) so that the text will not get pulled into the TOC. To apply the Normal paragraph style quickly after selecting the text, press **Ctrl Shift N**.

FURTHER CAUTION: The Style Separator has been known to cause problems with numbered headings in some situations. Specifically, inserting the Style Separator can result in paragraph numbers or even entire headings becoming "hidden" (invisible). This problem typically occurs in paragraphs where the numbered heading doesn't include any text or caption (for instance, it appears simply as "Section 1."—as opposed to "Section 1. Parties to the Agreement"). It is possible to work around this problem by using a TC code to mark the heading; you might also have to insert a second Style Separator to the right of the first one. Obviously, it's preferable to have text or a caption following a numbered heading, but if you ever need to insert numbered headings without any accompanying text, be on the alert for this issue.

---

[2] There is a feature in Word 2010 called "Linked Styles" that has been touted as a solution to the run-in paragraph problem. Linked styles are a sort of hybrid combination of a paragraph style and a character style. In theory, linked styles can be applied either to an entire paragraph or to selected text within a paragraph—such that you can apply one style to the heading and another style to the text that follows the heading. However, there are some reports on the web of problems with the linked styles feature. For now, it's probably better to disable linked styles by launching the Styles Pane and clicking the "Disable Linked Styles" checkbox at the bottom.

Tip: Adding Text to the TOC

Word 2010 also makes it easy for you to mark a paragraph (or other unit of text in the document) for inclusion in the TOC without applying a style to the text. First, select the text or, if you want to include an entire paragraph, simply insert the cursor somewhere within the paragraph. Next, click the **References tab**, **Table of Contents**, **Add Text**. From the Add Text drop-down, mark the text as a Level 1, Level 2, or Level 3 paragraph, which automatically un-checks "Do not show in Table of Contents."

Conversely, you can use the drop-down to mark a paragraph so that it does ***not*** appear in the TOC; however, doing so can have unintended consequences (similar to the Style Separator issues mentioned earlier). Use with caution.

Table of Authorities

(a)   Select (block, highlight) the citation.

(b)   While text is selected, press **Alt Shift I**, which brings up the "**Mark Citation**" dialog box. (If you prefer, you can click the "**Mark Citation**" **button** in the **Table of Authorities group** on the **References tab**.)

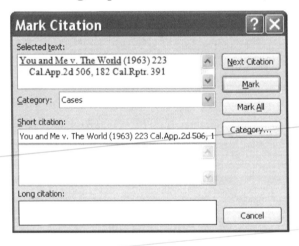

(c)   In the "**Selected Text**" **box**, make sure the citation looks the way you want it to look in the Table of Authorities. (This step is comparable to editing the Full Form of the citation in WordPerfect.)

(d)   Next, make sure the box reflects **the correct category** for that citation—Cases, Statutes, Treatises, whatever.

        NOTE: You can add a new category by **clicking on one of the numbers** in the Category field from 8 to 16, then **clicking on the Category button**, **typing a new name** in the "Replace with" box, and **clicking Replace**.

(e)   Then **edit the Short Citation**. This is the "nickname" Word will use when it searches for this citation throughout the document. It's usually a good idea to ***use*** *the most generic Short Citation possible* because Word searches for the exact text string in this box. Thus, for example, if you use C.C.P. in your Short Citation, it won't find—or mark—any instances of the citation that use California Code of Civil Procedure (or vice versa). Nor will it find or mark the word "section" if the Short Citation uses the section sign (or vice versa). You might find it works best if you use just the code section number (and letters, if any), such as 127.5(a).

(f)   When you have finished, click "**Mark All**" to mark all instances of the citation in the document.

(g)   If you need to mark an additional instance of a particular citation after you've generated the TOA, click to **position the cursor** just to the left of the citation. (You don't have to select the citation.) Next, either press **Alt Shift I** or click the "**Mark Citation**" **button** in the **Table of Authorities group** on the **References tab**. When the "**Mark Citation**" **dialog** appears, navigate to the "**Short Citation**" **box**, **click the nickname** for the citation, click "**Mark**," then click "**Close**."

Continue marking authorities in this fashion. (If you like, you can click the "Next Citation" button to move the cursor to the next citation, but this option is of somewhat limited utility, given that Word recognizes only a few of the "signals" commonly used in legal documents.)

3.   <u>**Generating the Tables**</u>.

This step actually includes "defining" the tables, too.

NOTE: Be sure to ***turn off Show Non-Printing Characters*** before generating the tables. Otherwise, because the Non-Printing Characters take up quite a bit of space in the document (and actually can bump text down a page), the TOC and TOA might not reflect the correct page numbers for headings and citations!

NOTE FURTHER: In Word, unlike in WordPerfect, you generate the TOC and TOA separately. You can also generate individual sections of the TOA separately, which can be useful—or confusing!

Let's start with the **Table of Contents**.

(a)   With the cursor at the exact spot where you want to generate the Table of Contents, click the **References tab**, **Table of Contents**, then click **Insert Table of Contents...** to open the TOC dialog box. (NOTE: You can add a TOC button to the Quick Access Toolbar if you like.)

(b)   Make sure you've selected the TOC format you want, and also that Show page numbers, Right align page numbers, Number of levels, and Tab leader are set the way you want. (The default settings are normally what you'll want, but check them anyway).

(c)   The next step, which is *critical*, is to click **Options**. You must check the Options tab because *Word marks TOC entries differently depending on whether you've used styles to create the headings or you've just typed headings from scratch*. If the former, be sure the "**Styles**" box under "Build table of contents from" is checked. If the latter, be sure the "**Table entry fields**" box is checked. (You don't need to do so if you have applied Outline levels to the headings as per the discussion on pages 503 and 504.) If you've created headings using both methods, you must check both boxes.

(d)   When everything is set right, click **OK**.

The process is basically the same for the **Table of Authorities**.

(a)   With the cursor at the exact spot where you want to generate the TOA, click the **References tab**, **Insert Table of Authorities** (the button at the upper right side of the Ribbon).

(b)   As with the TOC, make sure everything is formatted the way you want. *The most important thing to check before generating the TOA is that the Categories field says "All." If it doesn't, only a portion of the TOA will generate*.

(c)   When everything is set up right, click **OK**. The tables should generate properly, though you might need to do some "cleanup."

4.   Editing the TOC/TOA.

If you need to edit a heading or citation that you have already marked, you need to edit the **code** for that heading or citation, as well as the heading or citation itself. Normally the codes are hidden text, so in order to edit them, you have to turn on Show Non-Printing Characters (see page 185). When the codes are visible, *edit the text between the quotation marks*. (You can, if necessary, edit the heading level within the code, too. In the screenshot below, the heading level is the number "2" at the end of the TC code.)

C.→Plaintiffs·Have·No·Standing·to·Sue{·TC·"Plaintiffs·Have·No·Standing·to·Sue"·\f·C·\l·"2"·}·

Then regenerate the tables (quick method: **right-click** in the tables and click "**Update Field**" *or* select the entire document by pressing **Ctrl A** and then update all fields in the doc by pressing **F9**), and your changes will show up in the newly generated tables.

You might also want to modify the TOC and/or TOA style(s), although doing so can be somewhat complicated. For more detailed instructions, see the section entitled "Modifying TOC and/or TOA Styles in MS Word."

Modifying TOC and/or TOA Styles

After you have generated a Table of Contents and/or a Table of Authorities, you might notice that your tabs aren't exactly where you want them to be, that the table uses the wrong font, or that the headings don't look quite right. These elements of the TOC and TOA are determined by TOC and TOA *styles* that are pre-set in Word. You can, however, modify these styles and save your modifications--either in the particular document on your screen or, better yet, in the template on which your document is based. If you save the style changes to the template, all documents you create in the future that are based on that template will reflect those changes.

As you know by now, by default, Word saves your style changes **ONLY** in the specific document on your screen. To save those changes to the underlying template, you *must* click the "**New documents based on this template**" radio button on the Modify Style dialog box before clicking OK. If you forget to perform this step, you can do so at a later time—but you must have that particular document on your screen, or you'll have to modify the styles again from scratch.

There are two ways to modify the TOC heading styles, the TOA heading style, or the Table of Authorities (i.e., TOA text) style. The first way is to use the Styles Pane, as follows:

1. Insert the cursor into a heading or text whose style you wish to modify.

2. Launch the Styles Pane (using the dialog launcher or Ctrl Alt Shift S) and *right-click* the style name, then click **Modify**.

3. Click the **Format** button and then click the Font, Paragraph, or Tab button (etc.), and make all desired changes.

4. Remember to click (check) the **New documents based on this template** radio button if you want your changes saved to the template (for use in other documents), as opposed to saving them just in the current document. (You may or may not want to click the **Automatically update** box; because doing so can cause problems, as explained in the sidebar on page 366, it's probably best not to.) Once you've clicked the **New documents** radio button, click **OK**.

5. All instances of that style in your document should change to reflect the modifications you have made. If for some reason the style doesn't update, you can click **Ctrl Shift S** to open the **Apply Styles** box and click **Reapply**. Word should offer you two choices: (1) Update the style to reflect recent changes and (2) Reapply the formatting of the style to the selection. To ensure that the document reflects the modifications you've made, choose (2). (Otherwise, the style will be modified to reflect the formatting of the text your paragraph is in.)

The second method is to click the **References tab**, and then:

1.   To change a TOC style, click **Table of Contents**, **Insert Table of Contents**, **Modify**. **Select** the TOC style you wish to change and click **Modify** again. Then follow steps 3 through 5, above.

2.   To change a TOA style, click the **Table of Authorities** button (at the upper right side of the Ribbon), click **Modify**, and follow steps 3 through 5 above.

Tracking Changes[1]

Many attorneys like to keep track of edits they make while drafting their documents, a process sometimes referred to as "redlining" (or as "blacklining").

There actually are two different ways you can "track changes" in your documents in Word. One involves turning on the "**Track Changes**" feature (called "Revisions" in early versions of Word), which highlights any text you add to and/or delete from your document, as well as certain formatting changes, *as you type*. The other method, "**Compare Documents**," allows you to compare **two different drafts** of a document and produce a third, printable document that clearly displays all text that has been inserted into, deleted from, or moved in the more recent draft. The latter is the feature that is commonly called "redlining."

In both cases, when you are ready to finalize your document, you can go through it line by line and accept or reject individual changes (either your own or those made by another reviewer). This section of the book explains how to use the Track Changes feature; the following section discusses the Compare Documents feature.

When Track Changes is enabled, Word marks—with distinctive font colors, underlining, strikeout marks, and other formatting attributes—text that you insert, delete, and/or move from place to place within a document.

To start tracking changes, you can do any of the following:

1. Press **Ctrl Shift E**; *or*

2. Navigate to the **Review tab**, **Tracking group**, click the **Track Changes button**, and then click **Track Changes**; *or*

3. If you have added the "**Track Changes**" **indicator** to the **Status Bar**, click it once to turn Track Changes on. When you're ready to turn Track Changes off, click it again (it's a toggle).

    NOTE: In Word 2010, unlike in pre-Word 2007 versions, the Track Changes indicator is not displayed on the Status Bar unless you specifically add it. To do so, right-click the Status Bar and then click to put a check next to "Track Changes." (It's a good idea to put the indicator on the Status Bar because it can be difficult to tell if the feature is on or off otherwise.)

---

[1] **CAUTION**: Because Track Changes introduces a significant amount of "metadata" into your document, you need to be very careful to eliminate such hidden / confidential information before sharing the document with someone outside the firm (or anyone to whom you'd rather not reveal the metadata). There are a number of steps you can take to remove metadata from your documents, a few of which I'll discuss here.

Track Changes Options

Word is pre-configured to use certain colors and formatting attributes to highlight your edits. However, you can change the appearance of inserted and deleted text by clicking the **Track Changes button** in the **Tracking Group**, then clicking **Change Tracking Options**. (See the screenshot below).

As you can see, there are several different options you can set.[2] You can change the formatting and color for any or all of the following:

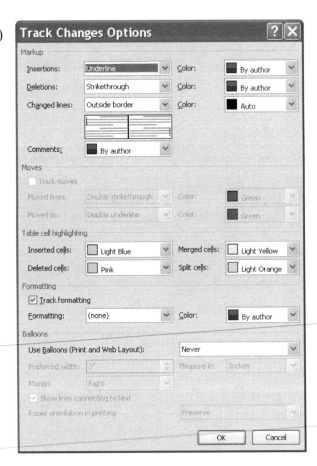

- **Insertions** (by default set to use underlining)

- **Deletions** (by default set to use strikeout marks, referred to as "strikethrough" in Word)

- The way that changes are flagged in the margins (labeled "**Changed lines**" in the dialog)

- **Comments**

- **Moves** (which includes marks indicating where text was moved *from* and marks indicating where text was moved *to*)

- Changes to **table cells** (this option was introduced in Word 2007)

- **Formatting** (e.g., bolding, underlining, italics)

Note that the default color setting for Insertions, Deletions, and Comments is "**By author**." That setting means that if several different individuals are working on the document, Word will assign different (unique) colors to different people to indicate each person's changes.

Even if you do not use the "By author" setting, you can determine who inserted, deleted, and formatted text by placing the mouse pointer over a particular revision; when you do, a pop-up will appear that shows the initials of the author, the date and time of the modification, the nature of the change (insertion, deletion, formatting, or comment), and the content.

---

[2] **NOTE**: These settings are specific to each individual user (i.e., the person whose name and initials are shown on the "**General**" page of **Word Options**).

To change the various settings, just use the drop-downs. (For example, I typically use the color blue plus double underlining for inserted text and the color red plus strikethrough for deleted text.) Once everything is configured to your liking, click **OK**.[3]

Balloons

Recent versions of Word allow you to display insertions, deletions, formatting changes, and comments in "**balloons**" in the document margins.

CAUTION: If this option is enabled, balloons not only appear in the document, but actually print with the document, which can be confusing, especially if you've never used this feature.

Note that there is a drop-down list in the **Track Changes Options dialog** that allows you to limit the use of balloons (to comments and formatting only) or to turn them off altogether (the "Never" option).[4] The Balloons options are as follows:

(1)   **Always**;

(2)   **Never**; and

(3)   **Only for comments/formatting**.

If you choose "**Always**," most of your changes—deletions, moves, formatting changes, comments, etc.—will appear in balloons in the margins. (Deletions will be indicated in the text by markers in the color you've selected for deletions.) Note that insertions will appear inline with the text, which makes perfect sense.[5]

If you choose "**Never**," your changes will be displayed in the body of the document only, without any balloons in the margins. (However, the vertical lines used to indicate which lines contain changes will continue to appear in the margins.)

If you choose "**Only for comments/formatting**," only formatting changes and comments will show up in balloons.

---

[3] You can change these settings again at any time.

[4] Word 2007 has a separate Balloons button in the Tracking group that you can use to configure settings for balloons. This button was removed from Word 2010; instead, there is a menu in the "Show Markup" drop-down that features various balloon options. The options, "Show Revisions in Balloons," "Show All Revisions Inline," and "Show Only Comments and Formatting in Balloons," are comparable to "Always," "Never," and "Only for comments/formatting."

[5] These generalizations assume you are using the **Final Show Markup** option in the **Display for Review drop-down** in the **Tracking group** of the **Review tab**. If you are using the **Original Show Markup** option, Insertions will appear in the margins and Deletions will appear inline.

Using the Feature

Once you've configured the options the way you want, turn on Track Changes (using any of the methods outlined above) and start typing. Word will keep track of your edits until you turn the feature off again.

Viewing Only Certain Types of Markup

If you don't wish to see revision marks for every type of edit, you can click the **Show Markup drop-down** in the **Tracking group** on the **Review tab** and turn off the display for one or more categories of "markup." These include: Comments, Ink (you can hand-write comments if you have a tablet PC), Insertions and Deletions, Formatting, Markup Area Highlight (i.e., the area where balloons display if you have balloons enabled), and Reviewers (if the document has been edited by more than one individual, you can selectively show or hide the markup by specific reviewers).

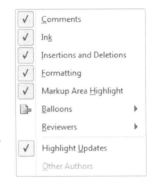

Previewing the "Final" Document / Viewing the "Original" (Unedited) Document

While you are revising a document, you can preview how the document would look if you accepted all the changes by navigating to the **Review tab** in the **Tracking group** and clicking the **Final** option on the **Display for Review drop-down** (the one at the top right of the group).

Alternatively, you can see how the document looked before you started making changes by clicking the **Original** display option. (Or you can see how the original and final drafts look with markings for insertions and deletions.) Keep in mind that these are *display* options only.

Finalizing Your Edits / Removing Markup From a Document

TIP: You can't undo finalization of a document, so if there's any chance you'll want to re-create your edits at some later date, you should save a copy of the document before proceeding to this next step.

When you have finished making changes and you are ready to finalize the document, navigate to the **Review tab, Changes group**. If you are satisfied with all of your edits (whether insertions or deletions), click the **Accept drop-down**, then click **Accept All Changes in Document**.

If, however, you aren't entirely certain you're happy with every revision, use the **Previous** and **Next** buttons to move to individual changes and click the **Reject drop-down**,

Reject Change to cancel the ones you don't want to retain, while clicking the **Accept drop-down**, **Accept Change** to confirm each of the others. Or you can use the **Reject and Move to Next** and **Accept and Move to Next commands** on the **Reject** and **Accept drop-downs**.[6]

Also, make a point of deleting any comments that you (or other reviewers) have inserted into the document.

After accepting or rejecting all of the changes and deleting the comments, *be sure to save the finalized document*.

And, of course, be sure to turn Track Changes off before you send the document to anyone else.

CAUTION: Be aware that selecting Final from the **Show Markup drop-down** in the **Tracking group** on the **Review tab** *merely alters the appearance of the document on your screen. It does not remove the Track Changes marks*. That means that if you forward the document to someone else, *they can view your edits simply by choosing a different option (such as Final Showing Markup) from the Display for Review drop-down*.

In order to remove the Track Changes marks from the document permanently—so that no one else is able to display them—you *must* accept or reject each individual change. If you fail to do so, you will leave metadata in your document.

_____

[6] **NOTE**: You can use this same process of going through the document and accepting or rejecting changes if you accidentally turn on Track Changes and can't figure out how to get rid of tracking marks you've inserted unintentionally.

SIDEBAR: What Does "Mark as Final" Do?

Word 2010 comes with a feature, introduced in Word 2007, called "**Mark as Final**." When Mark as Final is applied, no one can edit a document. Because of this fact, and because of the feature's name, it sounds as if it might be related to Track Changes. Indeed, Microsoft intends for this command to be used when you are collaborating with others in creating and reviewing documents. However, it is of somewhat limited utility, for the following reasons:

- It doesn't actually strip out revision marks, so it isn't a metadata removal tool and shouldn't be used as a substitute for accepting or rejecting all of the changes to a document.

- Although it makes the document read-only, anyone who receives the document can change the document status easily and make it editable again.

- And finally, if someone opens a "Marked as Final" document in an earlier version of Word, the read-only status is removed.

Still, you might find the feature useful as a reminder to others (or to yourself) that a document is a final draft and shouldn't be modified. To use it, click the **File tab**, **Info fly-out**, **Protect Document**, **Mark as Final**. A Marked as Final icon will appear in the Status Bar, and most icons in most tabs on the Ribbon will be grayed out, because you can't apply any formatting to the finalized document. But there's an easy workaround: Anyone who opens the document can just click the "**Edit Anyway**" **button** that appears in the Message Bar above the document or repeat the steps listed above in order to ***unmark*** the document.

Should you wish to ***password protect*** a document, restrict the type of editing someone else can do, and/or restrict the styles someone else can apply, use **Restrict Editing** (known as "Protect Document" in earlier versions of Word) instead of Mark as Final. Restrict Editing is on the **Review tab**, all the way to the right under **Protect**. Click to open the **Restrict Formatting and Editing Pane**. The first option on the pane lets you limit the styles other people working on the document can use (you choose allowable styles from a list). There is also an option to permit only certain types of editing: Tracked changes, Comments, Filling in Forms, or No changes (Read only). You can specify exceptions—i.e., individuals who are allowed to edit all or a portion of the document.

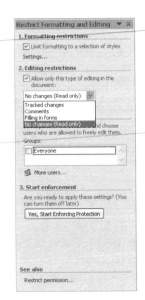

Check one or both of those options, then click the "**Yes, Start Enforcing Protection**" **button**. When the dialog opens, type and confirm a password and click **OK**. **CAUTION**: Be sure to make note of the password and keep it in a safe, easy-to-remember location.

To disable protection, open the document, navigate to the **Protect group**, click **Protect Document**, then click "**Stop Protection**." You'll have to enter the correct password and then click **OK** in order to remove the password.

Comparing Documents (Redlining)

To compare two different drafts of a document, click the **Review tab**, **Compare group**, **Compare button**, and click **Compare….** A **Compare Documents dialog** opens.

If you have used a version of Word older than Word 2007, you'll notice that this dialog has been redesigned to make it easier to determine which document you should identify first. On the left side, there is a drop-down plus a browse button for the ***Original document*** (i.e., the older draft—which might or might not be the first draft), and on the right side, there is a drop-down plus a browse button for the ***Revised document*** (i.e., the later draft).

Clicking the "**More**" button displays a number of comparison settings you can adjust. You can choose to have the redlined document display—or not display—moves, comments, changes to formatting, case changes, white space, modifications to tables, headers and footers, footnotes and endnotes, text boxes, and/or fields.

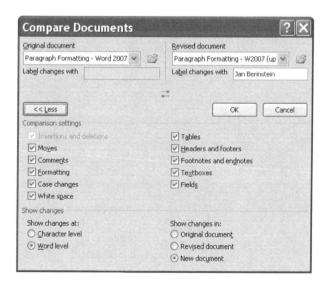

In addition, you can fine-tune the comparison to show changes at the character level (word level is the default). And, if you like, you can have Word show the changes directly in either the earlier (original) draft or the revised draft, although the default setting of "New document" has a compelling advantage: It prevents you from overwriting one of the existing drafts by accident.

Once you have verified that the comparison settings are to your liking, click **OK** to have Word compare the two drafts. The redlined document will appear on screen.

Unlike pre-Word 2007 versions of the program, Word 2010 shows the results in a split screen similar to that of some popular third-party document comparison programs. The left "pane" summarizes the changes; the middle pane displays the document with redlining, strikeout, and other markup[1]; and the right side is divided into two panes: one containing the older ("original") draft and one containing the revised document.

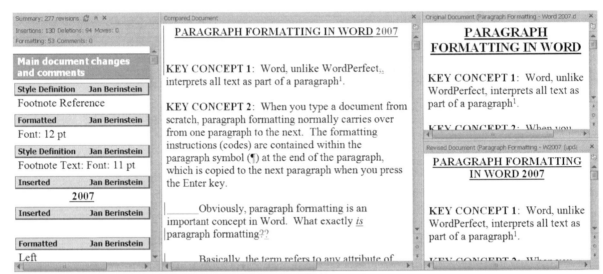

Compared Document

This profusion of screens can be somewhat overwhelming. Not to worry; you can close any (or all) of the side panes if you wish by clicking on the "X" in the upper right-hand corner.[2] Alternatively, you can make them narrower by dragging the vertical margin(s) to one side of the screen.

Accepting and Rejecting Changes

As noted in the "Tracking Changes" section, after performing a comparison, you can choose to go through the redlined document and selectively accept or reject changes that you or other reviewers have made to the document—or accept or reject all of those changes at once.

To accept or reject changes, you can do any of the following:

---

[1] The appearance and formatting of the markup—including whether or not any of it appears in "balloons" in the margin—depends on your settings under "**Change Tracking Options**" in the **Tracking group** on the **Review tab**.

[2] To re-display the left-hand pane, click **Reviewing Pane** in the **Tracking group**, and click **Reviewing Pane Vertical**. To re-display the right-hand panes, click "**Show Source Documents**" in the **Compare group**, then choose Show Original, Show Revised, or Show Both.

1.   Click the appropriate choice under **Accept** or **Reject** in the **Changes group** on the **Review tab**; *or*

2.   Right-click within the redlined text, then click **Accept Change** or **Reject Change**; *or*

3.   Right-click an item in the **Reviewing Pane**, then click **Accept Insertion** (or **Deletion**) or **Reject Insertion** (or **Deletion**).

Once you have finished reviewing the changes, you might decide to save the "redlined" version as a separate document. Click the **File tab**, **Save As**, and type a new name for the document (perhaps the document's name plus "Redline 1" or something similar to indicate that it's a redlined draft). You can, of course, print the redlined version without saving it, but attorneys frequently want to keep a redlined draft in the computer for future reference.

Comparing and Combining Documents (Formerly "Comparing and Merging")

Word actually offers two "comparison" options: (1) **Compare Documents** and (2) **Compare and Combine Documents**. The essential difference between the two is that option (1) typically is used for redlining sequential drafts of a document (ordinarily authored by a single individual) and option (2) typically is used for merging versions of a document worked on separately by different authors or reviewers in a collaborative environment.

The **Compare and Combine** process is very similar to that of comparing drafts of a document. One notable difference has to do with the way Word treats revision marks inserted into the documents before the comparison (i.e., as a result of a document author using **Tracked Changes**). When you use the simple **Compare Documents** feature, any markup existing in either the earlier draft or the revised draft *is blended into the redlined document as if you had clicked "Accept Change."* Also, Word labels insertions and deletions (etc.) as if all changes were made by one author.

By contrast, when you use **Compare and Combine**, the redlined document shows *all* markup, including markup that existed in one (or both) of the documents prior to the comparison. It also attributes changes (insertions, deletions, formatting, moves, comments, etc.) to the specific people who made those changes.

NOTE: Remember that which revision marks are visible in the combined (redlined) document depends in part on settings in the **Display for Review** and **Show Markup** drop-downs in the **Tracking group** of the **Review tab**. If for some reason you are seeing fewer changes than you anticipated, check the settings on both of those drop-downs to make sure that they allow for the display of all markup.

WHERE DID IT GO? Comment

The Comment feature, located on the Insert menu (and also available from the Reviewing Toolbar) in earlier versions of Word, is now on the **Review tab**, in the **Comments group**. To insert a comment, either select some text or position the cursor where you want the comment to appear, then click the "**New Comment**" button or press the key combination **Alt Ctrl M**.

To edit a comment, you can do one of two things:

- display the **Reviewing Pane** (click the drop-down in the **Tracking group** on the **Review tab**; you can choose to display it vertically or horizontally) and then click in the area of the pane where the comment is showing; *or*

- if balloons are displayed, just click in the balloon where the comment is showing. (If balloons are not displayed, click the **Track Changes drop-down** in the **Tracking group** on the **Review tab**, then click the **Change Tracking Options button** and configure balloons to show "**Always**" or "**Only for comments/formatting**." Be sure to click "**OK**" to save your changes.)

If you prefer not to show balloons, you can **right-click** within a comment indicator and then click "**Edit Comment**," and the **Reviewing Pane** will open so that you can make your changes. Click the "X" at the top right side of the **Reviewing Pane** to close it.

To view a comment without editing it, just position the mouse pointer over a comment indicator. A pop-up will appear with the name of the person who wrote the comment, the date and time the comment was created, and the text of the comment.

Troubleshooting Tips

Troubleshooting Tips and Best Practices

Troubleshooting can be tricky. Sometimes it's hard to figure out whether the problem you're experiencing is document-specific, is a bug in Word, is a Windows glitch, is the result of a hardware or software conflict, or derives from something else altogether. And even if you determine that the problem is confined to one ornery document, how do you know whether it's a simple formatting error or something more serious, like document corruption?

That is the crux of the matter: You have to isolate the problem, which essentially means focusing on the most likely causes and then testing each one in turn. To some extent troubleshooting is an art, and it involves a certain amount of educated guesswork, but you're more likely to get results if you proceed in a careful, methodical manner. These tips are intended to give you some guidance as you try to diagnose your issues with Word.

Consider the Context

The context matters. If a problem occurs only with one document, or only on one computer, that is an important clue. If it occurs only when you print, only when you print envelopes, or only when you exit from Word, that is an important clue. If it occurs only when you are working with styles, that is an important clue.

Under what circumstances do you experience the problem? Does it seem to be associated with one particular task? Does it trigger any error message? (If so, write down the message; if it's lengthy, write down only the first couple of lines. Then look it up on Google or some other Internet search engine.)

Do other members of your organization report the same type of trouble? If not, is there anything in their setup—their computer, their attached printer(s), other hardware (such as a scanner), the way they've configured Word, etc.—that might explain what's going on?

Does the problem occur only in documents that have been converted from WordPerfect? In documents that have been "round-tripped" between Word and WordPerfect?

Did the unruly document originate in house or at another company? Was it scanned in and converted from scanning software such as Omnipage?

Is it laden with a large number of styles or complex formatting, such as nested tables?

These sorts of questions can help you pinpoint the problem.

Test One Potential Cause at a Time

It is important to test, and rule out, ***one potential cause at a time***. Keep track of what you have tested so that you don't duplicate your efforts.

In addition, you need to narrow your focus to those items that are *the most likely reasons* for the specific problem you're dealing with. For example, if the way that a document appears on the screen has changed—if it suddenly seems larger or smaller than usual—it's probably just a display issue, and you should check the View tab (and possibly the Zoom dialog) to see if anything there is out of the ordinary. Has the Draft document view been enabled? If so, that might explain why you can't see the pleading lines and line numbers.

If underlining doesn't appear on the screen but does appear in the printed document, that probably is a display issue, too. Try changing the magnification of the document (zoom to about 115%) and see if that makes a difference.

Start With the Simple and Obvious Solutions

When you're troubleshooting, it's always best to start with the simplest and most obvious solution and work your way toward more complex fixes. More often than not, whatever is causing the problem is something fairly straightforward. (It's almost never something that can be solved by uninstalling and reinstalling the software; such a drastic move should always be a last resort.) In fact, formatting issues often can be traced to a setting in either the Paragraph dialog or the Page Setup dialog.

In the next few pages, I've listed some other common sources of formatting issues that you might want to check, depending on the symptoms.

The Paragraph Dialog

It can be a good idea to check the settings in the **Paragraph dialog box** first, depending on the symptoms. Review both the **Indents and Spacing tab** and the **Line and Page Breaks tab**. Look for any setting that doesn't seem "normal." Is there a hanging indent where you intended a first-line indent or no indent at all? Does the Spacing After box show 3 points instead of 12? Is "Page Break Before" checked even though the paragraph ought to be on the same page as the previous paragraph?

If nothing in those settings appears unusual or unexpected, display the **Non-Printing Characters (Ctrl Shift * [asterisk])** and/or invoke **Reveal Formatting (Shift F1)**. Again, look for anything out of the ordinary.

Line spacing and "Before" and "After" spacing can cause all kinds of havoc in your documents. As an example, last year one of my clients had an issue in a Word 2007 document that had been converted from WordPerfect. The document contained a table with text that was squished up toward the top of the cells. It seemed logical to deduce that the problem might have resulted from the vertical text alignment in the cell (Table Tools, Layout, Alignment). So I changed the text alignment so that it was centered vertically, as opposed to being at the top of the cell. No difference. I checked the row height (Table Tools, Layout, Cell Size dialog or Table Tools, Layout, Properties, Row tab) to make sure there wasn't a setting that was limiting the height of the cell such that it was too narrow for the text. There wasn't.

Finally, with my cursor in one of the problematic cells, I launched the Paragraph dialog. And voilà! As it turned out, the line spacing was set to 6 points—half the height of a standard single-spaced line. As soon as I changed that to single spacing (or 12 points), the text appeared normal.

Another client recently had a problem with a footnote that was too close to the pleading footer; the bottom line of the footnote was cut off. One of the staff members suggested changing the bottom margin (making it larger in order to accommodate all of the footnote text). That worked, but it affected every page of the document, leaving big gaps at the bottom of most of them.

I thought it might be preferable to add some extra white space after the footnote by using the "Spacing After" option. So we opened the Paragraph dialog and added 6 points of space after the footnote text. It was a great solution because it bumped the footnote text up enough to be completely visible without having an effect on any other pages.

Sometimes it takes a little imaginative thinking to figure out what's going on and devise an elegant solution—one that doesn't create new problems. (And the more you work with Word, the better you'll become at this sort of troubleshooting.)

The Page Setup Dialog

If nothing is amiss with the paragraph formatting, perhaps the problem lies with the page formatting. To rule out that possibility, take a look at the **Page Setup dialog**. Review both the **Margins** and **Layout tabs**.

In particular, check the **page margins**. In addition, note whether the **header** and/or **footer margin** (on the Layout tab) is larger (or smaller) than you meant it to be? And be sure to check the **Preview area (Applied to:)** toward the bottom of each tab to see if settings that should have been applied to the whole document were applied, incorrectly, to "This Section Only" or "This Point Forward"—or vice versa.

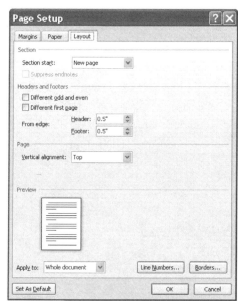

It might not occur to you to review the "**Multiple pages**" **option** in the "**Pages**" **section** of the **Margins tab**, but if your pleading looks funky, with a wide left margin on the odd pages and a wide right margin on the even pages, it's possible that this setting has gotten changed from "Normal" to "Mirror Margins." If so, change it back, then click "**OK**" to save your changes.

The Word Options

If you have reviewed both the Paragraph dialog and the Page Setup dialog, displayed the Non-Printing Characters, and checked Reveal Formatting and you're still stumped, take a look at the Word Options (**File tab**, **Options**). Unfortunately, these settings can be somewhat difficult to explore, not only because they're significantly more scattered (and require more clicking and scrolling) than in previous versions of Word, but also because there are a number of obscure configuration options in the Advanced category.

Still, it's possible that some setting buried in the Options is the reason your document is misbehaving. Be sure to check the following (if they strike you as possible culprits):

The AutoCorrect Options

AutoCorrect Options (under **Proofing**)—especially the **AutoFormat As You Type** tab. The settings for bulleted lists, numbered lists, border lines, and "**Set left- and first-indent with tabs and backspaces**" can cause unexpected behavior. In particular, if the latter option is enabled, pressing the Tab key will produce not a left tab, but a first-line indent (formatting that will carry over to the next paragraph automatically when you press Enter).

Set left- and first-indent with tabs and backspaces ⟶

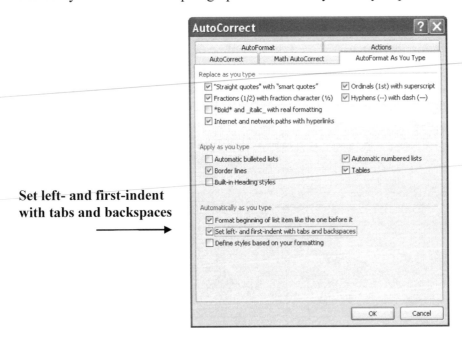

The Display Options

There are a couple of Display options that could throw you off your stride.

Many people don't realize that if any of the boxes under "**Always show these formatting marks on the screen**" is checked, those mark(s) will display in your document no matter whether you've manually toggled "Show Non-Printing Characters" on or off via the **paragraph symbol** in the **Paragraph group** (or by pressing **Ctrl Shift * [asterisk]**). In other words, the settings in Word Options take precedence over your manual settings.

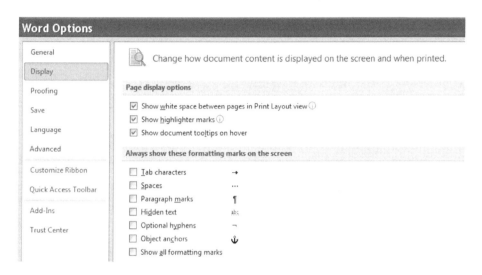

Also, if "**Update fields before printing**" is turned off (which it is by default), certain items in your document might not look correct when you print your document because the underlying field codes (SEQ codes, page number codes, cross-references, indexes, etc.) are not updating. To change this behavior, click to check (enable) the option.

Word Options, Display, Printing Options
"Update fields before printing"

Advanced Editing and Display Options

Under **Advanced**: Take a look at **Editing options** and, under the general heading of **Compatibility options**, **Layout Options**.

The main Editing option to watch out for is "**Typing replaces selected text**." If Typing replaces selected text is checked, you can delete text accidentally. For example, when you tab to the next column in a table, Word by default selects the text in the table cell to which you tab. If you then press a key (other than one of the arrow keys), Word will delete the selected text and replace it with whichever character is on the key you pressed.

Also under Editing, you'll find an option called "**Keep track of formatting**." This option isn't especially problematic, but it can be confusing. When "Keep track of formatting" is active, Word displays *manually applied formatting* (font attributes such as font size and bolding; paragraph formatting; and bullets and/or numbering) in the Styles Pane along with genuine styles.

"Keep track of formatting" offers significant benefits: It makes it easy for you to select text with similar formatting, an option that is available from the shortcut menu (under "**Styles**") when you right-click some text. Once the text is selected, you can change the formatting all at once either by applying a style or by manually applying various attributes such as bolding or italics.

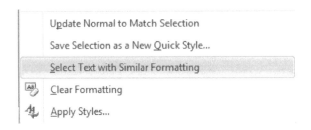

This Option Appears When You Right-Click Text, Then Click "Styles"

Also, when you enable this option, you can use the related option to "**Mark formatting inconsistencies**" (Word uses a blue squiggly line to flag such items), which can be valuable. Right-clicking the flagged text produces a context menu that prompts you to make the text consistent with the rest of the document text.

Although "Keep track of formatting" has its merits, many people turn this setting off because they find it somewhat distracting.

NOTE: If you disable this feature and Word still seems to be keeping track of manually applied formatting, open the **Styles Pane** (use the **Styles Pane launcher** or press **Ctrl Alt Shift S**), click "**Options**" in the lower right-hand corner, and when the Style Pane Options dialog opens, navigate to "**Select formatting to show as styles**" and *uncheck* all three boxes (Paragraph level formatting, Font formatting, and Bullet and numbering formatting). Then **OK** out of the dialog and close the Styles Pane. (Conversely, if you enable the feature and it doesn't seem to be working, take a look at the Style Pane Options and make sure the three boxes are checked.)

530

One Editing option you might want to enable—it is disabled by default in Word 2010—is "**Prompt to Update Style**." If the option is enabled, a message box pops up and warns you when you reapply a style to text after changing the formatting of the text. It lets you choose between updating the style to reflect the modifications you've made—which may or may not be a good idea—and reapplying the formatting of the style to the selected text. Note that the message box also gives you the option of automatically updating the style when you make manual formatting changes, which ordinarily you ***won't*** want to do because of the havoc that option can wreak with your documents.

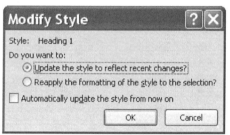

To enable the option, click the **File tab**, **Options**, **Advanced**. Under "**Editing options**" (which appears at the top of the Advanced category), navigate to and **click** to check the option labeled "**Prompt to update style**." Be sure to click "**OK**" to save your changes when you exit from the Word Options.

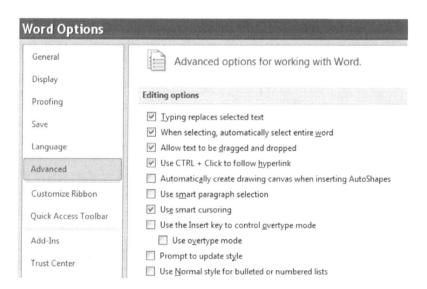

Word Options, Advanced, "Prompt to update style"

Layout Options

The **Layout Options**, which you'll find all the way at the end of the **Advanced tab**, are among the most complicated and inscrutable settings in Word. You might have to experiment to get these settings to work the way you want. If you get a chance, test some of them with a document that isn't critical (preferably, a copy of a document that contains complex formatting).

First, try changing the general **Compatibility** setting so that the document is laid out for **Word 2003** rather than Word 2010. Make note of what happens in the document, and make note of which specific Layout Options are checked or unchecked. Then change back to Word 2007 layout and observe what happens.

For a brief explanation of each of the layout options—at least, the ones available in Word 2003 (which are fairly similar to those in Word 2010)— see the following Microsoft Knowledge Base article:[1] http://support.microsoft.com/?kbid=288792

Perhaps the most important of these settings is the one labeled "**Use printer metrics to lay out document**." It's preferable to leave this option unchecked / disabled (which is the default) if you plan to print your document on multiple printers that aren't configured identically (for instance, if different people at your firm will be working on the document and sending it to printers that use different print drivers). When the option is disabled, Word lays out the document according to its own internal standards ("metrics"); when the option is enabled, Word lays out the document according to standards specific to the chosen printer and print driver. That means that the document—in particular, such critical aspects as the margins and page breaks— might not look the same when the document is printed on different printers.

Some other layout options you might want to test include the following:

Don't add automatic tab stop for hanging indent

By default, when you apply a hanging-indent format to a paragraph, Word inserts a tab stop at the position of the hanging indent. If the extra tab stop causes problems, you can disable (uncheck) this option.

Don't add extra space for raised / lowered characters

Worth testing if your text alignment seems off and none of the other potential solutions has helped.

Don't add leading (extra space) between rows of text

Worth testing if your text alignment seems off and none of the other potential solutions has helped.

Don't center "exact line height" lines

See the discussion about aligning text with pleading line numbers, starting on page 429. I have found that enabling this option sometimes resolves issues with text not aligning with the line numbers in pleadings that use "Exactly" line spacing. No guarantees, but it's worth a try.

---

[1] To the best of my knowledge, the article hasn't been updated for Word 2010.

Don't expand character spaces on a line that ends with SHIFT + RETURN

When you insert a line break (Shift Enter) in a justified paragraph, Word will add white space to stretch the line all the way across to the right margin unless this option is enabled. With the option enabled, the text acts more like left-aligned text (no extra white space in the line).

Split apart page break and paragraph mark

This option is important because when it is *disabled*, page breaks in a document might behave differently depending on whether you open the document in Word 2010 or a version of Word older than Word 2007. In pre-Word 2007 versions, page breaks and paragraph marks could not occupy the same line. In Word 2010 and Word 2007, they can share the same line, so if the option is disabled (meaning that the page break and paragraph mark are *not* split apart), a page break takes up less space than it would in an earlier version. (Unlike in pre-Word 2007 versions, the paragraph mark—representing one single-or double-spaced line, depending on your document—must be on the same page as the page break unless this option is *enabled*).

If you are experiencing problems with the way that page breaks in the same document work in Word 2010 and an earlier version of Word (and it isn't because you are using different printers or printer drivers), make sure this setting is *enabled* (checked).

See the following Microsoft Knowledge Base Article:
http://support.microsoft.com/kb/923183

(But note that the article erroneously says to *disable* the option. The option should be *enabled*.)

The **Suppress extra line spacing at bottom of page** and **Suppress extra line spacing at top of page** options are similar to what WordPerfect uses to ensure that there is no extraneous white space after (bottom of page) or before (top of page) text if the line spacing is set to a value higher than one. If they are not enabled and you are routinely having to delete extra space, particularly, at the top of a page, you might try testing to see if one or both of the options makes a difference.

These tips, while not exhaustive, should give you some useful ideas about how to begin the troubleshooting process, as well as some common sources of formatting problems. A solid understanding of Word's logic, as well as a methodical approach, will go a long way toward helping you to diagnose the occasional, but inevitable, difficulties that are endemic to working with computers.

SIDEBAR: Conflicts Between Word and Other Programs (Add-Ins)

Some problems can be traced to conflicts between Word and other software on your computer. In particular, there can be conflicts with the so-called add-ins, third-party programs that integrate with Word but that also—on occasion—can cause problems. These add-ins can include common programs such as Adobe Acrobat and, in my case, a program that I use to create screenshots for my books. Microsoft also creates its own add-ins for the Office programs.

One potential source of trouble, ironically, is the new Data Execution Prevention function (DEP) built into Office 2010. This important security measure, which helps to block so-called "overflow exploits" that allow viruses and worms to run on your machine also can cause add-ins to fail, which in turn can cause Word to crash. As explained in a Word 2010 "Help" article:

> "When Data Execution Prevention is enabled in Office 2010, Office programs may stop responding (crash) when an add-in tries to run in a manner that does not comply with the computer's security policy. When a Data Execution Prevention violation occurs, the Office program will stop responding to help protect your computer."

To locate this article, click the question mark at the right side of the screen, *or* press F1, *or* click the File tab, Help, and click Microsoft Office Help. When the Help dialog appears, type "DEP"—without quotation marks—in the search box and either press Enter *or* click the magnifying glass. The excerpt is from the article entitled "Why is my add-in crashing?"; see also "View, manage, and install add-ins in the Office programs."

If necessary, you can disable add-ins that might be causing Word to crash. (If you need to use both the add-in and Word, contact the add-in manufacturer; the company might have a patch that will resolve the issue. Also, sometimes a different version of the add-in program will run without problems.) For instructions on disabling add-ins, plus other useful information, see the following:

Microsoft Knowledge Base article, "How to troubleshoot problems that occur when you start or use Word 2010, Word 2007, Word 2003, or Word 2002" (instructions for disabling add-ins begin about 3/5 of the way down the page):
http://support.microsoft.com/kb/921541

CNET article, "A partial cure Microsoft Word 2007 crashes: disable add-ins" (the information also applies, in general, to Word 2010):
http://news.cnet.com/8301-13880_3-9874528-68.html

TechNet article (tailored for IT people), "Security Overview for Office 2010":
http://technet.microsoft.com/en-us/library/cc179050.aspx

Microsoft Knowledge Base article, "Word doesn't save changes…Adobe Acrobat 7":
http://support.microsoft.com/kb/906899

Preventing, Diagnosing, and Repairing Document Corruption

Because document corruption is a fact of life, the best strategy for dealing with it is a defensive one: namely, (1) practice good computer "hygiene" and (2) back up critical files frequently (and back them up to many different storage media, including external drives, USB drives, CDs and/or DVDs, online storage sites, and so forth). If you are diligent about both types of prevention, you are less likely to experience corruption, and you'll probably suffer less damage—and be in a better position to recover your work—if it does strike.

Common Causes of Corruption

Document corruption can occur for a wide range of reasons, including (but not limited to) the following: a sudden power surge or outage; saving a document while your computer resources are low; saving a file directly to or opening a file directly from a floppy disk , a USB drive, or another removable storage medium (rather than copying and pasting); "round-tripping" a document between Word and WordPerfect formats (i.e., saving the same document first in one format and then in another format); macro viruses; a corrupted printer driver; a bad sector on your hard drive; problems with / incompatibilities related to third-party "add-in" programs that work with Word; using the Master Document feature, Fast Saves, Versioning, Nested Tables, or certain other complex features (some of which are no longer available in Word 2010).

You can't prevent all of those events, but you can reduce the likelihood of at least a few of them. For ideas, see the section about good computer "hygiene" starting on page 538.

Symptoms of Corruption

First, it's worth pointing out that many phenomena besides corruption can produce unusual formatting or unexpected behavior. Before deciding that a file is corrupt, be sure to investigate other, less serious possibilities—and always try less drastic remedies first.

Suspect corruption if you experience one or more of the following problems:

- Difficulty saving a file;

- Inability to open a file;

- Opening a file causes Word to crash or freezes the computer;

- Uncontrollable cursor movement (and/or the cursor skips past certain sections or pages);

- Improper display of certain characters or the presence of "garbage" characters in the document;

- Constant repagination;

- Sudden changes in formatting;

- Error messages about document corruption;

- Error messages about "insufficient memory."

This is not an all-inclusive list, but it includes many of the most common symptoms of document corruption.

Some Possible Remedies and Workarounds

Depending on the problem(s) you are experiencing, you can try one or more of the following remedies or workarounds. They might help in some circumstances, although it is possible that they won't work for you.

CAUTION: To avoid making matters worse, always make at least one a backup copy of the problem document before attempting any repairs. That way, if the remedy doesn't work—or creates new problems—you can try something else.

If you are having trouble opening a Word document, use the "**Open and Repair**" **command** on the "Open" button at the lower right side of the Open dialog.

If you can work with a document but you are experiencing problems such as the cursor skipping certain sections of the document, turn on the non-printing characters (click the **paragraph symbol** in the **Paragraph group** on the **Home tab** or press **Ctrl Shift *** [asterisk]), and then select the entire document *up to, but not including, the very last paragraph symbol*. (The last paragraph symbol in a document can contain corruption.) Copy the selected portion and paste it into a new blank document screen, then save the copy with a new name.

Alternatively, try selecting the portion of the document up to the point where the cursor is skipping, copy that portion, and **paste it into a new blank document**. Then copy and paste the next "good" portion. Test to make sure the new document doesn't experience the same problem. If all seems well, save it with a new name. You might have to re-create the corrupted section of the original document from scratch, but at least you will have salvaged the bulk of the document.

Another possible solution is to copy the text of the document and paste into a blank document *as unformatted text*. Sometimes that strips out the corruption.

You can try saving the file **in a different format**—if the original file was saved as a .docx, try saving it as a .doc, or vice versa. Or try saving the file to RTF, which will preserve most of your formatting, or to Plain Text, which will discard your formatting (you'll have to reapply the formatting from scratch, a less-than-desirable option, but one that might be necessary under the circumstances). Then reopen the document in Word and check to see if the problem persists.

Type an "X" at the top of a blank document, then click the **Insert tab**, click the "**Object**" **drop-down**, and click "**Text from File…**" (to insert the text from the file into the

536

blank document). Then **delete the "X"** and **save the document with a new name**. This procedure (occasionally referred to as the "X-retrieve" method) sometimes removes corruption because it inserts the content of the file without the so-called "file header," which can become corrupted.

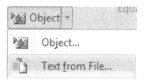

Some users have reported success using the word processing program **Open Office** to open corrupted documents that won't open into Word . Open Office is available as a free download from http://www.openoffice.org.

NOTE: It's probably a good idea to click the "I want to learn more about Open Office" link before downloading the software.

Deleting or Renaming the NORMAL Template

One common cause of document corruption in Word is a corrupted NORMAL template. If you have reason to believe your NORMAL template (normal.dotm) has become corrupted, try the following:

1. Exit from Word;

2. Locate the normal.dotm template;

3. Delete the template altogether *or*, if you haven't made a backup copy, rename it (perhaps giving it a name such as "normal-old.dotm")[1]; and

4. Reopen Word.

When you reopen the program, Word will re-create a *generic* NORMAL template (normal.dotm) from scratch. If having a new NORMAL template resolves the problems, you should be able to copy at least some of your customizations (styles and macros) from a backup copy, if any (or possibly from the original [renamed] NORMAL template), to the new template via the Organizer. For instructions on using the Organizer to copy customizations between documents (or templates), see the section starting on page 352.

---

[1] People often delete the normal.dotm rather than renaming it. However, the NORMAL template stores customized macros, styles, and AutoText entries; if you delete the template, those customizations will be lost—unless you had the foresight to create a backup copy of the template before problems arose. It's a good idea to *make a backup copy while the program is functioning normally* (and to create updated backups periodically). That way, if the original template becomes corrupted, you can delete it and copy any customizations from the backup copy to the new, generic template that Word will create the next time you launch the program.

If having a new NORMAL template ***doesn't*** resolve the problems, you can restore the original template (assuming you renamed it rather than deleting it) or the backup copy (if you deleted the original template).

To replace the generic new NORMAL template with the template containing your customizations, do the following:

- Exit from Word;

- Rename or delete the new normal.dotm template;

- Give the backup copy (or the original template) the name "normal.dotm" (without quotation marks); and

- Restart Word.

Good Computer "Hygiene"

There are several steps you can take to reduce the likelihood of computer problems and minimize the damage in the event of a serious issue such as a power outage. Some of these steps are fairly obvious, but I will point them out anyway because the consequences can be serious. As the saying goes, an ounce of prevention is worth a pound of cure. And on occasion, I have learned that lesson the hard way; my hope is that these gentle reminders will help you avoid similar ***tsouris*** (heartbreak, calamity, trouble).

- Don't place coffee cups or other beverages within spill distance of your computer keyboard. We've all done it, but it's better to learn from someone else's sad experience than from your own why it's not a good idea. The more important your document, the farther away the beverage should be.

- Invest in (or ask your firm to invest in) a heavy-duty surge suppressor so that normal power spikes don't damage your computer.

- If you work on a laptop, make sure your machine is plugged into an outlet (or, better yet, a heavy-duty surge suppressor that is plugged into an outlet) at all times and that the electrical connection is good.

- Save your documents frequently.

- Make copies of critical files, including the NORMAL template and any other template(s) that you've customized.

- Make frequent backups onto external media, such as an external hard drive, a USB drive, and/or a CD or DVD. However, be sure to do so with the next tip in mind.

- Never save a file directly to or open a file directly from a floppy disk, a USB drive, a CD, a DVD, etc. Instead, *copy the file to your hard drive*, then open it into Word *from the storage location on hard drive* via the File tab, Open or by pressing Ctrl O.

- Don't round-trip documents between Word and WordPerfect—or, for that matter, between Word and RTF.

- Watch for signs of macro viruses, including the inability to save a regular file (a .docx or a .doc) as anything other than a .dot, a .dotx, or a .dotm

Resources

In this section, I list a few selected articles about document corruption that you might find useful, as well as links to third-party companies that manufacture software designed to repair corrupted documents.

"How to troubleshoot damaged documents in Word 2007 and Word 2010":
http://support.microsoft.com/kb/918429

> This extensive article from the Microsoft Knowledge Base, which applies to both Word 2007 and Word 2010, offers a number of helpful suggestions about ways to try to diagnose and repair documents that appear to be damaged (corrupted). If you are experiencing any of the problems identified at the beginning of the article, or any other unusual behavior that you suspect is a result of corruption, read through each of the proposed solutions to try to determine which one(s) apply in your specific situation. Make a backup copy of the document, if possible, before attempting any repairs—just to be on the safe side.

http://word.mvps.org/FAQs/ApplicationErrors.htm

> The Microsoft MVPs (volunteer experts in the various Microsoft Office programs) have an entire page with links to articles about troubleshooting Word problems. Note that most of these articles deal with versions of Word prior to Word 2010.

http://word.mvps.org/FAQs/AppErrors/CorruptDoc.htm

> This article from the MVPs site discusses some causes of document corruption and a few remedies / workarounds. Note in particular the points they make about the features that increase the likelihood of corruption, as well as the fact that corruption often is stored in a section break or a paragraph symbol, especially the very last paragraph symbol in a document.

File Conversion Issues

Opening Word 2010 Documents
With Pre-Word 2007 Versions of MS Word

As you know, by default, Word 2010 saves documents in a new file format, ".docx," which is a form of Extensible Markup Language or XML. Microsoft chose that format in part to allow Word users to share documents with users of Open Office (another word processing program). Other reputed advantages of the .docx format are that it produces smaller files and supposedly is less prone to corruption than the standard file format used by earlier versions of MS Word (.doc).[1]

Unfortunately, the .docx format is not "backwards compatible" and won't open into any version of Word prior to Word 2007. That means you—and your clients and others with whom you share documents—won't be able to use Word 2003, Word 2002/XP, Word 2000, or Word 97 to open and read documents that were created in Word 2010 *unless you download and install a special converter*.

The converter (also referred to as a "Compatibility Pack") is available online from Microsoft free of charge. According to Microsoft, you should install all of the latest *Windows updates* (i.e., patches for your operating system) prior to installing and using the converter.

For more information and a link to the converter, see the Knowledge Base article, "How to use earlier versions of Excel, PowerPoint, and Word to open and save files from 2007 Office programs," available here:

http://support.microsoft.com/kb/924074

Note that you can configure Word 2010 to save all new documents in the old ".doc" file format. To do so, click the **File drop-down**, **Options**, **Save**, click the "**Save files in this format:**" **drop-down**, select **Word 97-2003 Document (.doc)** from the list, and **OK** out. That effectively changes the default file format for all future documents (although you still have the option of saving an individual document in a different file format *and* you'll still be able to read .docx files that other people send you).

As mentioned elsewhere in the book, when you use the .doc file format, you will not have access to certain of the program's new features, including Themes and Theme Fonts. And if you open a native Word 2010 file (.docx) in an earlier version of Word, some features will not work, or will work differently (many items that involve variables or placeholders in Word 2010, such as heading and body fonts and certain charts and diagrams, will become static text or images; text boxes that are positioned "relative to" an object and margins that change depending on which style is applied will take on an "absolute" position; text marked as "moved" in a document comparison will appear as an insertion or a deletion, since older versions did not have the ability to mark text as "moved").

---

[1] Or, at least, it reportedly does better at recovering and fixing corrupted files.

SIDEBAR: Third-Party Conversion Utilities

If you are migrating from WordPerfect to Word and you have a lot of files to convert, you might want to invest in a third-party conversion utility. There are a few available; I have limited first-hand knowledge of any of them, so I would suggest you do your due diligence before making a purchase decision. You might be able to obtain a trial version.

CrossWords

One of the best-known products is Levit & James's "CrossWords"; it has been around for more than a decade. You can request an online demo and/or an evaluation copy.

http://www.levitjames.com/crosswords/CrossWords.html

DocXchange

Another reputable third-party converter is "DocXchange" by Microsystems. There doesn't appear to be a link to a trial version, but you can contact the company via e-mail or phone (using information on their web site).

http://www.microsystems.com/products/docxchange.php

WordPerfect to Word Conversions

Word 2010 can "read" native WordPerfect files.[1] However, some features of WordPerfect won't translate perfectly into Word. In general, the more complex the formatting of the original document, the less successfully it will convert. Word just doesn't "get" all of WordPerfect's codes. And, of course, macros, QuickWords, and similar automated features won't convert at all.

Opening a WordPerfect File into Word With "File, Open" or "Insert, File"

When converting pleadings, you might find that Word knocks out the pleading paper lines and/or loses one or more of the line numbers. Word typically inserts section breaks where there are changes in page formatting (particularly where the pagination changes, but sometimes also before and after the pleading caption, which many WordPerfect users create with parallel columns rather than with tables). It also might lose a portion of a generated Table of Contents and/or Table of Authorities. However, in my (somewhat limited) tests, Word actually inserted TOA codes for many of the citations and was able to regenerate part of the TOA correctly.

In the past, consultants commonly advised people to use **Insert, File** (in the case of Word 2010, **Insert tab**, **Text group**, **Object drop-down**, **Text from File**, which I will refer to hereinafter as "**Insert, Object**") instead of **File, Open** (**File tab**, **Open** or **Ctrl O**) to pull a complex WordPerfect document into Word. When I tested opening two different WordPerfect pleadings into Word 2010, though, I found that the results were very similar and, if anything, File, Open actually produced slightly better results. (The operative word here is "slightly." It's something of a judgment call.) On the other hand, editing the documents opened with Insert, Object proved somewhat easier, and the results were reasonably good / acceptable.

Neither method produced ideally formatted documents. All of the converted docs had some of the same flaws:

The **pleading lines** on both the left and the right disappeared.

Word inserted **continuous section breaks** in numerous places where page formatting changed (as well as, mysteriously, in some places where page formatting *didn't* change).[2]

---

[1] Whether you use the File, Open method or the Insert, File (Insert, Object) method, you might find that only Word files are visible in the **Open dialog box**. In that case, navigate to the "**Files of Type**" field at the bottom of the dialog and, if necessary, change the drop-down to "**All Files**."

[2] The section breaks didn't cause any major problems, although they did make editing the footers more time-consuming. It's probably a good idea to delete any unnecessary section breaks, but be careful not to delete any **needed** section breaks (such as those required when you change the page number format from Arabic to small roman and vice versa).

The **horizontal line** at the bottom of the **case caption** in the WordPerfect pleadings appeared at the top of the caption in the Word docs.

On at least one page, the **left margin** was too narrow (the documents opened with File, Open used **mirror margins**—wide left margins on odd pages, wide right margins on even pages—and the documents opened with Insert, File had a narrow left margin on the first page, while the margins on the other pages were correct).[3]

Page numbers in the footers intruded slightly into the text area.

On the positive side:

The **caption** in both documents converted nicely from columns into a table.

The **alignment of the text with the line numbers** in both types of converted documents was fairly good, although in a few places I had to delete a single-spaced line and/or remove "before" and/or "after" paragraph spacing. Also, the footers came through the conversion relatively well; the font was slightly too small (9 points), however.

The **indentation** of the numbered paragraphs was fine in both types of documents.

Automatic paragraph numbering in the documents converted with File, Insert was fine; however, in the documents converted with Insert, Object turned into ListNum fields in Word, which unfortunately used the wrong list level (so that Arabic numerals turned into small roman numerals within a single end paren). (The easiest way to fix the numbering actually turned out to be to right-click within the number codes, click "Edit Field," and when the Field dialog appeared with ListNum selected, click "Outline" and make sure Level 3—corresponding to Arabic numerals in an Outline number style—was selected. I had to repeat this step several times to avoid applying numbering to unnumbered paragraphs.)

In both types of documents, the **pleading footers** came through reasonably well. They looked a bit funky because of the incorrect left margins, but the page numbers came in as codes and the horizontal line was intact. In some instances, the font size was acceptable (10 points or larger); other others, it was too small (9 points) to comport with the California Rules of Court.

In the documents opened with Insert, Object, the 28th line number was truncated. I had to go into the footer for each section of the document and drag the bottom margin of the shape (not

---

[3] The issue with **mirror margins** is one that I've observed with prior versions of Word, as well (i.e., when pleadings that originated in WordPerfect were opened into Word). To fix the problem in Word 2010 (or Word 2007): First, launch the **Page Setup dialog** (from the **Page Layout tab** or by pressing **Alt**, then **P, S, P**). CAUTION: Before proceeding, look at the very bottom of the dialog and make sure "**Apply to:**" is set to "**Whole document**." Next, locate the **Pages** section (about half-way down the Margins tab), change the **Multiple pages drop-down** from Mirror margins to **Normal**, and click **OK** to confirm your changes.

a text box!) down far enough to accommodate the number. This task was complicated by the large number of continuous section breaks that Word inserted during the conversion.

Cleaning up the converted documents took a fair amount of effort and time. In particular, I removed the extra section breaks; changed the "Mirror Margins" setting to "Normal" (via the Margins tab of the Page Setup dialog); adjusted the page margins where necessary (making sure to change the "Apply to:" drop-down so that the changes affected the whole document rather than the current section); and also adjusted the footer margin where necessary (i.e., the "**From edge**" setting in the "**Headers & Footers**" **section** of the **Layout tab** in the **Page Setup dialog**, and also available in the "**Header from Top**" and "**Footer from Bottom**" **options** in the **Position group** of the **Header & Footer Tools tab**).

To get the first line of text to align with the first pleading line number, I went into the Word Options (File, Options), Advanced, scrolled down and clicked Layout Options, checked "Don't center 'exact line height' lines," and then clicked "**OK**" to save my settings.

I didn't bother to insert the vertical lines, though I would have done so if I were working on documents that had to be filed with the courts.

In short, although the documents weren't pretty, they came across reasonably well. However, they required quite a bit of work to make them presentable. It might have made more sense simply to copy and paste the contents of the documents into a clean Word pleading (as discussed on page 549).

Ultimately, only you can decide which option is preferable, but the results of my tests should give you a sense of what you can expect if you open WordPerfect pleadings directly into Word.

Saving the WordPerfect File in Word Format, Then Opening into Word

The most recent version of WordPerfect (WP X5) allows you to save documents in Word 2007 format, i.e., as .docx files (by clicking File, "Save As," then choosing "MS Word 2007" from the "File type" drop-down).

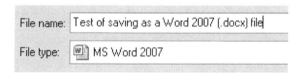

Several recent versions of WordPerfect, including WP X3, WP X4, and WP X5, also give you the option of saving documents in "MS Word 97/2000/ 2002/2003 for Windows" format, i.e., as .doc files.

You might consider asking people who send you WordPerfect files to save a copy as a Word document—either type—and then, when you receive the .docx or .doc files, try opening them directly into Word. In my (limited) tests, a couple of WordPerfect pleadings saved as

Word documents came through reasonably well. The caption looked fine, and the docs retained and the automatic paragraph numbering. However, there were a few glitches:

- the pleading lines disappeared;

- the text of the footer and the automatic page number came through, but the horizontal line disappeared;

- the header and footer margins were too big, and the footer intruded into the document text area;

- paragraphs with automatic numbering didn't have a first-line indent; and

- for some reason, Word applied a different header and footer for odd and even pages.

It was relatively easy to fix those items.

To add the pleading lines, I simply went into the header editing screen in a Word pleading (i.e., one that originated in Word), copied the first paragraph symbol in the header editing screen (which contains the formatting codes for the pleading lines), and pasted it into the header editing screen in the WP-to-Word doc. I had to paste the paragraph symbol into the header in the second section of the document, as well. (For a discussion about using this technique to reinsert disappearing pleading lines, see page 276.) Note that if you created your own pleading paper per the instructions in the section starting on page 419, you might have to copy and paste the first *two* paragraph symbols from pleading that originated in Word into the converted pleading.

The body of the document used regular Double line spacing; single-spaced portions used regular Single spacing. I had to select the double-spaced portions, open the Paragraph dialog, and change the drop-down to Exactly 24 points (to match the line spacing of the pleading line numbers in the header); for the single-spaced portions I changed to Exactly 12 points. You might have to use a fraction such as 22.75 points for double-spaced portions and 11.375 points for single-spaced portions. As you know by now, the measurement you use for double-spacing depends on (and should match) the line spacing of the pleading line numbers in the heading; single-spacing should be exactly half of that figure.

In both docs, I also had to go into the Compatibility Options (**File tab**, **Options**, **Advanced**, scroll all the way down to the bottom and click to expand the "**Layout Options**") and check "**Don't center 'exact line height lines'**" in order to move the first line of text on the second page down so that it aligned with the first line number. (For more about the ways in which the "Don't Center 'Exact Line Height' Lines" option can be helpful, see page 431.) If you make any changes to the Compatibility Options, remember to click "**OK**" to save your changes when you exit from the Word Options.

I had to reinsert the horizontal line in the footer, which took very little time.

I changed the header and footer "from edge" margins (i.e., I made both margins smaller), as well as the top and bottom page margins. It took some tweaking to get these settings just right.

On one page, the first line of text appeared below the first line of text on all the other pages (and below the first line number), even though I had taken care to apply the margin settings to the whole document. When I clicked in the first line text on the problematic page, then opened the Paragraph dialog, I discovered that the line spacing was set to "**At least** 24 points" rather than "**Exactly** 24 points." When I changed it to "Exactly 24 points" and OK'd out of the dialog, the text went back to the "correct" position at the top of the page, aligned perfectly with the first line number.

I unchecked the "Different Odd & Even Pages" option in the Header & Footer Tools tab.

Again, it wasn't a perfect conversion and it required some cleanup, but it wasn't overly burdensome or time-consuming. Knowing the trick about copying the paragraph symbol from the header of a good pleading and the trick about "Don't center 'exact line height lines'" helped.

Other Options

Sometimes WordPerfect documents just don't convert well. In those cases, the best solution might be to **copy the text** from the WordPerfect file and insert it into a blank Word document via **Paste Special**, **Unformatted Text** (also called "**Keep Text Only**" in this version of Word). Of course, that option transfers the text only, without any formatting. So you will need to go through the document and apply formatting line by line. It's a slow process, but depending on the circumstances—and, in particular, on the length and complexity of the document—you might find it preferable to struggling with the uncooperative codes that can result from a conversion. It gives you more control over the document formatting, and it also helps to prevent document corruption because it results in a "cleaner" document.

Another possibility is to save the WordPerfect file as RTF (Rich Text Format), an "intermediate" format invented by Microsoft that both Word and WordPerfect can read, and then open the file into Word. That didn't work very well with my WordPerfect pleading; when I opened the RTF into Word, the line numbering started with 2; the two vertical lines on the left turned into a fat single line and the single vertical line on the right disappeared; the formatting of the caption and the footer went haywire; and there was an Error! code in the header.

On the positive side, the automatic paragraph numbers appeared correctly (as Arabic numerals), with the exception of the fact that both the first and the second paragraph were numbered "1." That error was easy to change (by right-clicking the second "1." and then clicking the "Continue numbering" command.

However, the problems with the line numbering turned out to be much trickier than I had anticipated, and I gave up after a few minutes.

Despite the difficulties I experienced, saving a WordPerfect file as RTF and then opening the RTF file into Word might be a good choice in certain circumstances. It's something to keep in mind when you need to convert files. (You might want to make a copy of the document before experimenting, even though you're not likely to overwrite the original file when you save it as an RTF. [4])

---

[4] When you save a file in RTF format, it takes on the file extension .rtf, leaving the original file intact.

Word to WordPerfect Conversions

The first version of WordPerfect that is able to convert native Word 2010 files (i.e., .docx files or other Open Office XML file types) directly is WordPerfect X4 (14). If you use WordPerfect X4 or a later version, you should be able to open .docx files without difficulty either via File, Open or Insert, File.

If you have an earlier version of WordPerfect, you will have to do one of the following:

1. Save your Word file **as a .doc (a Word 97-2003 file)** and then open it into WordPerfect via File, Open or Insert, File; *or*

2. Save your Word document **in RTF format** (which preserves much of the formatting) or **as plain text (.txt)** (which will strip out all the formatting), and then open the converted file into WordPerfect; *or*

3. **Copy and paste** text from the Word document into WordPerfect, which will wipe out most or all of the formatting.

    CAUTION: You might get an error message if you try to paste text from Word 2010 into a legacy version of WordPerfect. If so, use the **Paste Special** command (found on the **Edit menu** in WordPerfect) and then paste the text either as **Unformatted Text** or, if it possible, as **Rich Text Format**. I say "if possible" because that option, despite being available in the Paste Special dialog, doesn't work in some older versions of WordPerfect, and you'll get an error message if you attempt to use it. (I had no difficulty pasting into WordPerfect X3, whether using the normal Paste command or using Paste Special, Unformatted Text.)

NOTE: Unlike Word 2007, Word 2010 does not list any version of WordPerfect in the "Save as Type" box. As a result, *you cannot save Word documents—whether .doc format or .docx format—in WordPerfect format*.

Typically, Word files (.docs) that are opened directly into WordPerfect bring a lot of extraneous codes with them, including First Ln Ind (First Line Indent) codes and Lft Mar Adj (Left Margin Adjustment) codes. If the profusion of codes is problematic, you can clean up the document with WordPerfect's **Find and Replace** feature, using either **Match Codes...** or **Type, Specific Codes...**, and replace each instance of a particular code with **<Nothing>** (the "**Replace All**" option makes relatively short work of this process). Note that you might have to run through the document more than once.

As with WordPerfect-to-Word conversions, the translation often leaves something to be desired. Still, in some situations it might be preferable to the tedious alternative of copying and pasting unformatted text and then reapplying formatting to the document line by line.

551

Avoid Round-Tripping Your Documents

One of the most important bits of advice consultants commonly offer to people who work in both Word and WordPerfect is not to "round-trip" documents between the two formats. In other words, avoid bringing a WordPerfect file into Word, saving it as a Word doc, and then pulling it back into WordPerfect. Doing so is a well-known—and a leading—cause of file corruption. A one-way conversion isn't particularly risky, but going back and forth is just asking for trouble.

Coping With Metadata

How Metadata Gets Embedded in Your Documents
and What You Can Do to Get Rid of It

Metadata: Definition and Origins

Metadata refers in part to information embedded automatically in a document by software,[1] as well as document properties and other information that can be inserted deliberately by a human author.

This information, much or all of which is "hidden" under normal circumstances—such that the person writing the document might not realize it exists—can include the identity of the author(s) and any reviewer(s), the company where the document author works, the software used to create the document, the computer and the exact path where the document is stored, the date and time the document was created and/or modified, the title of the document and any keywords or summary used to identify it, the amount of time spent on editing the document, the template on which it was based, and so on. If a document was routed by e-mail to other people in your firm, detailed routing information could be hidden in the document.

In addition, and of greater concern to many lawyers, revisions—insertions, deletions, and comments—can be stored in a document. Even if you are not seeing such "markup" on your screen, it may be possible for others to change configuration settings so that they can view that markup unless you take definite steps to remove material that has been superseded by later edits.

According to Microsoft:

"...hidden text, revised text, comments, or field codes can remain in a document even though you don't see such information or expect it to be in the final version. If you entered personal information, such as your name or e-mail address, when you registered your software, some Microsoft Office documents store that information as part of the document. Information contained in custom fields that you add to the document, such as an 'author' or 'owner' field, is not automatically removed. You must edit or remove the custom field to remove that information."

From "Remove personal or hidden information,"
http://office.microsoft.com/en-us/word/HP051901021033.aspx

Word 2010's Native Metadata Removal Tool: The Document Inspector

Word 2010 comes with a metadata removal tool called the Document Inspector. When you use this tool, it combs through the document, looking for comments, revisions, annotation, document properties, personal and company information, data in headers and footers (as well as watermarks), and hidden text. You can have the Inspector remove any or all of the items it finds.

---

[1] Some of this information is added/tracked by the operating system, as well as by the particular application used to create the document.

Before running the Document Inspector, ***make a copy of your document***. It's a good idea to create a backup (and possibly even search for and strip metadata from the copy) because once certain items are eliminated from the document, it can be difficult if not impossible to restore them without going through the laborious process of re-creating them manually.   In other words, some metadata removal can't be "undone." That can be problematic, especially because:

(1)   you can't see exactly which information the Document Inspector has identified before choosing to remove it;

(2)   you don't have an opportunity to pick and choose which items in any given category to remove (it's an all-or-nothing proposition); and

(3)   in an attempt to be meticulous, Word sometimes gets rid of innocuous information, such as entire headers and footers.

So try to get in the habit of copying your document prior to using the Document Inspector.

When you are ready to test the feature, click the **File tab**, **Info fly-out**, **Check for Issues button**, **Inspect Document**. You will see a dialog similar to the one below. It consists of checkboxes for various types of document content the Document Inspector can examine for metadata: Comments, Revisions, Versions, and Annotations; Document Properties and Personal Information; Custom XML Data; Headers, Footers and Watermarks; and Hidden Text.[2]

_____

[2] "Hidden Text" means text to which the "Hidden" property has been applied through the Font dialog. Note that the Document Inspector will ***not*** identify and remove text to which the color white has been applied (to make it invisible on a white background) or text that has been sized so small that it is not visible at normal screen magnifications.

All of the boxes are checked by default, but you can uncheck any types of content that you don't want the Inspector to review.

After you click "Inspect," the Inspector will go through the document, searching for various types of metadata. If it finds any, it will alert you with an exclamation point next to the type of content it located. See, for example, the next screenshot.

As mentioned above, the mere fact that the Document Inspector has found some "metadata" doesn't necessarily clue you in to what, exactly, that information includes. (In the screenshot, we see that Word found Revision marks, Comments, Document Properties including the Author name, and Custom XML Data, but we don't know the specifics.)

If you click the "**Remove All**" button next to a category of data, the Inspector will remove everything in that category. You can take an incremental approach and "Remove All" items in one category and then check the document, or you can click each of the "Remove All" buttons to scrub the suspect items in all of the categories tagged by the inspection utility.

Note that you can click the "**Reinspect**" button to have the Inspector go through the document again.

After you click "Remove All," the Inspector does its thing and then shows you the results, which might look something like the following (depending on whether you clicked "Remove All" for each category of metadata):

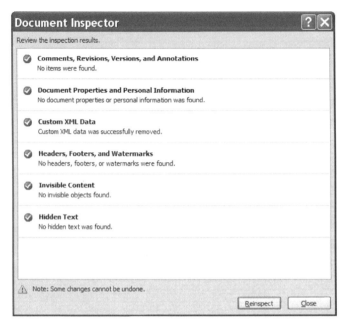

Document Inspector After Removal of All "Suspect" Items

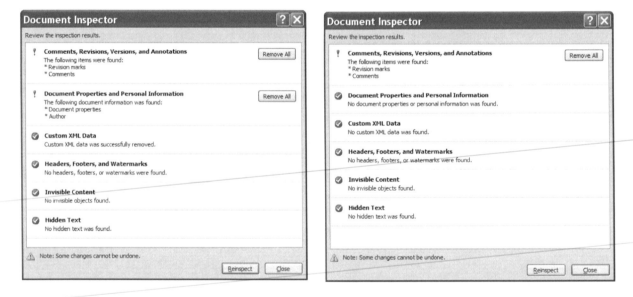

After Removal of Custom XML Data Only

After Removal of Custom XML Data and Document Properties / Personal Information

As you can see, the results appear to indicate that the items in question "were successfully removed" from the document.

In a test of a different document, when I went into the **Backstage View (Info fly-out menu)** and looked at the **Document Properties**, I saw that the Document Inspector removed my name from both the "Author" and "Last modified by" fields (leaving the fields empty); changed the total editing time from 45 minutes to 0 (zero) minutes; indicated the document hadn't been saved yet; changed the "Created" date from a date in 2009 to today's date; and changed the "Last printed" date from a date earlier this year to "Never."

CAUTION: Even after you use the Document Inspector, the document location (i.e., its path in the computer), as well as the document type, still appears when you click Advanced Document Properties and open the traditional Properties dialog.[3]

If you run the Document Inspector and are happy with the results, be sure to *SAVE the inspected document*. **ANOTHER CAUTION**: This is a critical step because if you close without saving, the metadata you thought had been removed will remain in the document!

Some Items That the Document Inspector Might Not Remove

Besides the above-mentioned items, there are other types of information or objects that can be embedded in your documents and potentially can be viewed by others. These additional items, which the Document Inspector might not flag or remove, include:

- Bookmarks
- Creation date
- Document variables
- Field codes
- Hyperlinks
- Linked objects
- Modified date
- OLE graphics
- Print date
- Smart Tags
- Text that is hidden by applying a very small font size (so that it is invisible, or nearly so, at a normal screen magnification)
- Text that is hidden by coloring it white (so that it is invisible on a white background)
- Unlink document property fields
- Unused styles
- Visual Basic for Applications (VBA)

Some of these items might not be problematic, but it's worth investigating further before deciding whether to rely exclusively on the Document Inspector or to invest in a third-party program.

---

[3] In one of my tests, the Document Inspector removed information from Advanced Properties, Statistics, as follows: it stripped out my name under "Last saved by"; changed the revision number from 11 to 1; and changed the total editing time to 0 (zero).

Third-Party Metadata Removal Programs

Because the Document Inspector doesn't eliminate all types of metadata from Word documents, you might want to consider purchasing a third-party metadata removal program and using it in conjunction with (or instead of) Word's built-in utility. There are several such programs available. I don't have enough personal experience with any of them to enable me to make a recommendation, but you can request evaluation copies (usually good for 30 days). That might be a good way to compare the various utilities.

Do ask about any possible incompatibilities with other software you have and make sure you can uninstall the trial versions easily. Also, you might want to install the trial versions on different computers, just in case they are incompatible with one another (and also to make it easier to differentiate among them).

There are a few articles on the web that discuss metadata in MS Office and the third-party metadata management utilities. See, for example:

Beverly Michaelis, J.D., "What You Don't Know Can Hurt You"
(Practical Paralegalism, March 24, 2010; also posted on eDiscovery Journal, March 24, 2010)
http://www.practicalparalegalism.com/2010/03/metadata-101-what-you-dont-know-can.html *or*
http://ediscoveryjournal.com/2010/03/metadata-101-what-you-don%E2%80%99t-know-can-hurt-you/

H. Craig Hall, Jr., "Dealing with Metadata in the Non-Discovery Context"
(Utah State Bar Journal, March 31, 2008)
http://webster.utahbar.org/barjournal/2008/03/dealing_with_metadata_in_the_n.html

"The Meta Monster: Hidden data in e-documents trips up GCs"
(Inside Counsel, July 2006)
http://www.insidecounsel.com/Issues/2006/July%202006/Pages/The-Meta-Monster.aspx?page=3

Links to Metadata Removal Product Web Sites

I've listed a few of the better-known programs below—in *alphabetical* order. Most of them remove metadata in Microsoft Office 2007 documents and other types of files (including PDF), but you should double-check to make sure they also work with Word 2010. **NOTE**: This list is not, and should not be construed as, an endorsement of any of the products.

iScrub (by Esquire Innovations)
www.esqinc.com

For more information, see this page on the company's web site:
http://esqinc.com/section/products/2/iscrub.html

To request an online demo or a 30-day evaluation copy, visit this page:
http://esqinc.com/section/howtobuy/product/2.html

MetaDact (by Litera, formerly known as Softwise)
www.litera.com (www.softwise.com redirects to the Litera site)

See also: http://www.litera.com/products/metadact.html

     Previously called Out-of-Sight. You can request a 30-day evaluation copy or an online demonstration of MetaDact from this page: http://change-pro.com/Demonstration.aspx

Metadata Assistant (by Payne Consulting):
www.payneconsulting.com

     Offers both a "retail" version and an "enterprise" version. The Payne Consulting site indicates that the Metadata Assistant "has been completely redesigned for Office 2007 and above" and integrates with "Microsoft Word, Excel and PowerPoint 2007 and above."

For more information about the retail version (single user license), see this page:
http://www.payneconsulting.com/products/metadataretail3/

For more information about the enterprise version (20 or more workstation licenses), see this page:
http://www.payneconsulting.com/products/metadataent3/

MetaReveal (by BEC Legal)
 www.beclegal.com/products.aspx?id=64

     Like the other companies, BEC Legal allows you to test-drive its product for 30 days and/or to request a demo.

Workshare Protect (by Workshare Technology):
www.workshare.com

     You can download a 30-day trial version from Workshare's site and/or request a demonstration. For more information, see this page:
http://www.workshare.com/solutions/featured/metadata-management.aspx

Resources

Tools to Ease the Migration to Office 2010

There are quite a few resources available to help people become comfortable with the new interface and other changes in Word 2010 and the Office 2010 programs. For one thing, Microsoft has created a number of reference guides, interactive tutorials, videos, help screens, and other educational materials. For another, you can take online classes via Lynda.com (a pay service, but one that is reasonably inexpensive) or via Hewlett-Packard's Learning Center (which is free but requires registration and enrollment). In addition, some third-party vendors offer utilities that emulate the familiar toolbars and menus from pre-Word 2007 versions of the program.

This section lists a few resources that you might find useful. Also, be sure to check out the web sites mentioned in the next section.

Online Classes

Lynda.com
www.lynda.com

> A pay site. Subscriptions start at $25.00 per month. However, you can watch a free introductory video for any course you're interested in to decide if you'd like to take the class.

HP Learning Center
www.hp.com/go/learningcenter

> This site offers many free classes; you do have to register with the site and enroll in individual classes. As of mid-May, 2010, as we are about to go to press, there are no Office 2010 courses listed on the site (although there are plenty of Office 2007 classes available), but presumably that will change before long.

Introductory Materials From Microsoft

Getting Started With Word 2010:
http://office2010.microsoft.com/en-us/word-help/getting-started-with-word-2010-HA010370239.aspx

Or use this "**tiny URL**": http://tinyurl.com/W2010Start

> An introductory site where people who have never used any version of Word, as well as people who have used a prior version, can click a link to find out what's new, how to use the Ribbon (and find out where familiar commands have gone), and how to perform basic tasks.

What's New in Word 2010
http://office2010.microsoft.com/en-us/word-help/what-s-new-in-word-2010-
HA010372687.aspx?CTT=5&origin=HA010370239

or use this "**tiny URL**":   http://tinyurl.com/NewW2010

> An overview of the new features in Word 2010. Just skims the surface, but
> includes links to more in-depth articles.

Product Guides

www.microsoft.com/downloads/details.aspx?displaylang=en&FamilyID=e690baf0-9b9a-4c47-
88da-3a84f3e9b247

Or use this "**tiny URL**":   http://tinyurl.com/Ofc2010Guides

> Microsoft has made available for download (for free) PDF versions of Product
> Guides for Office 2010 and for the individual Office 2010 programs: Word,
> Excel, PowerPoint, Access, Publisher, Outlook, OneNote, InfoPath, Office Web
> Apps, Office Mobile, and SharePoint WorkSpace.

Classic Menu Utilities and Ribbon Customizers

> Several companies offer "classic menu" utilities and/or Ribbon customizers that
> you can install if you want to emulate the pre-Word 2007 menus rather than (or as
> a supplement to) the new graphical user interface (GUI) with the Ribbon, the tabs,
> and the Quick Access Toolbar. For more information, see the sidebar on
> page 214.

Location of Commands in the Ribbon

> Microsoft has made available a few handy tools intended to help people locate commands
in the Ribbon.

Interactive Guides: Learn Where Menu and Toolbar Commands Are
http://office2010.microsoft.com/en-us/word-help/learn-where-menu-and-toolbar-commands-are-
in-office-2010-HA101794130.aspx?CTT=5&origin=HA010370239

Or use either of these "**tiny URLs**":
http://tinyurl.com/W2010WhereCommandsAre   *or*
http://tinyurl.com/W2010Interact

> As described in the section starting on page 61, Microsoft has also published
> **interactive guides** called "**Learn Where Menu and Toolbar Commands Are**."
> NOTE: For the guides to function properly (i.e., to be interactive), you must use
> a browser that is capable of working with Flash Player.

Word 2010: Menu to Ribbon Reference Workbook
http://office2010.microsoft.com/en-us/templates/CL101817133.aspx?CTT=5&origin=HA101794130

Or use any of these "**tiny URLs**":

http://tinyurl.com/W2010MtoR *or*
http://tinyurl.com/Ofc2010MtoR *or*
http://tinyurl.com/W2010Menu2Ribbon

> The "**Word 2010: Menu to ribbon reference workbook**" is an extensive, multi-page Excel spreadsheet that shows where menu commands in Word 2003 were moved in the Word 2010 Ribbon. A free download from Microsoft. The web site also offers similar workbooks for other Office 2010 programs, including Excel, PowerPoint, Outlook, and Publisher.

"Acquaint Yourself With the Ribbon"
http://office2010.microsoft.com/en-us/word-help/acquaint-yourself-with-the-ribbon-RZ101816356.aspx?lc=en-us&section=2

Or use this "**tiny URL**": http://tinyurl.com/AcqRibbon

> Microsoft also has put together a six-part video tutorial starting with a lesson called "**Acquaint Yourself With the Ribbon**." After viewing the videos, you can practice and, if you like, test yourself on what you've learned. Each lesson is relatively short (about 3 to 4 minutes).

Word 2010 Quick Reference Card
http://office2010.microsoft.com/en-us/word-help/quick-reference-card-RZ101816356.aspx?lc=en-us&section=11

Or use this "**tiny URL**": http://tinyurl.com/W2010QuickRef

> The Word 2010 Quick Reference card is a traditional help screen rather than an interactive tutorial. It provides some basic tips about working with the new interface and the new file formats in Word 2010.

SIDEBAR: Resources for IT People

I'm not an IT person, but in the course of my research for this book I have encountered a few terrific resources geared toward IT departments. This short list should get you off to a good start.

TechNet

Microsoft's TechNet site is a treasure trove of information for IT people. There are scads of useful resources for planning an upgrade to Office 2010, as well as for troubleshooting. The items listed below look particularly helpful.

Office Migration Planning Manager (OMPM)
http://technet.microsoft.com/en-us/library/ff453909.aspx

http://technet.microsoft.com/en-us/library/cc179179.aspx

OMPM is a file scanner, logging, and reporting tool to assist in analyzing an organization's computer setup and finding potential issues that might arise when converting from an earlier version of Microsoft Office to Office 2010.

Office 2010 Resource Kit
http://technet.microsoft.com/en-us/library/cc303401.aspx

Includes copious materials that cover assessing the compatibility of Office 2010 with an existing setup; planning the deployment; configuring and deploying the suite (installation, licensing, customizations, etc.); maintaining and updating the software; security and protection; troubleshooting; and a technical reference.

Microsoft

Hardware and Software Vendor Contact Information
http://support.microsoft.com/gp/vendors/en-us

List, in alphabetical order, of companies whose products integrate with Microsoft Office, with their contact information. This list can be very useful (for users as well as IT people!) because sometimes you can obtain patches or other updates from a vendor that will resolve a conflict with one or more of the MS Office programs. Last updated July 2009.

Selected MS Word Resources on the Internet

The following are a few selected Word 2010 (or general MS Word) resources that you might find helpful. Please let me know if any of the links don't work or turn out to be obsolete.

Microsoft's Knowledge Base (MS Word, Excel, Access, Windows XP, etc.):
http://support.microsoft.com/support/search

> On-line technical support for all Microsoft products. You can run searches (queries) using natural language or key words. (Note, for example, that searching for the word "pleading" returns several articles dealing with problems related to pleading paper.)

Microsoft Office 2010 (an official Microsoft site)
http://office2010.microsoft.com/en-us/office-FX101785584.aspx

> This site, run by Microsoft, is a central place for information about Office 2010, including free training materials. The materials include free tutorials from Lynda.com and free videos from BrainStorm. (As of this writing, only a few videos are available at the BrainStorm web site, but that probably will change, since Office 2010 is such a new product—in fact, it hasn't been released to the public just yet.)

> See also the additional pages from this site, listed below, for free Office 2010 training from Microsoft. Like the BrainStorm videos, the Microsoft training materials are sparse at the moment, but there should be a full complement of tutorials available over the next few months.

Getting Started With Office 2010 (part of the official Microsoft site)
http://office2010.microsoft.com/en-us/support/getting-started-with-office-2010-FX101822272.aspx

Free Office 2010 Training (part of the official Microsoft site)
http://office2010.microsoft.com/en-us/support/training-FX101782702.aspx

Word 2010 Training Courses (part of the official Microsoft site)
http://office2010.microsoft.com/en-us/word-help/CH010369478.aspx

> Self-paced tutorials walk you through the process of creating a Word 2010 document (changing the page margins, running the spell-checker, and adding formatting); using the new Navigation Pane feature; learning about the security-related features built into the program; and more. Microsoft suggests that most tutorials will take from 20 minutes to 45 minutes to complete. Some include tests at the end so that you can gauge your comprehension.

Note that you should click the "Show all categories" link at the left to see, and use, additional training materials (including traditional Help files). It's unfortunate that Microsoft doesn't display those links by default, since many users won't realize that there is much more information available than is apparent at first glance.

BrainStorm
http://cbt.brainstorminc.com/office2010/index.html

BrainStorm's computer-based training web site. A few of the Office 2010 tutorials are free; it appears that you have to register with the site and pay for some of the other available tutorials.

Microsoft Interactive Word 2010 Command Reference Guide
http://office2010.microsoft.com/en-us/word-help/learn-where-menu-and-toolbar-commands-are-in-office-2010-HA101794130.aspx?CTT=5&origin=HA010370239#

This tutorial is interactive in that you can point to a Word 2003 menu command to find out where the same command is in Word 2010. Clicking the command launches an animation that shows you the location of the command in the newer version.

Keyboard Shortcuts for Microsoft Office Word
http://office.microsoft.com/en-us/word/HP101476261033.aspx

Lengthy list of keyboard shortcuts for Word 2007, categorized by function. Most of these keyboard shortcuts also work in Word 2010. Be sure to click the "Show All" button toward the top right side of the article (Microsoft has a tendency to hide, or collapse, portions of its articles until / unless you take steps to expand them).

List of Keyboard Shortcuts for Word 2002, 2003, and 2007
http://support.microsoft.com/kb/290938

These shortcuts work with the U.S. keyboard layout, but not necessarily with keyboard layouts for other countries/languages. As far as I can tell, the article has not been updated yet to include Word 2010.

Word Viewer
http://www.microsoft.com/downloads/details.aspx?FamilyID=3657ce88-7cfa-457a-9aec-f4f827f20cac&displaylang=en

Downloadable Word Viewer available from Microsoft allows people who don't have Word to view Word files (including .docx format).

Microsoft Word MVP FAQ Site
http://word.mvps.org/FAQs/index.htm

> **Very** helpful site. Lots of tips and workarounds, as well as explanations of how Word works. (Note that if you type "html" instead of "htm," you'll get a "404 Not Found" error.) The site was redesigned a couple of years ago and isn't as user-friendly as it once was, unfortunately, and it needs updating, but it's still an excellent source of information.

Links to Web Sites of Various Word "MVPs":
http://www.mvps.org/links.html

> Scroll down almost to the bottom for links to web sites run by Word gurus.

Word FAQs site (by Suzanne Barnhill, Word MVP):
http://sbarnhill.mvps.org/WordFAQs/

> Barnhill is one of the best MVPs (and that's saying a lot). Her explanations tend to be unusually clear and readable.

Making the Most of Word (by Shauna Kelly, Word MVP):
http://www.shaunakelly.com/word/index.html

> Lots of terrific tips here. Kelly's instructions for using automatic numbering are especially useful, though she hasn't updated them yet for Word 2007/Word 2010.

Windows Secrets (formerly Woody's Office Portal)
http://lounge.windowssecrets.com/ or www.wopr.com

> Very helpful site started by Microsoft guru/gadfly Woody Leonhard. Offers hints and tips, downloads, bug alerts, a bulletin board, shareware/freeware, and links. The Word Processing section of the Lounge is a great place for posting questions about MS Word.

Woody's Office Watch:
http://office-watch.com

> Another of Woody Leonhard's MS Office sites, with assorted articles and tips.

An Expert's Guide to Word 2007 Numbering
http://www.beclegal.com/hot_topics.aspx?id=2994

> A white paper available as a downloadable PDF. From BEC Legal Systems (www.beclegal.com). Extremely thorough and helpful explanation of how multilevel lists work in Word 2007—and how to avoid possible glitches. Although the piece deals with Word 2007, the information applies to Word 2010, as well.

CompuSavvy's Word & WordPerfect Tips (blog)
http://compusavvy.wordpress.com

> My blog offering article-length tips, mostly about Word and WordPerfect. I try to add new posts at least once a week, sometimes in response to search terms people have used to try to find answers to their software questions. I also make an effort to write new material on a regular basis, rather than cribbing from existing handouts.

Hardware and Software Vendor Contact Information
http://support.microsoft.com/gp/vendors/en-us

> List, in alphabetical order, of companies whose products integrate with Microsoft Office, with their contact information. This list can be very useful because sometimes you can obtain patches or other updates from a vendor that will resolve a conflict with one or more of the MS Office programs. Last updated July 2009.

How to Import WordPerfect [for DOS] Files into Microsoft Word:
http://www.columbia.edu/~em36/wpdos/wptoword.html#2003word

> From Edward Mendelson's wonderful web site about WordPerfect *for DOS*. This particular page provides instructions for converting WordPerfect for DOS files to Word.

HotDocs Knowledge Base:
http://help.lexisnexis.com/tabula-rasa/hdknowledgebase/ home?lbu=US&locale =en_US&audience=all

> For help with issues having to do with the interaction between Word and the document assembly program HotDocs.

Where Important Word 2010 Files Are Stored

It can be helpful to know where key files—such as the NORMAL template and the template where Building Blocks / QuickParts (formerly called AutoText)—are stored in the computer. Because some of these files contain your customizations, you might want to create backup copies from time to time (and perhaps save them to a CD, a USB drive, an external hard drive, or a different computer). That way, if something happens to your computer and one of the files is damaged or is inaccessible, you don't have to re-create all of your customizations from scratch.

What follows is a list of some of the most important files and their typical locations.

NORMAL Template (Normal.dotm)

The NORMAL template (normal.dotm) is the basis for all new documents in Word. Each user has one. Many customizations are stored in the user's NORMAL template, including his or her default Normal Paragraph style, other styles he or she has created or modified, AutoCorrect entries, and macros (but *not* the user's personalized Quick Access Toolbar or Quick Parts / Building Blocks, which are located in separate files).

Ordinarily you will find the NORMAL template in the following locations:

In Windows XP:
C:\Documents and Settings\<User Name>\Application Data\Microsoft\Templates

In Windows Vista and Windows 7:
C:\Users\<UserName>\AppData\Roaming\Microsoft\Templates

Custom Templates

Each user's customized templates typically are stored in the same place as the NORMAL template:

In Windows XP:
C:\Documents and Settings\<User Name>\Application Data\Microsoft\Templates

In Windows Vista and Windows 7:
C:\Users\<UserName>\AppData\Roaming\Microsoft\Templates

Building Blocks

Word 2010 comes with two different Building Blocks templates. One contains items pre-formatted by Microsoft—various cover pages, footers, headers, page numbers, tables, text boxes, watermarks, and the like—and should not be edited directly; the other is a working copy that contains the custom Quick Parts / Building Blocks you create.

The template containing the pre-formatted content, called **Built-In Building Blocks.dotx** in this version of Word (unlike in Word 2007, where it had the same name as the user-customizable template), is stored in this location in Windows XP, Vista, and Windows 7:
C:\Program Files\Microsoft Office\Office14\Document Parts\1033\14

The user-specific copy, called **BuildingBlocks.dotx**, is located here in Windows XP:
C:\Documents and Settings\<User Name>\Application Data\Microsoft\Document Building Blocks\1033\14

The user copy is located here in Windows Vista and Windows 7:
C:\Users\<UserName>\AppData\Roaming\Microsoft\Document Building Blocks\1033\14

If something happens and the user-customized file becomes corrupted, Word creates a new customizable file based on the original template. (You likely will lose your Quick Parts if that happens, which is why it makes sense to make a copy of the customized file every so often.)

List styles gallery

The **ListGal.dat** file contains the user's customized gallery of numbered lists (i.e., it includes the lists that came with the program as well as any list styles you've created).

In Windows XP:
C:Documents and Settings\<User Name>\Application Data\Microsoft \Word

In Windows Vista and Windows 7:
C:\Users\User Name\AppData\Roaming\Microsoft\Word

Heading styles

Heading styles ordinarily are stored either in the NORMAL template (**normal.dotm**) or in the *document* in which they were created, although you can copy styles to (or create them in) your own custom templates. In fact, most built-in styles typically are saved in normal.dotm.

Note that whenever you create a new style or modify a built-in style, the default setting in the Modify Style dialog is to store the style *in the current document*. (WordPerfect works the same way). The only other choice available in the dialog box is to save to the NORMAL template, but you can use the Organizer to copy styles to other templates. (And you can copy styles between documents; see page 352 above.)

Quick Styles / Style Sets

Quick Styles and Style Sets are located in the following places:

Built-in Quick Styles and Style Sets are found here (in all three recent versions of Windows):
C:\Program Files\Microsoft Office\Office14\1033\QuickStyles

In Windows XP, user-customized Quick Styles and Style Sets are located here:
C:Documents and Settings\<User Name>\Application Data\Microsoft\QuickStyles

In Windows Vista and Windows 7, user-customized Quick Styles and Style sets are stored here:
C:\ Users\<User Name>\AppData\Roaming\Microsoft\Quickstyles

Themes

Theme files have the extension **.thmx**.

Built-in themes are located here in Windows XP, Windows Vista, and Windows 7:
C:\Program Files\Microsoft Office\Document Themes 14

Custom themes (i.e., themes that you create) are located here in Windows XP:
C:\Documents and Settings\<User Name>\Application Data\Microsoft\Templates\ Document Themes

Custom themes are located here in Windows Vista and Windows 7:
C:\Users\<User Name>\AppData\Roaming\Microsoft\Templates\Document Themes

AutoRecover Files

Temporary files that Word automatically recovers in the event of a "crash" or other serious problem have the extension .asd. Normally you don't have to look for them because Word opens them in a separate pane at the left side of the screen after a power outage or similar event. They can be found here:

In Windows XP:
C:\Documents and Settings\<User Name>\Application Data\Microsoft\Word

In Vista and Windows 7:
C:\Users\<User Name>\AppData\Roaming\Microsoft\Word

"Unsaved Documents" Temporary Backup Files ("Never-Saved Documents")

Note that actually there are two types of "Unsaved Documents"—what I have termed the "Never-Saved Documents" and the "Previously-Saved Documents—and the two types are saved in different locations.

In Windows XP, the "Never-Saved Documents" are located here:
C:\Documents and Settings\<User Name>\Local Settings\Application Data\Microsoft\ OFFICE\UnsavedFiles

In Windows Vista and Windows 7, you can find them here:
C:\Users\<UserName>\AppData\Local\Microsoft\Office\UnsavedFiles

"Unsaved Documents" Temporary Backup Files ("Previously-Saved Documents")

In Windows XP, the Previously-Saved Documents are stored here:
C:\Documents and Settings\<User Name> \Application Data\Microsoft\Word

In Windows Vista and Windows 7, they are stored here:
C:\Users\<User Name>\AppData\Roaming\Microsoft\Word

QAT (Quick Access Toolbar)

The QAT file, called Word.qat, is stored in the following locations:

In Windows XP:
C:\Documents and Settings\<User Name>\Local Settings\Application Data\Microsoft\ OFFICE\Word.qat

In Windows Vista and Windows 7:
C:\Users\<UserName>\AppData\Local\Microsoft\Office\Word.qat

Note that you can create a customized QAT for a particular document.[1] The settings for a document-specific QAT are stored in that document.

AutoCorrect Files

Unformatted AutoCorrect entries (i.e., those that consist of plain text—as opposed to, say, bolded text or text to which a different font color has been applied—and that use the default character set) are stored in files that use the extension .acl (for AutoCorrect List). They are located here:

In Windows XP:
C:\Documents and Settings\<User Name>\Application Data\Microsoft\Office

In Windows Vista and Windows 7:
C:\Users\<User Name>\AppData\Roaming\Microsoft\Office

Formatted AutoCorrect entries are stored in the user's NORMAL template (normal.dotm).

NOTE: I'm not sure if there is a way to migrate formatted AutoCorrect entries from an earlier version of Word to Word 2010 without overwriting the Word 2010 NORMAL template (and any customizations stored therein). One possibility is to make a copy of your old normal.dot

---

[1] When you customize the QAT, you'll see a drop-down on the upper right-hand side of the screen. By default it is set to save your customizations globally—i.e., to the Word.qat file (*not* to the NORMAL template, despite the wording of the drop-down). If you like, can click the drop-down and change it to save settings in the current document.

template (from the prior version) and put the copy into the Word 2010 Startup folder. Templates stored in the Startup folder, and the customizations in those templates, should be available globally in Word. For instructions about moving templates into the Startup folder, see page 344.

For instructions on copying AutoCorrect files from one computer to another, see:
http://support.microsoft.com/kb/926927

The article refers to Word 2007 but the information should apply to Word 2010, as well.

Custom Dictionaries

Custom dictionaries have the file extension .dic.

In Windows XP:
C:\Documents and Settings\<User Name>\Application Data\Microsoft\UProof

In Windows Vista and Windows 7:
C:\Users\<User Name>\AppData\Roaming\Microsoft\UProof

INDEX

X

XPS

DISCOUNT COUPON

This coupon entitles the bearer

to a *$50.00 discount*

on an on-site software training session
lasting six (6) hours or more*‡

* May not be used in combination with any other discounts

‡ One coupon per organization (or individual trainee)

20355902R00347

Made in the USA
San Bernardino, CA
07 April 2015